The Retirement Researcher's Guide Series

Retirement Planning Guidebook

Navigating the Important Decisions for Retirement Success

Wade D. Pfau, PhD, CFA, RICP

Published by Retirement Researcher Media, Vienna, Virginia.

For information about special discounts for bulk purchases, please contact Wade at wade@retirementresearcher.com

Library of Congress Cataloging-in-Publication Data:

Pfau, Wade Donald, 1977–

Retirement Planning Guidebook / Wade Donald Pfau.

pages cm

Includes index.

ISBN [978-1-945640-09-4] (paperback) - ISBN [978-1-945640-10-0] (e-book) - ISBN [978-1-945640-11-7] (hardcover)

Library of Congress Control Number: 2021912549

Retirement Researcher, Vienna, VIRGINIA

1. Retirement Planning. 2. Financial, Personal. I. Title.

Cover Design: Trevor Alexander

To those seeking to do something great with their retirement

Table of Contents

Preface

The book is designed to help readers navigate key decisions necessary for a successful retirement. The process of building a retirement income strategy involves determining how to best combine retirement income tools to optimize the balance between *meeting* your retirement goals and *protecting* those goals from the unique risks of retirement. I engage in a deeper exploration of retirement income tools, including investment-based approaches and insurance-based approaches such as annuities. Most books on retirement income are written from the perspective of one retirement income style. Here I adopt a more comprehensive approach since different styles are legitimate and the choice depends on personal preferences.

Additional chapters then dig deeper into other important aspects for a retirement income plan, including how to develop a strategy for claiming Social Security benefits, how to make decisions related to Medicare and other health insurance, how to structure a plan for managing long-term care needs, and how to choose your retirement housing and incorporate housing wealth into your planning. This is followed by a deeper investigation of tax issues and how to structure your retirement income to create the most tax-efficiency during your life as well as for your beneficiaries. With legacy planning, I also explore how to get your finances organized for incapacity and death.

After reading this book, I hope you will be able to identify your preferred retirement income style, understand retirement plan risks, and assess your retirement preparedness by comparing the value of your retirement assets and liabilities.

The focus then shifts to the non-financial aspects of a successful retirement, including the need to find your purpose and passion, to understand if there is a role for work in retirement, to enhance your relationships and social connections, and to maintain an active and healthy lifestyle.

The book includes detailed action plans to help with your decision making. The final chapter fits these pieces together into an integrated series of steps to achieve financial and non-financial success in retirement. Readers will come away with the detailed knowledge and planning steps needed to make the most of their retirement years. The simple act of proactively planning for retirement can improve retirement satisfaction and happiness. Risks become less nebulous, and those with a plan can feel more comfortable about what comes next.

Let me address the general philosophy that guides this book. I focus on creating efficiencies for your retirement to stretch your resources as far as possible. A retirement income plan should be based on planning to live, not planning to die. While a long life obviously involves more expense than a shorter life, this assumption should take precedence given that life spans are increasing and the risks involved of under-planning. Fight the impatience that could lead you to choose short-term expediencies carrying greater long-term costs. Many efficiencies can be gained from a long-term focus that supports a higher sustained living standard.

We will see many examples that focus on building a better long-term plan. These include delaying Social Security benefits, purchasing annuities with lifetime income protections, building a diversified portfolio offering long-term prospects for growth, choosing lifetime income options for defined-benefit pensions, identifying reserve assets, strategically paying more taxes to enjoy substantial future tax reductions, making home renovations and living arrangements with the idea of aging in place, planning for the risk of cognitive decline that will make it harder to manage your finances with age, developing an estate plan, and opening a line of credit with a reverse mortgage.

With respect to the non-financial aspects of a successful retirement as well, I do emphasize the dichotomy that develops. While on the financial side we must plan for the possibility of a long retirement, it is the non-financial side where we need to also better plan for the possibility of a short retirement. We do not know how long our health will remain, and we must prioritize making the most of our available time. It is also important to enjoy the present while being prepared for the future.

This book is current with tax and estate planning laws as of mid-2021. However, these are both areas with potential for major changes to be made over the coming years, and some sections could lose relevance. RetirementResearcher.com will provide a resource for updates on rules or laws impacting retirees until I can get an updated edition of this book released. Please visit **www.retirementresearcher.com** and sign up for our weekly newsletter with our latest articles, invitations to webinars, Q&A sessions, and more. The newsletter arrives to your inbox each Saturday morning.

I also welcome your feedback and questions. You can reach me at:

wade@retirementresearcher.com

Wade Pfau

Dallas, TX

August 2021

Acknowledgments

Writing a book is a major endeavor, and I have been helped along the way by countless individuals. First and foremost, I would like to thank my colleagues at Retirement Researcher and McLean Asset Management for providing the vision and resources to make this book possible. I am grateful for the leadership and willingness of Alex Murguia and Dean Umemoto to build a firm that turns my retirement income research into practical solutions for real-world retirees. I would also like to thank Trevor Alexander, Briana Corbin, Rob Cordeau, Bob French, Paula Friedman, Christian Litscher, Morgan Menzies, Kyle Meyer, Jason Rizkallah, and Jessica Wunder.

Furthermore, I am grateful to the American College of Financial Services for their leadership and focus on retirement income planning, particularly David Blanchett, Michael Finke, George Nichols, Kirk Okumura, Steve Parrish, and Art Prunier.

I am also deeply indebted to Don and Lynne Komai and the Watermark Design Office for inspiring the layout and design for this book.

I also wish to thank countless other practitioners, researchers, and readers who have helped me along the way. A partial list must include Dana Anspach, Rodney Bednar, Bill Bengen, Bill Bernstein, Jason Branning, Jason Brown, J. Brent Burns, Ian Cahill, Bill Cason, Curtis Cloke, Jeremy Cooper, Wade Dokken, Harold Evensky, Francois Gadenne, Jonathan Guyton, David Jacobs, Dean Harder, Rick Hayes, Jamie Hopkins, Robert Huebscher, Stephen Huxley, Michael Kitces, David Lau, David Littell, Kevin Lyles, Manish Malhotra, Ed McGill, Moshe Milevsky, Aaron Minney, Dan Moisand, Brent Mondoskin, Sheryl Moore, John Olsen, Emilio Pardo, Kerry Pechter, Robert Powell, John M. Prizer, Jr., Michelle Richter, Will Robbins, Jason and Art Sanger, Bill Sharpe, Jeff Smith, Larry Swedroe, Tomiko Toland, Joe Tomlinson, Bob Veres, Steve Vernon, and Bruce Wolfe. I also pay tribute to Dirk Cotton and Dick Purcell, who were both important influences on me and have passed away.

I also wish to thank my family for their support and the sacrifices made to help me get this book written, especially during the pandemic year.

Finally, I wish to thank everyone who has read and participated at RetirementResearcher.com since 2010.

Chapter 1: Retirement Income Styles and Decisions

When properly planned, retirement allows for the freedom and flexibility to focus on one's interests and passions after a lifetime of work. A successful retirement requires important planning and preparation on both the financial and non-financial sides of life. Complex and interconnected decisions are necessary.

At the same time, the traditional concept of retirement is increasingly unaffordable. People are living longer. If retirement ages do not change, the number of years of retirement will continue to increase. That also increases the costs of funding retirement.

An extended period of low interest rates has further complicated retirement. Interest rates reached new historic lows as part of the global pandemic in 2020. Unfortunately, low interest rates are another factor that increases the amount of assets needed to fund retirement spending.

Another concern is that many people are forced into an early retirement that constrains the options and decisions around retirement planning and saving. Whether it is due to a health problem, the need to care for a family member, or an unexpected job loss, repeated surveys show that more than 40 percent of Americans retire sooner than they had anticipated. These surveys were completed before the global pandemic, and it is possible that the percentage of people forced into an early retirement could rise. Retirement may occur earlier than anticipated.

We have also seen a shift in the United States away from traditional company pensions toward defined-contribution retirement plans. This shifts the burden of funding retirements from employers, who could pool risks regarding longevity and market volatility across all their workers, toward individual employees who are now expected to manage investment portfolios and to find the right asset drawdown strategy in the face of great unknowns about personal longevity and portfolio returns.

Without the relative stability provided by employment earnings, retirees must find a way to convert their financial resources into spending power that will last the remainder of their lives. For those who have been saving and accumulating in anticipation of a future retirement, the question remains about what to do with the accumulated wealth upon retiring. Retirees are more responsible than ever before for figuring out how to save, invest, and then convert these savings into sustainable income for an ever-lengthening number of retirement years. They may also have legacy goals and must consider how to structure additional asset reserves to help fund large potential spending shocks such as paying for long-term care.

This book provides a path forward for retirees. I aim to make this book as self-contained and comprehensive as possible, though I do identify additional resources for those wishing to dive deeper on certain retirement decisions. I will navigate through the important decisions, both financial and non-financial, for achieving retirement success. Action plans provide steps for making important retirement decisions in an efficient manner.

It is worth spending a moment to describe what I mean by efficiency, since this is such an important underlying concept in the book. I use the definition from economics. We all face resource constraints, and efficiency is about getting the most value out of a given set of resources. It is about doing more with less. In the context of retirement, efficiency is about how to obtain the most after-tax spending and legacy potential from one's assets. Retirement income planning is about finding efficient strategies. If one strategy allows for more lifetime spending and a greater legacy value for assets relative than another strategy, then it is more efficient.

We start our careers with a huge amount of human capital. This is the value of our future lifetime earnings from work. Over the course of our working years, our human capital is converted into income to cover both our current expenses and to provide a source of savings to fund future goals. We save to have resources for our spending needs during the years that we do not work. We must decide how to position those savings between different financial tools and products to support our future goals and to manage the risks confronting those goals.

Efficiency must be defined from the longevity perspective. This becomes an important theme throughout the book as well, as we will see time and again how certain strategies can enhance efficiency over the long term, but not necessarily over the short term. To get those long-term benefits, short-term sacrifices may be needed. Examples include spending other assets to delay the start of Social Security benefits, front-loading taxes to get the most after-tax lifetime spending power, and using annuities with lifetime spending protections.

Wealth management has traditionally focused on accumulating assets without applying further thought to the shifts that occur after retirement. But many things change. Spending must now be funded through distributions from accumulated assets rather than from employment earnings. Spending must be able to continue over an unknown period. The potential for spending shocks grows.

A mountain-climbing analogy is useful for clarifying the distinction between accumulation (the working years) and distribution (retirement). Ultimately, the goal of climbing a mountain is not just to make it to the top; it is also necessary to get back down safely. The skillset required to get down a mountain is not the same as that needed to reach the summit. In fact, an experienced mountain climber knows that it is more treacherous and dangerous to climb down a mountain. On the way down, climbers must deal with greater fatigue when facing a downslope compared to an upslope. Our bodies are designed in a way that makes it easier to go up than to go down, which creates risks of falling farther and with greater acceleration.

Exhibit 1.1
The Mountain-Climbing Analogy for Retirement

The retirement phase, when you are pulling money from your accounts rather than accumulating wealth, is much like descending a mountain. The objective of a retirement saver is not just to make it to the top of the mountain, which we could view as achieving a wealth accumulation target that we estimate will allow for a smooth transition to retirement. The real objective is to make it down the mountain safely and smoothly by spending assets in a sustainable manner for as long as we live.

Retirement planning is about identifying goals, analyzing the risks confronting those goals, and building a sufficient asset base to manage those goals. Retirees seek to sustain a living standard while spending down assets over a finite but unknown length of time, while also supporting goals related to legacy planning and providing liquidity to assist with unexpected expenses. Efficiency is important to the retirement plan because smart decision making facilitates the potential to achieve desired goals with fewer assets. We will navigate through decisions that become part of a comprehensive approach to making your best retirement.

Understanding Your Retirement Income Style

Before providing a summary of the decisions discussed in future chapters, I want to dig in immediately with this chapter's key retirement decision that will guide how you may think about numerous other issues and decisions that are part of your overall retirement plan. You should first determine your retirement income style. If you have spent much time reading about retirement income, it quickly becomes apparent that there are vastly different viewpoints about the best way to approach retirement spending. Some people love the stock market, others hate it. Some love annuities, others hate them. The same goes for life insurance, reverse mortgages, long-term care insurance, and various other products and tools. Commentators argue about questions such as whether there is such a thing as a safe withdrawal rate from an investment portfolio, whether annuities provide enough value for their costs, and whether it is better to start Social Security as soon as possible or to defer collecting benefits until closer to age 70.

In this regard, the financial services profession remains quite siloed. There is an old saying that if the only tool you have is a hammer, then everything starts to look like a nail. This tendency is alive and well within the financial services industry as those on the investments side tend to view an investment portfolio as the solution for any problem, while those on the insurance side tend to view insurance products as the answer for any financial question. Financial advisors and other pundits tend to support the approach they feel most comfortable with or are otherwise licensed or incentivized to provide, with little consideration for what may be best for any given individual. The prevalent idea is that there is one objectively superior retirement income approach for everyone, and anyone suggesting otherwise must be guided by a conflict of interest.

The reality is that there are competing viable approaches for retirement income. No one approach or retirement income product works best for everyone. There is room for nuance, and it pays to be agnostic. Understanding which approach is best for any given individual means knowing more about that individual's preferences and style. A vital first step in building a retirement income plan is to first identify the style that works for you. Defining a style and matching strategies to it provides an important step forward in aligning individuals with their retirement income strategies.

Understanding your style from the start can save time and money. Adopting a strategy that fails to align with your preferences can lead to a plan that is poorly implemented throughout retirement. Frequently revising a retirement plan is a potentially costly exercise that is prone to underperformance and inefficiencies. Retirees need to be comfortable and "buy in" into their strategy. Forcing the "wrong" strategy on someone is not appropriate. There are dangers to filtering strategies based on a financial professional or an investment media pundit's world view rather than seeking to better understand what strategies resonate with an individual's personal style. Meanwhile, financial advisors who work with retired clients can understand their own style and how that may impact the advice they provide, either by weeding out prospective clients who may not be aligned with the advisor's approach, or by being able to better serve clients by offering a broader range of strategies. Matching preferences with strategies will lay a foundation for achieving better retirement outcomes.

With "Professor of Retirement Income" as my formal academic job title, I have felt it to be my responsibility to understand the different strategies that exist around creating a retirement income plan. In 2012, I attempted to outline the characteristics of two fundamentally different philosophies for retirement income planning—which I called probability-based and safety-first. I still remember working on this during the subway rides back and forth to the university in Tokyo where I taught at that time. These philosophies diverge on the critical issue of where a retirement plan is best served: in the risk/reward trade-offs of a diversified and aggressive investment portfolio, or in the contractual protections of insurance products to fund key spending needs before turning to investments as well.

Strong disagreements exist about how to position a retiree's assets to best meet retirement goals. The guidance and strategies provided to retirees still largely depend on the viewpoints of the pundit, whether that person works in the media, the financial services profession, or as a personal finance blogger. What is missing is the concept that there are multiple appropriate ways to approach retirement. Each pundit will have a personal style that may be different from the style of the individual receiving that message, which creates misalignment. Individuals optimize for different outcomes based on personal styles. They have characteristics that can be determined to better position a strategy that is "right" for them rather than hoping for an alignment achieved through random matching with the viewpoint telling them what is objectively "right."

Different retirement income approaches are viable in the sense that they work best for individuals with a specific set of preferences and attitudes. When I described distinctions between probability-based and safety-first, they were based on observations about how different commentators in the retirement income space approached the matter of describing optimal retirement approaches. We now understand that these distinctions can be attributed to real and observable preferences.

Alex Murguia and I developed a survey which tested and quantified the role of six specific and distinct retirement income factors which make up a retirement income style. These factors identify a range of preferences around retirement finances. To do this, we reviewed a wide range of advisor and consumer-focused books and articles about retirement income written from different perspectives to identify factors representing a range of choices, either in terms of tradeoffs to be weighed or as different thought perspectives for making retirement decisions. From this review, we identified six factors that describe a range of potential preferences for retirees. Our statistical analysis determined that all six factors identify distinct preferences. Anyone interested in that statistical part can refer to the research article listed in the further reading section at the end of the chapter. It is worth discussing these factors because it is amazing how well they work together to define styles that directly translate into a taxonomy of specific retirement income strategies.

In conducting this survey with readers at RetirementResearcher.com, we were able to formally demonstrate the importance of two main sets of factors, as well as four additional supporting factors. We found that two factors can best capture an individual's retirement income style: Probability-Based vs Safety-First and Optionality vs Commitment Orientation. The other four factors play a secondary role through their correlations with the primary factors to help further identify retirement income strategies. These secondary factors include a Time-Based vs Perpetuity income floor, Accumulation vs Distribution, Front-Loading vs Back-Loading income, and True vs Technical Liquidity.

With the first factor, we use the probability-based and safety-first names. The *Probability-Based vs Safety-First* factor details how individuals prefer to source their retirement income from assets. Probability-based income sources are dependent on the potential for market growth to continually provide a sustainable retirement income stream. This includes a traditional diversified investment portfolio or other assets that have the expectation of growth with realized capital gains supporting retirement income. Meanwhile, Safety-First income sources incorporate contractual obligations. The spending provided through these sources is less exposed to market swings. A safety-first approach may include protected sources of income common with defined-benefit pensions, annuities with lifetime income protections, and holding individual government bonds to maturity. The safety-first approach does not depend on an expectation of market growth to provide capital gains as a source of spending, since the income is contractually driven. Though no strategy is completely safe, the inclusion of contractual protections implies a relative degree of safety compared to relying on unknown market outcomes.

The second main factor reflects the dimension of preferences for *Optionality vs Commitment*. This approach details the degree of flexibility sought with income strategies. Optionality reflects a preference for keeping options open for retirement income. Those with an optionality preference want to maintain flexibility with their strategies to respond to more favorable economic developments or to a changing personal situation. This preference aligns with retirement solutions that do not have pre-determined holding periods and are amenable to making changes.

Conversely, commitment reflects a preference for committing to a retirement income solution. There is less concern with potentially unfavorable economic developments or a worsening personal situation because the solution solves for a lifetime retirement income need. The security of having a dedicated retirement income solution outweighs missing out on potentially more positive future outcomes, and it may provide further satisfaction from having made decisions and not feeling a lingering sensation that this retirement income decision-making process must remain on one's to-do list. Planning in advance to manage potential cognitive decline and to protect family members who may not be as financially savvy can also be a source of satisfaction in this approach.

The other four factors we found play a more secondary role for understanding retirement decisions. First, with the *Time-Based vs Perpetuity* factor, retirees ultimately have two funding strategies for building retirement income floors. They may either fund an income floor for specific time periods or in perpetuity. Time-based funding strategies are used to fund fixed windows of time in retirement. Building floors in perpetuity involves using lifetime income protections through risk pooling.

Next is the *Accumulation vs Distribution* factor. Wealth management traditionally focuses on accumulating assets without applying further thought regarding the differences that may happen during retirement. It is possible that individuals may approach investing during retirement rather differently from investing for retirement, as retirees may worry less about maximizing risk-adjusted returns and worry more about ensuring that their assets can sustainably support their spending goals. The distinction for accumulation and distribution details a preference for portfolio growth while retired even though it will entail a more uncertain and lumpier retirement income stream (Accumulation), or a preference for a more predictable retirement income path to maintain a standard of living at the potential cost of foregoing the highest possible investment account value at death (Distribution).

Those with an Accumulation mindset will be more comfortable building a retirement portfolio using traditional investment tools designed for maximizing asset returns subject to an accepted level of short-term volatility as determined through risk tolerance questionnaires. Those with a Distribution mindset will be optimizing a different objective related to supporting spending goals in a sustainable manner. With a distribution mindset, investing during retirement is a rather different matter from investing for retirement. In this new retirement calculus, views about how to balance the trade-offs between upside potential and downside protection can change. Retirees might find that the risks associated with seeking return premiums on risky assets loom larger than before, and they might be prepared to sacrifice more potential upside growth to protect against the downside risks of being unable to meet spending objectives.

Next, the *Front-Loading vs Back-Loading Income* factor relates to the amount and pace of income to be received throughout retirement. This factor can be directly linked to the tradeoffs identified by the concept of longevity risk aversion. Longevity risk aversion represents a fear of outliving assets in retirement, and it will impact some individuals more strongly than others. Does a retiree feel more comfortable front-loading portfolio distributions with higher spending early in retirement to better ensure that savings can be enjoyed when one is more assured to be alive and healthy (Front-Loading)? Or does an individual prefer to spend at a lower rate in early retirement to better ensure that a particular lifestyle can be maintained without cuts during the later stages of a potentially long retirement horizon (Back-Loading)?

Those who fear outliving their assets will prefer back-loading income and will behave more conservatively.

An example may better illustrate this concept. Monte Carlo simulations are often used in financial planning contexts to gain a better understanding of the viability of a financial plan in the face of market and longevity risks. Monte Carlo simulations create randomized series of market returns to test the sustainability of financial plans through various market environments. The results are reported with a probability of success, which is the percent of cases where the plan meets the retirement goals without depleting assets. Suppose a Monte Carlo simulation identifies a retirement plan's chance of success as 90 percent. This means that 90 percent of the time the plan can be expected to work, but that 10 percent of the time the plan can be expected to deplete resources too early. While perhaps agreeing that this number is correctly calculated, the interpretation of what to do with it can be different. For those with a Front-Loading preference, a 90 percent chance is a more than reasonable starting point, and the retiree can proceed with this plan. The plan has a high likelihood of success. If future updates determine that the plan might be on course toward failure, a few changes, such as a reduction in spending, should be adequate to get the plan back on track. Those identifying with Back-Loaded spending, however, will be less comfortable with this level of risk. These individuals will want a greater assurance that the plan can work, as the thought of needing to make cuts to spending late in life is a greater source of stress.

Finally, the *True v Technical Liquidity* factor reflects differences between two ways that liquidity can be defined in financial planning. Those who prefer True Liquidity would like to have assets earmarked specifically as reserves for future unknown events that can derail a retirement income plan. To be truly liquid, assets must not already be matched to other financial goals such as planned retirement expenses or a specific legacy goal. True Liquidity can involve the use of cash set asides, buffer assets, and insurance. Those who prefer Technical Liquidity would rather raise cash from investments or assets already earmarked for other goals when necessary to fund unexpected expenses, with an understanding that cuts may then need to be made elsewhere. Technical Liquidity refers more to a general sense that there is a pot of assets to draw from for any type of expense. With a comfort around Technical Liquidity, fewer assets may be needed to feel comfortable with a retirement income plan because it is not necessary to have as much additional reserve assets to cushion the potential spending shocks that retirees face.

Another important element for this relates to income annuities, in which a retiree earmarks some assets to support lifetime spending. Annuitized assets are not liquid, but a true liquidity mindset would focus on how this decision could increase the level of true liquidity for other non-annuity assets that no longer need to be earmarked for the spending. A technical liquidity mindset would focus on how the income annuity is not liquid.

With the six factors introduced, we are now getting to the punchline for this discussion, which is how these factors correlate to help identify retirement income styles that will map to specific retirement income strategies. To explain this, Alex and I created the Retirement Income Style Awareness® (RISA®) Profiles as based on the RISA Matrix® shown in Exhibit 1.2. The RISA Profile® is effectively a replacement for measuring risk tolerance that is broader and includes more dimensions to be better suited to the complexities of retirement income planning. The RISA Matrix lays out how the scores calculated for each RISA factor can be utilized and matched to appropriate retirement income strategies.

Exhibit 1.2
The RISA Matrix

Optionality Orientation

	Safety-First & Optionality [Time Segmentation]	Probability-Based & Optionality [Total-Return Investing]	
Safety-First	Safety-First & Optionality [Time Segmentation]	Probability-Based & Optionality [Total-Return Investing]	Probability-Based
	Safety-First & Commitment [Income Protection]	Probability-Based & Commitment [Risk Wrap]	

Commitment Orientation

This process relies on the idea that even though these six factors are statistically distinct from one another and reflect unique characteristics, there are some correlations found between them. As those correlations work together, we can identify retirement income styles and strategies that match. I noted that the statistical analysis identified the two main factors as probability-based vs safety-first and commitment vs optionality. We create the RISA Matrix in the exhibit to show the intersection of these preferences. The scale for probability-based vs safety-first is aligned horizontally, and optionality vs commitment is aligned vertically. This creates four distinct retirement income strategy quadrants, each of which is based on an individual's scores for these two main RISA factors. Important to this as well is that the probability-based perspective is correlated with a preference for optionality, while those with a safety-first outlook also tend to be more commitment oriented. The four supporting factors are mixed in as well through their correlations with the main factors to identify strategies more strongly.

From the available retirement income strategies, we identify four main classes to match the four quadrants within the RISA Matrix. These are total return, risk wrap, income protection, and time segmentation (or bucketing). These strategies align closely with the common framework of systematic withdrawals (total return), time segmentation, and essential vs. discretionary (income protection and risk wrap). Although I am introducing these approaches now, I will describe these strategies in much greater detail later in Chapters 4 and 5.

Upper-Right Quadrant: Total-Return Investing

Starting at the upper-right quadrant of the RISA Matrix, these are individuals whose preferences lean toward both probability-based and optionality. Typically, individuals with these characteristics identify with drawing income from a diversified investment portfolio rather than using contractual sources to fund their retirement expenses. Investors rely on portfolio growth to sustainably support their spending and do not want to commit to a strategy. As for secondary characteristics in this quadrant, as identified through their correlations with the two primary factors, these individuals also tend toward an accumulation focus, technical liquidity, front-loading for spending, and time-based flooring. Those who value optionality wish to maintain the ability to consider retirement income withdrawal options on an ongoing basis. They are also more comfortable with seeking market growth despite the volatility for spending. The individual is likely to prefer a more variable income stream with the potential for investment growth rather than a stable retirement income stream with more muted potential growth. They want to enjoy their early retirement years and are willing to accept the risk that they may have to make spending cuts later.

This quadrant provides the combination of preferences that I have written about in the past as probability-based. These are investments-centric approaches that rely on earning the risk premium from the stock market. Stocks are expected to outperform bonds over sufficiently long periods, and this investment outperformance will provide retirees with the opportunity to fund a higher lifestyle. Should decent market returns materialize and sufficiently outpace inflation, investment solutions can be sustained indefinitely to support retirement goals. Those favoring investments rely on the notion that while the stock market is volatile, it will eventually provide favorable returns and will outperform bonds. The upside potential from an investment portfolio is viewed as so significant that insurance products are not needed. Investment approaches are probability-based in the sense that they will *probably* work.

The roots of this retirement income strategy originated from research conducted by California-based financial planner William Bengen in the 1990s. Bengen sought to determine the safe withdrawal rate from a financial portfolio over a long retirement. Though the term *safe withdrawal rate* uses the word *safe*, it is not part of the safety-first approach. The probability-based school uses "safe" in a historical context as based on what could have worked when tested with historical market returns. The question is: how much can retirees withdraw from their savings, which are invested in a diversified portfolio, while still maintaining sufficient confidence that they can safely continue spending without running out of wealth? Finding strategies that could have always worked with historical data make probability-based advocates feel comfortable.

The probability-based approach seeks to maximize risk-adjusted returns from the perspective of the total portfolio. Asset allocation during retirement is generally defined in the same way as during the accumulation phase—using the tools of modern portfolio theory to identify a portfolio on the efficient frontier in terms of single-period trade-offs between risk and return. Different volatile asset classes that are not perfectly correlated are combined to create portfolios with lower volatility. Investors aim to maximize wealth by seeking the highest possible return given their capacity and tolerance for short-term market volatility. Probability-based advocates are generally more optimistic about the long-run potential of stocks to outperform bonds, so retirees are generally advised to take on as much risk as they can tolerate to minimize the probability of plan failure. Answers about asset allocation for retirees generally point to holding around 40 to 80 percent of the retirement portfolio in stocks.

The "annuity puzzle" is described by academic economists who struggle to understand why commercial annuities are not more popular with retirees. The solution to this puzzle for those in this quadrant is that not everyone is optimizing for stable retirement income. There is an overlay of three distinct factors in which individuals can maintain preferences for an investment growth perspective, a willingness to accept volatile income with an accumulation mindset, and a desire for optionality. These individuals simply do not perceive a need for annuities as part of their planning.

The individuals whose style places them in this quadrant are more likely to subscribe to a systematic withdrawal strategy based on a total return investing approach for retirement income. Those who think this style is most applicable to their situations will want to focus on Chapter 4, which provides a deeper investigation of the issues that surround sustainable spending from investments.

Lower-Left Quadrant: Income Protection

The lower-left quadrant is home to individuals with a safety-first and commitment orientation. Other secondary factors also correlated with this quadrant include having a distribution mindset, a preference for perpetuity income flooring, a preference for true liquidity, and a desire to back-load spending to manage the fear of outliving assets. These characteristics align with retirement income strategies traditionally referred to as essential vs. discretionary or income flooring. Assets are positioned to match the risk characteristics of a spending goal. There is a preference for contractually-protected lifetime income to cover essential retirement expenses, while a more diversified total return portfolio is used for discretionary expenses. These characteristics associate with using income annuities through the annuitization of assets to provide greater downside spending protection with a lifetime commitment. We further describe income annuities in Chapter 5.

This quadrant reflects the set of characteristics that I have described as safety-first over my years of writing about retirement income. Safety-first advocates are generally more willing to accept a role for insurance as a source of income protection to help manage various retirement risks. For investments-only strategies, retirement risks are generally managed by spending less in retirement, as longevity risk is managed by assuming a long life, and market risk is managed by assuming poor market returns. But insurance companies can pool these market and longevity risks across a large base of retirees—much like traditional defined-benefit pensions and Social Security—allowing for retirement spending that is more closely aligned with average, long-term, fixed-income returns and average longevity. Those with average lengths of life and average market returns will have paid an insurance premium that is transferred to those who experience a more costly combination of a longer retirement and poor market returns. This could support a higher lifestyle than what is feasible for someone self-managing these risks and who is more nervous about the possibility of relying on market growth to avoid outliving assets.

Those more comfortable with the safety-first approach believe that contractual guarantees are reliable and that staking your retirement income on the assumption that favorable market returns will eventually arrive is emotionally overwhelming and dangerous. These individuals are more concerned about market risk, as a retiree gets only one opportunity for a successful retirement. Essential spending needs, at least, should not be subject to market whims. The safety-first school views investment-only solutions as undesirable because the retiree retains all the longevity and market risks, which an insurance company is better positioned to manage.

The safety-first school of thought was originally derived from academic models about how people allocate their resources over a lifetime to maximize their satisfaction. Academics, including many Nobel prize winners, have studied these models since the 1920s to figure out how rational people make optimal decisions in the face of scarcity.

Advocates of the safety-first approach view prioritization of retirement goals as vital to developing a good retirement income strategy. The investment strategy aims to match the risk characteristics of assets and goals, so prioritization is a must. Safety-first advocates move away from asset allocation for the investment portfolio to broader asset-liability matching, which focuses more holistically on all household assets.

With asset-liability matching, investors are not trying to maximize their year-to-year returns on a risk-adjusted basis, nor are they trying to beat an investing benchmark. The goal is to have cash flows available to meet spending needs as required. Contractual-based and committed income strategies that do not rely on market growth are viewed as appropriate for core retirement expenses.

For those in this quadrant, there is no need to discuss the "safe" withdrawal rate that dominates the probability-based world. Growth assets are only appropriate for discretionary goals where safety is less relevant. Safety-first advocates dismiss probability-based ideas about safe withdrawal rates by noting that there is no such constant safe spending from a volatile investment portfolio. But once the basics are covered, there is more flexibility to not worry about the performance of remaining investments.

Lower-Right Quadrant: Risk Wrap

The remaining two quadrants reflect hybrid styles that can better align with the preferences of retirees who may not hold all the natural correlations between different retirement income factors. Shifting to the lower-right quadrant of the RISA Matrix, we find individuals whose RISA Profile shows both a probability-based and commitment orientation. From the secondary factors, this quadrant is also associated with a preference for technical liquidity and for back-loading retirement income.

While individuals here maintain a probability-based outlook with a desire for market participation, they also have desire to commit to a solution that provides a structured income stream. Income annuities, which require an irreversible commitment and a lack of growth potential, tend to be non-starters for individuals in this quadrant. These individuals seek growth, and they think in terms of technical liquidity, but they also have more longevity risk aversion and are more comfortable with committing to strategies. For these reasons, using only unprotected investment portfolios is also not attractive.

Since the 1990s, the retirement industry has been creating structured tools that are more aligned with the combinations of preferences found in this quadrant. We use the term "risk wrap" as a general description of such tools. A risk wrap strategy provides a blend of investment growth opportunities with lifetime income benefits, generally through a variable or indexed annuity. Such tools can be designed to offer upside growth potential alongside secured lifetime spending even if markets perform poorly. Such tools also maintain technical liquidity for the underlying assets, as deferred annuity assets remain on the balance sheet and can be invested with their values shown on portfolio statements. There is commitment and back-loaded protection, but these strategies can also be reversed with remaining assets returned to those who decide they no longer want or need the lifetime spending protection. While the associated market exposure satisfies the probability-based dimension and the products offer technical liquidity, purchasing a more structured and secured retirement income guardrail through the lifetime income benefit addresses the commitment and longevity risk aversion dimensions at work within this quadrant. I will explain more about these tools in Chapter 5.

Upper-Left Quadrant: Time Segmentation

The upper-left quadrant identifies another hybrid case. These are individuals with both safety-first and optionality preferences. They like contractual protections, but they also prefer optionality. This quadrant is also correlated with preferences for true liquidity and front-loaded retirement spending.

Those whose factor scores place them in this quadrant reflect a desire for retirement income solutions that are characterized by contractually-driven income while still maintaining a high level of flexibility to change strategies or accommodate ongoing changes. It can be difficult to enter a contract while keeping options open, but the retirement world has addressed this challenge with strategies related to investment-based bucketing or time segmentation. These are also described in Chapter 4. Annuities with lifetime commitments are less likely to appeal to individuals in this quadrant, but these retirees may be satisfied with holding individual bonds to cover upcoming expenses with contractual protections.

A time-segmentation or bucketing strategy usually sources short-term retirement income needs with a rolling bond ladder or other fixed income assets. Bond ladders are frequently implemented with contractually-protected instruments (cash equivalents or government-issued securities) that can be used for shorter to intermediate income needs, with a diversified investment portfolio designed for longer-term expenses. That growth portfolio will be used to gradually replenish the short-term buckets as those assets are used to cover retirement expenses. Conceptually, some may also lump time segmentation together with the idea of holding additional cash reserves outside the investment portfolio to manage market volatility or for unexpected expenses. These strategies address the need for asset safety by including short-term contractual protections while maintaining high optionality for other investment assets.

There is much debate about whether these strategies are materially different from using total-return investing. In terms of behavior, these strategies do have an important difference from a total-return portfolio if they help people displaying this style's characteristics to be more comfortable with a growth portfolio. Short-term spending protections could help some retirees get through bouts of market volatility without panicking. That behavioral aspect is primarily where the value can lie. Much like risk wrap strategies, time segmentation reflects a hybrid approach that can match a less natural combination of preferences held by these retirees.

Discussions about retirement income planning can become quite confusing as there are so many different viewpoints expressed in the consumer media. Each individual investor must ultimately identify the style that can best support his or her financial and psychological needs for retirement. Financial service professionals and retirees should understand which style they most identify with to know how that impacts advice and whether retirees are speaking the same "language" as that guiding the advice they are receiving. The RISA Profile provides a way for people to quickly understand whether they are speaking the same language, and to find retirement income strategies that are best aligned with their style.

Invitation to Identify Your Retirement Income Style

I wear different hats as a university professor and a registered investment advisor. My intention is for this book to serve as a stand-alone educational tool. I learned my lesson with an earlier book that generated a few negative reviews from readers who interpreted it as a sales pitch for financial planning services. That makes me hesitant to start the book with a discussion of a commercial product.

I have outlined the types of preferences associated with each of four general retirement income styles. For this book to be standalone, you could simply think about your preferences related to the six retirement income factors and where that would place you on the RISA Matrix.

If you would like more guidance about how to find your style, we have created the RISA Profile questionnaire to quickly guide respondents toward an answer. It allows individuals to better understand their retirement income style and to align it with a strategy that will resonate.

I would like to offer you, as a reader, the opportunity to take this questionnaire and receive a free RISA Profile report. This will let you know where your preferences align in terms of the four quadrants of the RISA Matrix. That may help you to know whether to focus more on Chapter 4 or Chapter 5 as you read further.

To do this, please visit **www.risaprofile.com/guidebook** to take the questionnaire and obtain your RISA Profile results without cost or any further obligation. And please feel free to share your feedback with me as this is a new tool we are constantly striving to improve (**wade@retirementresearcher.com**). I will now hold off on any further promotion like this throughout the remainder of the book until the ending epilogue about opportunities for further engagement. We now resume this stand-alone educational resource.

Navigating the Decisions for Retirement Success

We continue to navigate through the important decisions for building a retirement income plan as efficiently as possible, seeking to meet spending and legacy goals with the intention of also preserving liquidity to serve as reserves for spending shocks. The thirteen chapters in this book provide an investigation into the key retirement decisions and a framework for putting them together.

Retirement Income Styles and Decisions (Chapter 1)

Identifying your retirement income style is a huge initial decision. In this chapter, I describe a set of scorable retirement income factors that define preferences for an overall retirement income style. The RISA Matrix provides a way for retirees to understand how a range of preferences exist and how those preferences can be identified and linked to appropriate retirement income strategies. This provides a way to make sense of the plethora of competing views about how to approach retirement income planning. The first key decision to navigate in retirement is to develop an understanding about your retirement income style. This helps with choosing from competing options and tools for building your plan.

Retirement Risks (Chapter 2)

Chapter 2 provides an overview of retirement income risks. Risk in this book means an inability to meet your financial goals. The three basic risks for retirees are longevity risk, market risk, and spending shocks. Longevity risk relates to not knowing how long you will live, and thus not knowing how long you must make your wealth last. Market risk relates to the possibility that poor market returns deplete available wealth more quickly than anticipated. Market losses in the early years of retirement can disproportionately hurt the sustainability of a retirement spending plan, creating sequence-of-return risk that amplifies the impacts of market volatility. Spending shocks are surprise expenses beyond the planned budget, such as for long-term care and major health expenses. Spending shocks require additional reserve assets to avoid having to spend assets intended to support the ongoing retirement budget.

For a planned retirement budget, the overall cost of retirement will be less with some combination of a shorter life, stronger market returns, and fewer spending shocks. But retirement could become quite expensive when a long life is combined with poor market returns and significant spending shocks. The danger is that a combination of risks contributes to an overall retirement cost that exceeds available assets. Developing strategies to manage retirement risks is an important theme in the book.

Quantifying Goals and Assessing Preparedness (Chapter 3)

Chapter 3 provides a framework to answer an important question many pre-retirees and retirees are asking themselves. That is, am I on the financial track toward supporting a successful retirement?

The first step to answering this question involves quantifying retirement financial goals. These goals define the retirement expenses, or liabilities, to be funded. Financial goals include to maximize spending power (lifestyle) in such a way that spending can remain consistent and sustainable without any drastic reductions, no matter how long the retirement lasts (longevity). Other important goals may include leaving assets for subsequent generations (legacy) and maintaining sufficient reserves for unplanned contingencies (liquidity). Lifestyle, longevity, legacy, and liquidity are the four Ls of retirement income. Effort is needed to figure out a realistic retirement budget, as well as placing a monetary value on legacy goals and reserves for contingencies.

A planning age and discount rate are then needed to quantify retirement assets and liabilities as single values for today, which includes converting future income and spending streams into their present value. The planning age can be determined as a conservative age one is unlikely to outlive. I also assume a conservative bond-like rate of return for the discount rate to determine if there are sufficient assets to meet the anticipated retirement liabilities through the planning age without requiring market risk.

Many assets can be used as part of the retirement income plan, and they can be generalized as reliable income assets, diversified portfolio, and reserves. Assets include investment accounts, retirement accounts, future work, Social Security benefits, home equity, life insurance and other insurance policies, and even family or community support.

The value of assets and liabilities can be compared by calculating the funded ratio. This is the ratio of assets to liabilities, assuming a conservative interest rate to translate future income and expenses into today's dollars. The funded ratio lets us know whether our plan will work by investing financial assets in bonds to meet future expenses. The hope is that assets exceed liabilities. The chapter concludes with a deeper consideration of funding levels for specific goals and possible actions to improve the funded status if assets fall short.

Sustainable Spending from Investments (Chapter 4)

The funded ratio provides a basic calculation about whether retirement is funded without accepting market risk. Those investing with a more diversified portfolio may feel comfortable relying on the stock market to provide a higher portfolio return than bonds alone. Chapter 4 describes the research-based approach for identifying the level of sustainable distributions from a diversified investment portfolio. This is the heart of the total-return investing quadrant of the RISA Matrix. It is also an important topic for anyone with investment portfolios covering a portion of retirement expenses.

I start by describing the origins of the 4 percent rule for retirement spending. The 4 percent rule is the starting point for how most probability-based thinkers view sustainable retirement spending. I then describe reasons why the 4 percent rule may be too high for today's retirees. Reasons include that it does not consider the international experience, that low interest rates and high market valuations create a situation that has not been tested in the historical data, and that retirees may deviate from its assumptions about earning the index market returns, maintaining an aggressive asset allocation, and using a total-return investing strategy. I also consider the impact of taxes, the desire to maintain a safety margin for assets, and the possibility that retirements may last longer than planned.

Then I shift to reasons why, despite the issues just mentioned, the 4 percent rule may still be too low. Reasons include that the retirement spending budget may not grow with inflation throughout retirement, that retirees may be able to put together a more diversified investment portfolio, that retirees may create a time segmentation or bucketing approach to asset allocation, that retirees may use a more dynamic asset allocation, that they are flexible about their spending, that they may have the capacity to accept greater risk for depleting their investment assets late in retirement, or that they may coordinate portfolio spending with distributions from a buffer asset to help manage sequence-of-return risk.

Annuities and Risk Pooling (Chapter 5)

Annuities serve as another retirement income tool that allows for greater spending than bonds alone. Annuities with lifetime income protections can provide an effective way to build an income floor in perpetuity for retirement. Annuities, as opposed to individual bonds, provide longevity protection by hedging the risks associated with an unknown retirement length. Annuities can be real or nominal, fixed or variable, and income payments can begin within one year or be deferred to a later age. The simplest type of annuity is an income annuity. I start with an exploration of these, and then continue to explore other types of more complicated annuities, including deferred variable annuities and fixed index annuities. Different annuities provide various combinations of guaranteed income, liquidity, and upside growth potential. Annuities used as tools to fund retirement spending will be especially attractive to those with the income protection and risk wrap retirement income styles.

After describing how different types of annuities work, the chapter continues with a deeper discussion of fitting annuities into a retirement income plan. Annuities with lifetime income protections provide a source for reliable income to fill any gaps in relation to the assets earmarked for longevity expenses. As for which annuity type is most suitable, the decision involves striking the desired balance between downside protection and upside potential with the annuity. I also discuss how to manage inflation risk with annuities, and how a partial annuity strategy impacts legacy and liquidity. Those purchasing annuities must also decide between selling stocks or bonds to fund the purchase, and I make the case for annuities as a bond alternative. The chapter concludes with a discussion of how to frame the issue of annuity fees with respect to the role that the annuities play within the plan, impacting the overall cost of retirement.

Social Security (Chapter 6)

Most households already have an annuity as part of their retirement income plan: Social Security. For most Americans, Social Security benefits serve as a core source of reliable income. As a government-backed, inflation-adjusted monthly income for life, Social Security benefits can help to manage longevity risk, inflation risk, and market risk. In addition to retired worker benefits,

Social Security also provides spousal, survivor, and dependent benefits from a worker's earnings record. For some households, the value of lifetime Social Security benefits could exceed $1 million. It is vital to understand that the Social Security claiming decision should be made independently from the decision to leave the labor force. Claiming decisions should not be taken lightly. It is possible to gain much from Social Security simply by understanding how the system works.

This chapter outlines the steps required to have a firm understanding about Social Security and how to approach your claiming decision. I will discuss how Social Security retirement benefits are calculated and how to factor in issues such a spousal and survivor benefit for couples, dependent benefits, and benefits for divorcees. I will also look at the earnings test, the windfall elimination provision and government pension offset. I also describe the basic philosophies about claiming Social Security, including to view it as insurance to protect for a long life, and breakeven analyses on when delaying benefits will pay off. The basic guideline is that at least the higher earner in a couple should consider delaying Social Security to age 70. I also describe the validity of arguments made in favor of claiming Social Security early, which includes a discussion of Social Security's history and potential reform options related to what may happen as the Social Security trust fund approaches depletion. My intention is to give you the knowledge and confidence to approach the Social Security claiming decision in the manner that can create the most long-term value for your plan.

Medicare and Health Insurance (Chapter 7)

Planning for retirement health expenses is an essential component in a comprehensive retirement income plan. Chapter 7 explores retirement health insurance options and retirement health expenses. Decisions made about Medicare or other health insurance can help mitigate the risks of large health-care spending shocks. The bulk of this discussion will be about Medicare, which is available to most Americans upon reaching age 65. It is by far the most important source of health insurance for retirees, and it requires numerous decisions regarding whether to use Original Medicare or a Medicare Advantage Plan, whether to use a Medicare Supplement with Original Medicare, and how to obtain prescription drug coverage. I also cover health insurance options for those retiring before reaching the Medicare eligibility age, and the rules about using other private insurance after reaching Medicare eligibility. I also discuss how to make ongoing annual decisions about Medicare. The chapter finishes with a deeper dive into budgeting for health care expenses and estimating reserves for retirement health care shocks.

Long-Term Care Planning (Chapter 8)

One of the largest spending shocks facing a retired household is the need to pay for ongoing long-term care. A retirement income plan must account for this risk, and various tools are available to help control the impacts of long-term care costs on family wealth. Physical and mental decline can lead to an inability to perform activities of daily living. This could create need for the provision of in-home care, adult day care, or a move to assisted living or a nursing home. Family members end up providing the bulk of long-term care, often at great cost to themselves in terms of their career, finances, and health. If family is not available, or if one is otherwise seeking to minimize the potential burden on family, then a plan is needed. The financial costs for funding long-term care expenses can be significant. Without further action, the default plan for long-term care is to self-fund any expenses or to receive care from family members until assets are sufficiently depleted to qualify for Medicaid. But other options exist, including traditional long-term care insurance and hybrid policies that combine long-term care benefits with life insurance or an annuity. Advanced planning for long-term care needs can help control the impact of spending shocks and cognitive decline. I conclude the chapter with a discussion about estimating the amount of reserve assets to hold for long-term care shocks.

Housing Decisions (Chapter 9)

Retirees must make numerous housing decisions related both to where they want to live and how to incorporate their housing wealth into their retirement plans. Chapter 9 includes background about whether retirees think they will move and whether they do move in retirement. I also identify characteristics of a good place to live in retirement, and considerations for when one is thinking about moving into a home on a more permanent basis. Most retirees wish to age in place, and I also discuss home modifications that can make it easier to accomplish this in the face of physical limitations. If one decides to live more permanently in a home which they own, housing wealth can be used in a variety of ways in retirement. Housing can provide inflation protection and some protection for the uncertain costs related to long-term care. With cognitive or long-term care needs, housing could be used to delay institutional living, and then housing wealth could be redeployed to cover the costs of institutional living if it becomes necessary. With a reverse mortgage, home equity can become a liquid buffer asset which can help reduce exposure to sequence-of-return risk or as reserves for spending shocks. I conclude the chapter with an explanation of the Home Equity Conversion Mortgage program, which is the most common type of reverse mortgage available.

Tax-Efficient Retirement Spending (Chapter 10)

An important aspect of creating efficiencies in the retirement income plan is to make sound decisions with respect to their tax implications. When should taxes be paid to generate the most after-tax spending and legacy for a given asset base? Answering this question requires digging into the intricacies of our progressive tax system. In Chapter 10, which is the longest chapter in the book, I describe tax-efficient retirement planning.

I start with the different tax advantages available in the tax code and how to create tax diversification between taxable, tax-deferred, and tax-exempt accounts. Then I describe asset location, or how to position assets between these different types of accounts. I also mention how to obtain tax advantages for taxable assets that go beyond the space available in tax-deferred or tax-exempt retirement plans.

I also describe important issues for tax-advantaged retirement accounts, including rules for required minimum distributions, early withdrawal penalties and their exceptions, rollovers, transfers, Roth conversions, and the pro-rata rules for IRAs with non-deductible contributions. I also cover the rules for net unrealized appreciation on employer stock.

Then I dive into tax-efficient retirement distributions, including tax bracket management, strategic Roth conversions, and long-term capital gains harvesting. I also cover the pitfalls involved in generating more taxable income, including the Social Security tax torpedo, increased Medicare premiums, and the net investment income surtax. I also describe tax strategies related to charitable giving, and I discuss the widow tax penalty regarding how taxes will likely increase after the death of a spouse. I finish with a detailed example to show how more tax-efficient retirement distributions using strategic Roth conversions can significantly extend retirement portfolio longevity. With the example, a tax-efficient strategy extends retirement sustainability by 5.63 years.

Legacy and Incapacity Planning (Chapter 11)

Chapter 11 shifts to the topic of preparing you and your family for end-of-life issues. I first discuss how to get your finances organized with easy access for those who need it in the event of an emergency. This includes personal and family information, contact information for professionals and service providers you work with, insurance information, medical history, and details about various financial accounts.

Then I shift to other important estate planning issues. The components of an estate plan involve tracking and organizing assets and taking a careful look at how they are titled and whether they include beneficiary designations. You will also want to create a will, decide about whether to create trusts, choose a financial power of attorney, create your advance health care directives, and outline your final wishes.

I then continue the discussion regarding tax-efficiency and tax-planning considerations as it relates to a legacy goal. Tax planning for legacy includes understanding aspects of the tax code related to the step-up in cost basis at death, considering the tax brackets of different beneficiaries, estimating estate taxes, using gifting strategies, and identifying roles for life insurance and irrevocable trusts. It is also important to understand the rules for required minimum distributions from various inherited retirement accounts and annuities as this may impact tax planning decisions such as whether to make strategic Roth conversions.

Non-Financial Aspects of Retirement Success (Chapter 12)

Though Chapter 12 is relatively short, it is vitally important to consider the non-financial aspects for enjoying retirement. Many retirees become bored with retirement because they did not prepare themselves sufficiently to cope with all the free time available in this phase of life. Retirees need to identify their purpose and passion that will provide a reason to get out of bed each morning. How will you like to spend your days in retirement? Retirees may also consider their relationship with work, as it is possible to work in retirement, either part time or even full time and possibly even in a new field. Retirement can provide the financial independence to work because you desire to do so, even at a lower wage or as a volunteer. Being financially independent offers the opportunity to pursue and prioritize work and activities that create meaning and value instead of those that provide the largest paycheck. Continuing to work offers many benefits aside from the income, in terms of staying active and engaged with your communities. Retirees must also plan to ensure that their relationships and social connections remain strong to avoid social isolation. Strengthened relationships with spouses, other family members, and friends deserve your attention and preparation ahead of retirement. Finally, enjoying a healthy and active lifestyle is an important part of enjoying your days and improving your health. An active mind may also help limit the onset of cognitive difficulties. Retirees who plan for these non-financial aspects can be better prepared to manage the various trials and tribulations of retirement and to enjoy stronger life satisfaction.

Putting it All Together (Chapter 13)

We have worked our way through the depths of decision-making for retirement income. We have covered the important decisions for navigating a successful retirement. Now it is time to fit these pieces together into an overall planning approach to achieve financial and non-financial success in retirement. In this chapter, I attempt to organize the previous discussion into an integrated series of steps to take in a somewhat chronological order to be prepared for your best retirement. The simple act of proactively planning for retirement can improve retirement satisfaction and happiness. This chapter puts together the various steps to take before retirement, at certain moments in the transition to retirement, and on an ongoing annual basis when updating your plan. It includes a discussion of the Retirement CARE Analysis™ to finalize answers for various retirement planning questions related to annuity use, asset allocation, and how much to spend from investments. I also include a discussion about working with a financial planner.

Action Plan

This chapter is introductory, laying the groundwork for the rest of the book. Nonetheless, there are a few important takeaways, including the very important matter of determining your retirement income style to guide your approach for sourcing retirement income. Key action items include:

- ☐ Understand the depth of decision-making for retirement.
    - ○ Determine your retirement income style
    - ○ Assess exposure to various retirement risks
    - ○ Quantify your financial goals and assess your preparedness with the funded ratio
    - ○ Understand strategies for sustainable spending from investments
    - ○ Understand strategies using annuities with risk pooling
    - ○ Develop a claiming strategy for Social Security
    - ○ Manage health care and Medicare decisions
    - ○ Plan for long-term care risks
    - ○ Decide about retirement housing and housing wealth
    - ○ Build tax-efficient retirement distribution plans
    - ○ Create plans for legacy and incapacity
    - ○ Prepare for the non-financial aspects of retirement
    - ○ Implement and monitor your retirement plan
- ☐ Understand the factors to identify retirement income preferences and how they interact to define retirement income styles.
- ☐ Determine your preferred retirement income style.

Further Reading

Murguía, Alejandro, and Wade D. Pfau. 2021. "A Model Approach to Selecting a Personalized Retirement Income Strategy." Available at SSRN: https://ssrn.com/abstract=3788425

Chapter 2: Retirement Risks

In this chapter, I review the major retirement risks. We must clarify the meaning of risk from the perspective of retirement and personal finance. When accumulating assets, the financial services profession generally defines risk as short-term market volatility. The ability of a risk-averse investor to stomach portfolio volatility is an important constraint for asset allocation decisions. But this is only part of the story for retirement income. More importantly, the fundamental nature of risk for retirees is the threat that events take place (unexpectedly long life, poor market returns, spending shocks) that trigger a permanently lowered standard of living for subsequent years. Risk for the household relates to the inability to meet financial goals over a long-term planning horizon. Retirees must decide how much risk to their lifestyle they are willing to accept, and this is a different decision than how much short-term volatility they can stomach.

Risk capacity becomes an important concept for retirees. Risk capacity refers to the ability of individuals to experience major portfolio losses without suffering too adverse of an impact on their standard of living. Retirees have less capacity to bear risk, as they become more vulnerable to a reduced standard of living when risks manifest. The first day of retirement can be the riskiest day of one's life. Stable earnings disappear, and it may be very difficult to obtain stable employment earnings again. The financial circumstances for retirees differ from pre-retirees.

As noted, retirement risks generally fall into three categories: longevity risk, market risk, and spending shocks. I will address these in turn. The practical impact of retirement risks is that the amount of assets needed to successfully fund retirement goals is unknown, which becomes a problem when the amount of assets falls short of what is needed.

Longevity Risk

The fundamental risk for retirement is unknown longevity. How long will your retirement plan need to support your budgeted expenses? Potential life spans are uncertain. A new 65-year-old retiree may live for anywhere from another year to more than 40 years. Longevity risk has a huge impact on the cost of sustaining a lifetime spending budget. It is the risk of living longer than anticipated and not having the resources to sustain spending over that longer lifetime.

We have a sense of life expectancies, or how long the average person lives. But the length of retirement could be much shorter or longer than the statistical life expectancy. A long life is wonderful, but it is also costlier and a bigger drain on resources. Half of the population will outlive their statistical life expectancy. And life expectancies continue to increase as scientific progress finds more ways to prolong life. For some retirees, the fear of outliving their resources may exceed the fear of death. This can create a paralyzing effect on retirement spending.

Moshe Milevsky coined the term *longevity risk aversion* to describe the emotions related to how one feels about the possibility of outliving one's retirement assets. Beyond the objective information available about mortality, longevity risk aversion is what will drive a retiree's decision about an appropriate planning age. Those with greater fear of outliving their wealth will seek to build a financial plan that can be sustained to a higher age for which there is a sufficiently low probability to outlive.

This gets to the heart of the retirement income factor related to Front-Loading vs Back-Loading income described in the previous chapter. Those with a Front-Loading preference believe it is optimal to enjoy a higher standard of living while one is still able to do so in early retirement. Later cuts to spending can be made as needed. Those with a preference for Back-Loading will want to assume the possibility of living much longer than average to feel comfortable with their plan, and that will mean either spending less early on to stretch assets out further or relying more on lifetime income protections. These individuals do not want to reduce their standard of living or to be a burden on their children at advanced ages.

This is about the tradeoff between maximizing today's lifestyle by accepting a shorter planning horizon, against protecting lifestyle in the future by spending less today and planning for a longer time horizon. While the probability of surviving to advanced ages is low, individuals must determine how low a level of spending they are willing to accept today in their effort to plan for a longer life and better ensure that they will not deplete their assets before death. Alternatively, as the worry about outliving assets increases, annuities with lifetime income protections will look increasingly attractive. While the annuity-based cost for lifetime income remains the same, the amount of assets needed to feel comfortable about funding retirement with investments will continue to increase as one becomes more longevity risk averse.

What is the optimal way to choose a planning age? When determining longevity, it may seem natural to base calculations on the aggregate US population, but clear socioeconomic differences have been identified in mortality rates. Higher income and wealth levels and more education each correlate with longer lifespans. This may not be a matter of causation (i.e., more income and education cause people to live longer), but perhaps an underlying characteristic leads some people to have a more long-term focus, and that, in turn, may lead them to seek more education and practice better health habits. Though accidents and illnesses will unfortunately lead to some exceptions, the very fact that you are reading this somewhat technical tome on retirement income suggests you probably have a longer-term focus and should at least expect to live longer than the average person. In this case, mortality data based on population-wide averages will underestimate your potential longevity.

It is also important to keep in mind that while life expectancy at birth is a more familiar number, it is of little relevance for someone reaching retirement. If you have reached 65, then an obvious point to note is that you did not die at a prior age. As obvious as it might be, this is important information. As you age, your subsequent life expectancy increases. The remaining number of years one can expect to live decreases, but not on a one-to-one basis with age. We do not say that 90-year-olds have a negative life expectancy, for instance. This matter also leads individuals to underestimate how long they may live in retirement.

There are tools available that provide more precise longevity estimates based on a person's circumstances. Some tools ask many questions about family history and current health to be quite precise, but I would like to describe a simpler tool that can provide a longevity estimate in minutes and without cost. The American Academy of Actuaries and the Society of Actuaries created the Longevity Illustrator [www.longevityillustrator.org] to help users develop personalized estimates for their longevity based on a few questions about age, gender, smoking status, and overall health. This is a simple way to allow for some fine-tuning with respect to longevity estimates. Exhibit 2.1 provides its output as an example for 65-year-olds based on their health assessment and smoking status.

This exhibit provides sufficient details for current 65-year-olds to decide about their planning ages. For example, a nonsmoking 65-year-old female in average health who is willing to accept a 10 percent chance for outliving her financial plan would want her plan to work to age 98. For a male with the same characteristics, age 96 corresponds to accepting the same amount of longevity risk. If these two individuals were married and therefore need to plan for the possibility that at least one of them is alive, then 100 becomes the age where there is a 10 percent chance of survival. With two people, the probability that at least one of them is still alive at an advanced age is higher than for just one person alone, as now there are two chances for this to happen.

In 1994, William Bengen chose 30 years as a conservative planning horizon for a 65-year-old couple when he discussed sustainable retirement spending. At that time, he assumed it was sufficiently unlikely for couples to have anyone live past 95. But as mortality improves over time, this planning horizon is becoming less conservative, especially for nonsmokers in reasonable health. In fact, we can see that the 50th percentile of longevity for a non-smoking couple in excellent health is age 94. This means that 95 is much closer to a life expectancy than to a conservative planning age needed to reasonably reduce the chance of outliving the retirement plan. For these couples, 25 percent will still have one member alive at age 98, and 10 percent of them will still have someone living at age 102!

Exhibit 2.1
Planning Ages for 65-Year-Olds from the Longevity Illustrator
Individuals born on January 1, 1956

	Males					
	Nonsmoker			**Smoker**		
Health Classification	Excellent	Average	Poor	Excellent	Average	Poor
Chance of Survival						
90%	73	72	70	68	67	66
75%	81	78	75	73	71	69
50%	88	85	82	79	77	74
25%	94	91	88	86	83	79
10%	98	96	93	92	89	84

	Females					
	Nonsmoker			**Smoker**		
Health Classification	Excellent	Average	Poor	Excellent	Average	Poor
Chance of Survival						
90%	76	74	72	70	69	67
75%	83	81	78	75	73	71
50%	90	88	85	83	80	77
25%	96	94	91	90	87	83
10%	101	98	96	96	93	88

	Couples - Either Individual is Alive					
	Nonsmoker			**Smoker**		
Health Classification	Excellent	Average	Poor	Excellent	Average	Poor
Chance of Survival						
90%	84	82	79	76	74	71
75%	89	87	84	81	79	75
50%	94	92	89	87	84	80
25%	98	96	93	92	89	85
10%	102	100	97	98	94	89

Source: American Academy of Actuaries and Society of Actuaries, Actuaries Longevity Illustrator, http://www.longevityillustrator.org/, (accessed February 8, 2021).

We can now return to the question of choosing a planning age. This is a personal decision to be based partly on objective characteristics: gender, smoking status, health status and history, family health history, and other socioeconomic characteristics that correlate with mortality. It is also based on an individual's answers to more subjective questions: how do you feel about outliving your investment portfolio, and what would be the impact on your standard of living if you outlived your portfolio? With the Longevity Illustrator, these subjective factors can point to which percentile of your estimated longevity distribution to use. As a general starting point, the 25th percentile survival ages may be more applicable to those with a reasonable Front-Loading preference, while the 10th percentile survival ages may be more applicable to those with a reasonable Back-Loading preference. One could consider going more extreme than this in either direction, but these values provided by the Longevity Illustrator are reasonable anchor points. The Longevity Illustrator or a related tool can also be used if you are at a different age than shown in the exhibit to get appropriate estimates for your personal circumstances.

Market and Sequence-of-return risk

A similar story exists regarding market risk. Markets are volatile. Market volatility causes investment returns to vary over time. Even with an average market return in mind, it is possible that markets could perform at a below average rate for a prolonged period. Related to this, market volatility is further amplified by the growing impact of sequence-of-return risk in retirement. This is the heightened vulnerability individuals face regarding the realized investment portfolio returns in the years around their retirement date—it adds to the uncertainty by making retirement outcomes more contingent on a shorter period of investment returns. What rate of return is one comfortable assuming for the investment portfolio during retirement? The lower is the assumed rate of return, the easier it will be for the financial plan to exceed that hurdle and to work. With a higher assumed return, it will be harder for the portfolio to keep pace and there will be greater risk for the plan to fail. The implications of market risk work in the same manner as longevity risk. That is, just as one seeks to plan for a long retirement with a low chance to outlive, one must also build a plan that will be robust to below average market returns. In this section, we explore the market risks for different investment options.

Risks for Fixed-Income Assets

Bonds and related fixed-income assets provide a starting point for thinking about funding retirement goals with investments. A bond is a contractual obligation to make a series of payments on specific dates. Typically, this includes interest payments made on a semiannual basis until the maturity date and the return of the bond's face value at maturity. Bonds are issued by both governments and private corporations to raise funds, and they are purchased by investors seeking an investment return on their capital. Bank

CDs also function as a type of bond in terms of providing cash flows at specified dates, though they are not traded on secondary markets.

Market risk is frequently considered as exclusively applying to the stock market, but bonds are also exposed to price volatility and the risk of capital losses. Bond interest rates—both coupon rates and the yields subsequently provided to investors—are determined by the interaction of supply and demand for the bonds as they continue to be traded. Rising interest rates will lower prices for existing bonds, so the subsequent return to the new purchaser can match the higher returns available on new bonds with higher interest rates. Conversely, lower interest rates will increase the selling price for existing bonds. If sold at their face value, these older bonds offer higher returns than newly issued bonds, and their owners will want to hold them. An agreeable selling price can only be found if the bond sells at a premium, and then the new purchaser receives a subsequent return on their purchase price that is in line with newly issued bonds. The price of a bond on the secondary market will fluctuate in the opposite direction of interest rates. Bond funds can therefore experience capital gains and losses in the same manner as stocks. This is called interest rate risk.

In the universe of bonds, there is not one single interest rate. Differences in interest rates among bonds reflect several factors that point to other types of bond risks:

- the time to maturity for the bond (longer-term bonds will experience more price volatility as interest rates change)
- the credit risk of the bond (bonds that are more likely to default on their promised payments are riskier and will have to reward investors with higher yields)
- liquidity (bonds that are less actively traded may offer higher yields as investors will demand an additional return premium for sacrificing liquidity)
- the tax status of the bond (municipal bonds from state and local government agencies are free from federal income taxes and thus offer lower interest rates to be more equivalent to taxable bonds on a net-of-tax basis)

Bond prices fluctuate as buyers and sellers shift to new equilibriums for pricing underlying risks related to maturity, credit, and liquidity. Bonds may also feature other options that affect the price an investor is willing to pay. For instance, if the bond is *callable* (meaning the issuer retains the right to repay it early if interest rates decline), the potential capital gains from a fall in interest rates are reduced, which lowers the price investors will pay.

US government treasuries are generally seen as having the lowest credit risk and high liquidity, and they will generally offer lower yields than corporate bonds with the same maturity date. They are less likely to default and create problems for borrowers to receive what is owed. They are backed by the full faith and credit of the US government. Treasuries are also free from state and local taxes.

As a bond provides a contractual right to a series of future payments received at specified points of time, the price for a bond is simply the present discounted value of its future cash flows. Bonds with more distant maturity dates typically offer higher interest rates than bonds with earlier maturity dates, since their prices (the present value of future payments) fluctuate more with changing rates, making them riskier to hold.

A *zero-coupon bond* provides only the bond's face value at maturity. It will be sold at a discount to the face value to provide a return and compensate for the risks related to holding it. A *coupon bond* provides the face value at maturity in addition to a series of coupon payments (often on a semiannual basis) until the maturity date. The *coupon rate* is contractually defined as a percentage of the face value.

The *yield to maturity* for a bond is the internal rate of return an investor will earn by holding the bond to maturity and receiving its cash flows. It is the return the investor would get for buying the bond today at its current asking price and holding it to maturity. If the price matches the face value, then the yield will be the same as the coupon rate. The yield to maturity for a new investor differs from the coupon rate whenever the bond sells for a different price than its face value. If the ask price is higher, then the yield will be less than the coupon, and if the ask price is lower, then the yield will be higher than the coupon. The *yield curve* shows the yields to maturity for a series of bonds—typically US Treasury bonds—with the same credit quality but different maturity dates.

It is also important to address inflation and how to think about bonds when they are meant to fund a liability, such as a retirement spending goal, that grows with the consumer price index for inflation. Fortunately, this is now practical as the United States began issuing Treasury Inflation-Protected Securities (TIPS) in 1997. The face value and coupon payments for TIPS are both indexed to keep pace with inflation and preserve purchasing power, and their yields are quoted in real inflation-adjusted terms. Whenever positive inflation (as opposed to deflation) is expected, real yields will be less than the nominal yields quoted on traditional bonds. As an approximation:

real interest rate = nominal interest rate − expected inflation rate

For TIPS, the nominal yields are not known in advance because they depend on the subsequently realized inflation experience. Conversely, we know nominal yields for traditional bonds, but their real yields can only be known after observing the realized path of inflation up to the maturity date. If inflation is unexpectedly high, then the real return on nominal bonds is less. TIPS, on the other hand, keep pace with higher inflation because it triggers a higher nominal return above their underlying real interest rate. Essentially, TIPS provide protection from unexpected inflation. They outperform treasuries when inflation exceeds the implied break-even inflation rate. This is a valuable attribute when spending is expected to grow with inflation. Retirees generally get more use from insurance that protects from *high* inflation, making TIPS a more natural candidate for retirement portfolios.

Investors may expect a positive nominal return on their investment (otherwise, there is no reason to invest), but that return may not offer the capacity to keep pace with inflation. Unlike traditional bonds, TIPS yields are quoted as real interest rates, and real interest rates can be negative. An auction for a five-year note held in October 2010 made headlines as the real yield dipped below zero (to -0.55 percent) for the first time. Though surprising at the time, negative yields for TIPS have become the norm in recent years. Even the 30-year TIPS yield fell below zero in March 2020.

With TIPS, we now have a better idea of market expectations for future inflation, though I would not call it perfect. TIPS offer a break-even inflation rate, defined as the difference in yields on the same maturity of traditional treasuries and TIPS. TIPS yields may not reflect the true underlying real interest rate because they have a few other components built into their pricing, including a premium for their relative illiquidity since they represent a smaller market than treasuries. Also, TIPs offer a potential additional premium for the protection they provide against unexpected high inflation. Nonetheless, the difference between Treasury and TIPS rates for the same maturity represents a reasonable market estimate of future inflation expectations.

We can also consider the distinction between holding bond funds and individual bonds. Holding individual fixed-income securities to their maturity provides a way to protect funds earmarked for upcoming expenses. This can be attractive to those preferring a time-segmented approach to retirement income. Time segmentation uses individual bonds to support short to medium-term spending, with a more aggressive investment portfolio with higher expected returns to be deployed for long-term expenses. Holding bonds to maturity avoids locking in any potential capital losses, as the cash flows provided by the bond, including the return of face value at maturity, are known in advance. With bond funds, the possibility of holding to maturity is not meaningful and capital losses can occur when shares are sold to cover spending.

One other risk that we should mention for bonds is timing risk. This is the risk of retiring in a low-interest rate environment that makes funding retirement more expensive. It is an important problem that today's retirees face. With less interest income, retirees will be forced to spend principal, meaning that a retirement spending goal cannot be sustained for as long as it otherwise would. It is important to emphasize that, as a retirement income tool, bonds of any type do not mitigate longevity risk. Creating a bond ladder to fund retirement expenses will eventually lead to the depletion of those assets. Low interest rates will cause this to happen sooner rather than later.

When current interest rates are lower than the historical averages, the historical average return is not relevant for someone seeking to estimate future market returns. Most retirement planning software gets this point wrong. The general problem with attempting to gain insights from the historical outcomes is that future market returns are connected to the current values for the sources of market returns, rather than to their historical performance.

Returns on bonds depend on the initial bond yield and on subsequent yield changes. Low bond yields will tend to translate into lower returns due to less income and the heightened interest rate risk associated with capital losses when interest rates rise. Historically, the relationship between interest rates and subsequent bond returns has been quite tight. Decreasing interest rates provide the only mechanism for bond returns to outpace bond yields. As interest rates have experienced a gradual decline since the early 1980s, this has been a common feature of bonds. But the possibility for further declining interest rates is limited when bond yields already start from a low point.

If the objective for an asset base is to fund a specific stream of spending on a year-by-year basis for a known length of time, the least risky way to accomplish this is to build a bond ladder. If the securities do not default, bond ladders provide intended cash flows to match spending liabilities at the appropriate dates. If spending grows with inflation, TIPS will provide protection from unexpectedly high inflation. Traditional bonds will work for spending that does not grow with inflation, or that otherwise grows at a fixed rate that is known in advance and can be incorporated into the ladder construction. Holding bonds to maturity avoids realizing interest rate risk, but if bonds are held as mutual funds, then the risk of capital losses may be realized when selling shares to fund expenses.

Risks for Stocks

Most people associate stocks with the asset class most exposed to market risk. The reason to include stocks in a retirement portfolio is their potential to generate higher returns than bonds. If this potential for higher returns is realized, the overall cost of retirement will be reduced based on the amount of assets that is needed at the beginning of retirement to avoid cutting spending later in retirement and/or running out of money in retirement. More of the future spending can be covered by portfolio gains than by the initial savings. Those comfortable with stock investments believe they will provide a risk premium, meaning that stocks will outperform bonds over reasonable lengths of time. The additional growth potential of stocks can then more easily support a lifetime spending goal than bonds alone. While the risk premium brings market risk back into the mix, the idea is that this risk is sufficiently low, and a diversified portfolio provides stronger performance.

The case for using an aggressive investment portfolio with a high stock allocation to fund retirement expenses rests on the idea that it will *probably* work, based on the premise that stocks have historically performed better than other asset classes, including bonds. Advocates for using aggressive investment portfolios as the primary way to fund a retirement plan often will allude to the concept of "stocks for the long run." There is a degree of comfort that an aggressive portfolio will provide sufficient returns in time to maintain retirement sustainability.

In terms of the RISA Profile and retirement income styles, I am describing preferences and attitudes associated with probability-based, optionality, front-loading, technical liquidity, and accumulation. Retirees with this style will often seek to create a diversified portfolio including higher allocations to riskier asset classes like stocks to provide growth for spending, liquidity, and legacy. Stocks are also important for other RISA Profiles, but in other cases such confidence about stock market growth is dampened and does not play such a pivotal of role in overall retirement funding.

Stocks are important for retirees, so this topic is worth a deeper exploration. Stocks simply provide an ownership stake in a company. They provide access to company earnings based on its future performance. Companies can pay dividends to their stockholders to distribute profits, or they can reinvest profits into the firm to lay the foundation for better performance and even larger dividends to owners in the future.

A company's stock price can rise when investors anticipate stronger future performance than they previously anticipated, which can serve as a source of capital gains for stock owners who sell shares. However, there are no contractual protections to receive either capital gains or dividends. In the ownership structure, stockholders are residual claimants, meaning that their rights to receive firm earnings or assets fall behind most other claimants like bond holders or lenders. A company could underperform relative to expectations, and the stock price could decrease in anticipation of a reduced ability for the company to pay dividends in the future. The returns from a stock over a specified holding period are the dividend payments it makes plus any capital gains or capital losses. For owners having to sell shares after a price decline, stocks could underperform relative to bonds.

The value of a stock can be estimated as the present value of its anticipated future dividend payments. This concept is the same as bond pricing, in terms of being a discounted present value of future cash flows, except that there are no contractual protections to support any anticipated dividends. Projections of company performance can change over time, leading to fluctuations in stock prices. With this price volatility, funding retirement expenses by selling stocks can be risky as stock prices may be in decline at the time they need to be sold, requiring more shares to be sold to meet an expense.

Mutual funds and exchange-traded funds (ETFs) provide a simple way for household investors to diversify across a broad range of company stocks. These same investment vehicles exist for bonds as well. Stocks ETFs and mutual funds provide a collection of securities that help to reduce the individual risks of companies by diversifying across a broader range of companies. By limiting exposure to individual companies, this also limits exposure to company specific risks. If company specific risks are independent from one another, then this diversification leaves investors exposed to the overall systematic market risk for the collection of stock holdings, but this diversification creates less overall volatility.

Investors prefer certainty to uncertainty. A bond provides a known yield with contractual protections helping to ensure that its return is realized if the bond is held to maturity. Stock returns are more uncertain, as they depend on the future performance of the company as well as on changing investor perceptions about the company. If a stock offered the same average return as bonds, but with greater volatility around that average, the typical risk averse investor would not be willing to purchase it. Risk averse individuals are willing to pay more to receive certainty, so less-volatile assets should have lower expected returns. To accept risk, investors will seek a higher expected return over time than they could receive from more reliable bonds. That higher expected return represents the risk premium. Stocks can generally be expected to outperform bonds over time, but such outperformance is not predictable and there can be reasonably long stretches in which stock returns lag bonds.

The potential risk premium to be earned by stocks provides the key for why retirees may want to own them. We need to measure that potential risk premium. There are a couple of ways to express average market returns when we consider the relative returns of stocks and bonds. The first is the *arithmetic mean return*. It is calculated by adding up all the annual returns from the historical data and then dividing by the number of years in the data set. The arithmetic mean represents the average historical growth rate over a single year, but it does not reflect the growth rate over a longer period. The *compounded return* represents the growth rate over multiple years, and it is always less than the arithmetic mean for any volatile asset. For long-term investors, it is the compounded return that matters.

To understand the volatility effect on compounded returns, realize that positive and negative returns do not create a symmetric impact on wealth. Negative returns must be followed by even larger positive returns to get back to the initial level. For instance, a 50 percent drop requires a 100 percent gain to break even. For this reason, wealth will grow at a lower compounded rate than the arithmetic average. Compounded returns take a larger haircut as the volatility of returns increases.

The volatility of returns is typically measured by the standard deviation, which quantifies the degree of fluctuations experienced around the average outcome. Approximately, two-thirds of the returns fall within the range of one standard deviation around the arithmetic mean. The remaining one-third of historical returns were even more extreme in either direction. Volatility reduces the predictability for realized returns. When thinking of risk as volatility, we generally care most about the risk for losses, but if market returns are symmetric around an average, then using standard deviation will work just as well.

With this understanding, we can consider returns from the historical data. A good starting point for understanding the risk premium offered by stocks is to consider the historical returns for different asset classes as determined with Morningstar and Ibbotson Associates data. They have compiled US financial market returns since 1926 in their *SBBI (Stocks, Bonds, Bills, and Inflation) Yearbook*. This data is usually the source for calculating average historical market performance and creating assumptions for future portfolio returns. We can use this data as a starting point for understanding about historical market performance. We will focus on two asset classes, large-capitalization US stocks and intermediate-term US government bonds, as these serve as the foundation for the 4 percent rule guiding total-return investment approaches and will be an important topic in Chapter 4.

For large-capitalization US stocks, as represented by the S&P 500 index since its creation in the 1950s, and a more general index of large companies in the years before that, the arithmetic mean return between 1926 and 2020 was 12.2 percent. As new data is added each year, this value tends to fluctuate around roughly 12 percent, which is why that number is used on occasion as an estimate for stocks returns. The historical standard deviation was 19.7 percent (roughly 20 percent). This suggests that roughly two-thirds of the historical annual returns fell between -7.5 percent and 31.9 percent. The volatility impact was such that these stocks grew over time at an average compounded rate of 10.3 percent over this 95-year historical period.

Moving to bonds, Morningstar data shows that since 1926, the arithmetic mean return from intermediate-term government bonds was 5.3 percent with a standard deviation of 5.6 percent. With the lower volatility, the compounded return is only slightly less at 5.1 percent. Among the universe of bond choices, retirement income studies generally show the most favorable results with intermediate-term government bonds. They provide an appropriate balance between generating higher yields while also maintaining lower volatility to avoid jeopardizing the spending goals for the portfolio. Including more types of bonds, such as corporate bonds, long-term bonds, or short-term bills, can be justified for reasons other than maximizing the sustainable spending rate from a portfolio.

We have described nominal historical returns, which include the historical average inflation of about 2.9 percent. The real historical returns after removing inflation put the analysis on a consistent basis over time so that the long-run spending plans can be discussed in terms of constant purchasing power. If we remove inflation from the historical data, the respective arithmetic real returns for this stock and bond data were 9.1 percent and 2.4 percent. The historical standard deviations for these real returns were 19.7 percent and 6.6 percent. For the compounded returns that reflect longer-term real growth rates, historically the S&P 500 provided an inflation-adjusted compounded return of 7.2 percent and intermediate-term governments bonds grew at 2.2 percent above inflation. The real historical risk premium for stocks over bonds with these asset classes is 6.7 percent in arithmetic terms and 5 percent in compounded terms.

These are the historical averages. For a lifetime financial plan, the most intuitive way to express a portfolio return assumption is as an inflation-adjusted (or real) compounding return. In the historical data, those were the 7.2 percent and 2.2 percent numbers mentioned. But simple analyses based on these returns as estimates for what retirees should expect in the future may provide an incomplete picture that overstates the potential for specific investment strategies. In addition to accounting for the impacts of volatility and inflation, it is also important to consider lower interest rates, investment fees, investor behavior, asset allocation, and taxes. Another important matter is to adjust to a lower-than-average return to allow for a higher probability of plan success. All too often, it seems that examples about retirement planning are based on assumptions that investments will grow at a fixed 8 percent or more. While not impossible, the reality is that such return assumptions are overly optimistic, especially for those approaching retirement.

The first issue to consider is the reality that interest rates are lower today than their historical averages. The real yield on a 5-year TIPS at the present has fluctuated around -1.5 percent. That is 3.7 percent less than the historical real compounded return we noted for intermediate-term bonds. Current interest rates are the best predictors for subsequent bond returns, so it will be difficult for bonds to achieve their historical averages. And if we believe that the risk premium for stocks should not be higher at the present, we might assume that stock returns will be lower in the future because of low bond yields. A common way to estimate stock returns is to add an equity premium to a bond yield. This technique for estimating returns is known as the capital asset pricing model. This model was developed by William Sharpe in the 1960s, and he was awarded a Nobel Prize in economics for his work in 1990 alongside Harry Markowitz.

The model posits that the expected return on a financial asset is equal to a risk-free rate of return plus a risk premium multiplied by a factor showing the relationship between the asset and the overall market portfolio. For an overall market index like the S&P 500, this suggests that its return should be equal to the return provided by low-risk assets like Treasury bonds plus a risk premium to account for the volatility of stocks. Adding the 5 percent historical compounded real premium from stocks to the lower TIPS yield suggests a forward-looking compounded real return of 3.5 percent for stocks. If stocks continue to provide their historical average returns while bond yields are lower, this implies that stocks are providing a higher than historical return premium over bonds. While this outcome is possible, someone developing conservative planning assumptions for their retirement would probably not be comfortable with such an assumption. Even if interest rates were to increase later in retirement, sequence-of-return risk describes how upcoming returns matter most. Therefore, it is a good idea to make an adjustment for returns necessary to obtain a more realistic picture about retirement sustainability.

Sustainable spending rates for retirees are intricately related to the returns provided by the underlying investment portfolio. And with sequence-of-return risk, the returns experienced early on will weigh disproportionately on outcomes. For those already spending, the assumption that returns will one day normalize to their historical averages is much less relevant than it is for accumulators who will rely on more distant market returns. Current market conditions are much more relevant in retirement, which means it would be a mistake to blindly apply a historical average return without further thought.

Also, while a risk premium must be expected to induce investors to position their assets into more volatile investments, there is no reason to necessarily believe that historical excess returns provide the best predictors about the future risk premium. The risk premium could be lower in the future. Reasons for this include the possibility for random differences, a realization that premiums could be more aligned with the lower international experience, or that higher stock market valuations could create less relative overperformance for stocks. Also, it may take longer than anticipated for returns on stocks to outpace bonds, and retirees who are taking distributions are vulnerable to this waiting game.

Another factor for making assumptions about net portfolio returns is fees. The assumed return may need to be reduced further to account for any fee drag associated with the management of the underlying investments. The index returns do not account for real-world investment expenses. It is possible to find index funds with low expense ratios, but the expenses for some actively managed funds can exceed 1 percent or even 1.5 percent per year. These are the operating expenses. There can also be an additional 12b-1 fee on some mutual funds to help cover marketing and distribution costs for the investment company. These expenses are listed separately from the operating expense ratio and must not be ignored.

Some mutual funds will also charge a front-end or back-end load as a percentage of the assets when mutual funds are bought or sold. Beyond these explicit expenses, mutual funds may underperform market indices on account of the transaction costs for trading inside the fund and for tax inefficiencies created by fund turnover. In a 2014 article for the *Financial Analysts Journal*, John Bogle estimated that the all-in expenses for actively managed mutual funds could add up to as much as 2.27 percent before the tax impact. Investment fees reduce portfolio returns accordingly. A 7 percent gross return with a 1 percent fee leads to a 6 percent net return, for instance. It is the latter number that matters.

A related matter is investor behavior. Are investors disciplined enough to stay the course with an investment strategy to earn the underlying index market returns? In times of market stress, it is important for retirees to stick with their financial plans and the asset allocation that matches their tolerance for market volatility. Studies on retirement spending from investment portfolios typically assume that retirees are rational investors who rebalance right on schedule each year to their rather aggressive stock allocations. They never panic and sell their stocks after a market downturn.

For many retirees, this may not describe their reality. Unfortunately, investors in financial markets tend to do the opposite of what happens in most other markets: they buy more when prices are high and sell when prices are low. This causes returns to drag behind what a "buy, hold, and rebalance" investor could have earned. To the extent that households fall victim to bad behaviors, the net returns and sustainable spending rates from their investments will be less than otherwise possible. The behavior gap refers to the concept that investor behavior may cause real individuals to underperform relative to index market returns.

This behavior gap has been estimated at a couple percentage points per year. For instance, Vanguard's study of Advisor's Alpha identifies the most important factor explaining investor underperformance is a lack of behavioral coaching to help investors stay the course and stick with their plans. They estimate that having the wherewithal to stay the course in times of market stress could add 1.5 percent of additional annualized returns to the portfolios of typical investors. In other words, without behavioral coaching, the typical investor could expect to underperform the markets by 1.5 percent per year due to poor decision-making.

Asset allocation decisions are also relevant. Though many articles about long-term investing will assume 8 or 12 percent returns, this implicitly suggests that the investor holds 100 percent stocks. That will rarely be the case, especially for retirees. As the asset allocation shifts from stocks to bonds, the portfolio returns and standard deviations both decrease. As retirees often seek to reduce their stock allocation in retirement, it becomes important to base return assumptions on a more bond-heavy portfolio that will have a lower expected return than a high-stock portfolio.

An asset allocation adjustment could also result in compounded returns that are larger than simple portfolios of just stocks and bonds. A more diversified portfolio including international assets, alternative investments, real estate, and small-cap stocks could serve to increase the arithmetic mean. Or diversification could reduce portfolio volatility, which can provide a lift for the compounded return even if the arithmetic mean does not change. Though it would entail risk, one might also wish to assign a premium to the return assumption to account for a belief that the investment manager can beat the returns on the underlying indices.

Another issue afflicting retirees is that tax drag will affect returns, as ongoing taxes for interest, dividends, and realized capital gains must be paid with the passage of time. Chapter 10 discusses these tax issues more deeply. Bogle estimated the tax impact for taxable assets as an additional 0.75 percent reduction in annual returns.

A final issue is that earlier we only identified average stock and bond returns. A simple approach for building a financial plan is to decide on a rate of return for the investment portfolio and to plug that value into a spreadsheet to represent an assumed rate of asset growth. When we wish for higher confidence that a plan will work, we do not plug in estimates for average returns. The average will only work half of the time. A lower return is assumed to have a plan that can work more than half of the time. In Chapter 3, I will discuss calculating a funded ratio using bond yields as the assumed return. Assuming a higher return than bonds requires risk.

More generally, Monte Carlo simulations provide an alternative that is now widely used in financial planning software. Simulations are used to develop sequences of random market returns fitting predetermined characteristics to test how financial plans will perform in a wider variety of good and bad market environments. The use of Monte Carlo tools has increased considerably over the past decades, which can likely be attributed to lower computing costs, increased recognition that returns are random, and the desire to provide more robust financial plans. A thousand or more simulations could be created to test the robustness of a retirement plan in many market environments. Historical data is commonly used to set these input characteristics. Most financial planning software works in this way. It is possible to adjust the inputs for the factors we covered, including fees, tax drag, and low interest rates. This is frequently ignored.

With Monte Carlo financial planning software, retirees generally focus on building a plan that achieves a high probability of success, such as 80 or 90 percent. This implicitly means the underlying assumed return is below average. But when thinking in terms of a fixed return assumption, we usually consider what we view as the best guess for future returns. Again, the best guess only implies a 50 percent chance for success. To be consistent with Monte Carlo planning based on a high probability of success, we must further scale down a fixed rate of return from our best guess estimate. This is a point which many investment management professionals have not internalized into their thinking, as they are conditioned to using their idea about average returns as the input.

Stock market risk relates to the idea that while stocks can be expected to provide higher average returns than bonds, they do create more risk. A retirement plan which relies on experiencing high market returns can fail when those returns are not realized, especially in the pivotal early years of retirement when the returns matter most. This creates the same general issue as with longevity risk in that retirees may feel forced to assume lower portfolio returns to ensure a sufficiently robust plan. When developing return assumptions, it is important to adjust returns for lower compounded growth, inflation, interest rates, fees, investor behavior, asset allocation, taxes, and a desire to be conservative. Only then can we have confidence in the viability of the retirement plan.

Lifetime Sequence-of-Return Risk

When seeking to use portfolio returns as a source of retirement spending, retirees must also deal with the sequence-of-return risk that amplifies the impact of traditional investment volatility. Financial market returns near the retirement date matter a great deal. Even with the same average returns over a long period of time, retiring at the start of a bear market is very dangerous because your wealth can be depleted quite rapidly, and little may be left to benefit from any subsequent market recovery. With sequence risk for portfolio distributions, the extra shares sold to meet a spending goal when markets are down are no longer available to experience the growth of any subsequent market recovery. The financial market returns experienced in the fragile decade around the retirement date matter a great deal more than retirees may realize.

Though sequence-of-return risk is related to general investment risk and market volatility, it differs from general investment risk. The average market return over a 30-year retirement period could be quite generous. But if negative returns are experienced when you start spending from your portfolio, you will face a difficult hurdle to overcome even if the market offers higher returns later in retirement. This matter increases the impacts of volatility risks described in the previous sections.

The dynamics of sequence risk suggest that a prolonged recessionary environment early in retirement could jeopardize the retirement prospects for a particular cohort of retirees. That scenario does not imply a large-scale economic catastrophe. This is a subtle but important point. Some retirees could experience very poor retirement outcomes relative to those retiring a few years earlier or later. Sustainable withdrawal rates can fall below what would be expected for average market returns over long periods of time, because the ordering of those returns matters.

Individual investors are vulnerable to the sequence of market returns experienced over their investing lifetimes. Individuals who behave in the same way over their careers—saving the same percentage of the same salary for the same number of years—can experience disparate outcomes based solely on the specific sequence of investment returns that accompanies their career and retirement. Actual wealth accumulations and sustainable withdrawal rates will vary substantially among retirees, as these outcomes depend disproportionately on the shorter sequence of returns just around the retirement date. Returning to the labor force becomes increasingly difficult and a market drop can be devastating.

Exhibit 2.2 attempts to give a clearer picture of how sequence-of-return risk impacts both the accumulation and distribution phases, and how the impact also grows with retirement distributions. The exhibit is based on statistical regression analysis, which determines how much of the outcome (wealth accumulation or sustainable withdrawal rate) can be explained by the returns experienced in each year of the investing life cycle. The exhibit isolates the impact of each year's return on lifetime outcomes using a larger sample of one million Monte Carlo simulations based on a 50 percent stock portfolio with the same characteristics as the historical data. For the first 30 years (when individuals are saving), the portion of the final wealth accumulation at the retirement date that can be explained continues to grow. With wealth accumulations at insignificant levels in the early part of one's career, the early returns have very little impact on the absolute level of wealth accumulated at the end of the savings period. But as retirement approaches, a given percentage return produces an increasing impact on the final wealth value in absolute terms as those returns impact more years of contributions.

Exhibit 2.2
Lifetime Sequence-of-Return Risk
50/50 Asset Allocation, Inflation-Adjusted Spending
1,000,000 Monte Carlo Simulations Based on SBBI Data, 1926–2020,
S&P 500 and Intermediate-Term Government Bonds

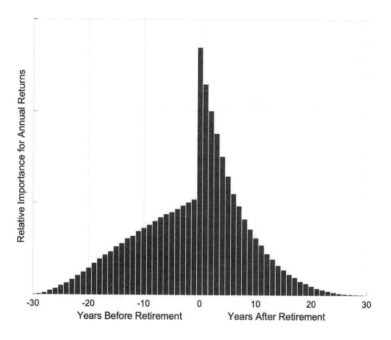

In years 31 through 60, during the retirement distribution phase, the exhibit shows the impact of each year's return on the maximum sustainable withdrawal rate. The return in the first retirement year has the biggest impact on the level of sustainable retirement spending. Retirees are extremely vulnerable to what happens just after they retire. As one moves further into retirement, returns have a rapidly decreasing impact, as the outcome for that retirement (high or low sustainable spending) was already set in motion during the first 5-10 years.

Sequence-of-return risk affects individuals throughout their entire investing lives. Individuals from different birth cohorts who otherwise behave in identical ways may experience dramatically different wealth accumulations and sustainable withdrawal rates. These outcomes are unpredictable. Strategies using a volatile portfolio to target a wealth accumulation goal or to sustain a constant spending strategy expose individuals to much greater risk than you might expect when thinking about average market returns over a 60-year investing cycle.

Spending Shocks and Other Surprises

If one could determine the precise amount to be spent in each year of retirement, with no spending shock surprises to increase the spending need, the risks for meeting that spending goal would reflect longevity and market risk. A third category of risks for retirees are those that could cause higher than anticipated spending needs. These are spending shocks. As we discuss these, there are a few that may not strictly be spending shocks, but they still fit well into this discussion because they shrink the asset base available to fund expenses. A primary example of this type of surprise is an involuntary early retirement or an inability to find work in retirement. Likewise, a risk like cognitive decline could be realized as an increase in unanticipated expenses, or it could simply lead to mistakes that reduce assets in unanticipated ways. The point is that the cost of funding retirement expenses, in terms of the assets needed at the beginning, may be greater than anticipated. Ultimately, retirees must preserve flexibility and liquidity to manage unplanned expenses. When attempting to budget over a long retirement, it is important to include allowances for such contingencies. Here we describe the different types of shocks for which retirees may include reserves as additional protection.

Long-term care needs

Perhaps the biggest potential spending shock for most retirees will be the need to pay for an extended stay in an institutional setting to help manage long-term care needs. As a result of physical and mental decline, retirees may eventually need assistance with performing the basic activities of daily living. Those with extended care needs could find significant costs added to their retirements. This risk is so significant that I devote an entire chapter to it (Chapter 8). To avoid being repetitive, please refer to that chapter for a detailed discussion of planning for long-term care risks.

Rising health care and prescription costs

Another important spending shock that receives an entire chapter devoted to it is health care expenses in retirement (Chapter 7). Health care prices tend to grow faster than consumer inflation, and it is hard to know how to plan for distant health care costs. Health care costs typically rise with age, but they can vary greatly based on how long one lives and what types of diseases or health risks impact an individual. Again, to avoid having overlapping discussions, please see Chapter 7 for a detailed discussion of managing health care expenses in retirement.

Inflation

Retirees face the risk that inflation will erode the purchasing power of their savings as they progress through retirement. Low inflation may not be noticeable in the short term, but it can have a big impact over a lengthy retirement, leaving retirees vulnerable. For instance, with 3 percent average annual inflation, the purchasing power of a dollar will fall by more than half in twenty-three years. That type of increase essentially doubles the cost of living. If we experience a bout of higher inflation, the risks are even greater that spending needs will grow in an unsustainable manner.

To manage inflation risk, retirees must ensure that they are including inflation in their projections for future expenses. This can be done by assuming a particular inflation rate for the retirement plan and then adjusting expenses over time for inflation, or by treating spending in today's dollars but then projecting assets at a real rate of return that has inflation removed. If realized inflation ends up lower than assumed, this will strengthen the plan as less spending will be needed and more will be left as legacy. However, inflation risk is manifested if realized inflation is higher than assumed. This would cause retirement spending to increase faster than anticipated, raising the overall costs of the plan. Higher inflation can be understood as a spending shock, as retirement expenses will grow larger than anticipated in the retirement budget.

Inflation can be easier to manage during the working years as salaries often increase with inflation. This can create a shock at retirement as most retirement assets, aside from Social Security, do not contain automatic increases to offset inflation. TIPS and I-bonds do provide an opportunity to manage inflation risk by providing a real rate of return with realized inflation added to the payments.

The common measure for inflation is the Consumer Price Index for All Urban Consumers (CPI-U). But it will not match the actual inflation experience of any individual household purchasing a different basket of goods than assumed in the government calculations. The Bureau of Labor Statistics has also created an experimental CPI for the elderly (CPI-E) that suggests their consumption basket cost may grow at a faster overall rate. One way to also deal with this issue in practice is to use different inflation rates for different types of expenses. For instance, health expenses could be projected to grow faster than the overall inflation rate. TIPS are presented by some as the perfect hedge for retirement spending, but that is only true if a retiree's spending grows at the same rate as the CPI-U and one also does have to worry about longevity risk.

On the other hand, the spending of many households will not keep pace with inflation in retirement as their consumption basket changes over time. Even though inflation will raise the costs of goods and services, a retiree may naturally consume less with age, which means their overall budget will not grow as quickly as the inflation rate. Strategies to help manage inflation include assuming a reasonable inflation rate for spending, deferring Social Security, using TIPS and I-bonds, choosing investments with growth prospects at least as strong as inflation, and holding additional reserve assets to treat high inflation as a spending shock.

Death of a spouse

Beyond the devastation of losing a loved one, significant economic risks can also surround the death of a spouse. Assets can decrease with the loss of Social Security and pension benefits, taxes can increase as the survivor transitions to filing as single, and household expenses may not decrease by enough to offset these other impacts. Though death is inevitable, the timing is unknown, and the financial impacts are hard to predict.

On the asset side, any pension or annuities that pay based on the single life of the deceased will end. As well, while Social Security has survivor benefits, the overall amount of benefits paid to the household will decrease by one-third to one-half. For single-earner households, benefits will drop by about 33 percent as the spousal benefit ends. If both spouses earned Social Security benefits based on their own records and had the same primary insurance amounts, the total benefits drop by 50 percent.

Naturally, spending needs may fall after the death of a spouse, but there is a danger that assets decrease faster than expenses. There are economies of scale from living together, as household expenses do not fall in half just because a two-person household becomes one. While some expenses may fall, like the total food budget, there are still fixed expenses that do not depend on the number of people in the household, such as home maintenance and utility bills.

Another issue is taxes. In the year following death, the survivor shifts from being able to file as married filing jointly to filing as a single. This reduces the thresholds for tax brackets, making it more likely to pay at higher marginal tax rates, to pay more taxes on Social Security benefits, and to pay surcharges on Medicare premiums.

Also, less risk pooling is possible within the household after the death of a spouse, such as having a healthy spouse to transport a sick spouse to doctor visits and so forth. The death of a spouse also implies the loss of a potential caregiver, which can then increase the likelihood of needing to pay for long-term care expenses for the surviving spouse. Loneliness can also harm health, leading to higher medical costs for the survivor.

Another risk is if the deceased spouse had handled the family finances. The surviving spouse may not even be aware of how to access everything, or how to manage the overall financial strategy. Surviving spouses may be more vulnerable to experiencing elder abuse and financial fraud.

The loss of a spouse disproportionately impacts women, as they tend to outlive their husbands. Women live longer on average, and they tend to marry individuals older than themselves. Older men who remain alive still tend to be with a spouse, whereas older women are much more likely to be single. Widows become vulnerable, especially when they served as a caregiver to the deceased spouse, which may have taken a toll on their finances and health. We can observe this among older age groups, as poverty rates are the highest for single women at advanced ages.

Some possible ways to manage the loss of spouse risk are to first recognize that it is inevitable and make sure that both spouses understand key aspects of the financial plan and can take control. This is discussed further in Chapter 11. As well, this risk can be managed by choosing joint-life options for annuities and pensions, having life insurance, planning for long-term care, having a plan for lost income sources, having the family finances clearly organized, and creating a proper estate plan well in advance. As well, one can plan to maximize the Social Security survivor benefit as explained in Chapter 6, which involves delaying Social Security for the high earner in the couple. When budgeting, it is important to think about how the budget may evolve after the loss of the spouse. Which expenses may decrease, and which may increase? Always keep this contingency in mind when planning.

Unexpected family-related financial responsibilities

Another family-related spending shock involves a need to help other adult family members in unanticipated ways. Retirees may find unexpected demands to help their parents, adult children, or even to become caregivers for grandchildren. The concept of the "sandwich generation" has developed as a name for the situation many near-retirees find themselves in with having to care for aging parents while also finding that their adult children are facing a more difficult time with leaving the home and becoming financially independent from their parents. Job loss and hardships related to the global pandemic may accelerate this issue for young adults who were less established in their careers. This is a difficult risk to manage other than to plan and budget for potential support to family as part of retirement expenses, as well as making an effort to discuss limits with family on providing support or co-signing on loans.

Divorce

A divorce can completely change the picture for retirement income. The concept of "gray divorce" refers to the increase in divorce rates happening at retirement ages. Divorce can be a spending shock in the sense that a couple loses the economies of scale from living together. Though it may not double costs, it is more expensive to pay for two separate homes after a couple splits. As well, attorney fees and other costs related to the divorce may be significant. This can be a difficult risk for spouses to discuss, but at least it is important to include in a list of potential spending shocks facing retirees.

When gray divorce happens in retirement, especially after a long and relatively happy marriage, it may be because the couple had different expectations about retirement and were not prepared for the potentially large increase in the amount of time spent with one another. As well, some couples just simply grow apart over time in ways that may be unavoidable. Though there is no easy way to mitigate the risk of divorce, the discussion in Chapter 12 will be the most relevant for helping to ensure that spouses have the same expectations and understandings for their retirements and have plans to fill their time with meaningful activities both separately and together.

As well, if divorce is imminent, it is important to understand the implications for Social Security, pensions, and other retirement assets. Finalizing a divorce within ten years of marriage, for instance, would remove the possibility of receiving Social Security benefits as an ex-spouse, as discussed further in Chapter 6. A divorce should also be followed by a careful review of estate planning documents and beneficiary designations to ensure that matters are aligned with the new reality (see Chapter 11).

Changing public policy and tax rules

Public policy risk refers to the idea that the government can change the rules. This makes planning harder as what may work best under current rules could be much less effective under a different set of rules. Important changes to the tax code and rules around tax-advantaged retirement accounts seem to arrive every few years and those planning for retirement face a constantly moving target. Possible changes include reduced benefits from Social Security or Medicare, changing rules about IRAs, an increase in income or estate taxes, and so on. Many expect an increase in taxes in the future, and the global pandemic made such outcomes more likely. Retirees must keep this in mind, realizing that it may be necessary to update plans over time to respond to changing policies, and to perhaps include a bit more for budgeted taxes that current law might suggest.

We can understand the nature of public policy risk just by looking at some of the significant recent policy changes that impact retirement planning:

- In 2013, the Net Investment Income Tax created the potential to increase marginal tax rates by 3.8 percent in various circumstances. (See Chapter 10)
- In 2015, Social Security began a phase-out of certain claiming strategies that could have provided married couples with up to $50,000 of additional lifetime benefits. (See Chapter 6)
- In 2017, rules for the Home Equity Conversion Mortgage (reverse mortgage) program were updated to increase the initial costs and reduce the growth potential of setting up a reverse mortgage line of credit. (See Chapter 9)

- In 2017, the Tax Cuts and Jobs Act provided a major overhaul of the federal tax system with many implications, including making it more difficult to itemize tax deductions and removing the ability to recharacterize Roth conversions. (See Chapter 10)
- In 2019, the SECURE Act changed the rules around required minimum distributions for inherited retirement accounts. In many cases, beneficiaries will have to fully distribute the accounts within ten years rather than being able to apply a lifetime stretch to the distributions. (See Chapter 11)

Business risks for annuities and pensions

It is common to view bonds, annuities, and pensions as being relatively free of risk. But an important risk to keep in mind is that corporations can go out of business. This can result in defaults by bond issuers, an insolvent annuity provider, a corporate pension plan which reneges on its promises, the loss of employer benefits such as for retiree health care and nonqualified executive compensation benefits, and the danger of holding too much employer stock in a 401(k) plan.

Retirement income tools that rely on risk pooling to fund retirement expenses, such as with traditional defined-benefit company pension plans or annuities supporting lifetime income, do rely on a centralized actor to manage the underlying funds to support these payments. Actuaries must make calculations regarding asset returns and longevity to know how much contributions or premiums are needed to cover the promised payments. Their projections can be hit by unexpected events.

Defined benefit pension plans of private employers have minimum funding requirements and contributions are made to an irrevocable trust. But the plans may still not have sufficient assets to fund all the promised benefits. Many plans are underfunded with respect to their obligations to pay pensions. The Pension Benefit Guaranty Corporation does provide a backstop to cover pensions from insolvent companies, but there are limits on the pension amount covered and a widespread pension default could overwhelm their resources. This pension insolvency risk can feed into the decision about whether to choose a lump-sum payment or lifetime income from the defined-benefit pension plan. Those who have more worry about the long-term viability for the pension to make its obligated payments would lean toward choosing the lump-sum option.

Also, a real concern to keep in mind is the long-term viability of insurance companies providing annuities with lifetime protections. Fear of an annuity company failure is a legitimate concern, though this risk can be overstated. It is an extremely rare event that annuity policy holders were not made whole on their promised payments in the past. Past performance does not guarantee the future, but if one focuses on highly-rated insurance companies and keeps premiums to any one company below their state's insurance guarantee limits, the risk of not being made whole on promised payments is very low.

A comment about defined-contribution plans such as employer 401(k) plans is also relevant. These plans do not promise payments through risk pooling, as the market and longevity risks are passed to the worker. Contributions are made to irrevocable trusts, so the assets are secure and protected from employer insolvency. However, market risk remains. This can impact individuals who invest heavily in their own employer stock, which reduces diversification and makes one more vulnerable to investment losses that could be correlated with business problems that also risk one's employment. Broader diversification is often a worthwhile pursuit for plan holdings, though before divesting employer stock, it is worthwhile to consider the potential for receiving net unrealized appreciation treatment as described in Chapter 10.

Not sticking to the plan – excess withdrawal risk

It is possible to work hard to create a sustainable retirement spending plan, only to see the plan fall apart due to general overspending not necessarily related to other identified spending shocks. A lack of discipline could lead to more spending for discretionary lifestyle expenses, or it could even take the form of excessive financial gifts to children or grandchildren. Another area where this risk can materialize is with the choice of a variable spending strategy that allows for higher initial spending because it calls for later cuts to be made that are not followed. The relevance of this risk can generally be understood by retirees who have a lifetime of experience to consider whether sticking to a budget is feasible. Those who struggle to stick to a spending plan may benefit from an income annuity which prevents overspending through the lack of liquidity and underlying access to funds. A retirement income plan will only be as strong as the commitment to maintain it.

Frailty and declining cognitive abilities

Frailty risk refers to the deterioration of mental and physical health that can happen with age. Frailty generally regards physical decline, while cognitive decline relates to the mental aspects. Retirees may increasingly struggle to take care of either their financial affairs, home and property maintenance, lawn care and snow removal, cleaning, and transportation needs, especially if they lose the ability to drive. Simple tasks such as replacing light bulbs can become a challenge. Declining abilities to engage in financial calculations and other types of cognitive impairment make it increasingly difficult to manage a complex investment and withdrawal strategy as aging progresses. This can increase retirement expenses either because services must be paid for which could have otherwise been handled before, or because individuals begin making mistakes, such as forgetting to pay bills and then incurring late fees, that lead to unnecessary expenses.

A retirement income plan must incorporate the unfortunate reality that many retirees will experience declining physical and cognitive abilities. Frailty and cognitive decline are risks that will impact most retirees to some degree over the course of a long retirement. Both can lead to an increased reliance on others, which can increase costs and exposure to elder abuse.

A vital way to help manage these risks is to anticipate them and to plan for them. Actions that can be taken in this regard include choosing housing where more of these issues are addressed, working with a trusted financial planning firm that can be on the lookout for cognitive impairment and help arrange for necessary additional help, relying on family members, a daily money manager, or a corporate trustee, and creating documents for power of attorney and a living trust.

While liquidity and flexibility are important, retirees should also prepare for the reality that cognitive decline will hamper the portfolio management skills of many as they age, increasing the desirability of advanced planning and automation for late-in-life financial goals. As well, allowing a trusted family member to handle your finances or working with a professional financial planner can be important, and these decisions need to be made in advance. The risk that an unprepared spouse will need to take over the finances can happen before death, as the spouse who has taken responsibility to manage the finances could develop reduced capacities that prevent the continuation of these tasks. For a deeper exploration of these issues, Chapter 9 covers retirement housing and Chapter 11 covers incapacity planning.

Financial elder abuse

As cognitive abilities decline and frailty sets in with continued aging, retirees are increasingly at risk of becoming victims of bad advice, fraud, or even outright theft. Culprits can include family members, neighbors, friends, financial professionals, paid caregivers, staff at institutional living facilities, and con-artists using phone, email, traditional mail, and in-person solicitations. Though there is a risk of strangers perpetuating fraud, most of this type of abuse is perpetuated by individuals known to the victim.

Retirees tend to have assets and savings that attract fraudsters, and they may be dealing with a variety of issues that can make them more vulnerable. This includes declining cognitive abilities, health problems, isolation, and loneliness. Victims may be unwilling to speak up and report abuse, as well, because of embarrassment, fear losing independence, or fear of causing trouble for the perpetrator. The danger is that nefarious individuals find a way to siphon off assets from the retiree, which then translates into another type of spending shock.

Ways to protect from elder abuse include staying organized, keeping track of possessions, locking up important documents, opening and sending one's own mail, signing one's own checks, freezing credit reports, and using direct deposit for Social Security benefits and other payments. It may also help to screen calls with voice mail rather than answering directly and being caught off guard by a scam. Screening caregivers and advisors is also important, as is including trusted family members in decisions. Ensure that any caregivers are licensed, bonded, and insured, and have gone through background checks. These matters require having a plan in place in advance for when one is less able to handle financial affairs and becomes more vulnerable to abuse.

Changing housing needs

Housing is a major retirement expense and housing needs can change in retirement. Issues related to housing pose a significant spending risk in that unexpected situations can result in substantial increases in retirement costs. Over time, retirees may need housing with greater accessibility or with ease of access by caregivers. Caregivers may not be available in the local area, and couples may need to be split when one spouse requires institutionalized care. Home repairs and home maintenance may grow in cost if one chooses to age in place and as frailty sets in. These risks are significant and are covered more thoroughly in Chapter 9.

Forced early retirement and reduced earnings capacity

The risk of forced early retirement relates to both the risk of losing your job before your planned retirement date or being unable to maintain desired part-time employment in retirement. This risk manifests as a shock to the asset side of the balance sheet, rather than as a spending shock. But the effect is the same: a worsening ratio of assets to liabilities and less funding for retirement.

For forced early retirement, a consistent finding from household surveys is that about half of the population ends up retiring earlier than anticipated. The Employee Benefit Research Institute has been tracking this for years with their Retirement Confidence Survey, and they reported most recently for 2020 that 48 percent of retirees had retired earlier than planned. Similarly, Prudential reported most recently in 2019 that 51 percent of respondents had retired earlier than planned.

Among those retiring earlier than planned, Prudential found that only 23 percent indicated it was because they had enough to retire and wanted to do so. The rest suggested that early retirement was involuntary and unanticipated. Reasons include 46 percent who retired for health reasons, 18 percent who were laid-off or otherwise lost their job, 12 percent who were offered an early retirement package, and 11 percent who had to care for a loved one. The differences in retirement ages were significant, as on average, individuals expected to retire at 65 but actually retired at 59.

Early retirement can have huge financial ramifications. Delaying retirement can serve as the best way to improve the funded status of a retirement plan. Naturally, the reverse is also true. Retiring earlier than planned means fewer years of working and saving, less time for assets to grow and compound before distributions begin, a longer retirement planning horizon to fund, and potentially smaller benefits from Social Security and traditional pensions. Early retirement can also mean a loss of employer health insurance benefits, necessitating finding other health insurance until reaching Medicare eligibility at age 65. These factors can all have a significant impact on the sustainability of a retirement plan.

This risk can extend into retirement if part-time work is necessary to help fund retirement expenses. The EBRI Retirement Confidence Survey found that while 79 percent expected to engage in part-time work in retirement, only 29 percent of retirees did work. Often such work is not feasible for any of the reasons mentioned regarding forced early retirement. Those who continue with some work, do find it to be a positive experience, as work also provides an opportunity to stay active and involved. Work can also help to provide purpose, fill time, or maintain a social network, and losing these things can be detrimental to health. Generally, it is important to try not to rely on significant employment income during retirement.

For those who are still somewhat far from their planned retirement date, it is important to incorporate the possibility that one must retire earlier than planned. For instance, one could plan for a reduced but adequate standard of living if needed at 10 years before the planned retirement age as a Plan B inside a broader plan. Also, for reasons related to involuntary job loss, it is important to maintain skills, education, and networks, in case it becomes necessary to seek new employment.

Maintaining a healthy lifestyle can also help to manage potential health risks that could force an earlier retirement. Also having long-term care plans in place for loved ones can help manage the risk that someone must give up their career to become the primary caregiver for a family member. As well, one can make efforts to manage a career to avoid burnout, such as taking time off, reducing responsibilities or making some cuts to the overall workload, so that it becomes more feasible to extend work for longer.

More broadly, retirement can lead to a discrete reduction to the value of human capital, which is an important risk. Retirees face reduced flexibility to earn income in the labor markets to cushion their standard of living from the impact of poor market returns. Risk capacity is the ability to endure a decline in portfolio value without experiencing a substantial decline to the standard of living. Prior to retirement, poor market returns might be counteracted with a small increase in the savings rate, a brief retirement delay, or even a slight increase in risk taking. Once retired, however, people can find it hard to return to the labor force and are more likely to live on fixed budgets. Retirees often experience large reductions in their risk capacity as the value of their human capital declines. As a result, they are left with fewer options for responding to poor portfolio returns.

Action Plan

The important concepts to incorporate into one's thinking about retirement are related to how retirement risks manifest. The amount of assets required to fund the financial goals of retirement depends on how long you live, your investment returns, and your exposure to various shocks. It is important to begin thinking about retirement risk exposure:

- ☐ Obtain longevity estimates using a tool such as the Longevity Illustrator [www.longevityillustrator.org].
  - o Those with a front-loading preference may prefer to use numbers closer to the 25th percentile of outcomes
  - o Those with a back-loading preference may prefer numbers closer to the 10th percentile of outcomes
- ☐ Market and sequence-of-return risk
  - o Understand your comfort level with market risk as it relates to your retirement income style
  - o Decide on reasonable net-return assumptions for your retirement portfolio
- ☐ Assess exposures to various retirement spending shocks and other surprises. As part of this assessment, consider the potential costs or impacts that these risks could create:
  - o Long-term care risks
  - o Health care and prescription costs
  - o Inflation
  - o Death of a spouse
  - o Unexpected family-related financial responsibilities
  - o Divorce
  - o Changing public policy and tax rules
  - o Business risk for annuities and pensions
  - o Excess withdrawal risk
  - o Frailty and declining cognitive abilities
  - o Financial elder abuse
  - o Changing housing needs
  - o Forced early retirement and reduced earnings capacity

Further Reading

Bogle, John C. 2014. "The Arithmetic of 'All-In' Investment Expenses." *Financial Analysts Journal* 70 (January/February).

Society of Actuaries. 2020. *Managing Post-Retirement Risks: A Guide to Retirement Planning*.

Society of Actuaries and American Academy of Actuaries. 2021. "The Longevity Illustrator." http://www.longevityillustrator.org.

Chapter 3: Quantifying Goals and Assessing Preparedness

An important question many pre-retirees and retirees ask themselves is whether they are on the financial track toward creating a successful retirement. This chapter provides a framework for determining the answer. Assuming a bond-like return on assets, we seek to determine if there are sufficient assets to meet the anticipated retirement liabilities, including desired reserves for spending shocks. We quantify the assets and the liabilities for the household and see which are larger.

I start by explaining how to quantify the financial goals for retirement. These goals define the expenses, or liabilities, to be funded. Effort is needed to determine a realistic retirement budget, anticipating the retirement spending to meet our ongoing needs and desires. I also estimate additional potential expenses for various contingencies that the retiree would like to have on hand to feel fully comfortable that the plan can also manage spending shocks and other retirement risks. I also consider legacy goals, which can be incorporated explicitly as a liability to fund, or which can be represented as the surplus wealth after sufficient assets have been earmarked for ongoing spending and contingencies.

Then I shift to assets, as we seek to construct the retirement balance sheet and to ultimately match assets with liabilities. What is available to manage retirement expenses? With assets and liabilities determined, we can calculate the funded ratio. This is the ratio of assets to liabilities, assuming a conservative interest rate to translate future income and expenses into today's dollars. The funded ratio lets us know whether the plan will work if retirees only invest in low-risk assets to meet their lifetime liabilities. It is a great result if assets exceed liabilities, with a funded status of over 100 percent, as it speaks to retirement preparedness. I also consider possible actions for when assets fall short of liabilities and retirement is underfunded.

The retirement income challenge lays out the broad retirement income problem we are attempting to solve. The process of building a retirement income strategy involves determining retirement goals and effectively meeting and protecting those goals from retirement risks. We must determine how to best combine retirement income tools and strategies to optimize the balance between these objectives in ways that align with our personal retirement income style. Exhibit 3.1 shows the retirement income challenge as a series of concentric circles. The innermost circle summarizes the overall process for retirement income. At the center, we must combine income tools to best meet goals and balance risks. Possible goals are listed in the next concentric circle. The third circle lists risks confronting those goals. The final circle shows available income tools for retirement. Do you have enough assets to fund tools that will help you meet your goals and manage your risks in retirement?

Exhibit 3.1
The Retirement Income Challenge

For the retirement income challenge, we start with the goals. The primary financial goal for most retirees relates to their annual spending: maximize spending power (lifestyle) in such a way that spending can remain consistent and sustainable without any drastic reductions, no matter how long the retirement lasts (longevity). This is the retirement budget. Other important goals may include leaving assets for subsequent generations (legacy) and maintaining sufficient reserves for unexpected contingencies that have not been earmarked for other purposes (liquidity). Lifestyle, longevity, legacy, and liquidity are the four Ls of retirement income. We describe how to quantify these goals, starting with the retirement budget.

Determining the Retirement Budget

The fundamental financial goal in retirement is to fund your ongoing budgeted expenses for the rest of your life. The budget, or spending plan, relates to longevity and lifestyle goals, though we will not make this distinction right away. Budgeting is not always enjoyable, but there are tools available to help simplify the process. Budgeting can help to increase your confidence and comfort about retirement if it helps you know you are on track.

It is common to be nervous about whether you have saved enough for retirement when you do not have a good idea about what you have been spending and what amount of spending will help you to support a comfortable lifestyle. By determining a budget, it becomes easier to assess retirement preparedness. Perhaps you already have sufficient savings, which could be a great comfort. If underfunded, you can design a plan for how to respond. Decisions include delaying retirement, reducing budgeted expenses, or assuming a higher rate of return on your assets. There will be more clarity. A significant source of uncertainty can now be better understood and managed.

The difficulty in budgeting for retirement, though, is that many expenses will change alongside the act of retiring. New retirees undergo a significant transition to their lifestyle. Even for those who have developed precise records about annual spending in their pre-retirement years, adjustments may be needed to account for changes happening at retirement. This is especially the case for those who move as part of retiring. Retirement budgeting requires tracking what you have spent and then planning for how those expenses are likely to change. You will need a reasonable estimate of the baseline expenses. How much do you anticipate spending on a year-to-year basis in retirement? As retirement continues, will your overall expenses grow by less or more than inflation?

Replacement Rates

As a brief starting point, one simple approach to avoid making a budget is to simply follow a replacement rate rule for retirement spending. An existing guideline is that retirees will spend 80 percent of their pre-retirement income when they retire. This held up well as a population average from a University of Georgia study conducted repeatedly since the 1970s. That study has not been updated since 2008, though. The intuition for the 80 percent replacement rate concept is that the retirement budget reflects salary less savings, taxes, and minor adjustments made for the reduction in work-related expenses. After these adjustments, the average household spends about 80 percent of what it earns.

Of course, even if this does reflect an average replacement rate, there is variation around this number in individual cases. It also works best when incomes are relatively stable, as when annual income is fluctuating the question quickly becomes: 80 percent of what? This guideline is also not relevant for those seeking to retire early and therefore use higher savings rates. It also does not consider the possibility of splurging in the first few retirement years. One must also factor in that pre-retirement spending may include mortgage payments and spending on children that will not be necessary after retiring. Those who were saving, paying a mortgage, raising children, paying payroll taxes, and facing some employment expenses may find that they can live comfortably on a much lower percentage of their pre-retirement salary. All considered, it is not a very helpful rule at all, as some basic planning can lead toward much more reasonable estimates for retirement expenses.

Tracking Recent Expenses

A better starting point is to build a retirement spending plan. For this, it will be helpful to begin with a look at actual spending over the previous few years. Your spending may change in retirement, but you need to know your starting point and to fully uncover any spending that you might not otherwise think about. Inflation has been low in recent years, but you might also adjust your past expenses to account for rising price levels and to make those expenses more reflective of today's purchasing power. Once you have an idea about your recent spending, it becomes easier to adjust these numbers for what can change in retirement.

We can consider a simple list of spending categories to include in your budget. This is a list of general expense categories and sub-categories that can be used to make a spreadsheet where you can fill in the appropriate numbers. You should feel free to customize these categories as you see fit. You could move expenses around, consolidate, or expand categories as appropriate for your situation. New categories could also be added as needed to cover special situations that are not otherwise easy to fit into these existing categories:

- Charity
- Clothing
- Credit card rewards (points for travel, cash back)
- Debt repayments (mortgage, car loans, education loans, credit cards, other loans)
- Entertainment (hobbies, leisure activities)
- Food (groceries, restaurants)
- Gifts (family support, education expenses)
- Health care (insurance and Medicare premiums, out of pocket expenses, dental, vision)
- Home maintenance (landscaping, snow removal, home security, pool, cleaner, pests, HVAC tune-up)

- Home expenses (rent, HOA dues, repairs)
- Insurance premiums (home, auto, umbrella, life, disability, long-term care)
- Memberships (fitness, civic organizations, warehouse clubs, season tickets)
- Miscellaneous household expenses (cleaning supplies, appliances, computers)
- Personal care
- Phone (cellular, landline)
- Subscriptions (newspapers, magazines, software, websites, music, cloud storage)
- Taxes (federal income, FICA, Medicare, state income, property & local taxes)
- Television and Internet (internet, cable TV, streaming services)
- Transportation (auto maintenance, fuel, parking, insurance, roadside assistance)
- Travel (flights, hotel, insurance, local transportation, admission tickets)
- Utilities (water, electric, gas, home oil, waste disposal, sewage)
- Special large expenditures (child wedding, automobile purchases, major home renovation, unique trip)

For examples about the flexibility for these categories, a mortgage payment or property taxes could be included in a general home expense category, as debt repayment, or as taxes, depending on what makes most sense to you. About a mortgage, it is important to remember that many mortgage payments include funds for property tax and homeowner's insurance which will need to be reflected in the budget after the mortgage is paid. Someone thinking to move and rent in retirement may think of those expenses as later translating into rent. Insurance is also a broad category with many of its expenses possibly showing up elsewhere instead. For instance, homeowner's insurance could go with home expenses, auto insurance with transportation expenses, life insurance in a separate category, and medical-related insurance could be classified separately as part of health expenses. Another problem could creep up when shopping at large box stores that offer groceries as well as other products. Trying to separate expenses may be a pain. My solution, for instance, it to count all spending at Costco as for groceries, though I know this is not the case. If one is consistent and has categories that capture all spending it is fine to develop a unique system that makes sense for you and helps to simplify your life. It is total overall spending that matters most.

In terms of consolidating expenses, I find in my own case that it is easier to have a general home expense category where I merge items like clothing, entertainment, gifts, memberships, miscellaneous household expenses, personal care, and subscriptions, which were all separate categories above. I feel that this works fine in my family, and it does make it easier to have fewer budget categories to manage. My personal budget includes the following categories: home repairs, HOA dues, cell phone, internet, television, utilities, insurance (car, home, umbrella, disability), groceries, restaurants, household expenses, transportation, health care, travel, business deductions, education and camps for children, credit card rewards, life insurance premiums, charity, and taxes (federal income, FICA, Medicare, state income, local property).

With the expense categories in place, you need a system for collecting your expenses. For those who can manage the responsibility to not overspend when using credit cards, they provide the opportunity to simplify the budgeting process. Credit card statements provide a clear record of expenses. Credit cards can also offer points and cash back opportunities to reduce expenses. For those who may have more trouble with controlling spending, using a debit card could be another alternative that also allows for expense tracking, though it may lack rewards and other benefits.

I treat credit card rewards as a negative expense category, providing an offset to reduce overall expenses. For cash back, this is easy to incorporate. Though it requires more work, it can be meaningful to also incorporate the value of plane or hotel benefits received through credit card rewards in order to have a better estimate of total travel expenses, if one is reducing them by using points that may not always be available. For instance, if I use points to pay for a flight ticket that would have cost $550, I will create an artificial transaction with my expenses for that plane ticket, and then create a second transaction with the points as a negative monetary value that offsets the ticket cost. This increases my travel expense category for budgeting purposes without increasing my total expenses. In later years I can just assume fewer credit card rewards.

Another issue relates to classifying expenses when paying for items with cash. Using cash requires more work in terms of needing to keep track of how the cash is spent. Because I do not use much cash, I simplify this process and just count any ATM withdrawals as part of general household expenses when the withdrawal is made. Because I personally use cash so rarely, this does not have much impact on how my budget looks by category, and the overall amount of expenses will still be correct. By tracking expenses from all bank accounts and credit cards, it can be easy to monitor total expenses and not experience leakages with spending from other places. Occasionally there might be other slight adjustments to make, such as if one receives cash or a gift card that does not otherwise show up with online transaction reports. Also, you should check your payroll stubs to make sure you are accounting for taxes and the full cost of any employer benefits that you may need to pay on your own after retiring. Those types of expenses would also not otherwise show up on credit card or bank statements.

Some may use budgeting to find and reduce unnecessary expenses. Working through your past expenses does provide an opportunity to catch recurring payments for services you no longer use and to cut other spending waste. In such cases, having more refined categories may help. For others, the goal is simply to determine overall annual spending. Fewer expense categories may be needed, other than to have separate categories for expenses that will change in retirement. For instance, in my own budget I have a separate category for education and camp expenses for my children, since these types of expenses can be substantial and will not continue after my children have grown. The category could also morph into gifts for adult children or grandchildren.

You can also decide about how to treat car purchases or other big-ticket items or home renovations that only happen occasionally but provide service to the owner over time. An easy way is to include purchases in the year made and then see what the average spending in that category works out to be over time. This speaks to another important point, which is that you will want to consider at least a few years of expenses to ensure that occasional big-ticket items are not missed. Such expenses increase average annual spending compared to only looking at a year without such expenses. In this regard, I find it more helpful to think about budgeting on an annual basis instead of a monthly basis, since monthly expenses can fluctuate so dramatically for the same sorts of reasons. Some large expenses like property taxes or insurance premiums may only show up once or twice each year. Of course, it may still be important to know when in the year large expenses happen to make sure enough funds are on hand, but otherwise the issue of fluctuating expenses tends to smooth out over the year. Also, if you have identified major one-time expenses for retirement, such as a home renovation or child's wedding, you might track these as separate liabilities outside your general budget.

I have referenced my own budgeting, and it may help to explain a bit more about how I do it. I use the free online tool at Mint.com to consolidate my credit card and bank accounts. Mint.com lets you then see the consolidated list of transactions. At the bottom of their webpage, they have a link to download those transactions to a spreadsheet. I do this and move them to a separate spreadsheet where I keep track of my expenses on an annual basis. With the raw downloaded numbers, I do adjust categories in my spreadsheet. I reclassify many expense categories because I find that Mint.com has them recorded wrong or at least not in the precise categories I like. I also remove credit card bill payments and transfers to savings, as those represent double counting or items that are not really expenses (unless you are paying interest on your credit cards). I try to update my spreadsheet of expenses at least once a quarter, as sometimes I must remember how certain expenses should be classified and waiting too long can make that hard. I also classify payments made by check into the right category, and as mentioned I treat ATM withdrawals as general household expenses. This provides me with a very good record of annual expenses that I can continue to build out and track over time.

Exhibits 3.2 and 3.3 show a hypothetical example for the process of tracking past expenses and then planning for retirement expenses. Exhibit 3.2 begins with the past expenses for a couple approaching retirement. We can note a few trends. First, the gifts / children's education category declines dramatically during these five years, as the youngest child finished college. We can also see expenses fluctuate quite a bit from year to year, and we can note a dramatic drop in expenses for 2020 as related to reduced discretionary spending opportunities during the global pandemic. There may not be a truly "normal budget" for this couple as unique circumstances are common. The best we can ultimately do will be to figure out reasonable average spending amounts for categories.

Exhibit 3.2
Tracking Recent Expenses

	Inflation Rate	2.11%	1.67%	2.29%	1.30%	
Nominal Expenses	**Cons. Price Index**	92.97	94.93	96.51	98.72	100.00
	AVERAGE	**2017**	**2018**	**2019**	**2020**	**2021**
Cell phone	$1,122	$996	$996	$1,627	$996	$996
Charity	$4,793	$3,864	$5,200	$5,000	$4,500	$5,400
Gifts / Children's Education	$9,777	$31,542	$17,292	$51	$0	$0
Groceries	$17,169	$17,633	$16,930	$17,142	$16,450	$17,690
Health Care (including insurance)	$8,110	$9,530	$7,337	$8,590	$6,668	$8,425
Household expenses	$26,079	$36,321	$27,551	$29,983	$17,100	$19,438
Housing (maintenance, furniture)	$902	$0	$0	$3,750	$0	$760
Housing (HOA dues)	$2,738	$2,690	$2,690	$2,690	$2,690	$2,930
Insurance	$3,228	$2,993	$3,150	$3,224	$3,360	$3,413
Internet	$954	$954	$954	$954	$954	$954
Property Taxes / Apartment Rent	$13,416	$12,545	$12,989	$13,419	$13,849	$14,279
Restaurants	$2,100	$1,750	$2,164	$2,927	$1,276	$2,385
Television	$671	$312	$526	$555	$980	$980
Transportation	$2,253	$2,033	$2,924	$2,467	$1,700	$2,139
Travel (International)	$6,278	$17,016	$0	$14,376	$0	$0
Travel (Domestic)	$3,109	$4,690	$6,123	$3,190	$0	$1,540
Utilities (gas, electric, water)	$3,124	$2,329	$2,896	$3,170	$3,512	$3,712
	$105,823	$147,199	$109,722	$113,115	$74,035	$85,041

The category of property taxes is included separately, as this couple currently owns their home with a fully paid mortgage, but they are thinking to move and rent in retirement. That category can evolve to represent home rent. Otherwise, we do not include taxes in this budget since taxes are so closely linked to work and income. Tax projections for retirement will need to be treated separately (see Chapter 10 for more on taxes). Knowing past taxes paid may not provide much insight into future tax bills, beyond property taxes. As well, transportation expenses were relatively low in these years, as the last car purchase was in 2016, a year that is not shown in the exhibit. This is something to consider when projecting future expenses. Finally, we note that these are raw expenses from each year in nominal terms, but that the consumer price index (with 2021 as a base year) is included at the top of the exhibit. This will become important for the next step of projecting retirement expenses.

Projecting Retirement Expenses

Once we have a grasp of what we have been spending, we can next turn to how spending might change in retirement. Some expenses will decrease after retiring. These include expenses related to child-rearing for children who have grown, the possibility for a mortgage to be paid off, the potential for lower taxes as work decreases, especially payroll taxes, and the lack of work expenses. Also, if moving to less expensive housing, home maintenance bills and property taxes may also decline.

On the other hand, other expenses may increase. There is a saying that every day is a Saturday in retirement, and leisure spending can be higher than when most of one's day was spent at work. One may wish to splurge a bit, at least in the early retirement years. As well, health care, health insurance premiums, long-term care expenses, and needing to outsource some services that may have previously been manageable could all raise the costs of retirement.

Exhibit 3.3 provides an example of the process for translating past spending into a retirement budget. For this case, the couple plans to sell their home and rent an apartment. The first thing to note about this exhibit is that the recent annual spending numbers have been adjusted upward to account for real spending in 2021 dollars based on the price index that was shown in Exhibit 3.2. This is an important adjustment, which ultimately increased the average annual spending for these five years from $105,823 in nominal dollars to $110,232 in real dollars. It is the real dollar amounts that are more relevant when projecting the retirement budget.

I have also added a column for the retirement budget next to the average amounts. This provides an easy way to see what has been spent so that we can adjust from a more relevant starting point. We can observe that some categories are quite close to the past averages with perhaps a slight upwards rounding as the household does not foresee changes in those categories. Other categories do have bigger changes. For instance, gifts drop dramatically as the household is no longer paying for education expenses, groceries are less to account for fewer mouths to feed, health care increases as the couple expects to pay more for health as they age and lose subsidized employer benefits (the specific method for calculating their health expenses is described in Chapter 7), housing increases to account for more furniture purchases to accompany the move, property taxes shift to an expected rent of $1,500 per month, restaurant spending increases as the retirees would like to go to more restaurants as a part of filling leisure time, transportation increases to budget in car purchases, and travel spending also increases to account for more leisurely travel in retirement. For this couple, the overall projected retirement budget is about $1,300 more than the average household expenses over the past five years. The couple anticipates spending $111,564 per year net of taxes. Taxes are not included here because that is a separate process going beyond basic budgeting and will be considered in Chapter 10.

Exhibit 3.3
Projected Retirement Expenses

Real Expenses (Today's Dollars)	RETIREMENT - PROJECTED -	AVERAGE	2017	2018	2019	2020	2021
Cell phone	$1,200	$1,162	$1,071	$1,049	$1,686	$1,009	$996
Charity	$5,000	$4,955	$4,156	$5,478	$5,181	$4,558	$5,400
Gifts / children's education	$3,000	$10,440	$33,928	$18,216	$53	$0	$0
Groceries	$18,000	$17,783	$18,967	$17,835	$17,761	$16,663	$17,690
Health Care	$11,464	$8,412	$10,251	$7,729	$8,900	$6,755	$8,425
Household expenses	$23,000	$27,184	$39,069	$29,024	$31,066	$17,322	$19,438
Housing (maintenance, furniture)	$1,500	$929	$0	$0	$3,885	$0	$760
Housing (HOA dues)	$0	$2,834	$2,894	$2,834	$2,787	$2,725	$2,930
Insurance	$3,300	$3,339	$3,220	$3,318	$3,340	$3,404	$3,413
Internet	$1,000	$988	$1,026	$1,005	$988	$966	$954
Property Taxes / Apartment Rent	$15,600	$13,878	$13,494	$13,683	$13,904	$14,029	$14,279
Restaurants	$3,000	$2,175	$1,883	$2,280	$3,033	$1,293	$2,385
Television	$1,000	$688	$336	$554	$575	$993	$980
Transportation	$7,500	$2,337	$2,187	$3,081	$2,556	$1,722	$2,139
Travel (International)	$10,000	$6,640	$18,303	$0	$14,895	$0	$0
Travel (Domestic)	$4,000	$3,268	$5,045	$6,450	$3,305	$0	$1,540
Utilities (gas, electric, water)	$3,000	$3,222	$2,506	$3,050	$3,285	$3,558	$3,712
	$111,564	**$110,232**	**$158,336**	**$115,586**	**$117,201**	**$74,996**	**$85,041**

For budgeting, it never hurts to round-up when projecting expenses to provide a more conservative target for future spending. It is easier to underspend and have leftover funds than to overspend. The budgeting process can be further refined with each passing year as new data on actual spending becomes available. Seeing realized retirement expenses and then comparing them to the projections can be illustrative in helping determine further adjustments.

When it comes to projecting retirement expenses, three of the trickier categories to estimate will be health care, housing, and taxes. These categories will receive more discussion in their own chapters. Medical costs and insurance (Chapter 7) can change dramatically in retirement, as most retirees will switch to Medicare at age 65. Housing (Chapter 9) may also change, especially if one moves. Moving can impact homeowner's insurance, utilities, property taxes, home maintenance and repair costs, and the cost-of-living in the new community. It may take a couple years to get a full picture about the changes to the budget caused by a move, but at least knowing this and planning for some flexibility can still guide you in the right direction. Finally, income taxes change in retirement (Chapter 10) as wages are replaced by distributions from assets that are taxed in a variety of ways. Tax bracket management becomes important to controlling the amount of taxes paid.

Lifestyle and Longevity Expenses

Another budgeting issue is the distinction between lifestyle and longevity expenses. Core retirement expenses are fixed and inflexible. But that may not represent the entire budget. Some expenses may be discretionary. Is there a baseline spending level you could manage comfortably and still feel that retirement is going well, even if it does not include everything?

Exhibit 3.4
Lifestyle and Longevity Expenses

	RETIREMENT - PROJECTED EXPENSES -	
Real Expenses (Today's Dollars)	FULL LIFESTYLE	LONGEVITY ONLY
Cell phone	$1,200	$1,200
Charity	$5,000	$3,000
Gifts / children's education	$3,000	$600
Groceries	$18,000	$12,000
Health Care	$11,464	$11,464
Household expenses	$23,000	$19,000
Housing (maintenance, furniture)	$1,500	$1,000
Housing (HOA dues)	$0	$0
Insurance	$3,300	$3,300
Internet	$1,000	$1,000
Property Taxes / Apartment Rent	$15,600	$12,000
Restaurants	$3,000	$2,000
Television	$1,000	$800
Transportation	$7,500	$6,000
Travel (International)	$10,000	$2,000
Travel (Domestic)	$4,000	$2,000
Utilities (gas, electric, water)	$3,000	$3,000
	$111,564	**$80,364**

In Exhibit 3.4, we extend our earlier example for a projected retirement budget by including a distinction between the full lifestyle ($111,564) and the longevity spending that one could accept as more of a bare minimum in retirement ($80,364). The $31,200 difference is based on the couple's assessment about where spending could realistically be cut. For this hypothetical couple, the biggest factors to reduce spending included less for charity, fewer gifts, less on groceries and household expenses, a less expensive apartment, fewer restaurant visits, and a substantial reduction to the travel budget that would likely be expressed as less frequent trips, such as an overseas trip once every few years instead of once per year.

Changing Expenses in Later Retirement

As if preparing a budget for retirement did not yet involve enough speculation, another important matter to address is how the retirement budget may evolve over a long retirement horizon. Exhibit 3.5 provides an example for this couple who anticipates spending adjustments starting at age 80.

Exhibit 3.5
Changing Expenses in Retirement

Real Expenses (Today's Dollars)	RETIREMENT - PROJECTED LIFESTYLE EXPENSES -		RETIREMENT - PROJECTED LONGEVITY EXPENSES -	
	Ages 65 - 79	Ages 80+	Ages 65 - 79	Ages 80+
Cell phone	$1,200	$1,200	$1,200	$1,200
Charity	$5,000	$5,000	$3,000	$1,000
Gifts / children's education	$3,000	$3,000	$600	$600
Groceries	$18,000	$12,000	$12,000	$10,000
Health Care	$11,464	$22,928	$11,464	$22,928
Household expenses	$23,000	$15,000	$19,000	$13,000
Housing (maintenance, furniture)	$1,500	$500	$1,000	$500
Housing (HOA dues)	$0	$0	$0	$0
Insurance	$3,300	$3,300	$3,300	$3,300
Internet	$1,000	$1,000	$1,000	$1,000
Property Taxes / Apartment Rent	$15,600	$15,600	$12,000	$12,000
Restaurants	$3,000	$600	$2,000	$600
Television	$1,000	$800	$800	$800
Transportation	$7,500	$3,000	$6,000	$3,000
Travel (International)	$10,000	$0	$2,000	$0
Travel (Domestic)	$4,000	$1,000	$2,000	$1,000
Utilities (gas, electric, water)	$3,000	$3,000	$3,000	$3,000
	$111,564	$87,928	$80,364	$73,928

Some retirees may avoid the issue of changing spending by assuming that the budget will simply grow with consumer price inflation throughout a long retirement. This is generally a conservative assumption that could also provide a way to budget in assets for spending shocks as overall spending for retirees will likely decline with age. But, as will be described further in the next chapter, most retirees do experience declining spending with age. Retirees may experience the Go-Go, Slow-Go, and No-Go years of retirement. Early on, retirees are more active and have higher discretionary expenses for categories such as travel and restaurants. Retirement spending tends to keep pace with inflation. But retirees will eventually begin to slow down and become less active. Spending no longer keeps pace with inflation and may even decline on a nominal basis. Our couple reflects this situation by estimating real spending declines starting at age 80. They reasonably anticipate a decline in groceries (less gourmet cooking at home), household expenses, home furnishings, restaurants, television, transportation, and travel.

They also plan for one category increase, which is to double the real cost for health expenditures after age 80 to account for rising health needs and the idea that health care inflation tends to exceed the overall inflation rate (health spending is discussed in Chapter 7). The anticipated overall spending decline will help to provide some relief for their retirement finances, though it will also point to a need for reserve assets to cover unanticipated late-in-life spending shocks that cannot be managed as easily by simply redirecting other spending. Doubling health expenses was one way to prepare, but there are also other possible expenses related to frailty and long-term care. The risks related to these unknown changes can be incorporated partially by leaning toward being conservative with the budget. For instance, the travel budget could be kept after age 80 with the idea that these funds could be easily redirected to other unexpected spending needs. To the extent that budgeted expenses decline, these risks must be managed separately.

Legacy

In addition to your budget, do you have quantifiable legacy goals? Is leaving a specific legacy important, or do you accept that legacy will be whatever happens to be left over at the end without necessarily needing to plan for a specific amount. Legacy goals can be defined for family, charities, or other institutions. Legacy can also be split between ongoing distributions as part of the budget, or as a specific amount to be provided at death. Life insurance can also be a useful tool for providing a specific legacy amount at death. To the extent that one has specific legacy goals in mind, it is important to be thinking about these at the same time one is engaging the budgeting process as legacy goals must also be funded to be fully prepared for retirement. With this sense of retirement spending in terms of longevity, lifestyle, and legacy goals, we can next turn to spending shocks and the impact they will have on retirement funding.

Liquidity

The fourth L for retirement financial goals is liquidity to cover spending shock contingencies. To feel comfortable about retiring, we need to determine an amount of reserve assets that are not earmarked for longevity, lifestyle, or legacy. These are reserves for spending shocks.

There are many potential spending shocks with different possible costs. It is difficult to protect against all of them individually as the total cost could become overwhelming. At some level, this discussion is about creating a bucket of reserves large enough to manage risks, without necessarily having enough to truly handle every possible risk happening all at once. This is especially the case for those with more of a technical liquidity mindset. Also, with the budgeting process, using higher spending estimates can be a way to incorporate a level of spending shocks within the budget. The more one targets to spend in the baseline budget, the less likely it becomes that the full budgeted amount is spent, and some of this excess can be redeployed for spending shocks.

Exhibit 3.6
The Liquidity Goal: Reserves to Cover Retirement Spending Shocks

Spending Shock	Liability Target Amount	Comments
Long-term care	$514,653	We do not have long-term care insurance and will investigate insurance options as we now realize the discomfort we have with this risk. We do not wish to rely on other family members for care. We recognize that some expenses will be offset in the budget in the event of long-term care needs, which partially helps to manage the risk, but nonetheless we feel the need to have a large set aside available to cover a lengthy long-term care need. This amount reflects our estimates for long-term care reserves identified in Chapter 8.
Health care (outside budget)	$83,012	We believe our health care budget is already relatively conservative, including the doubling in real value after age 80. Neither of us has significant health issues, however we do recognize this risk and wish to have an additional layer of funds set aside for unexpected health expenses that exceed what we have budgeted. We identify additional reserves following the process outlined in Chapter 7.
Inflation	$0	Inflation risk is being hedged through the retirement budget with the assumption that budgeted spending will grow with inflation.
Death of a spouse	$0	We have life insurance, and we plan to take care with tax planning, and look at joint-life annuity options to minimize the financial risks created by the death of a spouse. We do not feel a need for an additional set aside.
Family-related responsibilities	$50,000	Our children are establishing their careers and it is unlikely they will need our financial support. We have one living parent who is still able to live independently. We view this risk as relatively minor, but we would like to have some reserves available.
Divorce	$0	Though the risk is understood, we do not seek to set aside reserve funds specifically for this.
Changing public policy and tax rules	$0	We recognize this risk by assuming tax rates will increase in the future when we do our tax projections, and we will also assume a small reduction to our anticipated Social Security benefits to account for the risk of reduction. We feel these steps will properly cover this risk.
Business risks for annuities and pensions	$0	We recognize this risk but feel that our protected income sources will be sustainable.
Excess withdrawal risk	$0	By creating conservative spending estimates for our budget as based on our actual spending experience, we feel we are able to manage the risk of overspending.
Frailty and cognitive decline	$0	Our budget includes a spending increase on housing related expenses. In the early retirement years, this is meant to cover furniture, but over time it can be a resource to pay for additional home maintenance needs we cannot handle. Renting in retirement should also help to manage this risk.
Financial elderly abuse	$20,000	We find this risk to be difficult to quantify and will work to have plans in place to minimize this risk. However, we have decided that having a small set aside will help us to feel more comfortable.
Housing	$0	We are planning to rent in an active adult community and aim to manage our housing needs over time through our budget.
Forced early retirement	$0	We have reached our desired retirement date and do not include future work in our retirement plan.
Total	**$667,665**	

Exhibit 3.6 provides an example for how to manage spending shocks. I list each shock identified in Chapter 2, provide a numerical target for associated reserves, and then provide comments about the decision. This example does show the potential struggle we can have with trying to estimate the amount

of additional assets we seek for events that may not happen. In this example, the couple is quite concerned about long-term care risk. They plan for institutional care prices to rise faster than inflation and to last for multiple years. The couple views this as the biggest potential spending shock risk and would feel more comfortable if $514,653 of additional assets could be set aside at the start of retirement as reserves for potential long-term care expenses. Chapter 8 explains how they derived this number. They will also investigate long-term care insurance to see if it can be an option that would support a smaller reserve for out-of-pocket long-term care expenses. They also decide to include $83,012 for health care in addition to the already conservative amount of health care spending included in their budget. Chapter 7 explains how this number was derived. After also targeting $50,000 for family related responsibilities and $20,000 for elder abuse, they estimate that a contingency fund of $667,665 should be a reasonable amount of additional assets to have available for the unexpected in retirement. For the other risks, they do not anticipate a specific need to have additional reserves. If these reserve assets end up not being used for spending shocks or other unanticipated expenses that exceed the budget, they will likely become part of the eventual legacy for the couple.

Assessing Retirement Preparedness

After quantifying financial goals and their associated liabilities, we are ready to begin the process of assessing retirement preparedness. This process will be explained in terms of quantifying the funded status or funded ratio for retirement. We compare available retirement assets to retirement liabilities to determine whether there are sufficient assets to meet the goals. This can be a helpful starting point for understanding plan sustainability without the need to take market risk.

Retirement Income Optimization Map and Retirement Assets

The Retirement Income Optimization Map© (RIO-Map) illustrated in Exhibit 3.7 identifies the process of mapping assets into retirement liabilities. We have discussed goals and their associated liabilities already. We are now ready to focus on the assets column of the RIO-Map. Assets consist of more than just investment accounts, as we include every resource at the household's disposal for meeting retirement liabilities. Assets are divided between reliable income sources, the diversified portfolio, and reserves.

First, reliable income assets are used to draw consistent income to meet longevity goals by covering essential expenses. The idea for reliable income is to first build a floor of low-risk, contractually-protected income sources to serve basic spending needs in retirement. Reliable income answers the question, "How can I create a base of secure income in retirement that is safeguarded from market volatility?" Reliable income resources include Social Security benefits, annuities with lifetime income protections, traditional pensions, bond income ladders, cash accounts, and potentially continued employment. In some cases, access to home equity through a reverse mortgage may also provide reliable income. These income sources are not all inflation adjusted, which means you need to make sure the floor will be sufficiently protected from inflation, but the underlying idea for reliable income is to securely fund essential expenses.

The safety-first approach will put greater emphasis on ensuring that there is sufficient reliable income to meet longevity expenses. Those with a probability-based style will feel less compelled to match reliable income sources to longevity expenses, concluding that a diversified portfolio using a "safe withdrawal rate" can work out just fine for this purpose. That explains the probability-based arrow extending from the diversified portfolio to essential expenses. Safety-first individuals will be less comfortable treating a diversified portfolio as a source of reliable income.

Exhibit 3.7
Retirement Income Optimization Map©

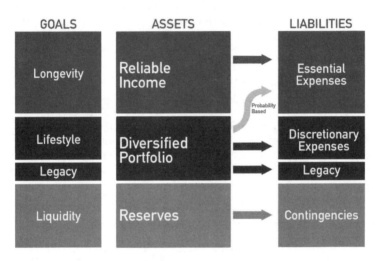

The next asset section of the RIO-Map is the diversified portfolio, which can be used most effectively to meet lifestyle and legacy goals. With the flooring in place for essentials, retirees can focus on upside growth potential with these assets. The diversified portfolio includes brokerage accounts, retirement accounts, and life insurance cash value. Since this extra spending (such as for nice restaurants, extra vacations, etc.) is discretionary, it will not be catastrophic if it must be reduced due to market losses. There is more at stake here than just identifying an asset allocation. We seek to determine how well you are positioned to effectively capture market rates of return, how you have practically managed your portfolio in the past, and what are your strengths and weaknesses in investment knowledge or application that could lead to good or poor outcomes. The diversified portfolio portion of the RIO-Map is about making sure that you have a unified strategy that maximizes your retirement preferences, which is well coordinated with reliable income and reserves.

The final component of assets is reserves. Reserves are aimed to meet the goal of supporting liquidity for contingencies in retirement. These are additional assets not already earmarked for other purposes, which can provide cash flows to fund unexpected spending. Reserves are unique as well in that many types of reserve assets may serve to reduce the potential size of the contingency liability box rather than increase the size of the reserve asset box. This means that we may not end up quantifying a dollar value for all potential reserve assets, but instead just note a smaller contingency liability when non-monetary reserve assets are available. For instance, having a strong network of family and community support in place reduces the need for large expenditures for care in the event of various long-term care, health, cognition, or frailty shocks. As well, a long-term care insurance policy can offset a portion of the tail risk for spending associated with experiencing a significant long-term care need, reducing the size of this contingency. That would lead one to reduce the monetary values identified when working through the spending shock risks outlined in Exhibit 3.6. If the size of the reserve asset box is aligned with the size of the contingency liability, the absolute size of these two boxes is less relevant. The idea is that reserve assets can be used to limit the impact of retirement spending shocks. Reserve assets may include varying combinations of cash and income, insurance policies, the ability to age in place, family assistance and obligations, taking care of one's health, and having a team of retirement professionals. Having extra investment assets available beyond what is earmarked to cover other goals is also a source of reserve assets providing true liquidity.

Viewing these reserves within the RIO-Map could help with psychological angst about feelings of "not having enough" to manage retirement risks. For those with a preference for true liquidity, for an asset to be available to fund contingencies, it cannot be earmarked to cover a different liability. Otherwise, if it is spent on something unexpected, it will no longer be available to cover its original intent. This is a subtle point that can also relate to longevity risk aversion. When relying on an investment portfolio to cover retirement expenses, another reason why people may spend less could be that they have a somewhat amorphous mental account in their mind about using assets. They have earmarked the same pool of investments to cover both lifestyle and liquidity, not clearly distinguishing how these objectives can be separated. Thus, in a sense, they worry that their investments must provide liquidity for contingencies, and they spend less in response. With the RIO-Map framework, we can be more explicit about the available reserve assets, which may allow retirees to feel more comfortable with supporting their lifestyle goals more completely. The next step is to quantify the size of the RIO-Map boxes by creating a retirement balance sheet that includes estimated values for the assets and liabilities.

Funded Ratio

With a budget in place, we next need to think about the overall cost of retirement. A problem with trying to determine the cost for funding financial goals in retirement is that retirees must manage a differing set of risks. Retirement risks include longevity risk, market risk, and spending shocks. Even if the planned budget is exactly right and the precise amount of future annual spending is known, retirees do not know how long they will live and what future market returns will be. The retirement budget will cost more to fund as one lives longer or experiences poor market returns. Spending shocks add further uncertainty around how much will need to be spent. When spending shocks are realized, the cost of retirement grows further. At some point, retirement costs may exceed the available assets.

The funded ratio provides a relatively simple way to understand if one is prepared to fund their lifetime retirement goals as based on their decisions related to these risks. One calculates if retirement assets are large enough to meet retirement liabilities using assumptions about future market returns, longevity, and spending shocks. A funded ratio of 1, implying a funded status of 100 percent, means that retirees have just enough assets to meet their liabilities. Overfunded and underfunded retirees have more or less than this, respectively.

The funded ratio is based on the value of assets and liabilities on the retirement balance sheet. It does not report a probability of success for the financial plan like many financial planning software programs. It is much simpler as it uses a fixed rate of return assumption as a "discount rate" that converts the value of future cash flows into today's dollars. When the discount rate is chosen conservatively, the funded ratio lets us see whether the goals of a retirement plan can be met without taking market risk. I will base the discount rate on long-term bond interest rates, which implies that plan assets will grow throughout retirement with a bond-like return. This can provide better context about how much investment risk one may desire or need when determining the right asset allocation for the plan. If you have already won the game by having sufficient assets without taking risk, this can be helpful in deciding just how much risk to take. A higher discount rate could be used to imply that market returns will be higher, but this also adds risk that poor market returns could reduce the funded status.

For the funded ratio, we must also choose a planning age to define the possible length of retirement. The planning age can be based on objective factors like your health status and subjective factors like your longevity risk aversion. The more one worries about outliving their wealth, the more conservative one must be with respect to assumptions about longevity and portfolio returns. This would raise the assumed cost of funding retirement, which would lead to accumulating more assets before one is comfortable transitioning away from work. The example I provide uses a planning age of 100 for the couple. They base their planning age on the 90th percentile for longevity for a couple in average health as was shown in Exhibit 2.1. Their concerns about longevity risk aversion are satisfied if they have a plan in place that can work until age 100. For this example, I assume that both members of the couple survive to 100, but the plan could be further tested for other scenarios in which one spouse dies sooner as well.

In the previous section, I describe how to develop your planned retirement budget. How will spending differ from preretirement, how will it adjust for inflation or otherwise evolve over time, and how is it divided between essential and discretionary expenses? We also need a proper accounting of any legacy goals and estimates for potential spending shocks and contingencies. These represent the liabilities for your retirement balance sheet. The next step is to gather information about your retirement assets.

The retirement balance sheet shows the assets and liabilities available for a retirement plan. It has a similar design as the RIO-Map, but the difference is that now we attempt to quantify monetary values for the assets and liabilities. The RIO-Map provided a visual illustration of how assets are mapped to liabilities, and that is ultimately the goal with creating the balance sheet for the funded ratio, but at a basic level it is not necessary to start with that mapping. First, we seek to assess the overall situation and then we can shift into examining the size of the boxes on your RIO-Map. This sets the stage for moving into the retirement income funding analysis by quantifying any gaps between the related asset and liability components in the map.

A funded ratio involves more than just financial assets. The retirement balance sheet is the starting point for building a retirement income strategy. At the core is a desire to treat the household retirement problem in the same way that pension funds treat their obligations. Assets should be matched to liabilities with comparable levels of risk. This matching can either be done on a balance sheet level, using the present values of asset and liability streams, or it can be accomplished on a period-by-period basis to match assets to ongoing spending needs. Structuring the retirement income problem in this way makes it easier to keep track of the different aspects of the plan and to make sure that each liability has a funding source. This also allows retirees to more easily determine whether they have sufficient assets to meet their retirement needs or if they may be underfunded. This organizational framework also serves as a foundation for choosing an appropriate asset allocation and for seeing clearly how different retirement income tools fit into an overall plan.

The process for collecting information on your assets is described in Chapter 11 as part of the discussion on getting your financial house in order. You might check that discussion to ensure that you do not overlook anything. We wish to identify the "present discounted value" of any assets that can be used as part of funding retirement liabilities. These present values include the current value of the financial portfolio (banking, brokerage, and retirement plan accounts) and other resources or property currently owned, such as the appraised value of real estate less estimated selling costs and taxes, which could potentially be sold to fund future spending needs. It also includes the present value of other income sources received over the lifetime, such as future employment income, Social Security benefits, an inheritance, pensions, and annuities. Meanwhile, liabilities include current debts, such as a mortgage or loan balance, and the discounted present value of expenditures related to the budget and taxes over the remaining lifetime, as well as contingencies and legacy goals. Such income streams and ongoing expenditures will need to be translated into a present value to add to the balance sheet.

We are separating assets and liabilities between amounts known today and present values of future streams of income or expenses. As for future income and spending, it may be easiest to keep track of these cash flows in inflation-adjusted terms because this provides a translation for the value of future amounts in terms of what can be understood today. To express matters in inflation-adjusted terms, future income and spending needs, as well as the discount rate used in the calculations, are all adjusted downward to account for inflation. If one is consistent about expressing all terms either with their real or nominal values, treating everything in either real or nominal terms is fine. But I find real terms to be the easiest to understand as inflation can just add confusion about the interpretation of future monetary values in terms of their purchasing power.

Returning to the discount rate, the fixed return assumption could be treated as bond yields, in which retirement income is based on building a ladder of individual bonds. In this case, the yield would reflect the average yield from the bond ladder if the yield curve were not otherwise flat. The rate could also reflect the return assumptions for a diversified investment portfolio. In this case, these returns would reflect the net compounding return assumption for the portfolio after fees. The rate can express either nominal or real returns. If nominal returns, then spending would also be nominal and would increase with inflation. But we will generally treat the retirement budget as a real spending value with the inflation effects removed. In this case, the discount should be treated as real returns net of inflation. As inflation is generally a positive number, real returns are less than nominal returns and so the retirement cost will be higher for real spending.

As we are expressing future values in inflation-adjusted terms, the rate of return or discount rate assumption I use reflects yields on Treasury Inflation-Protected Securities (TIPS). These are inflation-protected bonds issued by the US government which offer a real rate of return plus realized inflation. Using a discount rate based on TIPS implies that investment assets consist solely of TIPS, which is the "risk free" asset for an inflation-adjusted spending goal assuming longevity risk is not an issue. The long-term real interest rate on TIPS is approximately 0 percent at the time of writing. That becomes my baseline discount rate for this analysis, as again the starting point for the funded ratio will be to consider whether the retirement plan is funded without taking on additional market risk.

This leads to the example of cash flows for our retiring couple shown in Exhibit 3.8, identified through the planning age of 100. For this couple, two assets will be received as cash flows: a pension and Social Security benefits. The pension is $6,000 at age 65. It is the only cash flow assumed not to grow with inflation. The lack of inflation adjustments is reflected by having its real value decrease each year by an assumed 2 percent inflation rate. Social Security benefits begin at age 70 and provide $52,220 of annual real income, as the couple has decided to delay benefits and the low earner did not qualify for an own benefit (see Chapter 6). One spouse also holds a permanent life insurance policy with a death benefit that they conservatively project to be worth $450,000 at age 100 in terms of today's purchasing power with a 2 percent inflation rate. The death benefit at age 100 is relevant since that is the assumed age of death in the retirement plan. The couple may have other assets such as a vehicle and personal belongings, but these are not included as they will not be used to generate retirement income.

As for liabilities, we use the spending budget outlined in Exhibit 3.5, in which longevity expenses are targeted at $80,364, and lifestyle expenses represent an additional $31,200 for a total spending goal of $111,564 through age 79. Then, for age 80 and later, essential expenses are targeted at $73,928 with an additional $14,000 of lifestyle expenses. These expenses are expressed in real 2021 dollars with an assumption that these spending needs will grow with inflation. I also estimate annual taxes as 5 percent of the annual spending, which can be a reasonable estimate for a tax-efficient plan based on their assets, as will be further explored in Chapter 10. I assume they are in a state with no state income tax, but that would otherwise need to be added to their estimates. The taxes may seem low, but the funded ratio is calculated under the assumption that investments earn a low fixed rate of return matching inflation. There will not be much tax on investment gains. If investment returns end up higher, then more taxes will need to be paid, but the overall funded ratio would also increase if the tax rates on investment earnings are less than 100 percent.

With the cash flows in place and a planning age decided, the next step is to calculate present values for these cash flows for the balance sheet. The row with present values provides these calculations. Calculating these present values requires using a discount rate to reduce the value of future cash flows (assuming a positive discount rate) to account for needing less assets today to fund future expenses. If I know my assets will grow with interest, then I can set aside less today to cover future spending because the interim expected asset growth will cover part of my need. The present value is simply the amount of assets that would need to be set aside today to cover all the future cash flows through the planning age assuming those assets earn interest that matches the discount rate. A larger discount rate would mean less assets are needed today because we could expect greater growth on the assets before they are spent. It would also reduce the present value of assets arriving as future cash flows for the same reason. For instance, a Social Security benefit received in the future would be worth less today because if we had the benefit today, we could earn interest during the intervening years.

Exhibit 3.8
Determining the Present Values for Asset and Liability Cash Flows,
Real Discount Rate = 0%

		Income (Assets)			Spending (Liabilities)		
Year	Age	Pension	Social Security	Life Insurance	Essential living needs	Taxes	Additional Lifestyle
2021	65	$6,000	$0	$0	$80,364	$5,578	$31,200
2022	66	$5,882	$0	$0	$80,364	$5,578	$31,200
2023	67	$5,767	$0	$0	$80,364	$5,578	$31,200
2024	68	$5,654	$0	$0	$80,364	$5,578	$31,200
2025	69	$5,543	$0	$0	$80,364	$5,578	$31,200
2026	70	$5,434	$52,200	$0	$80,364	$5,578	$31,200
2027	71	$5,328	$52,200	$0	$80,364	$5,578	$31,200
2028	72	$5,223	$52,200	$0	$80,364	$5,578	$31,200
...							
2035	79	$4,547	$52,200	$0	$80,364	$5,578	$31,200
2036	80	$4,458	$52,200	$0	$73,928	$4,396	$14,000
...							
2051	95	$3,312	$52,200	$0	$73,928	$4,396	$14,000
2052	96	$3,247	$52,200	$0	$73,928	$4,396	$14,000
2053	97	$3,184	$52,200	$0	$73,928	$4,396	$14,000
2054	98	$3,121	$52,200	$0	$73,928	$4,396	$14,000
2055	99	$3,060	$52,200	$0	$73,928	$4,396	$14,000
2056	100	$3,000	$52,200	$450,000	$73,928	$4,396	$14,000
Present Values		$155,992	$1,618,200	$450,000	$2,757,948	$175,997	$762,000

We use a 0 percent real discount rate matching TIPS yields. The present values of real cash flows are simply the sum of those cash flows. But this would not be the case if the discount rate were different. We use 0 percent to discount the future cash flows which leads to the numbers shown in the present values row. The value of the pension in today's terms is $156k, while Social Security is worth $1.62 million if the couple lives to 100. As an aside, let that sink in... Social Security can be extremely valuable for retirees. As for liabilities, the present value to cover the core longevity expenses through age 100 is $2.76 million, while taxes add $176k and discretionary lifestyle expenses are $762k. With a 0 percent real discount rate, the life insurance policy death benefit at age 100 is also worth the same $450k in today's dollars. If you are interested to calculate present values for your assets and liabilities, you can use the *NPV* function in Excel, with inputs for the desired discount rate and the cells containing the cash flows to be discounted and summed.

The next step for the funded ratio is to add these cash flow present values with the current values of other assets and liabilities to make the overall retirement balance sheet. Exhibit 3.9 provides an example. To the present values of cash flows just described, we add additional assets and liabilities. Assets include $360k as a net sales value for home equity, $26k in checking accounts, $384k in brokerage accounts, $1.29 million of retirement plan assets, and $211k in a Roth IRA.

Exhibit 3.9
The Funded Ratio for the Retirement Plan

Real Discount Rate:	0.0%		
Assets		**Liabilities**	
Reliable Income	**$1,800,192**	**Longevity**	**$2,933,945**
Social Security	*$1,618,200*	Essential living needs	*$2,757,948*
Company pensions	*$155,992*	Taxes	*$175,997*
Checking accounts	$26,000	Debt repayment	*$0*
Diversified Portfolio	**$1,884,194**	**Lifestyle**	**$762,000**
Brokerage accounts	$383,961	Additional Lifestyle	*$762,000*
IRA / 401(k)	$1,289,500		
Roth IRA	$210,733		
Reserves	**$360,000**	**Contingencies (Liquidity)**	**$667,665**
Home Equity	$360,000	Long-term care	*$514,653*
		Health care	*$83,012*
		Other spending shocks	*$70,000*
NON-LEGACY ASSETS	**$4,044,386**	**NON-LEGACY LIABILITIES**	**$4,363,610**
FUNDED RATIO:	92.7%		
Additional Legacy Assets		Surplus (To Legacy) or Shortfall	
Whole Life Policy (Death Benefit)	$450,000	Legacy (+) or Shortfall (-)	$130,776

Note: assets and liabilities listed in italics represent present values for future cash flows; otherwise, they are current market values.

Not counting the life insurance, assets total $4.04 million. My decision to not count the life insurance is worth further discussion, as life insurance can be tricky. This couple has decided not to incorporate a specific legacy goal as a liability for their plan. Any surplus wealth at death will be treated as a legacy, and they will continue to monitor this value. They will think of their life insurance as a legacy asset for this purpose, though there is a possibility that if their plan is underfunded, they could potentially shift to including the cash value of the life insurance to become an additional asset used to fund their retirement liabilities. Life insurance is worth different amounts depending on whether the owner is still alive or has died, and the funded ratio could be explored using different approaches about how it is included. The smaller cash value is relevant if the policy will be used to fund expenses while the owner is alive, but the larger death benefit is relevant if the asset is incorporated into the plan at the owner's death.

On the liabilities side, in addition to the spending values described, which add up to $2.93 million of longevity expenses and $762k of lifestyle expenses, we add the $668k of contingencies calculated in Exhibit 3.6 for this couple as based on their analysis of exposure to spending shocks. These liabilities total $4.36 million. Not counting the life insurance, the present value of assets is about $319k less than the present value of liabilities. The funded status is 92.7 percent, suggesting that the couple is underfunded with respect to their overall goals for retirement. Adding the death benefit to their assets, they do now have a surplus of $131k, suggesting that one potential way to improve their funded status is to incorporate the cash value of the life insurance into the retirement income plan. If the cash value is at least $319k, then the plan is funded by treating the cash value as a funding mechanism for other liabilities. We will explore other options for improving the funded status.

In this example, the funded ratio is less than one (when life insurance is left out of the calculation), implying that the retirement is underfunded. A few natural approaches present themselves as potential responses to an underfunded status. Though perhaps easier said than done, options include to increase assets, decrease liabilities, or earn a higher investment return as expressed by using a larger discount rate for the calculations. Overfunded retirees could reverse some of these ideas.

On the asset side, one could decide to delay retirement and work longer. If it is feasible to continue working, delaying retirement is the most powerful way to improve retirement sustainability, as it allows for more savings and growth, a shorter subsequent retirement to fund, and a strengthened ability to delay Social Security and possibly even increase the primary insurance amount. Additional work impacts this plan by adding the present value for the future earnings as an additional asset. One could simply add these earnings net of taxes or add total earnings as an asset but increase the tax liability to account for the income and payroll tax on these earnings.

Another option for those with longevity risk aversion (which means using a high planning age and low discount rate to feel comfortable) is to include annuities providing lifetime income in the retirement plan. As will be described further in Chapter 5, annuity prices are based on objective measures for mortality and life expectancy for the underlying risk pool, while retirement plans with a conservative planning age assume that retirement lasts longer than average. When individuals live to the planning age, the annuity pays more by providing more spending through its mortality credits. In terms of the funded ratio, this would be expressed as the present value of the annuity payments through age 100 being worth more to the plan than the annuity premium, which increases the value of assets on the balance sheet.

As for decreasing liabilities, this could be reflected through updates for the retirement spending goals. Reducing the annual spending budget, either now or in the future, will have the effect of decreasing the present values for those spending streams. The amount set aside for spending shocks could also be reduced, but with the understanding that this would increase risk exposures for the retirement plan in terms of the potential for falling short in funding other goals after managing large contingencies. Finally, if the plan did include an explicit legacy goal, which this plan does not, that goal could be adjusted downward to reduce the overall cost for the retirement plan.

The third possibility is to assume a higher discount rate, which will usually improve the funded status of a retirement plan because it will typically lead to a bigger reduction in liabilities than in assets. Liabilities tend to be more backdated in retirement (in technical terms, they have a higher duration), especially if there is a legacy goal at the planning age or if there are significant amounts of financial assets available today. It is possible that a higher discount rate will reduce the funded status, perhaps in a rare case such as a very large inheritance that arrives in the future. But generally, a higher discount rate will improve the funded ratio and lead one to believe their financial plan is more sustainable. This may be an illusion, as a higher discount rate implies that underlying financial assets are invested more aggressively, leading to a wider range of planning outcomes on both the upside and downside. As the discount rate increases to include more volatility and upside, there is a greater chance that asset returns will fall short of the discount rate and subsequently reduce the funded status.

Assuming a higher discount rate is worth exploring further, because while it does suggest taking additional risks, most retirees do not plan to fund their retirement budget entirely with TIPS. Exhibit 3.10 shows the funded status of this plan for different real discount rates. In this example, increasing the real discount rate to a little over 1 percent would be sufficient to fully fund the plan with assumed assets and liabilities. Earning such a real rate of return in retirement is not an aggressive assumption, and some retires may be comfortable with the idea that the plan is funded as their expected portfolio returns will be sufficiently higher than what TIPS yields can provide. At least, this reflects a target rate of return that would be required to make the retirement plan work. To justify that assumption, an individual could increase the discount rate based on a healthy portfolio allocation to equities. But caution is suggested when moving in this direction, as any returns assumed above a risk-free rate will be further accompanied by a proportionate amount of volatility with respect to the outcome and a risk that the plan could shift to become underfunded with a market downturn.

Regarding the numbers in Exhibit 3.10, a few additional comments are warranted as the discount rate increases. The present values of any cash flows will decrease as the discount rate increases, which explains why asset values also decline. The values of Social Security, the pension, and the life insurance will decrease. The present values will be less, but these assets will still have the same future purchasing power. It is just a matter that less assets would be required today to provide that purchasing power. These calculations also assume that any financial or real assets that are not present values will appreciate at the same discount rate. In this example, an increase in the discount rate implies an unrealistic rate of return for checking account assets and potentially for home values as well. In addition, I did not re-calculate the tax liability for each discount rate. A higher rate of return would translate into more taxes due, which would offset some of the increase in the funded ratio.

Exhibit 3.10
Sensitivity of Funded Status to the Discount Rate

Real Discount Rate	Assets	Liabilities	Funded Status
-1%	$4,461,623	$5,096,169	87.5%
0%	$4,044,386	$4,363,610	92.7%
1%	$3,721,672	$3,791,422	98.2%
2%	$3,469,749	$3,339,797	103.9%
3%	$3,271,268	$2,979,588	109.8%
4%	$3,113,455	$2,689,294	115.8%

Individuals can decide to use different discount rates for different assets and liabilities with the idea of employing higher discount rates for less essential goals. For example, suppose the couple is comfortable assuming greater market risk is taken for the assets earmarked for contingencies. This would reduce the present value of the liability, which would improve the funded status of the plan. As will be discussed in Chapter 8, if we change the real discount rate for the long-term care contingency from 0 percent to 2 percent, the present value of this liability reduces from $515k to $306k. One could also reasonably use a higher discount rate for the lifestyle liabilities. For instance, a real discount rate of 2 percent values this liability at $578k instead of $762k This improves the funded status of the plan, with the understanding and acceptance of the risk that there are no contractual protections regarding the asset growth as would be the case with TIPS.

Exhibit 3.11 provides an example of the funded ratio with two changes made: the life insurance cash value is counted as a reserve and the lifestyle liability is discounted at 2 percent. This has increased the funded status to 101.2 percent, and now there is surplus wealth of $50k.

Another implication of the funded ratio is that asset allocation can relate to the funded status. Mathematically, the optimal allocation to volatile assets like stocks follows a U-shaped curve with a minimum stock allocation when the funded status is 100 percent. Stock allocations then become more aggressive as one moves further away in either direction. However, when the funded status is less than 100 percent, the mathematical optimization suggesting a higher stock allocation should be accepted with caution. While attempts to make a Hail Mary pass to salvage a financial plan may maximize the probability for a plan's success, matters could also just as easily backfire leaving the funded ratio in an even more dire condition.

Exhibit 3.11
The Funded Ratio for the Retirement Plan
Treat life insurance cash value as reserves and
use 2% real discount rate for lifestyle expenses

Real Discount Rate:	0.0%		
Assets		**Liabilities**	
Reliable Income	**$1,800,192**	**Longevity**	**$2,933,945**
Social Security	$1,618,200	Essential living needs	$2,757,948
Company pensions	$155,992	Taxes	$175,997
Checking accounts	$26,000	Debt repayment	$0
Diversified Portfolio	**$1,884,194**	**Lifestyle**	**$577,851**
Brokerage accounts	$383,961	Additional Lifestyle	$577,851
IRA / 401(k)	$1,289,500		
Roth IRA	$210,733		
Reserves	**$544,660**	**Contingencies (Liquidity)**	**$667,665**
Home Equity	$360,000	Long-term care	$514,653
Whole Life (Cash Value)	$184,660	Health care	$83,012
		Other spending shocks	$70,000
ASSETS	**$4,229,046**	**LIABILITIES**	**$4,179,461**
FUNDED RATIO:	101.2%	Legacy (+) or Shortfall (-)	$49,585

Meanwhile, in fortunate situations where the plan has excess funding, the implication is to think in terms of portfolio insurance in which investment risk can increase as the funded status increases. Options include either leaving the entire financial portfolio exposed to volatility or locking in the liabilities with laddered fixed income assets that meet spending needs on a rolling basis as new bonds mature, or otherwise with annuities that provide protected lifetime income through mortality credits. Then the surplus wealth could be invested for long-term growth. Those who are overfunded with a conservative funded ratio projection will find that their funded status tends to grow even stronger over time.

Probability-based thinkers feel comfortable with applying a distribution rate to an investment portfolio to cover the various types of expenses, while safety-first thinkers prefer reliable income to cover longevity expenses. The reliable income assets may not always provide further upside, but at least they prevent the potential downside tragedy of having achieved a goal and then letting it slip. The danger is that the funded ratio falls, and the retiree is subsequently unable to restore the funded status, which means that the individual had and subsequently lost their ability to meet their lifetime financial goals. To emphasize this point, having a fully funded plan at the present does not ensure retirement success as interest rates could decrease and market volatility may lead to losses. With reliable income, upside is still possible with the other discretionary investment assets that become part of the reserves and surplus wealth.

As an implication of the preceding discussion, one may naturally wonder about the probabilities involved with the evolving funded ratio status as life progresses. A market downturn could cause the funded status to transition from overfunded to underfunded when volatile investment assets are used to fund retirement liabilities. Using Monte Carlo simulations, it is possible to analyze the distribution for the value of the funded ratio at a future point in time, based on the starting point of today's funded ratio. Naturally, greater overfunding would also suggest a higher probability of success for the plan when a volatile investment portfolio is used. Assets, liabilities, and the funded ratio will fluctuate over time in response to portfolio returns, interest rates, inflation, or unexpected spending needs. Obviously, as the funded ratio drifts over time, it may be appropriate to adjust plans.

Finally, we can consider the funded status both from the perspective of the overall RIO-Map and for different subcomponents of the map. Even when the full plan is funded, there may be gaps in some categories, such as whether there is sufficient reliable income to cover longevity expenses. We do observe this happening with the example from Exhibit 3.9. The current reliable income assets fall short of the longevity liability ($1.8 million compared to $2.93 million), while the diversified portfolio exceeds the value of the lifestyle liability ($1.88 million compared to $762k). A probability-based couple may feel comfortable just considering the combined values (that is, $3.68 million of assets compared to $3.7 of liabilities), but a safety-first couple would consider converting part of the diversified portfolio into reliable income assets such as annuities to achieve a better matching for these sub-categories. They can also treat the excess portion of the diversified portfolio as part of their reserves to achieve better alignment with the contingency liability.

Building the retirement balance sheet is an important step in creating a retirement income strategy. Assets should be matched to liabilities with comparable levels of risk. Structuring the retirement income problem in this way makes it easier to keep track of the different aspects of the plan and to make sure that each liability has a funding source. This also allows retirees to more easily determine whether they have sufficient assets to meet their retirement needs or if they may be underfunded with respect to their goals. This organizational framework also serves as a foundation for choosing an appropriate asset allocation and for seeing clearly how different retirement income tools fit into an overall plan.

In subsequent chapters we move forward with refining the details from a funded ratio analysis. Looking ahead, Chapters 4 and 5 focus on different approaches for deploying assets to fund retirement expenses. Using a TIPS ladder, as is done with the funded ratio calculation, as a baseline starting point, greater spending may be possible with a broader approach that includes stocks and/or annuities. We cover sustainable spending from a diversified investment portfolio in Chapter 4 and look at the role for annuities to fund lifetime spending in Chapter 5. We also seek to monitor cash flows and to understand the distribution needs from the investment portfolio over time to monitor sequence-of-return risk and to ensure the timing of cash flows works out in terms of assets being available to fund liabilities at the right time.

Action Plan

We have covered the process of determining whether you have sufficient assets to fund your retirement goals. The following action items summarize the key steps for quantifying your goals and assessing your retirement preparedness:

- ☐ Estimate the Four Ls of retirement: longevity, lifestyle, legacy, and liquidity.
  - ○ Collect data on spending over the previous few years
  - ○ Use past spending as well as analysis of what will change in retirement to develop a baseline retirement budget
  - ○ Organize the retirement budget as essential longevity expenses and discretionary lifestyle expenses
  - ○ Project how spending needs may evolve
  - ○ Determine legacy goals
  - ○ Assess exposure to spending shocks to determine a target for reserves
- ☐ Build a retirement balance sheet by collating household finances and determining all assets and liabilities, including the present value for income and expenses that happen in the future.
- ☐ Choose a planning age and conservative discount rate to apply to the funded ratio calculations, and then calculate the funded ratio.
- ☐ If the plan is underfunded, take initial steps to determine a course of action to improve comfort that one has a reasonably funded plan.

Further Readings

Noonan, Timothy, and Matt Smith. 2012. *Someday Rich: Planning for Sustainable Tomorrows Today*. Hoboken, NJ: John Wiley.

Retirement Researcher. 2021. Take Our Funded Ratio Analysis.
   www.retirementresearcher.com/funded-ratio

Chapter 4: Sustainable Spending from Investments

In this chapter, we focus on the basics of sustainable portfolio distributions in the face of longevity and market risk, which is an important piece of any retirement plan that includes portfolio distributions as a spending source. This chapter provides a summary of the content in my book, *How Much Can I Spend in Retirement? A Guide to Investment-Based Retirement Income Strategies*. Those seeking a deeper dive into these topics may refer to the book for additional details.

The discussion begins with William Bengen's classic research from the 1990s that serves as the foundation for studying retirement spending using "safe" withdrawal rates as based on historical data. He provided us with the concept of the SAFEMAX, which is the highest sustainable spending rate from the worst-case scenario observed in the US historical data. The SAFEMAX was later re-framed in terms of portfolio success rates for different spending strategies, with the idea then becoming to focus on withdrawal rates that are sufficiently low to provide a high probability of success. With this historical data, the rule identified by William Bengen is that for a thirty-year retirement period, a 4 percent inflation-adjusted withdrawal rate using a 50–75 percent stock allocation should be reasonably safe for retirees to use.

Understanding the many assumptions behind the 4 percent rule are important, as suggested spending rates can vary dramatically by changing assumptions. After discussing William Bengen's work in more detail, we then investigate the implications of the many assumptions incorporated in the classic withdrawal rate studies. Some factors suggest that the estimates about sustainable spending provided by traditional studies are too optimistic, such as:

- US historical data is not sufficiently representative of what may happen in the future
- low interest rates and high stock market valuations jeopardize retirement spending in ways not tested by the historical data
- the portfolios of real-world investors – due to fees, asset allocation choices, or investor behavior – may underperform compared to the underlying index returns
- moving toward income-investing approaches can increase risks
- taxes can reduce the level of sustainable spending for a taxable portfolio

- there is a desire to build in a safety margin or bequest at the end of the thirty-year time horizon
- the retirement horizon may last longer than 30 years

However, other factors suggest that reasonable spending levels may be higher than traditional studies imply. Possible reasons include:

- actual retirees may reduce their spending with age
- retirees may build more diversified portfolios than used in the basic research studies
- retirees may benefit by managing downside risk with financial derivatives
- retirees may use bucketing or time segmentation strategies that can help manage sequence risk
- retirees may use a rising equity glide path instead of a fixed asset allocation during retirement
- retirees may have flexibility and are willing to adjust spending for realized portfolio performance
- some retirees may have the capacity and tolerance to accept higher portfolio failure probabilities because they have sufficient sources of income from outside their portfolios
- retirees may draw on uncorrelated "buffer assets" from outside their investment portfolio to support spending and provide relief to the portfolio at key moments

This chapter provides the details that are an essential part of the "probability-based" school of thought for retirement planning. This is especially relevant for people who plan to fund their retirements using an investment portfolio and those who are hesitant about using income annuities or other insurance products. The discussion also matters for the safety-first approach, since retirees will generally still seek to fund some discretionary expenses from investments after allocating sufficient reliable income assets to cover the basics. Ultimately, retirees face a tradeoff with investment spending in retirement as spending more at the present means creating greater risk for needing to reduce spending in the future. Retirees need to weigh the consequences between spending too little and spending too much—that is, being too frugal or running out of assets.

Origins of the 4% Rule - William Bengen's SAFEMAX

In the early 1990s, William Bengen read misguided claims in the popular press that average portfolio returns could guide the calculation of sustainable retirement withdrawal rates. If stocks average 7 percent after inflation, then plugging a 7 percent return into a spreadsheet suggests that retirees could withdraw 7 percent each year without ever dipping into their principal. Bengen recognized the naïveté of ignoring the real-world volatility experienced around that 7 percent return, and he sought to determine what would have worked historically for hypothetical retirees at different points.

For sustainable spending from an investment portfolio, William Bengen's work from the 1990s is the natural starting point on our journey. William Bengen's seminal study in the October 1994 *Journal of Financial Planning*, "Determining Withdrawal Rates Using Historical Data," helped usher in the modern area of retirement withdrawal rate research by codifying the importance of sequence-of-return risk. The problem he set up is simple: a newly retired couple plans to withdraw an inflation-adjusted amount from their savings at the end of every year for a thirty-year retirement period. What is the highest annual sustainable percentage of retirement date assets that can be withdrawn with inflation adjustments for a full thirty years? For a sixty-five-year-old, this leads to a maximum planning age of ninety-five, which Bengen felt was reasonably conservative.

To answer this question, Bengen obtained a copy of Ibbotson Associates' *Stocks, Bonds, Bills, and Inflation* yearbook, which provides monthly data for a variety of US asset classes and inflation since January 1926. He decided to investigate using the S&P 500 index to represent the stock market and intermediate-term government bonds to represent the bond market.

He constructed rolling thirty-year periods from this data (1926 through 1955, then 1927 through 1956, and so on), using a technique called "historical simulations." He calculated the maximum sustainable withdrawal rate for each rolling historical period. Such an approach helps illustrate the role of market volatility in a way that assuming a constant portfolio return does not. Though he did not create the following illustration, his spreadsheet calculations would have shown something like what we see in Exhibit 4.1.

To bring greater realism to the discussion of safe withdrawal rates in retirement, he focused his attention on what he later called the "SAFEMAX"—the highest sustainable withdrawal rate for the worst-case retirement scenario in the historical period. With a fixed 50/50 allocation for stocks and bonds, the SAFEMAX was 4.15 percent, and it occurred for a new hypothetical retiree in 1966 who experienced the 1966–1995 market returns. Searching for this "worst-case scenario" puts the focus on spending conservatively.

For the following discussion, I mostly will use the same assumptions as Bengen's original research, with one exception: I assume retirees make their withdrawals at the start of each year, while Bengen assumes end-of-year withdrawals. I think withdrawals at the start of the year are more realistic, since retirees need the funds in advance of spending them, and this assumption causes my SAFEMAX to be 4.03 percent, compared to Bengen's 4.15 percent.

Assume you start retirement with a $1 million portfolio; the 4.03 percent withdrawal rate means that you could withdraw $40,300 in the first year of retirement. In each subsequent year, you could increase that spending amount by the realized inflation rate from the previous year, and you would have been able to sustain these distributions for at least 30 years in each historical 30-year period of data. In all but this worst-case, you could have spent at a higher rate, or if you did use 4.03 percent then you would have had additional funds remaining at the end of 30 years.

Exhibit 4.1
Maximum Sustainable Withdrawal Rates
For 50/50 Asset Allocation, 30-Year Retirement, Inflation Adjustments
Using SBBI Data, 1926–2020, S&P 500 and Intermediate-Term
Government Bonds

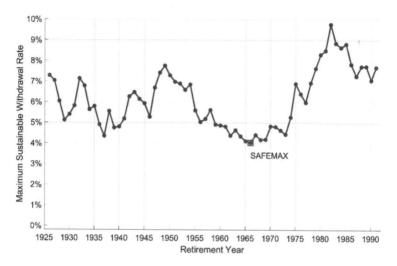

The highest sustainable withdrawal rate was only a little more than 4 percent with market returns from 1966 to 1995. This might be surprising as that 50/50 portfolio provided a 4.7 percent average inflation-adjusted return during those years. Accounting for volatility, the compounded real growth rate for the portfolio in these thirty years was 4.2 percent. If the portfolio could have grown at a fixed 4.2 percent for thirty years, someone withdrawing funds at the start of the year would have been able to use a sustainable withdrawal rate of 5.7 percent of initial assets. The actual withdrawal rate of 4.03 percent is quite a bit less. But why?

To be precise, a 1.3 percent fixed real return is all that is needed to make the 4 percent rule work for 30 years. The further amplifying effects of sequence risk on investment volatility made it seem like the compounded return was only 1.3 percent for retirees that year, instead of the actual 4.2 percent. Sequence risk amplified investment volatility, because the 30-year retirement could not rely on the average market return earned over the 30 years. The early part of the 1966 retirement was a tough time, with stock market losses in 1966, 1969, and 1973–74. This early period set the course for sustainable spending and caused spending to fall below what was implied by the average over the whole period. The markets boomed in the second half of this retirement period, but by then it was too late for the retiree. The portfolio was already on an unsustainable trajectory, leading to the lowest sustainable withdrawal rate in this historical period.

Bengen's work pointed out that sequence-of-return risk will reduce safe, sustainable withdrawal rates below what is implied by the average portfolio return over retirement. Bengen showed that, historically, a 4 percent initial withdrawal turned out to be much more realistic than higher numbers found when ignoring market volatility. Hence, 4 percent became the guideline for retirement withdrawals.

One other important factor from William Bengen's original study is asset allocation. In particular, he recommended that retirees maintain a stock allocation of 50–75 percent, writing in his 1994 article, "I think it is appropriate to advise the client to accept a stock allocation as close to 75 percent as possible, and in no cases less than 50 percent."

Higher stock allocations tended to support higher withdrawal rates, with little in the way of downside risk. The SAFEMAX does not appear to be that much lower with higher stock allocations, though the potential for upside with higher stock allocations is quite striking as higher sustainable withdrawal rates are possible with all but the worst-case outcomes.

Low stock allocations resulted in lower SAFEMAXs, with an all-bonds portfolio falling below a 2.5 percent spending rate. There is a sweet spot between about 35 percent stocks and 80 percent stocks where higher stock allocations have no discernable impact on the SAFEMAX. A 4 percent withdrawal rate tended to work historically no matter what stock allocation was chosen in this range. On the downside, retirees would have been just as well-off with 80 percent stocks as with 35 percent stocks.

Why, then, did William Bengen recommend 50–75 percent stocks? Because when discussing outcomes other than the worst-case, the upside potential was much greater with a higher stock allocation. Higher stock allocations historically led to little downside spending risk, but plenty of upside opportunity. With higher stock allocations, one could use higher withdrawal rates and would leave more legacy at any given rate.

Another of the classic studies in the field of financial and retirement planning is the "Trinity study," a nickname for the article "Retirement Spending: Choosing a Sustainable Withdrawal Rate," by Philip L. Cooley, Carl M. Hubbard, and Daniel T. Walz (all professors at Trinity University in Texas). It appeared in the February 1998 issue of the *Journal of the American Association of Individual Investors*. This study did help to popularize the concept after being discussed in Scott Burns' widely read columns for the *Dallas Morning News*.

Their research followed the same methodology used by William Bengen in his 1994 article. What was different in the Trinity study was the shift in emphasis away from William Bengen's SAFEMAX, or the highest withdrawal rate possible in the worst-case scenario from history, toward the idea of "portfolio success rates." The Trinity study tallied up the percentage of times that withdrawal rates fell below or above certain levels. They calculated these portfolio success rates for different withdrawal rates, for different time horizons, and for different asset allocations. What we can generally observe is that success rates increase for lower withdrawal rates, shorter time horizons, and higher stock allocations.

They also shifted from using intermediate-term government bonds to long-term corporate bonds, which increased the bond volatility and reduced the SAFEMAX below 4 percent in two historical periods for the 50/50 allocation and 30-year time horizon scenario. This reduced the success rate for the 4 percent rule to 95 percent, which made it sound like the result of a Monte Carlo simulation. Intermediate-term government bonds do provide the sweet spot in terms of risk/return tradeoffs to support the highest worst-case withdrawal rates.

An unfortunate side effect of the success rate redirection is that the meaning of these portfolio success rates has been widely misinterpreted. It meant that 4 percent worked 95 percent of the time in the historical data, but that does not necessarily translate into saying that 4 percent has a 95 percent chance to work for newly retired individuals. It is the latter group that people usually care about. One important issue today is that interest rates are so low relative to history, and this is a very important matter when assessing the viability of different withdrawal strategies. In fact, there are numerous underlying assumptions for the 4 percent rule that may vary in their appropriateness for different retirees.

Simplifying assumptions were used in early research, as the purpose was to provide a more realistic assessment of sustainable spending than found when assuming a fixed average investment return. But these studies subsequently took on a life of their own. The 4 percent rule has been widely adopted by the popular press and financial planners as an appropriate guideline for retirees. The 4 percent rule is so widely ingrained in the culture as a universal standard that people commonly think it must apply to any retirement, regardless of the planning horizon. The 4 percent rule is calibrated to a thirty-year retirement. It is not necessarily meant to apply to eighty-five-year-olds, nor can it be safely used by members of the Financial Independence Retire Early (FIRE) community.

The basic philosophy and assumptions behind the 4 percent rule include that the objective is to meet an overall lifestyle spending goal. Retirees are assumed to desire smooth spending, but they also have an appetite for market volatility. Retirees do not voluntarily reduce spending as they age or adjust withdrawals in response to realized financial market returns. Withdrawals are constant, inflation-adjusted amounts. Retirees earn the precise underlying investment returns net of any fees for a fixed asset allocation with annual portfolio rebalancing. The investment portfolio is either tax deferred or tax free. The two financial assets are large-capitalization stocks (S&P 500) and intermediate-term US government bonds. The 4 percent rule assumes the US historical experience is sufficiently representative of what future retirees may expect for their own retirements.

With this approach, failure in retirement is defined as not meeting the overall spending goal for the full assumed retirement time horizon. The underlying objective is to keep the failure rate (the probability of depleting investment assets) at a reasonably low level. For market risk management, retirees use a relatively aggressive diversified portfolio focused on total returns with spending from income and principal. For longevity risk management, retirees assume a planning horizon sufficiently beyond life expectancy, for instance 65-year-olds plan to live to 95. For management of spending shocks, retirees focus on precautionary savings. As the 4 percent rule is calibrated to be sustainable in the worst case from US history, it otherwise preserves assets that will generally gradually become available to be deployed for contingencies in other cases. These are a lot of assumptions. We should consider them more carefully.

Reasons Why the 4% Rule May Be Too High

We will start with considerations about why 4 percent may be too high as an estimate for a "safe" withdrawal rate in retirement.

The International Experience of the 4 Percent Rule

To begin, we should determine whether US historical data is sufficiently representative to have a clear idea of forward-looking "safe" spending rates. Classic safe withdrawal rate studies are largely based on the Ibbotson Associates' *Stocks, Bonds, Bills, and Inflation* (SBBI) data, which outlines total returns for US financial markets since 1926. This should be a concern for several important reasons. First, the period is too short to develop a wide perspective of possible outcomes. Looking at thirty-year retirements, there have only been about three independent observations since 1926.

Second, this period also coincides with the rise of the United States as a world superpower. The twentieth century was a rather remarkable and unparalleled era in the United States from the perspective of any country at any point in history. The US economic engine grew and produced extraordinarily during these years, which could give us overinflated estimates of how high the spending rates and stock allocations can safely extend for future retirees. Markets may behave differently in the future, so simply extrapolating this experience is problematic.

An argument in support of the 4 percent rule is that the post-1926 US historical period includes calamitous market events (Great Depression, Great Stagnation of the 1970s, etc.). As such, the argument goes, it is hard to imagine an even more dire situation awaiting future retirees. The historical success of the 4 percent rule suggests that we can reasonably plan for its continued success in the future.

But from a global perspective, asset returns enjoyed a particularly favorable climate in the twentieth-century United States, and to the extent that the United States may experience a more typical outcome in the twenty-first century, present conceptions of safe withdrawal rates may be less safe. Prospective retirees must consider whether they are comfortable basing retirement decisions on the impressive but perhaps anomalous numbers found in historical US data, or whether they should plan for something closer to the average international experience.

My first foray into researching personal retirement planning was a 2010 study of the sustainability of the 4 percent rule in other developed-market countries. The study is based on a data set providing financial market returns since 1900 for twenty developed-market countries plus GDP-weighted world and world ex-US indexes. The data is from the Dimson-Marsh-Staunton Global Returns Dataset provided by Ibbotson and Morningstar.

From an international perspective, a 4 percent withdrawal rate has been problematic. Updating that study and focusing on a 50 percent stock allocation based on local-country stock and bond markets, the 4 percent rule effectively survived historically only in Canada and the United States. Even allowing for a 10 percent failure rate, 4 percent made the cut only in Canada, the United States, New Zealand, and Denmark. In half of the countries, the SAFEMAX fell below 3 percent. In World War II–era Japan, the SAFEMAX was only 0.3 percent for 1937 retirees. The 4 percent rule would have supported expenditures for only three years. Meanwhile, hyperinflation in Austria led hypothetical retirees at the start of World War I to only sustain a 0.1 percent withdrawal rate from their portfolios. Shockingly, the 4 percent rule would have failed more than half of the time for countries including Spain, Germany, France, Italy, and Austria. Italians attempting to use the 4 percent rule in their domestic financial markets would have faced failure in 76 percent of the historical periods (24 percent success). Around the world, the 4 percent rule worked 68 percent of the time, and the withdrawal would have needed to be lowered to 2.8 percent to have a 90 percent success rate aggregated across all the international data.

From the perspective of a US retiree, the question is this: will the future provide the same asset return patterns as in the past, or should Americans expect lower asset returns to levels more in line with the experiences of other countries? International readers should keep in mind that the 4 percent rule is based on US historical data. Cautious retirees will wish to assume more conservative outcomes than what are found just with US historical data.

The Impact of Low Interest Rates and High Stock Market Valuations

Even if basing the spending analysis on this extraordinary period is otherwise sensible, current market conditions still outweigh the past events when developing sustainable spending rates. Rather than using historical averages to define our capital market expectations, we should be thinking about realistic assumptions based on what is possible for investors considering present conditions. Though forecasting is hard, clues to better ground us in the current reality can be found by looking at current interest rates and stock market valuations.

For those presently reaching retirement, this leads to a second concern beyond that suggested by the international data. US financial markets have entered uncharted waters now regarding the low bond yields and high stock market valuations facing investors.

Classic safe withdrawal rate studies investigate sustainable withdrawal rates from rolling periods of the historical data, giving us an idea of what would have worked in the past. For a thirty-year retirement period, we can learn about the historical sustainable withdrawal rates beginning up to thirty years ago (i.e., 1991). The question remains whether those past outcomes provide reasonable expectations for the future.

This is worth repeating, as it is important to remember and easy to forget. When looking at thirty-year retirements with historical simulations, we can only consider retirements beginning up to 1991. This is what we observed in Exhibit 4.1. With sequence-of-return risk, recent market conditions only show up at the end of these retirements and have little bearing on their outcomes. This matter extends beyond academic interest, as market conditions have witnessed historical extremes in recent years, in terms of both low interest rates and high stock market valuations.

The general problem with attempting to gain insights from historical outcomes is that future market returns and withdrawal rate outcomes are connected to the current values of market return sources. Future stock returns depend on dividend income, growth of underlying earnings, and changes in valuation multiples placed on earnings. If the current dividend yield is below its historical average, then future stock returns will also tend to be lower. When price-earnings multiples are high, markets tend to exhibit mean reversion, so relatively lower future returns should be expected.

Returns on bonds, meanwhile, depend on the initial bond yield and subsequent yield changes. Mathematically, if interest rates stay the same, then current interest rates will reflect the subsequent return on bonds. Low bond yields will tend to translate into lower returns due to less income and the heightened interest rate risk associated with capital losses if interest rates rise. This relationship is very tight. The early 1940s was the only other period where ten-year Treasuries fell to the 2 percent range. Rates are even lower now, and such low rates have not been tested by Bengen's historical simulations methodology.

Sustainable withdrawal rates are intricately related to the returns provided by the underlying investment portfolio. With sequence-of-return risk, the returns experienced in early retirement will weigh disproportionately on the retirement outcome. Current market conditions are much more relevant than historical averages.

This is a matter where Monte Carlo simulations shine, by allowing simulations to begin from today's starting point rather than incorporating historical outcomes generated from completely different market environments. We can consider an example about the sustainability of the 4 percent rule for different underlying assumptions about market returns.

We can use Monte Carlo simulations with the low interest rate world of today as a starting point for the simulations. We will not make any additional adjustments to reflect the high stock market valuation level, but we will preserve the historical equity premium that stocks have earned above bonds. So, when bond yields are low, stock returns must be less as well, as there is no reason to believe that stocks would offer even higher premiums above bonds than they have done in the past.

Exhibit 4.2 provides a way to compare the success rates for the 4 percent rule using Monte Carlo simulations that reduce bond yields at the start of retirement. This is compared with simulations calibrated to historical averages, as well as with the results of rolling period historical simulations. The simulations that start from lower yields reduce the average stock and bond returns by 3.4 percent to center the average real bond return for intermediate-term government bonds at -1 percent. This is a more appropriate real bond return for retirements beginning in 2021. This exhibit makes clear that the low interest rate environment creates additional stresses for the 4 percent rule that were not apparent in Monte Carlo simulations calibrated to historical data with higher bond yield assumptions than are available today. For a 50/50 asset allocation to stocks and bonds, these simulations indicate that the 4 percent rule worked 100 percent of the time in historical simulations, 97 percent of the time in randomized Monte Carlo simulations based on the historical data, and 56 percent of the time in simulations based on the lower average stock and bond returns. The 4 percent rule may work for today's retirees, but it is far from a sure bet or a "safe" spending strategy. In fact, the likelihood of success is much closer to the results of a coin flip.

With lower stock allocations, the 4 percent rule is even less likely to work, because it places demands on spending above what today's interest rate environment can easily support. It is wishful thinking to believe that bonds can earn higher rates of return than implied by today's low interest rate environment. Success is also less for higher stock allocations because of the assumption that the historical risk premium is maintained on top of a lower bond yield.

This exercise about looking at the impacts of interest rates illustrates that assumptions about future returns matter a great deal. Arbitrarily basing Monte Carlo simulations on historical averages, as many retirement planning calculators do, may lead to overly optimistic results. Unfortunately, this is a detail that is not widely understood to this day.

Exhibit 4.2
Portfolio Success Rates for a 4% Withdrawal Rate
Rolling vs. Monte Carlo Simulations
For a 30-Year Retirement, Inflations Adjustments

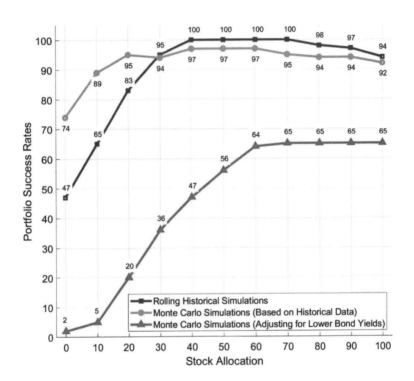

Do Retirees Earn Underlying Market Index Returns?

Another optimistic assumption of classic safe withdrawal rate studies is the assumption that retirees can precisely earn the underlying index returns on their investment portfolios. Three factors dispute that idea. First, expenses may reduce returns below the benchmark levels. Second, many investors may make behavioral and timing mistakes of buying high and selling low. Third, actively-managed funds do not precisely match the underlying benchmarks. As such, many investors will experience investment returns that lag the annually rebalanced and indexed portfolios enjoyed by the hypothetical retiree used in the safe withdrawal rate studies. It is important to consider the impact of account underperformance relative to benchmarks.

Consider if investors underperform the market index by 1 percent per year. With the index returns, a 1966 retiree could sustain withdrawals over thirty years using a 4.03 percent withdrawal rate. With 1 percent underperformance, the SAFEMAX fell by 0.47 percentage points to 3.56 percent. From the perspective of the SAFEMAX, 1 percent underperformance would have resulted in reduced potential spending power of 11.9 percent. Across the historical period, underperformance caused the maximum sustainable withdrawal rates to fall on average by 0.65 percentage points, or 10.9 percent of spending power.

Despite common misconceptions, a one-to-one trade-off between underperformance and withdrawal rates does not exist. As the portfolio decreases in size, underperformance impacts a smaller amount of wealth, while real withdrawal amounts for retirement spending do not change. This explains why the 4 percent rule did not become the 3 percent rule in response to the underperformance. Nevertheless, the potential to underperform indexed market returns does have an important impact on the sustainability of the 4 percent rule.

It is important to emphasize that this 1 percent underperformance should not necessarily be viewed as fund management or financial advisory fees. Doing that would confuse the reality that most investors, on their own, would not be able to earn the underlying benchmark index returns. Evidence on investor behavior suggests that investor returns trail behind overall market performance even net of investment costs. This broader impact can be ascribed to investor behavior and the tendency to buy high and sell low, as well as to use active funds that trade more and underperform relative to the market indices.

Should Retirees Use a Total-Return Investment Portfolio?

Total-return investing focuses on building diversified portfolios from stocks and bonds to seek greater long-term investment growth. By focusing on total return, the objective over the long run is to produce a greater and steadier amount of income relative to what could be obtained by investing for income by focusing solely on interest and dividends to support spending without the need for principal drawdown.

Nonetheless, investing for income is quite popular in practice. Many do-it-yourself retirees and advisors recommend investing for income in retirement, shifting away from a total-return perspective. Such methods have yet to receive much academic scrutiny, as it is difficult to obtain good data on historical returns for portfolios that tilt toward higher-yielding subsectors of the market.

Colleen Jaconetti, a senior investment analyst at Vanguard, has taken care to discuss the issues and pitfalls that come with investing for income. She explains that a retirement income strategy can be based on one of two things: total return or income. In some cases, these strategies are the same. If your asset allocation is designed from a total-return perspective and you can live off the income provided by the portfolio and other income sources from outside the portfolio (e.g., Social Security), then everything is fine.

The problem is what to do when the total-return portfolio does not generate the desired income, as may be common when dividend yields and interest rates are low. In such a situation, a total-return perspective would have you maintain your strategic asset allocation while consuming your principal or adjusting to lower spending. With an income perspective, the last thing you want to do is consume your principal, so you would instead rearrange your investments to provide enough income, so you do not have to sell any assets to meet spending needs. In other words, you chase higher yields than a total market portfolio that is weighted by the market capitalization of all investment offerings. Often this means either shifting to higher-yielding dividend stocks or to bond holdings offering either greater maturity or increased credit risk.

Shifting away from a total market portfolio comes with risk. For higher dividend stocks, the investment portfolio becomes less diversified relative to the total stock market. Dividend-based approaches tend to overweight value stocks relative to the broad market. Portfolios become more concentrated as the top ten holdings in a dividend fund take up a higher percentage of the total fund. It is also important to remember that dividend stocks are not bonds, and the value of these assets is highly correlated with the stock market. A stock downturn can decimate the portfolio value of dividend stocks.

Also, the misconception persists that higher dividends result in higher returns. In fact, the value of the portfolio drops by the amount of the dividend. Total wealth is not affected by a dividend payment. It may be worse, as the dividend may be taxed at a higher income tax rate rather than the long-term capital gains rate, if it is not a qualified dividend. This would diminish after-tax returns. Higher-yielding dividend stocks have historically provided about the same total return as lower dividend stocks before considering taxes.

As for higher-yielding bonds, the idea is to shift toward longer maturity bonds or bonds with greater credit risk. First, switching to higher-yielding, longer-term bonds leaves investors more exposed to capital losses if interest rates increase. Long-term bond prices are more volatile. With current low yields, a small increase in interest rates will result in capital losses that cancel out any higher interest income. As for higher-yielding corporate bonds, this leaves investors more exposed to default risk; when the stock market drops, corporate bond prices tend to do the same, as increased default risk works its way into higher interest rates. This credit risk must be considered alongside any potential for increased yields.

By reaching for yield, investors trade higher current income for a greater risk to future income. This risk must be accepted when moving away from a total-return portfolio. Despite the popular belief, investing for income is not necessarily superior to the total portfolio returns approach that backs the 4 percent rule.

Is Any of the Retirement Portfolio in a Taxable Account?

Most research on sustainable spending rates assumes spending is either from a tax-free account such as a Roth IRA or a tax-deferred account such as a traditional IRA. In the latter case, spending is assumed to be gross of taxes, as any taxes due must be paid from the distributions.

For a taxable account, sustainable spending rates would be negatively impacted by the need to pay ongoing taxes for interest, dividends, any capital gains distributions from mutual funds, and realized net capital gains when assets are sold or rebalanced. These taxes reduce the potential for compounding growth. Because the tax situations of individuals will vary so greatly in terms of tax rates, interest and dividends supported by the portfolio, and the cost basis of the taxable account, it is impossible to create one general number for a sustainable spending rate from a taxable account. This is an area, though, where William Bengen has extended his research to provide some guidance.

In his 2006 book on sustainable spending rates, *Conserving Client Portfolios during Retirement*, William Bengen attempted to estimate the impact of taxes on spending. He estimated that increasing the marginal income tax rate by 25 percent would approximate the impact of capital gains taxes. For instance, someone in a 25 percent tax bracket could estimate the impact of taxes using a 31.25 percent tax rate to approximate the total income tax liability.

Based on his historical SAFEMAX of 4.15 percent, Bengen provides comparisons for different effective tax rates. For a 20 percent effective tax rate (implying a marginal income tax rate of 16 percent), Bengen estimates that the SAFEMAX fell from 4.15 percent to 3.67 percent (a 12 percent decrease in spending power). If the effective tax rate is 35 percent, the SAFEMAX drops to 3.38 percent. With a 45 percent effective tax rate, the SAFEMAX is 3.2 percent. As tax rates increase, the stock allocation required to maximize spending increases as well. That 3.2 percent SAFEMAX number, for instance, requires a 90 percent stock allocation. One final point is that these new withdrawal rate numbers represent numbers net of taxes. Meanwhile, for a tax-deferred account, a SAFEMAX of 4.15 percent with a 25 percent tax rate would reduce the net spending rate to 3.11 percent.

While I cannot provide generalized numbers to show the impact of ongoing taxes on sustainable spending, basic estimates show that the impact can be substantial. Ultimately, the way to manage this tax issue is not necessarily to determine its impact on a sustainable withdrawal rate, but to test the circumstances of one's spending plan with a more complete model that accounts for the different tax treatment between different types of assets. Chapter 10 provides a focus on tax-planning for greater efficiency with retirement distributions.

Is the Retiree Willing to Plan for Complete Portfolio Depletion?

Traditional safe withdrawal rate research regularly assumes that retirees will choose a withdrawal rate that leaves nothing behind at the end of the retirement period. Retirees cling to inflation-adjusted withdrawal amounts, which leaves them playing a game of chicken as their wealth plummets toward zero. In addition, these hypothetical retirees do not make any adjustments for the fact that as their final planned year of retirement approaches, they are increasingly likely to live longer than their planning age. This also means that retirees have no desire to leave a legacy from their investments. The objective of the classical studies is to get a handle on the maximum sustainable withdrawal rate from a portfolio of volatile assets over a thirty-year retirement period without worrying about whether anything will still be left at the end. When we talk about using a safe withdrawal rate, we are describing a situation in which remaining wealth is potentially allowed to fall to zero.

The safe withdrawal rate approach is meant to typically provide leftover funds at the end of the time horizon when not in a worst-case scenario. But the analysis will be different if we specifically incorporate a desire that the worst cases still preserve some assets at the end of the time horizon either as a safety margin or for legacy.

Consider spending rates to maintain the *nominal* value of retirement date wealth at the end of the thirtieth year or maintaining the *real* value of retirement date wealth at the end of the thirtieth year. The value of wealth may decline and rebound in the interim, as I am only checking the value of wealth after the thirtieth year. With our baseline assumptions for a 50/50 portfolio, the classical wealth depletion assumption leads to the worst-case scenario withdrawal rate of 4.03 percent. Switching to an objective to preserve nominal wealth after thirty years, the SAFEMAX falls to 3.77 percent. The 4 percent rule would have been too aggressive to preserve nominal wealth at four historical starting points. When people say they want to preserve the value of their wealth, they are probably implicitly thinking in terms of preserving the real purchasing power of their wealth, even if they do not articulate it as such. People tend to suffer from "money illusion," in which they think in terms of nominal dollars when they really mean to consider the real purchasing power of dollars. The 4 percent withdrawal rate preserves the real purchasing power of initial wealth in about half of the historical simulations, but the SAFEMAX is only 2.72 percent for a retiree seeking to preserve the real value of their retirement date wealth in the worst-case. Any strategy that builds in an additional safety-margin for wealth will experience lower sustainable spending rates than if investment wealth may fall to zero.

What if Retirement Lasts Longer Than 30 Years?

The 4 percent rule is based on a planning horizon of thirty years. In 1994, Bill Bengen considered thirty years to be a reasonable planning horizon for sixty-five-year-old couples, resulting in a planning age of ninety-five. As discussed, the method for self-managing longevity risk is to select a horizon you are unlikely to outlive and then developing a plan which works that long. The horizon should be greater than life expectancy, as retirees have a 50 percent chance of living beyond the average. The conservative approach is to plan for a longer horizon and spend less so the money lasts.

Many people use different planning ages, such as 90 or 100. Those who are either younger or older than sixty-five may need to plan for more or less than thirty years. Even sixty-five-year-olds may wish to plan for different retirement durations depending on how conservative they wish to be and how fearful they are of outliving their investment portfolio. A sixty-five-year-old planning to live to 100 or 105 would need to plan for a thirty-five or forty-year horizon. For healthy individuals in their sixties, we are approaching the point where forty years must replace thirty years as a conservative planning horizon. A longer horizon means spending less to sustain the available resources.

If the retirement is longer than thirty years, the SAFEMAX declines, but at a decreasing rate. The historical SAFEMAX for forty years reduces to 3.72 percent, compared to 4.03 percent for thirty years. With US historical data, an approximation that develops about the historical SAFEMAXs for a 50/50 portfolio as they relate to the time horizon is that the SAFEMAX is about 8 percent for ten-year horizons, 6 percent for fifteen years, 5 percent for twenty years, 4 percent for thirty years, with a further reduction in the direction of 3.5 percent as the time horizon progresses toward an indefinite future. Longer time horizons will guide optimal retirement income solutions toward lower withdrawal rates, higher stock allocations, and a stronger case for guaranteed income retirement products.

Reasons Why the 4% Rule May Be Too Low

While we have covered issues that could lead to a lower sustainable spending rate from a diversified investment portfolio, there are other reasons to instead consider an even higher spending rate as we modify other assumptions regarding the 4 percent rule.

What Are Reasonable Spending Patterns for Retirees?

An important simplifying assumption in William Bengen's research is that retirees spend constant inflation-adjusted amounts throughout retirement. Their budget at the start of retirement always grows precisely for inflation. This behavior may be at odds with the actual spending patterns of many retirees. An exploration of the data should give us an idea of how people change their spending during retirement.

A well-known early example of spending changes over time for retirees can be found in Michael Stein's 1998 book, *The Prosperous Retirement: Guide to the New Reality*. Stein says retirement happens in three phases, popularly known as the Go-Go, Slow-Go, and No-Go years of retirement. He found retirement spending to be greatest in the early active phase of retirement through age seventy-five. In these Go-Go years, discretionary expenses for things such as travel and restaurants are high, and retirement spending tends to keep pace with inflation. Between the ages of seventy-five and eighty-five, retirees enter a transition phase (Slow-Go) in which they become less active and reduce discretionary expenditures. Spending no longer keeps pace with inflation and may even decline on a nominal basis. Finally, after age eighty-five, retirees enter the No-Go years, which are signified by a much more modest spending budget whose growth will generally also trail consumer price inflation.

A more recent contribution to the retirement spending debate is David Blanchett's work on the "retirement spending smile." He notes that spending tends to decrease both at and during retirement. While this again reflects the average outcome, Blanchett's data set provides some ability to follow the same households over time throughout retirement. He uses real household survey data to track the inflation-adjusted spending for retired households. Blanchett observes a "retirement spending smile" that varies slightly for retirees with different household spending levels. From age 65, a retiree might find that their real expenditures decline by as much as 26 percent by age eighty-four. After this point, average real expenditures increase, though they do not necessarily exceed their initial retirement levels until retirees reach their mid-nineties.

Exhibit 4.3
Understanding the Path of Real Retirement Spending by Age

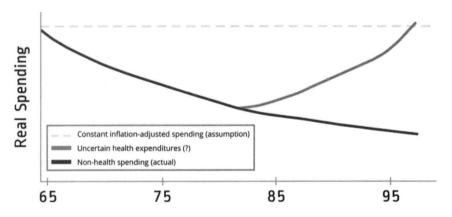

Blanchett observes that the spending smile reflects the same types of outcomes we have described thus far. At the start of retirement, retirees spend more as they enjoy traveling, eating out, and other types of discretionary expenses. As they continue to age, retirees tend to slow down and spend less. However, while discretionary expenses are declining, health costs tend to rise, and later in retirement these rising health costs offset reductions in other spending categories. Exhibit 4.3 provides a further illustration of this process.

The assumption of constant inflation-adjusted spending, according to Blanchett, will lead individuals to over save for retirement. The easiest way to understand this is to simply explore historical sustainable spending rates for different retirement spending patterns. As seen earlier, for a thirty-year retirement and 50/50 portfolio, 4.03 percent represents the historical worst-case sustainable spending rate. With the spending smile, the initial spending rate can increase to account for subsequent spending declines. In this case, I use Blanchett's spending patterns to estimate the worst-case initial spending rate as rising to 4.73 percent. For retirees basing their spending on these historical worst-case numbers, the retirement smile pattern would allow retirement to begin with almost 15 percent less accumulated wealth than otherwise on account of this higher sustainable withdrawal rate. This makes clear that retirement spending patterns are an important component of deciding on a sustainable spending rate. Constant inflation-adjusted spending is a simplifying and conservative assumption.

To decide on the right assumption between constant inflation-adjusted spending, decreased spending, or a retirement spending smile, the best approach will be to study the components of your spending during the budgeting process and do as best as possible to project how these expenses may change over time. One can err to the side of caution to assume that future expenditures will not drop by too much. Spending may decline, so I would not fault anyone for using assumptions of gradual real spending declines such as 10 percent or even 20 percent over the course of retirement. One may also assume a spending decrease but then add more to the spending shocks and contingencies to offset the risk that spending does not decline by as much as anticipated. Ultimately, I would avoid moving too far in the reduced spending direction as a baseline assumption. Though the inflation-adjusted withdrawal assumption could be improved, it builds in reasonable conservatism and may not be too far off for many retirees, even if the *average* retiree experience suggests otherwise.

Can Retirees Benefit from a More Broadly Diversified Portfolio?

Safe withdrawal rates are connected in vitally important ways to underlying asset class choices and their return/volatility characteristics. William Bengen's original research used large-capitalization US stocks and intermediate-term government bonds. Limiting the matter to two basic asset classes may underestimate the potential spending for a more diversified portfolio. Bengen even had ultimately concluded that with a more diversified portfolio including a disproportionate amount of small-capitalization stocks, 4.5 percent was a more reasonable SAFEMAX.

Expanding asset class choices can support a higher sustainable spending rate. A more diversified portfolio can adjust the risk and return tradeoffs. Even if the expected portfolio return does not increase, the sustainable withdrawal rate could be increased if portfolio volatility is less.

In my article, "Capital Market Expectations, Asset Allocation, and Safe Withdrawal Rates," from the January 2012 *Journal of Financial Planning*, I provide a framework for connecting portfolio returns and volatilities to identify sustainable spending rates more broadly. My article proposed a general framework for determining a safe withdrawal rate for a given retirement duration, acceptable failure probability, asset allocation, and capital market expectations. I used Monte Carlo simulations to calculate the combinations of real portfolio arithmetic returns and volatilities that would support different withdrawal rates for various retirement durations and acceptable failure probabilities. This can quantify the specific impacts on the "safe withdrawal rate" as the portfolio returns and volatilities adjust for different assumptions about the asset classes used as well as their characteristics. More generally, this is what is happening behind the scenes when one is calculating the sustainability of a specific retirement plan using software with a specific set of capital market assumptions and portfolio asset allocation. You will see this effect in terms of how changing portfolio returns and volatilities will impact the probability of success for the plan.

Of course, formulating appropriate capital market expectations is hard. Volatility especially complicates the process. A common view is that future stock returns will be lower than historical averages, but what about stock volatility? Would lower stock returns be accompanied by lower volatility, or is it reasonable to keep volatility the same? Might we even expect volatility to increase? Pinpointing the precise combination of expected returns and volatility is important for testing portfolio sustainability. The point of all this is to recognize that assumptions made about asset class characteristics is important in determining a spending rate, and that broader diversification can improve spending by reducing volatility even if returns do not increase.

The Use of Financial Derivatives

Related to the idea of a more diversified asset allocation, another approach that could potentially support a higher withdrawal rate is to change the downside and upside characteristics of portfolio returns with financial derivatives that sacrifice some of the potential upside growth by placing a floor on downside risk. Depending on the mix of changes to upside and downside, a higher sustainable spending rate is conceivable. Protecting from downside losses in the early retirement years will help to manage sequence-of-return risk, such that losing some exposure to upside growth can be justified. This is an area which has not been well studied, as whether outcomes are improved depend on whether the reduced downside losses create more overall benefits than the costs of missing some upside. This is an area in which we may see more developments in the future as ETFs are being developed to provide structured returns along these lines, and as the popularity of fixed indexed annuities and other structured annuities grow.

Can a Bucketing or Time Segmentation Approach Help?

For standard investment approaches, bonds are generally treated as a diversifying asset class that can help to reduce portfolio volatility. The standard accumulation investing philosophy does not consider how the nature of risk changes upon retirement. In short, it uses modern portfolio theory to choose an asset allocation strategy that includes bonds as part of a total-return investment portfolio. Bonds, with their lower expected returns and volatility, offer a way to reduce the portfolio's volatility to an acceptable level while still maintaining a sufficient return.

This approach to using bonds has been challenged by advocates of bucketing or time segmentation. The Financial Planning Association divides retirement income strategies into three categories: systematic withdrawals, time-based segmentation, and essential-versus-discretionary income. We also made this distinction with the RISA Matrix described in Chapter 1, in which those with probability-based and optionality preferences point toward total-return investing approaches, while those with safety-first and optionality preferences may consider bucketing and time segmentation approaches.

The defining characteristic of systematic withdrawal strategies is that rules are used to take distributions in a systematic manner from an investment portfolio designed with a total-return perspective spending consistently from both stocks and bonds. Time segmentation differs from systematic withdrawals in that fixed-income assets are held to maturity to guarantee upcoming retiree expenses over the short and medium term. A growth portfolio is also built with more volatile assets having higher expected returns, to be deployed to cover expenses in the more distant future. Assets are dedicated to the purpose they are best suited for: bonds generate predictable cash flows through their contractual protections, and stocks provide less predictability but more growth potential when left alone to perform. With the emphasis on optionality, those with a preference for time segmentation shy away from the lifetime commitments of annuities. Time segmentation simply involves investing differently for retirement spending goals falling at different points in retirement.

A retirement income bond ladder is the natural starting point for building a retirement income strategy. It can neutralize market-related risks for the retirement income plan by holding bonds to maturity, though it still exposes the retiree to longevity risk, as it is possible to outlive the end-date chosen for the bond ladder. If one seeks to spend more than the bond yield curve can support for a given ladder length, the two options are to seek a risk premium through stock market investments, or to pool longevity risk through insurance products. Time segmentation is comfortable with stocks, but it seeks risk management by having a time horizon built in for which stocks do not need to be sold so they will hopefully then have time to recover from any downturn.

In this regard, a selling point for time segmentation is that it avoids short-term sequence-of-return risk, as the volatile growth assets will not need to be sold immediately after a market drop to support retirement spending. The retiree can wait for markets to recover before selling stocks to extend the bond ladder. A retirement income ladder will naturally wind down if other assets from outside the ladder are not used to extend it further as time passes. That means assets must be sold at some point, and that means sequence risk may remain. But those comfortable with this strategy believe that this risk is quite limited because the windows created will provide the opportunity for growth with the long-term assets before they ever need to be sold. Its advocates are confident that sufficient upside growth will take place before growth assets need to be sold to support spending. Sequence risk only materializes when assets must be sold at a loss to support spending. Whether time segmentation can avoid sequence risk becomes the key to determining whether bucketing approaches might help to improve retirement outcomes relative to a total-return investing approach aside from any behavioral benefits the strategy can provide.

This becomes the primary question about time segmentation: is it a superior way for retirees to invest because it better manages sequence-of-return risk and can therefore support a higher spending rate? What I have found in simulating time segmentation strategies is that any claim that it can increase retirement spending must relate to the utilization of strategies that can increase the stock allocation when markets are going down. Then, the ability to invest more aggressively in market downturn leads to the improved outcome. The mechanism available to shift toward an increasing stock allocation is to simply avoid extending the bond ladder over time; maturing bonds are spent and are not replaced. If this is done when the portfolio looks to be in trouble, then time segmentation may help relative to a total-return portfolio with a fixed asset allocation through the ability to take on more risk.

But advocates of time segmentation may also argue that even if it is not a better pure investing strategy, it can at least lead to better retiree behavior because it is more easily understood. Time segmentation can be more intuitive than the blender approach of the total-return portfolio. People understand that certain assets are to be used for different time horizons in retirement. It is a form of mental accounting. When retirees instead have a front-end bond ladder, they know there is time for stocks to recover before they need to be sold. This provides the courage to leave stocks alone and focus on a more long-term investing approach. The approach is simple and clear to explain and understand.

In the end, appeals to time segmentation should be based as strongly on the behavioral aspects of the strategy as on its performance. For retirees who may struggle to stay the course with a total-return investing approach, the appealing logic of time segmentation could help them maintain better investment discipline in retirement. While time segmentation by itself may not provide a superior investing strategy when compared to a total-return approach with matching dynamic asset allocation, it is a viable strategy deserving of its place in the retirement income toolkit. Retirees must understand, however, that its implementation will mean dynamic asset allocations and adherence to a clear rule regarding when to extend the bond ladder during retirement. Time segmentation cannot generally be used to justify an increased withdrawal rate.

How Does a Rising Equity Glide Path Work?

Returning to total-return investing, a common assumption for withdrawal rate studies is that the asset allocation remains fixed throughout retirement and is rebalanced to the targeted allocation every year. Retirees may not maintain the same fixed asset allocation throughout their retirements for reasons separate from the time segmentation approach just discussed. Nevertheless, this discussion follows the time segmentation discussion as the strategies that I have found to work best in time segmentation will tend to mirror the idea of using a rising equity glide path throughout retirement.

Changing asset allocation over retirement within the context of a total-return investment portfolio can be understood as an attempt to reduce portfolio volatility at key points in retirement to decrease the retiree's exposure to sequence-of-return risk. Even if the average market return is decent, retirees are especially vulnerable to the impact of bad market returns in early retirement. Sequence risk is uniquely caused by the attempt to spend a constant amount each year from a volatile investment portfolio. Sequence risk can be dampened by either letting spending fluctuate or reducing portfolio volatility.

For reducing volatility, outside of just using a low-equity allocation throughout retirement (which comes with its own sets of risks in terms of being unable to support a spending goal beyond the bond yield curve), the rising equity glide path concept reduces volatility when most exposed to absolute wealth losses.

Rising equity glide paths for retirement aim to reduce portfolio volatility in the pivotal years near retirement when a retiree is most vulnerable to losing the most dollars of wealth with a given market drop. People are most vulnerable and have the most at stake when their wealth is largest, which generally happens around retirement. The suggested lifetime stock allocation path thus becomes U-shaped: stock holdings are higher when young, at their lowest around the retirement date, and higher again later in retirement. Exhibit 4.4 illustrates this general pattern.

The idea of a rising equity glide path in retirement is counterintuitive, as conventional wisdom says that stock allocation should decline with age. But the rising equity glide path is intended to be treated as a risk management technique in retirement. It may help support spending and wealth in retirement at times when retirement goals may be most at risk.

To understand the concept of rising equity glide paths, it is worthwhile to consider four general economic environments retirees may face. First, financial markets may do well throughout the entire retirement period. In this case, retirement should be successful regardless of asset allocation strategy, though more aggressive strategies will support a larger legacy. Next, the entire retirement may be confronted by poor market returns. In this case, no allocation strategy can save retirement. A rising stock allocation would at least fare better than a more aggressive asset allocation throughout. Third, financial markets may perform well in early retirement but poorly later in retirement. In this case, sequence risk will not manifest, and the sustainable withdrawal rate will be high. Rising equity glide paths will work, but they may leave less legacy than otherwise. Finally, the rising stock glide path excels in scenarios that have historically led to the worst outcomes for retirees. That is, markets fare poorly early in retirement and then recover later in retirement. These scenarios have created the lowest withdrawal rates for past retirees, and this is where a rising equity glide path can support improved retirement outcomes.

Exhibit 4.4
Stylized Lifetime Stock Allocation Glide Path with a Rising Equity Glide Path in Retirement

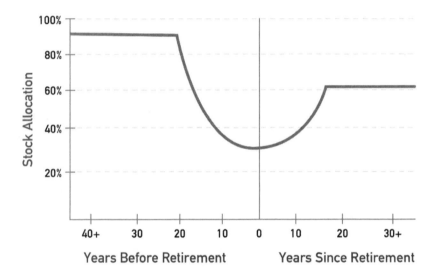

While the rising equity glide path idea is intended as a risk management technique, there are obvious real-world implications that may limit its usefulness. Primarily, it may be that as people age, it becomes increasingly difficult to stay the course in response to market volatility, and retirees who have experienced a period in early retirement where they dealt with less volatility may not be prepared to deal with volatility again late in life. Perhaps the best implication from research along these lines is to at least not think about continuing to reduce stock allocations throughout retirement, and that it may be okay to start retirement with a lower stock allocation than the traditional withdrawal rate studies suggest.

As well, when thinking about the entire retirement balance sheet, retirees may be using a rising equity glide path without even realizing it. If we think of Social Security, pensions, and annuities as bond-like assets whose remaining value declines with age, those who maintain a fixed asset allocation in their portfolios and who to do not experience the sequence risk that causes rapid portfolio decline may experience an increase in their allocation to stocks as their retirement progresses.

What if Retirees are Flexible About Their Spending?

William Bengen's 1994 article introduced the concept of the 4 percent rule for retirement withdrawals. He defined the sustainable spending rate as the percentage of retirement date assets that can be withdrawn, with this spending amount adjusted for inflation in subsequent years. In this scenario, the retirement portfolio will not deplete for at least thirty years with an allocation of at least 50 percent to stocks. Bengen's rule says to adjust spending annually for inflation and maintain constant inflation-adjusted spending until the portfolio depletes. Annual spending increases by the previous year's inflation rate. Spending does not respond at all to portfolio investment performance in retirement.

While this assumption may reflect the *preferences* of many retirees to smooth their spending as much as possible, real-world individuals will inevitably adjust their spending over time in response to performance of their portfolio. Cuts will be made if the markets are down. Retirees will not generally play the implied game of chicken by keeping their real spending constant as their portfolios plummet toward zero. It is an unrealistic assumption.

Being flexible with spending matters a great deal. Constant spending from a volatile portfolio is a unique source of sequence-of-return risk that can be partially alleviated by reducing spending when the portfolio drops in value. Traditional safety-first advocates would argue that the Bengen strategy is inherently flawed—those seeking constant spending should use a less volatile retirement portfolio, and those who accept portfolio volatility should also accept spending volatility.

Thus, an important mechanism for managing sequence risk is to allow spending to fluctuate over time. Reducing spending in the event of a market decline provides a release valve for sequence-of-return risk that can allow the initial withdrawal rate to increase. This is because the current withdrawal rate does not have to be increased by as much when the portfolio loses value. This allows for less shares to be sold at a loss and more assets to remain available in the investment portfolio to experience any subsequent market recovery. Managing sequence-of-return risk in this manner allows synergies to develop, making it possible to keep spending at a higher average level than a constant inflation-adjusted strategy without any flexibility, while maintaining the same overall risk for portfolio depletion. With spending flexibility, the initial withdrawal rate can increase by more than one might think on account of these synergies created through decreasing sequence risk. As such, estimates obtained with a constant inflation-adjusted spending assumption may be overly conservative for those willing and able to adjust their spending later.

While the constant inflation-adjusted spending strategy provides a useful benchmark and baseline for analyzing sustainable retirement spending strategies, it should probably not be viewed as a realistic or reasonable retirement income strategy. Efficient retirement strategies must adjust spending at least somewhat for portfolio volatility. The question then becomes how and when to make these adjustments.

On the spectrum of spending strategies, the fixed-percentage withdrawal strategy is the opposite of constant inflation-adjusted spending. The fixed-percentage strategy calls for retirees to spend a constant percentage of the remaining portfolio balance in each year of retirement. Occasionally the popular press will mistakenly define the 4 percent rule this way (a 4 percent fixed percentage strategy calls for withdrawing 4 percent of the remaining account balance each year), but the accepted definition of the 4 percent rule is the constant inflation-adjustment spending strategy described earlier. To be clear, with constant inflation-adjusted spending, the withdrawal rate will change throughout retirement as the portfolio value changes. The withdrawal rate adjusts, while spending stays the same. But with the fixed-percentage rule, the withdrawal rate stays the same, while spending adjusts.

An advantage of the fixed-percentage strategy is that, since it always spends a *percentage* of what remains, it never depletes the portfolio. Of course, spending could fall to uncomfortably low levels, but the concept of portfolio failure rates is inapplicable here. In addition, spending increases when market returns outpace the spending rate, and the portfolio grows. As well, this strategy eliminates sequence-of-return risk, as late and great Dirk Cotton first pointed out in 2013 at his Retirement Café blog. The fixed-percentage approach provides a clear mechanism for reducing spending after a portfolio decline. As with investing a lump sum of assets, the specific order of returns makes no difference to the final outcomes realized with this strategy. As such, we can expect the sustainable spending rate to be higher than with constant inflation-adjusted withdrawals.

As for disadvantages, when combined with volatile investments, spending can become extremely volatile with this strategy, making it difficult for retirees to budget for the future. For a fixed retirement budget, managing retirement with this rule could be a challenge. Those considering this rule should probably be thinking in terms of applying it to discretionary expenses that allow more flexibility for spending reductions that will not derail a retiree's standard of living.

With these advantages and limitations in mind, it is important to remember that the fixed percentage rule is the opposite extreme from constant spending. Most practical approaches to flexible retirement spending seek to balance the trade-offs between reduced sequence risk and increased spending volatility by only partially linking spending to portfolio performance. Variable spending strategies tend to seek a compromise between holding spending steady to avoid fluctuations in lifestyle and varying spending enough to adequately protect from the risk of portfolio depletion. Compromise strategies provide a mechanism to smooth spending adjustments made in response to market volatility. Many strategies seek to obtain some advantages of the fixed-percentage rule, while also reducing the frequency and size of spending adjustments and placing bounds on how far spending can increase or decrease.

For example, William Bengen has also described floor-and-ceiling withdrawals as one such spending compromise. This method begins by applying the fixed percentage rule, which allows greater spending when markets do well, and which forces spending reductions when markets do poorly. Bengen also adds hard dollar ceilings and floors on spending. Spending is not allowed to fluctuate outside of a specified range. So, the fixed-percentage rule is applied when spending falls inside the bands and a constant amount strategy is applied at the ceiling or floor when the fixed-percentage rule would force spending outside of this range. This keeps spending from drifting too far from its initial levels, helping to smooth spending fluctuations while helping to manage sequence risk and allowing for a higher initial spending rate.

There are also countless other examples of variable spending strategies that apply different approaches to adjusting spending. Jonathan Guyton and William Klinger, for instance, developed a series of decision rules that allow for a higher initial spending rate but provide guardrails around spending to keep the ongoing distribution rate from rising too high as a percentage of remaining assets. For another example, David Zolt introduced the Target Percentage Adjustment method. It provides a rule for determining when spending adjusts for inflation or remains fixed in nominal terms.

Another style of spending rule involves using actuarial methods. Actuarial methods generally involve retirees recalculating their sustainable spending annually based on the remaining portfolio balance, remaining longevity, and expected portfolio returns. This approach uses an increasing percentage from the remaining portfolio over time to accounting for the shortening remaining life expectancy as one ages. A simple form for the actuarial method is to use the Internal Revenue Services' required minimum distribution (RMD) rules (these spending rules always use Table III for RMD rates, see Chapter 10 for more on this) as a more general guide for sustainable spending. For the purposes of tax collection, the RMD rules indicate a by-age percentage that must be withdrawn from tax-deferred accounts.

The RMD rule contains the actuarial components of spending a percentage of remaining assets, which is calibrated to an updating remaining life expectancy. Its deficiency is that it does not provide a mechanism for users to adjust their portfolio return assumption beyond what government policy makers initially assumed when developing the by-age RMD rates. The RMD rules assume investment returns of 0 percent, so they do not reflect asset allocation or other market return assumptions. With this conservative return assumption, some retirees may decide the RMD strategy provides overly conservative spending rates. Another possibility, then, is to increase all the RMD rates by a chosen factor to increase spending. Any of these variable spending strategies will reduce sequence risk in retirement and allow for higher initial spending rates, potentially higher average spending amounts, and a generally more efficient spenddown of assets than the baseline constant inflation-adjusted spending strategy associated with the traditional 4 percent rule.

How Does an "Optimal" Withdrawal Rate Relate to a "Safe" Withdrawal Rate?

The Trinity study that we mentioned earlier had established the idea of focusing on success rates and failure rates, building into our psyche the idea that one's retirement is a failure if the investment portfolio depletes. This has put too much emphasis on the portfolio and on spending conservatively to keep failure rates low. This is not the whole story, as certain circumstances may allow retirees to accept a higher probability of "failure" and spend more aggressively from their investment portfolio. Depleting the investment portfolio is not always catastrophic.

We must evaluate the trade-off between reducing spending today to better protect future spending potential and seeking to enjoy the highest possible living standard today even if that creates greater risks for having to make cutbacks later in retirement. This speaks to the RISA Profile factor of Front-Loading or Back-Loading retirement income. Withdrawal rate studies have typically focused on the probability of depleting the portfolio while still alive, without considering what is lost in terms of life satisfaction by using a lower withdrawal rate and spending less, implying a strong Back-Loading preference. When using low withdrawal rates, retirees will typically leave behind a large pot of wealth (unless their retirement returns sequence matches the worst-case scenario). Less retirement spending and unintendedly large legacies are not the goals for most retirees.

When taking portfolio spending out of the vacuum, there are four interrelated factors that we must consider:

- Reliable income sources: what proportion of your retirement spending is covered through reliable income sources from outside the investment portfolio?
- Longevity risk aversion: how fearful are you about outliving your investment portfolio in retirement? This is an emotional characteristic unrelated to whether you may outlive your portfolio in an objective sense. It reflects a preference for Back-Loading.
- Spending flexibility: is it possible to reduce portfolio distributions without creating significant harm to your standard of living?
- Availability of reserves: what other resources are available that have not been earmarked to manage spending and can be used to cover contingencies?

These factors all relate to what is an acceptable probability of success, or probability of failure, for the retirement plan. For someone who worries and loses sleep about outliving his or her portfolio, does not have much additional income from outside the portfolio, mostly faces fixed expenses without much room to make cuts, and does not have much in the way of backup reserves, it may be necessary to plan for a quite high probability of success. This will imply using a lower stock allocation and a lower spending rate.

However, for someone who has less fear about outliving his or her portfolio, has additional income sources from outside the portfolio that reduce the lifestyle impact of depleting investments, has the flexibility to cut portfolio distributions without adversely impacting lifestyle, and has sufficient additional reserves, a higher spending rate accompanied by a lower probability of success can be "optimal."

To be more explicit about what all of this means, we must distinguish between "safe" withdrawal rates and "optimal" withdrawal rates. While we discussed earlier how the 4 percent rule may be too high for those focused on identifying a sustainable withdrawal rate that will not deplete the portfolio over a thirty-year period, this does not necessarily forbid the use of 4 percent or higher. Retirees may still choose higher withdrawal rates as a part of downplaying the potential impact of investment portfolio depletion. A higher withdrawal rate may be optimal in some cases even though it is associated with a high probability of failure. A simple focus on a retirement income strategy that applies a low failure rate for the investment portfolio is woefully incomplete. Retirees need to be thinking about a more complete model that incorporates these factors.

How Might Using a Buffer Asset Help?

There are four general ways to manage sequence of returns and longevity risk for a retirement spending budget. These include spending less, being flexible with spending and reducing it after downturns, reducing the sensitivity of spending to portfolio volatility, and strategically drawing from non-correlated buffer assets held outside the investment portfolio. We now consider that fourth approach.

Buffer assets are held outside the financial portfolio and can be drawn from to cover retirement spending when the portfolio is in danger. Returns on these assets should not be correlated with the financial portfolio, since the purpose of these buffer assets is to support spending when the portfolio is otherwise falling short. Buffer assets must be liquid and must not decline in value along with a general market downturn. In other words, buffer assets should have non-negative returns. Buffer assets are conceptually different from time segmentation and as such are held outside of the portfolio. They will only be employed temporarily under certain market conditions. However, in terms of the RISA Profile and the RISA Matrix, strategies that involve a heavy use of buffer assets will mostly fit best in the time segmentation quadrant. The three buffer assets that have been described are cash holdings, cash value for whole life insurance, and a growing line of credit for a Home Equity Conversion Mortgage (reverse mortgage).

The original buffer asset is to maintain a separate cash reserve, perhaps with two or more years of retirement expenses, separate from the rest of the investment portfolio. Harold Evensky was an early adopter of the cash reserve strategy, having developed the "five-year mantra" for his clients in the 1980s. Writing about it in the 2006 book, *Retirement Income Redesigned*, Evensky extolled the behavioral benefits of his approach, as it helped his clients to avoid panic during downturns and to stay the course with up to five years to wait for market recovery. While this might sound like time segmentation, the difference is that this cash is not spent on a consistent basis. It is set aside as a spending resource only for when the portfolio looks to be in danger. Cash can be a drag on portfolio returns, and in recent years more attention has focused on other alternatives such as the reverse mortgage and life insurance to be used in the same general way as buffer assets or volatility buffers.

In isolation, using buffer assets may look expensive. With cash holdings, yield is sacrificed. Reverse mortgages and whole life insurance include notable set-up expenses and do reflect using loans that will accumulate interest. But buffer assets should not be viewed in isolation. They are a piece of a larger puzzle that retirees are trying to solve. The costs can be offset by gains elsewhere in the overall financial plan through their ability to help manage sequence-of-return risk. Buffer assets can work to protect the investment portfolio from incurring excessive distributions. That helps to manage sequence risk, which allows for the portfolio to maintain a higher long-term balance exceeding the buffer asset costs. This creates an overall net benefit through the synergies of better managing sequence-of-return risk.

In my simulations, I have found that the benefits for the portfolio from reducing the sequence risk were more than able to offset the costs for setting up and using either a reverse mortgages or whole life insurance as a buffer asset in a coordinated strategy. The benefits from reducing distribution pressures on the investment portfolio more than offset the costs of spending from these buffer assets. Buffer assets provide a sophisticated technique to grapple with sequence-of-return risk by only spending from the buffer when the retiree is vulnerable to locking in portfolio losses.

As for how to implement a decision rule for when to spend from the buffer asset, practitioners of these approaches describe many different approaches. I have tested numerous possibilities and found a very simple rule to use which works just as well as any of the more complicated systems out there. It involves considering the size of the investment portfolio at the beginning of retirement. At subsequent points, whenever a distribution is sought to cover spending, compare the nominal value of the portfolio at that point to its initial retirement level. If the portfolio is larger than at the start of retirement, then spend from it. But if the remaining portfolio balance is falling short of where it started, then take the distribution from the buffer asset. If the portfolio subsequently recovers and exceeds its starting level, one then has discretion about whether to voluntarily pay down the loan balance on the buffer asset to preserve its potential use again later in retirement. This is not necessary though, since loan balances on buffer assets do not have any set repayment schedule and can be deferred to death or to when otherwise leaving the home in the case of a reverse mortgage.

Action Plan

We have described the assumptions and evolution of the 4 percent guideline for spending from investments in retirement, and then we considered a series of factors explaining why retirees may wish to use either a lower or a higher spending rate from their own investments. The action items for this discussion relate to how one goes about fitting these factors together to determine an overall strategy for the diversified portfolio component of retirement spending.

However, while it is important to include this discussion early in the process of retirement income planning, these determinations should be made later in the planning process when it comes time to fit all the pieces together. For example, you cannot really decide on a withdrawal rate before you have considered whether to use an annuity. I developed the Retirement CARE Analysis™ as a framework for incorporating this discussion into planning so that one can determine appropriate investment spending and asset allocation strategies for the retirement income plan. We will return to this topic in Chapter 13 as part of putting these pieces together. For this reason, I am holding off on providing a list of action items for this chapter.

There is a key point with which to finish the chapter. I have developed a reputation as being quite concerned about using the 4 percent rule in practice. Especially with low interest rates, I am concerned that 4 percent is too aggressive for a retiree who really wants to meet the rule's underlying assumptions. But retirees can implement a variety of techniques described here that can increase withdrawal rates, such as reducing their spending later in retirement, using a broader asset allocation, adjusting spending in response to portfolio performance, tapping into buffer assets from outside the portfolio, and accessing reliable income from outside the portfolio that reduces the harm created if the 4 percent rule does not work. With all these factors at play, a retiree might still find it to be appropriate to use a withdrawal rate of 4 percent or higher at the start of retirement even if the 4 percent rule, as strictly defined, is not safe.

Further Reading

Bengen, William P. 1994. "Determining Withdrawal Rates Using Historical Data." *Journal of Financial Planning* 7 (4): 171–180.

Bengen, William P. 2006. *Conserving Client Portfolios during Retirement.* Denver: FPA Press.

Bengen, William P. 2012. "How Much Is Enough?" *Financial Advisor* (May).

Blanchett, David. 2014. "Exploring the Retirement Consumption Puzzles." *Journal of Financial Planning* 27 (5): 34–42.

Cooley, Philip L., Carl M. Hubbard, and Daniel T. Walz. 1998. "Retirement Savings: Choosing a Withdrawal Rate That Is Sustainable." *American Association of Individual Investors Journal* 20 (2): 16–21.

Cotton, Dirk. 2013. "Clarifying Sequence of Returns Risk (Part 2, with Pictures!)." Retirement Café (blog), September 20.

Finke, Michael, Wade D. Pfau, and Duncan Williams. 2012. "Spending Flexibility and Safe Withdrawal Rates." *Journal of Financial Planning* 25 (3): 44–51.

Guyton, Jonathan T., and William J. Klinger. 2006. "Decision Rules and Maximum Initial Withdrawal Rates." *Journal of Financial Planning* 19:49–57.

Huxley, Stephen J., and J. Brent Burns. 2004. *Asset Dedication: How to Grow Wealthy with the Next Generation of Asset Allocation*. New York: McGraw-Hill.

Jaconetti, Colleen. 2012. "Investing for Income in Today's Environment." The American College–New York Life Center for Retirement Income Video Series. https://retirement.theamericancollege.edu/video-library/investing-income-todays-environment.

Pfau, Wade D. 2010. "An International Perspective on Safe Withdrawal Rates: The Demise of the 4% Rule?" *Journal of Financial Planning* 23 (12): 52–61.

Pfau, Wade D. 2012. "Capital Market Expectations, Asset Allocation, and Safe Withdrawal Rates." *Journal of Financial Planning* 25 (1): 36–43.

Pfau, Wade. 2017. *How Much Can I Spend in Retirement: A Guide to Investment-Based Retirement Income Strategies*. McLean, VA: Retirement Researcher Media.

Pfau, Wade D., and Michael E. Kitces. 2014. "Reducing Retirement Risk with a Rising Equity Glide Path." *Journal of Financial Planning* 27 (1): 38–45.

Stein, Michael. 1998. *The Prosperous Retirement: Guide to the New Reality*. Emstco Press.

Chapter 5: Annuities and Risk Pooling

Annuities are another important tool for funding retirement spending. They are contracts which can be structured to provide a series of payments from an insurance company, either for life or for a fixed period. Lifetime income protections available through annuities can support a retirement income goal through risk pooling and mortality credits. The contract owner is the one who buys and makes decisions about an annuity contract. The annuitant is the person or persons on whose age and survival is used to determine annuity payments. The contract owner is often also the annuitant, but this is not strictly necessary. The beneficiary is the one who will receive any death proceeds from the annuity.

A Caveat on Annuities

In this discussion, I am mostly making an implicit assumption that the annuity is competitively priced. Fees reflect what is needed to support the guarantees provided by the insurance company and to keep the company profitable. But fees are not excessive such that the value to the consumer is eliminated. Not all annuities are created equally in this regard. Deferred annuities, especially, can be complex financial instruments. That complexity can hide a lack of competitiveness in the pricing of individual products. An annuity that is pitched along with a free dinner presentation is possibly not the type of financial product I have in mind. One should tread carefully. Due diligence and a comparison with other annuity options is necessary to ensure that the product is priced fairly and aligns with the purchaser's expectations. I do not want the "bad" annuities out there to catch a free-ride off of my explanations about "good" annuities.

Many types of annuities exist. Our focus will be on immediate and deferred income annuities, deferred variable annuities, and deferred fixed index annuities. In providing an overview of annuity types and how they can be incorporated into retirement planning, this chapter provides a summary of the content from my book, *Safety-First Retirement Planning: An Integrated Approach for a Worry-Free Retirement*. Readers seeking a deeper dive into these topics may refer to that book for additional details.

We now will discuss the basic logic behind annuities, how different types of annuities work, and how annuities can fit into a retirement income plan.

The Fundamental Logic of Annuities with Lifetime Income

Before digging deeper into different types of annuities, it is worth first focusing on how a basic life-only income annuity works and how it fits into retirement planning. A simple annuity can effectively replace bond holdings in a retirement plan that are earmarked to meet the lifetime spending goal. The question is why should a retiree hold any bonds in the portion of their asset base designed to cover ongoing retirement spending goals?

Premiums for the income annuity are invested in bonds (the insurance company adds your premium to its bond-heavy general account). The annuity then provides payments precisely matched to the length of time they are needed. Stocks provide opportunities for greater investment growth. Individual bonds can support an income for a fixed period, but they do not offer longevity protection beyond the horizon of the bond ladder created. Bond funds are volatile, exposing retirees to potential losses and sequence risk while still not providing enough upside potential to support a particularly high level of spending over a long retirement. Risk pooling with an income annuity can support a higher level of lifetime spending compared to bonds. Stocks also offer the opportunity for higher spending, but without any guarantee that stocks will outperform bonds and provide capital gains during the pivotal early years of retirement.

Income annuities can be viewed as a type of coupon bond which provides payments for an uncertain length of time in which the principal value is not repaid upon death. Another way to think about income annuities is that they provide a laddered collection of zero-coupon bonds that support retirement spending for as long as the annuitant lives. Much like a defined-benefit pension plan, income annuities provide value to their owners by pooling risks across a large grouping of individuals.

Longevity risk is one of the key risks which can be managed effectively by an income annuity. Investment and sequence risk are also alleviated through the more conservative investing and asset-liability matching approach on the part of the insurance company for the underlying assets held in the insurance company's general account. The payout rates for an income annuity assume bond-like returns and longevity is further supported through risk pooling and mortality credits, rather than by seeking outsized stock market returns.

Longevity risk relates to not knowing how long a given individual will live. But while we do not know the longevity for any one individual, insurance company actuaries can estimate how longevity patterns will play out for a large cohort of individuals. The "special sauce" of the income annuity is that it can provide payouts linked to the average longevity of the owners because those who die early end up leaving money on the table to subsidize the payments to those who live longer. Though it may seem counterintuitive to subsidize payments to others, this act can allow all owners in the risk pool to enjoy a higher standard of living than bonds could support. All annuity owners know that the mortality credits will be waiting for them if they do end up living beyond life expectancy.

Meanwhile, sequence risk relates to the amplified impacts that investment volatility has on a retirement income plan that seeks to sustain withdrawals from a volatile investment portfolio. Even though we may expect stocks to outperform bonds, this amplified investment risk also forces conservative individuals to spend less in case their early retirement years are affected by a sequence of poor investment returns. Many retirement plans are based on Monte Carlo simulations with a high probability of success, which implicitly assumes lower investment returns. An income annuity also avoids sequence risk because the underlying assets are invested by the annuity provider, mostly into individual bonds which create income that matches the company's obligations for covering its promised annuity payments.

In hindsight, those who experienced either shorter retirements or who benefited from retiring at a time with strong market returns would have probably preferred if they had not purchased an income annuity. Income annuities are a form of insurance. They insure against outliving assets due to some combination of a long life and poor market returns. In the same vein, someone who purchased automobile insurance might wish they had gone without if they never had an accident. But this misses the point of insurance. We use insurance to protect against low probability but costly events. In this case, an income annuity provides insurance against outliving assets and insufficient income late in retirement.

Income annuities offer an important benefit to those who do not make it long into retirement, especially for those who are particularly worried about outliving their assets. That benefit can be seen when comparing the income annuity to the alternative of basing retirement spending strictly on a systematic withdrawal strategy from an investment portfolio. To "self-annuitize," a retiree must spend more conservatively to account for the small possibility of living to age ninety-five or beyond while also being affected by a poor sequence of market returns in early retirement. The income annuity supports a higher spending rate and standard of living than this from the outset. All income annuity owners, both the short-lived and long-lived, can enjoy a higher standard of living during their life than they would have otherwise felt comfortable with by taking equivalent amounts of distributions from their investments.

Upon entering retirement, a retiree has several options regarding allocations between stocks, bonds, and income annuities. Let us consider a simple example with four different approaches. With the basic understanding in place, we can then dig in deeper.

Bonds

Suppose a retiree wants to stretch the nest-egg over twenty years and will earn 0 percent returns by investing in bonds. We could assume higher bond returns, but that would simply complicate the math without changing the intuition behind the example. Since insurance companies also invest in bonds, higher interest rates would increase the annuity payout rate as well. With 0 percent returns, these bonds allow for spending at 5 percent of the initial portfolio balance—the sustainable spending rate—every year for twenty years. With this spend rate, bonds will leave nothing to support spending beyond year twenty.

Income Annuities

Now suppose life expectancy is twenty years and longevity risk is added to the equation. Some will not make it twenty years; others will live longer. With the 0 percent returns the annuity provider earns from bonds, the provider could still support this 5 percent spending rate through risk pooling and mortality credits no matter how long the annuitant survives.

"Self-annuitization"

Now suppose the retiree "self-annuitizes" instead by managing this longevity risk without insurance. This requires picking a planning age one is unlikely to outlive. Suppose the retiree decides to plan under the assumption that retirement will last for thirty years. In this case, to spread assets out over thirty years with a 0 percent investment return, the spending rate must fall to 3.33 percent. Note as well, the spending rate could only be 2.5 percent to support expenses for forty years. In this situation, there is a direct relationship between a longer life and a lower rate of spending. Retirees are forced to spend less to the extent they worry about outliving their portfolio. In terms of an unintended legacy, if one did live for twenty years, then a third of the assets would remain with a thirty-year plan, or half of the assets would remain with a forty-year plan. Compared with an annuity, using bonds leads to a lower than possible retirement lifestyle and potentially an unintentionally large legacy, but with risk for shortfalls for an even longer than planned lifetime.

Stocks

Alternatively, one could seek an investment return higher than 0 percent by including stocks. With a fixed annual investment return of 3.1 percent, the retiree could support the 5 percent spending rate for thirty years. With a 4.2 percent investment return, spending could be supported for forty years. The question then centers around how likely it is for the portfolio to earn these higher rates of return through a stock-heavy focus.

Stocks create risk. Seeking this higher investment return requires the retiree to accept portfolio volatility with a growing allocation to stocks. Spending from investments further heightens sequence risk. A few poor returns early on could easily derail the attempt to support that 5 percent spending rate for as long as the plan targets. While it is possible to obtain the higher returns necessary to support a bigger spending level in this way, there is no guarantee that this approach will be successful. The stocks strategy provides greater upside potential for wealth to grow, but it also creates greater downside risk that the retiree will not be able to meet the spending goal throughout retirement. The range of potential outcomes widens.

The introduction of stock market risk requires two additional elements for the decision-making of our risk averse retiree. What failure probability does she comfortably and willingly accept that her portfolio will not be able to support spending through the planning age? As well, how high of stock allocation is she willing to accept, in terms of her ability to stomach the daily volatility experienced by her investment portfolio? With volatile investments and a fixed spending goal, some probability for portfolio depletion must be accepted by anyone seeking upside growth potential through the equity risk premium.

Annuitized assets do not provide upside in the sense that a legacy would be left when markets do well, but they also eliminate downside spending risk. The long-lived do receive a form of upside through mortality credits. The effective return from the annuity matches what the stocks needed to earn to support those longer retirements. For our example in which we said that stocks required a 4.2 percent return to fund a 5 percent distribution rate for 40 years, an annuity is providing this same return to an owner who happens to live this long.

"Self-annuitizing" requires lower spending, and stocks could support higher spending with upside growth, but that adds risk as well. As for bonds, ultimately, the question is this: why hold any bonds in the part of the retirement portfolio designed to meet spending obligations? The income annuity invests in bonds and provides payments precisely matched to the length of retirement, while stocks provide opportunities for greater investment growth above bonds. Bonds alone hold no advantage.

The income annuity provides a license to spend more from the start of retirement due to the insurance company's ability to pool risk. Supported spending from an income annuity is higher because it is based on reaching life expectancy, and should the retiree live beyond life expectancy, the higher income continues to be sustained because of the subsidies arriving from those who died early. The expectation that subsidies will arrive as needed allows spending to increase for everyone from the very start of retirement. Exhibit 5.1 highlights how mortality credits represent a third source of spending with an income annuity beyond the spenddown of principal and the interest generated by that principal.

Regarding sequence risk, for those who "self-annuitize," there are two options for deciding how to spend from investments. One is to spend at the same rate as the annuity with the hope of either dying before running out of money, or the hope that the investments earn strong enough returns to sustain the higher spending rate indefinitely. This approach requires acceptance of the possibility that the standard of living may need to be cut later in retirement should the hopes for sustained investment growth not pan out. The alternative is to spend less early on and, should good market returns materialize, increase spending later or leave a bigger legacy. The problem with intending to increase spending over time is that it is the reverse of what most people generally wish to do, which is to spend more early in retirement and cut back as life slows down at more advanced ages.

Exhibit 5.1
Sources of Income Annuity Payouts

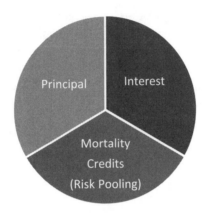

Overview of Annuity Types

The previous explanation about how an annuity can contribute to a plan was based on the simplest form of an annuity: A life-only income annuity. Now we are ready to step back to describe the broader annuity universe.

A fundamental aspect that defines an annuity is that it is a contract which can be annuitized to provide a series of payments from the insurance company, either for life or for a fixed period. However, today there are many annuities that downplay this aspect of annuitization. As the tax code in the United States provides tax-deferral advantages for annuities, other forms of annuities have evolved with a greater emphasis on providing tax-deferred growth for the assets in the annuity with a de-emphasis on their income-generating abilities. As well, more recent developments include optional riders that can be added to annuities to support a lifetime income without having to annuitize the contract.

Two broad classifications for annuities exist: fixed and variable. Simply, fixed annuities credit interest to the underlying assets in the annuity at a fixed rate (which can change over time), while variable annuities position the premiums into subaccounts that allow for investments into different funds earning a variable rate of return. Fixed annuities pool assets in the insurance company's general account, while variable annuities hold assets in separate investment subaccounts that are like mutual funds. Since variable annuities behave more like investments, those selling them need to be properly licensed in most states to sell both insurance and investments.

This definition about fixed and variable annuities can be confusing. First, income annuities are fixed annuities, but they do not show an underlying account balance to which interest is credited. Rather, the insurance company determines the payout rate based, in part, on the interest it projects to earn on the underlying premiums held in its general account.

Second, fixed index annuities can be structured to credit interest based on the performance of a volatile investment index. This can make them sound more like a variable annuity, but technically it is just a matter that fixed interest is being credited based on outcomes for a volatile index. Fixed index annuities provide principal protection, which means that one cannot experience any capital losses from negative market returns. Unlike a variable annuity, fixed index annuities do not provide subaccounts in which investments are made. They only credit interest based on the performance of a linked index. Variable annuities subaccounts can experience loss.

An even more recent development is structured annuities that behave a lot like index annuities, but which can experience losses. These are technically a type of variable annuity, and they go by many names including buffered annuities, variable index annuities, or registered index-linked annuities (RILAs). Finally, variable annuities could include subaccount options that provide fixed returns in the same manner as a fixed annuity, but the distinction is that variable annuities position the assets in investment subaccounts, unlike fixed annuities that hold them as part of the insurance company's pooled general account.

One other potentially confusing way to classify annuities is whether they are immediate or deferred. This distinction is relevant because it affects the tax treatment for annuities, as will be discussed in Chapter 10. The confusion relates to how these terms are used in two different ways with annuities. Formally, the classification is not related to when guaranteed income begins, but rather to when the act of annuitization takes place. Some deferred annuities could provide income immediately through structured lifetime payments, while some immediate annuities may defer income payments. For the former, the variable annuities and index annuities with income riders that we discuss are both types of deferred annuities, even if guaranteed distributions start immediately. The reason they are still called deferred annuities in this case is that technically the contract does not annuitize unless the contract value of the underlying assets has fallen to zero.

Meanwhile, for immediate annuities the act of annuitizing the assets takes place at the time the premium is paid. There is no liquidity for the underlying premiums past that stage. "Immediate" immediate annuities, such as single-premium immediate annuities (SPIAs), begin income payments within one year of annuitization, while deferred immediate annuities begin income payments at least one year past the date of annuitization. Since the name "deferred immediate annuity" is so confusing, a more common alternative name for them is deferred income annuity (DIA). Regarding the more confusing name, though, the immediate part of the name refers to immediate annuitization, and the deferred part of the name refers to the delay in starting the annuitized payments.

Annuities for Accumulation

For retirement income, the discussion of annuities naturally tends toward using them for systematic payouts in retirement, either for a lifetime or for a fixed period. However, through their ability to provide tax deferral for gains, annuities can also be used as pure accumulation tools. Though every annuity, by definition, must include a means to convert into a guaranteed income stream, this is not the priority when used for accumulation. Owners may plan to eventually have the lump-sum contract value returned after it has provided tax deferral. Chapter 10 dives deeper into the tax aspects of annuities.

Deferred fixed annuities (DFAs), or multiyear guaranteed annuities (MYGAs), are the annuity equivalent of holding CDs or other shorter-term fixed-income investments to a targeted maturity date. Their objective is to seek competitive after-tax fixed income returns for assets. This may be possible through their principal protection and lack of interest rate risk (they do not lose value when interest rates rise) and their tax deferral.

Fixed index annuities (FIAs) can also be used in a similar manner. We discuss FIAs later with an optional lifetime withdrawal benefit included. But when such benefits are not included, FIAs can be treated as another alternative to a taxable bond portfolio providing principal protection, tax deferral, and some exposure to market upside which could make them competitive with the after-tax returns on bonds.

A low-cost deferred variable annuity may also be used for tax deferral rather than thinking of it as a source for lifetime income. Deferred variable annuities were created in the 1950s in the United States as a tax-deferred vehicle for accumulating assets. They grew in popularity after the Tax Reform Act of 1986 limited the opportunities for tax-deferred savings in qualified retirement plans. Such a deferred variable annuity with low costs and de-emphasized guarantees provides tax deferral for those investors who have already filled other options and seek to invest further in tax-inefficient asset classes that may generate ordinary income and short-term capital gains. To benefit from tax deferral, it is vital that the annuity costs are less than the tax benefits.

Income Annuities – SPIAs and DIAs

We now shift to longer discussions for the key types of annuities used for retirement income planning. For those seeking to spend more in retirement than the bond yield curve can support, the alternative to seeking risk premium through an aggressive asset allocation is to use risk pooling.

Income annuities are the simplest type of insurance products which trade a lump-sum payment for protected lifetime income. The ability to convert a portion of assets (as it is not an all-or-nothing decision) into a guaranteed income stream is a fundamental retirement income tool which contrasts with an investment portfolio in terms of the advantages and disadvantages for managing retirement risks. Income annuities are fixed annuities, and they are annuitized at the time of contract issuance and premium payment. This means they are immediate annuities, even if the start date for payments is deferred.

We start our discussion of annuities with the income annuity because it is the most straightforward and easy-to-understand way to convert a pot of money into a guaranteed stream of spending for life. Income annuities are also known as immediate annuities, single-premium immediate annuities (SPIAs), deferred income annuities (DIAs), qualified longevity annuity contracts (QLACs), or longevity insurance.

Risk pooling and mortality credits are the drivers of value from an income annuity. The annuitant accepts the risk of dying early and receiving fewer payments from the annuity in exchange for the ability to continue receiving payments no matter how long one ends up living. By pooling longevity risk with a collection of individuals, an income annuity allows its owners to earmark assets by only needing to fund retirement as though they will earn fixed income returns and live to their life expectancy. Those who end up living beyond their life expectancy will have their continuing benefits subsidized by those who die before life expectancy. While this clearly benefits the long-lived, we can also conclude that it benefits the short-lived as well by allowing them to enjoy a higher standard of living than they might have otherwise been comfortable supporting from an unguaranteed investment portfolio. This can allow for more spending and a more satisfying retirement experience, and more peace of mind compared to those self-managing longevity risk by spending less and then leaving too much behind at death.

Menu of Income Annuity Features and Options

Income annuities can be either immediate or deferred in terms of when their payments begin, though as noted these are all technically immediate annuities because the contract is annuitized. An immediate income annuity begins income payments within one year of the purchase date, while a deferred income annuity does not begin payments until at least one year after the purchase date. A deferred income annuity purchased at retirement with income beginning at age eighty or eighty-five is also referred to as *longevity insurance*.

After the Treasury Department updated regulations in 2014 to facilitate the use of longevity insurance inside retirement plans, longevity insurance is now also known as a qualified longevity annuity contract (QLAC). In practice, deferred income annuities are used less as a form of longevity insurance and more for prepaying retirement and removing market risk in the pivotal preretirement years. In such a case, one might purchase a deferred income annuity at age fifty-five or sixty, for instance, for income to begin at sixty-five.

Single life income annuities only cover one person's life. With such an annuity, income payments continue until the annuitant's death. A joint life annuity, on the other hand, continues payments for as long as at least one of two annuitants survives. Often joint annuities are set up for two spouses, but marriage is not a requirement for two annuitants to be included on a joint life contract.

Since payments are expected to last longer when two lives are covered, the joint protection comes at the cost of a lower initial payout rate. A joint life and 100 percent survivor annuity provides the same payment as long as one annuitant is alive. This is the most popular option in practice. With a joint life and 67 percent survivor annuity, for instance, the payment would reduce by 33 percent upon the first annuitant's death, allowing for a higher initial payment.

A life-only income annuity is the Platonic ideal, offering the highest payout and the most mortality credits. Payouts are highest because the purchaser is taking the most "hit by a bus risk"—the common fear of signing an annuity contract and then being hit by a bus and killed on the way out of the office. Life-only annuities are popular with academics because acceptance of this risk makes more funds available to the longer-surviving members of the risk pool, allowing one to buy protected lifetime income at the lowest possible cost. In practice, many annuity buyers will be uncomfortable with a life-only annuity. CANNEX, a firm providing annuity quotes, finds that only about 15 percent of the inquiries it receives are for life-only options.

A variety of other flavors will lower the payout rate but may otherwise make the income annuity a more palatable choice. By offering less mortality credits to the risk pool because you want some protection for your beneficiary in the event of an early death, you should, in turn, expect to receive less mortality credits back from the risk pool in the event of a long life. This is the nature of the trade-off that results in a lower payout rate for added protections. Other flavors of annuities that lower the payout rate in exchange for providing protections to a beneficiary for an early death include:

- Cash refund provision: Provides a cash refund of the difference to the beneficiary if death happens before the owner receives cumulative payments from the annuity that add up to the initial premium payment. CANNEX reports that about half of the requests it receives include the cash refund.
- Lifetime with ten-year period certain annuity: Pays for life. If death happens before annuity payments were made for at least ten years, the beneficiary continues receiving payments for the full ten years. These period-certain guarantees can also be arranged for any number of years, such as five, fifteen, or twenty.

- Installment refund: Works very similarly to the cash refund, except beneficiaries receive the difference as continued annuity payments in installments until the full premium has been returned, rather than receiving a one-time refund.
- Period certain: An income annuity does not require lifetime payments. It may just make payments for a set period. This works the same way as building a bond ladder and can be an alternative to individual bonds when considering retirement income bond ladder strategies.

As well, there are generally three options regarding payments:

- Fixed or level income annuity: These annuities will pay the same amount on an ongoing basis for as long as the contract requires. The purchasing power of the income payments will decrease over time as there is no adjustment made for inflation. CANNEX notes that most requests it receives are for this option.
- COLA: A cost-of-living adjustment (COLA) provision allows payments grow at a fixed compounding rate each year. For instance, if I decide that 2 percent is a reasonable assumption for future inflation, I might choose a COLA of 2 percent with the intention of preserving the purchasing power for my annuity income. If realized inflation ends up being higher, I will lose purchasing power over time, but purchasing power would increase if realized inflation ends up being lower. COLAs can only approximate the inflation experience in retirement. With payments increasing over time, the initial payment will be less than with a fixed or level annuity.
- CPI: One could add a provision that the income growth rate of the annuity payments precisely matches the Consumer Price Index (CPI). When inflation is low, income grows more slowly, as do living costs for the retiree. When inflation is high, income grows more quickly to better support the increasing cost of living. CPI-adjusted income annuities hedge inflation risk in the same manner as TIPS. These have been offered in the past, but since January 2020 no company has been offering CPI-adjusted income annuities in the United States.

Income Annuity Pricing

Pricing income annuities is not as hard as one might think, as the basic recipe requires just three ingredients:

1. Mortality rates (which vary by age and gender) impact how long payments will be made. Younger people will have longer projected payout periods, which means that payout rates must be lower.

2. Interest rates impact the returns the annuity provider can earn from investing the annuity premiums. Higher interest rates imply higher payout rates because the insurance company will be able to earn more interest on the premiums in their general account supporting the annuity payments.
3. Overhead costs relate to extra charges an annuity provider seeks to cover business expenses and to manage risks related to the accuracy of their future mortality and interest rate predictions.

Including mortality rates in the pricing is the secret sauce of the annuity. Retirees could just build a bond ladder on their own and set aside the full present value of their lifetime spending. But because a retiree does not know how long she may live, it becomes necessary to plan for an age well beyond average life expectancy. Annuity owners obtain a discount on the bond ladder pricing because the survival probabilities to each subsequent age indicate whether these payments will need to be made. The annuity price is a survival-weighted present value of potential lifetime payments. Any one individual is either alive or dead. But for a large pool of individuals representing the customer base of the annuity provider, the company can rely on the law of large numbers to evaluate what percentage of customers will remain alive at each subsequent age. If there is only a 10 percent chance that someone is alive at age 100, the insurer only needs to set aside 10 percent as much for that payment as someone who self-manages the risk. This is risk pooling.

The bond ladder costs more, with the benefit that the bond ladder supports some legacy if retirement is shorter than assumed with the ladder construction. But the bond ladder does not provide any additional longevity protection beyond the end date of the ladder as assets are fully depleted at that time. With the income annuity, that longevity protection can be provided while devoting less funds to the goal.

The life-only income annuity offers the highest payout because it creates the most risk about receiving fewer payments for any beneficiary in the event of an early death. Adding a period-certain payment or a cash refund reduces the potential mortality credits that the annuity owner offers to the risk pool. The higher payout on a life-only income annuity provides compensation for accepting the risk of an early death.

Academics who study income annuities generally suggest a life-only income to fully maximize the income-producing power, with legacy goals covered through other means. But cash refund and period-certain provisions are quite popular in practice. Psychologically, for many it is too difficult to overcome the perceived lack of fairness with a life-only income annuity in which one could die shortly after paying the premium and then receive back little in return.

Payout Rates and Rates of Return for Income Annuities

The pricing of an income annuity is typically described using either the monthly income amount it generates, or as the annual payout rate of the income received as a percentage of the premium amount. For instance, an income annuity might offer $481.67 per month for a $100,000 premium. For twelve months, that sums to $5,780, which is 5.78 percent of the initial premium amount. The annuity payout rate is 5.78 percent. After aligning with assumptions about how spending may grow with inflation, this payout rate is directly comparable to a sustainable withdrawal rate from initial retirement date assets for an investment portfolio. Both rates incorporate the idea that principal is spent in addition to any investment returns.

It is important to recognize that the payout rate is not a *return* on the annuity, which may create some confusion. It is wrong to compare the payout rate to an interest rate that involves the subsequent return of principal. For instance, if you can earn 1 percent by holding a CD and 5.78 percent from an income annuity, the income annuity is not almost six times more powerful than the CD.

The problem is that the 1 percent number for the CD only represents its interest payments. The principal value is returned at maturity. Meanwhile, a 5.78 percent payout from an annuity includes interest and principal payments (as well as mortality credits—the true source of additional returns beyond that provided by a fixed-income alternative). Principal is being spent as well, and so the comparison to the CD rate is neither fair nor meaningful.

The annuity does have a return, but it is less straightforward to calculate. To know the annuity *return*, it is necessary to know how long the annuitant will live and how many annuity payments will be generated. Or, at least, returns can only be calculated by assuming how long income payments will be received. A longer life means more payments from the annuity, which helps to increase the return it provides over time. And if the underlying investments in the general account provide a higher return, that feeds into a higher annuity payout rate, which helps to boost the annuity's return more quickly as well. For life-only annuities, returns start out negative, as cumulative payments fall short of the premium paid. The return crosses from negative to positive when the total payments received exceed the premium paid. With enough time, the return can eventually exceed the payout rate. A competitive income annuity will provide a return matching bonds at around the owner's life expectancy. Eventually those continuing cash flows will imply returns that are competitive with stocks.

An income annuity is designed to provide a higher return to people who live longer and therefore need higher returns to fund their retirements. Though tragic to consider, those who do not live as long do not end up needing strong returns to fund their retirement. This is how annuities can better match to the funding needs of a retirement plan.

Money's Worth Measures for Income Annuities

Annuities have a reputation for being a high-fee financial product. Is this reputation deserved? We will address this for different types of annuities, starting first with income annuities. It is a bit complicated to answer this for income annuities because they do not have visible fees. There are no fees extracted from the quoted payout rate, as the payout rate is already a net number after fees have been deducted internally. Simply, with the internal fees, the quoted payout rate is lower than otherwise possible.

Fortunately, we can reverse engineer the fair price for an income annuity without fees and then compare it with real-world annuity payout rates to obtain a money's worth measure for the income annuity. The "fair price" without overhead costs just involves using interest rates and mortality rates to calculate the survival-weighted present value of the potential lifetime payments. The additional complication relates to making reasonable assumptions for interest rates and mortality rates.

In determining the money's worth for an annuity, we must consider three issues: could the retiree earn the same returns from her own fixed-income investments with the same risk level, how does the retiree's objectively determined longevity prospects compare with that of the overall risk pool, and how much does the retiree value mortality credits as based on her longevity risk aversion and subjective views about how long she might live. Purchasing income annuities can be a win-win situation both for the consumer and the insurance company when the benefits created through risk pooling are shared between both parties in the transaction.

First, can a retiree invest in the same fixed-income portfolio and earn the same returns as the insurance company can obtain for its general account? We note that the insurance company may be able to obtain higher investment yields because of its ability to diversify among higher-yielding bonds with greater credit risk, to use asset-liability matching to hold less liquid and longer-term bonds, and to receive institutional pricing on purchases which avoids the pricing mark-ups faced by retail investors.

Second, it is important to be realistic about longevity when determining whether an income annuity is priced fairly. Someone who can reasonably expect to live longer than average should not try to calculate a fair price using population-average mortality. If annuity prices are simulated with mortality rates for the general population, that will cause the money's worth measures to be lower and annuities to look more expensive. My readers will tend to display characteristics that are associated with increased longevity, such as higher education levels, more income, greater wealth, and a stronger health focus. When this is the case, money's worth estimates based on mortality tables reflecting the longer lifespans of annuitants are more reasonable to use.

Third, separate from the objective money's worth measure, it is important to also consider the subjective value being received by the annuity owner. For those with longevity risk aversion, the prospects of spending from investments may be such that an income annuity could still support more spending than the retiree otherwise would be comfortable taking from investments. With an investments-only strategy, longevity risk aversion is manifested through a lower spending rate from investment assets. Because income annuities pool longevity risk, they can help to reduce the worry individuals have about outliving their assets.

The income annuity payout is based on objective mortality statistics rather than subjective fears. The case for an income annuity becomes stronger for individuals more worried about longevity. Such individuals may value income annuities at more than their fair price. For instance, if my life expectancy is 85, but I build a financial plan to work until age 95, adding an income annuity to the plan will improve my funding status. The present value of the annuity payments is greater when I plan to live to 95, because the annuity is priced with objective mortality data where people do not live that long on average. The income annuity provides risk pooling and mortality credits that individuals cannot create on their own. Just because money's worth measures imply underlying costs to the owner does not necessarily mean that annuities are a bad deal for anyone who experiences longevity risk aversion.

For example, a $100,000 premium may be quoted as supporting $600 per month for life. Without any built-in fees, perhaps the fair monthly income could have been $610 or $620. This reverse engineering process lets one estimate the costs built into an income annuity. If an income annuity provides $600 per month, but we simulate that a fair price is to provide $610 per month, then the money's worth of the annuity is $600 / $610 = 0.9836. In this case, the commercial annuity pays 1.64 percent less than the fair price. We could interpret this 1.64 percent as an upfront transaction cost or one-time fee for purchasing the annuity. At the same time, perhaps the household could not invest for as much yield as the insurance company or might have an unusually long expected lifespan, such that a more personalized fair monthly income is only $580 or $590. In this case, the annuity provides a great deal. These matters are not transparent. We must calculate the actuarially fair price for an annuity and then compare it to the actual price. Then we have a better sense of the "money's worth" from the annuity.

Deferred Annuities with Lifetime Income Benefits

Generally, the most efficient means for balancing protected income and investment upside is to use annuities as a replacement for bonds and combine life-only income annuities with aggressive stock portfolios. However, this requires a degree of investor self-control and long-term focus that may be difficult to achieve in practice. It requires accepting both the loss of liquidity as annuity assets disappear from the portfolio balance, as well as accepting a more aggressive asset allocation for what remains in the portfolio. Many retirees are nervous about these trade-offs.

As a means for accommodating the concerns of real-world retirees, deferred variable annuities (VAs) and fixed index annuities (FIAs) with lifetime spending protections have developed as a more palatable compromise. In practice, sales of deferred annuities dwarf sales of immediate annuities.

With deferred annuities, owners continue to see the annuity assets on their financial statements as part of the overall portfolio balance. As well, those assets maintain exposure to market upside that is not provided within an income annuity. The appeal to retirees is based on the combination of downside protection with a protected income stream, upside growth potential through their underlying investments (or links to investment indices in the case of fixed index annuities), and liquidity for the underlying assets, while also offering the potential for tax-deferral. Retirees can see their account values, they can continue to make choices about how their funds are invested, they can access their funds, and any funds remaining at death are generally available to beneficiaries as a death benefit, all while ensuring protected income through the inclusion of an optional guaranteed living withdrawal benefit (GLWB) rider on the contract.

Nevertheless, the features and workings of deferred annuities with lifetime income benefit riders can be rather complex. For those just starting to investigate deferred variable or index annuities, complexities relate to understanding how returns are calculated for the contract value, how the income guarantees work, and how fees are structured.

Contract Value Growth

The underlying contract value of deferred annuity assets can grow (or shrink, with variable annuities) throughout the life of the contract. With variable annuities, the process is straightforward and comparable to how most will understand investing with brokerage accounts. VAs allow for the direct investment of premiums into subaccounts representing different asset classes and their investment performance less distributions and fees will determine the value of remaining assets over time. Variable annuity subaccounts are subject to capital losses.

Since FIAs are fixed annuities, *crediting interest* is the technical term for the returns generated by their contract value. FIA premiums are added to the general account of the insurance company and credit interest to the owner based either on a fixed return or on the performance of a linked market index. FIAs offer index-linked interest, but they are not invested directly into the underlying index. There are no subaccounts. They simply pay interest to the owner using a formula linked to the index performance.

With FIAs, the credited interest (or returns) can be structured more precisely in terms of controlling downside and upside exposures. FIAs protect principal in the sense that 0 percent interest is credited even if the underlying index declines significantly in value. To obtain this protection, FIA owners should expect to receive only a portion of any positive gains experienced by the index. Overall, FIAs may reduce the volatility of the underlying contract value relative to a variable annuity.

For FIAs, insurance companies generally offer access to different index options as well as a fixed interest option. Contract owners can often combine these options in any way they choose and can change the allocations at the start of each new term. Common index choices include the S&P 500 for large capitalization US stocks, or the MSCI EAFE index that provides representation for international stocks. Only the price returns (capital gains or capital losses) matter with these indices as dividends are excluded from the returns when determining credited interest. This is because financial derivatives are used to link performance rather than owning the underlying assets, so dividends are not available.

Almost countless crediting methods are used in practice and there is a trend to increase the complexity of the methods used. With the chosen index, interest crediting will generally be based on a formula that can include floors, caps, participation rates, and spreads. As an example, we will consider an *annual reset one-year term point-to-point crediting method with a participation rate*.

The one-year term and the point-to-point method means that the changes in the index values on one-year contract anniversaries will be used to calculate interest. Annual point-to-point looks at the change in the index at two different dates, one year apart. At the end of each yearly term on the anniversary date of the contract, the interest-crediting formula uses the index gain for that year (the price return, not including dividends) to credit interest. A floor of 0 percent is protected, and a participation rate determines the percentage of upside gains that are credited.

As for the annual reset design, this reflects how interest crediting calculations start fresh for each term. If the index lost 10 percent in the previous year and the FIA credited 0 percent interest for that year, it is only the new point-to-point change for the current year that matters to calculate the new term's interest. There is no need for cumulative gains to make up for previous losses when the annual reset provision is included.

A simple way to think about the downside protection with the guaranteed floor is that the insurance company buys enough bonds with the annuity contract value that the growth of that portion with interest will match the original contract value at the end of the term. With what is left after purchasing bonds to protect the principal, the insurance company keeps a portion to cover company expenses and profit motives, and the remainder is the "options budget" used to purchase upside exposure to the index.

When the FIA offers a *participation rate* on upside, the insurance company can use the "options budget" to buy a one-year at-the-money call option on the S&P 500 index. This is a financial derivative that provides its owner with the right, but not the obligation, to buy shares of the S&P 500 at the option's strike price. The option is at-the-money if the strike price matches the current value of the index. If the index loses value during the term, the option expires worthless, and principal was protected with the bonds. If the index experiences capital gains (not including reinvested dividends) during the term, the owner receives exposure to the upside through the call option. The participation rate is the ratio of the "options budget" to the price of the call option, which provides the percentage of index gains received.

Because there is a cost for creating protection for the contract value against a loss when the index declines in value, one should not expect to receive the full upside potential from the index. The call options will generally cost more than the size of the options budget. FIAs do *not* provide a way to get the returns from the stock market without accepting the risk of the stock market.

The parameters offered by an FIA will depend in large part on the level of interest rates and the cost of financial derivatives for the associated index. Higher interest rates mean that principal can be protected with less assets, which then leaves more for the options budget used to purchase upside exposure. Less expensive call options will also allow for more upside participation to be purchased. Factors that reduce the options prices include less implied volatility for the underlying index, an increase in the strike price for the option relative to the current index price, a lower risk-free interest rate, and a shorter term to maturity. Participation rates can conceivably be higher than 100 percent if interest rates are high enough and the call options are cheap enough. On a related point, it should also be clear that if the owner is willing to accept a lower floor, it would be possible to gain more upside potential since less is needed for bonds and more is available to purchase call options.

It is also vitally important to understand that the amount of upside potential that can be offered by an FIA will vary over time as interest rates and call option prices change. With an annual reset design, the insurance company must repeat the process each year and will face different interest rates and call option pricing as these variables change values over time. More upside potential is possible with higher interest rates and cheaper call options, and vice versa. This is the reason why insurance companies maintain the freedom to change the contract parameters (such as the fixed rate, participation rate, cap rate, or spread) at the beginning of each new term, subject to a minimum or maximum value allowed for each parameter within the contract.

With indexed annuities, the floor could be negative or there may be other mechanisms that allow for capital losses on the contract value. If the floor is less than zero, then the annuity is technically a variable annuity that maintains most characteristics of the FIA except that it is also regulated as a security because it can experience losses. These types of structured annuities are growing in popularity and go by various names including registered index-linked annuities. Aside from a negative floor, these annuities may also have buffers. For instance, a product that provides a 10 percent buffer would mean that the interest credited is zero percent for index losses of up to 10 percent. If the index loses more than 10 percent, then this approach would credit the amount of the loss exceeding 10 percent. An 18 percent loss on the index would lead to an annuity loss of 8 percent, but an 8 percent loss for the index would lead to no loss. Accepting this greater downside risk can support more upside potential, which contributes to their growing use in the marketplace.

Lifetime Income Benefits

We have just described contract value growth for deferred annuities. For deferred annuities offering guaranteed lifetime withdrawal benefits, there can be a separate and parallel set of calculations to determine a benefit base and guaranteed income amount. We must consider how guaranteed income is determined for both the growth during the deferral and distribution periods.

Before going further, I must emphasize that obtaining guaranteed income through a lifetime income rider is not the same as annuitizing the contract. The contract is still technically deferred after lifetime income begins. The benefit rider supports an allowed annual distribution amount for the lifetime of the annuitant, or annuitants in the case of a joint contract. Ultimately, while the underlying contract value of assets remains positive, retirees are spending their own money. The insurance company then pays from its own resources after the contract value depletes. Contract value depletion is what eventually triggers annuitization.

First consider the growth process for the guaranteed benefit base during the deferral or accumulation period before distributions begin. This growth is important because it is subsequently used to determine the amount of guaranteed lifetime income provided by the annuity. The deferral period can be skipped if the retiree starts lifetime distributions immediately.

There are two general ways that lifetime income benefits can grow in a deferral period before the lifetime income commences. The first is a more complicated method that includes a benefit base, a rollup rate, and the possibility for step-ups. Deferred annuities with income guarantee riders generally support the ability to lock-in a guaranteed growth rate on the benefit base during the accumulation period, and also offer the ability to define the benefit base as the high watermark of the contract value of the underlying assets on anniversary dates if that growth is higher than the guaranteed rate. The benefit base is a hypothetical number used to calculate the amount of guaranteed income paid during the withdrawal phase. It is distinct from the contract value of assets, which is what the owner could access based on actual account growth net of fees and any surrender charges.

For this method, a guaranteed lifetime withdrawal benefit rider supports an income for life at a fixed withdrawal percentage (based on the age when distributions begin) of the guaranteed benefit base. It initially equals the premium paid into the annuity, which is also the initial contract value for the assets. Over time, the contract value of assets can rise or fall depending on realized investment returns and as fees and distributions are taken from the asset base. On any contract anniversary, if the contract value of the underlying assets has reached a new high watermark and exceeds the guaranteed benefit base, that base is stepped up to the new high watermark value. This increases the subsequent amount of guaranteed income. During the deferral period before distributions begin, an annuity may also offer a guaranteed rollup rate to increase the benefit base automatically over time if the value of the underlying contracted assets has not otherwise grown larger on its own. Generally, the benefit base can grow at the higher of either a guaranteed rollup rate or the high watermark achieved through contract value growth.

Roll-up rates are often misunderstood as guaranteed returns for the annuity. These rates do not impact the contract value of assets. Their role is only to determine the hypothetical benefit base that is combined with a guaranteed withdrawal rate to determine the guaranteed lifetime income. It is the interaction of these two components that matters.

At some point, the owner may stop deferring and turn on their lifetime distributions. If the retiree does not take out more than the guaranteed withdrawal amounts, guaranteed withdrawals never decrease, even if the account balance falls to zero. One exception to this is that some companies market a feature that allows for higher distributions when assets remain and lower distributions after assets deplete. The contract may be terminated at any point with the contract value of the remaining assets, net of any potential surrender charges, returned to the owner.

Deferred annuities generally make a distinction between distributions that are covered by the lifetime income guarantee rider, and one-time distributions that are not covered by the guarantee. Non-lifetime distributions may be allowed before guaranteed income begins. That distinction is important, as it would generally allow rollups to continue, as rollups mostly end once guaranteed distributions begin. As well, non-lifetime distributions beyond the guaranteed level are allowed after the guaranteed distributions begin, but this will reduce subsequent guarantees.

The deferral period ends once guaranteed lifetime distributions commence, beginning the distribution period. Guaranteed income will be set using an age-based guaranteed withdrawal or payout percentage rate applied to the value of the benefit base. The guaranteed withdrawal rate multiplied by the benefit base sets a guaranteed distribution amount supported for life, even if the contract value of the underlying assets is depleted. Guaranteed distributions may even increase through step-ups if new high watermarks are reached for the underlying asset base on the designated dates when this is checked.

For a simple example, a company might offer the following payout rates to single individuals based on the age that lifetime withdrawals begin: 4.5 percent for ages fifty-nine to sixty-four, 5 percent for ages sixty-five to sixty-nine, 5.5 percent for ages seventy to seventy-nine, and 6.5 percent for ages eighty and over. For couples, payout rates would generally be 0.5 percent less and would be based on the age of the younger person. For couples, another possibility could be that the payout rates remain the same as for singles, but that a higher fee is charged to support the guarantee over the longer expected joint lifetime. GLWB annuity payouts generally do not make a distinction between genders, which would provide benefit to longer living women relative to men.

There is another way that lifetime income benefits can be structured that moves away from the hypothetical benefit base and the rollup rate. This alternative approach is more commonly found with FIAs, while the method just described is more common for variable annuities. In the alternate formulation, a lifetime withdrawal percentage, which is still defined by age bands, is determined at the time the GLWB is added to the annuity. In this case, it is the age that the benefit is purchased rather than the age that income begins. Then, rather than using a rollup rate with a benefit base, there is a deferral credit that increases the withdrawal rate for each year that the owner defers the start of their lifetime income distributions. When lifetime distributions begin, they are set as a percentage of the contract value at that time, where the percentage is rising over time on account of the deferral credits.

For example, suppose a fifty-five-year-old purchases an FIA that includes this type of income rider. For this contract, the withdrawal percentage when purchased at fifty-five is 4.5 percent, and the deferral credit is 0.3 percent for each year that the individual delays the start of income. The individual plans to retire at age sixty-five, which would provide ten years of deferral. That would mean that the lifetime withdrawal percentage is 7.5 percent (4.5 + 0.3 x 10) of the contract value at that age. In this case, principal is protected only on a gross basis before the rider fee is applied at the end of each year. Principal would be protected in terms of zero interest being credited when the index lost value, but the optional benefit charge could then reduce the value of the principal.

Moshe Milevsky has described the separate presentation of rollup rates and guaranteed withdrawal rates as telling consumers the temperature in Celsius when individuals can only make sense of temperatures provided in Fahrenheit. In this case, what a retiree will understand is the amount of income guaranteed by the annuity. It may not be immediately obvious to someone whether an annuity with a 5 percent rollup rate and 5 percent withdrawal rate is better than an annuity with a 4 percent rollup rate and a 6 percent withdrawal rate.

Many consumers misinterpret the guaranteed growth rate on their benefit base as a guaranteed investment return, not realizing that it is the combination of a growth rate on the benefit base and the withdrawal rate applied to the benefit base that determine the level of guaranteed income. These two factors cannot be disentangled. A higher rollup rate combined with a lower payout rate does not necessarily leave consumers in a better position. For these reasons, the second deferral credit method is easier to understand and has a more direct correspondence to how the payout rate on a deferred income annuity increases with the length of deferrals.

With either method, the payouts on deferred annuities at different ages will generally be less than the payouts offered by an immediate annuity purchased at the same age. This can be expected since deferred annuities provide the advantages of liquidity and potential for upside growth in the guaranteed income. However, there can be exceptions. For instance, especially with a long deferral period, the insurance company can expect that some FIA owners will lapse and not take the guaranteed distributions from the FIA despite paying for the income rider. This takes the insurance company off the hook for making good on its guarantee, and through competitive pricing some of this benefit is returned to the other owners in the risk pool. With an income annuity, there is no flexibility and so no possibility for mistakes on the part of owners.

As well, one difference from VAs is that upside potential for step-ups with FIAs may be more limited. The interest crediting method might even prevent the possibility of a step-up during the accumulation period with the rollup rate and benefit base approach. This could happen when a cap on credited interest is less than the rollup rate, especially when the optional rider fee would reduce the net cap applied. With the distribution phase as well, the capped gains could be less than the guaranteed withdrawal amount plus the rider fee, preventing the possibility for step-ups. For this reason, greater focus with FIAs should be on their minimum guaranteed protections without necessarily thinking that step-ups will provide further increases.

The practical impact of the optional rider fee will be to reduce the contract value a bit more quickly leading to a lower death benefit than otherwise. But with the focus on income rather than accumulation, the rider fee is of secondary importance. The goal is not to find the lowest rider fee, as it would generally support a less generous guarantee, but to find the annuity that offers the most value through lifetime income to the individual for a given rider cost. When the individual survives long enough that the annuity contract value is depleted, the benefit continues to support lifetime income and the previous fee drag becomes irrelevant.

The income riders on deferred annuities provide the ability to receive mortality credits, which can reduce the asset base required to support a lifetime spending goal. The rider fees paid for the income guarantee provide insurance that the spending will be protected in case someone experiences a combination of either living too long or experiencing sufficiently poor market returns that they outlive their underlying investment assets and cannot otherwise sustain an income for life.

Death Benefits

The standard death benefit for a deferred annuity is the greater of the contract value of any remaining assets at death, or the total premiums paid less distributions received by death. It is provided to the beneficiary. In addition to optional GLWBs (also called living benefits), deferred annuities also offer optional death benefit riders that create an opportunity for more than the standard death benefit. One should look carefully at these as they could be counterproductive for those focusing on getting the most guaranteed income from their variable annuity. For instance, a common death benefit rider could support a death benefit equal to the full value of the annuity premiums if at least one dollar remains in the contract by an advanced age. One must consider whether it is a wise choice if the focus is otherwise placed on maximizing the spending power afforded by an income guarantee, which can involve spending down the contract value completely to trigger the lifetime income protection. Nonetheless, retirees may consider these optional enhanced death benefits on deferred annuities as an alternative to life insurance for funding legacy goals.

Fees

Providing a guaranteed lifetime withdrawal benefit is a risky endeavor for the insurance company. The insurance company is obligated to provide lifetime income payments at the guaranteed level if the underlying assets held within the annuity have been depleted. Variable annuities with living benefits require managing market risk in addition to longevity risk. For FIAs, because of principal protection, the rider fees for living benefits only need manage longevity risk. The greater the investment volatility and the higher the guaranteed withdrawals that the insurance company allows, the greater is the cost for creating a risk management framework to support that guarantee.

When people mention that annuities have high fees, they generally have variable annuities in mind. Deferred variable annuities generally have several types of ongoing fees. The first relate to the underlying funds expenses that would be included with any mutual fund investment. The only issue to consider here is whether the funds within the subaccounts have elevated fees due to the inclusion of 12b-1 fees in their expense ratios, and whether investment options available to the individual outside of the variable annuity also include 12b-1 fees. These fund fees are charged on the contract value of underlying assets.

The second type of fee relates to mortality and expense charges for the insurance company. These fees help to support the risk pooling and business costs of the insurance company as well as a basic annuity death benefit. These fees are also generally charged on the contract value.

A third type of fee that may exist in the short run are contingent deferred sales charges (or surrender charges) for those seeking non-lifetime distributions above the allowed levels in the early years of the contract. Surrender charges receive much of the criticism related to the fee levels for annuities. Deferred annuities are liquid in that they may be surrendered with the contract value returned as an excess distribution above the guaranteed distribution level. But in the early years of the contract, surrender charges may limit the portion that can be returned without paying a fee. For instance, surrender charges could work on a sliding scale basis starting at 7 percent in the first year the annuity is held, and then gradually reducing by 1 percent a year down to zero after the seventh year that the annuity is held. In this case, after the seventh year the surrender charges end, and the contract value will be fully liquid in all subsequent years. Deferred annuities are meant to be long-term holdings and surrender charges help to recoup the fixed set-up costs to the insurer for those who leave early.

Finally, optional GLWB riders or enhanced death benefits require an additional ongoing charge. Rider charges end after the account is depleted, though this is the source of lifetime protections. Rider charges can be confusing because they may be charged in three different ways. The most expensive option is to have the rider charged on the annuity's benefit base. As the contract value approaches $0, this will increase the rider cost as a percentage of remaining assets and work to deplete the contract value more quickly. Two other options include charging the rider on the contract value of assets and charging the rider on a declining benefit base equal to the benefit base less cumulative guaranteed distributions.

With these various fees, it is possible that total variable annuity fees could add up to more than 3 percent. This, along with surrender charges, is how variable annuities have developed a reputation as being a high-cost product.

We can compare this to fixed index annuities, or fixed annuities more generally. FIAs with living benefits do not require market risk management since principal is protected and the general account of the insurance company is designed with asset-liability matching. Only longevity risk must be managed with the rider fees. FIAs also differ from VAs in that, as with an income annuity, FIA fees tend to be structured internally to the product such that there are no observable fees to reduce the contract value. Fees can be kept internal because they are based on a spread between what the insurer earns on the assets and what it pays out. The insurance company earns more from investing the premiums than it pays to the owner. As with income annuities, it is also possible to reverse engineer and estimate the internal costs and "money's worth" for an FIA. This process does get more complicated because financial derivatives are being used behind the scenes to provide exposure to market upside. Internal fees are reflected through the limits placed on the upside growth potential. Of course, upside growth potential must be limited to support the downside risk protections. The internal fees for the FIA just mean that upside growth potential is less than it could have been if the insurance company did not need to cover its expenses and profit needs.

At the same time, though, households may not be able to earn the same rates of returns on their funds as an insurance company that obtains institutional pricing on trades, improved diversification, and longer-term investment holding periods. The living benefit also provides risk pooling and mortality credits. It is not always the case that households could easily replicate on their own what the FIA provides as an accumulation tool even before adding the longevity protection.

FIAs do not have subaccount charges or mortality and expense charges. The exceptions to the lack of external fees include that FIAs may still have a surrender charge schedule in the early years for excess distributions. This is done to allow the insurance company to invest the premium in longer-term assets and to cover the company's fixed expenses for providing the annuity. These surrender charges will gradually disappear for long-term owners. As well, any optional lifetime income benefits or enhanced death benefits added to the contract have observable fees that will be deducted from the contract value. Though otherwise protected, the contract value of the FIA could decline on a net basis after accounting for optional rider fees.

Fitting Annuities into a Retirement Plan

A retirement income strategy can extend beyond traditional investment management to also use insurance and risk pooling with annuities as a part of managing the changing risks of retirement. The process of building a retirement income strategy involves determining how to best combine retirement income tools to optimize the balance between *meeting* your retirement goals and *protecting* those goals from the unique risks of retirement. Retirement risks come in many forms, including unknown planning horizons, market volatility, inflation, and other spending shocks. Each of these risks must be managed by combining different tools and tactics, each with different relative strengths and weaknesses.

Retirement spending goals can be met through distributions from the investment portfolio, through annuitized income annuities, and through lifetime distribution provisions from deferred annuities. Product allocation is about how to combine these different tools into an overall plan. With this approach to retirement risk, it becomes hard to counter the notion that risk pooling and insurance have an important and valuable role to play. But this still leaves many questions about what type of annuity to use and what specific contributions an annuity can make.

Filling an Income Gap with an Annuity

A common question about annuities is how much should be allocated to them. The question is often framed as though the annuity is another asset class in an asset allocation problem. What is the right asset allocation between stocks, bonds, and annuities? A better way to approach this question is to ask how much annuity income is needed to meet the longevity (and potentially lifestyle) retirement expenses.

The Retirement Income Optimization Map™ (RIO Map™) framework described in Chapter 3 provides a summary for how to approach retirement income. Retirement assets are matched to the liabilities connected to the four L retirement goals (longevity, lifestyle, legacy, and liquidity). Assets are positioned in three general categories: reliable income resources, the diversified portfolio, and reserve assets. Reliable income includes Social Security and pension benefits, individual bonds, and different types of annuities providing lifetime income protections. The diversified portfolio is the traditional investment portfolio and can also include life insurance for matching to a legacy goal or for coordinating with investments to cover spending. Reserves are remaining assets that have not been earmarked to cover other goals and are truly liquid and available to help support retirement contingencies.

With this framework, the amount of portfolio assets to earmark as an annuity premium is based on how much is needed to support at least the longevity goals after accounting for the other reliable income resources. For example, suppose an individual reaches retirement with $1 million in an IRA and a $30,000 Social Security benefit. This retiree seeks to spend $70,000 per year, of which $45,000 is deemed as essential expenses. After Social Security, there is a $15,000 gap for reliable income. Suppose the retiree is considering an annuity with a 5.78 percent payout rate for lifetime income. The cost of filling the income gap is the $15,000 gap divided by 0.0578, which is $259,516. This represents 25.9 percent of portfolio assets, and it would serve as the starting point for analyzing the annuity allocation decision. The retiree must evaluate whether this is a reasonable portion of the overall asset base to devote toward an annuity. To make the decision more precise will require tax considerations as well as a strategy for managing inflation for the spending goal. But this process is the easiest and most practical way to think about allocating assets to annuities with income protections.

Upside Exposure, Downside Protection, and Liquidity Provisions

Given a targeted amount of annuity income, the next question becomes what type of annuity to use: income annuities, variable annuities, or index annuities? Each provides a different balance among the tradeoffs between upside potential, downside protection, and liquidity provisions.

As a simple starting point, income annuities, when treated as bonds, will frequently be the most efficient way to incorporate lifetime income into a plan. This was a conclusion I have reached when exploring the efficient frontier for retirement income where I look at performance of various combinations of asset classes and annuities. I found that stocks and income annuities replace stocks and bonds on the efficient frontier for retirement income planning. The efficient frontier is about the tradeoffs between risk and return and finding asset and product allocations that cannot provide greater advantage for one without creating loss for the other. For retirement, that involves the trade-off between satisfying spending goals for life and preserving financial assets for legacy and liquidity. Deferred annuities with lifetime income provisions also tend to beat bonds for retirement income because of the mortality credits they provide to help support spending in the event of a long retirement.

In practice, it is uncommon to find someone who is comfortable with the combination of a life-only income annuity and very aggressive asset allocation for the remainder of the investment portfolio. The math shows this to be the most effective combination, but it is not the most palatable as retirees have concerns about both life-only annuities and high stock allocations for the rest.

Deferred variable annuities and fixed index annuities play a role for those attracted to the upside and liquidity features they offer compared to income annuities. In some circumstances, they may even make it to the efficient frontier of options by providing higher protected income levels or a better overall asset allocation for retirees struggling with the concept that income annuities should replace bonds. Deferred annuities also offer greater flexibilities for the income start date and the opportunity to exchange into a different annuity or even no annuity in the future, as there is less lock-in when the contract has not been annuitized.

In theory, simple income annuities should offer the highest guaranteed payout rates. Their simple design lacks any special features like liquidity and upside potential that require additional cost. The income annuity can offer the most downside protection but no upside potential. Even though that downside benefit may be less, an important selling point of deferred annuities is that they potentially provide more than just a minimum guaranteed withdrawal benefit. More generally, fixed annuities should offer higher guaranteed withdrawals than variable annuities because fixed annuities do not need to manage market risk in addition to longevity risk. With principal protection, the worst-case scenarios for fixed annuities can be known. FIAs will fall in between income annuities and variable annuities both in terms of their downside protections and upside potential. Variable annuities will require the greatest costs to provide protection, since they also manage market risk, and this will generally lead them to offer the least downside protection in terms of guaranteed lifetime withdrawal benefits. But competitive variable annuities will provide the most upside potential, especially with lower costs, higher quality investment choices, and investment freedom to choose an aggressive asset allocation.

Generally, as just described, accepting less upside potential allows for the possibility of more robust downside protections. But there can be exceptions. FIAs can occasionally have higher guaranteed payout rates than income annuities, as deferred annuities provide discretion to owners to make irrational decisions. Not everyone takes advantage of distributing the full allowed guaranteed amounts from deferred annuities, which reduces the odds for the contract value to deplete and eases pressure on the insurer. Through competition, this can lead to a higher payout rate on the living benefit for an FIA. There can also occasionally be exceptions in which variable annuities can offer comparable guarantees to fixed annuities, particularly in cases where the VA may have very limited bond subaccount options for investments that lead to less downside risk. Indeed, the type of annuity offering the most guaranteed income can vary depending on household characteristics, the length of deferral, and potential future changes in pricing and product offerings. Shopping around between different types of annuities to obtain the best deal available at any given moment is a worthwhile endeavor.

This provides a framework for choosing between annuity types. It is worthwhile to first investigate what the guaranteed income levels are with different annuities at the targeted retirement date if purchased today. The annuity offering the most guaranteed downside income then becomes the baseline. Then consider whether there are additional reasons to choose a different annuity with less guaranteed income but with attractive liquidity provisions, upside growth potential, or even a better death benefit. When comparing deferred annuities with income annuities, including a cash refund provision for the income annuity would provide the closest approximation to the standard death benefit of deferred annuities. The difference in worst-case guaranteed income levels from different annuities reflects the effective cost of these other features. Especially, with upside, if growth potential is achieved for deferred annuities, then step-ups may be realized, and lifetime income could be higher than the minimum guaranteed level.

With the investment options and annuity features, how likely is it that the contract value can grow, and how important is it to the retiree to maintain the liquidity provided by the contract for those assets? About liquidity, we must remember that deferred annuities may not provide true liquidity if those assets are earmarked for income because excess distributions beyond the guaranteed amount will reduce the subsequent amount of guaranteed income provided. One application of deferred annuities, though, is to pay for the income protection to manage sequence risk and then if sequence is not realized in the early retirement years, one may decide to drop the guarantee from their plan. If a retiree values this liquidity and optionality about changing the decision later, then comparing the amount of guaranteed income lost to provide the liquidity (and upside) helps to quantify the tradeoff for the decision between income annuities and deferred variable annuities with income guarantees.

To summarize, but with a reminder that there are exceptions to these trends, the variable annuity maintains a contract value that can rise and fall with the markets, creating more upside potential and downside risk than other annuities. The fixed index annuity offers upside potential and liquidity, but generally less upside potential than a variable annuity and less minimum guaranteed income than an income annuity. It falls in the middle. Income annuities do not offer liquidity or upside, but they are usually the most efficient way to secure a stream of protected lifetime income with the least amount of assets. The idea would be to then use other non-annuity assets as the source for liquidity and upside, which leads to the next section.

Annuities, Asset Allocation, Legacy, and True Liquidity

The next important detail is deciding which investment assets should be sold to fund the annuity purchase. The potential benefit from annuities depends in part on how they are treated as part of asset allocation. Annuities have a better chance to work when they are treated as a bond and funded through the sale of bonds. Annuities become a bond replacement. That is the idea of the efficient frontier for retirement income mentioned in the previous section: stocks and annuities, instead of stocks and bonds. Over the long term, this can lay the foundation for greater legacy and liquidity for the retirement plan after also providing a stronger foundation to meet spending goals.

Annuities are not the intended source for legacy or liquidity. Income annuities do not provide liquidity or legacy without adding provisions which reduce the value of their mortality credits. As well, for deferred annuities with income benefits, the point is to use these assets to support spending and the liquidity and legacy potential of the assets is of less importance even though it may be a behavioral selling point for the annuity. These assets can be spent down because they continue to provide income even after they are depleted, and this can provide relief for other non-annuity assets to have less commitment to funding spending and more opportunity to grow.

There is more to the story about liquidity and legacy as relates to how an annuity fits into an overall plan. Often the discussion around annuities frames the matter incorrectly, as if it is an all-or-nothing decision. Partial annuity allocations let us think about how we allocate assets toward meeting different goals.

Annuities will work best when their owners view them as part of the "bond" allocation for retirement, so that overall stock holdings do not decrease with a partial annuity strategy. To keep the value of stock holdings the same, this does suggest that the stock allocation will be higher for the remaining portfolio assets outside the annuity. While this can cause some behavioral concerns, treating the annuity as a bond is justified.

In the discussion about "optimal withdrawal rates" from the previous chapter, we noted that for someone who worries about outliving his or her portfolio, does not have much additional income from outside the portfolio, mostly faces fixed expenses without much room to make cuts and does not have much in the way of backup reserves, it may be necessary to spend and invest quite conservatively to achieve a high probability of plan success. This individual has less capacity to bear financial market risk because their lifestyle is more vulnerable to a market downturn. In an investments-only world, such individuals would look to using a lower stock allocation and a lower spending rate.

Meanwhile, someone who has less fear about outliving his or her portfolio, has additional income sources from outside the portfolio, has the flexibility to cut portfolio spending without adversely impacting the living standard, and has sufficient additional reserves, a higher spending rate and more aggressive asset allocation could be quite satisfactory and optimal. Repositioning a portion of assets into an annuity offering lifetime income protections will contribute to better achieving these characteristics.

First, reliable income is increased through the annuity. More of the spending goal is now covered by reliable income assets that are not exposed to downside market risk. I use the term GRIP, or Guaranteed Retirement Income Percentage, to describe this concept. When the GRIP increases, more of the total spending budget is covered by resources with lifetime protections. This reduces the harm of investment portfolio depletion because more retirement spending is available outside the portfolio. With less exposure to downside market risk, the retiree has greater risk capacity and can rest more easily with a higher stock allocation for what remains. Adding protected lifetime income provides a stronger GRIP on retirement.

Second, for those with longevity risk aversion who are planning for a retirement lasting beyond life expectancy, using annuities with lifetime income benefits can mean that the present value of annuity benefits in the financial plan is greater than the annuity cost. With this subjective view toward longevity, the annuity asset is worth more than the premium, and this increases the funded ratio for the plan. Though the annuity does not increase plan assets in the objective sense, it does increase assets in the subjective sense that the plan is aiming to work to an advanced age, and people who live longer will receive more from the annuity. The remaining portfolio is available for more discretionary uses since the mortality credits of the annuity are covering more of the spending goal in the long run. The retirement is more secure, justifying a higher stock allocation for the portfolio piece of the asset base.

The third factor is the availability of reserves. What other resources are available that have not been earmarked to manage spending and can be used to cover contingencies? Having more reserves available means less reliance on the assets covering other goals to outperform and to create reserves through market gains. By helping to meet spending goals with less assets, the annuity creates additional reserves that provide true liquidity. With this added flexibility, the retiree can feel more comfortable with the aggressive asset allocation because there is less exposure to the possibility of having to sell assets at a loss to cover contingencies, and then not having enough left to cover other subsequent spending needs.

Finally, traditional risk aversion is the countervailing force for all of this, and this is the factor that may receive the most attention. Though the investment portfolio is a smaller portion of the overall asset base after some of it is sold to purchase the annuity, the retiree must still be comfortable with the greater short-term portfolio volatility that a more aggressive asset allocation will imply. Conceptually this is justified, as we have discussed. But the retiree must accept and understand these points to avoid the potential of panicking and not following the strategy during market downturns. An income annuity is still an asset even though it does not appear on the portfolio statement. To be effective, retirees should view the annuity as part of their bond holdings and adjust their portfolio accordingly. This is also an area where deferred annuities can help with the psychology behind holding annuities. If retirees cannot overcome the psychological hurdle to adopt a higher stock allocation after adding an annuity, the likely outcome will be a reduction in their overall allocation to stocks, which will undermine the effectiveness of a partial annuity strategy.

To better make this case, we can also discuss why annuities are "bond" like in their characteristics. First, income annuities provide bond-like returns with an additional overlay of mortality credits. The insurance company providing the annuity is investing those funds primarily in a fixed-income portfolio. For someone wishing to spend at a rate beyond what the bond yield curve can support, bond investments will essentially ensure that the plan will fail. Income annuities are *actuarial bonds*. They provide longevity protection which is unavailable with traditional bonds. Income annuities are like a bond with a maturity date that is unknown in advance, but which is calibrated and hedged specifically to cover the amount of lifetime spending needed by retirees.

Likewise, fixed index annuities that are linked to stock indices will also be more effective for those who treat them as part of their bonds. With principal protection, FIAs have less downside risk than either stocks or bonds. Bonds, of course, can experience capital losses when interest rates rise. But can enough upside be captured with the FIA to beat either stocks or bonds on a risk-adjusted basis? Though the interest they credit may be linked to a stock index, the returns on FIAs will be closer to bonds than to stocks. Owners should not think about FIAs as an alternative to owning stocks but rather as another option for fixed-income assets that protects principal and has the potential to outperform bonds when considered net of taxes and fees. With their principal protection, retirees may even consider increasing their stock allocation when replacing bonds with an FIA. The point is that FIAs provide returns comparable to bonds and can be treated as such even when linked to a stock index.

For variable annuities, the discussion is more complex as these annuities allow for stock investments to be held in the subaccounts. But when providing for lifetime spending, the guaranteed living withdrawal benefit serves as a "put option" on the stock market. Put options are financial derivatives that provide upside exposure while protecting from downside risk. When the stock market drops, even though the contract value declines, a GLWB protects lifetime retirement spending from this downside risk. This can allow retirees to feel more comfortable increasing their stock allocation in the variable annuity relative to an unprotected portfolio, or to otherwise view the variable annuity as a bond-like asset when framing retirement risk as the ability to meet financial goals rather than the underlying volatility of assets.

Moshe Milevsky and Vladyslav Kyrychenko have provided research based on over one-million variable annuity policy holders showing that those with optional income guarantees were willing to have about a 5 percent to 30 percent higher stock allocation than those without guarantees on their variable annuities. For instance, someone willing to hold 30 percent stocks without a guarantee may increase their stock allocation to between 35 percent and 60 percent with an income guarantee in place. This demonstrates an understanding and willingness in practice to view stocks held inside the variable annuity as being less "risky" to spending goals.

Having the income guarantee supported with actuarial bonds increases the risk capacity of retirees, as their retirement standard of living is less vulnerable to a market downturn. This can provide the capacity to use a higher stock allocation when a guarantee is in place, both inside and outside of a variable annuity. This works inside the variable annuity because the income guarantee protects income on the downside while still offering upside potential. Outside the variable annuity, the income guarantee reduces the harm created if portfolio assets deplete, providing increased risk capacity.

There are situations when variable and index annuities might help to achieve more efficient outcomes in retirement in terms of the combination of spending and legacy over retirement portfolios without a variable or index annuity component. These relate to asset allocation and whether it may change when an income guarantee is in place. Income guarantees provide greater relative benefit to retirees who are either willing to invest more aggressively because of the guarantee, or who would otherwise be uncomfortable using stocks in retirement.

Those who accept the notion that the income guarantee increases risk capacity and are willing to use a more aggressive asset allocation than otherwise both inside and outside of the annuity, could find that the additional exposure to the stock market equity premium more than offsets the annuity fees when markets perform well in retirement. The guarantee is also valuable if it otherwise stops retirees from panicking and selling stocks after a market drop. And when markets perform poorly, by paying an insurance premium for the income protection, one should anticipate depleting the underlying asset base sooner than with a lower-cost, investments-only strategy. But because the annuity still includes a lifetime guarantee, retirement spending will be supported after assets deplete.

Variable and index annuities could also create better outcomes for those who would simply use a lower stock allocation no matter the chosen retirement strategy, but who are unwilling to sacrifice the liquidity foregone with an income annuity. With a low stock allocation, investment assets are more likely to deplete, as there is only so much spending that bonds can support. The annuity provides the opportunity to continue with income for life even after the contract value of assets is gone. Without exposure to the risk premium, the contract value of underlying assets is more assured to deplete in the event of a long retirement. With investments-only, asset depletion ends the ability to spend, but an income guarantee assures this continued spending ability for life.

When allocating from bonds to annuities with lifetime income protections in the retirement income plan, the risk pooling from annuities can lay the foundation for more legacy (at least after life expectancy) and liquidity in the financial plan. In early retirement, legacy will naturally be less with partial annuitization or with a deferred annuity with surrender charges. But for conservative spenders where the payout rate from the annuity is higher than the initial withdrawal rate, with partial annuity use there is less pressure on the portfolio in the early retirement years. This allows non-annuity assets to grow more over time as mortality credits reduce the need to spend these other investment assets. The remaining investment assets may eventually grow to catch up with where an investments-only strategy would have been at about the life expectancy. Beyond that age, the increasing role for mortality credits allows the partial annuity strategy to get further ahead with legacy compared to an investments-only strategy.

When retirement is short, partial annuity strategies often lead to a smaller legacy, though the remaining legacy from investment assets is still reasonably large. For longer retirements, partial annuity strategies provide sound spending support while also fortifying a larger legacy. By requiring less assets to meet spending, risk capacity increases and the withdrawal rate from remaining assets decreases. Non-annuity assets can grow with less sequence risk, creating better long-term opportunities for legacy. Short-term sacrifice supports long-term gain.

As for true liquidity in the plan, consider a couple who believes that the 4 percent rule serves as an appropriate guide for their retirement spending. They seek to spend $40,000 per year with inflation adjustments, and they have $1 million invested in stocks or bonds through their brokerage account. Does this couple have any liquidity? Yes, technically, since they do have $1 million of liquid financial assets. But in a meaningful sense, this couple does *not* have liquidity. They are not free to use that $1 million for other purposes. The full amount must be tied up to support their spending objectives. An investment portfolio is a liquid asset, but some of its liquidity may be illusionary if those assets are already earmarked for specific goals. This distinction is important because there are cases when tying up a portion of assets in something illiquid, such as an income annuity, may allow for the household liabilities to be covered more cheaply than could be done when all assets are positioned to provide technical liquidity.

Many real-world retirees end up earmarking more assets than necessary to support income, and therefore spend less than possible because there is no guarantee component with investments, and they worry about outliving their assets. In simple terms, an annuity with lifetime income benefits that pools longevity risk may allow lifetime spending to be met at a cost of twenty years of the spending objective, while self-funding for longevity may require setting aside enough from an investment portfolio to cover thirty to forty years of expenses. The amount to be set aside with investments grows with the longevity risk aversion of the retiree. Because risk pooling allows for less to be set aside to cover the spending goal, there is now greater true liquidity and therefore more to cover other unexpected contingencies without jeopardizing core-spending needs. True liquidity will be larger whenever the payout rate for the annuity is greater than the determined "safe" withdrawal rate from investments as based on the retiree's risk aversion. As this will be the case for risk averse retirees who plan for living longer than average while earning below average portfolio returns, allocating to an annuity to cover an income gap can create more true liquidity for the overall retirement plan. Risk pooling and mortality credits allow for less to be set aside to cover the spending goal, creating greater true liquidity to cover other unexpected contingencies without jeopardizing core spending needs. Liquidity, as it is traditionally defined in securities markets, is of little value as a distinct retirement goal. The distinction between technical and true liquidity is important.

Inflation Risk Management and Annuities

A common question about annuities relates to inflation protection and whether it should be incorporated into the annuity. We can distinguish between whether the retiree *needs* the annuity to provide inflation protection and whether the retiree *wants* the annuity to provide inflation protection. With a lower payout rate, an income annuity providing income growth and inflation protection will require a larger premium to build up the same initial spending power. Alternatively, the same premium amount will buy less initial income when this income grows over time. Obtaining inflation protection means trading less spending early on for more spending later. Likewise, many deferred annuities with GLWBs may offer the potential for step-ups to keep pace with inflation, but retirees should recognize that the probability this will happen could be low as the retirement gets longer.

The tradeoff is that with level annuity spending, the remaining investment portfolio must also cover the subsequent inflation adjustments that the level annuity does not provide. Less can go into the annuity initially, leaving more in the portfolio, but the subsequent demands on the portfolio will be greater to also cover the missing inflation adjustment for the annuity portion. As it turns out, the lower withdrawal rate from investments can help assets to grow and to manage sequence risk, such that the higher spending need later in retirement can be more effectively managed. For this reason, I do not think it is necessary to include inflation protection into the annuity. I think that the common concern about annuities not providing inflation protection is framing it as an all-or-nothing decision, rather than recognizing that the annuity facilitates the use of other non-annuity assets as a source of inflation protection.

Meanwhile, the decision about whether the retiree will *want* inflation protection for the annuity is a different matter. Some worry quite a bit that inflation will be much higher in the future than it is today. The possibility of high inflation would make the inflation-adjusted annuity a more attractive choice. At the present, CPI-adjusted annuities are not available, and having a fixed COLA will not really help with an unexpectedly high inflation rate. If CPI-adjusted annuities were available, the retiree must decide whether it is worth paying the additional cost to obtain contractually protected lifetime inflation-adjusted income beyond what Social Security provides, or whether to instead use a lower initial premium to obtain level income from the annuity. The retiree can then try to manage the inflation risk through the investment portfolio and through the synergies of reducing sequence risk by being able to use a lower distribution rate from the remaining investments. While there is a risk because there is not an asset specifically linked to inflation, my research suggests that the latter approach is generally worthwhile.

One additional important point about this discussion is that it has presupposed that retirees desire their overall spending to consistently keep pace with inflation. The reality is that the inflation-adjusted spending for many retirees can be expected to decline with age. Other income sources, such as Social Security, will adjust their benefits with inflation. And as partial annuity strategies mean that only a fraction of overall income is provided by the annuity, it may be the case that an income annuity with level payments will match the spending needs of real retirees more precisely. In other words, having those inflation adjustments may not even be necessary in many cases. If retirees do find that their inflation-adjusted reliable income is falling short of their longevity spending goals, it is always possible to ladder in additional annuities to support more reliable income.

Framing Annuity Fees

We have described the fees for different types of annuities, and it is worth returning to this issue. As we noted, fees for fixed annuities are often less and are based on spreads between what the insurer can earn on the assets and what is credited as interest. They must be reverse engineered since there are not always explicit fees beyond those on optional benefits.

This discussion is mostly about variable annuities. Their fees are often presented as one of the biggest objections to annuities, and sometimes fixed annuities get caught in that crossfire. Variable annuities have generally come under attack for the higher internal costs relative to an unprotected investment portfolio.

It is important to frame the issue of variable annuity fees in terms of the potential value the variable annuity can provide to a retirement income plan. Variable annuities may have higher ongoing charges than non-annuity investment portfolios, but a portion of those fees are to pay for the assurance of a lifetime income in the face of longevity and market risk.

It may be easiest to think about the fee issue by comparing to simple income annuities. Income annuities do not include transparent fees, as the fees are internal to the product and the payout rate is provided on a net basis. Money's worth measures can be used to back out the implied fees for an income annuity. But if we frame the income annuity in the same way as a variable annuity, we conclude that the income annuity has a 100 percent fee at the time the contract is signed, and the premium is paid. Once an income annuity is purchased, assets are relinquished to the insurance company and will be inaccessible at any point in the future when the annuitant remains alive (there could be a cash refund provision at death). There is no contract value.

In contrast, deferred variable annuities provide liquidity through the contract value. Variable annuity liquidity allows for the guarantee to be ended at any time, returning any remaining assets. Excess distributions are allowed with a proportional reduction to the guarantee. The fee drag will work to gradually reduce the contract value over time rather than eliminating it immediately.

In practice, we do not describe the income annuity as having a 100 percent fee. Rather, we focus on the role its guaranteed income can play in the overall financial plan. Variable annuities maintain a contract value which has a higher cost associated with it, but the focus should be on how much must be earmarked to fund different retirement goals. With risk pooling, an income rider may allow fewer assets to be earmarked to meet retirement spending needs, which supports the annuity's value proposition. Also, if fewer assets are needed to comfortably meet the spending goal, then even a higher fee drag on a smaller asset base may not lead to more overall fees.

More broadly, in the context of the retirement income plan, focusing on the internal costs of a variable annuity is not the best way to frame the problem we are attempting to solve. Is an investments-only strategy with lower internal fees preferable if that approach to managing longevity and sequence risk translates to spending less or delaying retirement? That is the context in which to assess fees: can they support better outcomes through risk pooling that reduce the overall costs of the plan in terms of the asset base required to meet the financial goals of retirement?

There is also another aspect of variable annuities related to asset allocation. If one maintains the same asset allocation both inside and outside of the variable annuity, then the additional fees for a variable annuity can be expected to deplete the underlying value of the assets more quickly than if they were held in an unprotected investment account with lower fees. However, this outcome changes since an income guarantee can support using a higher stock allocation within a variable annuity. In this case, when markets do well in retirement, the additional exposure to the risk premium can more than offset the higher costs of the variable annuity to allow for greater overall growth in assets. This can support greater legacy after meeting the same spending goal. If markets perform poorly in retirement, the additional costs within the variable annuity could cause depletion of assets sooner than otherwise. But with poor returns, the investments-only portfolio will be on track to depletion shortly thereafter. With the variable annuity assets, at least, the income guarantee continues to support spending after the contract value depletes. With investments-only, spending power ends. The simple argument that higher fees makes annuities unattractive is not the whole story.

Action Plan

For retirees who view annuities as a bond replacement and whose overall spending goal implies a lower withdrawal rate than the annuity payout rate, partial annuity strategies can increase success rates, raise the proportion of lifetime spending goals that can be covered, and improve legacy outcomes especially for those living beyond life expectancy, relative to an investments-only strategy. The mortality credits provided through risk pooling provide relief for the distribution needs from non-annuity assets, giving them more potential to grow. But not everyone will need or want an annuity. Some retirees may already have plenty of lifetime annuity income through Social Security and traditional defined-benefit pensions. The action items for determining whether and how to include annuities within your retirement income plan include:

☐ Assess whether your characteristics and preferences are aligned with obtaining greater value from an annuity.
  - Your RISA Profile suggests that your preferences align with income protection and risk wrap strategies.
  - You have an income gap in which there is not enough reliable income to cover your longevity expenses.
  - Your risk tolerance limits your comfort with stocks in retirement. The case for annuities is stronger for those with a lower stock allocation.
  - You have greater longevity risk aversion. Concerns about outliving retirement assets lead to more relative benefits from annuities as the alternative is to spend even less from investments.
  - You view annuities as a replacement for bonds and are comfortable using a higher stock allocation with remaining investment assets.
  - You seek protection from making behavioral mistakes with your investment portfolio, you lack self-control for spending, or you find investments intimidating. Annuities may also protect less financially savvy family members.

☐ Learn about the features and mechanics of different annuities.
  - When comparing annuities for lifetime income, it is essential to first focus on the minimum guaranteed withdrawals for your purchase age and anticipated income starting age.
  - Consider your preferences for tradeoffs between upside and downside, the desire for liquidity, and the types of asset allocations you would use both with and without income protections.
  - Determine whether there may be an annuity option with other attractive features that make it worth accepting even if it does not have the strongest downside guarantees.

- ☐ Determine the income gap you are seeking to fill and decide whether the amount of assets needed to fill that gap with annuities is reasonable. Decide on a premium amount.
- ☐ Take your time with making this purchase decision.
  - ○ Discuss the decision with family members to coordinate both with the spouse and with any potential heirs.
  - ○ Work with someone who is familiar with the vast array of available annuities and understands which work better for different purposes, ages, and deferral periods.
  - ○ Make sure you understand how the annuity works with respect to its various features and fees.
  - ○ Understand how the annuity taxes work (see Chapter 10).
  - ○ Only add living or death benefits that you intend to use.
  - ○ Consider diversifying purchases between different companies and even different types of annuities.

Further Reading

Milevsky, Moshe A., and V. Kyrychenko. 2008. "Portfolio Choice with Puts: Evidence from Variable Annuities." *Financial Analysts Journal*, Vol. 64, No. 3 (May/June), p. 80–95.

Olsen, John L. 2020. *John Olsen's Guide to Annuities for the Consumer, 4th Edition*. St. Louis: John Olsen.

Pfau, Wade D. 2019. *Safety-First Retirement Planning: An Integrated Approach for a Worry-Free Retirement*. Vienna, VA: Retirement Researcher Media.

Chapter 6: Social Security

Social Security retirement benefits support a lifetime income in the same way as an annuity. For most Americans, Social Security benefits serve as the core component of retirement income. About 90 percent of retirees in the United States will be eligible for Social Security. As a government-backed, inflation-adjusted monthly income for life, Social Security benefits help to manage longevity risk, inflation risk, and market risk. In addition to retirement worker benefits, Social Security also provides spousal, survivor, and dependent benefits from the retired worker's earnings record. Social Security benefits also receive preferential tax treatment.

This makes the Social Security claiming decision very important. It is vital to understand that the decision for when to start Social Security should be made independently from when one decides to leave the labor force. Claiming decisions should not be taken lightly. It is possible to gain much from Social Security simply by understanding how the system works.

This chapter will walk you through the steps required to have a firm understanding about Social Security claiming. I will discuss how Social Security benefits are calculated and how to factor in issues such as spousal and survivor benefits for couples, dependent benefits, and benefits for divorcees. I will also look at the earnings test, and the windfall elimination provision and government pension offset for those spending a portion of their careers outside of the Social Security system. I will also explain cases where benefits may be suspended for strategic reasons.

I also consider the philosophies about claiming Social Security, including its insurance value to protect for a long-life, breakeven analyses on when delaying benefits will pay off, and the validity of arguments made in favor of claiming Social Security early. The latter involves a discussion of Social Security's history, and potential reform options related to what may happen as the Social Security trust fund approaches depletion. The intention for this chapter is to give you the knowledge and confidence to approach Social Security to create the most long-term value for your retirement income plan.

Introducing the Social Security Claiming Decision

Any discussion of life annuities would not be complete without discussing a life annuity that will be available to most Americans: Social Security. The Social Security claiming decision should be made independently from when one decides to quit working and retire. Too many people believe they are related and that a visit to the Social Security office is an automatic part of leaving work. It is perfectly okay to retire and to wait until a later date to begin Social Security benefits.

Deciding when to claim Social Security benefits is complicated. Entire books are available for those who really want to dig deep into this subject (see Further Reading at the end of the chapter for my favorites). I will take the approach of summarizing the key issues and ideas at work to give readers a good understanding about how to proceed, and to know which specific special cases may apply to their situation that could require a deeper dive.

A key idea in this chapter is that because Social Security is so complicated, it is worthwhile to take the time to investigate your situation with a comprehensive Social Security claiming software package. Even with a small nominal cost, the difference in lifetime outcomes between good and bad claiming strategies could add up in some cases to be more than $100,000 of additional lifetime benefits. There are a lot of special circumstances that could otherwise be too easily overlooked.

I do not have any affiliation with the following software programs, and these are not endorsements, but I do have respect for their creators. Any of these programs are available to consumers, as opposed to financial advisors, and should provide a good idea about a proper course forward:

- Mike Piper's *Open Social Security* (https://opensocialsecurity.com/) is a free open-source online calculator.
- Larry Kotlikoff's *Maximize my Social Security* (www.maximizemysocialsecurity.com) offers an annual household license for $40.
- William Reichenstein and William Meyer's *Social Security Solutions* (https://www.socialsecuritysolutions.com/) offers various pricing options starting from $19.95 for a year of access and a detailed custom report.

If you are ambitious and test your case in all three programs, you may find slight differences in the recommended claiming strategies. These will result from different assumptions used regarding longevity and interest rates. Making sure that the assumptions used in each program are the same should close any gaps. Especially, longevity assumptions can create a big impact on which strategy works out best. But overall, the optimal strategies from each program will ultimately lead to similar outcomes and the differences between strategies that are close to optimal will be small enough that you have some flexibility for your choice. The difference in lifetime outcomes between "good" and "bad" strategies can be massive.

Another key point is that the Social Security claiming decision must be made as part of an overall plan and not in isolation. It is important to coordinate with investments or other assets in terms of building a Social Security delay bridge if retiring before claiming, to coordinate on the tax side to pay less taxes over time by better managing tax brackets (see chapter 10), and to coordinate with respect to how Social Security impacts the Retirement CARE Analysis™ by providing more capacity to bear financial market risk (see chapter 13).

In January 2021, the Social Security Administration reported that the average monthly Social Security benefit for retired workers is $1,543 per month, or $18,516 per year. For a couple, total benefits would be larger if two people are eligible for benefits, either on their own work records or as a spouse. Individuals with above average lifetime earnings will be entitled to even larger benefits, and the average benefit received is less than otherwise possible because most Americans claim benefits before their full retirement age and are subject to benefit reduction factors. Delaying the start of your benefit would also help to provide a larger amount.

The Social Security Administration's online calculator shows that individuals turning 70 and claiming at this age in 2021, and who earned the maximum taxable earnings over their career up to this point, will be entitled to a maximum possible benefit of $3,895 per month or $46,740 per year. Over 20 years, that is $934,800 of real spending power just for the worker's benefit. It will exceed $1 million including spousal benefits or for a retirement lasting beyond 20 years.

The full retirement age has been 66 in recent years, applying to those born between 1943 and 1954. As of 2021, the full retirement age begins increasing by two months each year until it reaches 67 in 2027 for those born in 1960 and later. In 2021, those turning 62 face a full retirement age of 66 and 10 months, and anyone 61 or younger faces a full retirement age of 67. Since we are getting close to that point and to simplify the math around not having to factor in benefits for partial years, I will treat 67 as the full retirement age for examples used in this chapter. Nonetheless, individuals can claim their Social Security retirement benefits as early as age 62 (with reductions) and will receive delay credits for their own benefit after the full retirement age for waiting up to age 70. There is no reward provided for delaying beyond age 70.

To the extent that wages will grow faster than consumer prices, current Social Security rules support further benefit growth for wage earners born at later dates. And it is also important to remember that benefits will grow with inflation throughout retirement.

I will also use an additional simplification about birth dates. A quirky aspect of Social Security is that one is assumed to reach an age on the day before their birthday. Someone born on January 1 is treated as being born in the previous year. In the previous paragraph, when I refer to those born in 1954, for instance, I mean born between January 2, 1954, and January 1, 1955. To facilitate the discussion, I keep this as simple as possible, but it is important to remember for those born on the first day of the month.

Social Security is a significant retirement asset. The present value of Social Security benefits at retirement, which can total hundreds of thousands or even millions of dollars, joins home equity as the top two assets available for most American retirees, easily dwarfing the value of investment portfolios. Especially for lower- and middle-income Americans, Social Security may end up supporting most retirement spending.

For higher lifetime earners and savers, the relative importance of Social Security will be less. Nonetheless, for those experiencing a sufficiently long retirement, total Social Security benefits could easily exceed $1 million, and optimal Social Security claiming decisions could end up supporting more than $100,000 of *additional* retirement income, relative to less effective claiming choices. It is hard to find people wealthy enough that this is not a big deal.

It is also important to recognize that case workers at Social Security offices may not know about sophisticated claiming strategies, as they otherwise generally assume that the reason for visiting them is because you want your benefits to start sooner rather than later. They cannot advise you on your decision.

Social Security claiming strategies involve deciding on which age to claim retirement benefits. Those benefits can be claimed starting at age 62, and additional credits are available for delaying benefits up until age 70. For a single person, the claiming decision is a matter of picking the start date for benefits. The decision is more complicated for couples or singles with dependents, though. For couples, each spouse must consider when to claim their own benefit, when to claim their spousal benefit (for the few left that can make this distinction), and the impact of their claiming decision on whether their spouse has access to a spousal benefit and the size of a survivor benefit. Any potential benefits for dependents must also be factored into these decisions as well.

Brief History of Social Security

Recipients of Social Security benefits today include not just retirees, but also disabled workers, spouses, and young children of deceased or disabled workers, and the spouses, dependents, and survivors of retirees. However, this was not always the case. In fact, the original Social Security Act of 1935 created retirement benefits for only the retired worker, who became eligible at age 65. In 1939, Congress passed amendments to extend benefits to spouses and minor children of retired workers, as well as to the widows and minor children of deceased workers. Disability insurance arrived in 1954, and in subsequent years, the disability program expanded to include the families of disabled workers. In 1972, Congress passed legislation to create annual cost-of-living adjustments for benefits. Prior to that time, benefit increases were subject to the whims of Congress and happened only intermittently.

The 1975 Social Security Trustee's report estimated that the Old-Age, Survivors, and Disability Insurance (OASDI) Trust Funds would be depleted by 1979. Administrators generally desire to have the Trust Fund be on track to cover net outflows (given all the expected future tax collections and interest less benefit payments) for at least 75 years. This was a serious problem. In 1977, Congress enacted amendments to deal with the impending financial problems. The amendments increased the payroll tax, increased the amount of income that was eligible for the payroll tax, and reduced benefits slightly. The economic slowdown in the early 1980s again left the Trust Fund with serious funding problems.

Alan Greenspan, who would later gain greater fame as a long-serving chair of the Federal Reserve Board, headed a commission to examine this problem in 1983. The Greenspan Commission called for, and Congress subsequently passed into law, an increase in the full retirement age to gradually extend from 65 to 67, increases in Social Security tax rates, and the addition of new taxes on the benefits of the wealthiest individuals. The goal was to solve the immediate financial problems and to build up a surplus over the next few decades in anticipation of the inevitable Trust Fund drain resulting from the coming baby boomer retirements.

Under the current law, the combined employee/employer tax rate for the Old-Age, Survivors, and Disability Insurance (OASDI) fund is 12.4 percent. Medicare adds another 2.9 percent to this, bringing the total to 15.3 percent. This amount is split equally between employers and employees, or is paid entirely by the self-employed, up to a maximum taxable limit for the OASDI part that is $142,800 in 2021. The Medicare part does not have an upper limit and there is an additional 0.9 percent Medicare surtax on higher earners. As noted, the full retirement age is now slowly ascending toward 67 for those born in 1960 and later.

That Social Security is expected to again undergo funding shortages at some point in the future should come as no surprise. Social Security in the United States is meant to be pay-as-you-go, meaning that each generation of current workers pays for the benefits of current beneficiaries. Three trends, though, make this an increasingly difficult task despite the present surpluses. First, the baby boomer cohort is of unprecedented size and is now in the process of reaching traditional retirement ages. Second, life spans are becoming longer, meaning that the retiring baby boomers will enjoy longer retirements and receive more benefits. The third important trend is the decrease in fertility rates. During the height of the baby boom, women, on average, were having between 3.5 and 4 children each during their lifetimes. The 2021 *Trustee's Report* expects the long-run fertility rate in the United States to be just 2.0.

Combining these three trends means that there will be fewer workers available to support retirees. Throughout Social Security's history, the ratio of covered workers contributing to Social Security relative to the number of retirement and survivor beneficiaries has witnessed gradual decline. Still though, in 2000 there were 3.9 workers per retired beneficiary. In 2020, the Social Security Trustees estimate only 3.2 covered workers per beneficiary, and the best guess is that by 2030 there will be 2.7 workers per beneficiary.

If we add recipients of spousal, child, survivor, and disability benefits to the calculation as well, the Trustees expect there to be only 2.4 workers per Social Security beneficiary by 2030. New contributions will not be able to pay for promised benefits due to the misalignment of the worker to beneficiary ratio.

This poses a clear problem. As indicated, a legacy of the 1983 Greenspan Commission is that the Trust Fund accumulates more each year than it spends to build a buffer. However, the size of the Trust Fund for retirement and survivors benefits peaked in 2010 and is now in decline. The current best guess in the 2021 *Trustee's Report* is that the combined Social Security Trust Fund will be depleted by 2034. The report's release was delayed until August 31, 2001, and now accounts for impacts related to the global pandemic. Subsequent years will be met with cuts in benefits, increases in taxes, or borrowing from the rest of the government's budget. This is not to say that near retirees should expect Social Security to disappear, as there are a variety of reforms which could be implemented to get the system back on track. As well, even if no action is taken, the inflows of new payroll taxes and taxes on benefits will be sufficient to cover more than 75 percent of benefits due. I discuss reform options further near the end of the chapter.

Calculating Social Security Retirement Benefits

It is meaningful to consider how retirement benefits are calculated. The Social Security Administration has now followed the same approach for calculating benefits since 1979. Necessary ingredients in the benefit computation include finding the average indexed monthly earnings (AIME), converting this into the primary insurance amount (PIA), using the primary insurance amount to calculate the starting benefit for all relevant family members, checking to ensure that the total benefit payments do not exceed the family maximum, and then increasing the annual benefits using the cost-of-living adjustment for all remaining years of the recipient's eligibility. With more details, the steps for determining one's Social Security benefit are as follows:

Determine Eligibility. To be eligible for retirement benefits, a minimum amount of taxable earnings must be recorded for at least 40 quarters (10 years). In 2021, a quarter of coverage is provided for $1,470 of eligible earnings, so that income of $5,880 of covered earnings would provide a year of credits. The Social Security Statement shows the lifetime taxable earnings for a worker. This statement used to be mailed annually. It is now mailed every five years. One can obtain a copy of their statement online by following the links at http://www.ssa.gov/myaccount. This is a useful document to help you budget for what your Social Security benefits will be, and it is otherwise important and worthwhile to check this document to make sure that Social Security has a proper recording of your earnings history. Keep in mind that the earnings listed are only up to each year's maximum taxable amount (which is $142,800 in 2021 but has been rising faster than inflation and used to be much less). Projected benefits on the statement assume no future inflation or wage growth, and that you continue to work until the age that you begin benefits.

Calculate Average Indexed Monthly Earnings (AIME). The AIME is the average of the top 420 months of earnings up to maximum taxable amounts. That is 35 years, and earnings are only tracked at the annual level. Past earnings through age 60 are indexed to higher amounts to account for economy-wide average wage growth. After age 60, earnings still count but are not indexed. This makes the Average Wage Index at age 60 very important for determining benefits. For someone whose career was shorter than 35 years, the AIME can include years with $0 earnings. For someone who has already logged 35 years of earnings, payroll taxes continue for additional work, but new wages must be high enough to displace other wages from the list of the top 35 years to have an impact on benefits. As well, even for those who still work while receiving benefits, payroll taxes continue and the AIME can subsequently be increased to reflect new earnings that enter the top 35 years. That can increase subsequent benefits beyond the amount of cost-of-living adjustments.

Calculate Primary Insurance Amount (PIA). Next, the PIA is calculated to determine the available benefits at the full retirement age (FRA). Until 2020, the full retirement age is 66. It now begins a gradual increase of two months per year toward 67 in 2027 for those born in 1960 and later. The PIA calculation translates the AIME using a progressive benefit formula which provides a higher percentage of the AIME to lower-wage workers and a lower percentage for higher-wage earnings. The PIA formula provides a 90 percent replacement rate for the lowest range of the AIME, a 32 percent replacement rate for a middle range, and a 15 percent replacement rate for an upper range. The ranges used to calculate the PIA are based on the year that the worker reaches age 62 and are linked to the average wage index at age 60. For those reaching 62 in 2021, the 90 percent factor applies to the first $996 of the AIME, 32 percent applies to the range of AIME between $996 and $6,002, and 15 percent applies for the amount of the AIME over $6,002. The PIA is then lowered to the closest multiple of 10 cents.

With the different percentage bend points in the formula, higher AIME values will translate into a lower overall replacement rate for benefits. This works out to the average benefit being about 40 percent of average wages each year, though Andrew Biggs of the American Enterprise Institute has pointed out that this widely publicized 40 percent number is not how most people think about replacement rates. He calculates that the average benefit replaces about 53 percent of average inflation-adjusted lifetime earnings. Because of the progressive nature of the benefit formula, those with less than average earnings, or with higher earnings for a smaller number of years, would experience higher replacement rates, while those with a lengthy record of above average earnings would experience a lower replacement rate.

Translate the PIA into a benefit amount based on claiming age. The PIA provides the benefit available at the full retirement age. Benefits adjust upward or downward depending on when they start relative to the full retirement age. For each month of delay beyond the full retirement age, the benefit increases by 0.67 percent. This sums to an 8 percent increase in benefits per year (not compounded). For each month of early uptake relative to the FRA, the benefit reduces by 0.56 percent per month for the first 36 months of early uptake, and by an additional 0.42 percent for any months beyond that.

Since claiming earlier means more years of benefit receipt while claiming later means less years, these adjustments were designed to be actuarially fair. This means it should not matter what age one claims their benefit for single individuals who live to their life expectancy. However, those calculations for actuarial fairness were made in the early 1980s and they no longer hold for today's retirees who live longer and face lower interest rates. Retirement benefits can be claimed as early as age 62, and delay credits are provided up to age 70. Exhibit 6.1 summarizes how the claiming age adjusts the PIA to determine the actual retirement benefit in inflation-adjusted terms. Actual benefit increases would be even larger to account for annual cost-of-living adjustments provided after age 62.

Exhibit 6.1
Social Security Benefit Adjustments by Age

Adjustments by Age		
Claiming Age	Full Retirement Age = 66	Full Retirement Age = 67
62	75%	70%
63	80%	75%
64	87%	80%
65	93%	87%
66	100%	93%
67	108%	100%
68	116%	108%
69	124%	116%
70	132%	124%

Account for additional spousal and dependent benefits. A worker's record can also be used to support spousal, dependent, and survivor benefits. Dependent benefits are available to children under 18, children who became disabled before 22, and even parents who rely on the earner for more than 50 percent of their income. Divorcees who were married for at least 10 years are also eligible for benefits based on an ex-spouse's record. These additional benefits are provided up to a family maximum, which is the highest total amount of benefits that one worker's earnings record can support to individuals other than the worker. There is an exception for divorce benefits, which exist outside of these limits.

Adjusting benefits for inflation. It is easier to refer to Social Security benefits in terms of their value expressed in today's dollars rather than inflated future values that include those inflation impacts. In practice, Social Security retirement benefits will grow in nominal terms to reflect changes in consumer prices. Social Security benefits adjust for the Consumer Price Index for Urban Wage Earners and Clerical Workers (CPI-W) starting at the age of eligibility, which is 62 for retirement benefits. These increases apply to subsequent benefits even for those who have not yet claimed.

Philosophy and Practicalities of Claiming Strategies

Social Security claiming strategies can be extremely complicated. Treatises on this topic provide page after page of details, nuances, and exceptions. When you consider all the possible strategies for a couple given that each person can claim for each of 96 months between the ages of 62 and 70, there are millions of potential claiming strategies with spousal and survivor benefits mixed in. Very few people in the world fully understand all the Social Security rules that have accumulated since 1935. In fact, many case workers at Social Security offices are not trained in the nuances of the system and may tell you that you are unable to do something which is permitted under the rules. While it is best to prepare in advance for a visit to the Social Security Office, and even to take written explanations with photocopies from the Social Security handbook suggesting what you want to do is allowed, it is not necessarily practical or a good use of time to become an expert on all the nuances of Social Security claiming.

Rather, it is vital to use robust software which can maximize the Social Security claiming decision for your personalized situation. The costs for using software could help to provide more than $100,000 in net gains over a household's lifetime. Readers may use such software either directly on their own, or may choose to work with a financial advisor who maintains a license to test their clients' situations with such software. I provided the names and web addresses for three options in the introduction to this chapter. It is best to use a comprehensive program like the ones suggested, rather than a more basic calculator that does not cover all possible angles, especially regarding dependent and disability benefits or matters like the Government Pension Offset and Windfall Elimination Provision. I will provide a basic introduction to claiming Social Security with an overview of the main issues and possible special cases. The software will have you covered on these issues if you understand how to enter the inputs correctly and do not overlook the relevant tabs.

Keeping matters as simple as possible, eligibility for retirement benefits requires reaching age 62 and having at least 40 quarters (10 years) with sufficient Social Security covered earnings. Full retirement age comes later and as mentioned it is shifting from age 66 to 67. Important items to keep in mind about the full retirement age include:

- It is the age that one is entitled to the full retirement benefit (PIA)
- The earnings test ends so that one can receive Social Security without reductions even while continuing to work
- Some of the more creative strategies that became available at full retirement age have been scaled down, but there remain a few possibilities around suspending benefits or filing a restricted application that become available at full retirement age

Single Individuals

For single individuals with no dependents, Social Security claiming is an easier endeavor, though it is probably worthwhile to still double check one's strategy using a high-quality software program. That is just to make sure that one has not missed out on any special opportunities, such as a possibility for an ex-spouse or survivor benefit as well. This could also help to avoid a surprise with the Windfall Elimination Provision for those who worked in noncovered jobs for a part of their careers. Otherwise, a single individual only needs to decide on a claiming age. Unless one is in such dire circumstances that he or she simply does not have assets to fund a delay in benefits, or unless one has a valid medical opinion that he or she is unlikely to live beyond age 80, it is important to seriously consider the possibility for delaying benefits to support a permanently enhanced lifestyle and to obtain the full insurance value from Social Security.

Couples

Those with spouses and dependents face a more complicated decision-making process. For couples, the claiming decision is more difficult, especially when both spouses are eligible for benefits based on their own earnings records. Each spouse is potentially eligible for benefits based on:

- their own work record (plus your spouse is also eligible for a benefit based on your record)
- a spousal benefit based on a living spouse's record
- a survivor benefit based on a deceased spouse's record

One is eligible for spousal benefits at age 62 if married for at least one year. The spousal benefit is up to 50 percent of the spouse's primary insurance amount. Claiming a spousal benefit before full retirement age results in a reduction. At age 62, the percentage is 35 percent for those with a full retirement age of 66 and 32.5 percent for those with a full retirement age of 67. There are no delay credits for a spouse to extend claiming the spousal benefit beyond his or her full retirement age.

As well, to be clear, the spousal benefit is based on the worker's primary insurance amount and is based on the age that the spouse claims but not on the age that the worker claims. Unlike the survivor benefit, the spousal benefit is not impacted by the age that the worker claims his or her own benefit, however it is *necessary* for the worker to have claimed before the spouse is able to claim a spousal benefit on that earnings record. This could affect older spouses who are not eligible for benefits on their own record. For example, a 70-year-old who did not work is married to a 60-year-old-worker. The 70-year-old cannot obtain a Social Security spousal benefit until the younger spouse claims.

Except for the rare case that one can still file a restricted application (see callout box on the Bipartisan Budget Act of 2015), an individual is now deemed as always filing for both their own worker benefit and their spousal benefit. It is no longer possible to file for one without filing for the other. If the spouse has not yet claimed, then any additional spousal benefits will not be added until that time. But then they will automatically start. In that case, the claiming age for the spousal benefit will adjust to the age that the benefit payment begins.

If one is claiming before full retirement age, the process for determining the full benefit received is a bit complicated. The benefit has two components: the worker's own benefit first, and then any additional top-off to the benefit that represents the difference between the spousal benefit and the own benefit. Each of these portions will then separately be subjected to any reductions for claiming early. Also, claiming after the full retirement age would increase one's own benefit, but the spousal benefit does not receive any further increases for delayed claiming. The spousal benefit is based on the spouse's primary insurance amount and so the age that the worker claims is not directly connected to the amount of the spousal benefit. As mentioned, it is necessary for the worker to claim before the spouse can receive. And while delaying claiming does not directly lead to a bigger spousal benefit (unless it relates to continued work that increases the AIME and the PIA), it will feed into the opportunity to potentially receive a larger survivor benefit.

Spousal benefits are complicated, so it is worth summarizing the previous discussion with different wording that can highlight key points. The worker needs to have filed for their own benefit before a spouse can claim the spousal benefit. A spouse at full retirement age is eligible for up to 50 percent of the worker's primary insurance amount. Having that worker claim early or late does not impact the amount of the spousal benefit. Finally, if the spouse claims before full retirement age, then the benefit is reduced, but there are no delay credits for extending the spousal benefit past the full retirement age.

I will provide an example for a married couple who are the same age, because this is complex. The PIA for the husband at full retirement age is $2,500. The PIA for the wife at full retirement age is $900. Their full retirement age is 67. The husband plans to claim at full retirement age and the wife plans to claim five years earlier at age 62. We want to determine the amount of the wife's benefit now and later.

The wife's total benefit at full retirement age is $1,250, or 50 percent of the husband's benefit. This consists of $900 of her own benefit and a $350 top off for the spousal benefit. She claims five years earlier and this is before her husband claims. So, she receives 70 percent of $900, or $630 as a benefit until full retirement age. Then at full retirement age her husband claims, and she is now eligible for the spousal benefit. Since she begins receiving her spousal benefit at full retirement age, she is eligible to receive that full $350 top-off amount without reduction, which is added to her own reduced $630 benefit for $980 total.

This is only a simple introduction to the complex world of Social Security claiming for couples. A further relevant factor is the ratio of primary insurance amounts for each spouse, as this impacts the relevance for both own worker and spousal benefits. If the primary insurance amount for the lower earning spouse is at least half of the primary insurance amount for the higher earning spouse, then spousal benefits are not relevant. That can further push the high earner to delayed claiming. But if one spouse could receive very little from his or her own benefit, there could be an advantage for the high earner to claim sooner to allow for more years of spousal benefit to be received. Especially, as delay credits are not available for spousal benefits, these benefits could simply be lost. This loss must be balanced against the potential gains for increasing the survivor benefit through deferral. Another matter relates to age differences between the spouses. If the higher earner is also older, this strengthens the case for delay as that benefit has a greater opportunity to be obtained for longer through the survivor benefit. This aspect is weakened when the higher earner is younger.

We are getting a taste of Social Security's complexity when it comes to spousal benefits. It is worth repeating, again, that the minimal expenses required to test one's situation with a high-quality comprehensive Social Security calculator is incredibly worthwhile, as such software could provide a strategy that garners significant additional benefits over one's lifetime. These decisions are not easy to figure out on one's own, and this is a matter for which a basic investment of time and energy can lead to meaningful improvements for one's retirement finances.

Bipartisan Budget Act of 2015

Social Security claiming strategies became a hot topic in the early 2010s. Larry Kotlikoff's book, *Get What's Yours: The Secrets to Maxing Out Your Social Security*, was the #3 best-selling book at Amazon in early 2015, and this was not just for a short period after its initial release.

The interest in Social Security dropped off dramatically after the unexpected provisions included in the Bipartisan Budget Act of 2015 began a phaseout for newfound and sophisticated claiming strategies to wring more out of Social Security. By allowing for the voluntary suspension of retirement benefits at full retirement age, the Senior Citizens' Freedom to Work Act of 2000 had created some likely

---

unintended opportunities to get an extra windfall out of Social Security. Legislators intended to lessen the Social Security penalty for people who work through age 70. Loopholes developed that allowed retirees to take advantage of the new provisions even if they had already left the labor force.

In one strategy for couples, after reaching the full retirement age, someone could file a restricted application for their spousal benefit without having been deemed as filing for their own retirement benefit as well. For those whose spouses had already claimed benefits, this gave the higher earner in a couple a chance to get spousal benefits for the four years they are waiting to begin collecting their own benefits at 70. This option is no longer available for those born after January 1, 1954, meaning that anyone still eligible to do this is at least 67 in 2021. There may still occasionally be someone under age 70 who could benefit from this. For those too young to be eligible, the rule today is that one is automatically deemed as having filed for their own retirement benefits and any spousal benefits they are eligible for and cannot do this type of restricted application from among these two options. By 2024 there will not be anyone left who could possibly benefit from this restricted filing.

Alternatively, after the full retirement age, someone could file for and then suspend their own benefit. This allowed spouses and dependents to begin claiming benefits on the worker's record, perhaps but not necessarily with the restricted application just discussed, while the worker continued to earn delay credits up to age 70. Such action might provide an additional $50,000 just for a spouse over four years that is otherwise lost for those who were not aware of this option. This was the subject of Chapter 1 in the old edition of Larry's book. It is no longer possible to use this strategy at all. Suspending benefits after full retirement age is still allowed, but the new rule is that one cannot receive spousal or dependent benefits from another's record if that person has suspended his or her benefit.

Survivor Benefits

Regarding survivor benefits linked to a retirement benefit, a few additional comments are worthwhile. The first is that full retirement ages for survivor benefits can be slightly different than for retirement benefits. To be eligible for the survivor benefit, the marriage must have generally lasted for at least nine months. Generally, the scheduled increases in full retirement ages for survivor benefits lag retirement benefits by about two years. As well, early claiming for survivor benefits can began at age 60. There are reductions for survivor benefits when claiming before full retirement age and survivor benefits are also subject to the earnings test before full retirement age.

The survivor benefit at full retirement age is equal to the deceased spouse's benefit if that spouse has already claimed. If the deceased spouse did not yet claim, the survivor benefit is the larger of the deceased spouse's primary insurance amount or the benefit that the deceased spouse would have received if claiming at the time of death. That increases the survivor benefit above the deceased worker's primary insurance amount for those delaying benefits past the full retirement age. Unlike spousal benefits, survivor benefits reflect the delayed retirement credits earned by the deceased worker.

There is a provision that the survivor benefit when claimed at full retirement age is at least 82.5 percent of the deceased's primary insurance amount. This could result in a slight increase to survivors for workers who claimed at closer to age 62. Nonetheless, delaying benefits can generally support a larger survivor benefit from that worker's record.

Survivor benefits can be available before age 60 as well in cases where the surviving spouse is disabled or is caring for children under 16. In such cases, the benefit would end once the qualifying condition ended, and the survivor would become eligible again for the "retirement version" of the survivor benefit at age 60.

Another important point about survivor benefits is that they do allow for a separate claiming decision. A restricted application is possible for survivor benefits. With spousal benefits, except for the rare remaining exception mentioned in the call-out box, one is deemed to have filed for their own benefit to get access to spousal benefits. Restricted applications are mostly phased out for spouses. But that is not the case with survivor benefits. This allows for special coordination opportunities for widows, depending on the relative size of their benefit options.

For instance, if the worker benefit would ultimately be larger, one could claim the survivor's benefit early and delay their own worker benefit to age 70 to take advantage of delay credits. Survivor benefits do not increase with delay credits past the full retirement age, but for those whose survivor benefits are significantly larger, it could be worthwhile to begin the worker's benefit at age 62 and then switch to the survivor benefit at full retirement age. Again, this is a subtle and confusing point: the survivor benefit increases if the deceased worker had delayed beyond full retirement age but not if the survivor delays claiming the survivor benefit beyond full retirement age. There are more possibilities to explore with Social Security claiming for younger widows. A good Social Security claiming software program can help make better sense of these options.

Because of survivor benefits, the case for the higher earning spouse to delay benefits becomes even stronger because the delay credits will feed into both retirement and survivor benefits. The survivor benefit is the full amount that the deceased worker is receiving or would receive if claiming at the time of death. Thus, the relevant age for the higher earning spouse extends beyond his/her own age of death to his/her age when the last surviving member of the couple passes away. For a couple, joint survivorship is higher. As well, if the higher earning spouse is significantly older, their record could generate survivor benefits for many years, making Social Security delay extremely attractive. To reiterate, the higher earner claims based on number of years benefits will be generated by the earnings record for the longest living member of the couple.

Matters are different for the lower earning spouse, and the claiming decision for the lower earning spouse is also impacted by the differences in their lifetime earnings and primary insurance amounts. There are many circumstances when the lower earning spouse might claim at a younger age, with considerations about how each of the spouses may receive some short-term benefits from the lower earner's record. Generally, the case for delay until 70 is weaker for the lower-earning spouse, because the relative length for these benefits is when both spouses remain alive. Once one spouse has passed away, only the higher earner's benefit is relevant: either the higher earner lives and continues receiving their own retirement benefit, or the lower earner lives and can switch to a survivor benefit based on the higher earner's record.

Dependent Benefits

Other dependents may also be eligible for Social Security benefits as based on a retired worker's earnings record. A family maximum limit applies to the total benefits paid on a worker's record (excluding benefits paid to ex-spouses) that will fall around 150 to 187.5 percent of the primary insurance amount. When the family maximum is reached, all benefits except for the worker's own benefit (if alive) will be reduced proportionately so that the total amount matches the maximum.

When the family limit has not been reached, dependent children are eligible for 50 percent of their retired parent's primary insurance amount, and 75 percent is available as a survivor benefit from a deceased parent. These benefits are available to unmarried children under 18, 18 and 19-year-olds who are attending primary or secondary school, and those 18 and older who are disabled when the disability happened before age 22. Spouses are also entitled to the full spousal benefit when caring for children under 16 or when caring for the disabled adult child of the worker. Once there are not eligible children, the dependent spouse benefit stops until the spouse becomes eligible for retirement benefits. This creates a distinction between a spousal benefit when caring for dependents and a spousal benefit for retirement. Dependent parents who are age 62 and older when the primary supporter dies and when that primary supporter provided at least half of the parent's support are also eligible. For one parent, the benefit is 82.5 percent of the primary insurance amount, and two parents can each receive 75 percent of the primary insurance amount.

Dependents do add a complication to the claiming decision. Early claiming may be wise in some cases where not claiming means permanently losing access to the dependent benefits. One might also consider claiming before full retirement age to obtain these dependent benefits and then suspending again after full retirement age to collect some delay credits. But the decision is complicated and certainly worth testing with software to compare the tradeoff with receiving more dependent benefits versus losing the opportunity for higher future retirement and survivor benefits.

Divorce

Divorced individuals are also eligible for benefits on an ex-spouse's earnings record provided the marriage lasted at least ten years and the individual is not currently married. If an individual has multiple ex-spouses where eligibility for a benefit is in place, then the individual can receive the largest of these benefit options. If the divorce was finalized within the past two years, then the ex-spouse must have filed already for the divorced spouse to receive benefits, as is the case with spousal benefits. But this requirement ends two years after divorce. A divorced person can receive benefits even if the ex-spouse has not yet claimed, though that ex-spouse must be at least 62 years old. As well, divorce benefits are not counted as part of the family maximum benefit limits for one person's earnings record. Otherwise, rules for divorced spouse benefits are comparable to the rules for spousal benefits.

As for survivor benefits, these are also available to divorced individuals. An individual can re-marry after age 60 (or after 50 if disabled) and still be eligible for a survivor benefit from an ex-spouse's record even though they would not be eligible for the divorced spouse benefit. As ex-spouses pass away, individuals can switch to survivor benefits from ex-spouses offering the highest overall benefit. Divorced individuals should monitor this situation since the Social Security Administration may not proactively reach out regarding a higher benefit possibility once an ex-spouse has passed away.

Earnings Test

Those who continue to work while collecting Social Security before their full retirement age may find that they must return their benefits if they earn too much. In 2021, those under the full retirement age will have to return $1 of benefits for every $2 earned above $1,580 per month or $18,960 per year. This changes in the year one reaches full retirement age and only for the months before reaching that age. During this short period, $1 of benefits is withheld for each $3 of earnings above $4,210 per month or $50,520 per year. Upon reaching full retirement age, the earnings test ends and full benefits are available without any offset.

Benefits lost to the earnings test are not necessarily permanently lost. After reaching the full retirement age, the claiming age is adjusted upward to account for the number of months of benefits lost to the test, which will reduce the degree of the reduction one had for claiming early. Subsequent benefits will be larger. Nonetheless, it may not be wise to claim early while working as this permanently affects survivor benefits if death occurs before full retirement age.

One other important point to make is that continued work can increase benefits if the total covered earnings in a year can replace an old year from the top 35 used for the AIME calculation. For those continuing to work, it is possible to increase the primary insurance amount even after benefits have started. The Social Security Administration automatically recomputes benefits each year even after benefits start. Earnings would need to displace one of the top 35 years to have an impact, but this can become more likely as wages past age 60 are not indexed and have a chance to be larger if they are growing with economy-wide average wages. For those with less than 35 years of earnings, any new earnings will replace a $0 from the calculations to create an obvious benefit.

Windfall Elimination Provision and Government Pension Offset

Not all employment in the United States is covered under the Social Security system. Some state and local government agencies, federal civilians who began employment prior to 1984, railroad workers, and non-profit organizations may provide separate pensions and are exempt from collecting Social Security payroll taxes from their employees. For those who spend a portion of their career at a noncovered job that provides a pension and a portion of their career earning Social Security credits, it could be possible to earn additional lifetime payments in a way that most would feel is unfair. This relates to the progressive nature of the Social Security benefit formula. Since Social Security considers the top 35 years of earnings, those working only a part of their career in covered employment will appear poorer and will receive a higher replacement rate on their average indexed monthly earnings. Combined with their other pension from noncovered work, this individual could receive more total pension income than Social Security would have provided if the whole career had been in covered work.

To help remedy this situation, Social Security created the Windfall Elimination Provision (WEP) and the Government Pension Offset (GPO) as part of their 1983 reforms. The WEP reduces one's primary insurance amount from Social Security for those receiving a pension from noncovered work. This leads to a lower Social Security benefit for the worker and any spouse or dependents receiving benefits from that worker's record. It is important to note that while the WEP reduces benefits when the worker is alive, the WEP is not applied to any survivor's benefits generated by that worker's record. It applies for those with less than 30 years of substantial earnings that were subject to the payroll tax. Note that substantial earnings are different from the earnings needed to earn full Social Security credits in a year. In 2021, the substantial earnings threshold was $26,550.

The WEP works by impacting how average indexed monthly earnings are translated into the primary insurance amount. As explained, for the first portion of income, the primary insurance amount receives a 90 percent replacement rate. For those in noncovered work who have 20 years or less of substantial Social Security earnings, that 90 percent is reduced to 40 percent. That leads to a maximum reduction of the primary insurance amount of $498 in 2021. The factor adjusts from 40 percent up to its original 90 percent as the years of earnings increases from 20 to 30. There is no reduction for anyone who has a noncovered pension and still has more than 30 years of substantial earnings covered by Social Security. Also, the benefit reduction from the WEP cannot be greater than half of the pension received from noncovered work. Finally, the WEP can lower spousal and other dependent benefits because of the reduced primary insurance amount, but survivor benefits are not impacted by the WEP.

Meanwhile, the GPO affects spousal, divorce, and survivor benefits that an individual would have been eligible for when receiving pensions from outside work not covered by Social Security. For those earning a pension from noncovered work, any spousal and survivor benefits this person could receive are reduced by two-thirds of the pension amount. With a large enough pension, this could eliminate the ability to receive these benefits through someone else's earnings record.

A Spousal Benefit Less Than 50 Percent of the Worker's Benefit?

For those who have already claimed Social Security and have read that spousal benefits are equal to 50 percent of the worker's benefit, one might be puzzled to find a different situation in which the spousal benefit is less. To review, I have identified several reasons why a spouse's benefit could be less than 50 percent of the worker's benefit:

The spouse claimed before the full retirement age. Doing so will lead to a reduction factor being applied to the spouse's benefit.

Before full retirement age, benefits are subject to the earnings test if the individual is still working.

The worker delayed past his or her full retirement age. This will provide delay credits to the worker, but the spousal benefit is based on the worker's primary insurance amount and would not receive those delay credits. The value of a worker's delay to the spouse is not through the spousal benefit, but through the survivor benefit. Also, though not directly relevant to this point, this is a good chance to provide a reminder that spouses and survivors do not obtain delay credits for beginning past their full retirement age.

A spouse who is impacted by the government pension offset could see a reduction to the entitled spousal benefit.

Finally, for workers with multiple dependents receiving benefits, the family maximum limits may apply and reduce the benefits received by each of those dependents, including the spouse.

Disability Benefits

Some individuals may already be receiving disability benefits from Social Security as they approach retirement. The disability benefit is equal to the primary insurance amount for that worker. After reaching age 62, disabled individuals can also receive spousal benefits from spouses who have claimed if the spousal benefit is greater than the disability benefit. Spouses can also file for spousal benefits based on the disabled worker's primary insurance amount. When the disabled individual reaches the full retirement age, the disability benefit is automatically converted into a retirement benefit equal to the primary insurance amount. There is no disability benefit beyond that age. Individuals do have the option to suspend their benefit at the full retirement age. In this case, a disabled beneficiary could suspend the new retirement benefit at full retirement age to get delay credits for the years up to age 70 and then start again. Another point about disability benefits is that those who are disabled for 24 months will automatically be enrolled in Medicare even before age 65.

Suspending Benefits and Redo Opportunities

Though the Bipartisan Budget Act of 2015 eliminated the file and suspend strategy as a path to additional spousal benefits, redo and suspend strategies are still available. Redo opportunities where suspending benefits could come in handy include:

- You can withdraw your application for retirement benefits and repay any benefits received during the 12 months after benefits begin. This provides a way to change your mind and delay further. This is allowed once in a worker's lifetime.
- For those who claimed early, it is also possible to suspend benefits after the full retirement age to earn some delay credits.
- Those who were disabled before the full retirement age are automatically converted to retirement benefits at that time. These individuals could then suspend their benefits to subsequently earn delay credits past the full retirement age.
- For those who regret claiming early, going back to work before full retirement age can trigger the earnings test that operates in practice as a forced suspension of benefits.

Remember, unlike the old file and suspend strategy, spouse and dependent benefits are stopped during the suspension period. The purpose of these strategies is to try to create some delay credits if one regrets having claimed too early. Suspending benefits at or after the full retirement age allows for delay credits and higher subsequent lifetime benefits in inflation-adjusted terms. Inflation-adjusted longevity insurance is extremely valuable and should not be overlooked.

One other related point is that when filing for retirement benefits after the full retirement age, one can request that benefits begin up to six months before the filing date, but not before the full retirement age. In fact, the Social Security Administration may assume this retroactive filing is desired, such that someone claiming at age 70 might be pushed to 69 and 6 months unless they firmly state that they do not want this to happen. Any retroactive benefits that are sought will be received as a lump-sum and subsequent benefits would be reduced to account for the earlier claiming age. Those past full retirement age who wanted to delay further, but who find themselves in need of cash for an expected situation, could file and suspend to claim this six months of benefits as a lump sum. This would lead to a loss of six months of delay credits, but it may be a worthwhile opportunity for those in a bind.

Taxes on Social Security Benefits

Making a portion of Social Security benefits taxable for federal income tax purposes started as part of the 1983 Social Security reforms. At first, up to 50 percent of benefits were taxable. Since 1994, up to 85 percent of Social Security benefits are taxable when incomes exceed certain thresholds. Managing the portion of taxable Social Security benefits becomes an important part of managing a tax-efficient retirement distribution strategy. Retirees can work to avoid the Social Security tax torpedo, which is an increase in marginal tax rates paid when a dollar of income also uniquely generates additional taxes on Social Security benefits. This important matter will be addressed as a part of the tax planning discussion in Chapter 10.

When are People Claiming Social Security?

One of the hottest topics in retirement income planning over the past ten years has been how to help individuals strategize their Social Security claiming decisions. These discussions used to delve into the intricacies of approaches like "file and suspend" or "file a restricted application" that could provide higher benefits but were phased out starting in November 2015. The general theme emerging from these discussions is that there can be value in delaying the start of benefits past the earliest allowed ages.

This message has been getting through to the public. Using numbers reported in the 2020 *Annual Statistical Supplement to the Social Security Bulletin*, I find that the last year the percentage of nondisabled Social Security retirement beneficiaries who claimed benefits at 62 was over 50 percent was in 2011. It fell from 50.5 percent that year to 32.7 percent in 2019. Meanwhile, those who delayed claiming until past their full retirement age was still under 6 percent until as late as 2009. It has been steadily climbing since, reaching 19.5 percent of new beneficiaries in 2019. This historical data is provided in Exhibit 6.2, demonstrating a clear change in claiming patterns for more recent years. The reason to exclude disabled individuals from these calculations is that those receiving disability benefits will automatically transition into retirement benefits at their full retirement age, which artificially increases cases where there was not discretion available regarding the choice. In recent years, about 16 to 17 percent of new retirement beneficiaries have represented these conversions from disability benefits.

Exhibit 6.2
Age distribution of new Social Security retirement beneficiaries
Excluding individuals on disability who transition into retirement benefits at
Full Retirement Age (FRA)

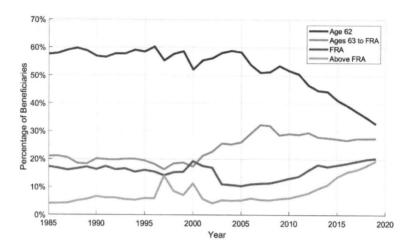

Source: Own calculations using Table 6.B5 from the 2020 *Annual Statistical Supplement to the Social Security Bulletin*

It is hard to be certain whether education on Social Security claiming is responsible for these recent shifts, or whether other factors may be at work. Nonetheless, as these trends continue, it is reasonable to think that education is an important factor. With an understanding about how benefits are calculated and how different benefits work, we now shift our attention to that education about choosing a claiming strategy.

Social Security as Insurance

We can think about the Social Security claiming decision in terms of how it plays out in the event of a short or long retirement. How do the consequences of claiming interact with longevity risk? We can think of four general outcomes for Social Security: claim early and experience a short retirement, claim early and experience a long retirement, claim late and experience a short retirement, and claim late and experience a long retirement. The consequences of these different outcomes are summarized in Exhibit 6.3.

It is surely unfortunate to experience a short retirement. In relation to Social Security, claiming early would have gotten the most out of the program. But claiming late would have resulted in minimal harm. Less would be obtained from Social Security, but there would have also been less pressure on the investment portfolio and other assets. A short retirement is less costly and so beneficiaries will still receive plenty of leftover assets even if Social Security is delayed.

Consequences become more severe with longer retirements, and this is where the focus of decision-making should be placed. When claiming early, a retiree is setting up conditions for a permanently reduced standard of living in retirement. A long retirement combined with Social Security delay supports a permanently enhanced lifestyle. The point is that greater emphasis should be placed on what happens in longer retirements, since the financial consequences are more severe, and this is when delaying Social Security provides a clear positive impact.

Exhibit 6.3
The Outcomes for Social Security Claiming Decisions

	Claim Early	Claim Late
Short Retirement	Worked Out	Minimal Harm Done
Long Retirement	Permanent **Reduced** Lifestyle	Permanent **Increased** Lifestyle

This discussion points to Social Security being viewed as insurance. Social Security retirement benefits are inflation-adjusted, and government backed. With lifetime cash flows, they mitigate longevity, inflation, and market risk for retirees. For risk-averse retirees who would otherwise invest more heavily in bonds, which do not provide longevity protection, the insurance value of Social Security becomes even stronger because there would otherwise be less potential for upside growth. Social Security also provides spousal and survival benefits, as well as benefits for dependent children. Importantly, survival and disability benefits are also available for pre-retirees, which is extra insurance value provided before retirement begins. Any discussion about Social Security as an investment should not forget about this insurance value.

It is a bummer to die early. But regret about Social Security claiming does not exist after death. Avoiding premature death is outside of our control, apart from taking care of our health. The real concern and focus that we can better control is to avoid a situation in which we outlive our assets. A bit of patience with Social Security can really help individuals to manage their longevity risk. The view of Social Security as insurance is to delay claiming and to take advantage of the delay credits that will really pay off if one experiences a long retirement.

Social Security as an "Investment"

The alternative to treating Social Security as insurance is to view it as an investment, or as a gamble on how long one lives. This can be problematic. The investment approach focuses more on the breakeven age for when it finally pays to delay benefits. With inflation-adjusted discount rates of 0 percent to 2 percent, the breakeven age is around 80 to 84. Though these ages are within the range of life expectancies for 62-year-olds, they *appear* to be high, and retirees start to worry that they may not live long enough for delay to be beneficial. People start to worry about losing out on potential benefits if they delay and then die early, rather than emphasizing the consequences of depleting assets if they live a long time.

As well, sometimes it is financial advisors who get ahead of themselves, thinking that they can invest the early Social Security benefits better and provide more lifetime wealth to their clients. I have seen advisors say that it makes no sense to delay Social Security, because the advisor can invest the benefits and earn a higher return for their clients over the long run.

Certainly, if realized investment returns are high enough, then claiming early is advantageous. But the odds are not in favor of getting that sort of investment return over the eight-year delay period, especially in our current world of low interest rates. As well, one might be surprised about just how high the implied return on delaying Social Security can be.

The confidence involved in thinking that one can claim early and invest the benefits for greater returns requires amplifying risk for an asset that should otherwise be treated as a true backstop and safeguard for retirement income. It is difficult to fathom how the additional upside potential outweighs the downside risks from claiming Social Security early and investing the proceeds in the stock market, except possibly for those who are sufficiently overfunded that they simply have no need to spend from their Social Security benefits and are purely focused on legacy.

Nevertheless, while I prefer thinking of Social Security delay as a form of insurance, I think we *can* reframe the discussion to view Social Security delay as a rather attractive "investment" proposition as well. This involves better understanding the additional credits provided by delaying Social Security benefits, which were meant to be "actuarially fair."

For someone living to their life expectancy, it should not matter in principle what age they claim their benefits. The increase in benefits from delay should precisely offset the fewer number of years that benefits will subsequently be received. However, these calculations about actuarial fairness for the delay credits were made as part of the 1983 Amendments to Social Security. The calculations are close to 40 years old, and changes since that time suggest that delaying now provides net advantages.

First, Social Security actuaries calculated the delay factors assuming that the real interest rate is 2.9 percent. Recently, the yield on 30-year TIPS is about 0 percent. It is negative for shorter-term TIPS. As an inflation-adjusted bond, TIPS are the closest type of investment to what Social Security provides as an inflation-adjusted income (though TIPS do not support this income over an unknown lifetime). Lower interest rates today mean that we should expect lower returns on other types of investments, which supports delaying Social

Security to obtain higher overall returns for the assets on the retirement balance sheet.

The second change relates to longevity, which continues to improve. Retirees are now living longer than they were in 1983. This also favors delaying Social Security, as it improves the odds for living long enough to enjoy positive net benefits from delayed claiming. On a related note, Social Security actuaries considered aggregate longevity for the population of Social Security participants, and people who read books about retirement planning are not average. My readers can expect to live for longer than the average Social Security participant.

A simple example can help to illustrate how delaying Social Security can work as an "investment" which helps to improve portfolio sustainability for retirees. What follows is not an effort to optimize any decision-making, but rather to observe the long-term impacts of two different claiming strategies.

Consider a single 62-year-old with no eligible dependents who has already left the workforce. This leaves out additional complications, though having a spouse entitled to survivor benefits would further strengthen the case for delay, while having dependent children might weaken the case. This individual is simply thinking about the decision between claiming Social Security at 62 or at 70.

Someone aged 62 in 2021 would experience a full retirement age of 66 and 10 months. To avoid the complication of dealing with partial years, I consider the case for someone who turns 62 in 2022 such that the full retirement age is 67.

Exhibit 6.4
Claiming Social Security Early at 62

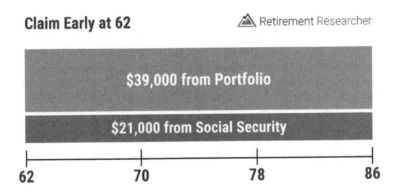

For the example, the overall annual spending goal is $60,000 in today's terms. Future spending grows with inflation. Her full retirement age is 67, and her PIA is $2,500 per month or $30,000 per year in today's dollars (all dollars are expressed as their age 62 values, though in subsequent years cost-of-living adjustments would be applied both to the overall spending goal and Social Security benefits). Should she claim at 62, her benefit would be reduced by 30 percent to $1,750 per month or $21,000 per year. Should she delay until 70, her benefit grows by 24 percent from the PIA to $3,100 per month or $37,200 per year. Inflation-adjusted Social Security benefits are 77 percent larger when claimed at 70 relative to 62.

To meet her $60,000 spending goal, any amount above what is provided by Social Security will be funded by withdrawals from an investment portfolio worth $866,000 today. This creates two lifetime spending scenarios. By claiming at 62, Social Security provides $21,000 of income, and $39,000 is withdrawn from the investment portfolio (see Exhibit 6.4).

Meanwhile, when claiming at 70, $60,000 will have to be supported by the portfolio for the first eight years of retirement. Starting at 70, Social Security then provides $37,200 with the remaining $22,800 coming from the portfolio (see Exhibit 6.5).

Exhibit 6.5
Delaying Social Security to 70

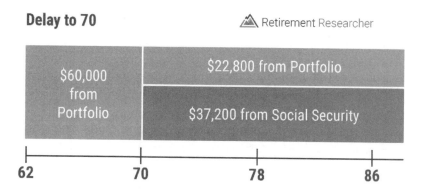

One way to compare these strategies is with the implied withdrawal rate needed from the portfolio after accounting for Social Security. By claiming at 62, the inflation-adjusted withdrawal rate to meet the spending goal is:

Withdrawal Rate = ($60,000 − $21,000) / $866,000 = 4.50%

When claiming at 70, there could be two different withdrawal rates for before and after 70. However, it would not be wise to use a volatile investment portfolio for the full spending amount when Social Security is delayed, as that would magnify sequence risk. Instead, I assume that eight years of age 70 Social Security benefits will be set aside from the portfolio at age 62 and earn a 0 percent real interest rate. This used to be a conservative assumption, but today TIPS yields are negative so some risk would need to be taken. This means that $37,200 x 8 = $297,600 will be set aside as a Social Security delay bridge illustrated in Exhibit 6.6, leaving the other $568,400 for withdrawals.

The required withdrawal rate to meet the spending goal throughout retirement is now:

Withdrawal Rate = ($60,000 – $37,200) / ($866,000 – $297,600) = 4.01%

Exhibit 6.6
Social Security Delay Bridge

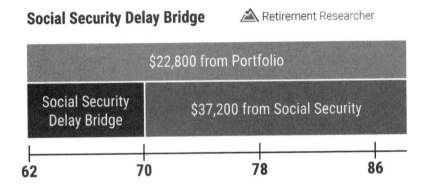

In this example, Social Security delay allowed the withdrawal rate to drop from 4.50 percent to 4.01 percent. This improves retirement sustainability. The investment portfolio is less likely to be depleted *and* more income remains available through the higher Social Security benefit if the portfolio depletes. In other words, running out of financial assets is both less likely to happen and less damaging when it does happen.

Allowing for the same probability of portfolio depletion by matching up the withdrawal rates, total spending could be increased by about 5 percent to $62,778 to use the same 4.5 percent withdrawal rate as when claiming early. The magnitude of the difference would be larger if the retiree's spending goal and asset base were smaller relative to the Social Security benefits, and vice versa. And remember, 77 percent more income is still available than otherwise in the event of portfolio depletion. This is the permanently enhanced lifestyle possible with Social Security delay. The basics of this example are illustrated in Exhibit 6.7.

For this strategy to work effectively, the overall spending goal cannot be too large relative to the size of the financial portfolio. For instance, if the portfolio is $300,000, there would hardly be enough to create the delay bridge.

Otherwise, a large enough portfolio will allow for Social Security delay to reduce the required portfolio withdrawal rate. And if the portfolio is not large enough, it is more of a reflection that the overall spending goal is not realistic, rather than an indictment against Social Security delay. Though, as will be pointed out later, severely underfunded retirees without alternatives may be forced to claim Social Security early and accept a permanently reduced lifestyle.

Exhibit 6.7
Impact of Social Security Delay on Retirement Withdrawal Rates

Impact of Social Security Delay on Retirement Withdrawal Rates

	Claim at Age 62	Claim at Age 70
Spending Goal	$60,000	$60,000
Social Security Benefit	$21,000	$37,200
Portfolio Withdrawal	$39,000	$22,800
Investment Portfolio	$866,000	$866,000
Set Aside for Social Security Delay	$0	$297,600
Remaining Portfolio	$866,000	$568,400
Withdrawal Rate	4.50%	4.01%

The previous discussion has demonstrated how delaying Social Security receipt can improve the sustainability of a retirement income plan. It is necessary to withdraw more until Social Security starts, but retirees can then withdraw less after starting Social Security. The strategy is not fool proof with only a volatile investment portfolio as a backstop, because a bad sequence of returns early in retirement could cause the portfolio to drop in value, locking in losses. But assets can be carved out of the main investment portfolio to create a Social Security delay bridge. Possibilities for this bridge include structuring a bond or CD ladder or using a fixed-term income annuity. Another alternative for retirees is to use other buffer assets from outside the financial portfolio, such as home equity through a reverse mortgage or the cash value from a life insurance policy.

A second way to understand the delay of Social Security benefits as an investment is to calculate the implied rate of return on the cash flows that Social Security provides for different claiming strategies. I now look at the internal rates of return on the cash flows that Social Security provides. The "investment" value of delaying Social Security can also be seen through these internal rates of return since they will represent return hurdles that other investments would need to beat to provide better outcomes.

Exhibit 6.8
Impact of Social Security Delay on Retirement Withdrawal Rates

Age	Real Benefits with Age 62 Start	Real Benefits with Age 70 Start	Difference	Real Return on Delaying by Age
62	$21,000	$0	-$21,000	
63	$21,000	$0	-$21,000	
64	$21,000	$0	-$21,000	
65	$21,000	$0	-$21,000	
66	$21,000	$0	-$21,000	
67	$21,000	$0	-$21,000	
68	$21,000	$0	-$21,000	
69	$21,000	$0	-$21,000	
70	$21,000	$37,200	$16,200	
71	$21,000	$37,200	$16,200	
72	$21,000	$37,200	$16,200	-22.2%
73	$21,000	$37,200	$16,200	-15.5%
74	$21,000	$37,200	$16,200	-10.9%
75	$21,000	$37,200	$16,200	-7.6%
76	$21,000	$37,200	$16,200	-5.1%
77	$21,000	$37,200	$16,200	-3.2%
78	$21,000	$37,200	$16,200	-1.7%
79	$21,000	$37,200	$16,200	-0.4%
80	$21,000	$37,200	$16,200	0.6%
81	$21,000	$37,200	$16,200	1.5%
82	$21,000	$37,200	$16,200	2.2%
83	$21,000	$37,200	$16,200	2.8%
84	$21,000	$37,200	$16,200	3.3%
85	$21,000	$37,200	$16,200	3.8%
86	$21,000	$37,200	$16,200	4.2%
87	$21,000	$37,200	$16,200	4.5%
88	$21,000	$37,200	$16,200	4.8%
89	$21,000	$37,200	$16,200	5.1%
90	$21,000	$37,200	$16,200	5.3%
...	...	...	...	...
95	$21,000	$37,200	$16,200	6.1%
...	...	...	...	...
100	$21,000	$37,200	$16,200	6.6%

Exhibit 6.8 provides this information for the same example with someone whose full retirement age is 67 and whose primary insurance amount is $30,000 of annual benefits. Delaying Social Security from age 62 to age 70 can be reviewed as making an investment of $21,000 annually for eight years which provides a payment of $37,200 annually starting at age 70 and continuing for life. Because these are real purchasing values at age 62, the returns implied by these cash flows are real returns and realized inflation could be added to them to get the total nominal return. These real returns become positive at age 80, reflecting the breakeven age when delaying starts to pay off. The real return is 3.8 percent by age 85, 5.3 percent by age 90, 6.1 percent by age 95, and 6.6 percent by age 100.

For government-backed, inflation-adjusted income, this can be compared to TIPS yields which have been hovering around 0 percent or less. Looking not far beyond life expectancies, these returns from Social Security delay even become competitive with the historical compounded real returns provided by the stock market. Again, one would need their investments to beat these returns for early claiming decisions to pay off.

The real-world *caveat* to consider, of course, is whether a high portfolio return assumption can be justified, as it would require taking substantial market risk. The probability that you could consistently earn a compounded real return of 6 percent is rather low, and to have *any* opportunity to achieve this return would require retirement assets to be mostly invested in stocks.

Though it depends on survival, delaying Social Security offers attractive investment returns compared to safe alternatives available today. It can really pay to spend down other assets more quickly until age 70. Though the portfolio will be smaller at 70, the reduced spending needs after 70 – because Social Security is paying 77 percent more in real terms – will leave you increasingly better off forever after. Those lucky enough to live far into retirement will preserve more of their portfolio for their heirs and be thankful they delayed Social Security.

Social Security: The Best Annuity Money Can Buy

A final frame for viewing the Social Security claiming decision is as an annuity purchase. By starting at age 70 instead of 62, the retiree misses eight years of receiving a benefit of $21,000. But starting at 70 provides the retiree a net increase in benefits of $16,200 per year for as long as he or she lives. The eight years of lost benefits could be viewed as a premium payment for a $16,200 inflation-adjusted lifetime income starting at 70.

By not claiming until 70, the eight-year loss of Social Security benefits sums to $168,000, which would also be its present value with a 0 percent real interest rate. We could view that $168,000 as the approximate premium to buy a deferred income annuity with inflation-adjusted annual income of $16,200 beginning at age 70. The implied payout rate on the "annuity" provided by delaying Social Security is 9.64 percent.

This is quite attractive when compared to commercial annuities. The current marketplace does not even offer an inflation-adjusted income annuity at the time of writing. Social Security is inflation adjusted. We can only approximate inflation by choosing a fixed cost-of-living adjustment for the annuity, though this would not protect spending power if actual inflation rose higher. As well, the $16,200 difference in benefits is measured in today's dollars and it would grow with inflation for the next eight years. We are forced to also assume an inflation rate for the next eight years to properly discount the income to be received from a commercial annuity.

For the comparisons, we must assume an inflation rate to have the annuity benefit grow by each year, and to also reduce the purchasing power for the first payment received in eight years so it is expressed in today's dollars. I will assume a 2 percent inflation rate, and it is important to note that the commercial annuity would look increasingly worse as the assumed inflation rate increases.

In April 2021, the best available deal at immediateannuities.com for an eight-year deferred income annuity with a $168,000 premium for a 62-year-old with a 2 percent cost-of-living adjustment on payments is $12,612 of annual income for men, $11,280 for women, and $9,384 for couples with a 100 percent survivors benefit that would be the closest match for Social Security survivor benefits to the high earner. With eight years of 2 percent inflation, the real purchasing power for these spending numbers are $10,764 for males, $9,627 for females, and $8,009 for couples.

These represent payout rates of 6.41 percent for men, 5.73 percent for women, and 4.77 percent for couples. Each of these three numbers can be compared to the 9.64 percent payout implied by treating Social Security delay as purchasing an annuity. Social Security delay provides a higher payout rate *and* stronger inflation protection than commercially available annuities. Delaying Social Security should be the first step for anyone considering annuities as part of their retirement income plan. Commercial annuities do not beat the implied payout rates on delaying Social Security.

Arguments for Claiming Social Security Early

Legitimate arguments do also exist for claiming Social Security early. Some individuals simply need the funds to survive and have no other income alternatives to cover delaying their benefits. Delaying retirement would be a better option, but it is not always possible. Claiming early in such circumstances may be unavoidable.

Another reasonable situation to claim early is for individuals with legitimate medical reasons to believe they will not live to their 80s. This should be based on a medical diagnosis and not just on a hunch. In this instance, it is important to consider survivor and dependent benefits based on the earnings history. Age of death is not the only factor in determining the optimal household solution. Related to this point, a spouse who will be impacted by the government pension offset for spousal and survivor benefits might decide against delay.

Some strategies also legitimately call for the spouse with a smaller primary insurance amount to start benefits earlier as part of maximizing lifetime household benefits. As I discussed, the benefit for the low earner is only relevant until the age that the first member of the couple passes away. Claiming software will often report optimal results for the high earner to delay, but the low earner to start earlier.

The higher earner might also occasionally claim earlier to take advantage of benefits for dependent children, a spouse caring for dependent children, or dependent parents, or to otherwise allow a spouse to claim the spousal retirement benefit sooner. Especially in cases with dependent children who will grow past their eligibility, it is possible to claim at an earlier age to tap into these ephemeral dependent benefits and then suspend again after full retirement age to gain some delay credits toward age 70. With so many options and so much money at stake, I cannot emphasize enough the importance of testing individual situations using comprehensive Social Security planning software that includes all relevant variables.

Other reasons can be used to justify claiming Social Security early, but I generally find them less compelling. For instance, some have made the rather dubious claim that an investment portfolio can be expected to produce higher returns than those offered by Social Security delay. While portfolios could produce higher returns, it is unwise to count on it, especially this close to retirement.

This uncertain quest for upside growth means giving up a valuable, lifelong, inflation-adjusted income stream. To make risks comparable, the appropriate investment would be TIPS. To generate the returns needed to beat Social Security delay would require a high tolerance for risk and an aggressive asset allocation, not to mention plenty of discretionary wealth. People tend to be overconfident about their investing prowess, making it easy to fall into a behavioral trap. Earlier I described the investment return hurdles that exist to justify claiming early from an investment perspective. Beyond life expectancy, those hurdles are tough to beat.

The Social Security claiming decision can also be viewed in terms of the breakeven age you have to reach before the delay decision pays off. This causes some to feel like they are gambling their savings by delaying, considering that they could die before the strategy pays off. But it is important not to view the Social Security decision this way. The breakeven age analysis misses the insurance value provided by Social Security. What matters more is the possibility of outliving your assets, and this is where Social Security can really help. If you choose to delay and then die before collecting or breaking even, you will not be around to regret it. Regret comes when you live a long life and think about how you could have been better off if you had delayed.

If someone dies early in retirement, they leave a larger nest egg to the next generation. Being the bigger of two already large numbers may not have much of an impact on the financial circumstances for heirs who are already receiving a large and unexpected bequest.

The nature of the legacy changes for longer and more expensive retirements. Delaying Social Security lowers the likelihood of depleting your financial assets, meaning less strain on any potential heir to provide *reverse support*. The potential to leave a larger relative legacy is higher with delayed Social Security in these long-retirement cases when the available bequests will otherwise be less. This is when each dollar of additional bequest will count for more. It may seem counterintuitive, but a retiree may be doing their beneficiaries a favor by delaying benefits.

A final reason for claiming early is the idea that Social Security will go away, which can create an urgency to claim early to obtain benefit from the system before it is too late. This matter is addressed in the next section.

Potential Directions for Social Security Reform

A Retirement Researcher reader eloquently stated what I find to be a common sentiment:

> I'm cynical; for my retirement planning I assume that I'll pay into Social Security until I stop working and I assume that I'll draw nothing out i.e all cost, no benefit. This is a 'worst case' so anything else with any benefit will be a pleasant surprise.

A common argument for claiming Social Security early is that the program is about to be dramatically overhauled in a way that leaves retirees attempting to get a little out of the system before it disappears. But it seems rather unlikely that any impending reforms would leave at least near retirees with significant reductions to their benefits.

The widespread belief that Social Security is bankrupt and about to disappear has existed for a long time. I can remember walking around Washington, D.C., in the late 1990s and receiving a pamphlet on the National Mall suggesting that there are more Americans who believe that UFOs visit us on earth than who believe that Social Security will be there when they retire.

I commonly hear from individuals that they will plan for retirement assuming there will be no Social Security, and any benefits they do get will be icing on the cake. While I generally support conservative assumptions for planning purposes, I think this viewpoint takes matters too far. For my own personal planning, my conservative planning assumption is that I will receive 75 percent of my presently legislated projected benefits, and I am much further away from collecting benefits than today's near retirees.

While Social Security has funding problems, the situation is not quite so dire as to think it will disappear entirely or otherwise be converted into a pure welfare program. The general goal of reforming Social Security is to help place the Trust Funds into 75-year actuarial balance.

The 2021 *Trustee's Report* estimates that the combined Social Security Trust funds (OASDI) are not generating enough revenue to stay in balance past 2034, and that an immediate increase in the payroll tax of 3.54 percentage points (shared between employees and employers) would be needed for the Social Security system to maintain its solvency for the next 75 years.

If no action is taken, Social Security benefits would have to receive an across-the-board 22 percent reduction so that the inflows of new contributions from workers could cover the outflows of benefit payments starting in 2034.

The Congressional Research Service provides an interesting report to explain what happens if the Trust Funds deplete and the full legislated benefits could not be paid. It notes how there are two conflicting laws: the Social Security Act requires benefits to be paid, but the Antideficiency Act says that the government cannot spend more than its available funds. The lack of funds to pay the benefits does not remove the obligation to pay entitled benefits and lawsuits about this would surely happen. For there to really be an across-the-board benefit cut, Congress would have to step in to legislate it, rather than a cut becoming the default through inaction. In the process of creating such legislation, Congress would probably find a compromise between benefit cuts and tax increases as happened in 1983. It is not hyperbole to suggest that a major reduction to benefits would be very unpopular with the public. A big across-the-board reduction to benefits is unlikely.

The presently legislated course for Social Security includes a continued increase in the full retirement age to 67, an OASDI payroll tax of 12.4 percent, the use of CPI-W to make annual cost-of-living adjustments, and the use of the average wage index for indexing benefits at the age of first eligibility. There are a multitude of ways in which Social Security reform could proceed to get Social Security back on track to a 75-year actuarial balance. Exhibit 6.9 provides a list of various reform options.

Many reform options would have minimal impact on current or near retirees. Options include an increase in payroll tax rates, or a lift in the ceiling on maximum taxable earnings. With payroll tax increases, only those still in the workforce would be impacted at the end of their careers.

A gradual increase in the full retirement age consistent with the 1983 reforms would also not affect those already near retirement. After all, the individuals first impacted by the full retirement age increase to 67 were only 23 years-old when the reform passed. Retirement age increases could be accomplished in a fixed manner, such as gradually shifting the full retirement age to 69 or 70. Another possibility is to calibrate the full retirement age to match the shift in longevity. As the population naturally lives longer, the full retirement age automatically adjusts to match the changes. One problem with increasing the full retirement age, though, is that it can be considered as a regressive reform. The gains in longevity are not shared across the population, and those groups with lesser longevity prospects or who find it difficult to continue to work at later ages would be unduly impacted by such a reform.

Exhibit 6.9
Social Security Reform Options

Reforms Impacting Current or Near Retirees	Other Reforms
Use a smaller COLA	Increase payroll tax rate
Use more than top 35 years of earnings	Increase maximum taxable earnings
Link benefit reductions to longevity improvements	Gradually raise full retirement age
Means testing for benefits	Switch from "wage indexing" to "price indexing"
Make Social Security benefits fully taxable	Expand Trust Fund beyond US Treasuries

Another popular reform idea is to switch from "wage indexing" to "price indexing" when calculating Social Security benefits. Though this sounds somewhat technical, it would allow current or near retirees to escape the burden of reform. Instead, reform would compound over time so that younger people will eventually receive lower and lower benefits relative to their wages and payroll taxes. Benefits would effectively be frozen at today's levels even if the standard of living continues to improve in the future as expected. As an attempt to look out for young people, I oppose this reform for its particularly stark intergenerational impacts.

Finally, a reform that would not affect benefits is to expand the investment approach of the Social Security Trust Fund to include additional investment options beyond the current specially issued non-tradable Treasury bonds. This reform was discussed during the 1990s, though nothing ever became of it. A related reform idea popularized by President Bush in the 2000s was to carve out a portion of Social Security payroll taxes to create Personal Retirement Accounts. This reform also did not make it far into the legislative process.

There are other reform ideas which could also impact current or near retirees today with the introduction of near-term benefit reductions. For instance, Social Security benefit growth could be linked to a new price index which grows less rapidly, or the cost-of-living adjustments (COLA) could be set at one percent less than the consumer price index. The impact of this reform would be to gradually reduce the real purchasing power of benefits over time. The justification for such a reform is that the current CPI-W measure used by the Social Security Administration may overstate inflation and that people tend to spend less as they age. Objections to this reform include that it would leave the extreme elderly and widows more vulnerable to poverty, and it may be the case that expenses for some vulnerable elderly rise faster than the CPI-W.

Another reform which would lead to benefit reductions is to increase the number of years used to calculate the average-indexed monthly earnings. This would bring in more years with lower earnings to reduce the calculated average lifetime wages that enter the benefit formula.

A popular reform internationally is to provide a more direct and automated link between longevity improvements and the full retirement age. But another variation is to link longevity improvements to benefits paid by reducing benefits to account for a longer period of receipt.

A reform which could have a bigger impact on wealthier individuals who are about to retire is the introduction of means-testing for benefits. Those with sufficient means, represented either through other income sources or wealth accumulations, would no longer be eligible to receive Social Security benefits. Such a reform would run counter to the entire history of the Social Security program, which has always sought a clear link between benefits and contributions. Means testing would convert the Social Security program into a welfare program. In this regard, it seems unlikely that such a reform could happen, though politicians do discuss this possibility from time to time. For those deemed as wealthier by the law, this is the only type of reform that could lead to a more significant reduction in benefits for some members of the population.

To be clear, there are stealthier ways to create means testing than doing it outright. The progressive benefit formula could be made more progressive, for instance, by reducing the replacement rate for higher earners. Also, taxing Social Security benefits was a way to move toward means testing in a sneakier and less direct manner. Social Security benefits could still be made fully taxable. This provides a push toward means testing without being as explicit about it.

While higher income individuals may have some justification to worry about means testing, it seems incredibly unlikely that a wholesale reduction in benefits would be enacted for the general population of current and near retirees. It is overly conservative for near retirees to be worried that Social Security will disappear entirely. It is tough to justify the idea that one should claim early to get something before it is too late.

Social Security still requires significant reform, but it is by no means on the road to disappearing. Other structural changes will be needed in the coming years, but Social Security will still be around. This is a clear example of "public policy risk," in which changing tax and entitlement laws can throw a wrench into the planning process. Congress is free to change Social Security benefits at any time, but it will surely remain as a core resource to support retirement spending. Retirees should take care to develop a proper claiming strategy that provides long-term benefits under the assumption that Social Security will exist.

Action Plan

Choosing your Social Security claiming strategy is a key part of building a retirement income plan. The benefit application can be done online, by phone, or in person at a Social Security office. Though Social Security claiming is just one step in building a retirement income plan, the value of lifetime Social Security benefits can dwarf many other retirement assets. Thought and care are needed to determine how to claim Social Security in the most effective manner for the household. Here are key steps to take:

☐ Obtain your updated Social Security Statement at ssa.gov
☐ Check your statement's earnings history for accuracy and understand the assumptions used for estimating your benefits
   o future covered earnings
   o economy-wide wage growth and inflation
☐ Familiarize yourself with the basic claiming philosophies
   o View Social Security as longevity insurance
   o Analyze Social Security from breakeven age perspective
☐ Understand basic Social Security rules
   o Worker benefits, spousal benefits, survivor benefits, ex-spouse benefits, and benefits for other dependents
   o Consider applicability of the earnings test when claiming and working before full retirement age
   o Identify exposure to windfall elimination provision and government pension offset
   o Those collecting disability benefits should understand the transition to retirement benefits
   o Identify possibilities for suspending benefits
☐ Collect the relevant information for making a claiming decision
   o Benefits from your earnings record: spouse & dependents
   o Your eligibility for benefits from other's earnings records: spouse, ex-spouse, survivor
   o Role of earnings test, windfall elimination provision, government pension offset, disability benefits
   o Availability of resources to support delayed claiming
   o Dependence on Social Security as reliable income
   o Risk tolerance
☐ Use software to calculate the optimal claiming strategy and compare with other options
☐ Build a strategy to support deferring benefits when applicable

- o Identify how to meet spending goals before benefits begin (portfolio distributions, part-time work, reverse mortgage, life insurance cash value)
- o Consider tax planning opportunities while deferring (see Chapter 10)

Further Reading

Biggs, Andrew. 2014. "Better no Social Security Replacement Rates than Wrong Replacement Rates." AEIdeas Series (September 3).

Congressional Research Service. 2020. *Social Security: What Would Happen If the Trust Funds Ran Out?* Available from https://crsreports.congress.gov/product/pdf/RL/RL33514

Kotlikoff, Laurence J. Philip Moeller, and Paul Solman. 2016. *Get What's Yours: The Secrets to Maxing Out Your Social Security*. Simon & Schuster.

Piper, Mike. 2017. *Social Security Made Simple*. Simple Subjects.

Reichenstein, William, and William Meyer. 2017. *Social Security Strategies*. CreateSpace.

Chapter 7: Medicare and Health Insurance

Planning for retirement health expenses is an essential component in a comprehensive retirement income plan. This chapter explores retirement health insurance options and retirement health expenses. The bulk of this discussion will be about Medicare, which is available to most Americans upon reaching age 65. As the most important source of health insurance for retirees, decisions must be made regarding whether to use Original Medicare or a Medicare Advantage Plan, whether to use a Medicare Supplement with Original Medicare, and how to obtain prescription drug coverage. A lack of understanding about the rules of Medicare can lead to gaps in coverage, overpayment on services or coverage, and unanticipated outcomes. I also cover health insurance options for those retiring before reaching Medicare eligibility age, and the rules about using other private insurance after reaching Medicare eligibility. I also discuss ongoing annual Medicare elections as well as how to develop a budget for retirement health expenses. I discuss budgeting towards the end of the chapter because retirement health care costs will closely relate to decisions made regarding insurance. I will finish with an action plan for health care in retirement.

Health Insurance Options Prior to Medicare Eligibility

Medicare qualification typically occurs at age 65; non-citizens must be 65 and legally resident in the United States for at least five years. There are a few exceptions where coverage can begin before age 65, including qualification after receiving Social Security disability benefits for 24 months (or immediately if the disability benefits are triggered by the onset of amyotrophic lateral sclerosis), or by a determination of end-stage renal disease.

Otherwise, anyone who retires prior to age 65 must obtain health insurance elsewhere. I consider the options generally available here. Early retirees must also determine how to get health insurance for their family members and to decide on the best option. Factors that play into the decision about health insurance include premiums, deductibles, coinsurance and copayments, out-of-pocket maximums, covered providers, prescription coverage, supplemental benefits like dental care, and availability for family members.

Many individuals who otherwise might retire early may remain in the workforce due to the high cost of insurance outside of the employer-provided insurance ecosystem. Despite this constraint, the Affordable Care Act remains a way to obtain health coverage, especially if none of the other methods we describe are available, including coverage through a spouse, retiree health coverage, or COBRA. Though not technically insurance, members of faith-based communities may also consider healthshare programs.

Coverage Through a Spouse

When one spouse has retired but the other is still working, the best approach may be to obtain health insurance coverage through the spouse or domestic partner's health plan. This coverage is often subsidized by the employer and may be more cost effective than other options when it is available. It may also provide more options for prescription drugs and other services like dental care. When available, this coverage can be the starting point for comparisons with other potential options.

Another consideration for obtaining coverage through a spouse that must also be coordinated is when that spouse becomes eligible for Medicare. If the working spouse changes to Medicare and drops the coverage at work, the previously retired spouse (assuming this spouse is still under 65) and any dependents would lose their coverage. Medicare is only for individuals, not family members.

Employer-Provided Retiree Health Insurance

Employer benefits for some retirees may include retirement health insurance that can fill the coverage need in the years leading up to Medicare enrollment at age 65. Retiree coverage may also be available through other work-related organizations like unions or professional societies. This type of coverage is becoming less common as employers move away from these types of offerings. Government employees are much more likely to have access to these benefits than those employed privately, as 65 percent of public employers and 13 percent of private companies offer retirement health insurance to at least some employees in 2019. It is also important to investigate how the coverage interacts with other aspects of employer benefits. For instance, a decision about a defined-benefit pension could impact whether retirement health coverage is available. Even when offered, though, the retired employees may be paying an increasing portion of the costs for these benefits. You may still wish to compare the costs for this coverage with other options. Nonetheless, when it is available, this is an important coverage option for earlier retirees waiting for Medicare to begin.

Coverage through COBRA

Those working at employers with 20 or more employees may continue their same group health insurance coverage through COBRA for up to 18 months after leaving work, if the departure was for reasons other than gross misconduct. For coverage to continue, one must already be enrolled in the plan before leaving work. This could help fill a short gap in coverage for those close to age 65. This coverage may be costly, though, as the individual will need to also pay for the portion of coverage that had been paid by the employer in addition to the employee portion, plus another 2 percent for administrative costs. For many employers that subsidize coverage, this could represent a very large increase in total premiums.

Coverage through other means may be cheaper, especially through income-based subsidies available through the Affordable Care Act. Nonetheless, for those who may be just a few months away from Medicare eligibility, temporarily paying a higher premium through COBRA may be a better option than trying to find alternative coverage that includes preferred in-network health providers. Deductibles play an important role in this decision, potentially offsetting at least some of the higher cost of COBRA if deductibles have already been met earlier in the year.

Coverage through the Affordable Care Act or Private Market

Health insurance may also be obtained through the state and federal exchanges created by the Affordable Care Act that began operating in January 2014, or through the private insurance market. The Affordable Care Act made it dramatically easier for those retiring before 65 to find health insurance coverage without the risk of rejection for pre-existing conditions. Information about how and when to sign up, as well as the available coverage and costs, is available at HealthCare.gov. Plans are available as Bronze, Silver, Gold, and Platinum, with premiums generally increasing and out-of-pocket costs decreasing as one progresses through the list.

Early retirees may also be able to benefit from subsidies for coverage that are available to those whose modified adjusted gross incomes are less than 400 percent of the federal poverty level. The poverty level varies by household size, and in 2021, for example, the 400 percent ceiling is $69,680 for a two-person household. The American Rescue Plan Act of 2021 passed in March 2021 does temporarily increase access to subsidies above the 400 percent limit in 2021 and 2022. Chapter 10 provides more discussion about the tax-planning implications for these subsidies. It is important to note that the provisions of the Affordable Care Act are politically contentious, and the program could experience drastic changes in the coming years. Early retirees may not wish to become too dependent on obtaining coverage this way over a multi-year period, in case such coverage is not always available, its subsidies are reduced, or its costs otherwise become unaffordable. Insurance can also be purchased from companies outside of the Affordable Care Act exchanges, but this type of coverage will not be eligible for the subsidies.

Healthshare Programs

One other option that is not insurance, but which is growing in popularity with over one million participants in the United States, is a healthshare program. These are typically operated through Christian organizations. These programs often look like insurance, but they are not regulated like insurance and do not have contracts that require that health bills be covered. They may also require the acceptance of specific religious principles and cost-sharing may not be provided for certain health issues related to activities that are deemed to be against the religious beliefs. These aspects may be attractive to some members, but the main benefit is financial, as the costs to participate may be less than with other health insurance options.

The ABCDs of Medicare

Medicare is a health insurance program primarily available to those aged 65 and older. Created in 1965 as part of Lyndon B. Johnson's Great Society, it is administered through the federal government's Centers for Medicare and Medicaid Services in the Department of Health and Human Services. Its funding sources include payroll taxes, earnings on its trust fund, premium payments, and taxes on Social Security benefits. Medicare is not designed to cover all health expenses for retirees, but it is an important program that serves as the primary insurance for most retirees.

Those eligible for Medicare must make a variety of decisions related to Parts A, B, and D of the program, along with the possibility of using Part C in place of A, B, and sometimes D, as well as having supplement choices with plans ranging from A to N. There really is an ABCs of Medicare to consider. Parts A and B operate through the federal government, while Medicare Advantage, supplement plans, and Part D are made available through private insurers.

Medicare Part A – Hospital Insurance

Part A of Medicare is hospital insurance provided through the federal government. It covers inpatient care in hospitals, inpatient skilled nursing facility care (but not custodial care or long-term care), hospice care, and home health care. For inpatient hospital care in semi-private rooms, this includes meals, nursing care, drugs, and other hospital services. Inpatient psychiatric care is also available for up to 190 days in a lifetime.

There is usually not a specific premium to be paid for Part A, as it is covered through the payroll taxes from your working years, like with Social Security. Receiving Part A without a premium is linked very closely to how one qualifies for Social Security by having 40 or more quarters of Medicare-covered employment or being entitled to Social Security benefits based on a spouse or ex-spouse's earnings record, and that spouse is at least 62. Also, in rare cases where someone did not qualify for Part A through payroll taxes, it is possible in 2021 to purchase Part A coverage with a $471 monthly premium for those who have less than 30 quarters of coverage and $259 per month for those with 30 to 39 quarters.

Part A does include deductibles and co-payments as determined through benefit periods, which are different from calendar years. A benefit period for hospital coverage provides a fixed amount of coverage that resets when a new benefit period starts. A benefit period begins on the first day of a hospital stay and ends once 60 days have passed since receiving inpatient care at a hospital or skilled nursing facility. The start of a benefit period triggers a new deductible to be paid, which makes it possible that a deductible may need to be covered twice (or more) in one year. For hospital stays in 2021, there is a $1,484 deductible applied to each benefit period. After meeting the deductible, the rest of the costs for those first 60 days of inpatient hospital care is covered. Then, for days 61 to 90, inpatient stays have a daily $371 copayment. After receiving 90 days of inpatient care, coverage for the benefit period ends, but one also has access to an additional 60 lifetime reserve days. On these days, there is a daily $742 copayment. Beyond this point, the individual will face all costs from the hospital stay during a given benefit period. Again, a new benefit period will start once 60 days have passed since receiving inpatient care.

Part A also includes some care at a skilled nursing facility provided that many conditions are met. Skilled nursing care can be available for up to 100 days for a need related to an inpatient hospital stay for at least three days and is certified by a doctor that the care is needed. When a hospital stay may only last three days, it is important to clarify that you have been admitted for inpatient care rather than considered for outpatient observation even if staying overnight. For the first 20 days of skilled care, there is no additional charge once the deductible has been covered, but days 21-100 require an additional daily copayment of $185.50. No benefits are available beyond 100 days. A limited amount of home care is also available through a Medicare-certified home health agency under limited circumstances.

Medicare Part A also covers hospice care with certification of a terminal illness with less than six months to live. Hospice care includes comfort care instead of attempting to cure your illness. Benefits include pain relief, symptom management, medical, nursing, and social services, medical equipment, and spiritual and grief counseling for you and your family.

These are the only types of Medicare coverage that relate to what people may have in mind about long-term care. But Medicare is not a provider of traditional custodial care for those with long-term needs. We discuss this further in the next chapter.

Medicare Part B – Medical Insurance

Part B of Medicare is for the basic medical insurance for preventative care including vaccines and wellness visits, doctor's visits, outpatient care, medical equipment, home health services, ambulance services deemed necessary, mental health services, and other eligible types of care not involved with hospital stays. These services must be medically necessary. Specific coverage exceptions, though, include dental care, dentures, vision care, cosmetic surgery, and hearings aids. With a few exceptions, prescription drugs are not covered, though one can also obtain a Part D plan for this coverage. Part B is funded through premiums and general tax revenues rather than payroll taxes, and it is also administered through the federal government.

Part A and Part B coverage for Medicare allows an individual to use any doctor, hospital, or service provider that accepts Medicare for payment. Most medical professionals (98-99 percent) do accept Medicare, so this is typically not a concern. There is no need to choose a primary care physician and referrals to specialists are generally not necessary.

Medicare Part B includes a $203 deductible in 2021 and a 20 percent coinsurance rate for most doctor's services and outpatient care. There is no out-of-pocket maximum payment with this coinsurance. As medical bills can be costly, even a 20 percent coinsurance rate could lead to significant strains on retirement assets.

Part B requires a monthly premium along with the deductible and coinsurance or co-pay amounts. The base monthly premium for Medicare Part B in 2021 is $148.50 per month. When modified gross adjusted incomes from two years prior exceed certain thresholds, the Part B premiums increase according to an Income Related Monthly Adjustment Amount (IRMAA). This becomes an important tax-planning implication for retirement and is discussed further in Chapter 10.

There is a hold harmless provision for baseline Part B premiums for those who are already receiving Social Security benefits. It says that net Social Security benefits cannot decrease after accounting for Medicare Part B premiums. This means that Part B premiums cannot increase by more than the Social Security COLA amount for existing beneficiaries. This creates a problem for those not yet receiving Social Security; they must bear the full costs for additional premiums needed to cover expenses. When Social Security COLAs are low, those not yet on Social Security may have to pay more. This can be counted as a slight knock against delaying Social Security, and it really is a problem with existing law that should be fixed, but it generally would not overturn the arguments for delay provided in the previous chapter. I estimated that the cumulative impact of low COLAs in 2015 and 2016 was about $550 of total additional Part B base premiums for those who had not claimed Social Security.

Medicare Advantage Plans – Part C

"Original Medicare" refers to someone enrolled in Parts A, B, and possibly D of Medicare. There is an alternative to Original Medicare called Medicare Advantage. It is Part C. Presently about one-third of Medicare enrollees choose Medicare Advantage, while two-thirds stay with Original Medicare.

Medicare Advantage plans are provided through private insurers rather than directly from the federal government. Medicare regulates the services they must provide, which generally include anything provided through Medicare Parts A and B. Medicare Advantage can also provide additional services, such as for dental care, vision, hearing, nutrition services, in-home support, home modifications, or fitness plans, and most Medicare Advantage plans provide prescription drug coverage. Those who do not receive prescription drug coverage through their Medicare Advantage plan can use a Part D plan or other creditable coverage instead. About the added benefits, it is important to examine them carefully as they may be limited in their practical use.

A key difference for Medicare Advantage is that it is less universal, as users are generally limited to in-network doctors, hospitals, and providers. Referrals may be needed to see specialists. Medicare Advantage plans are focused on specific service areas and may have few in-network options outside those geographic areas. There can be additional charges for out-of-network care, which is reminiscent of how many private health insurance plans work but is not an issue with Original Medicare. An exception to this is made for emergency care, which will be considered in-network anywhere in the United States.

Medicare Advantage plans are structured in any variety of ways including as health maintenance organization (HMO) plans, preferred provider organization (PPO) plans, fee-for-service plans, special needs plans, and medical savings account plans. Depending on where one lives, there may be around 33 Medicare Advantage choices. HMOs are the most popular advantage option. They limit care to in-network providers and charge lower premiums. PPOs, in contrast, allow for out-of-network visits as well, but at a higher cost. Some Medicare Advantage plans are group plans made available to retirees through certain employers and unions.

For those covered by Medicare Advantage, one still pays the usual Medicare Part B premium plus an additional premium charged by the Advantage plan. In 2021, the Kaiser Family Foundation reports that 54 percent of Medicare Advantage plans did not require an extra premium, and the extra premium amount averaged $21 per month across all plans, or $46 per month among those plans charging a premium. Medicare then also pays a fee to the Advantage plan to share some of the premium it collected from you. As well, just like with Original Medicare, Medicare Advantage plans can require deductibles, coinsurance, and copayments. How these are structured can vary between plans.

A benefit of Medicare Advantage, unlike Original Medicare, is that it offers a maximum out-of-pocket expense limit for costs related to Medicare Part A and Part B benefits. For 2021, these out-of-pocket maximums can be at most $7,550 for in-network care and $11,300 for out-of-network care. After those limits are reached, Medicare Advantage will cover all eligible costs for the rest of the year.

An important choice that individuals will make when enrolling in Medicare is to choose between Original Medicare and Medicare Advantage. As based on our summary, reasons that individuals may lean toward choosing Original Medicare include:

- Live in two parts of the country throughout the year, such as those spending the winter in a warmer climate, which makes finding in-network providers more difficult with Medicare Advantage
- Preferred health care providers would not be in-network

- Tend to use more health care services and see more specialists
- Value the options provided by Original Medicare to not be restricted to in-network providers from a limited-service area
- Desire to have a comprehensive supplement to help limit out-of-pocket costs
- For those traveling internationally, including a supplement can provide some international coverage that is not generally available with Medicare Advantage

Meanwhile, those who may lean toward choosing Medicare Advantage may be attracted to:

- Lower overall premiums compared to adding Part D and a comprehensive supplement with Original Medicare
- Preferred health care providers are all in-network for the plan
- Tend to use less health care services so that the copayments and coinsurance costs will be less of an issue and overall out-of-pocket costs may be less
- Find value in the additional benefits such as dental, vision, or hearing
- Some individuals with chronic conditions may find special needs Medicare Advantage plans that are better tailored to their situation
- Appreciate the all-in-one aspect of not needing to differentiate between A, B, D, and a supplement plan.

Comparing the overall cost differences between Original Medicare and Medicare Advantage can be complicated because costs will depend on the amount of health care services used and on the choice of a supplement with Original Medicare. There will be tradeoffs between paying higher premiums to reduce the potential long tail of high uncovered expenses. A lower premium is not the only objective, as overall costs may end up higher as more care is used. Original Medicare with a comprehensive supplement will result in higher overall premiums but less subsequent out-of-pocket costs and more stable overall spending on health care. Total out-of-pocket costs with a comprehensive supplement can be less than with Medicare Advantage. In the absence of a supplement, however, costs with Original Medicare will be much more dependent on the amount of health care used, as compared with Medicare Advantage that offers an annual cap on expenses.

Meanwhile, Medicare Advantage can provide lower overall premiums, but then higher costs as health care is utilized, until finally reaching an out-of-pocket maximum for the year that could be higher than Original Medicare with a comprehensive supplement. This can mean fewer overall costs for those not using much health care, but then eventually higher overall costs as more health care is utilized, though at least there is a ceiling on how high those costs can go.

It is not an easy decision, and you may benefit from speaking about your specific situation with someone who is familiar with the various options available in your area and who can help to analyze your potential overall costs for different options as based on the types of health care you typically need. Of course, as new medical problems develop, this sort of look-back process on the health care you have used may be less helpful, but comparing different programs based on past health care needs is certainly a valuable starting point to understanding the implications of your choices.

Medicare Part D – Prescription Drug Coverage

Medicare Part D is the source of prescription drug coverage for those enrolled in Original Medicare. It is also available to those who choose a Medicare Advantage plan that does not include drug coverage. Much of the discussion about choosing among Part D plans applies as well to analyzing the drug coverage provided by Medicare Advantage.

Part D plans are provided through private insurers. Depending on where you live, there could be 30 or more available plans from which to choose. Plans vary in numerous important ways that can dramatically impact an individual's total prescription costs for a given year. The details which vary between Part D and Medicare Advantage plans include:

- Monthly premium amounts
- Amount of annual deductible, copayments, and coinsurance
- The formulary, or list of drugs covered, which can be changed from year to year and even during a year
- The breakdown of tiers and costs for covered drugs
- Lists of pharmacies that are preferred in-network, standard in-network, or out-of-network
- Whether prescriptions can be filled by mail order
- Step therapy rules, where lower tier drugs need to be used first
- Whether prior authorization is required before filling a prescription
- Quantity limits on prescriptions
- Medicare star ratings for plan quality, ranked from one to five stars

Part D plans charge premiums, include a deductible, and have coinsurance rates for prescription purchases. When choosing among plans, it is the total costs for covering one's prescriptions that matters, and that is the sum for these different components. One cannot look at any of these issues in isolation.

Plans charge a monthly premium that can vary widely by plan, though Medicare identifies that the average base premium amount nationally in 2021 is $33.06 per month, or about $397 per year. As with Part B, Part D premiums are also exposed to the income-related monthly adjusted amounts that can raise premiums for those with higher incomes in retirement. Planning for this situation is described in Chapter 10.

The costs for prescriptions depend on the plan's formulary, which lists the drugs covered by the plan and classifies them into different cost categories. Plans may also vary by their list of covered pharmacies as well as whether prescriptions can be filled through the mail, as this will be a consideration for those wishing to use a specific pharmacy. For those using a specific list of prescriptions, studying these formularies becomes important in estimating the total prescription costs under different plans. As a first step, make sure the plan you are considering covers the prescriptions you use. Then consider the out-of-pocket costs for each prescription with the plan, and any quantity or purchase limits.

Prescription costs also depend on total spending over a year's time. The cost for a particular prescription depends on which of three phases of coverage you are current in: the initial coverage phase, the gap coverage phase, and the catastrophic phase.

This can get complicated, but it is summarized nicely in the *Medicare and You* handbook for 2021: "Once you and your plan spend $4,130 combined on drugs including the deductible, you will pay no more than 25 percent of the cost until your out-of-pocket spending is $6,550. Then you receive "catastrophic coverage" in which you pay no more than 5 percent of the cost for covered drugs for the rest of the year."

In other words, the initial phase applies until spending (not counting premiums) reaches $4,130. The gap coverage phase then applies until your spending gets to $6,550. Beyond this amount, you have entered the catastrophic coverage phase. Individuals may also be using drugs that are not covered by their Part D plan and do not count as part of these thresholds.

In the initial phase, the standard or minimum coverage required through a Part D plan is a $445 deductible in 2021 before coverage begins, but this deductible may be less and even $0. After the deductible, plans can charge differently for different tiers of drugs and whether they are brand-name or generic. The coinsurance rates can be set high or low, or there may be copayments. When the coverage gap phase begins, coinsurance rates cannot be more than 25 percent. But again, they can be less. Finally, in the catastrophic phase the results are more standard: the coinsurance rate is 5 percent but not less than $3.60 for a generic prescription and $8.95 for a brand-name prescription.

Exhibit 7.1
Example of Part D Drug Costs Using Medicare Plan Finder

Tiers	Initial coverage phase	Gap coverage phase	Catastrophic coverage phase
Preferred Generic	$5 copay	$5 copay	Generic drugs: $3.60 copay or 5% (whichever costs more)
Generic	$10 copay	$10 copay	
Preferred Brand	$47 copay	For all other drugs, you pay 25% for generic drugs and 25% for brand-name drugs	Brand-name drugs: $8.95 copay or 5% (whichever costs more)
Non-Preferred Drug	50% coinsurance		
Specialty Tier	33% coinsurance		

Exhibit 7.1 provides an example showing how a randomly chosen plan structured its coverage. This information is provided for all plans using Medicare's important Plan Finder tool (Medicare.gov/plan-compare) which is explained later in this chapter. The point to take from the exhibit is there are many components to pricing and these numbers can vary by plan and can be presented as copays or coinsurance. As well, each drug may be in a different tier for different plans, and some plans may not even include the drug. If left to one's own devices, it could be a nightmare to compare plans for a specific set of medications.

Medicare Supplement (Medigap) Plans

For those enrolled in Original Medicare, optional Medicare Supplement or Medigap insurance policies are available from private insurers to cover some or most of the deductibles, coinsurance, and copayments for Medicare Parts A and B. These plans are only an option for Original Medicare and may **not** be used with Medicare Advantage.

The premiums for these policies vary by company and coverage plan. The methods used for determining premiums also vary, which can be an issue for those planning to keep the supplement throughout retirement. Some cost structures start higher but then grow more slowly, while others start lower but include larger anticipated increases over time.

Premiums based on attained age are most common, probably because they start the lowest. For these plans, prices vary based on your age at the time of enrolling in the plan, and they also increase as you age, and your costs of care are expected to rise. After enrolling, it is the only method that uses your current age as part of determining ongoing premiums. Premiums adjust over time to reflect the costs of claims for the insurance company, but everyone with the same attained age and same starting age will have the same premium. Next, community-based premiums have a single price for a service area regardless of age. This approach has less growth in premiums since your premiums do not increase specifically because you get older. Potential premium increases instead reflect the overall costs in the community to the insurer. This approach is how Medicare Advantage plans are priced. Finally, issue-age policies are based on when you first purchase the plan, and the price does not specifically change because you get older.

Despite the different premiums and methods for determining them, plans of the same type offer standardized coverage. States regulate coverage and so there could be slight differences between states, but within a state the coverage is fully standardized for each plan type. Plans are also guaranteed to be renewed for your lifetime once in place if you continue paying the premiums. These plans provide benefits only for costs related to Parts A and B. They do not cover other types of missing benefits such as dental care and they do not cover out-of-pocket costs for prescription drug coverage. Another point of comparison for supplement plans is whether your preferred health care providers will process the paperwork for the plan you choose, or whether you will have to do the paperwork yourself. You may ask your preferred care providers about this.

There are currently eight supplement plans available to new enrollees, along with two more for those who enrolled in Medicare before January 1, 2020. Each provides standardized coverage according to the terms of that type of plan. Exhibit 7.2 provides details about the ten types of plans.

Exhibit 7.2
Medicare Supplement (Medigap) Plan Options

Benefits	Premiums	A	B	C*	D	F*	G	K	L	M	N
	$864	$1,188	$1,476	$1,344	$1,488	$1,152	$492	$828	$1,224	$948
Part A co-insurance and hospital costs up to 365 days beyond initial Medicare benefits	Yes	Yes	Yes	Yes	Yes	Yes	Yes	Yes	Yes	Yes
Part B co-insurance and co-payments	Yes	Yes	Yes	Yes	Yes	Yes	50%	75%	Yes	Yes
Blood (first 3 pints)	Yes	Yes	Yes	Yes	Yes	Yes	50%	75%	Yes	Yes
Part A hospice co-insurance or co-payment	Yes	Yes	Yes	Yes	Yes	Yes	50%	75%	Yes	Yes
Skilled nursing facility care co-insurance	No	No	Yes	Yes	Yes	Yes	50%	75%	Yes	Yes
Part A deductible	No	Yes	Yes	Yes	Yes	Yes	50%	75%	50%	Yes
Part B deductible	No	No	Yes	No	Yes	No	No	No	No	No
Part B excess charge	No	No	No	No	Yes	Yes	No	No	No	No
Foreign travel exchange (up to plan limits)	No	No	80%	80%	80%	80%	No	No	80%	80%
Out-of-pocket limit	n/a	n/a	n/a	n/a	n/a	n/a	$5,880	$2,940	n/a	n/a

* Plan C and Plan F are not available to those newly eligible for Medicare after January 1, 2020.

Note: As an example, premiums reflect the lowest annual premium for a 65-year-old non-smoker female in Fairfax County, Virginia, for 2021. Personal pricing options are at Medicare.gov/plan-compare

The more comprehensive plans are more popular in practice. In recent years, Plan F is the most comprehensive available supplement. It covered the deductibles and coinsurance for Parts A and B completely so that there will not be any out-of-pocket costs. This will lead to higher premiums but less overall costs when adding those additional expenses related to high health care usage in a year. Starting for those newly eligible for Medicare after January 1, 2020, it is no longer possible to have the Part B deductible covered through a supplement. Those already covered with Plan F or Plan C can keep it, and those who first enrolled in Medicare before this date can still switch to these plans, but otherwise Plan G is now the most comprehensive plan for new enrollees. It covers everything included with Plan F except for the $203 Part B deductible. Some states do also offer high-deductible versions for Plan F and Plan G. These require paying all costs up to $2,370 in 2021 and then the plan pays. The tradeoff is that these plans will have lower premiums.

Average premium costs do not bear out the idea that more comprehensive coverage is always more expensive. This may be due to the lack of plan availability in different regions or different pricing formulas. There may also be more competition for some types of plans in your area. The purpose of including an example of premiums is to provide a sense of what these premiums may be on an approximate basis. It is important to shop for different plans available where you live and to not be intimidated about looking at more comprehensive plans because you are worried about costs. It is also important to remember that premiums are for individuals and plans must be purchased separately for each member of a couple. Each spouse is also free to choose a different plan based on their differing health characteristics and preferences.

Potential benefits are completely standardized across insurers for each plan type. All supplement plans cover coinsurance amounts for Part A as well as an additional 365 days of hospital coverage. Plans K and L are higher-deductible style plans and only cover a portion of the next three benefits but with out-of-pocket limits, while the remaining plans otherwise cover Part B co-insurance and co-payments, 3 pints of blood, and Part A hospice coinsurance and copayments. Plan A offers the least additional coverage, with only these first four benefits provided. The remaining benefits on the list are only available with certain plans. These include the co-insurance for skilled nursing care, the Part A deductible (and Part B with earlier enrollees), and foreign travel benefits.

The Part B excess charge refers to whether a medical provider has "accepted assignment" from Medicare. This means the medical provider has agreed to be paid directly by Medicare and to accept the Medicare approved payment amount. The medical provider will not charge more to the patient than the Medicare deductible or co-insurance amounts. Most medical providers do accept assignment, but you are welcome to ask about this before receiving care. Those who do not accept assignment may charge up to 15 percent more than the Medicare allowed amount. For expensive care, this can add up to a lot. The Part B excess charge benefit then covers the additional costs for care that exceed what Medicare pays for medical providers who have not accepted assignment.

Exhibit 7.3 provides more detail about the potential value for these different types of benefits. The choice between supplement plans involves the premiums as well as the self-assessed likelihood of using the benefits provided through different plans.

Not everyone using Original Medicare will need a Medicare supplement plan. Some of the most risk tolerant may prefer to take the risks related to potential health care costs based on the amount of care used, while others may obtain this type of additional coverage through their retiree health insurance plans or other secondary coverage options.

Exhibit 7.3
Medicare Supplement (Medigap) Plan Benefits

Benefit Type	Potential Monetary Value of Coverage (2021)
Part A co-insurance and hospital costs up to 365 days beyond initial Medicare benefits	Covers $371 copay for days 61-90, then covers full cost beyond 90 days for up to 365 days
Part B co-insurance and co-payments	Covers the 20% coinsurance rate for care received after deductible is met
Blood (first 3 pints)	Covers when a hospital buys blood for you, otherwise you pay the hospital costs for the first three units of blood in a calendar year
Part A hospice co-insurance or co-payment	Covers $5 copayments for prescription pain and symptom management drugs, and 5% coinsurance for Medicare-approved inpatient respite care
Skilled nursing facility care co-insurance	Covers the $185.50 copayment per day for days 21-100
Part A deductible	Covers the $1,484 deductible per benefit period
Part B deductible	Covers the $203 per year deductible
Part B excess charge	Covers charges exceeding Medicare reimbursement rates for health care providers who do not "accept assignment" from Medicare
Foreign travel exchange (up to plan limits)	Medicare generally does not cover health care while traveling outside the United States. This covers foreign travel emergency care if it begins during the first 60 days of the trip, and covers 80% of billed charges for certain medically necessary emergency care outside of the US after a $250 deductible (lifetime limit = $50,000)
Out-of-pocket limit	Original Medicare does not have out-of-pocket maximums

For the risk averse, Original Medicare alongside a comprehensive Medicare supplement may be the best option. Though premiums will be higher, most health expenses will be covered through benefits instead of paid out-of-pocket. This combination alleviates potential concerns about staying in-network because care can be obtained from any medical provider who works with Medicare. There is also no need to worry about whether a provider accepts assignment from Medicare because coverage is standardized along with the ability to maintain the same type of plan for life. In terms of annual updates, the only ongoing decision relates to choosing a Part D plan to prove the most cost-effective coverage for the following year. It is not necessary to keep up with changes in Medicare Advantage plans. You can switch to a Medicare Advantage plan later in retirement if you wish to, but if you instead use Medicare Advantage from the start, you may not be able to later switch to coverage from a desired supplement. This is a detail I will address later.

Using the Medicare Plan Finder

Medicare provides the Plan Finder (Medicare.gov/plan-compare) to help participants learn more about the various options in their community for Part D prescription plans, Medicare Advantage plans, and Medicare supplements. The tool is probably the most useful for analyzing prescription drug costs, while it provides the least amount of information for Medicare supplements. We will discuss this tool, but one additional detail worth noting first are the star ratings. Each plan includes a star rating for the plan quality and performance. It is based on whether members were getting preventative care, how they manage chronic conditions, member survey results, member complaints, and customer service outcomes. The results range from one to five stars, with five being the best. It is not necessary to log into your Medicare account to use the tool.

Medicare Part D Plans

If we could make the heroic assumptions that an individual knows their exact list of prescriptions for the following year and that no changes to the formularies are made mid-year, it is possible to use the Plan Finder tool to calculate total costs for your list of prescriptions per plan and to then choose the one supporting the lowest overall costs. We do not know this information with certainty, but it can still be helpful as a start.

Regarding mid-year changes to formularies, this is especially hard to predict, and we may not be able to plan for it. When it happens, the plan should provide a reasonable alternative option at similar cost. We might lean toward a plan with a higher star rating under the assumption that the plan will be more cooperative to help with these situations.

The other input, which is our list of medications used in the next year, does require some guesswork on our part. To estimate this, it is worthwhile to begin accumulating a detailed list of your prescriptions each year to help refine and estimate your needs for the coming year, hoping that no new conditions develop to throw off your plans (among other downsides from new health problems). If you already have a sense that new medication will be needed in the following year, you might test plan options with and without the medication. You might also compare generic and brand name options for medicines. The goal is to see how much different plans will cost to meet your anticipated prescription needs in the following year.

With this list of anticipated prescriptions, we are now ready to sit down with Medicare's Plan Finder. At this website, you can select to view the Part D plans, and enter your zip code and county of residence. Choose "yes" if you want to see your drug costs when you compare plans. To get the widest analysis, choose both mail-order and retail pharmacy options for how you normally fill prescriptions. You can then enter your list of prescription drugs you wish to test, as well as all the potential pharmacies you could consider. You are only allowed to enter five pharmacies at a time, which could require re-running a few times to make sure you have been able to consider all the viable pharmacy options. Calculated costs can also vary quite dramatically by pharmacy. If you have chosen pharmacies that are generally being included as a preferred-provider for your available plans, then you may have a good idea about your options with just five pharmacy choices. After entering this information, you will receive a list of insurance plans that you can rank by:

- Lowest yearly drug deductible
- Lowest drug and premium cost
- Lowest monthly premiums

The only one of these choices that really matters is the middle one: how much will you pay in total for your annual prescriptions after accounting for both premiums and the costs you pay toward each prescription. Knowing who has the lowest deductible or lowest monthly premiums is not helpful since this is just one component of costs. You may also filter the results by having drug coverage accepted across the US, by the star rating of the insurance plan, and by individual insurance carriers.

To provide a sense of the possible outcomes, I tried using the Planner with a few random prescriptions. Thirty plan options were available in my search. Total drug and premium costs ranged from $1,359.42 for the least expensive plan (which included $85.80 for monthly premiums, using a retail pharmacy, a $435 deductible, and a 3.5-star rating) up to $3,119.77 for the most expensive plan (which included $86.80 for monthly premiums, using mail-order pharmacy, a $250 deductible, and a 3-star rating). Monthly premiums ranged from $13.20 at the lowest (but with a $2,898.81 total cost) to $147.20 at the highest (but with a $1,522.62 total cost). Deductibles ranged from $0 to $435. If I limited options to those providing national coverage, the lowest total cost was $1,850.98. There were no 5-star plans, but if I instead limited options to 4 stars and higher, the lowest total cost was $3,091.11.

Results varied widely in this simple example, which leads to a few conclusions about finding a Part D plan:

- Focus on total costs for your estimated prescriptions, not lowest premium or deductible. Plans with higher premiums or deductibles may offer lower total costs for your prescription needs.
- If you are finding that your prescription drugs are not covered or may be covered in a more expensive tier, discuss with your health care provider about whether there are more affordable options.
- If you do not use prescriptions at all, you might focus on plans with lower premiums, but make sure to study how the charges work in the initial coverage phase of the plan.

- Make sure to include options for mail-order as well as at least a few local pharmacies, as the results can vary between these options. If none of the pharmacies you enter regularly shows up as a preferred option, then consider expanding further with your retail pharmacy choices to find a preferred pharmacy that is popular with your local plan options.
- Consider how much you value having either national coverage or a high star rating if it leads to greater costs.

I think it is worth checking up on your Part D choice annually. If you are already updating your list of medications throughout the year, this whole review process can be done in a couple of hours each autumn and could lead to substantial cost savings for the following year.

Medicare Advantage

The Medicare Plan Finder provides a similar system for comparing Medicare Advantage plans both with and without prescription drug coverage. For drug coverage, the process is quite similar as with Part D plans. Select to find health and drug plans, view Medicare Advantage plans, provide your zip code and county of residence, and select "yes" for viewing drug costs when comparing plans. Again, you may enter to use both mail and retail pharmacies, select up to five pharmacies, and enter your prescription drugs.

When I did this for the 22182 zip code, I was provided a list of 26 plans. The plans could be sorted by their drug deductible, health plan deductible, drug and premium cost, or monthly premium. The most useful of these metrics is the combined drug and premium costs. You might also consider copays and coinsurance rates, but the tool does not otherwise allow you to input medical procedures to estimate costs of care in the same way as can be done for prescriptions.

The results can be further filtered for various options related to whether the plan is a health maintenance organization (HMO) or a preferred provider organization (PPO), and what additional benefits are available regarding vision, transportation, dental, fitness or hearing. Plans can also be considered as based on their star rating, specific insurance carrier, or whether you want to remove plans that include the drug coverage.

With a simple test I tried that included medications for both high blood pressure and cholesterol, the total yearly costs for premiums and drug expenses ranged from $2,342.76 to $5,056.20 across the plans. The least costly plan included $84 for monthly premiums, a $0 health deductible, $360 drug deductible, and health out-of-pocket maximums of $7,550 for in-network and $10,000 for out-of-network. It included a variety of supplemental benefits, except for transportation, in-home support, home safety devices and modifications, and an emergency response device. Primary doctor visits have $15 copays and specialists have $50 copays. Linking to this plan for further details does provide a great deal of information related to plan benefits and costs, extra benefits, optional packages, drug coverage and costs, star ratings, and contact information. The tool does provide a link that allows for online enrollment in the plan.

Medical information is less comprehensive than with Part D. Prescription costs are shown in the same way as with Part D plans, but out-of-pocket costs for health care services cannot feasibly be shown. This makes it harder to compare plans as it relates to the types of doctors and specialists you see. The Plan Finder does not confirm what medical providers are covered by the plan, so this information will need to be obtained separately on the insurance company's website or by asking your preferred providers. While the Medicare website offers details about the types of coverage and the associated out-of-pocket costs, you may also have questions for the insurer about the specific nature of these benefits.

Medicare Supplement Plans

The Plan Finder information provided for Medicare supplements is not particularly useful. The tool does allow you to search for a list of available plans in your zip code. It also provides the range of premiums for available plans with each plan letter as based on information you provide about your age, gender, and tobacco use. It also does provide other information about plan coverage as discussed earlier, but since these details are all standardized by plan type there is nothing new to learn.

The problem with the tool is that when you click to view policies for a given plan type, you do not receive helpful information to choose among the companies. For instance, when I clicked to view the available Plan G options in the 22182 zip code, I received a list of 48 supplement plans arranged by insurance company. The only information provided is contact information by insurance company and how the plan is priced in terms of attained age, community pricing, or issue age. The actual plan premiums are not shown, so there is no way to know how to begin your search. In addition, clicking on web links may lead you to the insurance company's general webpage instead of their supplement page, while a further search of the website is not clear as to whether that the company even offers supplement plans. In some states you may have to make a phone call to gather specific information.

As I investigated the tool, I did find one large insurance company that provides premium quotes as well as an online application process for the fifth state I tried (the first four states indicated that state law prohibited sharing this information through the webpage). Then I found another company which did offer online premium information and online enrollment in all these states. It is possible to successfully use the Plan Finder tool to enroll in a Medicare supplement. But it may not always be easy, and in some states in may be necessary to call companies to get information about their options.

Because supplements should be treated more as a lifetime commitment, you may wish to work with an independent broker to review your options and save time. Alternatively, it is just a matter of doing the legwork of connecting with each company and discovering their options. Since the benefits are standardized by plan type, the only two variables that matter are the premiums and the choice of the insurance company. The major questions to answer are your comfort level with the company's stability, the company's customer experience and whether your health providers have relationships with the company such that they are willing to handle the billing and claims paperwork.

Getting Additional Help

If you would like help regarding Medicare beyond what is available with the Plan Finder, there are various other options. The Center for Medicare Services does provide these tools:

- Physician Compare (https://www.medicare.gov/physiciancompare/)
- Hospital Compare (https://www.medicare.gov/hospitalcompare/)

The physician compare tool includes information about whether providers accept assignment from Medicare along with other demographic information and specialties, but it does not include whether they work with different Medicare Advantage plans.

Medicare personnel are also available 24 hours a day by phone for counseling (1-800-633-4227), and you can also talk to knowledgeable volunteers through the Medicare Rights Center (www.medicarerights.org) and your state's State Health Insurance Assistance Program (www.shiptacenter.org). Finally, you may wish to speak to a professional who can help you select the right Medicare option. Captive agents can help with specific plans from an insurer, and independent brokers may provide access to a variety of plans. Brokers are generally paid through a commission from the Advantage, supplement, or drug plan you choose, rather than being paid directly by you. As such, from your perspective, their services are free, as you would not pay less by enrolling directly with the insurer. With drug plans and Medicare Advantage, the Plan Finder can be more helpful to narrow the options. But Medicare supplements require more effort to find out premium rates, which is where a broker may be especially helpful. A good broker can also serve as a check to make sure you have not overlooked any issues discussed in this chapter, especially regarding decisions you may still make for other primary or secondary coverage, or when you may have to be underwritten as part of joining a supplement.

Upon Reaching the Medicare Eligibility Age

In this section we examine the process for your initial enrollment into Medicare, including when it will happen, when you might be able to delay, and what decisions you will need to make. Most individuals reach Medicare eligibility when they turn 65. More precisely, Medicare can begin as early as the first day of the month in which one reaches 65. Those born on the first day of the month can begin Medicare at the start of the previous month. We mentioned the exceptions to be able to qualify before 65, which include having end-stage renal disease or receiving Social Security disability benefits for at least two years. To simplify the discussion, I will focus on when it is the act of reaching age 65 that makes one eligible.

Enrolling at Age 65

For those who become eligible at age 65, the *initial enrollment period* for Medicare is the seven-month window which includes the three months before reaching age 65, the month that one reaches 65, and then the three months after reaching age 65. If you want to have Medicare begin precisely in the month you turn 65, you need to enroll in the three months before reaching 65. Practically speaking, this makes sense because otherwise coverage will not begin immediately. Initial enrollment involves making decisions about Medicare Parts A, B, and D, Medicare Advantage, and a Medicare supplement plan.

Each of these components for Medicare has subtle distinctions about how their precise initial enrollment period is defined. I just outlined the initial enrollment period for Parts A and B. As a practical matter, you will likely be best served to act during the earlier three months so that your coverage for all the different components you want can begin when you reach 65. This also avoids any hassles related to the possibility you might not have a primary insurance provider immediately after your 65th birthday. You do not want other health coverage to end before your Medicare coverage begins.

If you decide to use a Medicare Advantage plan, you can enroll so it begins coverage at the same time as Part A and B. When first turning 65, Medicare Advantage also provides a one-year trial period that allows changing to Original Medicare and choosing a supplement without underwriting. You may decide instead to use a supplement and/or a Part D plan. With Part D, you must be enrolled in either Part A or Part B already (or both), but the initial enrollment period otherwise matches A and B.

As for a supplement, its open enrollment period technically begins on the first day of the month after turning 65 and being enrolled in Medicare Part B. It lasts for six months. This is the case when enrolling in Part B during the initial enrollment period or the special enrollment period, but not the general enrollment period (more on these later). This is called the Medigap Open Enrollment Period. In many states you may be able to apply in advance so that your coverage can start at the same time as Part B. This is the best opportunity to choose a supplement because individuals cannot be denied coverage or charged a higher monthly premium during this period for existing medical conditions. Afterward, if you wish to join or exchange a supplement, you will need to have your coverage underwritten by insurers, which may result in either higher premiums or the denial of coverage.

If you are already collecting Social Security benefits or railroad retirement benefits at age 65, you will be automatically enrolled in Medicare Parts A and B at 65. You can opt out of Part B, but those collecting Social Security cannot opt out of Part A. If you are not collecting Social Security yet, the enrollment process is not automatic. You must take action to enroll in Medicare. This is important to remember, since as the full retirement age for Social Security is no longer age 65, it is easy to lose track that Medicare is still based on turning 65. Enrolling can be done online (socialsecurity.gov/benefits/medicare), by phone, or in person at a Social Security office. Contact Medicare three months before reaching age 65 if you will not be automatically enrolled. Filing for Social Security benefits forces enrollment in at least in Part A at age 65. If you do want to defer enrolling in Medicare, it is another reason to delay Social Security claiming.

Upon reaching age 65, many individuals decide to terminate other health insurance coverage and switch fully to Medicare. With one exception, Medicare becomes the primary payer by law at age 65, with any other coverage as secondary. Secondary insurance will only pay toward costs not covered by the primary payer and it may not pay anything if one does not enroll in Medicare and therefore has no primary coverage. It is also important to make sure that your pre-65 health insurer does not automatically enroll you in their Medicare Advantage plan, as this would take away the potential value from investigating your options.

Not everyone will enroll in Medicare at 65. Some can be allowed to delay because they maintain active employment and receive primary employer coverage, but everyone else is taking a risk by not having primary health insurance. Enrolling in Medicare is not mandatory, but if you wait beyond initial eligibility and you do not otherwise have a primary payer for health insurance or creditable coverage for prescription drugs, then you may face medical bills and gaps in coverage. If you subsequently enroll, your premiums may also include a penalty.

Working Past Age 65 with Employer Coverage as Primary Payer

As more people work past age 65, enrollment issues related to Medicare get more complicated and confusing. Not everyone has to enroll in Medicare. But delaying Medicare enrollment without creating coverage gaps and potential premium penalties is only possible if you or a spouse are actively working at a company with 20 or more employees and are covered through that company or union's group health insurance plan that remains by law as a primary payer. This coverage must be based on *active* employment at the company. This is the circumstance under which you can delay Medicare without loss of primary coverage.

If you or your spouse meet this very specific requirement, you are eligible to wait on enrolling in Medicare. You should check with your benefits administrator to confirm precisely how your insurance works with Medicare. You may also wish to confirm these points by investigating the plan's summary of benefits section on interactions with Medicare. Assuming your insurance does maintain a primary payer status, there are a few additional matters to consider.

But first, to be clear about this point and to provide further emphasis about its importance, I provide a list of cases where the health coverage mentioned is **not** a substitute for enrolling in Medicare at age 65:

- Covered by an employer health insurance plan, but the employer has less than 20 employees
- Continuing to work but covered by an Affordable Care Act health plan from an insurance exchange or private insurer
- Retired but receiving health insurance through a retiree health insurance plan from a previous employer
- Receiving coverage through a religious-based healthshare plan
- Receiving coverage as a VA benefit or through TRICARE for Life
- Receiving coverage through COBRA from a previous employer
- Receiving health coverage through Medicaid

Unfortunately, many in these circumstances do not realize that they must enroll in Medicare to obtain primary coverage. For those who have formally confirmed that they can truly defer Medicare without risk, the first decision is whether to go ahead and enroll in Medicare at 65 or wait for your special enrollment period after you end work. Enrolling in Medicare Part A does not create any premium or cost, and it may help to cover some hospital expenses not covered by your employer health insurance. Most will want to enroll in Part A without delay for these reasons. One exception is that enrolling in Part A means that you can no longer contribute to an HSA even if your employer health insurance is a qualified high-deductible plan. Aside from this consideration, there is no other reason to delay enrolling in Part A. One other complicated note about HSA plans is that Part A coverage can be applied retroactively for up to six months if you are waiting past age 65, so it is best to stop making HSA contributions if you intend to enroll in Medicare in the next six months.

As for Part B, consider whether it is worth keeping your eligible employer plan or switching to Part B. Relevant issues for making this decision include the relative costs and range of coverage for the two plans, whether you have already met deductibles with the employer plan, and whether there are other family members (spouse or dependents) who maintain coverage through the employer plan that will lose their coverage if you switch to Medicare.

Remember, Medicare is for individuals. It does not provide family coverage. With a younger spouse who cannot qualify for Medicare, you may compare options for an Affordable Care Act policy against maintaining employer insurance for broader family access. As well, when you are still working, it may be more likely that you will exceed income thresholds that result in higher Part B premiums, which would impact the relevant costs for your choices. Of course, for those who decide not to maintain the eligible employer plan, it is important to follow through and complete your Medicare enrollment.

Coordinating with Secondary Health Coverage Past Age 65

Many retirees will have access to valid types of secondary health coverage in retirement that can potentially serve the role of a supplement or as creditable prescription drug coverage to take the place of a Part D plan. You may have aspects of these two types of coverage through Medicaid, an employer or union health plan, COBRA, the Federal Employee Health Benefits program, Christian-based healthshare programs such as the Senior Assist program offered through Medi-share, Veterans programs, TRICARE for the military, various health programs for Native Americans, and even some older supplement plans (which are no longer available to new enrollees) include drug coverage.

According to a Vanguard study from 2018, which we describe further in the section about health care costs, the most common approach with Medicare is to use secondary coverage for filling gaps. Their study notes that 12 percent of Medicare enrollees choose Original Medicare and a Part D plan without a supplement or secondary coverage, 21 percent of enrollees choose Original Medicare with a Part D plan and a supplement, 32 percent choose Medicare Advantage with drug coverage, and 35 percent used Original Medicare along with other secondary coverage.

Deciding about whether to use secondary coverage (especially if it is not free) or to choose a Part D or supplement (or Advantage) plan can be quite complex and it will likely be worth talking through all the options with a professional who is up-to-date on both your secondary coverage as well as the Medicare options for your area. If you have coverage through an employer or union, you should also check with the benefits administrator about the potential need or other implications (such as losing the employer coverage) for signing up with a Part D plan or a Medicare Advantage plan. Indeed, maintaining the outside insurance may also be necessary to keep other family members covered, and you will want to take care that your decisions regarding various aspects of Medicare do not impact your ability to maintain this outside coverage for your family.

If there are no other family members needing the coverage, the choice otherwise relates to premiums and all the different aspects of coverage regarding out-of-pocket expenses, the possibility to receive benefits for items not covered by Medicare, and access to doctors and health providers. Determine how much of the Medicare Parts A and B deductibles, coinsurance, and copayments will be covered by your secondary source.

It may be the case that Medicare offers better opportunities than any other coverage you have, especially if you are paying premiums for the other coverage. But it is impossible to figure this out without a careful comparison of the options. It is also important to obtain a letter from the insurer stating that the plan qualifies as creditable prescription drug coverage to avoid penalties if you choose to later enroll in a Part D plan. As a final comment, if health or prescription bills are becoming onerous, financial assistance is also available through programs such as Extra Help for prescription drugs, various Medicare Savings Programs, Medicaid, and Supplemental Security Income.

Enrolling Later During a Special Enrollment Period

For those who meet the coverage requirement for delaying enrollment at age 65, it is possible to wait until the *special enrollment period* to first register with Medicare, or to sign up for Part B if already enrolled in Part A. The special enrollment period for Part B is the eight months that begin the month after either eligible active employment ends or health insurance coverage from that employer ends, whichever happens first. There is also the ability to enroll at any time before this as well, as in practice this exception extends the initial enrollment period through the start of the special enrollment period.

Enrolling during the special enrollment period is more complex because you will need to demonstrate qualifying coverage during the period after 65 up until your special period started. Those required to enroll during the special enrollment period but who fail to do so will lack a primary payer and face potential premium penalties.

As soon as you discontinue primary active employer coverage, the enrollment deadlines for switching to Medicare include eight months for Part B, 63 days for Part D, the date that Part B is effective for Medicare Advantage, and six months after Part B is effective for a supplement. To simplify your options and avoid a lapse in coverage, decide on what coverage you want, and put those coverages into effect the day after your employer coverage ends.

There are also special enrollment periods available when certain events happen for those who are already enrolled in Medicare but may have had secondary coverage to help with prescription drugs or in place of a supplement. Medicare Advantage also offers special enrollment periods to select a Medicare Advantage plan outside of open enrollment periods under certain conditions. During special enrollment periods, it is possible to change from Medicare Advantage to Original Medicare, to switch from Original Medicare to Medicare Advantage, and to switch from one Medicare Advantage plan to another.

For Medicare Advantage, situations that trigger these special enrollment periods include moving to a new residence, experiencing a change in Medicaid status or other low-income subsidies or assistance, moving in or out of a skilled nursing care facility, leaving a PACE program (in selected states), losing creditable prescription drug coverage, losing employer-sponsored health insurance coverage, having your Medicare Advantage plan canceled, wanting to switch to a five-star Medicare Advantage plan, or other special circumstances.

When you are in a special enrollment period, you may also be able to select from a subset of supplement plans without underwriting if you are otherwise outside of the initial period and might otherwise be denied coverage. In these special cases, guaranteed issue of coverage is available for plans A, B, G, K, and L only. There are also other exceptions in some states, as rules for supplements are created at the state level.

These special enrollment periods for Medicare supplements can be triggered by events including losing coverage through Medicare Advantage because the plan ends or you move out of its service area, you had other secondary health coverage that ends, and other various cases. In this regard, having other retirement health coverage that is cancelled could allow for more opportunities with choosing a supplement plan.

Though there are exceptions as noted that can vary by state as well, there is a risk that you cannot obtain a Medicare supplement if you do not choose it initially and do not experience a valid trigger that creates a special enrollment period. This aspect of Medicare supplements creates an important planning issue because it is possible to permanently miss the chance for a Medicare supplement.

Enrolling in Medicare at Other Times

While there is no requirement to enroll in Medicare once eligibility is triggered, potential costs include the lack of a primary insurance carrier to pay for health expenses. We now discuss what happens when people miss enrolling in Original Medicare during either the initial enrollment period or during the special enrollment period (if applicable).

If you miss the initial and special enrollment periods, you must then wait until the next *general enrollment period* to sign up. These only happen from January 1 and March 31 of each year, with coverage then beginning on July 1 after enrolling. With these provisions, someone who decides they want to enroll in April would have to wait a full 15 months before their coverage can begin. This could lead to a large gap of time without sufficient health coverage or even a primary insurer. For any health issues arising during this time, costs of care could be quite high. In addition to being responsible to provide full payment for your health expenses during the delay while you wait for coverage, you may face medical underwriting with Medicare supplements, and you may have to pay penalties for your subsequent Medicare premiums. We have described many different enrollment periods now, and it can be confusing. Exhibit 7.4 provides a summary of these details.

The premium penalty results in a permanent increase in the Part B premiums. Premiums increase by 10 percent for each full 12-month period when coverage should have existed, based on the length from the end of the allowed enrollment period until the time you sign up. For those who do have to pay premiums on Part A coverage, there is also a temporary 10 percent penalty applied to premiums that lasts twice the length of the period of delay.

Exhibit 7.4
Initial and Ongoing Enrollment for Medicare

Which	When	What
Initial Signup for Medicare		
Initial Enrollment Period	7 months beginning 3 months before the month you turn 65	Signup for Part A and Part B, as well as Medicare Advantage Plan and/or Part D
Special Enrollment Period	Anytime while actively employed with primary coverage plus 8 months beginning after employment or coverage ends, whichever is first	For those who did not have to sign up during initial enrollment period because they held active employer group health plan coverage that maintained primary payer status. Signup for Part A and Part B, as well as Medicare Advantage Plan and/or a Part D plan
Medigap Open Enrollment Period	6 months beginning on the first day of the month you turn 65 and are enrolled in Part B	Allows for enrollment in Medicare supplement without underwriting. The Part B signup must happen during the initial or special enrollment period, not the general enrollment period
General Enrollment Period	Jan. 1 to March 31, with coverage starting July 1	For those who did not sign up during initial period or special enrollment period (if applicable). Can sign up for Part A, B, D, Medicare Advantage, and/or a supplement (subject to underwriting)
Making Changes to Medicare		
Open Enrollment Period	October 15 - December 7, with changes effective on Jan. 1	Change between Original Medicare and Medicare Advantage; Change Medicare Advantage plans; Change Part D plans; Change supplement plans (subject to underwriting)
Medicare Advantage Open Enrollment Period	January 1 - March 31	Those with Medicare Advantage can switch their plan or change to Original Medicare and choose Part D plan and supplement (subject to underwriting)
Medicare Advantage Special Enrollment Periods	Meet a trigger requirement	May join, switch, or drop Medicare Advantage throughout year if a special trigger is met
Part D Special Enrollment Periods	Meet a trigger requirement	May make changes to Part D plan throughout year if a special trigger is met
Medigap Special Enrollment Periods	Meet a trigger requirement	Certain Medicare supplement plans will be available with guaranteed issue to avoid underwriting, accessibility varies by state
5-Star Special Enrollment Period	Dec. 8 to Nov. 30	May switch to a 5-star Medicare Advantage or Part D plan

As well, if you are eligible for Medicare, you must have creditable prescription drug coverage from a secondary coverage source to avoid paying penalties on Part D premiums should you ever wish to sign up in the future. If delaying prescription coverage through Part D or Medicare Advantage, then you should obtain and keep a letter each year from your provider stating that it provides "creditable coverage" for prescriptions. If this coverage ends and new coverage is not obtained within 63 days, then penalties for Part D begin to accumulate. The penalty for not signing up for Part D and having a period of non-coverage after the initial or special enrollment period ends is calculated as one percent of the national base beneficiary premium ($33.06 in 2021) multiplied by the number of full uncovered months for drugs and then rounded to the nearest ten cents. The penalty increase for premiums is permanent.

Annual Open Enrollment Options Review

Medicare choices can be overwhelming. Many treat Medicare as a one-time decision made at initial enrollment, and then never revisit whether they are still receiving the best available coverage for their situation. Plans and personal needs change. Each year Medicare provides an open enrollment period to make changes. If you do not act during this period, you will keep the same plan choices for the following year.

The annual open enrollment window for Medicare occurs yearly from October 15 and December 7 for those who are already enrolled in Medicare. When changing plans, new coverage begins on January 1 of the following year. The options available include changing Part D plans, changing Medicare supplements, changing Advantage plans, or switching between Original Medicare and Medicare Advantage. At least for prescription drugs, annually reviewing options to see if there are better choices available is a good idea. Medicare also provides a broader open enrollment opportunity throughout the year to switch to a Medicare Advantage or Part D plan with a five-star quality rating.

Each year, Medicare Advantage and Part D plans send out documentation, which details the coverage you received in the current year and how it might change in the following year. Changes will be outlined in the Annual Notice of Change and the Evidence of Coverage, both of which should arrive in time to digest for open enrollment decisions. Items that were covered may be lost. Other plan options may also change, such that your best coverage choices can differ. Each year you can review your available options the using Medicare Plan Finder tool (Medicare.gov/plan-compare).

Changing Part D Plans

While it is possible to change Part D plans annually, inertia tends to set in after initial enrollment. Many never check to see if there are better options available for their Part D coverage even as available plans and their own personal needs change. This can be a costly mistake. For Part D, changes to your plan coverage will be outlined in the Annual Notice of Change and the Evidence of Coverage. These detail the formulary of drugs covered by your plan, their tiers, how much you pay, and any changes in coverage, costs, provider networks, service area, and other features for the upcoming year.

It is important to consider the available options on a regular basis for reasons related to changes in the types of prescriptions you use, as well as changes in the formularies, premiums, deductibles, and drug costs covered under each available plan. A change may also be needed if you move to a new area or if your plan is discontinued. You will want to determine if there is a more cost-effective option for the medications you expect to use in the following year. A couple hours of effort with the Plan Finder could save hundreds or even thousands of dollars.

Changing between Medicare Advantage and Original Medicare

During the annual open enrollment window for changing between Medicare Advantage and Original Medicare, it is possible to move in either direction. Those enrolled in Medicare Advantage also have the option to switch to a different Medicare Advantage plan. With Medicare Advantage, make sure that your preferred doctors, hospitals, and other care providers will remain on the covered list. When the provider network changes to remove preferred care providers, you may either work with the insurer to find acceptable alternatives, or you may look for a new plan.

As well, for Medicare Advantage plans covering prescriptions, the same issues apply regarding changes to the formularies and costs of drugs. Insurers could even decide to stop offering your plan, which will require choosing another or returning to Original Medicare. Again, the goal of this exploration is to see if there are changes to either your situation or the available options that will lead to more cost-effective solutions.

A second window also opens from January 1 to March 31 only for those using Medicare Advantage. You can drop a Medicare Advantage plan to return to Original Medicare and choose a Part D plan and a supplement, or you can switch to a different Medicare Advantage Plan. This provides some extra flexibility for those using Medicare Advantage to be comfortable with their choices.

Changing Medicare Supplements & Reduced Options

We have explained that you may not have all the supplement plan options available after your Medigap Open Enrollment Period, which is the six months after turning 65 or signing up for Part B during a special enrollment period. This can limit your options during the annual open enrollment period (which has a similar name but is not the same). Though state law manages this and there can be exceptions, including that certain events can trigger a special enrollment period with guaranteed issue for some options, the default assumption is that those seeking to join a supplement plan after the initial period should expect to face medical underwriting with their application. This underwriting can result in either higher premiums or declined coverage. Even if your application is accepted, you may experience a six-month period where pre-existing conditions are not covered as well. A professional may be able to help you strategize about which company to apply for the best opportunity to pass the underwriting.

During the annual open enrollment period, be cautious about dropping a Medicare Advantage plan until you know that you will be covered by the supplement you want at a premium you can accept. As well, if you are seeking to switch from Original Medicare to Medicare Advantage, it is important to understand that there is a possibility you may not be able to someday return to the supplement plan you gave up.

For those who have a supplement already, since benefits within a particular supplement are standardized, the only item that changes on an annual basis is its premium. The Annual Notice of Rate will also arrive before open enrollment to notify you of any premium changes. You can expect rates to increase over time, even more quickly if you choose the attained-age option. One will not be switching supplements regularly.

These issues create an important complication for Medicare planning. You might want to use Medicare Advantage in early retirement when expenses are lower, but then switch to Original Medicare with a comprehensive supplement later in retirement to have stronger overall coverage. This can be risky because if you do not start a Medicare supplement during your initial period of eligibility, you may not be able to qualify to receive it in the future. This contrasts to Medicare Advantage and Part D plans that can be easily changed each year. This creates additional value to start with a Medicare supplement in that you can always decide to drop it, but if you do not choose it initially then it may not be available later.

Budgeting for Retirement Health Care Expenses

How much should a retiree budget to cover remaining lifetime health expenses? This can be a complicated question to answer. We will first take a brief look at estimates of total lifetime expenses for the average retiree, and then we can consider more deeply how individuals can develop more personalized annual estimates for their retirement budgets.

The components for medical expenses in retirement include premiums for health insurance, including the various components of Medicare and any other primary or secondary coverage, plus deductibles and co-payments for covered care, plus costs for non-covered care including dental care, eye exams, and certain types of drugs and care that fall outside of Medicare coverage. In these discussions of health care cost estimates, we do *not* include long-term care spending. Long-term care is an entirely separate topic covered in the next chapter.

We can tackle the health care spending plan by creating a budget for health expenses, projecting how much they may grow throughout retirement, and deciding how much to pad the budget with conservative projections about future spending. As an alternative to being more conservative within the budget, we could also set aside a larger reserve for health spending shocks.

Existing Lump-Sum Estimates of Average Costs

Several organizations provide estimates for the total lump-sum amount needed by an average retiree to cover remaining lifetime health care expenses. Two of the most well-known studies that are frequently updated include those from Fidelity and the Employee Benefit Research Institute. Their estimates differ quite dramatically.

For instance, Fidelity creates an annual Retiree Health Care Cost Estimate. In 2020, they estimated that the average couple in retirement will need $295,000 set aside at the start of retirement to cover medical expenses, excluding long-term care. This breaks down to $140,000 for a man and $155,000 for a longer living woman. These estimates are updated annually, and the estimates do tend to grow faster than overall inflation. In 2014, for instance, their estimate was $220,000 for a couple.

The Fidelity estimates are based on a couple each at age 65 in 2020 who will live to their median life expectancies, rather than to a conservative planning age. They estimate average spending, such that half of retired couples could expect to spend more than the projected amount, but half could expect to spend less. Longevity, as well as health status and geographic location will all play a role in determining an individual's or couple's costs. Fidelity divides the $295,000 cost estimate as 39 percent for Medicare Part B and D premiums, 42 percent for other medical expenses including co-payments, co-insurance, and deductibles for doctor and hospital visits, and 19 percent for drugs. Their assumption is that the couple uses Original Medicare and a Part D plan without a supplement. These estimates do not include over-the-counter medications or dental care.

The Employee Benefit Research Institute (EBRI) is another source of estimates. They create an ongoing study that estimates retirement health care expenses. The expenses include premiums for Medicare Parts B and D, premiums for the comprehensive Plan G supplement plan, and other out-of-pocket health and prescription expenses. In 2020, they estimate lifetime costs for 65-year-olds based on a Monte Carlo simulation. The median cost (which means having at least enough 50 percent of the time) for health and prescription drug expenses is $73,000 for men, $95,000 for women, and $168,000 for a couple. This estimate is dramatically less than the one provided by Fidelity, which may be partly explained by the supplement plan preventing large out-of-pocket costs. It is hard to be precise because neither study clarifies their assumptions about important details such as health care cost growth and the discount rate applied to future expenses. To increase the chances for having enough, EBRI also reports on the thresholds for higher expenses, with either health expenses or prescription expenses at the 90th percentile of the cost distribution. If both health care expenses and drug expenses are on the high side, the total costs for the couple grow to $325,000.

A Broader Model for Refining Annual Expense Estimates

These lifetime expense estimates can be useful as a starting point. But the estimates are full of assumptions regarding current costs, inflation rates applied to future costs, discount rates applied to future costs, and the length of retirement. These assumptions can be difficult to unravel, which in turn makes it hard to know how much to set aside annually.

In practical terms, it will be more useful to develop personalized estimates for a retirement health care budget, and to then project how that budget may evolve. This will still require assumptions, as predicting future medical expenses and inflation is inherently complex and uncertain. But we can surely develop more personalized spending estimates.

To start, Vanguard and Mercer developed a more refined model to estimate annual health care costs in their 2018 article, "Planning for Health Care Costs in Retirement." They note that personal cost estimates will relate to factors including health status and risks, the presence of chronic conditions in one's family history, coverage choices regarding Medicare options and other primary or secondary health insurance, the degree of subsidies provided through one's insurance choices, age, location, and whether one pays the IRMAA surcharges on Medicare premiums.

They also emphasize the importance of considering how expenses change after switching to different insurance in retirement, and the potential loss of employer subsidies for insurance. One cannot simply extrapolate pre-retirement health spending into retirement. For example, those using ACA marketplace plans and who do not receive subsidies may see their health spending fall dramatically when switching to Medicare, while those who have highly subsidized employer-based insurance before retirement may not see much change in total health spending.

Geographic location can also have an important impact on costs. Location does not impact Medicare Part B premiums, but Part D, Medicare Advantage, and Medicare supplement premiums can all vary in price by zip code. The Vanguard study found that the cheapest Plan F supplement available by zip code ranged from $1,488 to $3,348 per year in 2017. As well, out-of-pocket care expenses are also linked to local costs-of-living. It will be important to plug in realistic premium and cost estimates as you develop your budget.

Vanguard also considered three risk levels for health spending as based on the presence of twelve chronic health conditions. These twelve conditions include hypertension, high cholesterol, rheumatoid arthritis or osteoarthritis, heart disease, diabetes, chronic kidney disease, depression, Alzheimer's disease or other related dementia, chronic obstructive pulmonary disease, cancer, asthma, and osteoporosis. The study considers the presence of these conditions both in the individual and their parents' medical histories.

Chronic conditions along with smoking status and the number of doctor visits are used to identify high, medium, and low risk categories. High risk characteristics include smoking, frequent doctor visits, and two or more chronic conditions. Low-risk individuals are free of any chronic conditions and do not smoke. Medium risk falls somewhere in between as possible smokers with one chronic condition.

Regarding Medicare Part B and Part D premiums, they do vary by income levels. This becomes an important issue with tax-efficient retirement planning that we discuss further in Chapter 10. There, Exhibit 10.15 shows combined premiums for various incomes levels. In 2021, individuals with modified adjusted gross incomes two years prior of less than $88,000 for singles and $176,000 for those married filing jointly, will face annual Medicare Part B and D premiums of about $2,179 per person, or $4,358 for a couple. The Part B portion is fixed, but the Part D portion varies, and this estimate is based on its average value. Approximately five percent of Medicare recipients are paying higher than this baseline premium level, and so the general cost estimates for health care spending in retirement use these baselines. But at the extreme for the highest income earners, these Medicare premiums alone could be $7,381 per individual or $14,762 for a couple in 2021.

Vanguard models costs for health insurance premiums and out-of-pocket health expenses including dental and vision. They consider cases where an individual uses Original Medicare without a supplement or other secondary coverage, and Original Medicare with a comprehensive supplement. Vanguard models for women because their costs tend to be slightly higher than men, though they note that the gender difference in health costs is less than two percent. They provide results for 65-year-olds.

Exhibit 7.5 provides a summary of their study results. Expenses vary by risk categories as well as whether more comprehensive insurance is used to control out-of-pocket costs. You may wish to inflate these numbers by about 10 to 20 percent to update for today, as the study is from 2018, but these numbers may help you to determine where along the spectrum you may fall before doing a deeper dive to estimate your actual expenses. Vanguard provides the median health spending as well as the distribution of possibilities for different levels of risk when using Original Medicare either with no supplement or with the most comprehensive (at the time) Plan F supplement. As we understand, the higher premiums for Plan F do raise total costs when less health care is needed, but the point of insurance is to reduce the potential costs at the higher percentiles of the distribution. Nonetheless, we do also see that it is only for the higher risk cases that the Medicare supplement helps control costs, as out-of-pocket spending is not otherwise high enough for those falling in the lower and medium risk categories.

This exhibit exposes the tradeoffs that retirees face with their health decisions: pay for comprehensive coverage and your costs are likely to rise on average, though in cases with extremely high expenses you may find a large benefit. We see with Vanguard's study that the cost benefits from a comprehensive supplement do not arise until one is in the higher risk categories. This might speak to the idea of switching to a comprehensive supplement later in retirement, but we have discussed how that may not be possible due to the underwriting. One cannot simply wait until health expenses start to rise and expect to be accepted for a comprehensive Medicare supplement.

Exhibit 7.5
Vanguard Study on the Range of Annual Health Care Costs for a 65-Year-Old Woman with Baseline Medicare Premiums in 2018

Health risk	Low	Medium	High	Low	Medium	High
Geography, cost-of-living	Low	Medium	High	Low	Medium	High
Supplemental coverage	None	None	None	Plan F	Plan F	Plan F
Median	$3,300	$3,900	$7,700	$4,700	$5,200	$6,900
10th percentile	$3,000	$3,200	$3,500	$4,700	$4,900	$5,500
25th percentile	$3,100	$3,400	$4,700	$4,700	$5,000	$5,900
75th percentile	$3,700	$4,900	$13,500	$4,800	$5,600	$8,700
90th percentile	$4,200	$6,600	$21,800	$4,800	$6,000	$11,000

Source: Vanguard, "Planning for Health Care Costs in Retirement"

A retiree must decide whether to obtain a supplement at the beginning and pay the higher premiums for years in anticipation of future benefits when health problems arise. There is no simple answer about how to decide this, as it ultimately depends on your preferences and level of risk aversion. More risk averse individuals would choose a comprehensive supplement to be protected from the beginning, while less risk averse individuals may take their chances with an approach that has lower average costs but more exposure to spending shocks. One may also factor in the degree of set-aside reserves needed for health, which would certainly be less if one chooses to pay for a comprehensive supplement. For those worried about not having enough, skipping the supplement does not necessarily lower the assets one needs to feel comfortable about affording health care. It just shifts more to a need to hold additional reserves outside of the budget.

The other aspect of health expenses is how they will evolve during retirement. Health expenses tend to grow faster than overall inflation. Health care utilization also tends to increase with age as well, separately from inflation, which causes a further increase for the health budget over time. An inflation rate for health care expenses is often estimated at 5 to 7 percent. For Medicare enrollees, Vanguard uses an inflation rate of 5.6 percent for health expenses, compared to 2.6 percent for overall inflation. This indicates a 3 percent real growth rate for health expenses, which would double the real cost after 23 years. Incorporating the idea that health usage tends to also increase with age, it makes sense to build in an assumption that the real cost of health spending will double after 15 to 20 years.

But while health expenses grow, there will likely be offsetting effects as spending in other categories tends to fall over time. David Blanchett has written about the retirement spending smile to explain the patterns of expenditures for typical retirees. At the start of retirement, retirees spend more as they enjoy traveling, eating out, and other types of discretionary expenses. As they continue to age, retirees tend to slow down and spend less. While discretionary expenses are declining, health costs tend to rise, but the overall impact may still be a decline in real spending until very late in retirement. Exhibit 7.6 provides a hypothetical illustration of this process.

Exhibit 7.6
Understanding the Path of Real Retirement Spending by Age

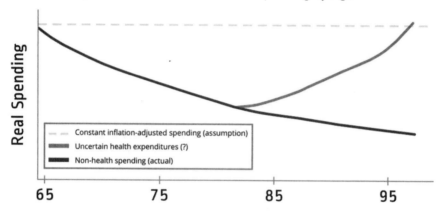

When you create your retirement budget, if you simply assume that your overall budget will grow along with consumer price inflation throughout retirement, then you may already have a sufficiently conservative spending assumption. Even though health expenses can be expected to rise, perhaps at around 5 to 7 percent annually, those increases may be more than offset by declines in other categories, relative to an overall assumption that all expense categories in retirement stay fixed in inflation-adjusted terms. Constant inflation-adjusted spending is a simplifying and conservative assumption that can more than handle the issue of health expense growth in retirement. In other words, you have taken care of this aspect of health spending risk already if you use a simplified assumption that your overall retirement budget will grow with consumer price inflation. If your budget does incorporate reduced spending in other categories with age, then you may find it more important to include an increase in health expenses with age.

Tracking Past Expenses

As a part of the budgeting process described in Chapter 3, it can be helpful to carefully track past expenses related to health care. This includes any out-of-pocket expenses found as you analyze your expense history, including over-the-counter medications or other health expenses that do not go to insurance. But when it comes to expenses reflecting what you paid out of pocket on insurance-covered health care, to get a better sense of overall costs, you may also include a separate accounting for the component of costs that went through your health insurance.

Your insurance documentation will generally provide this information. You might keep detailed information on your health care expenditures in your pre-retirement years: not just the amount you paid, but the amounts covered by the plan and what the costs would have been without health insurance coverage that may have negotiated for a lower rate. Information from the insurer usually indicates the amount billed, the insurance plan discount, the amount paid by the plan, and the out-of-pocket cost. For expenses through health insurance, you could prepare separate lists for prescriptions, health care services, and Medicare non-covered items like dental, vision, and hearing.

Knowing the details around total costs in addition to what is left as an out-of-pocket expense can help you to better understand what your health expenses could be with different coverage. A complication is that many insurers negotiate prices with the health providers (reflected in the insurance plan discount), so that it is hard to know what you might end up paying in the future, but at least tracking this information can give you a better sense about the possibilities. Many insurer websites will provide a straightforward way to download these details into a spreadsheet.

Using past expenses to extrapolate future health expenses has its limitations. New or different health problems may develop, or past health problems may be resolved. Moving to a new location, or even just obtaining insurance from a difference source, can lead to a complete rearrangement regarding the nature of health costs. Subsidies (either from employers or the government) for your coverage can change. Nonetheless, having a better sense about past spending is an important starting point to help clarify the presence of chronic conditions, the use of various medications, the frequency of medical visits, and your typical health expenses.

Creating a Budget and Reserves Estimate

In budgeting for retirement health expenses, we have three levers to adjust when deciding how to manage expected expenses and potential surprises:

- Create a baseline annual budgeted amount to cover health expenses in retirement. Though health spending will fluctuate over time, finding an appropriate average amount should work well as a budgeting device, especially if there is additional insurance to help control the size of spending shocks. The baseline number can be increased to build greater conservatism into the budget.

- Estimate how health costs will change over time both in terms of an overall inflation rate and a potential growing need for care. This can be complicated, but assuming real health expenses will double over 15 to 20 years is a reasonable starting point. Also consider how other budgeted expenses might naturally change over time, especially if health expenses increase. For instance, a travel budget could potentially be tapped for health expenses since the ability to travel may be compromised if severe health situations arise. For most retirees, just having an overall assumption that the budget grows with inflation will be sufficient to handle rising health expenses through offsets in other categories.
- Include a pool of reserve funds that can be tapped to cover unexpected health expenses that exceed the budgeted amounts.

We can develop assumptions for a spending budget with a desired amount of built-in conservatism, and we can also earmark reserves to manage health care spending shocks that extend beyond our assumptions. We can also consider that as health expenses start to increase, this may naturally reduce other expenditures in the budget such as travel and leisure. These natural types of expense offsets may help to control the overall impact of rising health costs. While these costs vary based on personal characteristics, the range of potential costs can be controlled somewhat by using more insurance such as a comprehensive Medicare supplement. That would exchange a fixed premium amount for reduced volatility around the amounts of deductibles, co-payments, and co-insurance paid for health expenses. Regarding reserves set aside for unexpected expenses, they can naturally be less as greater conservatism is otherwise built into the budget and use of insurance. For reserves, keep in mind that the lump-sum estimates for retirement costs we started the section with (such as the $295,000 number for couples from Fidelity) include amounts in the budget already, so health care reserves would not need to be as large.

We now walk through the questions to be answered as a part of making your retirement budget and reserves for health care expenses:

- ☐ Will you use Medicare Part A? Will you pay a premium? Do you have a supplement or other secondary coverage to help with deductibles, co-payments, and co-insurance? What is a reasonable amount to budget for hospital out-of-pocket costs?
- ☐ Will you use Medicare Part B? Will your premium be subject to income related Medicare adjustment amounts? Do you have a supplement or other secondary coverage to help with deductibles, co-payments, and co-insurance? What is a reasonable amount to budget for out-of-pocket costs related to medical expenses?

- ☐ Will you be covered through active employer primary health insurance in retirement? How long might this last? What are your premiums? What is a reasonable amount to budget for out-of-pocket costs related to health expenses? As well, if you are retiring before reaching Medicare eligibility, this category also reflects your pre-retirement health insurance.
- ☐ Will you use a Medicare Advantage plan? Is there an additional premium? Does it include prescription drug coverage or is that needed elsewhere? What is a reasonable amount to budget for out-of-pocket costs related to health expenses?
- ☐ Will you use Medicare Part D? Will your premium be subject to income related Medicare adjustment amounts? What is a reasonable amount to budget for out-of-pocket costs related prescription drugs?
- ☐ Will you use a Medicare supplement plan? What is the premium? The impact on out-of-pocket costs should be reflected through lower cost estimates for Part A and Part B.
- ☐ Will you be covered through other secondary coverage in retirement? How long might this last? What are your premiums? Will it work in place of either prescription coverage or a supplement plan? The impact on out-of-pocket costs should be reflected through other categories.
- ☐ Will you have other noncovered health-related expenses in retirement. This can include items such as dental, eyewear, or hearing aids, over-the-counter medications or other noncovered prescriptions, or other health spending not covered by insurance.
- ☐ Remember, long-term care expenses are a separate topic that will be covered in the next chapter. They are not part of this budget.

Exhibit 7.7 provides an example for how to identify a budget for health expenses. It includes various categories and crosses out the ones not relevant for the example. In this hypothetical example, the couple is not exposed to IRMAA increases for Part B and D premiums. The first spouse chooses Original Medicare with a comprehensive Plan G supplement with estimated premiums of $2,000. Alongside Part B and D premiums, this individual also anticipates $1,200 of out-of-pocket prescription expenses and another $1,000 for noncovered care. This was based on assessments from tracking past health expenses. The second spouse decided to use a Medicare Advantage plan including prescription coverage with $720 of annual premiums. Along with the Part B premium, this spouse anticipates $1,500 of health and prescription out-of-pocket expenses related to Medicare and sets aside another $1,000 for noncovered expenses. Together, this couple budgets $11,464 for retirement health spending. Their budget will use the simplification that these expenses grow for overall inflation, but they will revisit this budget over time as they learn more about their health expenses in retirement and will assume that this budget doubles in real terms starting at age 80.

Exhibit 7.7
Hypothetical Household Budget for a Couple's Health Expenses

	Premiums	Out-of-Pocket Costs
Medicare Part A	$0	$0
Medicare Part B (factor in IRMAA)	$1,782	$0
~~Active Employer-Based Primary Coverage~~	-----------	-----------
~~Medicare Advantage (Part C)~~	-----------	-----------
Medicare Part D (factor in IRMAA)	$480	$1,200
Medicare Supplement	$2,000	(impacts in Part A & B)
~~Other Secondary Insurance Coverage~~	-----------	-----------
Other noncovered health-related expenses	n/a	$1,000
TOTAL		$6,462
Medicare Part A	$0	$0
Medicare Part B (factor in IRMAA)	$1,782	$0
~~Active Employer-Based Primary Coverage~~	-----------	-----------
Medicare Advantage (Part C)	$720	$1,500
~~Medicare Part D (factor in IRMAA)~~	-----------	-----------
~~Medicare Supplement~~	-----------	-----------
~~Other Secondary Insurance Coverage~~	-----------	-----------
Other noncovered health-related expenses	n/a	$1,000
TOTAL		$5,002
TOTAL (Couple)		$11,464

This couple has tried to be conservative with their projected health care expenses. Nonetheless, it can be hard to overcome a nagging feeling that savings are insufficient to overcome whatever retirement throws their way. To help build additional comfort with their planning, the couple decides to earmark additional funds as reserves to cover unexpected health care expenses. The nature of uncertain expenses is difficult to quantify, but to help organize their thinking, Exhibit 7.8 provides a basic calculator to determine how much reserves they wish to set aside at retirement to cover unexpected health care expenses. They are 65 and decide they would feel better if starting at 80 they could handle an additional $2,000 of health expenses through their planning age of 100. The $2,000 of expenses is identified in today's dollars, but the couple includes an assumption that the $2,000 need grows with 5 percent inflation to match health cost growth, while the overall consumer price inflation is 2 percent. Thus, the health care spending amount is growing at about 3 percent faster than the overall inflation rate, which matches the assumption used in the Vanguard study. They also think in terms of the funded ratio from Chapter 3, in which they use a conservative 0 percent real discount factor to determine how much to set aside today to cover this additional expense starting at age 80. The calculation identified that to be comfortable meeting this additional spending need, they would like to have $83,012 of additional reserve assets at the start of retirement to manage their health care spending risk. These inputs we have discussed, including the health care budget and health care reserves estimate, are then used in the overall retirement preparedness calculations in Chapter 3.

Exhibit 7.8
Health Care Reserves Estimator

Current Age	65
Age that Additional Expenditure Begins	80
Age that Additional Expenditure Ends	100
Additional Annual Health Care Expenditure (Today's Dollars)	$2,000
Inflation Rate for Health Care	5%
Overall Inflation Rate	2%
Real Discount Rate	0%
Health Care Reserves (Today's Dollars)	**$83,012**

Action Plan

Health expenses are a major component of retirement spending. Precise expenses can be hard to estimate and become more uncertain because of health spending shocks not covered through insurance. The action plan for health care in retirement relates to finding the appropriate health care and prescription drug coverage throughout retirement and having a plan to cover health care related expenses. This action plan can be organized into several phases: before Medicare eligibility, at Medicare eligibility, and ongoing decision making.

The most risk-averse action plan for retirement health care is generally to enroll in Original Medicare, choose a comprehensive Medicare supplement plan (Plan G for new enrollees), and choose a highly rated Plan D prescription drug plan with reasonable costs for your expected prescriptions. Then each year during the annual open enrollment period, you simply review Plan D options and pick a new plan as desired. Variations for this conservative baseline strategy include foregoing a supplement or secondary coverage plan with Original Medicare, choosing a Medicare Advantage plan, or using other retirement health coverage as a secondary payer or as creditable prescription coverage.

In the years before Medicare eligibility:

- ☐ If retiring before age 65, make sure you have considered how to obtain health insurance and what health costs you will face until reaching Medicare eligibility age
- ☐ Coverage may be available through an employer, a spouse's plan, the Affordable Care Act marketplace, other private insurance, retiree health insurance, a healthshare plan, or COBRA

- ☐ Make sure that spouse and dependents have coverage if you are retiring and leaving your employer plan
- ☐ Develop estimates for a baseline health care budget, how it may grow, and potential cost shifting from other categories
- ☐ Make sure you have budgeted for dental, vision, hearing, or other types of health-related needs that may not be covered by your insurance choices
- ☐ Decide on an amount of reserves to help with higher than anticipated expenses

As you reach Medicare eligibility age:

- ☐ If you would like professional assistance, identify an independent broker specializing in Medicare to guide you
- ☐ If you or your spouse is still actively employed, determine whether your employer health insurance can be counted as primary insurance after you reach age 65
- ☐ If Medicare will become your primary insurance, plan for timely Medicare enrollment to avoid penalties and a lapse in coverage
  - o Read *Medicare and You* book at Medicare.gov
  - o Choose Original Medicare or Medicare Advantage
  - o Choose a Part D drug plan, drug coverage through Medicare Advantage, or coverage through other secondary health insurance with creditable coverage
  - o With Original Medicare, decide whether to purchase a Medicare supplement plan or whether other secondary retirement health insurance can play this role
  - o Determine whether there are any impacts from Medicare decisions on any of your other employer benefits
  - o If thinking to switch from secondary coverage to a supplement later, determine if you will potentially be eligible for a special enrollment period at some point to provide access to some plans without underwriting
  - o Use Plan Finder tool at Medicare.gov/plan-compare
- ☐ Make sure that spouse and dependents have coverage if you are switching your coverage to Medicare
- ☐ Enroll in Medicare online, by phone, or at your local Social Security office
- ☐ Open account at MyMedicare.gov to keep track of your Medicare claims and obtain information about your coverage
- ☐ Medicare personnel are available 24 hours a day by phone for counseling (1-800-633-4227), and you can also talk to knowledgeable volunteers through the Medicare Rights Center (www.medicarerights.org) and your state's State Health Insurance Assistance Program (www.shiptacenter.org)

Ongoing annual decisions:

- ☐ Update health care budget and reserves based on recent spending and health care usage
- ☐ Maintain a list of prescription drugs to use with testing for the best personalized prescription drug plan during each open enrollment
- ☐ Check each year during open enrollment (October 15 to December 7) about a new drug plan and other options
  - o New Part D prescription plan
  - o Move from Medicare Advantage to Original Medicare or vice versa
  - o Choose a new Medicare supplement plan with Original Medicare (be aware of underwriting and the potential denial of your application)
- ☐ Use preventative care benefits and maintain a healthy lifestyle

Finally, I conclude this chapter with a list of potential Medicare mistakes that have arisen in this discussion. Double check that you understand the following points and do not make mistakes in relation to any of them:

- ☐ Medicare coverage is based on individuals. Medicare does not provide family benefits or benefits to a younger spouse. Each spouse can make separate decisions about their own coverage.
- ☐ If you have not claimed Social Security before age 65 (which the lessons of this book suggest should generally be the case), your Medicare enrollment is not automatic. Plan to act.
- ☐ By law Medicare becomes the primary payer for health coverage upon reaching the age of eligibility except for those who can maintain coverage through active employment (by yourself or a spouse) at a firm with at least 20 employees.
- ☐ For those with secondary coverage through other health insurance, it is important to enroll at least in Parts A and B, and then carefully analyze the costs and coverage for different options related to using the secondary insurance or using Medicare for prescription and supplemental coverage.
- ☐ Understand that using only Medicare Parts A, B, and D can lead to significant exposure to uncapped medical expenses if you experience costly health events.
- ☐ Especially if you have secondary coverage that provides primary coverage for other family members, be careful about making decisions that could have unintended consequences as based on the rules of your health plan.
- ☐ Understand that if you do not have primary coverage by law after turning 65 and do not enroll in Medicare, you may find yourself without health coverage and may have to wait up to 15 months to begin coverage during a general enrollment period.
- ☐ When comparing different health options, do not make decisions based solely on which option has the lowest premiums or deductibles. Instead, consider the full costs under various options.

- ☐ Medicare is not meant to be set-it-and-forget-it. Each year you can review your options and make changes to some aspects of your health care coverage as your needs or program benefits change.
- ☐ Understand that outside of the initial enrollment period and somewhat with special enrollment periods, applications for Medicare supplements will be underwritten and potentially denied. Those wanting a comprehensive supplement should consider enrolling during their initial Medigap Open Enrollment Period.
- ☐ Taking care of your health and using preventative care can provide long-term cost savings and a higher quality of life.

Further Reading

Department of Health and Human Services. 2021. *Medicare and You: The Official U.S. Government Medicare Book*. Available at https://www.medicare.gov/Pubs/pdf/10050-Medicare-and-You.pdf

Guyton, Derek, Jennifer Leming, Stephen Weber, Jacklin Youssef, and Jean Young. 2018. "Planning for Health Care Costs in Retirement." Vanguard Research (June).

Oh, Jae W. 2020. *Maximize Your Medicare: Qualify for Benefits, Protect Your Health, and Minimize Your Costs*. 2020-2021 Edition. New York City: Allworth Press.

Moeller, Philip. 2016. *Get What's Yours for Medicare: Maximize Your Coverage, Minimize Your Costs*. New York City: Simon & Schuster.

Chapter 8: Long-Term Care Planning

Most of the research about retirement income planning focuses on two of the three major retirement risks: market volatility and longevity risk. The question to be answered is how well does a predetermined spending plan work in the face of low returns and a long life? The third major risk of spending shocks receives less attention. Being able to meet a predetermined spending plan alone is not sufficient. There must also be mechanisms in place to deal with the various contingencies and unexpected spending shocks that may arise during a long retirement.

Long-term care (LTC) spending represents perhaps the most severe spending shock that can impact retirees. Long-term care is a general category for care related to physical, mental, social, and medical needs in the event of significant physical or mental decline. The potential for such decline accelerates with age. This is a distinct matter from general health care expenses which were covered in the previous chapter.

Lifetime long-term care expenses for retirees are uncertain. About half of retirees may be able to make it through retirement without facing even $1 of long-term care expenses. But at the extreme, long-term care costs can exceed $1 million. An expensive LTC event could derail an otherwise well-built retirement plan. This problem is growing as people live longer, since it becomes more likely that care will be needed for longer as well. Older individuals suffer from higher rates of physical and cognitive problems, and they may have fewer family members or friends who are positioned to provide sustained daily assistance.

Because costs for care are high, and the probabilities that care will be needed are not particularly low, most long-term care funding strategies will add significant expenses to a retirement plan. These expenses can manifest in the form of insurance premiums or as additional reserve assets to be set aside beyond assets needed for lifestyle, longevity, and legacy.

Planning for how to manage these potential expenses is an important part of a retirement income plan. However, it is often overlooked or avoided. Many are unwilling to confront the questions and possibilities related to losing their own independence. Psychologically, it can be difficult to face morbidity as no one likes thinking about the possibility of being unable to effectively handle the basic activities of daily living. It is a natural response to think that this is something that only happens to other people.

A common misperception also remains that Medicare pays for long-term care. It does not. Few people make proper plans for long-term care. This lack of planning can create strains as long-term care expenses deplete household assets, bankrupt a surviving spouse, or add burdens for other family members who may end up making large sacrifices to provide care.

The default long-term care plan will be to self-fund expenses until assets are depleted and to then transition into Medicaid. But there are other possibilities. No retirement income plan is complete without a proper consideration of how to plan most effectively for potential LTC expenses.

Defining a Long-Term Care Need

Long-term care is generally defined as requiring assistance with normal activities of daily living (ADLs) for more than 100 days. Any event lasting less than 100 days, such as recovery after a surgery, is not considered to be a long-term care need and would also have a smaller financial impact on the household. However, common statistics about how most people will need long-term care, such as the oft-cited number at longtermcare.gov that at least 70 percent of people aged 65 and older will need long-term care services during their lifetimes, also generally include short-term care.

More specifically, especially when it comes to qualifying for long-term care benefits, a long-term care need is defined as requiring help with two or more of six common ADLs: bathing, continence (maintaining control of bowel and bladder functions), dressing, eating, toileting, and transferring – such as to or from a bed. Difficulties with dressing and bathing generally develop first. Defining exactly when long-term care is needed to qualify for benefits can become a rather technical issue, and it is generally determined by a physician or other medical professional. Cognitive impairments such as dementia may also serve as an indicator for a long-term care need, even if the impairment does not immediately lead to an inability to perform ADLs. Triggers for requiring long-term care can relate to both physical and mental decline.

Higher order activities which may require assistance without necessarily qualifying for long-term care benefits include managing household finances, driving, and housecleaning. This assistance would more commonly be provided by family and friends, rather than formally hired caregivers. These are called incidental activities for daily living (IADLs).

Costs and Prevalence of Long-Term Care

How likely is a person to experience a need for long-term care? Long-term care needs are a possibility which should be planned for, so the specific probability with which they happen is less important. Nonetheless, it is understandable to want to know more about the possibilities. This is a challenging question, and we can find occasional research reports that address it. Fortunately, to avoid having to use even older reports, the

Department of Health and Human Services (DHHS) issued a research brief on this topic in January 2021, which provides information and estimates for individuals turning age 65 in the years 2020 to 2024. They estimate forward-looking lifetime long-term care needs and costs for this population.

Exhibit 8.1 show the DHHS estimates that 51 percent of men and 61 percent of women in this age group will need long-term care at some point, and that the average lengths for care are 2.3 years for men and 3.2 years for women. They also estimated that 41 percent of men and 50 percent of women will require care for one year or longer, while 18 percent of men and 26 percent of women will need care for at least 5 years. Across the population, 56 percent will need care for an average of 2.8 years, with 22 percent of the population requiring care for at least 5 years. Those who will experience long-term-care needs are not an insignificant portion of the population. Many retirees will require long-term care support during their lifetimes, so careful planning is warranted.

Exhibit 8.1
Projected Long-Term Care Needs, Persons Turning 65 in 2020-24

	Men	Women	Combined
Percentage who will need care	51%	61%	56%
Average number of years	2.3	3.2	2.8
Percentage needing no care	49%	39%	44%
Percentage needing 1 year or less	10%	11%	10%
Percentage needing 1-2 years	9%	9%	9%
Percentage needing 2-5 years	14%	16%	15%
Percentage needing 5+ years	18%	26%	22%

Source: Department of Health and Human Services, January 2021

The estimates in Exhibit 8.1 include time spent receiving care at home from unpaid caregivers, which is a substantial portion of the care received. Exhibit 8.2 provides numbers that are less dire, as it looks only at the need for *paid* long-term care, with unpaid care provided by family and friends at home excluded from the estimates. With this adjustment, 41 percent of men and 53 percent of women will use paid care during their remaining lifetimes. Average durations are much less, as men use paid care for an average of 0.9 years while women need 1.3 years of care. Only 5 percent of men and 9 percent of women will use paid care for 5 or more years. Combined, 47 percent of the population turning 65 in 2020 to 2024 are projected to use paid care for an average of 1.1 years, with 7 percent requiring paid care for at least 5 years.

Exhibit 8.2
Projected Use of Paid Long-Term Care, Persons Turning 65 in 2020-24

	Men	Women	Combined
Percentage who will need paid care	41%	53%	47%
Average number of years	0.9	1.3	1.1
Percentage needing no paid care	59%	47%	53%
Percentage needing 1 year or less	18%	21%	20%
Percentage needing 1-2 years	8%	9%	8%
Percentage needing 2-5 years	10%	15%	12%
Percentage needing 5+ years	5%	9%	7%

Source: Department of Health and Human Services, January 2021

As for the costs of lifetime care, DHHS uses cost estimates for the Genworth study we discuss shortly, and projects them to the future with assumptions that institutional care prices will grow at 3.8 percent annually and home care prices will grow at 3.2 percent annually. Their modeling estimates long-term care utilization at different ages. Discounting at their 2.5 percent assumed rate of consumer price inflation (which means a real discount rate of 0 percent) to be consistent with our descriptions about discounting future costs into today's dollars, they estimate that average lifetime expenditures for the 41 percent of men needing paid care are $142,200 in 2020 dollars. For the 53 percent of women needing paid care, the average lifetime cost in 2020 dollars is $175,500. Averaging between genders, those needing paid care over their lifetime would require an average of $161,400 to be set aside by the age of 65. These expenditures do include amounts from Medicaid, which can provide relief for those with an expectation that Medicaid will be a necessary funding mechanism. For others, these amounts are paid out-of-pocket or through insurance.

Long-term care planning is an especially important consideration for women. Wives tend to be younger than their husbands and tend to also live longer. Women are more likely to experience a period of widowhood. They are more likely to serve as long-term caregivers for the men in their lives, and they are then more likely to be widowed and alone by the time they need their own care. The DHHS estimates show that on average women will require $33,300 more to be set aside by 65 to cover their additional long-term care expenses. Women may have fewer financial assets remaining by the point they need care as well, especially in cases when a spouse required care earlier.

The need for long-term care can be triggered by accidents, chronic illness, or conditions such as Alzheimer's disease. The need for care increases with age, though accidents and illness can cause younger people to also need care. With age, the odds for needing care increase as debilitating conditions like strokes and dementia leave more individuals vulnerable. At a personal level, the odds for needing long-term care are higher for individuals with greater longevity in their family history and for those with a family medical history including dementia, Alzheimer's disease, and neurological disorders. Healthy individuals might ironically be more in need of care, as living a long life also means experiencing greater odds for physical or mental decline near the end.

I just provided lifetime care cost estimates from DHHS. Those estimates were based on the annual *Cost of Care Survey* from Genworth, a major provider of long-term care insurance. The most recent version of this study is for costs in 2020, and their estimates are shown in Exhibit 8.3. Costs for long-term care vary by geographic region, type of facility and services used, and reasons for care. Genworth provides estimates at the local level, but I will describe the national median costs. Annual care costs for those remaining at home average $53,772 for those needing homemaker services (assistance with cooking, cleaning, and errands), $54,912 for those needing a home health aide (personal care to help with ADLs, but not medical care), and $19,236 for adult day care services. For those requiring institutionalized care, the median annual costs in the United States are $51,600 for an assisted living facility, $93,072 for a semi-private room in a nursing home, and $105,852 for a private nursing home room.

Exhibit 8.3
Median Costs of Long-Term Care in the United States, 2020

	Daily	Monthly	Annually
Homemaker services	$147	$4,481	$53,772
Home health aide	$150	$4,576	$54,912
Adult day care	$53	$1,603	$19,236
Assisted living facility	$141	$4,300	$51,600
Nursing home (semi-private room)	$255	$7,756	$93,072
Nursing home (private room)	$290	$8,821	$105,852

Source: Genworth Cost of Care Survey, 2021

It is important to emphasize that these are median values at the national level. Median costs in specific states vary widely. For instance, a private room in a nursing home generally exceeds $100k per year in the northeast, the upper midwest, the west coast, Alaska, and Hawaii. Alaska is an anomaly, with a $436,540 median annual cost. Within the continental United States, Connecticut is most expensive state with a $172,280 median annual cost. The cheapest state is Missouri, where the annual median cost is $68,985. Annual median costs in 2020 also fell below $80k in Arkansas, Texas, Louisiana, and Oklahoma.

It is also important to consider inflation for long-term care costs, as these reported costs are only for a calendar year. Generally, the cost of long-term care has risen faster than overall consumer price inflation. Cost increases stabilized in recent years as more facilities have opened, but the demographic trends show more people needing care and fewer people available to provide it, suggesting that cost increases could be substantial in the coming years as baby boomers approach their 70s and 80s. For the Genworth cost surveys from 2014 to 2020, the 5-year annualized growth rates for median costs across the United States were 3.8 percent for homemaker services, 3.71 percent for home health aides, 1.45 percent for adult day care, 3.62 percent for assisted living, and 3 percent for nursing home facilities. This is a period where overall inflation averaged about 1.8 percent per year. Those who may not need long-term care support until 20 to 30 years from now should surely anticipate that the costs they will face are going to grow faster than the overall inflation rate.

Demographic Challenges

The need for long-term care will continue to grow as baby boomers start to reach more advanced ages and people continue to live longer than ever before, requiring a longer period for care. As one example of the growing trend, the number of Americans afflicted with Alzheimer's disease could triple by 2050 without significant medical advances to stop the disease.

Changing demographics also feed into this concern, as the proportion of older people relative to younger people continues to increase. As Americans are having fewer children, and as dual-income households in which both spouses maintain careers have become the norm, there will be fewer opportunities to obtain long-term care support from children or other family members as well as fewer people in the labor force who could be paid to provide care. Family members who are ultimately forced to leave the workforce to provide care will sacrifice lost wages, Social Security benefits, and savings. Additionally, the stress from providing such care could also lead to greater health problems for the caregiver.

An aging population with fewer younger family members to provide care, coupled with fewer young people in general who can serve as paid providers for long-term care services, will likely continue to increase the future costs of quality care. The impacts of increasing demand for care and the decreasing supply of caregivers means inevitably higher prices unless new technological improvements and automation can be developed to allow more care needs to be met without human intervention.

Different funding sources for long-term care needs will be discussed shortly, but an immediate implication for these demographic trends is that the idea of planning ahead to spend down assets to receive long-term care services through Medicaid may become an increasingly unattractive option for those who can otherwise afford to avoid it. With fewer available workers, there is a risk that care quality provided through Medicaid facilities may decline in the future.

The Continuum of Long-Term Care

Many receive long-term care at their homes or at community centers or adult day care centers. Institutionalized living is not always required, and proper long-term care planning may allow one to remain at home for longer than otherwise possible. For many, staying at home will be preferable during the transition when more long-term care assistance starts to be needed. However, additional options along the continuum of care include assisted living facilities, continuing care retirement communities, and nursing homes. Though some of these options may be skipped for any individual, long-term care needs generally progress along these lines:

- Assistance provided by friends and families at home
- Home visits from health care aides
- Adult day care centers
- Assisted living
- Nursing home
- Hospice

It is important to distinguish between two types of care: *skilled* and *custodial*. Skilled care is for when intensive medical attention is needed, generally for less than 100 days as it results from a short-term medical condition from which the patient is expected to recover. Private health insurance and Medicare may both cover short-term skilled care needs when certain conditions are met.

Custodial care – also known as "non-skilled care" – is for patients with a chronic condition from which recovery is not expected. This care is mostly for help with activities of daily living (ADLs), rather than providing specific medical treatments. Custodial care does not require a professional and can be provided by family members or unlicensed workers. Most long-term care falls into the category of custodial care.

Health insurance and Medicare do not cover custodial care, as they are reserved for care relating to acute medical conditions and short-term needs with expected recovery. Custodial care must be funded by other means such as personal savings, Medicaid, or long-term care insurance.

When looking for specific care options, it may be helpful to work with a geriatric care manager or care coordinator who knows the options in your area. These are paid professionals who can help guide you through the various care options and supporting services. Some long-term care insurance policies will provide a care coordinator as a policy benefit.

Home Care

Long-term care generally begins with receiving some assistance at home, especially with proper planning to make funding for this possible. Home care is typically provided by unpaid family members, though care from paid providers such as home health aides is also a common approach. Many businesses offer home care services, making the option to stay at home more viable today than in the past. Even with family members available to provide care, enlisting paid support can reduce family stress and help family members focus more on social interactions and less on care needs.

The "aging in place" movement has risen from growing recognition that it will ultimately be cheaper for society if individuals can stay at home longer instead of moving to an institution. Staying at home also generally helps to support the physical and emotional health of the care recipient if the individual does not become too socially isolated. More resources are available to support aging in place. Homes can be retrofitted in many ways to allow for better support and to make homes safer. Community services are available that provide meals, social interaction, and transportation to doctor appointments. Medicaid is also simplifying the process to cover home care especially as part of the response to the global pandemic.

Adult Day Care, Community Centers, and Other Respite Support

When unpaid family members serve as the primary long-term care providers, services such as adult day care centers can give caregivers the freedom to go to work or otherwise take a break from the ongoing demands of providing care. Services providing respite support allow a primary caregiver to have short breaks. Visits to such centers can also benefit the patient, as regular social interaction can help sustain the patient's ability to live at home longer, thus delaying the transition to a more institutionalized living environment. Such services are becoming more popular to help facilitate the growing demands of the aging population. Many communities will also provide senior community centers that offer a variety of resources and social activities for the community.

Assisted Living Facilities

Next are assisted living facilities for individuals who still maintain some independence, but who do also need more assistance. Support and services vary widely among different assisted living facilities, but they usually provide meals, help with medication, housekeeping, transportation, daily assistance for ADLs at scheduled times, and recreational and social activities. Many assisted living facilities are equipped to provide varying degrees of care up to the point of requiring full-time nursing care.

Generally, one must pay out-of-pocket to live at an assisted-living facility, especially if the move is made before the requirements to trigger benefits from long-term care insurance have been met. Costs may involve an upfront fee and ongoing monthly fees. Assisted living facilities tend to be less regulated and it is important to review their contracts with an elder law attorney. Important questions to ask a facility include what the monthly fees cover and how they may change in the future. Important non-financial questions when considering assisted-living facilities include:

- Who assesses what care is needed and when needs change?
- What limits are placed on the amount of care received?
- What is the process for determining when conditions have worsened so that care can no longer be provided at the facility?
- What happens if the resident runs out of funds to pay the ongoing fees?
- How are grievances handled with respect to issues about joining meals, taking medication, moving around inside or outside the community, and so on?
- What is the housekeeping schedule, and how is assistance for various activities of daily living scheduled?
- Are the staff properly trained and what qualifications do they hold?
- Does the facility have resources to provide sufficient support to residents who may show initial signs of dementia or confusion about their circumstances?

Nursing Homes

When most people think of long-term care, their image probably involves care at a nursing home. More options are available today for home care and assisted living, which will help many avoid ever having to use the nursing home option. But nursing homes serve as a last resort for those requiring extensive long-term and medical care services in the final months or years of life. The quality and costs of nursing homes vary, and those who can pay through means other than Medicaid may find they receive better arrangements.

Nursing homes are state-licensed facilities providing residents with skilled and custodial care services. They tend to provide the most expensive level of care services but can offer 24-hour care to residents. Some nursing homes may have specific wings for Alzheimer's patients. Medicare provides a Nursing Home Compare service at their website (www.medicare.gov) to help learn about certified options in your local community. Certified nursing care facilities are eligible to receive Medicare and Medicaid payments, which is important if you run out of funding during your stay and need support from Medicaid.

Hospice Care

Hospice care is available at the end of life to relieve discomfort for terminally ill patients who are not expected to recover. Hospice care can be provided in one's home or at an institution. Medicare may cover hospice care if a doctor certifies that the patient is expected to live for less than six months.

Continuing Care Retirement Communities (CCRCs)

Another option for long-term care is a continuing care retirement community (CCRC). These begin with independent living and provide a full range of long-term care services from active and independent living to assisted living to nursing care in the same community. CCRCs provide the option to increase care as needed over time. With all levels of care provided, CCRCs are meant to be a permanent solution for retirement living needs. It can be challenging or costly to modify a CCRC contract if one decides to leave.

Most CCRCs will require that new residents can still live fully independently upon moving in. If greater care is already needed, the application to the CCRC may be rejected. CCRCs also generally require an entrance fee and monthly payments. Entrance fees can be high, even up to $400,000. These fees can be structured as all-inclusive or paid on a fee-for-service basis as needed with a smaller upfront fee. The all-inclusive version can be viewed as an alternative way to obtain long-term care protection, such that also having long-term care insurance may mean doubling up unnecessarily if choosing a full-service CCRC option. The initial contract should state the nature of housing and long-term care services to be provided for life.

An important distinction for CCRCs is that future nursing home care services are included as part of the initial package, which reduces the need to find a new facility in the future. This can be convenient for spouses and friends in the community to make visits after nursing home care is needed, since the facility is close by. Some CCRCs require the purchase of a group long-term care insurance contract as an entrance requirement.

Important questions to ask when considering CCRCs include:

- What is the entrance fee and is it refundable?
- What do the monthly fees cover?
- What are other possible expenses in addition to monthly fees?
- What is the nature of accommodations, and do these accommodations change if one member in a couple transitions to nursing care?
- Can monthly fees increase and under what circumstances?
- What types of long-term care services are provided and what is the cost for additional services?
- Does the facility require a long-term care insurance policy?
- Is there a waiting list for entering?

Long-Term Care and the Global Pandemic

Incidence of COVID-19, visiting restrictions, and threats to their financial sustainability have placed long-term care facilities at the center of the news about the global pandemic in 2020. This may lead to permanent changes in how long-term care institutions fit into retirement planning. It is possible that such institutions will play a smaller role in the future. Individuals may be less comfortable with financial models that involve paying a large upfront fee for the provision of lifetime care. We may see an even faster shift toward the provision of care at home as individuals may view long-term care institutions as riskier places to live.

With CCRCs, the resident must trust that the managing company will remain in business to provide the contracted services over the long term. This is a reasonable concern, so it is acceptable and important to vet the financial strength of the facility to help determine if it is on a sustainable trajectory. Having a well-qualified elder law attorney review the stipulations in any contract is important.

Options for Funding Long-Term Care Expenses

The four general ways to finance long-term care expenses include:

- Self-funding with personal assets
- Medicaid
- Traditional long-term care insurance (LTCI)
- Hybrid policies combining long-term care with life insurance or annuities

To better understand the options, the overall cost of long-term care can be defined as:

LTC Cost = LTC Expenses + LTCI Premiums – LTCI Benefits

This equation highlights that the overall cost of funding long-term care is comprised of the actual expenses for care plus any premiums paid for long-term care insurance, less any benefits received (including death benefits or other auxiliary benefits, when applicable) from the insurance policies. For this formula, one may consider Medicaid payments as a type of insurance benefit that reduces out-of-pocket expenses. It is the net out-of-pocket expenses that matter. When experiencing LTC spending shocks, the formula suggests that insurance has positive value if its benefits exceed the premiums to help reduce the overall care costs.

Before we go any further, notice that Medicare and health insurance are *not* on the above list of funding options. The misperception that Medicare provides long-term care support is common. But Medicare provides support only in limited situations when an individual spent at least three days in a hospital and is then confined to home or an institution, requires skilled nursing or rehabilitative care for the same condition from a Medicare-certified professional as prescribed by a doctor, and is expecting a full recovery. When these conditions apply, full benefits last 20 days and partial support ends after 100 days. For eligible veterans, benefits from the Veterans Administration may provide a care option.

Numerous considerations are involved in deciding between the four funding options: age, health, ability to receive help from family or friends without overburdening them, wealth levels and how they may relate to Medicaid qualifications, legacy objectives, risk tolerance related to the financial impact of unknown long-term care events, and the costs and benefits of different types of insurance. As far as funding is concerned, developing a written plan, and sharing it with family members can help to avoid misunderstandings about providing and paying for care. You should also ensure family members know about any funds set aside or any insurance policies designed to support care in case you are incapacitated when care needs arise.

Self-Funding

Self-funding means long-term care expenses will be paid through distributions from household assets. Potential funding sources could include investments, cash value in life insurance policies, or home equity. This strategy keeps the full risk for long-term care spending on the household and results in the widest range of potential spending outcomes. If no long-term care event occurs, there is no cost for self-funding. Any reserves that had been set-aside for long-term care will likely wind up as part of a larger legacy. But without any risk-sharing, the full burden of potentially very high expenses remains as a risk for the retirement plan.

Risk-averse individuals may prefer to pay a premium to better protect wealth in the event of an expensive long-term care event, even if this carries a loss should no long-term care event arise. Risks of self-funding include potential high costs, investment risks for the underlying assets, and difficulties with managing investment assets after a long-term care need begins. Unknown spending needs also require setting aside reserve assets to feel comfortable that there will be enough to self-fund care, which raises the amount of assets required to feel financially independent.

For self-funding, ask yourself if you have sufficient financial resources to cover an expensive long-term care shock and still meet the remaining financial goals for retirement. Which specific resources could be used for long-term care expenses? How will they be invested? What impact would these expenditures have on the standard of living for remaining household members and potential beneficiaries? Is this a risk that can be accepted, or could insurance provide a positive impact by helping pool this risk and reduce the potential size of the shock?

When discussing the budget in Chapter 3, I provided an example for a couple that did not have other forms of long-term care protection and included about $500,000 as a contingency liability to cover long-term care expenses after also considering other offsets to the budget created by an LTC need. We will walk through the example for obtaining that estimate near the end of this chapter. It provides a framework for thinking about self-funding. Though it is hard to be precise with this quantification, the budgeted amount should be in the ballpark of providing a 90 percent chance that enough is being set aside to cover the eventual long-term care expenses if both members of a couple require paid care. When considering whether self-funding is the right approach, one might also estimate how much those reserves could be reduced while still feeling comfortable with the plan if insurance benefits are also available. Clearly, the self-funding option is only possible for those with sufficient discretionary assets to meet potential expenses. With sufficient assets, those with high risk tolerance may prefer the increasing variability in net care expenses from self-funding. Others with a lower risk tolerance might choose to pool some of the risks through an insurance company.

Another risk tolerance consideration with self-funding is what kind of investment returns can be earned by the reserve assets. The more conservatively the assets earmarked for long-term care are invested, the less potential upside growth they can obtain. Those with a greater risk tolerance who invest more aggressively may find that self-funding fits their circumstances, though they are taking on risk about the amount of available funds, while those who would otherwise invest the assets more conservatively – in cash or CDs, perhaps – may benefit more from an insurance solution that is priced assuming similarly low underlying returns.

The self-funding route may also be more attractive to individuals with a family history free of health problems that result in the need for long-term care. Also, those with the potential to receive care from family or friends without creating an excess burden may feel that self-funding is a safer bet as overall costs will be less even with a greater care need.

Along these lines, self-funding could force a retiree to rely more greatly on family care, which introduces potential opportunity costs not included in formal cost calculations. Up to 70 percent of long-term care may be supported informally by family members. Caregivers often experience increased stress and health problems, and they could be forced to make sacrifices in their careers that could result in substantially reduced lifetime earnings. The health problems created by providing long-term care could potentially result in the caregiver eventually also needing long-term care.

One other matter that should be mentioned about self-funding is the potential psychological risk of feeling guilty about spending on long-term care when it is needed. Even without explicit pressure, there is a natural hesitancy that some may have about spending assets on their own long-term care needs. There can be feelings of guilt related to the perception of spending someone else's inheritance. In some cases, family pressure may be explicit, resulting in less long-term care usage to preserve funds for an inheritance. This issue may be important with second marriages and conflicts between children from earlier marriages and the new spouse. Having long-term care insurance can solve for this potential problem, even for the wealthy who could afford to self-fund, as one rarely would feel guilty about spending the insurance company's money.

We can also briefly mention another more imprecise long-term care funding source. Some individuals view qualified longevity annuity contracts or other deferred income annuities as a funding means for long-term care. This is an imprecise method based on the idea of planning to have increased sources of income starting at around age 80 or 85, which corresponds to when one is more likely to face long-term care expenses.

Medicaid

Medicaid is the most common funding option for paid long-term care in the United States. It generally serves as a last-resort once assets and income decline to sufficiently low levels. Medicaid is the main option for those entering retirement with little savings. It is also the go-to for continuing with care after available resources have been depleted.

The qualifications for Medicaid – assets, income, and medical need – vary widely by state. This makes it hard to generalize about the process. Some states require relative impoverishment to qualify for Medicaid, while others allow substantial assets to be set aside for a spouse through the community spouse resource amount. As well, some states allow qualification only for the "categorically needy" whose income and wealth falls below thresholds without considering medical bills, while other states have more generous "medically needy" rules that allow for benefits when LTC expenses otherwise push higher incomes below the thresholds.

To a limited extent, it may be possible to reposition assets with the aid of an elder law attorney to work around Medicaid rules and gain access to care with some assets still protected. This is a controversial strategy known as "Medicaid planning." Some view it as unethical, while others say they are entitled to the welfare benefits through their lifetime tax payments.

For this process, there are countable and non-countable assets when determining Medicaid eligibility, which can differ by state. A simple part of the planning process is to move assets from countable categories to non-countable categories, or to simply spend from countable categories on items not covered by Medicaid such as hearing aids or a specialized wheelchair. Other ideas include paying down a mortgage, making home improvements, or purchasing a new car. Spousal retirement plans are non-countable in some states, which suggests trying to preserve those. Some states do not count the primary residence, an automobile, assets belonging to a family business, furniture, or other personal belongings. Spouses also have protections to maintain some assets for their own use.

Medicaid is making such planning increasingly difficult by limiting the ability to transfer assets so that they do not get used to pay for long-term care. There is now a five-year look-back period on any asset transfers to determine if they are acceptable or if Medicaid eligibility will be delayed to account for the transfers. Any invalid transfers will delay Medicaid benefits by the number of months equal to the transfer amount divided by the average monthly nursing facility cost in the state. Invalid transfers may also include annuity purchases or moving assets to a trust. Transfers made at least 60 months before care is requested are allowed, which can benefit those making plans well in advance. Also, efforts to recover Medicaid benefits from the estates of beneficiaries have increased as states work harder to reduce overall Medicaid expenditures. This can include placing a lien on the home that was considered as a non-countable asset during life. A specialized elder law attorney can guide this planning.

Medicaid planning may be helpful for those with limited resources and health problems preventing them from qualifying for long-term care insurance. Available resources may still need to be spent on long-term care needs, and qualification for Medicaid could occur if long-term care needs persist. The perception that wealthy individuals are qualifying for Medicaid while protecting significant assets is likely overstated.

Because Medicaid reimbursement to long-term care facilities is generally lower than the true cost, self-funding patients may receive priority admission – and potentially higher-quality care – over Medicaid patients. It can be helpful to enter a nursing home or other institution before beginning Medicaid receipt. Also, understand the institution's procedures for what happens if you switch to Medicaid after care begins, as you may be moved to a less desirable room. As an increasing number of people require long-term care, making it difficult for everyone to receive the same high quality, those who would otherwise be able to cover their bills outside of Medicaid may come to regret using Medicaid planning techniques that lead to lower quality care. Nonetheless, Medicaid remains as an important funding source for those lacking other options.

Traditional Long-Term Care Insurance

The traditional health-based long-term care insurance (LTCI) strategy involves paying an ongoing premium for long-term care insurance until a long-term care event takes place, and then gaining eligibility to receive a defined amount of long-term care benefits for a defined period as care is received. Estimates from the National Association of Insurance Commissioners in 2018 suggest that less than six percent of the population aged 50 and older in the United States have a LTCI policy. While it is not popular in practice, a description of this tool is worthwhile to ensure that the option is understood and utilized when helpful.

At the point that one can set aside enough reserve assets to feel comfortable, wealth becomes sufficient to self-fund long-term care expenses. But reasonable individuals may still decide to include insurance in their plans as part of an overall risk management strategy. The potential benefits from having LTCI include the risk management aspect that overall costs can be reduced when significant long-term care needs happen. This leverages the potential value of long-term care dollars by incorporating risk pooling to extend their reach through the benefits. With LTCI, less reserves need to be set aside for the purpose of funding long-term care. Long-term care insurance can also help with maintaining independence by allowing for the receipt of care without burdening family members and being more willing to receive care without the guilt of spending someone's inheritance. Many long-term care policies will also include the provision of a care coordinator who can help manage the long-term care process and gain access to the best facilities or home-care programs. Beneficiaries from these policies may receive better guidance about finding good care, and they may receive better opportunities to enter high-quality facilities.

Wealth levels can be too low to benefit from insurance. Premiums may not be affordable, and there could be a risk of lapsing on the policy if premiums become too much of a burden. There may be little that can be done to avoid the eventual need for Medicaid. It may make less sense to purchase insurance if there is not much wealth to protect and Medicaid will ultimately pay for care. One might hold a small amount of insurance as part of a transition into Medicaid eligibility.

Some states also have state partnership programs in which qualified insurance policies can help to protect assets from subsequent Medicaid eligibility. The amount of insurance benefits become a protected amount of non-countable household assets for Medicaid qualification, once the full benefit amount of the policy has been received. These policies are only relevant for individuals who may need Medicaid at some point. As these decisions depend upon the varying rules for each state, seeking guidance from a local elder care law attorney will be valuable.

There are risks for owning long-term care insurance. Risks include the potential for premium increases, the possibility that long-term care costs will exceed available benefits, and the possibility that claims will be denied or that certain expenses are not covered by the policy.

Variables to consider when determining whether to purchase a long-term care policy include age, health status, and family medical history. These factors help to determine the probability for requiring care as well as the level of policy premiums. Naturally, the odds for needing care rise at higher ages, for those with poor health, and for those with a family history of dementia or other debilitating conditions.

Consider available financial resources when thinking about long-term care insurance. Can you comfortably pay the premiums, and is it reasonable to expect that premiums can be paid even with premium hikes? In terms of total assets, are you able to self-fund long-term care? If so, are you willing to take the risk about the total cost for self-funding, or would you rather use insurance to help narrow the tails for potential costs? In this context, risk tolerance can be measured as your degree of willingness to subject your standard of living and/or legacy objectives to the risk of substantial long-term care spending shocks. Risk averse individuals are more willing to pay an insurance premium to offset the impact of a significant long-term care shock.

Upon deciding to purchase an insurance policy, it is best not to wait too long before doing so. A general guideline is that it is appropriate to start a policy while in your 50s, though there can be valid reasons to start sooner or later. Generally, you do not want to wait too long to start because premiums can increase with age at rates faster than the savings from not starting sooner, and because there is a growing risk that you will develop health problems that will disqualify you from initiating coverage. The process requires underwriting, and once health conditions have developed which make the need for care more likely, it may be too late to qualify.

Nonetheless, at younger ages there may be other insurance needs which weigh more heavily when determining how to allocate a limited pool of dollars. For a young person with a family to support, life insurance and disability insurance may be more important than long-term care insurance. It is important to find the balance between being old enough that other insurance needs have been sufficiently met, while being young enough to still be in good health to qualify for coverage with reasonable premiums.

Some policies offer a shared benefits rider for couples, which can be substantially cheaper than buying two separate policies. A joint policy can provide lower costs because it is less likely that two spouses will require expensive care, and because one spouse will often provide care to the other, which reduces claims on the insurance policy. There is a risk, though, that one spouse uses up all the available benefits.

How much does LTCI cost? When searching for current prices, the only online calculator I could find is at the Mutual of Omaha website. Exhibit 8.4 provides examples of premiums from their cost calculator as based on starting age for the policy. The policy I checked provides a $4,500 monthly benefit and a 36-month benefit period, for a total benefit pool of $162,000. There is no inflation adjustment for the benefit, and benefits begin after a 90-day wait period. The couple's premium reflects purchase by each spouse with a 15 percent discount for both using insurance. It is not a pooled benefit though, as each has a separate three years of coverage.

Exhibit 8.4
Annual Premiums for Mutual of Omaha Long-Term Care Insurance
Cost for Monthly Maximum Benefit of $4,500, 36-month Benefit Period

Initial Age	Male	Female	Couple
45 years old	$1,884	$3,096	$4,233
50 years old	$2,076	$3,432	$4,682
55 years old	$2,304	$3,876	$5,253
60 years old	$2,664	$4,536	$6,120
65 years old	$3,336	$5,592	$7,589

Note: For residents of Virginia. Rates may vary by state. Quotes obtained on March 15, 2021. Policy provides 36 months of benefits ($162,000 total coverage per person). https://www.mutualofomaha.com/long-term-care-insurance/calculator

We can further analyze these numbers to better understand the potential value proposition of the insurance. The sooner LTC is needed so that premiums end and benefits start, the better is the financial outcome from the insurance. Suppose that premiums do not ever increase and that a LTC need begins at age 85 allowing for maximum benefits to be received for next three years. As the 50-year-old mark is a commonly suggested age for starting insurance, I will use this as an example. The 50-year-old pays premiums for 35 years through age 85. For men, this sums to $72,660, and for women it is $120,120. Then, $54,000 is provided annually as benefits from age 85 through 87. The internal rate of return on these premium and benefit cash flows are 3.9 percent for men and 1.5 percent for women. For couples, it is 3.4 percent, if both members of the couple independently experience LTC events at age 85. These are nominal returns, rather than real returns, because none of these monetary values receive inflation adjustments.

Especially for women, it may be reasonable to assume that these rates of return could be beaten with reserve assets invested relatively conservatively, even if interest rates never increase from today's levels. The idea is that instead of paying premiums, the assets are kept and invested as reserve assets. Returns are low even without premium increases and assuming the full benefit pool is received for care. If the LTC event happens sooner, it improves the outlook for insurance. For example, if the care need otherwise starts at 80, returns are 5.3 percent for men, 2.6 percent for women, and 4.7 percent for the couple. With care coming sooner, the household is less at risk anyway as their overall retirement with likely be shorter. The value proposition is less if the LTC event happens even later, and that corresponds to when assets may be at greater risk of depletion.

With these return estimates, we can at least note that LTCI provides higher net-of-tax returns. Benefits are received tax-free and there is implied tax-deferral on premiums compared to investing in a taxable account requiring ongoing taxes on interest. There may also be opportunities to deduct the insurance premiums, though this is less likely after retirement as it becomes harder to itemize beyond the standard deduction. Nonetheless, this LTCI policy does not fully cover the spending risk as the total benefit pool is capped and bills could easily exceed these thresholds when care is needed. These cost-benefit considerations may explain why LTCI is held by relatively few Americans.

Long-term care insurance has traveled along a rocky road since its inception. When people entered a nursing home after a hospital stay, early long-term care insurance policies of the 1960s generally only supported stays in nursing home facilities that required skilled care rather than custodial care. This is exactly what Medicare covers, and since skilled care is rarely needed for longer than Medicare provides, these types of policies rarely provided benefits and left a stain on the industry.

By the 1990s, new policies covered an increasingly general range of long-term care needs, including help with activities of daily living and/or cognitive decline. Coverage is generally for skilled care, intermediate care, and custodial care. The typical policy today covers nursing homes, assisted living, and home care. It may also cover other needs like homemaker services, hospice care, adult day care, international coverage, respite care (temporary care from others to provide a break for informal caregivers), bed reservation (which holds a spot at an institution while away for a hospital stay), care coordination, caregiver training, and supportive equipment. The range of expenses covered by long-term care insurance varies, and it is important to understand what exactly is covered by a contract.

The long-term care insurance market expanded rapidly during the 1990s. However, many companies entering the market offered a level of benefits which could not be supported by premiums. Some companies overestimated lapse rates as more contracts were held longer than expected. With medical improvements, people were also living longer than anticipated when under claim. Insurers also underestimated the recent decline of interest rates, which meant they were earning less on their invested premiums to pay claims. State insurance regulators must approve premium increases, which may be necessary if the alternative is that insurers are unable to pay claims. As it stands, even with substantial premium hikes, older policies may have lower premiums than if the same policy was issued today. Some companies simply priced policies too low to generate more sales in the ongoing battle between the marketing departments and actuaries at insurance companies.

The contracts usually offer guaranteed renewal or are defined as having level premiums. This does not guarantee against increasing premiums. It only means that premiums do not increase solely because of changes in age or health status. Level premiums require only that the company must charge the same premium to everyone who bought policies within the group at a point in time, not that premiums remain at the same level. If the insurance company convinces the state insurance commission that higher premiums are needed to support the promised benefits for that group, all policyholders within a group may experience the same increase in rates.

The financial strains created by these underpriced insurance contracts have led to dramatic consolidation in recent years, with fewer insurers writing new policies today. Those still issuing new policies have had to raise premiums and reduce benefits. Research by Christopher Finefrock, Suzanne Gradisher, and Caleb Nitz from 2015 found that among 58 companies that had written long-term care insurance policies, only four never initiated a rate increase. They also found that, for instance, only 12 carriers were actively selling new long-term care insurance policies in California. Meanwhile, an additional 46 companies with existing policies had stopped issuing new policies.

For many retirees on a fixed budget, premium increases became unaffordable and countless policies lapsed. These premium increases left many Americans nervous about purchasing traditional long-term care insurance. In the future, premium increases may be less common as companies have a better grasp on how to price their policies, and as interest rates are unlikely to fall dramatically lower than their current low levels. Nonetheless, it is wise to at least anticipate a possibility that premiums could increase by 50 percent or more during the period leading up to a benefit claim. It is important to shop around between different providers as the ability to qualify and the health classification for premiums may be different between companies. Buying based on who offers the lowest premium is risky, since the company may be seeking upfront sales and may be less stable.

Public hesitation about long-term care insurance stems from numerous concerns. As with many other insurance options, people struggle to place appropriate value in something they may not end up using. Consumers fear future rate increases could affect their ability to keep paying for the policy. They have concerns about underwriting and the lack of standardization among contracts making it difficult to know what is and is not covered, as well as the finite coverage provided by contracts which may still leave them with expenses extending beyond coverage limits.

Another important concern for traditional long-term care insurance is the possibility of inadvertent lapsing. The Center for Retirement Research at Boston College released a troubling study in 2015 which found that about 25 percent of policy holders who entered a nursing home had let their policy lapse during the preceding four years, resulting in loss of benefits they had supported with premiums earlier in their lives. The troubling implication of this research is that two of the top hardships experienced in the years leading to entering a nursing home – financial strain and cognitive decline – led to a lapse in coverage when it was most needed. By following households over time, they learned that lower scores on cognitive tests increased the likelihood of needing long-term care *and* increased the odds for lapsing their existing long-term care insurance policies. The importance of having family, friends, or professional assistance during this time cannot be overstated.

Hybrid Insurance Policies

Attempts to combat concerns about traditional long-term care insurance have resulted in combination or hybrid products using an asset-based approach to fund long-term care. These new approaches generally combine long-term care funding with life insurance or an annuity. Annuity products are rare, as low interest rates have made it hard to offer additional long-term care benefits on top of a guaranteed return for the annuity. But the use of hybrid life insurance products has grown rapidly in popularity. Even for those who cannot obtain long-term care benefits through their life insurance, another option may be a life settlement or viatical settlement that can provide more than the cash value of the policy to cover expenses, though this would require giving up the policy's death benefit.

There are two general types of life insurance approaches to long-term care. The first is most like a traditional permanent life insurance policy, except that it includes an optional rider allowing the death benefit to be received on an accelerated basis to pay for qualifying long-term care needs. These types of policies do not provide more than the death benefit and will include different provisions about how the death benefit can be received in advance for long-term care. The rules will generally require standard eligibility for two ADLs or cognitive impairment, will include an elimination provision, will not provide inflation protection, and will provide the full benefit amount as a cash payment rather than requiring reimbursement for expenses. Since these policies do not provide support beyond the death benefit, they may be more suitable for individuals expecting shorter long-term care needs.

The second option is an asset-based approach linking a long-term care policy to life insurance. These can be viewed foremost as intended for long-term care, with the ability to extend long-term care benefits beyond the amount of the life insurance death benefit. For instance, one asset-based strategy involves the purchase of a long-term care insurance policy bundled with whole life insurance. This may be accomplished with a single upfront premium, a set of premiums for a fixed term, or ongoing premiums. The cash value generally grows at a low fixed rate and is liquid after surrender charges.

Long-term care expenses are first subtracted from the cash value before the insurance company must cover care expenses with other resources, which allows these policies to be viewed as high-deductible policies. These policies generally provide a death benefit for a fixed amount, less any long-term care claims. To be clear, there are additional charges for the life insurance benefit. The death benefit is available for long-term care, and an optional continuation of benefit rider for the policy could allow for long-term care benefits to continue even after the death benefit depletes.

When choosing large upfront premiums, these policies may provide an outlet for funds that would have been invested in short-term fixed income reserve assets anyway, so the opportunity costs from potential lost investment growth are less. When compared to low-yielding short-term fixed income assets, a competitive return is provided by the death benefit in the event of a long-life and unused long-term care benefits. The internal rate of return, however, could be significantly higher if the long-term care benefits or death benefit are received earlier in retirement. As well, it is important to remember the tax advantages related to tax-deferral inside the contract as well as receiving the death benefit and long-term care benefits on an income tax-free basis.

Conceptually, households may view the hybrid policy as part of their reserve assets which provide leverage for the assets if there is a long-term care need. This can support a reduced overall need for reserve assets to fund spending shocks related to long-term care. If no care is needed, then the death benefit provided to the estate may imply returns that are similar to having just invested the reserve assets conservatively throughout retirement. But the point is that less assets may have been needed to feel comfortable when having the LTC risk covered by the policy.

To consider a basic example for how these policies may be structured, suppose a one-time $70,000 premium is placed into a life insurance contract that provides a death benefit of $125,000. The death benefit can be spent down in advance at a set rate for qualified long-term care expenses, and the unused cash value of the contract remains liquid (after surrender charges) while growing at a modest rate similar to short-term fixed income investments after deducting insurance charges. Tapping the cash value for non-qualified expenses would negate the value of the insurance, though. Of importance is that those insurance charges were guaranteed in advance as part of the policy and cannot be increased, unlike the case with traditional long-term care insurance.

A continuation of benefit rider may be added, which can even allow for lifetime benefits after the maximum benefit period for the base policy has been reached. Underwriting is generally slightly easier than traditional LTCI. In some cases, a phone interview or basic health questionnaire and no medical exam is sufficient. Simplified underwriting makes this option available to those who may not otherwise qualify for traditional long-term care insurance. Some policies are also issued jointly for spouses to share, with the death benefit provided at the second death.

Many hybrid policies also offer return-of-premium provisions if the owner decides not to hold the contract through death. Such provisions can be expensive to include, which reduces the leverage that assets can provide for long-term care. But this is another feature that must be balanced against a potential future need for funds to pay for long-term care.

These newer approaches have sought to eliminate the perceived disadvantages of traditional long-term care insurance, such as premium hikes, finite benefit periods, fears about not making it through the underwriting process, and the general use-it-or-lose-it nature of insurance products. The death benefit is provided when the assets are not used for long-term care expenses. Premium increases can be avoided by paying with a single premium or with a guaranteed set of premiums for a finite time. Versions are available that lock costs in at the start, which alleviates the concern of holding traditional long-term care insurance that can inadvertently lapse in the period leading up to needing care.

Long-Term Care Insurance and Taxes

Long-term care insurance can also provide tax benefits. First, long-term care benefits are generally received tax-free. All benefits from reimbursement policies are tax free, while cash benefit payments are tax-free up to a limit of $400 per day in 2021. This is generally true for both traditional long-term care insurance and hybrid policies.

As for premiums, qualified traditional long-term care insurance policies can be tax deductible. Most policies issued today are qualified, which means they meet certain requirements including that the insured cannot perform at least two ADLs or faces a several cognitive impairment for at least 90 days. Most hybrid policies do not qualify for premium deductibility, except possibly for the portion of premiums going to the continuation of benefits, as one requirement to be qualified is that any death benefit on the policy cannot exceed the aggregate premiums paid.

Regarding premium deductibility, two frameworks exist. For employers paying premiums on behalf of employees, or for the self-employed, premiums can be fully deductible as an above-the-line business expense up to limits. There are many exceptions for this deductibility that relate to different types of corporate structures. Therefore, it is important to discuss your situation with an accountant.

For others with qualified policies, including those paying premiums themselves when employed by others or those who are retired, premiums are not deductible as an above-the-line expense. But they can be included with other eligible medical expenses as a below-the-line deduction when itemizing and when exceeding 7.5 percent of adjusted gross income. A deeper discussion of tax planning to clarify this terminology is provided in Chapter 10. Some states also provide tax deductions or even tax credits for long-term care insurance premiums.

There are age-based limits on the amount of premiums that can be deducted for qualified policies. These are spelled out in Exhibit 8.5. These limits also apply to the amount of long-term care insurance premiums that can be paid annually as an eligible expense from a health savings account.

Exhibit 8.5
Tax Deductibility Limits for Long-Term Care Insurance Premiums in 2021

Taxpayer (Age at End of Tax Year)	Deductible Limit
40 or younger	$450
Between 41 and 50	$850
Between 51 and 60	$1,690
Between 61 and 70	$4,520
71 and older	$5,640

For those with existing life insurance and annuity policies, it may be possible to engage in a 1035 exchange to a new policy that includes long-term care protections without triggering a taxable event. This could serve as another source of funds to provide long-term care protections.

Coverage Options for Long-Term Care Insurance Policies

Both traditional and newer hybrid insurance policies provide numerous options. At the most basic level, these include:

- How much time passes before benefits start?
- How much benefits are provided per period?
- How long are benefits provided?
- What is the total benefit pool available?

There are other important considerations as well, which we delve into.

Elimination or waiting period

First, what is the initial elimination period before benefits begin? This choice could be viewed as a deductible, with longer elimination periods serving as the equivalent of a less costly high-deductible policy.

Since many long-term care events have short durations, a short elimination period could substantially raise the cost of insurance. It may also not be necessary. In certain circumstances, Medicare or health insurance may cover a portion of the costs for short-term events.

Elimination periods in the range of two to three months may be a reasonable compromise for those with sufficient assets to fund the initial care. A common elimination period is 90 days. Elimination periods of up to one year may work best for retirees who can afford to fund short-term events themselves and wish only to protect themselves from the risk of more serious and costly events while helping to lower insurance costs.

Another important detail about the elimination period is whether it is defined in terms of calendar days or service days. Calendar days begin the count as soon as eligibility is determined. Service days only count days when care is received. This could substantially lengthen the elimination period if, for instance, care is only received two days per week. All else being the same, service day elimination periods will increase the time before benefits are received, which should lower the premiums.

Monthly or daily amount, period of coverage, and total benefit pool

Most benefits are defined in terms of a monthly or daily maximum payable benefit amount. Determining the appropriate level depends on the cost of care in your community, your ability to partially fund some expenses in other ways, and the affordability of the premiums.

The period of coverage indicates how long benefits are available. As most policies allow the period to be extended when less than the full periodic benefit amount is used, a key consideration for the periodic amount and period of coverage is the total benefit pool available to be used. For instance, a $150 daily benefit provided for five years would provide maximum benefits of 150 x 365 x 5 = $273,750. Or, in our example of coverage from Exhibit 8.4, the policy provided a $4,500 monthly benefit for three years, for maximum benefits of 4500 x 36 months = $162,000. Long-term care benefits up to these total amounts are available. Coverage ends without further benefit payments when the total pool is spent. If less than the full amount of coverage is received each period, the total length of coverage can be extended until the total pool of funds is used.

Most traditional insurance policies allow for care coverage from one to five years. Lifetime coverage is now rare for traditional policies, though some hybrid policies may still offer lifetime continuation of benefit riders.

Inflation protection

Long-term care benefits may be calibrated to the costs of care at the present, but those costs will grow over time. Should the long-term care benefit grow over time as well? This is an important question, as the long-term care benefits may not be received until 20 or 30 years later and long-term care costs often grow at a faster rate than overall consumer price inflation. Today's cost of care may only be a fraction of future care costs. But inflation protection may increase premiums substantially.

Common options for inflation include no benefit growth, a simple growth rate, or a compounding growth rate. Growth rates may be 3 percent or 5 percent. Some policies may even link coverage growth to the consumer price index. Generally, at the start of each anniversary for coverage, the daily or monthly benefit amount and any remaining portion of the total benefit pool are increased by the policy's inflation rate.

Exhibit 8.6
Tracking Growth for a $5,000 Monthly Benefit Using Different Inflation Factors

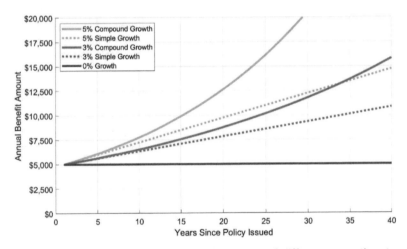

Exhibit 8.6 provides an example of the impact of different growth rates for a baseline monthly benefit amount of $5,000. With no growth, the benefit amount remains at $5,000. With a simple growth rate, a fixed amount is added to the benefit each year. For instance, 3 percent simple growth adds $150 to the monthly benefit amount each year. After 40 years of coverage, monthly benefits grow to $10,850. Meanwhile a 5 percent simple growth rate adds $250 per year. After 40 years, the benefit is $14,750. With compounding growth, the amount of growth increases over time as the rate is applied to the latest benefit amount rather than the initial amount. With 3 percent compounding growth, the benefit is $15,835 after 40 years (which is more than with 5 percent simple), as opposed to $33,524 with 5 percent

compounding growth. It takes about 33 years for a 3 percent compound growth rate to catch up to and exceed a 5 percent simple growth rate, making the choice among these options less than obvious. Compounding growth should better reflect the pattern of cost growth in the future, but simple growth may be a more affordable option.

The choice is also complicated because there is no way to know when you will need care and how inflation will impact costs then. Simple growth may not be able to keep pace with long-term care costs, but it at least provides some growth relative to a flat benefit.

Another option to support a growing benefit amount over time is a provision within the contract that allows the periodic purchase of additional coverage. This provides an opportunity to obtain more coverage in the future in exchange for additional premium without overcoming the hurdle of additional underwriting and without an initial commitment to the additional expenses involved in purchasing additional insurance or an inflation rider.

How benefit amounts are determined and paid

Several options are available for benefit payments. The reimbursement method requires paying the provider and then submitting a claim for reimbursement from the insurer. It requires more effort to keep track of and submit receipts. The indemnity method pays the beneficiary a specific benefit amount for any period that services are received, which could be more than actual expenses. The cash method provides payments even when receiving unpaid informal care from family or other volunteers.

By better matching up with actual expenses, the reimbursement method is usually the most cost effective for premiums because it will result in smaller claims that only cover paid expenses. Paying more for benefits that can exceed the actual costs for care may not make sense. Nonetheless, an advantage for cash-based methods is that benefits can be used to pay informal caregivers as well.

One other related issue is whether the benefit period is daily or monthly. For those receiving different amounts of care each day, a monthly benefit period can potentially provide flexibility for covering more of the costs. This can be understood with a simple example by comparing a $150 daily policy with a $4,500 monthly policy. Suppose an individual receives care for 20 days in the month, and each day of care costs $200. With the daily policy, only up to $150 is reimbursed per day, so the total benefit received for the month is 20 x 150 = $3,000. For the monthly policy, up to $4,500 for the month is reimbursed, and so the full $4,000 of expenses in this example would be covered.

Qualifying expenses

It is also important to consider which expenses qualify for benefits. Early policies only supported skilled nursing home care after a qualifying hospital stay. New policies are less restrictive, but standards may vary about what is covered. Identify whether a policy will cover home care, assisted living, and nursing homes. Additionally, do expenses for adult day care or other respite care qualify? What about care options that have not been invented yet? The ability to receive care at home is important because the alternative would involve moving out to qualify for benefits from the insurance policy. Home care and respite care benefits also provide relief for family members serving as caregivers, making it possible to delay moving to an institution for a longer period. Some policies may even provide benefits to pay for informal caregivers such as family and friends who do not normally live in the same home. Having more comprehensive coverage provides greater flexibility.

In terms of what qualifies for benefit coverage, the standard has become that you need to either be unable to perform two of six standard Activities of Daily Living (ADLs) or be cognitively impaired as determined by a qualified physician or other licensed health care practitioner. But qualifications may differ between companies and policies, so it is important to consider this issue carefully.

For example, a policy requiring two ADL limitations to qualify for benefits is of little value if bathing is missing from the list, as that is often the first ADL requiring help. Also, bathing could be defined in different ways, such as being able to get into a bathtub or being able to conduct a sponge bath. Standard definitions or fixed lists of ADLs do not exist, so you must be careful when comparing different policies. It is also important to make sure that cognitive impairment is a qualifying condition, especially if an impaired individual can still perform ADLs.

For an example, this is how the Federal Long Term Care Insurance Program, which serves federal employees and military, defines their benefit coverage: "when a licensed health care practitioner certifies, and we agree, that you are unable to perform at least two of six activities of daily living without substantial assistance for a period expected to last at least 90 days or you require substantial supervision to protect yourself due to a severe cognitive impairment, such as Alzheimer's disease." Their six activities are bathing, dressing, toileting, continence, eating, and transferring (from bed to chair).

Option for pooled benefits for a couple

It can be cheaper for spouses to buy a joint policy than for each spouse to buy a separate policy. For example, the premiums for six years of benefits to be jointly shared will be cheaper than two separate policies each with three years of benefits. Even if benefits are not shared jointly, lowered premiums can be attributed to a better chance that claims will be less because one spouse cares for the other, and because of the reduced probability that *both* spouses will experience conditions which qualify for expensive long-term care benefit payouts.

Underwriting requirements

Another consideration is the degree of underwriting and the health classification provided for insurance premiums. It is worthwhile to shop among different companies, as they may arrive at competing conclusions about appropriate premiums based on their underwriting. Those in good health will likely benefit from more stringent underwriting that can result in a lower premium. Everything else being the same, those in poorer health would prefer a less rigorous underwriting process.

Hybrid policies generally have fewer underwriting requirements, as a questionnaire and telephone interview may be sufficient without needing an additional medical examination. A hybrid policy may be the only insurance option for those with health conditions that prevent them from qualifying for a traditional insurance policy. It is important to remember that the risk for an application to be rejected grows with age as one is more likely to experience disqualifying medical conditions.

Other considerations

A few other considerations for comparing different policies include issues such as secondary benefits. Does the policy include liquidity or death benefit options for unused coverage? How frequently are premiums paid? Is there is a one-time premium option? Can premiums be increased in the future? Is there a waiver of premiums once benefits begin? If coverage is received and the need ends, can premiums and coverage be renewed? Does the policy pay any dividends? Are benefits available if one chooses to live abroad? Does the policy offer the services of a care coordinator who can help to answer questions and develop a plan for your specific needs? Also consider the viability of the insurer to pay claims, as determined through credit rating, past involvement with the long-term care industry, and experience with claims payouts and customer complaints.

Finally, the lack of standardization among long-term care insurance policies means that you should be careful about the specifics for each individual contract under consideration. Does the policy cover the variety of potential living arrangements or care you may need or want to receive in the future? Some policies may only cover care at home or at certain institutions, while a comprehensive policy will cover any type of care no matter where it is received. It is surely worthwhile to have a qualified elder law attorney study the contract for any potential issues or misunderstandings.

With these considerations when designing a long-term care insurance policy, we can provide a summary of ways to lower a policy premium. These include reducing the level of inflation protection, reducing the periodic benefit and total benefit amounts, adding longer elimination periods before benefits begin, using a shared policy for spouses, initiating the policy when younger, and keeping initial coverage low but including a rider to allow for future insurance purchases.

Budgeting for Long-Term Care Expenses

We end the chapter with a discussion about budgeting for long-term care expenses. When we described budgeting for health care expenses, that involved a combination of building annual expenses into the budget and creating a reserves set-aside for spending shocks. Long-term care is different because the baseline budget will not need to include long-term care spending beyond any long-term care insurance premiums.

Long-term care funding is otherwise a problem of managing reserves for potential expenses that range from $0 (the outcome for half of the population) to more than $1 million. How much of a reserve is needed for long term care depends on the types of scenarios you want to be financially equipped to handle in the future. When might a long-term care event happen, how long might it last, what will the out-of-pocket expenses to cover care be, how much might other budgeted spending drop if long-term care is needed, what is the inflation rate for long-term care as well as the overall price level, and what discount rate will be used to convert future expenses back into the reserve amounts needed today?

An important factor that will help with managing long-term care expenses is the reduction in other expenses that will naturally occur following a move into an institution. When you see the costs for long-term care, it is important to recognize that they are not fully additive to your existing budget. If you are spending $90,000 on nursing home care, some other expenses in your budget would reduce in response to offset some portion of these costs in terms of net household expenses. For couples there is the possibility that one spouse requires extended long-term care in an institution, while the other remains at home with a similar overall budget, but if you are projecting out prolonged long-term care events for two spouses, at some point there may not be a family home and much of the existing budget could be redirected to long-term care. By redeploying some of the existing budget to cover long-term care expenses, the additional reserve assets desired may be less than expected.

Exhibit 8.7 extends the budget described in Chapter 3 to provide estimates for this couple's budget after age 80 when one spouse moves to a nursing home, and then later if the surviving spouse also moves to a nursing home. These estimates involve speculation as they are experiences one has not had, and you might be conservative regarding estimates about how much other expenses will be reduced. But it is important to recognize that the quoted cost of nursing home care would not simply be added on top of the existing budget. There will be offsets. In the exhibit, the couple estimates their total spending at $87,928 in today's dollars once they reach age 80. Working through this exercise, they estimate that if one spouse moves to institutional living, the budget for everything else will reduce by $23,600 to $64,328. Later, if that spouse were to pass away and the surviving spouse then also moves to a long-term care institution, then other spending will fall by $71,714 to $16,214. With a long-term care need, the couple estimates major reductions for charity, gifts, groceries, household expenses, housing, insurance, property taxes (for the survivor), television, travel, and utilities.

Exhibit 8.7
Retirement Budget with and without Long-Term Care Events

RETIREMENT - PROJECTED LIFESTYLE EXPENSES -

Real Expenses (Today's Dollars)	Ages 65 - 79	Ages 80+	Budget After Long-Term Care For First Spouse	Long-Term Care (Last Survivor)
Cell phone	$1,200	$1,200	$1,200	$750
Charity	$5,000	$5,000	$1,000	$0
Gifts / children's education	$3,000	$3,000	$600	$0
Groceries	$18,000	$12,000	$7,000	$500
Health Care	$11,464	$22,928	$22,928	$11,464
Household expenses	$23,000	$15,000	$7,500	$2,500
Housing (maintenance, furniture)	$1,500	$500	$500	$0
Housing (HOA dues)	$0	$0	$0	$0
Insurance	$3,300	$3,300	$3,300	$0
Internet	$1,000	$1,000	$1,000	$0
Property Taxes / Apartment Rent	$15,600	$15,600	$12,000	$0
Restaurants	$3,000	$600	$500	$0
Television	$1,000	$800	$800	$0
Transportation	$7,500	$3,000	$3,000	$1,000
Travel (International)	$10,000	$0	$0	$0
Travel (Domestic)	$4,000	$1,000	$0	$0
Utilities (gas, electric, water)	$3,000	$3,000	$3,000	$0
	$111,564	$87,928	$64,328	$16,214
Reduction to Ages 80+ Budget			$23,600	$71,714

With these estimated inputs, we can now shift to the long-term care reserves estimator shown in Exhibit 8.8. Each spouse is 65 when making these projections. After considering possible care scenarios and their probabilities, they would like to be prepared for a scenario in which the first spouse spends two years in a semi-private room at a nursing home starting at age 80, and the second spouse spends three-years in a semi-private nursing home starting at age 97. For the cost of this care, they input the national median average for semi-private nursing home care in 2020, though this could be further refined as based on where they expect to live when care is needed. As well, they do not have other long-term care insurance so the full costs will be paid out of pocket. They also do not anticipate using Medicaid to fund their care.

The care cost will grow at the inflation rate for long-term care, which they input as 4 percent as based on our earlier discussion. They also include the budget offsets from Exhibit 8.7, which they project to grow at an overall consumer price inflation rate of 2 percent. They are not assuming constant inflation-adjusted spending throughout retirement because we already did adjust their budget downward to reflect the slow-go years starting at age 80. Finally, they discount this future spending using the same 0 percent real discount rate from the funded ratio analysis in Chapter 3. They wish to see the costs for funding their plan without assuming stock market gains. With these inputs, they estimate a reserves requirement today of $203,903 for the first spouse and $310,750 for the second spouse. The total reserves needed to feel comfortable with their plan is $514,653. This is a large number they would like to have set aside to feel financially independent and ready for retirement. It is quite sensitive to assumptions.

Exhibit 8.8
Long-Term Care Reserves Estimator

	First Spouse	Second Spouse	Total
Current Age	65	65	
Age that Long-Term Care Need Begins	80	97	
Duration of Long-Term Care Need	2	3	
Annual Out-of-Pocket Long-Term Care Cost (Today's Dollars)	$93,072	$93,072	
Assumed Reduction to Other Budgeted Spending (Today's Dollars)	$23,600	$71,714	
Inflation Rate for Long-Term Care	4%	4%	
Overall Inflation Rate	2%	2%	
Real Discount Rate	0%	0%	
Long-Term Care Reserves	$203,903	$310,750	**$514,653**

Because care is received so far in the future, the value of the discount rate and the difference between long-term care inflation and overall inflation become very important. A higher discount rate and a smaller differential between the cost-growth rates will both contribute to much lower reserve needs. For example, if we simply shift the inflation rate for long-term care to 3 percent, total reserves fall to $337,174. Moving that back to 4 percent, if we use a real discount rate of 1 percent, the total reserves reduce to $394,558. At 2 percent, reserves fall to $305,532. For someone investing their long-term care reserves in a diversified portfolio, it could be justified to use a higher discount rate, especially since Medicaid can always serve as a back-up if one did end up without enough reserves to cover long-term care expenses. I would not fault anyone for using a higher discount rate for their long-term care reserves than they use for other retirement liabilities, but I do keep the 0 percent discount rate for the discussion in Chapter 3. This decision depends on the comfort level with a future ability to reasonably manage a relatively significant long-term care event. That is a personal matter, which also depends on whether there are insurance options that could also be tapped or whether Medicaid can be a back-up plan if the perfect financial storm of a bad sequence of returns, a long life, and an expensive long-term care shock were to all strike simultaneously. Cumulatively, this is a low-probability event.

Action Plan

These are the key steps to manage long-term care risk in retirement:

- ☐ Identify the long-term care options and costs in your community. Consider how other budgeted expenses, such as travel, may be reduced if long-term care is needed. Decide where you would like to receive care. Determine whether CCRCs are a consideration.
- ☐ Understand what your default plan of care will be if you do not take further action. This includes taking an inventory of what you have at the present:
  - o traditional long-term care insurance policies
  - o permanent life insurance with long-term care benefits or other hybrid policies
  - o family members who may be willing and able to help without creating too much burden
  - o reserves that can be earmarked to cover long-term care expenses
  - o the level of countable assets that would be spent before reaching Medicaid eligibility in your state
- ☐ Identify the potential to self-fund long-term care expenses and the potential impacts this could have on other family members.
- ☐ Identify a reasonable amount of reserve assets to set aside as a funding source for long-term care.
  - o Is this amount realistic?
  - o How will it be invested?
  - o Do any family members expected to provide care understand and accept the obligation?
- ☐ Determine whether Medicaid may be unavoidable as part of a long-term care plan. Consult with an elder law attorney to assist with Medicaid planning as needed.
- ☐ If interested to offset some of the spending risk related to self-funding, explore a variety of options to include traditional long-term care insurance or hybrid approaches.
  - o Will your health allow you to qualify for coverage?
  - o How much of the long-term care spending risk would you like to offset through insurance?
  - o How much of the risk can you afford to offset?
  - o Will you pay for coverage with investment assets or through the exchange of existing insurance policies?
  - o How much would the coverage lower your need to hold reserves for self-funding while still feeling comfortable?
- ☐ When considering insurance, determine what makes the most sense regarding the tradeoffs between premiums and the periodic benefit amount, total coverage, inflation adjustments, and elimination period?

- o Traditional long-term care insurance may appeal to those who can obtain tax deductions for premiums, may use a partnership plan to provide further asset protection for Medicaid, and wish to include inflation protection riders.
  - o Hybrid policies may appeal to those seeking stability for premium amounts, protections for the use-it-or-lose-it aspect, have health issues that make it hard to qualify for traditional insurance, and have existing insurance available that could be exchanged to these policies.
- ☐ Provide family members with your written plan for long-term care so they can easily implement it if you are cognitively impaired. The plan includes details about sources of care, sources of funds, insurance policies, and any professionals who may be available to answer questions, such as a care coordinator provided by an insurance policy.
- ☐ Periodically review the plan to make updates or changes.
- ☐ Take care of your health and stay active to help avoid the development of conditions that trigger long-term care needs.

Further Reading

Department of Health and Human Services. 2021. "Long-Term Services and Supports for Older Americans: Risks and Financing, 2020." ASPE Research Brief (January).

Finefrock, Christopher, Suzanne Gradisher, and Caleb Nitz. 2015. "Long-Term Care Insurance: Comparisons for Determining the Best Options for Clients." *Journal of Financial Planning*. 28 (2): 36-43.

Genworth. 2021. *Genworth 2021 Cost of Care Survey*. https://www.genworth.com/aging-and-you/finances/cost-of-care.html

Hou, Wenliang, Wei Sun, and Anthony Webb. 2015. "Why Do People Lapse their Long-Term Care Insurance?" Boston College Center for Retirement Research Working Paper #15-17.

Matthews, Joseph L. 2020. *Long-Term Care: How to Plan and Pay for It*. Berkeley: NOLO.

Chapter 9: Housing Decisions in Retirement

Developing a plan to meet housing needs throughout retirement is an important decision. Most retirees will continue to live at the same home as before retirement, but the thought of moving is a consideration for many and a reality for some. Some retirees will move multiple times throughout retirement. Housing options do multiply for retirees with greater flexibility to consider RV living, active adult communities, continuing care retirement communities, and living abroad, among other possibilities.

As part of this process, retirees should think about how housing needs may change during retirement in response to physical and cognitive decline. One or more moves may become necessary in retirement for health-related reasons, but planning can reduce both the need for, and the impact created by moving.

While a home provides an emotional anchor of daily comfort, shelter, memories, and proximity to both friends and community, it is also a major source of wealth for retirees and near retirees. For many Americans, home equity provides a substantial part of their net worth. The home's value is often greater than that of the household's investment portfolio. This is an asset that can also be treated in a strategic manner as part of retirement income.

As well, expenses related to the home (property taxes, utility bills, home maintenance, and upkeep) can add up to a significant portion of the overall household budget. The Center for Retirement Research at Boston College analyzed numbers for retired couples aged sixty-five to seventy-four and found that housing expenses represented 30 percent of the typical household budget.

In this chapter, we consider retirement housing in greater detail. We consider the characteristics for a good home in retirement. For homeowners, we also consider planning aspects related to being able to age in place, to generate income through the home, and whether to carry a mortgage into retirement.

Do Retirees Move?

New retirees frequently feel more freedom and flexibility to live where they wish. While working and raising children, families are more firmly locked in place by proximity to employment and schools. Upon retirement, a move to a community with a less highly rated school and no daily commute could mean lower property taxes and increased savings for the retirement budget. There is the potential to improve finances by moving to a state with a more tax-friendly environment for retirees. This newfound freedom can create a whole new set of options that might not have been realistic in the past.

Nevertheless, most retirees do choose to stay put. Richard Green and Hyojung Lee studied households and found that the propensity to move peaks in an individual's twenties and then declines until about fifty. Moving then stays at these lowest relative levels for higher ages. Older individuals are less likely to move, and the rate of moving does not rise at typical retirement ages. There is an uptick in moving at more advanced ages, but this reflects a need to move for health-related reasons, such as to assisted living or a nursing home.

In Spring 2016, the American College of Financial Services conducted a survey of 1,003 people between the ages of 55 and 75 with at least $100,000 of investment assets and $100,000 of home equity. When asked a question about whether you plan to remain in your current home for as long as you possibly can, 60 percent said yes, 23 percent said maybe, and 17 percent said no.

As well, in a Merrill Lynch Retirement Study conducted in partnership with Age Wave and published in 2015, the results showed that among retirees aged fifty and older, only 37 percent had moved in retirement, while another 27 percent anticipate moving at some point, and 36 percent of retirees had no plans to move. The most popular reason to not move was loving one's home, while important reasons for moving were listed as being closer to family, decreasing home expenses, fulfilling health needs, and changes in marital status.

The decision to move or stay put relates to decisions about priorities and preferences among numerous characteristics. We will return to topics relevant for those who choose to remain in the same home, but first we review relevant considerations for new retirees thinking about the best place to live.

Characteristics of a Good Place to Live in Retirement

Joseph Coughlin, the director of the MIT AgeLab, created three basic questions to identify quality-of-life issues for retirement:

- Who will change my lightbulbs?
- How will I get an ice-cream cone?
- Whom will I have lunch with?

An essential part of answering these questions involves solving for the right type and location of housing. These questions illustrate how our lives will change as our bodies slow down and health issues or other aspects of aging make us less mobile.

For some early retirees, moving around frequently and traveling may be common, but these are important considerations for anyone considering settling down more permanently in one location.

These questions focus on whether we can continue to live in and properly maintain the same home, whether we have access to a community that lets us continue to enjoy basic conveniences even if we stop driving our own cars, and what will happen to our social lives and opportunities to remain active as old friends also become less mobile or move away.

Will we live in communities that keep these key aspects of quality living accessible to us? For new retirees, any difficulty with answering these questions may still reside in the distant future, but the major life changes associated with retirement provide a good opportunity to reflect on the different possibilities and develop a set of contingency plans.

Ultimately, one of the greatest dangers to quality of life in retirement is the risk of becoming increasingly isolated with only television or web surfing to pass the time. On the emotional side, the housing decision may relate in large part to figuring out how to best answer Coughlin's three questions over the long term.

Because of its important connection to the emotional and financial aspects of retirement, it is worthwhile to think carefully about housing options and potential uses for home equity. The importance of living somewhere with social connections, transportation options, quality health care, and long-term care services increases with age. In the more immediate present, you need to think about where to live, how long to stay there, and whether to move later in retirement. Plenty of justifications exist for staying put or for moving early in retirement.

It is important to anticipate changing life needs in advance, as moving becomes more difficult as we age. Putting off these matters may result in the need to make quick and suboptimal decisions in the face of impairments that may arise. Planning around finding a good place to live and making the necessarily modifications in advance can allow for more desirable long-term outcomes.

Decisions to move must not be taken lightly. It is easy to make a move based on a vision that does not become reality. It is worth conducting a trial move by renting for a few months during different seasons to make sure that the move feels right. This way, if things do not work out as planned, you have avoided a potentially costly and difficult situation.

We consider reasons for moving, which can also relate to reasons for staying put if these priorities are already fulfilled. Issues relate primarily to the changing emphasis of life's priorities and needs. There are numerous considerations that each retiree will need to prioritize to decide on the best options. The media provides rankings about the best places for retirees to live, which may involve different combinations of these factors. Such lists may be helpful with ideas and important considerations, but the article's methodology may not match your priorities. Let us consider some of the important matters.

Affordability

First, affordability and retirement sustainability on the financial side are important. Housing is a major expense, and the current home may be larger and more expensive than necessary. Empty nesters may no longer require a home large enough to accommodate an entire family. Large homes require more cleaning, maneuvering, heating, cooling, and maintenance.

Many retirees will consider downsizing as one way to free up home equity for other retirement expenses. Downsizing does not necessarily mean moving to a physically smaller home; it can mean moving to a similar-sized home in a less expensive area. The arithmetic of converting home equity through downsizing is straightforward. If you pay off the mortgage on a $300,000 home, sell it, and move into a $200,000 home, you have freed up $100,000 of home equity for other uses. This may also reduce housing-related expenses for the budget.

An important caveat about downsizing is that it can be dangerous to assume that it will provide an important source of retirement funding. The same study of retirees conducted by Merrill Lynch and AgeWave also found what they refer to as a "downsize surprise," where many retirees who planned to downsize ended up not wanting to do so once they retired. For those who had moved since retirement, 51 percent moved to a smaller home, 19 percent to a same-sized home, and 30 percent to a larger home. For those who chose to upsize, the most important reason given was to have more space for family members (including grandchildren) to visit. The AgeWave study makes clear that downsizing is not the only moving option for retirees, and it should not be viewed as a given.

Besides housing costs, one can also consider other cost of living expenses. How would the basic costs of daily living change in a new location? Are homeowner's insurance policies and utilities more expensive? Is it necessary to pay for trash pickup and other services? Consider as well that health insurance, health care, and long-term care costs can vary dramatically by location.

Furthermore, what is the tax situation? Tax considerations include state income tax rates and whether some retirement income sources such as Social Security are excluded from state income taxes. State and local sales taxes, state inheritance taxes, and local property taxes are also important considerations to factor in the retirement budget with a move. With sales tax, one may also consider if certain categories of expenses, such as food or prescriptions, are exempt. As well, there may be local government programs to provide property-tax relief for the aged.

Home Ownership vs. Renting

Another consideration related to moving in retirement is simply selling your home and then renting a new place. This frees up home equity and provides the flexibility to make more frequent moves before settling down. Renting provides the option to change the living situation more frequently, and some retirees may value this and wish to move multiple times during retirement.

As for financial considerations, the home is a large, undiversified asset that may not appreciate over time. Many retirees will find themselves fortunate if their home value can maintain pace with inflation, though there are certainly opportunities for faster home appreciation in some parts of the country. By selling, home equity can be re-invested into a more diversified investment portfolio that may have the potential to earn higher long-term investment returns.

As well, though there will now be a rental expense, other retirement costs will reduce. First, property taxes are gone. Rent for an apartment may even be comparable to what was paid in property taxes on a family home in a good school district. As well, there will be savings on home maintenance, repairs, and homeowner's insurance. Deciding whether to own or rent is an important consideration for retirees on the move.

Proximity to Family and Friends

Another important issue that becomes very personal is the location of family and friends. Does moving mean leaving such individuals behind? What are the odds of making friends in the new location? Alternatively, children may have moved to other parts of the country, and new retirees may wish to move to be closer to their grandchildren. If children and grandchildren live elsewhere, the choice may become more related to remaining near friends or moving to be close to family. As today's new retirees are also called the sandwich generation on account of their potential need to care for both their aging parents as well as their adult children or grandchildren, moves may also be related to these needs.

Maintaining social ties and not becoming isolated is important in retirement. Being close to family and friends can help in this regard. As well, meeting new people and developing a social network in a new community can fulfill this same purpose. It is important to have someone who can provide occasional checks and help you avoid isolation. As aging progresses, obtaining trusted support for lawn care, snow removal, home maintenance, cleaning, and food delivery services can be very helpful. These are important considerations, especially for retirees who lack friends and family nearby to help with these matters.

Agreeable Climate, Community, & Leisure Activities

When considering a move, many opportunities exist for retirees to find communities with active networks for social activities related to specific hobbies or interests.

There are various living options for retirees during their more active years of retirement. Aside from continuing in the same home, opportunities include extensive traveling by RV or living abroad. They can involve communities organized by age, religion, lifestyle, recreational interests, or hobbies. Think, for example, of a neighborhood organized around a golf course. It could also be a college or university town which may allow cultural opportunities and the ability to take courses or engage in other educational activities. Naturally occurring retirement communities are neighborhoods in which the residents gradually shifted toward being retirees over time who may work together to provide social support or other services for residents.

Active adult communities are another option. They are available both for age 55+ (in which 80 percent of residents must be at least 55) and 62+ (in which all residents must be at least 62). These are the only housing options allowing for age discrimination. They can provide organized activities and social support. These types of communities generally do not provide health care or assisted-living options. But they are increasingly available in areas with favorable climates, in university towns, or in other places attractive to retirees.

When making a big move, it is important to consider the year-round climate. A place that was nice to visit in the winter may be unbearably hot in the summer. As well, tourist areas that may be lively during their peak seasons can be dramatically different during the off-season. Especially when moving for reasons discussed here, a trial-run of renting in the area for a more extended period can be valuable to ensure that it is the right fit.

Continuing-care retirement communities are another option that can provide social networking benefits as well as covering potential long-term care needs. These can be an option for those seeking only to make one move who do not want to move again later for health reasons. These are described in more detail in the previous chapter about long-term care.

Opportunities for Part-Time Work

Anyone interested in working part-time, full-time, or in volunteering, needs to consider whether a specific locale is conducive to these opportunities.

Health Care and Long-Term Care Options

Another consideration is the availability of high-quality medical facilities in the area. Those with specific health conditions may already understand the need to live close to specific medical facilities providing the needed care. For others, it is important to recognize that care needs may grow over time and so choosing a place located near first-class hospitals and medical facilities is an important part of aging in place.

When considering relocating, remember that Medicare Advantage and some other types of health insurance are location-specific for in-network care. Relocating may require changing Medicare options. Original Medicare may be a better choice for retirees who are frequently on the move.

Diverse Transportation Options

For long-term planners, it is important to consider the availability of transportation options outside of using your own car, such as public transportation, taxis or services like Uber, or volunteer services from non-profit organizations. Is the location walkable and accessible? An important part of planning involves less dependency on your own ability to drive a car. Being isolated in the suburbs could accelerate any decline experienced, and this can subsequently make a move more difficult. The aging process will slowly reduce mobility. Moving with long-term needs in mind will increase your chances of aging in place and maintaining quick access to important medical care.

Considerations for Settling More Permanently in a Home

Many retirees have family, community ties, and friendships that they do not wish to leave behind. Many have significant memories and good feelings about their homes and wish to maintain this stability and familiarity. A home can be an important part of one's emotional identity, so many choose not to leave that anchor behind. Homeowners tend to take pride in ownership and might not care to go through the moving process again. New technologies and the possibility of renovating one's home can also make aging in place easier than in the past. After considering the points from the previous section, most retirees will decide that the best option is to remain in place in retirement. We look now at some issues to help ensure the best outcomes for this decision.

Aging in Place

Staying at home over the long-term requires anticipating future potential needs related to physical and cognitive limitations and making sure that life can continue comfortably at the same home. *Aging in place* refers to the growing industry around helping members of the aging population remain in their homes despite functional or cognitive impairments. New technologies and services are always coming on the market designed to support those wishing to age in place. By renovating an existing home to age in place, retirees can maintain familiarity and comfort, delaying or potentially avoiding any future move to institutional settings.

Merrill Lynch and AgeWave conducted a survey of retirees aged fifty and older and found that 85 percent viewed their own home as the preferred location for receiving long-term care. Beyond this, 10 percent were looking at assisted living facilities, 4 percent considered moving in with other family members, and 1 percent expressed interest in nursing homes. Home care is often the more desirable and less expensive option, and it can be extended with sufficient planning. As well, government agencies have expressed support for the idea and have promoted the concept, as aging in place often requires less contribution from government programs like Medicaid than do nursing homes or assisted-living facilities.

Professionals can provide guidance about specific home renovations to better support aging in place. Universal design features and other characteristics that can lay a stronger foundation for aging in place include:

- Walk-in showers, grab bars, and other bathroom safety features
- Single-floor living with no stairs (kitchen, bathing facility, and bedroom are all on one floor), or an elevator allowing access to other floors
- Wheelchair accessibility: ramps to the home, wide doors and hallways that can fit a wheelchair, and at least one wheelchair-accessible entrance to the home
- Levers for door handles and faucets rather than a twisting knob
- Good lighting in case sight is diminished
- Accessible cabinets and closets as well as lowered counters to allow for cooking while sitting
- Softened non-skid flooring to help cushion any falls, but no rugs or other floor items that could create a tripping hazard
- Accessible electric controls and switches that are not too high off the ground
- New technologies to monitor health status and medicine use

The planning required to age in place offers several potential paths depending on your specific desires and needs. If you stay put, renovating your home can make it livable even if you have physical or cognitive impairments. If you move, you can look for a new home with the necessary renovations already in place and a community where many types of care are readily accessible. By ensuring that these steps are taken, it will be easier to avoid future health-related moves, which is an important goal for most retirees.

Generating Income Through the Home

For those seeking additional income, there are a few options that can be considered with one's primary residence. For extra income, a room or a portion of the home could be rented to a traditional renter. One might even add a rental apartment to the home, such as above a detached garage. On a short-term basis and when allowed by local regulations, this type of approach could also be used with services such as Airbnb. Such an approach will not be for everyone, but some retirees may desire the potential for more social interactions that could occur with additional people in the home.

Carrying a Mortgage into Retirement

More Americans are now entering retirement while still carrying a mortgage. In 2014 (which remains their most recent study of this), the Consumer Finance Protection Bureau reported that the percentage of Americans aged sixty-five and older with a mortgage rose from 22 percent in 2001 to 30 percent in 2011—a rise from 3.8 million to 6.1 million. Among individuals over seventy-five, those who still had mortgages rose from 8.4 percent to 21.2 percent. This is consistent with the Merrill Lynch and Age Wave survey which determined that 81 percent of the respondents owned their homes, and among homeowners, 28 percent still held a mortgage.

For those approaching or already in retirement with a mortgage, it is worth considering whether to accelerate payments on the mortgage. This decision involves the general points made about pre-paying a mortgage earlier in life, but the decision may come out differently as the nature of investment risk and volatility grows as one approaches retirement. Another option is to refinance a mortgage into a reverse mortgage, which we consider later in the chapter.

When we think about risk tolerance and asset allocation in a broader perspective beyond just an investment portfolio, a mortgage is effectively a "negative bond." It represents a bond you have issued instead of a bond you own. Instead of receiving interest like a typical bond, interest is charged to the borrower on the outstanding mortgage balance at the rate set by the mortgage. Paying down mortgage principal means reducing the amount of "assets" held that pay a negative interest rate. In other words, it can be viewed as investing in an asset yielding a rate of return equal to the mortgage rate. A mortgage is a liability, of course, so this is just a theoretical exercise to think more broadly about the mortgage decision.

Consider a very basic example of a fixed rate mortgage with a 3.5 percent interest rate. After making my obligated mortgage payment, suppose I have an extra $1,000. For this example, there is already an established emergency fund and no other debt, such as credit cards or student loans, with higher interest rates. If I use the $1,000 to make a voluntary principal payment on the mortgage, it reduces my interest growth on $1,000 of principal on an annual basis by 3.5 percent. I can compare that to other investment alternatives. If I were to invest that $1,000 in a CD paying 1 percent, then I would be better off paying down the mortgage instead. If there were another safe investment paying 6 percent, then I would be better off investing in the asset earning 6 percent instead of voluntarily pre-paying down the mortgage balance that would "earn" 3.5 percent.

An important consideration, though, is that the potential to earn a higher return than the mortgage interest rate will generally require accepting risk. There will rarely be a safe investment earning more than mortgage interest rates, except perhaps if someone locked in a mortgage at a low rate and then interest rates later rise.

When it involves taking risk, the decision to pre-pay a mortgage requires a consideration of risk tolerance. Holding a mortgage means holding a negative bond and leveraging the home equity to seek the potential for a higher investment return. The asset allocation is effectively more aggressive with a mortgage. Risk tolerance guides this pre-pay decision, with the understanding that risk tolerance can decline at retirement, and investment volatility can have a bigger impact at retirement with the amplified sequence-of-return risk that distributions create.

Another factor impacting those near retirement is the decline in human capital. Income from working is often also viewed as a more bond-like asset. Pre-paying a mortgage can serve to reduce the overall risk of the household balance sheet to align better with the risk tolerance as one approaches retirement and has less bonds in the form of human capital. Psychologically, this can also make near retirees more comfortable to know that the stress of paying a mortgage is no longer an issue.

As well, once work stops, paying a mortgage requires taking distributions from assets. If this involves distributions from a tax-deferred account, then adjusted gross income may be increased in ways that cause other undesired tax consequences, such as triggering taxes on Social Security benefits. Tax planning for retirement will be considered in much greater detail in the next chapter.

Another matter relates to the potential tax advantages of holding a mortgage. Interest on acquisition debt, which is debt to build, acquire, or substantially improve a home, can be deducted. But to be deductible, itemized deductions need to exceed the standard deduction. After the changes to the tax code made in late 2017, it has become increasingly difficult to itemize. When the standard deduction is taken, there is no tax benefit provided from mortgage interest deductibility. Even when one itemizes, only the amount that exceeds the standard deduction is receiving any real tax benefit.

As well, individuals must understand that the portion of mortgage payments allocated to interest declines with mortgages as the principal is re-paid. An example of this is shown in Exhibit 9.1, in which a $300,000 home is purchased with a 30-year fixed 3.5 percent rate mortgage and a 20 percent down payment. Annual mortgage payments sum to $13,049.12, and initially a large portion of payments are for interest on the loan balance. As time passes, interest payments decrease as the balance gets smaller, and a larger portion of the payment is used to cover principal. Late in the mortgage period most of the payments are for principal and are not deductible. This reduces potential to receive a tax benefit from the mortgage over time. Retirees with a mortgage may find that this large expense in early retirement forces them to take portfolio distributions that they may have otherwise avoided, which can also avoid tax headaches.

Exhibit 9.1
Interest Portion of Mortgage Payments for Fixed 3.5% Rate 30-Year Mortgage on a $300,000 Home with 20% Down Payment

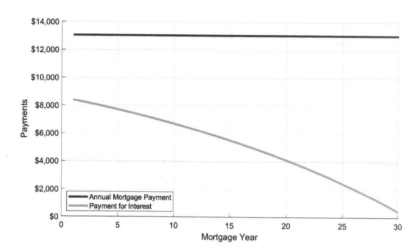

Reverse Mortgages

After considering other housing options, if you have decided to remain in an eligible home (or move into one), you may want to consider a Home Equity Conversion Mortgage (HECM–pronounced "heck-um"). These are commonly known as reverse mortgages. This is another topic that I have written a full book about. Here I am providing a brief overview of my first book, *Reverse Mortgages: How to use Reverse Mortgages to Secure Your Retirement*, which is available for those seeking a deeper dive.

Reverse mortgages have a relatively short history in the United States, originating with a Maine bank in 1961. The 1987 Housing and Community Development Act saw the federal government systemize reverse mortgages through the Home Equity Conversion Mortgage program under the auspices of the US Department of Housing and Urban Development (HUD).

Today, most reverse mortgages in the United States are HECM reverse mortgages, which are regulated and insured through the federal government by HUD and the Federal Housing Authority (FHA). Options outside of the federal program are becoming more common, such as jumbo reverse mortgages for amounts exceeding federal limits. As well, there are fixed-rate HECMs without a line of credit option. But I will focus here on the most common type of reverse mortgage: the variable-rate HECM.

In the past, any discussion of reverse mortgages as a retirement-income tool typically focused on real or perceived negatives related to traditionally high costs and potentially inappropriate uses of funds. These conversations often included misguided ideas about the homeowner losing title to the home and hyperbole about the "American Dream" becoming the "American Nightmare." Reverse mortgages have been portrayed as a desperate last resort option.

However, recent developments have made it harder to dismiss reverse mortgages outright. Especially, since 2013, the federal government has been refining regulations for its HECM program to improve the sustainability of the underlying mortgage insurance fund, to better protect eligible nonborrowing spouses, and to ensure that borrowers have sufficient financial resources to continue paying their property taxes, homeowner's insurance, and home-maintenance expenses. The thrust of these changes has been to ensure that reverse mortgages are used responsibly as part of an overall retirement-income strategy rather than to fritter away assets.

On the academic side, recent research articles have demonstrated how responsible use of a reverse mortgage can enhance an overall retirement-income plan. Importantly, this research incorporates realistic costs for reverse mortgages, both in relation to their initial up-front costs and the ongoing growth of any outstanding loan balance. Quantified benefits I describe here are understood to exist only after netting out realistic costs associated with reverse mortgages.

Reverse mortgages give responsible retirees the option to create liquidity for an otherwise illiquid asset, which can, in turn, potentially support a more efficient retirement-income strategy (more spending and/or more legacy). Liquidity is created by allowing homeowners to borrow against the value of the home with the flexibility to defer repayment until they have permanently left the home.

Regarding the intuition for why reverse mortgages may be a useful tool, we have described how retirees must support a series of expenses—longevity and lifestyle spending goals, unexpected contingencies, legacy goals—to enjoy a successful retirement. Suppose that retirees only have two assets—beyond Social Security and any pensions—to meet their spending obligations: an investment portfolio and home equity. The task is to link these assets to spending obligations efficiently while also mitigating retirement risks like longevity, market volatility, and spending surprises that can impact the plan.

The fundamental question is this: How can these two assets work to meet spending goals while simultaneously preserving remaining assets to cover contingencies and support a legacy? Spending from either asset today means less for future spending and legacy. For the portfolio, spending reduces the remaining asset balance and sacrifices subsequent growth on those investments. Likewise, spending a portion of home equity surrenders future legacy through the increase and subsequent growth of the loan balance. Both effects work in the same way, so the question is how to best coordinate the use of these two assets to meet spending while also preserving reserves and legacy.

When a household has an investment portfolio and home equity, the "default" strategy tends to value spending down investment assets first and preserving home equity, with the goal of supporting a legacy through a debt-free home. A reverse mortgage is viewed as an option, but it is only a last resort once the investment portfolio has been depleted and vital spending needs are threatened.

Recent research on this matter has generally found this conventional wisdom constraining and counterproductive. Initiating the reverse mortgage earlier and coordinating spending from home equity throughout retirement can help meet spending goals while also providing a larger legacy. That is the nature of retirement-income efficiency: using assets in a way that allows for more spending and/or more legacy.

Legacy wealth is the combined value of any remaining financial assets plus any remaining home equity after repaying the reverse-mortgage loan balance. Money is fungible, and the specific ratio of financial assets and remaining home equity is not important. In the final analysis, only the sum of these two components matters. For heirs wishing to keep the home, a larger legacy offers an extra bonus of additional financial assets after the loan balance has been repaid. The home is *not* lost.

While taking money from the reverse mortgage reduces the home-equity component, it does not necessarily reduce the overall net worth or legacy value of assets. Wanting to specifically preserve the home may be a psychological constraint which leads to a less efficient retirement.

There are two potential benefits involved in obtaining a reverse mortgage earlier in retirement that offer the potential to improve retirement efficiencies despite their costs. First, coordinating withdrawals from a reverse mortgage reduces strain on portfolio withdrawals, which helps manage sequence-of-return risk. This is the buffer asset concept at work; reverse mortgages sidestep the sequence risk created by spending from a volatile portfolio by providing an alternative source of spending after market declines. If not used as a buffer asset, continually funding part of retirement spending from the reverse mortgage reduces the distribution rate from remaining assets and a lower distribution rate means less exposure to sequence risk.

The second potential benefit of opening the reverse mortgage early—especially when interest rates are low—is that the principal limit or borrowing capacity will continue to grow throughout retirement. Reverse mortgages are nonrecourse loans, meaning that even if the loan balance is greater than the subsequent home value, the borrower does not have to repay more than the home is worth. Sufficiently long retirements carry a reasonable possibility that the available credit may eventually exceed the value of the home, especially if the home value stagnates. The borrower and/or estate will not be on the hook for repaying more than the value of the home when the loan becomes due. In these cases, mortgage-insurance premiums paid to the government are used to make sure that the lender does not experience a loss. This line-of-credit growth is one of the most important and confusing aspects of reverse mortgages.

Research reveals the possibility of sustaining a spending goal while also leaving a larger legacy at death. Strategically using home equity can lead to a more efficient strategy than the less flexible option of viewing the home as the legacy asset that must not be touched until everything else is gone. This analysis provides a way to test whether the costs of the reverse mortgage— in terms of the up-front costs and compounding growth of the loan balance— are outweighed by the benefits of mitigating sequence risk. Strategic use of a reverse-mortgage line of credit is shown to improve retirement sustainability, despite the costs, without adversely impacting legacy wealth. Next, we will consider how this all works.

How the HECM Program Works

There are many aspects involved in understanding how reverse mortgages work. We will consider the eligibility requirements, how the borrowing capacity is determined, the upfront and ongoing costs for using a reverse mortgage, the spending options, why the line of credit for a HECM grows, why it generally makes sense to open a reverse mortgage line of credit before it may be needed, and repayment and tax issues for reverse mortgages.

First, basic requirements to become an eligible HECM borrower include:

- age (at least sixty-two)
- equity in your home (any existing mortgage or loan can be refinanced with HECM proceeds)
- financial resources to cover tax, insurance, and maintenance
- no other federal debt
- competency
- receipt of a certificate from an FHA-approved counselor for attending a personal counseling session on home-equity options

HUD provides a list of approved counselors on its website. For your *property* to be eligible, it must:

- serve as your primary residence
- meet FHA property standards and flood requirements
- be an FHA-eligible property type
- pass an FHA appraisal
- be maintained to meet FHA health and safety standards

If your home does not meet all standards, some home improvements may also be required before you can initiate a reverse mortgage. As well, the obligations to pay property taxes, homeowner's insurance, and home maintenance should not be viewed as extraordinary, as they are required for any type of mortgage. This protects the lender by keeping up the value of the collateral for the loan.

Next, consider how the initial borrowing capacity for the HECM is determined. The *principal limit* represents the credit capacity available with a HECM reverse mortgage. It is based on the principal limit factor (PLF) table published by HUD. The table shows the percentage of the home equity up to the lending limit that can be accessed initially. Because HECMs are nonrecourse loans, the principal limit that can be borrowed must be less than the home's value to reduce the potential for the loan balance outgrowing it. The available credit amount is determined primarily by the appraised home value, the homeowner's age (or, for couples, the age of the younger eligible spouse—and one spouse must be at least sixty-two), a lender's margin, and an expected interest rate that has been the ten-year LIBOR swap rate but is currently undergoing a transition to Treasury rates. The PLF determines the borrowing amount as a percentage of the appraised home value, up to the FHA mortgage limit of $822,375. If the home's appraisal value exceeds $822,375, this serves as a maximum to which the PLF is applied.

When setting up a HECM, up-front costs for reverse mortgages come in three categories. First, the mortgage lender can charge an origination fee. These are related to the home value and are capped at $6,000 for homes worth more than $400,000. These fees are the maximum allowed by the government. Lenders have discretion to reduce or waive these fees. A second source of up-front costs is the initial mortgage-insurance premium paid to the government, which is 2 percent of the home value. Its maximum value is $16,448 for homes appraised at or above the $822,375 limit. The purpose of the mortgage-insurance premium is to cover the guarantees provided by the FHA to the borrower and lender. Finally, there are traditional mortgage closing costs. These include the costs of the FHA-mandated counseling session, a home appraisal, credit checks, and any costs related to titling. If the appraisal shows shortcomings of the home that could impact health or safety, then additional home repairs may be required as part of setting up the reverse mortgage. The up-front costs could be paid from other resources or financed from the proceeds of the reverse mortgage loan and repaid later with interest. You should plan to stay in your home long enough to justify payment of any up-front costs.

The ongoing costs for a reverse mortgage relate to the interest accruing on any outstanding loan balance, as well as any servicing fees. Servicing fees can be up to $35 per month, though they are generally now incorporated into a higher margin rate rather than charged directly to the borrower. The principal limit grows over time at the effective rate, which consists of a variable short-term interest rate such as the one-month or one-year LIBOR rate or Treasury rate, a lender's margin, and an annual mortgage-insurance premium of 0.5 percent.

The short-term rates are the only variable part for future growth. The lender's margin rate and ongoing mortgage-insurance premium are set contractually at the onset of the loan and cannot change. The margin rate charged on the loan balance is the primary way that the lender—or any buyer on the secondary market—earns revenue, especially lenders who have forgone the origination and servicing fees. Estimates for reasonable margin rates are generally between 1.75 percent and 4.5 percent, with higher numbers typically being associated with lower origination and/or servicing costs.

The principal limit, loan balance, and remaining line of credit all grow at the same variable rate. The sum of the loan balance, line of credit, and any set-aside is the principal limit. Interest and insurance premiums are charged on the loan balance, but not on set-asides or the line of credit. Set-asides are not part of the loan balance until they are used, but they limit access to the line of credit. Though interest and insurance premiums are not levied on set-asides or the line of credit, both components grow as if interest and premiums were charged. This is the key.

When funds are borrowed, the line of credit decreases and the loan balance increases. Conversely, voluntary repayments increase the amount of the line of credit by transferring funds from the loan balance, which will then continue to grow at the effective rate, allowing for access to more credit later.

The overall principal limit consists of the loan balance, remaining line of credit, and any set-asides. These factors grow at the same effective rate, which increases the size of the overall pie over time. If no further spending or repayment happens over time, the proportions of each of these components of the principal limit remain the same since they all grow at the same rate.

Having unused line of credit growth is a valuable consideration for opening a reverse mortgage sooner rather than later. It is also a detail that creates a great deal of confusion for those first learning about reverse mortgages, perhaps because it seems that this feature is almost too good to be true.

I believe that the motivation for the government's design of the HECM reverse-mortgage program is based on an underlying assumption that borrowers will spend from their line of credit sooner rather than later. Implicitly, the growth in the principal limit would then reflect growth of the loan balance more than the growth of the line of credit. In other words, designers assumed that the loan balance would be a large percentage of the principal limit.

The line of credit happens to grow at the same rate as the loan balance, and, if left unused, it can grow quite large. There was probably never an expectation that such open lines of credit would just be left alone for long periods. However, as I will discuss, the bulk of the research on this matter since 2012 suggests that this sort of delayed gradual use of the line of credit can be extremely helpful in prolonging the longevity of an investment portfolio. This could be viewed as a financial planning trick to create an unintended advantage through government rules.

A simple example may help illuminate the concept further. Consider two individuals. Each opens a reverse mortgage with a principal limit of $100,000. For simplicity's sake, assume that ten years later, the principal limit for both borrowers has grown to $200,000.

Person A takes out the entire $100,000 initially from the reverse mortgage (100 percent of the principal limit is the loan balance). For this person, the $200,000 principal limit after ten years reflects a $200,000 loan balance (the loan balance is still 100 percent of the principal limit), which consists of the initial $100,000 received plus another $100,000 divided between accumulated interest payments and insurance premiums.

Person B takes a different route and opens a reverse mortgage but does not use any of the credit, so the $200,000 principal limit at the end of ten years reflects the value fully of the line of credit. The principal limit was still 100 percent in the line of credit. This value was calculated with an implicit assumption that interest and insurance payments have been accruing, even though they have not.

Person B can then take out the full $200,000 after ten years and have the same loan balance as Person A, but Person B has received $200,000 rather than $100,000. At this point, Person B has bypassed the accumulation of interest and insurance during that period.

Generally, opening the line of credit earlier allows for greater availability of future credit relative to waiting until later in retirement to start a HECM. Had Person B waited for the ten years before opening the line of credit, that $200,000 available would have surely been less unless the home value dramatically appreciates, or interest rates experience a large decline during that ten-year period.

With that information in place, we can begin looking at HECM strategies. The proceeds from the variable-rate HECM can be taken out in any of four ways. First is a lump-sum payment. One can take out a large amount initially, though not necessarily the full amount available. Second, the tenure payment option works similarly to an income annuity, with a fixed monthly payment guaranteed to be received while the borrower remains in the home (which, to be clear, is not the same as dying, as the borrower may leave the home while still alive or otherwise fail to meet homeowner obligations). Tenure payments allow for additional spending from the HECM even when the line of credit has been fully used. The mortgage-insurance fund bears the risk that payouts and loan growth from the tenure-payment option exceed the subsequent value of the home when the loan becomes due. This creates a type of "mortality credits" like with an annuity. Third, the term payment is a fixed monthly payment received for a fixed amount of time.

Finally, users have the line of credit. Home equity does not need to be spent initially—or ever. The line of credit can be open and left to grow at a variable interest rate as an available asset to cover a variety of contingencies later in retirement. Distributions can be taken from the remaining line of credit whenever desired until the line of credit has been used in its entirety.

Repayment of a HECM loan balance may be deferred until the last borrower or eligible nonborrowing spouse no longer meets the terms for maintaining the loan, either through death, moving or selling the home, or failing to maintain the homeowner's obligations such as paying property taxes. Prior to that time, repayments can be made voluntarily at any point, with no penalty for early repayment, to help reduce future interest due and allow for a larger line of credit to grow for subsequent use.

The HECM is a nonrecourse loan. The borrower (or borrower's estate) is not obligated to pay the lender more than the smaller of the loan balance or 95 percent of the home's appraised value at that time. When the final repayment is due, the title for the home remains with the borrower or estate. Should beneficiaries wish to keep the home, the smaller of the loan balance or 95 percent of the appraised home value can be repaid with other funds. Heirs can also refinance the home with a traditional mortgage should they wish to keep it. If they decide to sell the home, they keep anything beyond the outstanding loan balance. Should the loan balance exceed what the home can reasonably be sold for, heirs can simply give the home to the lender through a deed in lieu of foreclosure without worrying about selling it themselves.

Generally, the borrower or heirs have up to 360 days to sell the home or refinance when the loan comes due, but this requires a few extensions from the lender. If you intend to use the full 360 days, it is essential that you maintain regular contact and work with the lender during that time.

As for taxes, distributions from reverse mortgages are treated as loan advances and do not reflect taxable income. They are not included in adjusted gross income and do not impact Medicare premiums or the taxation of Social Security benefits. In this regard, proceeds from a reverse mortgage behave the same way as Roth IRA distributions. They can provide a way to increase spending power without pushing you into a higher tax bracket.

A more complex area relates to eligible deductions on interest payments for reverse mortgages. If the interest is related to acquisition debt, it can be deductible when itemizing. Acquisition debt is debt to build, acquire, or substantially improve a primary residence. This includes refinancing a mortgage that was for acquisition debt. If the reverse mortgage is used for general retirement spending, its interest will not be deductible. Interest deductibility is also based on the year it is repaid, not when it is incurred. This can lead to a potentially large tax deduction if the loan balance is paid all in one year, and it is important to strategize around making sure the deduction can provide value. For example, an interest payment may provide the opportunity for a strategic Roth conversion to create income that offsets the deduction.

HELOC vs. HECM

Either a traditional home-equity line of credit (HELOC—pronounced "*he*-lock") or a HECM can serve as a source for contingency funds in retirement. Both cannot be combined on a given home. People often think that they should just use a HELOC and not bother with a HECM, but there are important differences to consider between the two options.

A HELOC may have lower start-up costs, but in most other ways the advantage is with a HECM. With a HELOC, repayments are required sooner. Users of a HECM can voluntarily repay sooner but are under no obligation to make any repayment while eligible for the loan.

In addition, retirees may not qualify for a HELOC if they do not have regular income. Though HECMs added new safeguards in 2015 to make sure that they are not used solely as a last resort by those who have otherwise depleted their resources, the qualification requirements are less stringent than for a HELOC. A HECM may still be available with set-asides included to cover tax, insurance, and maintenance obligations.

A HECM also differs from a HELOC in that its line of credit cannot be canceled, frozen, or reduced. This was a large problem with HELOCs during the 2008 financial crisis and the global pandemic in 2020. With a HECM, borrowers are ensured access to their line of credit. No such protections are available with HELOCs. One also should not forget that the principal limit and line of credit for a HECM will grow throughout retirement, unlike the fixed amount available with a HELOC.

The HECM is noncancelable, it has flexible payback control, and the line of credit grows over time independent of home value. If your goal is to set up a liquid contingency fund, make sure that you examine these important distinctions between HECMs and HELOCs.

Potential Strategies for a HECM

With this background, we now consider the many ways to use a HECM in retirement. Exhibit 9.2 provides a framework for organizing potential strategies. These are ordered from ways that spend available credit more quickly to ways that open the line of credit as a type of insurance backstop that may never need to be tapped. We consider these in turn.

First, coordinating housing-related issues with the investment portfolio and a reverse mortgage can be a critical step in a structurally sound retirement plan. Briefly, for those not carrying a substantial mortgage into retirement, a simple HECM use is to fund home renovations to better support the ability to age in place. This may help retirees to remain in their homes for longer, reducing pressure to move into an institutionalized setting. Other options include providing an alternative to carrying a traditional mortgage into retirement or using the HECM for Purchase program to purchase a new home in retirement.

Exhibit 9:2 The Spectrum of Reverse-Mortgage Strategies

Spend Down Credit (Favors Low Margin Rate / High Upfront Costs)

Portfolio/Debt Coordination for Housing	Refinance an Existing Mortgage
	Transition from Traditional Mortgage to Reverse Mortgage
	Fund Home Renovations to Allow for Aging in Place
	HECM for Purchase for New Home
Portfolio Coordination for Retirement Spending	Spend Home Equity First to Leverage Portfolio Upside Potential
	Coordinate HECM Spending to Mitigate Sequence Risk
	Use Tenure Payments to Reduce Portfolio Withdrawals
Funding Source for Retirement Efficiency Improvements	Tenure Payments as Annuity Alternative
	Social Security Delay Bridge
	Tax Bracket Management or Pay Taxes for Roth Conversions
	Pay Premiums for Existing Long-Term Care Insurance Policy
Preserve Credit as Insurance Policy	Support Retirement Spending After Portfolio Depletion
	Protective Hedge for Home Value
	Provides Contingency Fund for Spending Shocks (In home care, health expenses, divorce settlement)

Preserve Credit (Favors High Margin Rate / Low Upfront Costs)

As well, mortgage debt in retirement presents an additional planning challenge. For retirement distributions, additional fixed payments related to paying off debt create a strain for retirees due to the heightened withdrawal needs triggering greater exposure to sequence-of-return risk. Exposure rises because the debt payments are fixed and require greater distributions than otherwise, so if there is a market decline early in retirement, the portfolio is further strained as an even greater percentage of what is left in the portfolio must be taken to meet these fixed expenses.

The general idea is that a reverse mortgage used primarily to refinance an existing mortgage creates more flexibility for distributions from the investment portfolio by removing a fixed expense from household budgeting in the pivotal early-retirement years. During preretirement, it is common to pay off the mortgage more slowly in hopes that investment returns will outpace the borrowing costs on the mortgage. As we discussed, this approach becomes riskier in retirement, as distribution needs heighten the retiree's vulnerability and exposure to market volatility.

For retirees still carrying a traditional mortgage, two options are to use a HECM to refinance the existing mortgage and then not worry about repaying the loan balance until it becomes due, or to use the HECM to refinance an existing mortgage and then continue making voluntary payments to reduce the size of the loan balance and increase the available line of credit throughout retirement. Both options performed well in my simulations against options to either pay off the mortgage at the start of retirement with financial assets or to continue making payments on the traditional mortgage in retirement from the financial portfolio, and then only treating a reverse mortgage as a last resort option if investment assets deplete. The ability to mitigate sequence-of-return risk by refinancing the mortgage with a HECM is beneficial enough to offset its costs.

When purchasing a new home in retirement, the HECM for Purchase program provides a funding option that can be compared against alternatives such as paying cash for the home or obtaining a fifteen-year traditional mortgage. Again, the question becomes whether the benefits created through the HECM by reducing demands on the portfolio to pay for the retirement home are valuable enough to offset the HECM's costs. I have found that using the HECM for Purchase to reduce the distribution rate from investment assets is a powerful way to manage sequence-of-return risk that creates net advantages after considering the reverse mortgage upfront and ongoing costs.

The second category of uses is to coordinate spending from investment portfolios with the reverse mortgage when funding the retirement spending goal. Sequence risk increases with higher withdrawal rates. Drawing from a reverse mortgage has the potential to mitigate this aspect of sequence risk for an investment portfolio by reducing the need for portfolio withdrawals either generally, or just at inopportune times. Coordinating potential spending with distributions from a reverse-mortgage line of credit can be an effective way to help manage the sequence-of-return risk in retirement. This has been demonstrated in a series of research articles since 2012 highlighting how the strategic use of a reverse mortgage can either preserve greater overall legacy wealth for a given spending goal, or otherwise sustain a higher spending amount for longer in retirement.

The conventional wisdom on how to treat housing wealth in retirement was to preserve it as a last-resort asset for when all else has failed. But this failure to coordinate home equity with the investment portfolio or to attach a growing line of credit to home equity leads to less efficient retirement outcomes by not fully realizing potential ways to manage sequence risk. A reverse mortgage can reduce the need to maintain a larger cash buffer, provide the flexibility to hold on to investments during bear markets, allow flexibility to use home equity as a source of spending, and improve portfolio survivorship rates without an adverse impact on legacy.

For the third category, a reverse mortgage may be a helpful resource to support certain strategies that require paying short-term costs to obtain long-term benefits, such as:

- to fund the creation of a Social Security delay bridge

- to use the tenure-payment option as an alternative to purchasing an income annuity
- to use the reverse mortgage as a longevity insurance alternative
- to pay for the taxes on strategic Roth conversions
- to help avoid falling into a higher marginal tax bracket when sourcing income to meet spending obligations
- to maintain an existing long-term care insurance policy by paying insurance premiums from the line of credit

The final category of use for a HECM is to preserve the line of credit as an insurance policy against a variety of retirement risks. Preserving credit as insurance involves setting up a HECM as early as possible and then leaving it unused until needed. The up-front costs for the reverse mortgage could be treated as an insurance premium that may never need to be used if everything else goes well in retirement. However, a variety of potential pitfalls face retirees, and implementing a reverse mortgage earlier in retirement could support a sizeable pool of contingency assets. Potential insurance provided by the growing line of credit in this context includes protection from declining home values, funds to pay for in-home care to avoid, or at least delay, the need to move to an institution, or as a tool for splitting the home equity in the event of a divorce.

If you think a reverse mortgage may be worth considering, a next step can be to discuss options with a lender. Finding a trustworthy reverse-mortgage lender is not necessarily easy for those beginning the process, but you might seek referrals from your financial advisor, or from friends or family who have felt satisfied with their lenders. It is important to speak with a few different lenders and to get a sense of the range of possibilities regarding the options in terms of up-front costs, the lender's margin, and ongoing costs, and whether the lender can serve as a resource to address any servicing issues after the loan is initiated. Costs will vary and can depend on how the loan is used: those wishing to set up a line of credit as a later resource may have to pay a higher up-front cost than those who plan to spend more quickly from the HECM by refinancing a mortgage. It is important to consider more than just who offers the lowest up-front costs, because having a personal connection to the lender can be important for any subsequent servicing issues or questions, and because the interaction of up-front and ongoing costs can be complicated.

Action Plan

Housing decisions are an important aspect of retirement planning. The following action plan can ensure that housing decisions are made to better support long-term retirement success.

- ☐ Identify the aspects of retirement housing that are most important
- ☐ Begin thinking about housing options in advance of retirement and determine whether a move will be part of your plan

- Conduct trials in any new area to make sure that moving there is the right decision
- Make housing decisions in anticipation that physical and mental impairments may happen with age that impact what you need
- Understand how housing decisions could be impacted by long-term care needs and how moving becomes more difficult with age
- Some retirees will want to move frequently in retirement, while others may wish to stay put or to only move once. Once one gets to the stage of thinking that their current or next home will be more permanent, it is important to consider whether:
    - The home is affordable and the home-related costs, as well as how they may change with age, are budgeted
    - The home is near family, friends, or a social network that can help prevent growing isolation in retirement
    - The home provides an agreeable climate with the right blend of activities and opportunities to have an enjoyable retirement lifestyle
    - The home is in a location that supports any desired work or volunteer opportunities
    - The home is accessible to health facilities and long-term care opportunities
    - The community provides a diverse set of transportation options beyond self-driving
    - Home renovations are done to support aging in place
- For those owning an eligible home, consider whether it is worthwhile to incorporate a HECM early on as part of an overall strategy rather than treating it as a last-resort option

Further Reading

Center for Retirement Research at Boston College. 2014. *Using Your House for Income in Retirement.*

Coughlin, Joseph F. 2013. "3 Questions Predict Future Quality of Life." *MarketWatch RetireMentors Series* (April 17).

Giordano, Shelley. 2019. *What's the Deal With Reverse Mortgages? 2nd Edition.* Washington, DC: Rethink Press.

Green, Richard. 2013. "Who Moves? Not Old People." *Forbes* (July 23).

Merrill Lynch and Age Wave. 2015. "Home in Retirement: More Freedom, New Choices."

Pfau, Wade D. 2018. *Reverse Mortgages: How to Use Reverse Mortgages to Secure Your Retirement.* 2nd Edition. McLean, VA: Retirement Researcher Media.

Chapter 10: Tax Planning for Efficient Retirement Distributions

Tax planning for retirement is as complicated as the ever-expanding tax code might suggest. But applying some key principles can lay a foundation for more tax-efficient distributions that will prolong the sustainability of retirement assets. These efficiencies result from the progressive tax system used in the United States. Tax rates increase with income, such that managing taxable income in a strategic manner over time can help with paying taxes when tax rates are low, while avoiding the need to realize more taxable income when tax rates are high. Tax planning can help improve the efficiency of a portfolio distribution plan by taking advantage of tax diversification, asset location, and tax bracket management. With the complicated tax code, there are many pitfalls and opportunities to consider, and this chapter provides an overview of tax-related issues for retirement distributions.

Incorporating tax planning is a very important part of building an efficient portfolio distribution strategy. For those still in the pre-retirement years, we will discuss how to set up investments for tax efficiency in retirement. After that, we move into managing taxes during retirement. We will consider how to get more spending power without pushing the tax bill too high, and how to take advantage of any leftover tax bracket capacity. This discussion is about strategically controlling taxes to pay them at times when the marginal tax rate is lower. This often involves front-loading some tax payments in retirement, which becomes another example of short-term sacrifice for long-term gain.

We will finish the discussion by also including the impact of taxable income on Social Security and Medicare premiums and consider some other tax strategies to lay the foundation for enhanced after-tax spending. This discussion is meant as an overview of tax considerations and does not consider every nuance of the tax code. While we highlight big picture issues, you should also rely on a tax professional to help develop and confirm specific tax strategies.

The Basics of Income Taxes

Like many countries, the United States has a progressive tax system. This means that the income tax bill increases in a more than proportional way as income increases. Because this process starts fresh for each tax year, it is the foundation for strategizing about greater tax efficiency in retirement.

Tax Brackets, Marginal Tax Rates, and Effective Tax Rates

When considering taxes, we must distinguish between marginal tax rates and effective tax rates. The marginal tax rate is tax paid on last dollar of income. It will be higher at larger taxable incomes due to the progressive tax rates. Generally, it is the tax bracket that your taxable income reaches, though there can be exceptions when more income uniquely also makes Social Security taxable, increases the premiums for Medicare, or eliminates one's ability to qualify for various tax deductions or tax credits. When looking at an additional dollar of income, it is the marginal tax rate that matters.

We will focus on federal income taxes, but many states have their own progressive income tax frameworks that would apply on top of federal income taxes. Some states with income taxes do offer relief for certain types of retirement income, such as Social Security benefits or pension payments. For states with income taxes, these same principles will apply as with federal income taxes, and the advantages of strategic tax planning can be even greater.

To figure out what marginal tax rates apply to income, we must consider the tax filing option. The five filing options in the United States are:

1. Single
2. Married Filing Jointly
3. Married Filing Separately
4. Head of Household
5. Qualifying Widow(er) with Dependent Children

Our discussion will focus on the single or married filing jointly options, as these are likely the most relevant for retirees. The filing option does not affect the tax rates, but it does affect the income brackets on which the tax rates are applied. The current structure for marginal tax rates was created by the Tax Cuts and Jobs Act (TCJA), which was passed in December 2017. The tax rates are 10%, 12%, 22%, 24%, 32%, 35%, and 37%.

Exhibit 10.1 shows the tax rates and the taxable incomes to which they are applied for singles and those married and filing jointly in 2021. These taxable income thresholds represent the tax brackets for federal income taxes. This system has applied for taxable income since 2018. Each year the thresholds for each tax bracket tend to get adjusted upward slightly to account for inflation. The equivalent tax brackets for married individuals filing jointly are higher than for singles. This accounts for the larger household size. In most cases, the tax thresholds for couples are double those for singles. The tax filing status is based on marital status and family situation at the end of the tax year, but one exception is that it is possible to file as married filing jointly for a final time in the year of a spouse's death.

This tax regime will remain until 2026, when taxes are scheduled to revert to their pre-TCJA levels. The tax rates and brackets were higher before, and it is a common belief that tax rates are currently as low as they will ever be.

Therefore, it is a good idea to anticipate a larger tax burden in the future to fund the growing government debt.

Exhibit 10.1
Federal Income Tax Brackets and Rates in 2021

Tax Rate for Taxable Income Over:

Tax Rate	Single Individuals	Married Filing Jointly
10%	$0	$0
12%	$9,950	$19,900
22%	$40,525	$81,050
24%	$86,375	$172,750
32%	$164,925	$329,850
35%	$209,425	$418,850
37%	$523,600	$628,300

Exhibit 10.2 provides details about what the tax rates and tax brackets would have been in 2018 before and after the TCJA.

Exhibit 10.2
Federal Income Tax Brackets and Rates with the Tax Cuts and Jobs Act

Tax Rate for Taxable Income Over:

New Tax Brackets in 2018		Pre-TCJA Tax Brackets for 2018, Set to Resume in 2026	
Tax Rate	Single Individuals	Tax Rate	Single Individuals
10%	$0	10%	$0
12%	$9,525	15%	$9,525
22%	$38,700	25%	$38,700
24%	$82,500	28%	$93,700
32%	$157,000	33%	$195,450
35%	$200,000	35%	$424,950
37%	$500,000	39.6%	$426,700

Tax Rate	Married Filing Jointly	Tax Rate	Married Filing Jointly
10%	$0	10%	$0
12%	$19,050	15%	$19,050
22%	$77,400	25%	$77,400
24%	$165,000	28%	$156,150
32%	$315,000	33%	$237,950
35%	$400,000	35%	$424,950
37%	$600,000	39.6%	$480,050

This is the regime set to resume in 2026 with inflation adjustments made to the numbers. This exhibit reveals the impact of inflation in the comparison between the higher tax brackets from 2021 to their 2018 values. That difference is accounted for solely by the three years of inflation adjustments in 2019, 2020, and 2021, compared to 2018. As for the previous law set to resume, the tax rates applied to different income levels were mostly higher, and these will also surely be adjusted for inflation when they are re-introduced as scheduled in 2026.

These exhibits provide the marginal tax rates applied to various tax brackets. The taxes due and the effective tax rate are determined by adding up the taxes paid for each portion of income up to its total level. Effective tax rates can be much less than marginal tax rates. The typical way to define effective tax rates is the total taxes paid divided by taxable income. In retirement, though, we might consider other ways to define an effective tax rate, such as taxes paid divided by total spending. This is because spending is what retirees care about, rather than the precise definition of taxable income. Many assets provide spending to retirees without increasing taxable income. Making the adjustment to consider taxes relative to spending may be a more meaningful way to understand the tax efficiency of a strategy.

Exhibit 10.3 shows how to calculate income taxes for a single filer in 2021. The idea is that total income taxes due increase as different tax rates are applied to different portions of the income. For example, consider a single filer in 2021 with $164,926 of taxable income. This is $1 into the threshold above $164,925, which is in in the 32 percent tax bracket. Accounting for the lower tax rates before that point, the tax bill is $33,603.00 for income below that bracket plus another 32 cents for the last dollar of income. The total federal tax bill is $33,603.32. As a percentage of taxable income, this is an effective tax rate of $33,603.32 / $164,926 = 20.4 percent. With the progressive tax code, the effective rate is generally the same or less than the marginal tax rate. In this example, we are defining the effective tax rate in terms of taxable income, but this is not the most relevant consideration for retirees. When we know the total spending for the year, we might also investigate the effective tax rate as a percentage of total spending.

Exhibit 10.3
Federal Income Taxes Due for Single Filers in 2021

Tax Rate	Single Individuals	Taxes Due	
10%	$0	$0	plus 10% of income over $0
12%	$9,950	$995.00	plus 12% of income over $9,950
22%	$40,525	$4,664.00	plus 22% of income over $40,525
24%	$86,375	$14,751.00	plus 24% of income over $86,375
32%	$164,925	$33,603.00	plus 32% of income over $164,925
35%	$209,425	$47,843.00	plus 35% of income over $209,425
37%	$523,600	$157,804.25	plus 37% of income over $523,600

Determining Taxable Income

To understand tax planning, it is also important to understand how taxable income is determined and how it relates to total income and adjusted gross income. These are different types of income as defined in the tax code.

We start with total income. It includes salary and wages, self-employment income, interest income, dividend income, rental or other passive income, and short-term capital gains. Total income also includes retirement specific income sources such as distributions from qualified tax-deferred retirement plans, pension income, a portion of distributions from non-qualified annuities, and a portion of Social Security benefits. As well, qualified dividends and long-term capital gains also count as part of total income, but they are subject to a different set of tax rates that we will discuss momentarily. There are some other minor income categories as well. Other issues for total income include that wages, salary, and self-employment income also require payroll taxes to cover Social Security and Medicare, in addition to income tax. As well, some bonds provide interest that is tax exempt, and interest from Treasury bonds is subject to federal income tax, but not state or local income tax.

From total income, we subtract any above the line tax deductions to get to adjusted gross income (AGI). Common above-the-line deductions include contributions up to limits made to tax-advantaged retirement plans such as Individual Retirement Accounts (IRAs) and 401(k)s, but not their Roth counterparts, contributions to Health Savings Accounts, the deductible part of the self-employment payroll tax, and student loan interest deductions. There are several other less common above-the-line deductions as well. Removing these deductions leads to AGI:

Adjusted gross income = total income – above-the-line deductions

The AGI is an important measure, as there are various modified adjusted gross income measures (MAGI) based on AGI used to calculate related taxes and subsidies such as the portion of taxable Social Security, Medicare premiums, Affordable Care Act health care plan subsidies, and so forth. The definition of MAGI varies for almost every application in which it shows up in the tax code, but it generally involves adding a few items to AGI that are not part of the AGI definition. The subsequent below-the-line deductions we discuss can reduce taxable income but not AGI, and therefore do not reduce exposure to these auxiliary tax issues. But one has some control over AGI by contributing to savings plans that provide tax deductions or by limiting distributions from accounts that generate taxable income.

From AGI, we subtract the below-the-line deductions to calculate taxable income. Below-the-line deductions equal the larger of two options: the standard deduction amount or the total of allowed itemized deductions. Subtracting the larger of these choices leads to taxable income:

Taxable income = adjusted gross income – below-the-line deductions

Taxable income is the amount used in the previous exhibits to calculate the taxes due. The Tax Jobs and Cuts Act of 2017 raised the standard deduction and removed exemptions. The standard deduction amount in 2021 is $12,550 for individuals and $25,100 for married couples filing jointly. An additional standard deduction amount for those aged 65 and older or the blind is $1,700 for singles and $2,700 for married filing jointly.

If itemizing deductions can allow for values that exceed these standard amounts, then itemizing will reduce taxable income. However, with the increase in the standard deduction, fewer households will likely benefit from itemizing in the future. As well, changes in the Tax Cuts and Jobs Act make itemizing harder by reducing options.

First, the home mortgage interest deduction has been modified. One may only deduct interest on acquisition indebtedness – a mortgage used to buy, build, or substantially improve one's home - up to $750,000 for joint filers. For mortgages taken out before December 15, 2017, the limit is $1,000,000 for joint filers. Keep in mind, as retirement approaches, mortgage debt is less likely; those who have mortgage debt typically plan to pay it off soon. As well, because a larger portion of the payment is applied to principal as a mortgage gets closer to pay-off, there is less to potentially deduct.

Next, a significant change also took place with state and local taxes. Deductions for state and local sales, income, and property taxes remain in place but are now limited. The cap on claiming for all state and local sales, income, and property taxes together may not exceed $10,000 for joint filers. As for medical and dental expenses, the "floor" is 7.5 percent of AGI in 2021. The portion of qualifying medical expenses that exceeds 7.5 percent of AGI are the only deductible part of those expenses that can count as an itemized deduction. Finally, charitable donations are another important deduction category. Charitable donations are also only deductible up to certain limits as a percentage of AGI.

A final note is that for high-income taxpayers who itemize their deductions, the Pease limitations previously capped or phased out certain deductions. Under the current tax law, these Pease limitations no longer apply, but they could return along with personal exemption phaseouts when the pre-2018 tax regime returns as scheduled in 2026.

We have discussed the categories for below-the-line deductions. To be clear, they only provide value when their total exceeds the standard deduction. If the standard deduction is larger than the itemized deductions, then the itemized deductions do not have any impact and do not help to reduce the tax bill. They are effectively wasted in this regard. This creates room for some planning strategies such as deduction bunching that we will consider in greater detail later in the chapter. This situation is the first of several nonlinearities in the tax code we address in this chapter that make planning more important. By a nonlinearity, I mean that the impact varies in a way that is not a straight line. The nonlinearity for deductions is that they have no impact when they add up to less than the standard deduction, and that only the portion of itemized deductions exceeding the standard deduction creates any real value to reducing taxes.

Payroll Taxes

There are a few more related issues to consider. If you continue to work in retirement – in the form of salary, wages, or self-employment income – you must pay payroll taxes. They are not applied to other sources of total income. For salary and wages, the tax is split between the employee and employer. It is 6.2 percent for Social Security and 1.45 percent for Medicare. This totals 7.65 percent from each. For the self-employed, the full amount must be paid by the individual, adding up to 15.3 percent of these income sources. The portion of the payroll tax that applies to Social Security is only charged on up to the maximum wage base limit, which is $142,800 in 2021. The Medicare portion of the tax applies to these income sources without a cap and there are additional surcharges at higher income levels. Payroll taxes will continue to impact earned income if paid work continues during retirement.

Taxes for Long-Term Capital Gains and Qualified Dividends

As mentioned, special tax rates apply for qualified dividends and long-term capital gains (LTCGs). Exhibit 10.4 shows the tax rates and tax brackets for these income sources in 2021. Capital gains are realized when an asset is sold for more than its cost basis, which is usually closely related to how much was paid for the asset including its purchase price and any brokerage commissions. Regarding long-term vs short-term capital gains, the difference is that long-term gains are for assets held for more than one year and short-term gains apply for assets held less than a year. LTCGs are taxed at lower rates, and they are only taxed when realized. This is a benefit gained from holding the security for at least a year. Mutual fund owners may find that their tax forms include capital gains even when no shares were sold, because the underlying funds may be buying and selling securities throughout the year.

Exhibit 10.4
Federal Tax Rates for Qualified Dividends and Long-Term Capital Gains in 2021

Tax Rate for Taxable Income Over:

Tax Rate	Single Individuals	Married Filing Jointly
0%	$0	$0
15%	$40,400	$80,800
20%	$445,850	$501,600

Assets can suffer from capital losses as well as enjoy gains. When losses and gains are realized, the method for determining taxable income is that first any short-term losses offset short-term gains and any long-term losses offset long-term gains. If there are net gains for both short-term and long-term holdings, then each is added to taxable income accordingly. If one of these categories has a net loss, then the short-term and long-term outcomes offset each other. When the resulting value is positive, that income is taxed according to whether it was the short-term or long-term gain that was larger. With a net loss at the end, up to $3,000 of a capital loss may be deducted from ordinary income in a given tax year. Any remaining capital loss can be carried forward to deduct in future years.

If there are net gains, then we can consider how long-term capital gains (as well as qualified dividends) are applied to the calculation of taxable income. These preferential income sources are added to taxable income on top of all the other taxable income sources. For example, suppose a single individual has a taxable income of $42,000, which consists of $38,000 of income sources taxed at regular rates and $4,000 of LTCGs and qualified dividends. The $38,000 is taxed according to the tax schedule from Exhibit 10.3. This individual is in the 12% tax bracket for that last dollar of income. The remaining $4,000 is added on top of this amount and taxed with the tax schedule in Exhibit 10.4. The first $2,400 is still in the 0% tax bracket and the remaining $1,600 falls into the 15% tax bracket. Notice that a 0% tax rate applies for taxable income amounts that are close to the top of the 12% federal tax brackets. Even though the combined taxable income looks to place the individual in the 22% federal income tax bracket, this is not the case after separating out the income taxed at preferential rates, adding it to the top of other taxable income, and then applying those preferential rates to this portion of income.

Capital Gains Exclusion for Selling Home

While discussing capital gains, it is worth mentioning another area that can impact retirees, which is the exclusion of a portion of capital gains on the sale of a home when certain conditions are met. Single individuals may be eligible to exclude up to $250,000 of long-term capital gains on the sale of a home, and this can be up to $500,000 for couples. A surviving spouse may also receive the full couple's exclusion for two years following a spouse's death.

Qualifying for the full exclusion amount requires meeting several tests. These include both an ownership and use test. The ownership test requires being an owner of the property for at least two years over the previous five years before the sale. The use test is similar in terms of requiring using the home by living in it as the main home for at least two years over the previous five years. For couples, the use test requires both spouses to use the home while the ownership test only requires one spouse to own. There is also an eligibility test stating that the exclusion may not have been received for at least two years. There are exceptions to these rules including a shorter time for the use test or being able to receive a partial exclusion if forced to leave the home for unforeseen circumstances or due to a health or cognitive issue that may involve the need to move to assisted living or a nursing home. This ability to exclude potentially large capital gains on a home sale is an important advantage of home ownership, though it is worth pointing out that those incurring a loss on a home sale are not able to use that loss to offset other gains.

Tax Diversification

We can now dive deeper into strategies for obtaining greater efficiency from retirement distributions. We will start with pre-retirement strategies designed to provide optimal preparation for retirement. These include tax diversification and asset location.

Regarding tax diversification, investment accounts fall into three main tax categories: taxable accounts, tax-deferred accounts, and tax-exempt accounts. As will become clear with the discussion of planning, tax diversification will be a general goal for retirees, as there are benefits to have some assets in each of these types of account structures. This is beneficial because we do not know what future tax rates will be and when we will experience events that could either lead us to generate taxable income at low tax rates or be forced to generate taxable income at high tax rates.

Taxable Accounts

Taxable accounts are standard brokerage accounts and bank accounts. They are funded with after-tax money, meaning that taxes have already been paid on any income before it is invested. Some important features of taxable accounts include that ongoing taxes must be paid on interest and dividends as they are received, as well as any realized capital gains from pooled investments like mutual funds. Qualified dividends and realized long-term capital gains are taxed at lower rates. As well, taxable accounts have a cost basis which can be spent tax free. For legacy purposes, the cost basis receives a step-up at death to match the value of the assets at that time, avoiding potential capital gains tax for beneficiaries.

When selling shares, there are three options that may be used to determine the cost basis of the shares sold. The average cost basis for all shares can be applied, shares can be sold on a first in, first out basis with the oldest shares being sold first, or one can specify which specific share lots are being sold to better control the amount of capital gains generated. The latter option provides the most flexibility to identify and control the amounts of gains and losses, but it requires the most effort to keep track of all purchases and reinvested interest or dividends.

Ongoing taxation on account growth is not an attractive feature because taxes subtract from the value of the account and leave less for subsequent growth. For a very simple example to illustrate this idea, consider a $1,000 account that grows at a 5 percent compounded growth rate for ten years. Consider a 20 percent tax rate on account earnings that can either be applied on an ongoing basis or can be applied once to cumulative earnings at the end of ten years. First, if there was no tax, the $1,000 would grow to $1,628.90 after ten years of 5 percent annually compounding growth. If a 20 percent tax is applied to the growth just at the end of ten years, the post-tax account balance would be $1,503.12. But if the 20 percent tax is applied annually to earnings, the ending after-tax account balance would be just $1,480.24. The impact would be larger as the length of the investment horizon increases, as the investment return increases, or as the tax rate increases. Allowing for tax-deferred growth is a valuable attribute.

Tax-Deferred Accounts

Tax-deferred accounts are qualified retirement savings accounts such as employer-sponsored retirement plans and traditional Individual Retirement Accounts (IRAs). Specifically, employer-sponsored retirement plans include 401(k) plans for private for-profit employers, 403(b) plans that are typically associated with educational institutions and other tax-exempt organizations, 457 plans for state and local government employees and other nonprofits, as well as the Federal Thrift savings plan at the federal government level. Employer plans also include traditional defined-benefit plans that structure benefits as an annuity payment to the participant. Defined benefit plans also include profit sharing or cash balance plans. These plans are also referred to as either employer plans or qualified plans throughout the book. As for IRAs, this includes traditional IRAs as well as SEP or SIMPLE IRAs that can function as employer plans but are structured more like IRAs in terms of their options and rules. Some small employers may offer SIMPLE IRA plans instead of 401(k) plans. For the self-employed, options include SEP IRAs, a solo 401(k), or a defined-benefit plan (though these are not common).

These plans are funded with pre-tax money, which means that money invested in these accounts provides an above the line tax deduction to reduce adjusted gross income for the year it is invested. Tax deductible contributions are most common, but it is also possible in some circumstances to make nondeductible contributions as well. Nondeductible contributions are treated as cost basis in the plan and may be made to IRAs when income exceeds thresholds for deductions, and some employer plans may allow for after-tax contributions to be made as well. Life insurance cannot be held in IRAs, but it can be found in some qualified plans.

Money, including both the deductible contributions and account growth, is taxed upon withdrawal, generally at ordinary income tax rates. Any nondeductible contributions from the accounts are treated as cost basis and may be distributed without taxes. The ordinary income tax rates, which are often higher, are applied to all taxable distributions, including what would have been counted as long-term capital gains and qualified dividends if the assets had been held in a taxable account.

Tax deferral has value. Allowing assets to grow tax free and then paying once at the end, rather than chipping away at their compounding growth potential by forcing ongoing taxes to be paid on the interest, dividends, and gains, can frequently lead to greater after-tax values for the assets. Though it depends on the assumptions, this is frequently true even after considering that income which might have counted as qualified dividends or long-term capital gains is forced to be taxed at ordinary income tax rates when held inside of the tax-deferred account.

There are limits on contributions that can be made to these accounts. These limits can apply both to the amount of the contribution and to the income levels that will still allow for the deduction. In 2021, IRA contribution limits were 100 percent of employment earnings up to a maximum of $6,000 with an additional $1,000 catch-up contribution allowed for those aged 50 and older. One must have earned income in an amount at least equal to the contribution. An exception is made for non-working spouses who are filing jointly. They may contribute based on the working spouse's earnings.

As well, the contribution only provides a tax deduction when income falls below certain levels for those who are also eligible for a retirement plan at work. If income exceeds these thresholds, the contribution to the IRA can still be made, but it is not deductible. These phaseouts for deductibility begin at modified adjusted gross incomes of $66,000 for singles and $105,000 for couples filing jointly in 2021. If a person is not an active participant in an employer plan but the spouse is, then the phaseout for the non-active person begins at $198,000. For those not eligible to participate with an employer retirement plan, the income limits do not apply.

As for retirement plans such as 401(k)s and 403(b)s, employee contribution limits are $19,500 in 2021, with a catch-up total of $26,000 for those who are 50 and older. Employers can also make contributions of up to $38,500. These employer contributions may be provided independent of any action from their worker, or they may be provided as a company match on worker contributions that become available after meeting eligibility and vesting requirements. There are no income limits.

If one can choose whether to contribute to an employer plan or an IRA, there are a few issues to consider. The first detail to note is that many employer-sponsored retirement plans will offer an employer match for a portion of employee contributions. It is generally best to first contribute at least enough to benefit from the full company match. Otherwise, this is free money that will be left on the table. Beyond this, some employer 401(k) plans may have high fees and limited investment options compared to IRA plans. As well, it can be more difficult to tap into an employer plan while still employed. Some may offer hardship withdrawals or participant loans, but not all plans have this flexibility. This must be evaluated as part of the tax diversification decision. When employment ends, options for retirement account assets include potentially keeping them in the employer plan, rolling them over to an IRA, or taking as a taxable distribution with possible penalties if done before age 59.5.

Tax-Exempt Accounts

Tax-exempt accounts include Roth IRAs, Roth 401(k)s, or Roth 403(b)s. They are funded with after-tax money, meaning that any income invested in these accounts has already been taxed. The contribution limits are the same as with tax-deferred accounts. Contributions are not tax deductible. However, their great advantage is that no taxes are owed on qualified distributions from the accounts. This protects investment gains from tax.

Roth IRA accounts do have income limits that may prevent direct contributions. In 2021, the full contribution is allowed for singles whose modified adjusted gross income is under $125,000 and for married filing jointly cases with modified adjusted gross incomes under $198,000. Unlike with traditional IRAs, these rules are not related to whether one is an active participant in an employer retirement plan. Once incomes exceed these levels, Roth IRA contributions are quickly fully phased out by MAGIs of $140,000 and $208,000, respectively. When exceeding these limits, the IRS does allow what is known colloquially as a backdoor Roth contribution. In this case, the individual makes a nondeductible contribution to an IRA, waits a few days, and then converts this amount to the Roth account. This approach works without a hitch when any IRAs owned are otherwise empty before the contribution. Otherwise, with other account assets, the pro-rata rules for the Roth conversion will apply and the transaction will not be tax free. These pro-rata rules are discussed later in the chapter.

Some employer plans may offer Roth versions. With Roth accounts, Roth contributions are only available on employee contributions. The employer contribution cannot be made to a Roth account.

There are no age limitations on making contributions to Roth IRAs. One can always contribute any earned income up to the limits when incomes are below the thresholds. With the SECURE Act passed in 2019, this is also now true for traditional IRAs as well.

Choosing Between Tax-Deferred and Tax-Exempt Accounts

An important part of tax diversification is that over time it can be helpful to accumulate assets in a variety of account types to create more flexibility about the sources of retirement spending as a control for taxes. To plan for diversification, in any given year we must decide where to place our savings. When deciding between tax-deferred and tax-exempt options, the goal is to pay taxes at the time that one is subject to a lower marginal tax rate. Tax-deferred accounts are most useful for those who may be in peak earnings years and expect to be in lower tax brackets in the future. The idea is to get the tax deduction today when the tax rate applied would be higher, and then pay taxes on the distributions later at a lower tax rate.

Roth accounts have the opposite characteristic. Individuals can pay taxes and contribute to Roth accounts today because they anticipate a higher tax rate will be applied to their future distributions. For this reason, Roth contributions can make sense for younger individuals who have not yet reached their full earnings potential, as well as during years that taxable income is unusually low. Roth contributions are also a consideration for those who are worried that the tax code of the future could include substantially higher tax rates than today.

The discussion here is about where to place new contributions between tax-deferred and tax-exempt. This comparison of tax rates now and in the future also applies to making Roth conversions for tax-deferred assets. A Roth conversion triggers taxable income as a distribution, which is transferred to a Roth account. This creates taxable income during the current year but then allows subsequent qualifying Roth distributions to be made without generating taxable income. The idea is to make Roth conversions when the tax rate applied is relatively low compared to what it may be in the future. This comparison also applies to the tax rates for beneficiaries who may receive the retirement account as an inheritance.

To summarize, the conventional wisdom around choosing between traditional and Roth accounts is that the choice does not matter if the tax rate is the same both today and in retirement. If the tax rate will be higher in the future, then contribute to the Roth IRA today or consider a Roth conversion for existing tax-deferred assets, and if the tax rate will be lower in the future, then contribute to the traditional IRA today and hold off on making a Roth conversion.

Advantages of Tax-Exempt Accounts for Retirement Income

There are a few reasons to consider contributing to the Roth even if the tax rate is expected to be a bit lower in the future. First, since the government technically has claim over part of the tax-deferred account, the Roth allows its owner to obtain tax deferral on more assets. William Reichenstein of Baylor University has described tax-deferred accounts as a type of limited partnership in which the account owner really only owns $(1-t)$ percent of the account, and the government owns the other t percent of the account. The t is the marginal tax rate at the time that funds are distributed.

Rather than think of tax-deferred accounts as tax-deferred, it is really the case that the portion of the account owned by the investor is tax-exempt. For this portion, the owner experiences the full return and the full risk. The issue is that the government is entitled to a share of the distributions to be paid as taxes, and the owner of the account has some discretion about when to take these distributions to minimize the portion of the account that goes to the government.

Suppose someone contributing is in the 22 percent tax bracket. She could contribute $1,000 of after-tax tax money to the Roth account and have no current tax savings, or she could contribute $1,000 to the traditional IRA and have $220 of tax savings. But the government will receive a portion of the traditional IRA in the future, so the owner does not really benefit from the full contribution amount. If the owner is still in the 22 percent tax bracket when the distribution is taken, then the owner receives 78 percent of the distribution after taxes are paid. To make up this difference, she may invest the $220 of current tax savings in a taxable account, which is then subject to ongoing taxes on its compounding growth potential. Investors do not receive all the returns from assets held in taxable accounts because of this ongoing need to pay taxes which, if paid from the investments, means that less is subsequently retained to benefit from compounding growth. Together, this means that even with a lower tax rate in retirement, contributing to the Roth and having full access to the contribution and its growth could still provide net benefits.

As well, in terms of tax diversification, Roth IRAs provide benefits by giving access to contributions without penalty prior to age 59.5. After age 59.5, distributions are tax free if the account has been open for at least five years. Roth IRAs can also help to cover large, unexpected expenses in retirement without triggering higher taxes as would be the case when pulling from a tax-deferred account to cover an unexpected spending need. Traditional IRA distributions count as part of adjusted gross income, as mentioned, while Roth distributions do not show up as income at all in tax calculations. Roth IRAs are also very efficient tools for providing legacy as they do not result in taxable income for their beneficiaries.

While Roth accounts provide many advantages, a reason for diversification relates to the possibility of future law changes. Roth distributions will likely never be taxable, but Congress could enact reforms that would reduce the value of Roth accounts. Two possibilities include adding required minimum distributions (RMDs) for the accounts or including the distributions in measures of modified adjusted gross income or provisional income for determining other taxes such as on Social Security or triggering higher Medicare premiums. With required minimum distributions, the Roth distributions would not necessarily need to be spent, but they would have to at least be reinvested into a taxable account and the assets would lose their tax advantages. Already, Roth 401(k)s do have RMDs, but these can be avoided by rolling the assets over to a Roth IRA before the year that one turns age 72.

As part of the tax diversification discussion, another critical matter for qualified retirement accounts such as 401(k)s and IRAs is that they will eventually be subject to required minimum distributions (RMDs) that generate taxable income. Since the passing of the SECURE Act at the end of 2019, RMDs now begin at age 72 instead of 70.5. The CARES Act that was part of the response to the global pandemic did temporarily remove the need to take RMDs in 2020, but they are back in 2021. Roth IRAs do not experience required minimum distributions during the owner's lifetime, and this can be a very valuable attribute for making tax-strategic distributions.

Having too much in tax-deferred accounts can provide an RMD surprise by pushing people unexpectedly into higher tax brackets. This is the retirement tax cliff. RMDs generate taxable income and cannot be avoided even when one has no interest in spending these funds. This is a key reason to diversify and not hold too much in qualified retirement plans.

Exhibit 10.5 provides an idea about required minimum distributions at different ages and for different account balances. Approximately, having

$500,000 in qualified plans will mean that RMDs remain less than the standard deduction for married filing jointly couples until more advanced ages are reached. This could be an important part of a lower overall tax level in retirement. Besides tax diversification, this can be a justification for tax bracket management and making Roth conversions especially in the years before RMDs begin. Maintaining high balances in tax-deferred accounts subject to RMDs can lead to a lot of taxable income later in retirement that may exceed what is needed to support retirement expenses. Especially as one ages and remaining life expectancies get shorter, the RMD percentages, which are one divided by remaining life expectancies, increase. This triggers more taxable income from a given account balance. Such distributions could be reinvested into taxable accounts (as one cannot do Roth conversions on RMD amounts), but taxes would have to be paid at higher rates than may have been necessary with more careful planning.

Exhibit 10.5
Taxable Income Generated by Required Minimum Distributions

IRA Balance	RMD @ 72	RMD @ 75	RMD @ 80	RMD @ 90
IRS Life Expectancy	25.6	22.9	18.7	11.4
$100,000	$3,906	$4,367	$5,348	$8,772
$500,000	$19,531	$21,834	$26,738	$43,860
$1,000,000	$39,063	$43,668	$53,476	$87,719
$2,000,000	$78,125	$87,336	$106,952	$175,439
$3,000,000	$117,188	$131,004	$160,428	$263,158

Asset Location

The next important tax-planning issue is asset location. In a similar manner to diversification between different account structures, asset location addresses the issue of which assets should be held in each type of account. Asset allocation addresses how to allocate the overall financial portfolio between different asset classes like stocks, bonds, real estate investment trusts, and so forth. Asset location addresses where different asset classes should be held among taxable, tax-deferred, and tax-exempt accounts.

Exhibit 10.6 ranks different assets in terms of their tax efficiency. Determining the appropriate asset allocation should always be considered before asset location, but once asset allocation is determined, this exhibit prioritizes tax efficiency regarding asset location. All else being the same, more tax efficient assets should be held in taxable accounts and less tax-efficient assets can be held in accounts providing tax advantages. This applies to the extent possible with the capacity constraints for each account type.

Starting at the top, tax-exempt bonds should always be held in a taxable account. They offer a lower yield because their tax advantages make them more equivalent to taxable bonds on a net-of-tax basis for those paying taxes on bond interest at higher tax rates. Placing tax-exempt bonds in a tax-advantaged account would just lead to a lower return without any offsetting tax benefits.

Exhibit 10.6
The Spectrum of Tax Efficiency for Asset Classes

Most Tax Efficient

Taxable Accounts — Tax-Exempt Bonds

US Stock Index Funds

International Stock Index Funds

Cash

Actively Managed Stock Funds

Government Bond Funds

Corporate Bond Funds

Commodities

Tax-Advantaged Accounts — Real Estate Investment Trusts

Least Tax Efficient

Next, stocks tend to lean toward taxable accounts, especially index funds. They provide preferable tax treatment for long-term capital gains and qualified dividends. Unrealized capital gains also naturally receive tax deferral since taxes are not paid until assets are sold. Taxable assets also provide a step up in basis at death, which eliminates capital gains taxes for beneficiaries. They also provide the ability to harvest losses to offset gains. And one can donate appreciated shares with the most long-term capital gains to charities to obtain more tax benefits than just donating cash. With capital gains taxes, the government partly shares the risk of investing in equities in taxable accounts since capital losses reduce taxes.

For stocks, US stock index funds are listed first because the dividend yield tends to be less than international stocks at present, which will help to lower their ongoing taxes. Also, index funds are more tax efficient because they involve less trading and asset turnover, resulting in less realized capital gains on shares that one continues to own.

Next on the list is interest on cash holdings. This is taxable, but cash tends to have low yields at present, so there may not be much taxable interest.

Actively managed stock funds come next. They are less tax efficient than index funds. Capital gains and losses reported by mutual funds can differ from the change in fund value because it depends on sales of underlying assets held in the funds. Active funds that trade more frequently will trigger more taxes through these realized gains or losses on sales even when the fund owner holds onto the shares. Active funds may also trigger more short-term gains through their internal buying and selling, and these taxes are passed to the owner of the fund.

Moving along, government and corporate bond funds are next. More of their returns are generated through the payment of interest, and tax deferral can help to avoid paying ongoing income taxes on that interest. This can leave more in the account to remain invested and to grow.

Asset Location in a Low Interest Rate World

As interest rates have fallen so low, one consequence could be the shifting of some of the advice around asset location. Since they pay so little in interest, bonds might also be held in taxable accounts with minimal tax implications.

Finally, some asset classes like commodities or real estate investment trusts are particularly known for tax inefficiency. They are good candidates for tax-advantaged accounts.

Besides the issue of tax efficiency and placing assets into taxable or tax-advantaged accounts, decisions must be made about the placement of tax-advantaged assets between tax-deferred and tax-exempt accounts. When deciding on an asset location between IRA and Roth IRAs, for instance, the suggestion is to locate higher expected-return assets in the Roth accounts and lower expected-return assets in traditional accounts. In this case, bonds would be targeted first for tax-deferred accounts. A disadvantage of having stocks in tax-deferred accounts is that their long-term capital gains and qualified dividends that would have been taxed at lower rates, end up being taxed as ordinary income. Instead, Roth accounts could be the place to hold less tax-efficient stocks with high growth prospects such as small value, emerging markets, and so forth. Such gains will not be taxed with qualifying distributions from the Roth. Holding assets in this manner will also accommodate the withdrawal order sequencing issue that we will address for retirement distributions as Roth distributions will tend to happen later in retirement, facilitating a higher level of risk.

Exhibit 10.7 provides a summary of this asset location discussion. Taxable accounts hold the most tax-efficient assets. Tax-deferred accounts hold less tax-efficient assets with lower expected returns. Tax-exempt accounts hold less tax-efficient assets with higher expected returns.

Remember, asset allocation decisions comes first, even if it means holding assets in accounts that are not necessarily suggested by our discussion. For example, an individual portfolio may contain more bonds than available capacity in tax-deferred accounts. This does not mean the amount of bonds owned should be limited. Rather, it means owning bonds in taxable or tax-exempt accounts as well. The guidelines we offer are meant as suggestions in terms of where assets should be placed when the capacity is available, but asset allocation should rank ahead of asset location in terms of deciding which assets to own. When tax-inefficient assets are held in taxable accounts because there is not enough spare capacity available in tax-advantaged accounts, there are other financial tools that can provide additional tax advantages as we will consider briefly in the next section.

Exhibit 10.7
Asset Location Characteristics

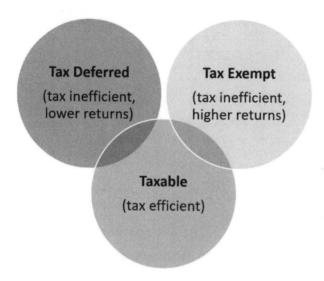

Obtaining Tax Advantages for Taxable Assets

To summarize the tax diversification discussion, there are three potential ways to obtain tax advantages in the tax code:

1. Receiving a tax deduction for contributed funds, which reduces current taxable income.
2. Gains could accumulate on a tax-deferred basis.
3. The distribution of gains could be obtained free of additional taxes.

Tax-deferred and tax-exempt accounts provide attractive options to consider before placing assets into a taxable account. The ongoing taxes for a taxable account will chip away at its after-tax growth. But tax-deferred and tax-free retirement plans have limits on how much can be contributed on an annual basis. For those who exceed these limits, various financial tools exist to obtain tax advantages for assets that would otherwise be held in taxable accounts.

Exhibit 10.8 shows more about the three beneficial tax properties and a more complete list of different types of assets that may provide them. First, taxable brokerage accounts do not provide any of these benefits. Qualified retirement plans provide a tax deduction and tax deferral. Roth accounts provide tax deferral and tax-free distributions. The exhibit also lists other potential options.

Exhibit 10.8
Tax Advantages for Different Types of Assets

	Tax Deduction	Tax Deferral	Tax-Exempt Distributions
Brokerage Accounts			
IRA, 401(k), & Other Qualified Plans	Yes	Yes	
Roth IRA, Roth 401(k)		Yes	Yes
529 Plans	Yes, in some states	Yes	Yes, for qualified education expenses
Health Savings Accounts	Yes	Yes	Yes, for qualified medical expenses
I-Bonds & E-Bonds		Yes	
Tax Exempt Bonds			Yes, though interest is counted toward Social Security benefit and Medicare premium taxation
Nonqualified Annuities		Yes	
Cash Value Life Insurance		Yes	Yes, when structured properly

Education 529 Plans and Health Savings Accounts

Two additional tax vehicles for specific expenses include 529 plans and Health Savings Accounts (HSAs). 529 plans work similarly to Roth accounts when used for qualified education expenses. They provide tax deferral and tax-free distributions. And though they do not offer deductions for federal income tax, some states do provide a deduction for state income taxes. Next, health savings accounts are a special type of tax vehicle that can provide all three tax benefits. This is a rarity. Health savings account contributions are tax deductible, grow tax deferred, and can be distributed tax free for qualified medical expenses. For other expenses, taxes must be paid along with a 20 percent penalty. At age 65, the penalty goes away when used for non-medical expenses, but taxes will still be due, meaning the treatment is same as with an IRA. To contribute to an HSA, you must be enrolled in a qualified high deductible health plan. In 2021, the limits on HSA contributions are $3,600 for individual health plans and $7,200 for family health plans. Those over 55 can make a $1,000 additional catch-up contribution.

Fixed Income Assets with Tax Advantages

In the realm of fixed income, for individuals who have filled their tax advantaged accounts and still seek more tax benefits on bond holdings, additional options include I-Bonds or E-Bonds, and tax-exempt municipal bonds. I-Bonds and E-Bonds provide tax deferral and I-Bonds provide a real yield plus realized inflation. The interest on these bonds is taxed when the assets are distributed. There are annual contribution limits for these types of bonds. As well, municipal bonds pay interest that is not counted as taxable income when determining total income. They do have an important caveat for retirees though, as their interest is included in modified and provisional income measures that are used to determine how much Social Security benefits are taxed and whether additional Medicare premiums are required.

Nonqualified Annuities

Another major product category with tax advantages is the nonqualified annuity, which offers tax deferral and can be incorporated into financial plans in different ways. It is worth having a basic understanding about how the taxes for annuities work when they are being used by households as a source of ongoing spending during the owner's lifetime. A great resource for more in-depth treatment of annuity tax issues is John Olsen and Michael Kitces' book, *The Advisor's Guide to Annuities*.

When it comes to basic tax treatment for annuities, we distinguish between annuities held in nonqualified or taxable accounts, and annuities held in qualified retirement plans such as IRAs and 401(k)s. As well, we must distinguish between annuities that have been annuitized into a stream of payments and annuities that remain in the deferral stage, which includes non-lifetime distributions and lifetime distributions obtained through an optional guaranteed lifetime withdrawal benefit.

Income annuities, including single-premium immediate annuities and deferred income annuities, are already annuitized and provide the ability to lock in income. Deferred annuities such as variable and index annuities provide more flexibility because they are not annuitized. They offer upside potential, the ability to annuitize within the contract, and many offer an option to add a lifetime income benefit that will support guaranteed lifetime distributions without annuitization.

In taxable accounts, the basic idea for annuities is that distributions representing return of premium are not taxed, but distributions representing any interest or gains through market growth or mortality credits are taxed. Taxation occurs at the point of distribution rather than when interest is earned, which allows for continued tax deferral for the underlying annuity assets until distributions are made.

For income annuities and other annuitized contracts that were purchased in a taxable account, meaning that they are nonqualified annuities, the portion of payments representing interest and mortality credits is taxed as income, and the portion representing the return of premium is received tax-free. To determine how much of the annuity payment is classified as the return of the initial premium, the IRS provides details for how long an annuitant should expect to receive payments from the annuity. The portion of each annuity payment considered to be a return of principal is the amount of the premium payment divided by the total annuity income to be received during the expected lifetime. This provides an exclusion ratio for the contract as the portion of payments excluded from taxable income.

Once the full amount of premium has been returned as income at the life expectancy, subsequent annuity income then becomes fully taxable for the remaining lifetime. This process helps to defer some taxes to the latter part of retirement after surpassing the IRS measure of life expectancy. This concept also applies to deferred income annuities, as annuitized assets grow tax deferred within the contract and then the exclusion ratio is applied once payments begin. This also helps to defer tax payments into the future.

For immediate and deferred income annuities with lifetime payments, income payments can begin before age 59.5 and are exempt from an early withdrawal penalty. For period certain annuities that only pay for a fixed period without a lifetime component, immediate annuities are also exempt from the penalty, but deferred income annuities will trigger the penalty for the taxable portion of the payments if they begin before age 59.5, unless there is some other reason for the distributions to be exempt. We discuss early withdrawal penalties later in the chapter.

This nature of taxation for annuitized annuity contracts can be beneficial when combined with other strategies, such as Roth conversions, that lead to generating more taxable income in early retirement to take advantage of the exclusion ratio, so that there can be less taxable income from other sources later in retirement when the annuity income switches to become fully taxable.

Deferred annuities, meaning that the contract has not yet been annuitized, also provide tax deferral for assets that would otherwise experience ongoing taxation in a taxable account. But they have a different tax structure as they do not apply an exclusion ratio. Both types of annuities will provide the return of premium tax-free, but rather than having premium returned as an ongoing part of the distributions, a deferred annuity is taxed on a last-in-first-out (LIFO) basis. Any distributions from the deferred annuity, either as guaranteed distributions through a living benefit rider or unguaranteed distributions, are treated first as gains from the contract. The original principal is received only when there are no remaining gains to be taken. When a deferral period has been used, this pushes larger taxable income distributions toward the early part of the contract distribution period, rather than later like with the exclusion ratio for annuitized contracts.

This tax deferral is subject to the usual limitations the government provides, which are that all subsequent gains, even long-term capital gains, are taxed at ordinary income tax rates. This could be an issue for variable annuities that invest in subaccounts with stocks and assets that could have qualified for preferential tax rates outside of the annuity. For this reason, it is best to locate less tax-efficient asset classes in the variable annuity. A 10 percent penalty also applies for distributions taken prior to age 59.5 if there is not an exception.

Tax deferral can be a powerful benefit for annuities in taxable accounts. This tax deferral has motivated the use of annuities as accumulation vehicles with a de-emphasis on their original purpose of providing periodic distributions on fixed dates. If annuities are used for less tax-efficient asset classes that mostly generate ordinary income rather than long-term capital gains, then this tax deferral could provide net positive value for the owner. A low-cost investment-only variable annuity has become a popular tool and costs must be kept low so that the benefits of tax deferral can exceed the annuity costs.

One other point that is relevant for deferred annuities is that the IRS allows for 1035 exchanges. These rules prevent the creation of a taxable event when exchanging a life insurance policy into an annuity, or for exchanging from one annuity contract to another. This can provide a way to switch to an annuity offering more attractive guaranteed income payments or other features.

For example, if a variable annuity with a guaranteed lifetime withdrawal benefit has experienced strong growth in its investments such that the contract value is worth about the same amount as the benefit base, it may be possible to exchange that variable annuity into a more attractive annuity. Options could include a fixed annuity contract with better annuitization rates, a fixed index annuity, or another type of variable annuity with more attractive withdrawal benefits. This can occur without creating a taxable event. This feature of the tax code only applies to deferred annuities since annuitized contracts are not liquid and cannot be exchanged in such a way.

Life Insurance

Finally, cash value life insurance can potentially provide tax-deferred growth, tax-free distributions, and a death benefit free from income tax. There are ways to access the cash value on a tax-free basis through appropriately structured policy loans. After Roth contributions are exhausted, permanent life insurance becomes the primary tool to obtain both tax-deferral and tax-free distributions for after-tax dollars.

Among life insurance advocates, there are a strain of supporters who focus a great deal on promoting the tax advantages of life insurance to minimize taxes paid in retirement. In explaining their views and approach to retirement income, these advocates first tend to focus on how tax rates are presently at historic lows, and that one should expect much higher tax rates in the future.

These advocates explain that you will be better off paying taxes now at lower rates to avoid paying taxes in the future at higher rates, which naturally leads to advocating for tools that support tax deferral and tax-exempt distributions. Life insurance allows for practically unlimited contributions, which can serve as an important tool for obtaining additional tax-advantages for savings and wealth.

An ideal financial plan for these advocates would involve having just enough saved in qualified retirement plans such as a 401(k) that required minimum distributions do not push these taxable income amounts above the level of standard deductions, then perhaps have some funds in taxable investment accounts from which taxable long-term gains can be drawn without pushing the tax rate out of the 12 percent level (which keeps the tax rate on long-term capital gains at zero), and then taking other income as distributions from Roth accounts or policy loans from life insurance. One could potentially fund a quite sizable amount of spending power in retirement without having to pay any federal income taxes.

Withdrawals from Tax-Advantaged Retirement Plans

There are two types of tax-advantaged retirement plans we have described so far. First, tax-deferred accounts such as IRAs, 401(k) employer plans, or solo 401(k) plans for the self-employed, allow for a tax deduction on contributions up to a limit, tax deferred growth, and then distributions are treated as taxable income. Tax-exempt accounts, such as Roth IRAs, Roth 401(k) employer plans, and solo Roth 401(k) plans for the self-employed do not provide a deduction on contributions, but they do provide tax-deferred growth and tax-exempt distributions. The reality is that things can be more complex than this simple overview, and these complexities are the focus of this section. In this chapter we are focusing on tax issues during the lifetime of the owner, and the next chapter will extend this discussion to inherited accounts after the death of the account owner. This discussion will lay the groundwork for better understanding tax-efficient retirement distributions.

Choosing Distribution Options from Employer Plans

A first consideration with tax-advantaged plans is what to do with assets accumulated in employer-based plans (defined contribution 401(k), 403(b), 457 plans, or other defined-benefit pension plans) when an employee leaves the firm. Subject to plan rules for what is allowed, when individuals change employment or retire, they may rollover the lump-sum value in the plan to another retirement account, they may keep the plan in place with the previous employer, or they may decide to withdraw the amount as a taxable distribution (which could also create a 10 percent penalty if under age 59.5). When rolling over assets to another account, a direct transfer of assets can be used as the simplest and most secure method. Employer plans are required to provide a notice to participants noting that these direct transfers or direct rollovers to another plan are allowed. With a direct transfer, the plan assets are moved to another tax-advantaged plan such as an IRA. For employer-based Roth accounts, the transfer may be to a Roth IRA. Transfers could also go to Roth IRAs as taxable Roth conversions.

Indirect transfers are allowed, in which the funds are provided to the participant, except for a 20 percent withholding requirement, and then the individual is required to finish the rollover within 60 days to avoid having the amount become a taxable distribution. This would also require replacing from elsewhere the 20 percent of assets that were withheld. A direct rollover avoids the withholding that applies to an indirect rollover and can be the safer approach to avoid any possibility for mistakes.

An important question then arises as to whether it makes sense to keep the assets in the employer plan or to roll the assets to another account. For defined-contribution plans, the employer plans may have more limitations than IRAs, suggesting an advantage for a rollover. This includes, first, the type of distributions allowed. Qualified plans generally will not offer discretionary withdrawals. Distributions may be taken through the form of different types of immediate annuities, as a lump-sum, or as a series of installment payments. As for investment options, qualified plans may have a more limited selection of investment funds offered within the plan and may not allow deferred annuities or other financial products. The investment options may also include higher fees than options available outside the plan. IRA plans are generally much more accommodating both for the types of withdrawals and investment options. Owners can take discretionary withdrawals as desired and will not be limited by the list of options in the employer plan. IRAs also provide much greater depth to the types of annuities that can be purchased as well as greater discretion about the timing for the purchase date.

For defined contribution plans, the starting point is the lump-sum account value, but it may be possible to purchase some types of annuities within the plan from private insurance companies. For those interested in an annuity, it is worthwhile to compare pricing both in the plan as well as with outside options available in IRAs. The employer plan may offer more competitive institutional pricing on annuities, or it may be the case that a better deal could be obtained through rolling the assets to an IRA and purchasing the annuity there. One further consideration is that employer plans must offer unisex pricing on annuities, which could give an edge to women who live longer and may find higher costs with the gender-specific pricing used outside the plan.

Many participants may find it worthwhile to make rollovers of eligible distributions from their qualified plans to IRAs. These eligible amounts include account assets except for any required minimum distributions due in the year, 401(k) hardship withdrawals, or periodic payments lasting for 10 years or more (including life annuities). A few reasons not to make a rollover include that more cost-effective options are available in the employer plan, or the potential to retain net unrealized appreciation tax advantages (discussed later in this section). For those with after-tax contributions in their employer plan, another idea relates to rolling over all but these amounts to avoid the pro-rata rules around distributions that exist in IRAs and will be discussed later in this section. We described how IRAs are generally more flexible, but this is an area where employer plans have an edge. They allow more flexibility about what is distributed, so that deductible contributions and earnings can be earmarked for the rollover and only the cost basis from after-tax contributions (if there is any) can be kept in the employer plan and then distributed tax free or rolled over to a Roth account without triggering taxes. IRAs do not provide this flexibility.

Defined Benefit Pension Plans: Lump-sum or Annuity?

For those with defined benefit plans, an important decision is whether to take a lump-sum distribution from the plan (either as a taxable withdrawal or as a rollover to another plan) or to choose an annuity option from within the plan.

The standard form for the pension option is a life annuity and any other distribution options provided will be actuarially equivalent amounts, except in some cases where large employers may subsidize benefits for early retirees by not making a full actuarial reduction to an early payout. For married individuals, the default is a joint annuity with survivor benefits, providing a smaller payment because it will last for the lifetime of both individuals. The spouse must waive the right to a joint pension if another option is chosen.

Many plan participants will decide to take a lump-sum option as a rollover instead of an annuity. This decision should be made carefully. Participants should determine whether there is a role for annuity income in their retirement plan and what distribution options are available from the plan. This includes determining whether the right type of annuity is available and if the timing for annuity payments aligns. For instance, if the participant wants deferral for when annuity payments begin, this may not necessarily be an option provided by the plan.

If an annuity makes sense, and the plan offers the right annuity for the participant, a further consideration involves whether more income is available from the plan directly, or through a lump-sum rollover and subsequent purchase of a commercial annuity in an IRA. The approach that will offer the most income varies on a plan-by-plan basis and may also change over time as changing interest rates can impact both the lump-sum amount from the plan and the cost of annuity income outside the plan. One should also consider the security of the annuity, comparing credit risk for the commercial annuity with any risks in the employer plan and the protections provided for defined-benefit pensions through the Pension Benefit Guaranty Corporation. Couples might also consider a possibility for pension maximization strategies: will it be better to take a joint life annuity from the plan or to take a higher-paying single life option and use the difference to purchase life insurance designed to protect the surviving spouse?

Another consideration involves whether the pension decision impacts other benefits such as retiree health care insurance. For example, choosing a single-life pension may eliminate retiree health care benefits for a spouse, or choosing a lump-sum option may eliminate the possibility of receiving retiree health care benefits from the employer. These benefits could also be lost due to retiring early or deferring a pension. It is important to also check carefully about whether the pension choice affects other types of benefits and to include that information in your decision.

Finally, for those approaching retirement, it is important to consider the timing of retirement and how that affects a contribution credit for that year of work. Benefit amounts are often based on years of service and a measurement of income. Receiving the credit for a year of service could require a certain number of hours worked in the year or could require employment through the end of the year. The potential value of the credit and how much it would increase the value of a pension might make it worth delaying retirement. In a related matter, it is important to consider how income is defined for the purposes of determining the pension amount. This definition can include whether it is base pay or total income including overtime or other extra compensation, as well as which years of employment are counted in the calculation. Depending on the formulas used, there may be incentives to maximize income during certain key years of employment.

Required Minimum Distributions from Retirement Accounts

For retirement plans providing tax deferral, such as traditional IRAs and qualified retirement plans, the required minimum distribution (RMD) rules are meant to ensure that the government will be able to collect taxes at some point. There are different rules regarding RMDs for the original owners and for beneficiaries. Here we describe RMDs during the owner's lifetime, and in the next chapter we will extend the discussion to beneficiaries of tax-advantaged retirement plans with RMDs. Also, RMDs are not required for Roth IRAs. They are required for Roth accounts in employer plans, but the RMDs can be avoided by rolling those Roth accounts into a Roth IRA. When Roth accounts do have RMDs, the amount must be distributed but no taxes are due. The distributions could be reinvested in a taxable account if they are not needed for spending. RMD rules also reflect only the minimum that must be withdrawn, and individuals could always decide to withdraw more than the required amount. Having RMDs in retirement without other taxable income subject to withholdings could also create a need to pay quarterly estimated taxes.

As part of the SECURE Act from 2019, RMDs begin at 72 for anyone who turns 70 on July 1, 2019, or later. Previously, RMDs began at age 70.5. In 2020, the CARES Act removed RMDs for that calendar year as a response to the global pandemic. They are back as of 2021. Distributions are required in each distribution year past the relevant starting age for the account owner.

For the first year that an RMD is due, the individual has until April 1 of the following year to take the distribution. In subsequent years, the distribution must be taken by December 31 of the same calendar year. Individuals who do wait into the new year to take their first RMD would then have to take two RMDs in the same calendar year, which would increase taxable income for the year.

For qualified plans where an individual continues to work past age 72 and is not a 5 percent owner of the company, RMDs for just that employer account can be delayed until the year that the individual retires from that employer. This exception only applies for the employer plan where the individual continues to work, but if that account accepts rollovers, it may be possible to make rollovers to that account to delay other RMDs.

Taking RMDs is a serious matter, as the penalty tax applied for distributions not taken in their required years is 50 percent of the amount that should have been withdrawn in addition to the taxes due on the distribution. This makes it very important to not skip RMDs.

The method for calculating RMDs for a given year is relatively straightforward. RMDs are based on the individual's age at the end of the calendar year and the account balance on December 31 of the previous calendar year. That account balance must include any indirect rollover amounts that were initiated before December 31, even if the rollover was not completed until the new year. Also, a deferred annuity with optional benefits may need to add a valuation of those benefits to the contract value as a part of determining the account value for the RMD.

There are three relevant life tables for calculating RMDs. The most common one during the lifetime of the owner is the uniform lifetime table (Table III). This table is for unmarried owners, married owners whose spouses are not more than ten years younger, and married owners whose spouses are not the sole beneficiaries of the IRAs. Table II is used for owners whose spouses are more than ten years younger and who are the sole beneficiary of the IRAs. This is a larger table providing joint life expectancies for all combinations of ages 20 and older. The marriage situation for determining if Table II can be used is based on January 1 of the year. If married on that date and the sole beneficiary status is maintained for the year, then Table II can be used for that year even if a divorce or spouse's death happens in that year. Finally, Table I provides single life expectancies and is used for some types of beneficiaries of retirement plan assets. This table becomes more relevant for the discussion in the next chapter about beneficiaries, but it is relevant to just take note for now that the single life table provides smaller life expectancies and higher distribution rates than the uniform life table.

A selection of RMDs is provided in Exhibit 10.9. An additional note about this exhibit is important. We are currently undergoing a change in the RMD tables with a new set of numbers available for years 2022 and later. I have chosen to provide information from the new 2022 tables in Exhibit 10.9. If you happen to be taking a distribution for 2021, this exhibit does not have the right information. The new tables note that people are living longer, and the life expectancies are increased by approximately two years for ages up until the early 70s, after which point the differences between the old and new tables are less.

As noted, the uniform lifetime table is commonly used for RMDs during the owner's lifetime, with the exception noted about when Table II is applied. Because the uniform table is constructed assuming there is a spouse who is ten years younger than the participant, even when the individual is single, this table does provide relatively conservative RMD rates. As seen, at age 72 the rate is just 3.65 percent. This corresponds to the old RMD distribution rate at age 70 for 2021 and earlier.

As an example, suppose it is 2022 and a retiree's IRA balance was $130,000 at the end of 2021. The retiree will turn 85 in November 2022. This individual is not married. What is the RMD for the year? The relevant life expectancy is for age 85 from the uniform lifetime table, which we can see in the exhibit is

16 years. The RMD amount is $130,000 / 16 = $8,125. This amount must be distributed by December 31.

Exhibit 10.9
Life Tables for Requirement Minimum Distributions, Starting in 2022

	Uniform Lifetime Table (Table III)		Single Life Table (Table I)	
Age	Life Expectancy	Distribution Rate	Life Expectancy	Distribution Rate
20			65	1.54%
30			55.3	1.81%
40			45.7	2.19%
50			36.2	2.76%
60			27.1	3.69%
70			18.8	5.32%
72	27.4	3.65%	17.2	5.81%
75	24.6	4.07%	14.8	6.76%
80	20.2	4.95%	11.2	8.93%
85	16	6.25%	8.1	12.35%
90	12.2	8.20%	5.7	17.54%
100	6.4	15.63%	2.8	35.71%
110	3.5	28.57%	2	50.00%

If an IRA account has non-deductible contributions or other cost basis, RMDs do also apply to these amounts. But only a portion of the RMD will be taxable. The pro-rata rules for determining this are described later in this section.

Another important matter for RMDs is about knowing when account aggregation rules apply if there are multiple retirement accounts. These rules can be complicated regarding what types of accounts can be aggregated. IRAs can be aggregated together as can 403(b) plans. If an individual owns multiple IRAs, this person may determine the RMD for the combined account balances and then take the distribution from only one of the accounts if desired. About aggregating IRAs, this means only traditional IRAs, not inherited IRAs or Roth IRAs. Also, I must emphasize that spouses cannot aggregate their accounts. Each spouse needs to take their own separate RMDs from their own separate retirement accounts. Also, other types of plans may not allow aggregation. When aggregation is not allowed, RMDs would need to be taken separately from each relevant account.

A plan of action for RMDs, then, is to make inventory of all plans subject to RMDs, determine RMD amounts each year for each account, determine which accounts may be aggregated to provide flexibility for the account that the RMD is taken from, and then make sure that all RMDs have been distributed by December 31.

Required Minimum Distributions from Annuities

Annuities can be owned in qualified retirement plans such as employer plans and IRAs, as well as in Roth IRAs. With Roth accounts there will not be taxes, and for tax-deferred accounts, annuity distributions are taxed at ordinary income tax rates as they are received. This is straightforward. The aspect that can get trickier relates to determining RMDs for the annuity assets. The approach is different for annuitized contracts and for deferred annuities.

For annuitized contracts, the RMD calculation does not include any annuity premium or present value of payments. The annuity income is accepted as covering the RMDs for the annuitized assets. At younger ages, annuity income might be larger than the RMD that would have been required for those assets, but the annuity income could be less than the RMD at later ages. These differences are assumed to balance out over time, though, since the annuity is treated as an accepted way to spend down the assets over retirement.

To be clear, in the early years, when the annuity income is larger than the RMD would have been on the annuitized assets, the retiree does not get to use the annuity income to cover the RMDs on other assets remaining in the qualified plan. This could be viewed as a disadvantage with a partial annuity strategy, as the retiree pays taxes on the annuity distributions and the annuity distributions cannot be counted against any other RMDs due on remaining assets, which could increase the overall taxable income generated by the retirement accounts in those early years.

Though the tax treatment is relatively simple for an immediate annuity in a qualified plan, there are problems with using a deferred income annuity in a qualified plan when income is to begin past the starting date for RMDs. Such a situation creates a technical violation for RMD rules as annuity income covers the RMDs for the annuitized assets, but there is no annuity income when that income is deferred for too long. In July 2014, the Treasury Department created new regulations for qualified longevity annuity contracts (QLACs) to help rectify this problem. Qualifying contracts for annuitized premiums up to $135,000 or 25 percent of the combined balances held in qualified plans, whichever is smaller, can now delay annuity income to age eighty-five without violating the RMD rules. The total limit applies across all plans and the 25 percent rule applies to each account, though IRAs can be aggregated. Only deferred income annuities are eligible to be QLACs, not other deferred annuities. RMDs for this portion of annuitized assets can be deferred past 72.

Not many 401(k) plans or other qualified retirement plans that are set up by employers offer the ability to purchase annuities. This may become more common in the future as the SECURE Act simplified the process for employers to include deferred annuity options. For those who do have this option, it is worth exploring whether the annuities inside the employer plan may provide a better opportunity than annuities outside the plan. Women can particularly benefit from the unisex pricing that is required for annuities held inside employer retirement plans. If good annuity choices are not available in the 401(k), then the common process after retiring would be to rollover the 401(k) assets into an IRA and then purchase the annuity inside of the IRA. When these steps are correctly followed, no taxable events have transpired until distributions are received.

With deferred annuities in qualified plans, distributions from the annuity are treated as taxable income when they are received. This is the same as for annuitized contracts. It is important to emphasize that since retirement plans already provide tax deferral, this is not a distinct advantage of holding an annuity inside a qualified plan. There must be some other benefit from the annuity, such as the desire to receive protected lifetime income, to justify its placement this way. For lifetime income, a reason why the annuity may be more attractive inside a retirement plan, despite already having the benefit of tax deferral, is that taxable investment holdings may have embedded capital gains that would trigger a large tax bill if sold to pay the annuity premium. There is no 1035 exchange for moving assets from a taxable portfolio to an annuity.

For deferred annuities, the contract value of the annuity remains liquid, and RMDs are calculated on it. Unlike with annuitized contracts, deferred annuities allow their distributions to be aggregated into the overall RMD calculations. This can be a benefit at younger ages, when the distribution from the annuity under a guaranteed living benefit may exceed the RMD on the underlying contract value, so that part of the annuity income can also be counted against the RMDs for non-annuity assets. In cases where the contract value declines over time, this benefit could even increase further as the annuity income may be much larger than the RMD on the smaller remaining contract value. This can help to lower the need to take distributions from the remainder of the IRA to cover RMDs, which could prove useful in managing sequence-of-return risk.

However, there are complications related to this point because the RMDs on a deferred annuity contract may not only be applied to the contract value. RMDs may also be due on the present value of any living or death benefits in the contract. Two simplifications provided about this are that the actuarial value of these benefits can be ignored if they are worth less than 20 percent of the contract value, and a standard return of premium death benefit can also be ignored for these calculations. These requirements can complicate taxes because it is necessary to obtain estimates for the actuarial present value of the annuity benefits to determine the total RMDs for the annuity.

This taxation matter also speaks to the value of not placing all retirement plan assets into a deferred annuity. One potential calamity could relate to an optional death benefit rider that only paid a death benefit if the contract value exceeds zero. If the contract value is close to zero, one might wish to stop taking distributions, but the RMD required on that death benefit could exceed the remaining contract value and require a complete liquidation of the annuity if there were no other assets that could be used to cover the RMD. Having other IRA assets can be an important way to manage tax surprises related to this complex aspect of calculating RMDs for deferred annuities.

Qualified Charitable Distributions

Another idea relates to Qualified Charitable Distributions (QCDs) from IRAs. For IRA owners who are at least 70.5 (this age remains with the SECURE Act, even though the start age for RMDs changed), QCDs allow for up to $100,000 from the IRA to be distributed directly to a charity without any tax consequences. QCDs are even allowed for amounts that would otherwise need to be distributed as RMDs. The SECURE Act now allows for contributions to IRAs for those still working past age 70.5, and the QCD annual limit is reduced by the accumulated contributions made to traditional IRAs after 70.5.

The benefits for this strategy are significant – even though there is no tax deduction, the amount of the donation does not count as income but does count as that year's RMD. For non-QCD donations, even if the donation could be itemized, it shows up in the adjusted gross income because it is a below-the-line deduction. This means that it could create vulnerability to the auxiliary taxation issues related to AGI and MAGI (more on these later in the chapter) that are determined before deductions are considered. For those who are not otherwise itemizing, a non-QCD donation would not allow for a tax deduction anyway.

In comparing a QCD with instead donating appreciated securities from a taxable account, the appreciated securities donation can permanently avoid capital gains on the donated securities. A tax deduction can be received when itemizing. But for those waiting to receive a step-up in basis on the taxable assets at death, the advantage of avoiding capital gains taxes through the donation would be neutralized. Which approach is best does depend on specific circumstances, but the QCD for tax-deferred accounts is a valuable tool for making charitable contributions that is now a permanent part of the tax code.

Early Withdrawal Penalties and Their Exceptions

Retirement plans are provided with tax advantages to encourage retirement savings. As such, distributions that occur before age 59.5 may be penalized with an additional 10 percent penalty tax applied to the distribution amount in addition to any other income taxes due. There are exceptions where early distributions can be made without incurring the penalty. The situation becomes more complicated because different rules apply for traditional IRAs, employer plans (except 457 plans), Roth IRAs, and Roth accounts in employer plans. We cover Roth accounts in the next section. Section 72(t) of the tax code covers IRAs and employer plans.

Regarding exceptions, first, both traditional IRAs and employer plans provide exceptions for the death of the participant. Beneficiaries do not have to worry about early withdrawal penalties. Spouses have a unique situation in which they can rollover the inherited account to their own IRA. Doing so would remove the ability to avoid the penalty, but the penalty can be avoided if the account remains in the name of the decedent. A surviving spouse considering early distribution may keep the account in the name of the decedent until age 59.5 when a rollover can be made.

Next, an exception is also applied for a participant's permanent disability. The disability exception is strict, as the individual must be deemed as unable to engage in any substantial gainful activity for the indefinite future. Third, distributions that add up to less than the taxpayer unit's deductible medical expenses for the year (qualifying medical expenses that exceed 7.5 percent of adjusted gross income) are allowed without penalty. These expenses do not have to be deducted if the standard deduction applies, but they must just be deductible expenses. Fourth, up to $5,000 of expenses related to a newborn birth or adoption are allowed. This is a new exception created by the SECURE Act.

Finally, both types of accounts also provide an exception for distributions that are deemed to be substantially equal periodic payments (SEPPs) from the account as described by Section 72(t) of the tax code. The rules around these payments are complex and must be considered carefully, as modifying one's scheduled distributions under these rules can lead to severe additional penalties. Even though they are calculated as based on lasting for a lifetime, the SEPP payments must continue for the longer of at least five years or until reaching age 59.5. Then they may be changed or stopped. For example, someone beginning a SEPP at 50 must continue it to 59.5, and someone beginning at 58 must continue to 63.

Three methods are available for calculating SEPP payments: the amortization method, the annuitization method, or the life expectancy method. The amortization and annuitization methods lock in a number that must be used precisely in subsequent years, while the life expectancy method is similar to RMDs. The highest distribution amount is provided with the amortization approach, and the annuitization approach may be close behind. Both amounts will be fixed values. The life expectancy approach will lead to lower and more variable amounts, as it updates each year for changing account balances and distribution rates. For those wishing to reduce their distributions, a one-time switch to the life expectancy method is allowed during the time that the SEPP must continue.

The maximum SEPP amount will be available assuming the highest account balance allowed (based on date used), the highest interest rate allowed, and the amortization method for a single life. There is flexibility to reduce the amount with assumptions for account balances and interest rates as well as using a joint-life calculation. A separate IRA can also be carved out and the

SEPP can be applied just to this separate account as there is no need to aggregate across IRAs.

In fact, carving out an IRA for the SEPP is generally a good idea. The SEPP unravels if one accidently changes the payment amount, or transfers funds in or out of the IRA. Carving out the separate account and being very careful with it can help avoid violations. The penalty is harsh, as in the year a distribution is modified, the 10 percent penalty on all past SEPP distributions plus interest all become due in the current tax year.

Continuing with exceptions, traditional IRAs provide three additional exceptions not found in qualified plans. Up to $10,000 can be used toward the purchase of a home and the distribution must happen within 120 days before the home purchase and used for the payment to qualify. For the home purchase, it does not necessarily have to be for a first-time home buyer, as it can be applied if a home has not been owned over the previous two-year period. The $10,000 is a lifetime limit for this. Distributions up to the amount of qualifying higher education expenses for the participant or eligible family member can also be made without penalty. These distributions do not have to go directly to the educational institution, so having eligible expenses in the same year can allow for a penalty-free distribution of up to the amount. Third, distributions to pay for medical insurance premiums when unemployed for oneself and eligible family members are also allowed.

Exhibit 10.10
Exceptions for the Early Withdrawal Penalty

Exceptions	Traditional IRAs	Qualified Plans	Roth Accounts
Death of participant	Yes	Yes	Yes - Qualifying
Permanent disability of participant	Yes	Yes	Yes - Qualifying
Distributions less than deductible medical expenses for the year (over 7.5% of AGI)	Yes	Yes	Nonqualifying- but no penalty
Substantially equal periodic payments	Yes	Yes	Nonqualifying- but no penalty
$5,000 of newborn expenses	Yes	Yes	Yes - Qualifying
$10,000 for first-time home buying expenses (must be within 120 days of home purchase and used for payment)	Yes	No	Yes - Qualifying (for Roth IRA)
Distributions less than qualifying higher education expenses for participant or eligible family members	Yes	No	Nonqualifying- but no penalty
Medical insurance premiums for unemployed participants and eligible family members	Yes	No	Nonqualifying- but no penalty
Exception for employer plan if employment ends after age 55	No	Yes	No

Finally, there is one additional exception for qualified plans that is not available to traditional IRAs. If employment ended after age 55, then distributions can be taken from the one qualified account associated with that employer without penalty. This is only allowed if employment ended after age 55 though, so that the exception does not start at 55 for those who ended employment at an earlier age. This exception may not always be useful as many employer plans do not allow discretionary withdrawals.

Exhibit 10.10 summarizes these exceptions, including the information for Roth accounts that will be discussed in the next section.

Potential Penalties and Taxes on Roth Distributions

We do think of Roth distributions as being tax free (and, by association, penalty free). This is only completely true for qualifying distributions. Beyond this, matters get more complicated. One simplification to first note is that contributions to Roth accounts can be distributed at any point without penalty or tax. Then we must determine if the withdrawal is qualifying and therefore exempt from tax and penalty, or if the withdrawal is nonqualifying but still exempt from penalty, or if the withdrawal is subject to both tax and penalty. It is important to keep track of differences for Roth IRAs built from new contributions, Roth IRAs created from conversions, inherited Roth IRAs, and designated Roth accounts in qualified plans.

Qualified distributions are not subject to penalty or tax. A Roth distribution is qualified if it passes the five-year rule *and* meets another triggering event. A first requirement for a Roth IRA distribution is that at least five years have passed since January 1 of the first year that any Roth IRA was set up with a contribution. There is aggregation with this requirement, as the owner just needs to have any Roth IRA open for at least five years before making a distribution. It is important to note, however, that this requirement always applies no matter the age, which speaks to the importance of at least opening a Roth IRA as soon as possible to get the countdown started. Also, this aggregation does not apply for Roth employer plans. With them, each plan must be opened for five years before their distributions can become qualifying. An easy fix for this, assuming a Roth IRA has already been opened for five years, is to first rollover the Roth account to the Roth IRA and then take the distribution.

Assuming this five-year requirement is covered, we then look for a further triggering event to make the withdrawal qualifying. The distribution is qualified if the individual is at least 59.5 years old at the time of the distribution, or if one of four exceptions are met with the same criteria as described in the previous section about traditional IRAs: death of the owner, permanent disability of the owner, the $10,000 exception for a first-home purchase, or $5,000 for a newborn or adoption in the same year.

If these two requirements are not met, then the distribution is nonqualifying. To understand the implications, we next keep track of what the distribution represents as there are ordering rules for withdrawals. First, for Roth IRAs, the first dollars distributed represent contributions. Contributions can always be received on a tax-free and penalty-free basis even if they are nonqualifying distributions. Once contributions are removed, we look to any dollars in the Roth IRA representing Roth conversions. For any Roth conversions, the taxed amount of the conversions is removed next. For these amounts, no taxes are due, but the distribution is exposed to the 10 percent penalty if it has been less than five years since the conversion took place, the individual is under 59.5, and there is no other exception about nonqualifying distributions that remove the need for a penalty. Once the individual is over 59.5, there is no need to wait five years since the Roth conversion to make a distribution, assuming any Roth IRA has been open for at least five years. These exceptions are also related to the discussion about traditional IRAs including for deductible medical expenses, substantially equal periodic payments, qualifying educational expenses, or medical insurance premiums when unemployed. Next, if there are any nontaxed amounts from Roth conversions, representing the conversion of nondeductible contributions, these are distributed without tax or penalty. Finally, earnings are distributed from the Roth IRA. Nonqualifying distributions of earnings are taxed and are exposed to the 10 percent penalty tax unless there is an exception for the same reasons as just described for taxed conversion amounts.

This ordering for distributions is a bit different for Roth accounts within qualified plans. Roth employer accounts are subject to a pro-rata rule with proportional distributions from contributions and account gains as reflected by their portions in the account. Contributions are not subject to tax or penalty, but gains are. Also, as noted, Roth accounts from qualified plans are also different because they do have RMDs and the five-year rule about having the account open to make a distribution qualifying applies to each account and not just when the first account was created.

Rollovers, Transfers, and Roth Conversions

Account owners may shift assets between different types of retirement plans and IRAs without generating taxes. These transactions are called rollovers or transfers. Usually, the term transfer is used for a direct rollover, in which assets move directly from one account to another. Rollovers can be direct or indirect, though, with indirect rollovers being the case when the individual receives the funds and then has 60 days to complete the rollover before it becomes a taxable distribution. For indirect rollovers from qualified plans, there is a mandatory 20 percent withholding, though this withholding does not apply to indirect rollovers from IRAs. Generally, except for those seeking specific short-term access to the funds, direct rollovers are encouraged to avoid any issues with not completing an indirect rollover within 60 days and making the distribution fully taxable and potentially subject to early withdrawal penalties.

Roth conversions are also allowed, in which funds are transferred from an IRA or qualified plan into a Roth account. Roth conversions are allowed from a traditional IRA or other plans like a SEP IRA or a SIMPLE IRA (after two years), as well as employer and self-employed retirement plans.

Beneficiaries of qualified plans can also make a Roth conversion, though this is not allowed for beneficiaries of IRAs. Roth conversions are technically taxable rollovers and can be direct or indirect. Conversions can be made by re-designating an IRA as a Roth IRA, by doing a trustee-to-trustee transfer from an IRA or a direct transfer from a qualified plan, or by doing an indirect rollover.

With conversions, income tax is paid on the taxable amount of the conversion as though it is being withdrawn from the account. For those younger than 59.5, there is no 10 percent penalty applied on Roth conversion amounts. The amount of the taxable income is the fair market value of the converted assets on the date of the conversion, which is straightforward for most investments but can create complications for annuities with additional benefits. The conversion deadline for a tax year is December 31. Indirect rollovers initiated before the end of the year and then completed in the following year are counted as happening in the initiation year.

Partial rollovers, transfers and Roth conversions are allowed if the distributed amount is eligible. The ability to make partial conversions allows for better control over the tax situation and is a key part of strategic Roth conversions. Eligible amounts include the account balance except for distributions coming out as a series of payments such as with a SEPP, required minimum distributions, hardship withdrawals, or other corrective or deemed distributions. When there are RMDs, conversions may only be done on amounts exceeding what must be distributed as an RMD.

In the past, Roth conversions could be recharacterized or undone by October 1 of the following year. This was ended with the Tax Cuts and Jobs Act in 2017. There were some planning opportunities with recharacterization that may still be mentioned in older materials but are no longer available. One was to convert different types of assets and then recharacterize conversions of assets that subsequently lost value and keep the conversions on assets that gained value. Another was to convert too much and then recharacterize as necessary to fully control the tax bracket one sought to manage. Since this is no longer possible, tax planning around tax bracket management becomes more complicated, especially as one gets close to thresholds that trigger jumps in Medicare premiums, as recharacterization is no longer a relief valve to reduce taxable income.

Non-Deductible Contributions in IRAs and the Pro-Rata Rules

We mentioned before that while employer plans provide flexibility in controlling what is distributed between taxable amounts and any cost basis, such flexibility does not exist with IRAs. Any cost basis in IRAs, including nondeductible IRA contributions and after-tax contributions to employer retirement plans that were rolled over to the IRA, must be distributed using a pro-rata rule. They cannot be specifically chosen for a distribution to reduce taxable income.

In a case where a person has more than one IRA, the IRAs must be aggregated for applying pro-rata rules. These aggregation rules do not apply to other types of retirement accounts. One cannot carve out their nondeductible contributions into a separate IRA and then convert or distribute them tax free.

Nondeductible contributions may exist when a contribution is made to an IRA, but income exceeds the thresholds for making the contribution deductible. They may also exist when a person made after-tax contributions to an employer plan that they had subsequently rolled over to an IRA. Such after-tax contributions may exist when the plan allowed it because the individual was seeking additional tax deferral even after exceeding the limits for deductible contributions.

For example, consider an individual who has two IRA accounts. The first has $10,000 of nondeductible contributions and $30,000 of deductible contributions and account earnings. The second IRA has $60,000 of deductible contributions and account earnings. This individual would like to do a Roth conversion of $5,000 from the first IRA account. The question: how much of this conversion represents taxable income? The answer is that the nontaxable portion is the $10,000 of nondeductible contributions found in the accounts divided by the combined $100,000 balance of the two accounts, or 10 percent. $500 of the conversion is tax-free and the other $4,500 represents taxable income. Again, the answer is not that $0 is taxable because there is no option to just choose to convert the nondeductible portion, and the answer is not that $3,750 is taxable because the nondeductible portion of that first account is 25 percent of its value. Aggregating across the IRAs we see that 10 percent of the account balances are nondeductible contributions and that becomes the portion of the distribution that is not taxed. This issue applies in the same manner for both distributions and Roth IRA conversions.

This issue is relevant for the backdoor Roth contribution strategy that we mentioned earlier. If there are no other IRA accounts, the nondeductible contribution to the IRA can be converted to the Roth IRA after a few days without creating a taxable event. But if there were already IRA accounts that had deductible contributions and earnings, then the pro-rata rule applies, and a portion of the conversion is taxable. This provides a reason to delay rollovers from employer plans when possible to preserve the option for backdoor Roth contributions in the future.

These pro-rata rules do not apply to other types of retirement plans. After-tax or non-deductible contributions can be carved out from the rollover and then distributed tax free or converted to a Roth account without taxes. This means that one may be strategic about when to do rollovers and what to rollover.

Net Unrealized Appreciation on Employer Stock

One of the rare exceptions regarding distributions from tax-deferred accounts being taxed at income tax rates is the possibility for those who own employer stock in their retirement plan to have gains on the stock taxed at long-term capital gains rates. This is called Net Unrealized Appreciation (NUA). The NUA rules are complex, and it may or may not always be a good idea to use this tax treatment depending on individual circumstances.

The long-term gains tax treatment is available if these conditions are met:

- The entire amount from the employer plan is distributed within one year. The opportunity is lost with only a partial withdrawal or an in-service distribution.
- This distribution must follow a triggering event, which includes reaching 59.5, dying, or ending employment.
- The treatment is only relevant for the actual employer stock in the plan from that employer.
- The distribution can be divided between withdrawals and rollovers to an IRA, but the shares of employer stock in which one is seeking NUA treatment must be distributed and not rolled over.
- The employer stock must also be distributed in kind as the shares rather than taken as cash.
- Any employer stock that is rolled over or sold and distributed as cash loses the potential for this tax treatment.

For the employer stock that is distributed, income tax will be due on the cost basis for that stock, based on its value when provided from the employer and as determined by the employer. The gains on the stock will then obtain long-term capital gains treatment when the stock is subsequently sold. The net unrealized appreciation is this difference between the value of the stock when distributed and its costs basis. For example, suppose employer stock worth $100,000 is distributed and has a cost basis of $40,000. $40,000 is taxed as income that year and the NUA is $60,000 that will be taxed at long-term capital gains rates whenever it is subsequently sold. If the stock is held longer, any subsequent gains above the NUA amount will be treated as short-term gains if sold within a year from the distribution date and long-term gains if held longer.

Is it a good idea to get this tax treatment for employer stock, or is it worth sacrificing the tax treatment? The obvious benefit is getting the lower tax rate on the stock's gains, which of course is more valuable the larger the gains are relative to the cost basis. With a large cost basis and small amount of gains, the disadvantage of taking the distribution and generating taxes may outweigh the small benefit of a reduced tax rate on the NUA. Nonetheless, for those who otherwise want to take the distribution now, this can be a good opportunity to obtain some tax benefit. And it is not necessary to apply NUA treatment for all the employer stock, as the owner can choose a portion to distribute and a portion to roll over. Only the distributed portion receives the tax benefit.

There are disadvantages as well. First, if the distribution is triggered because employment ends before age 59.5, then the cost basis that is taxed during the year is also subject to the 10 percent early withdrawal penalty when no other exception applies. The NUA is not exposed to this penalty, but the cost basis is. As well, holding the employer stock means less diversification and a relevant asset allocation question relates to whether the investor is better off by diversifying away from the employer stock. Another consideration relates to the idea that by taking the distribution, it changes the composition of taxable assets and tax-deferred assets. These assets no longer receive benefits from tax deferral and for younger people that loss may outweigh any benefits.

To summarize, the best candidates for seeking the NUA treatment are those who are close to retirement, who are seeking the distribution anyway, and who have a large NUA build up. Younger individuals are less likely to benefit from the NUA treatment as they face the 10 percent penalty on the cost basis, lose opportunities for subsequent tax deferral, face holding a less diversified portfolio, and may not have much NUA build up anyway. The rules around NUA are complicated and it is worth discussing this issue with an accountant for those who hold large quantities of employer stock in their retirement plans.

Tax-Efficient Retirement Distribution Strategies

With the technical tax discussion complete, we next look at how to source distributions during retirement in a tax-efficient manner. This discussion is about withdrawal sequence ordering and tax bracket management. Most people do not think about these issues, but your distribution strategy in retirement and the resulting taxes you pay can have a significant impact on how long your money lasts and how much you can spend, especially if you have taken care to set up options and flexibility through tax diversification.

A basic guideline around withdrawal order sequencing is to first consider any income you receive from Social Security, pensions, and so forth, as well as any required minimum distributions you must take from qualified retirement plans and other tax-advantaged accounts. Then the order of spend down for covering remaining spending is taxable accounts, then tax-deferred accounts, and then tax-exempt accounts. Taxable assets create a drag on returns because taxes must be paid annually on interest and dividend payments. They are spent first while tax-advantaged accounts are given more time to grow with tax deferral. This guideline is directionally correct, but it can be further refined for greater impact through tax bracket management and strategic Roth conversions.

Tax Bracket Management and Withdrawal Sequence Ordering

The ordering of taxable, tax-deferred, and tax-exempt, is a reasonable starting point, but it is possible to do better. Taxes are unavoidable, but what we really seek to do with tax planning for retirement income is to pay taxes at the lowest possible tax rates to generate the most lifetime spending and legacy power net of taxes from the retirement asset base. This leads to tax bracket management to manage tax efficiency with the progressive tax code. The planning potential can be greatest when significant assets are held in tax-deferred accounts.

The objective is to try to fill up lower tax brackets with taxable income and then potentially take from areas with better tax treatment to fill any spending gaps without moving unnecessarily into a higher tax bracket. As well, in cases where spending needs have been met while additional capacity remains in a lower tax bracket, it may be worthwhile to fill that bracket with taxable income and pay tax at lower rates to help avoid the possibility of being pushed into a higher tax bracket in the future.

Each retiree's situation is different in this regard, but one threshold that creates a big advantage for strategic management is the divide between the 12 percent and 22 percent tax bracket. That reflects the biggest jump in tax rates, and in 2021 the taxable income levels where this shift happens are $40,525 for singles and $81,050 for joint filers. These thresholds are also quite close to where the tax rate for long-term capital gains and qualified dividends jumps from 0 percent to 15 percent. For singles this happens at $40,400 of taxable income and for married couples filing jointly it is $80,800.

If there is spare capacity for taxable income in a lower tax bracket after meeting spending goals, the idea is to fill up the bracket with taxable income. In the early years of retirement, three options for generating more taxable income include:

1) Spend less from taxable accounts and more from tax-deferred accounts to cover the spending goal in a way that increases taxable income toward the desired level.

2) Cover the spending goal from taxable accounts, but then increase taxable income by doing Roth conversions with assets from the tax-deferred account.

3) Generate taxable long-term capital gains by selling and then immediately re-purchasing assets in taxable accounts, especially when still in the 0 percent tax bracket for these preferential income sources.

These ideas are for creating more taxable income to fill up a particular bracket. But for those whose spending goals are pushing them into a higher than optimal level of taxable income, this process could work in the opposite direction where distributions from tax-deferred sources could be reduced and replaced with spending from sources that do not generate taxable income.

Exhibit 10.11 divides potential sources of retirement spending by their tax treatment. There are sources that count as ordinary taxable income using the income tax rates, sources that receive preferential tax rates, and sources that do not count as taxable income and do not show up on the tax return. Taxable income sources are the usual items we discussed before, including any wages or earnings, distributions from qualified retirement plans like IRAs, short-term capital gains, interest, dividends not qualified for special tax treatment, pensions, rental income, and a portion of cash flows received from nonqualified annuities and Social Security.

Exhibit 10.11
Tax Characteristics for Various Retirement Spending Resources

Increases Taxable Income	Taxable income with preferential tax rates	Spending Sources -- Not Taxable Income
Wages, salary, and self-employment earnings*	Qualified dividends	Cost-basis of taxable investments
Qualified retirement plan distributions (IRAs)	Long-term Capital Gains	Roth IRA distributions
Short-term capital gains		A portion of nonqualified annuities
Interest		A portion of Social Security benefits
Dividends		Health savings accounts (qualified)
A portion of nonqualified annuities		Reverse mortgage proceeds
A portion of Social Security benefits		Cash value of life insurance (cost basis or loan proceeds)
Pensions		Benefits from long-term care insurance
Rental or other passive income		

* Also subject to payroll taxes

The spending sources with preferential tax rates include qualified dividends and long-term capital gains. Sources that can support spending without generating taxable income include the cost-basis of taxable investments, Roth IRA distributions, a portion of the income from Social Security and nonqualified annuities, qualified distributions from health savings accounts for medical expenses, proceeds from a reverse mortgage, and partial surrenders of cost basis or policy loans from life insurance policies.

Strategic Roth Conversions

When one is generating more taxable income from tax-deferred accounts to fill a tax bracket, the options are either to reduce other spending sources and cover spending with these distributions, or to engage in Roth conversions for these additional distributions. The Roth conversion approach can often provide an edge in creating greater long-term benefits as will be shown later with an example.

Roth conversions are accomplished by taking funds from qualified tax-deferred accounts and transferring them into a tax-exempt account. This triggers a tax payment on the amount of deductible contributions and account gains that are converted. Ideally, the taxes would not be paid from the distribution itself, but from other sources outside of the tax-deferred account. This would especially be the case before age 59.5, as paying taxes on the conversion from the tax-deferred account could trigger an additional 10 percent penalty. The penalty does not apply to converted amounts, but it would apply to any distributions that are not converted to the Roth, such as for paying the tax.

By doing this strategically, the retiree can pay a lower tax rate on the converted amount, and then have that money grow tax free in the future. This can help to avoid paying higher tax rates on the assets in the future, especially after required minimum distributions begin.

Roth conversions can be especially useful in years when taxable income is low, such as years after work has ended but before Social Security benefits have started, or in years with large tax deductions that offset a higher adjusted gross income.

As well, Roth conversions could be used after a market downturn to get more shares shifted over to the Roth at a "discount" without generating as much taxable income. A concern with this would be if it is necessary to pay taxes on these conversions from assets that have also declined in value with a market downturn. This could be an opportunity for buffer assets that have not declined in value to be a resource for paying taxes and obtaining the conversion benefits without triggering sequence risk.

The SECURE Act passed at the end of 2019 further increased the potential opportunities and value for Roth conversions. First, by raising the start age for required minimum distributions from 70.5 to 72, there is more opportunity and time to engage in Roth conversions before required minimum distributions begin. Conversions can only be done on amounts that exceed the RMDs. The SECURE Act also changed rules about RMDs for beneficiaries of retirement accounts which may speed up the need for distributions. That could more easily force beneficiaries into higher tax brackets, especially if they are otherwise in their peak earnings years when receiving the inheritance. This could guide toward greater use of Roth conversions when intergenerational tax planning is considered, which is a subject explored more deeply in the next chapter.

Long-Term Capital Gains Harvesting

The third concept for generating more taxable income as a part of tax bracket management is to harvest capital gains. This is especially valuable when still in the 0 percent tax bracket for long-term capital gains. Long-term capital gains could be harvested up to the top of the 0 percent bracket without generating taxable income. The assets could then be immediately reinvested, resetting the cost basis to a higher level. Wash sale rules exist when harvesting losses, which are rules about not purchasing a substantially identical asset within 30 days of the date sold to allow the loss for tax purposes. But there are no such rules for harvesting gains.

Pitfalls to Monitor When Generating More Taxable Income

There are potential pitfalls regarding efforts to increase taxable income as a part of managing taxes. These pitfalls make the process more complicated as there is more to pay attention to than just the federal or state income tax brackets. Taxable income can uniquely generate a need to pay taxes on more of Social Security benefits and can raise Medicare premiums. It can also trigger the net investment income surtax. After 2026, it may lead to phaseouts for personal exemptions and itemized deductions. In special cases, there could also be additional tax deductions and tax credits with income limits that could be lost. For those retiring before Medicare eligibility, taxable income could also impact the availability of subsidies for health insurance coverage. Here we will emphasize a few of these key issues. Perhaps the most important of these for typical retirees will be the Social Security tax torpedo.

The Social Security Tax Torpedo

Having more income can uniquely generate a need to pay taxes on Social Security benefits. Up to 85 percent of Social Security benefits can be counted as taxable income. The rules for Social Security benefit taxation create what is known as the "tax torpedo." Once benefits begin, each $1 of additional income from qualified plan distributions and the like will require taxes on that income as well as taxes on up to 85 percent of a corresponding $1 of Social Security. Wealthier individuals may find that avoiding taxes on 85 percent of Social Security benefits is impossible, but those with relatively more modest resources might be able to set into motion a plan that can reduce or even completely avoid the tax torpedo for life, while following conventional wisdom strategies could leave them mired in paying more taxes through the torpedo. Presently around 50 percent of Social Security beneficiaries will pay taxes on at least a portion of their Social Security benefits.

Exhibit 10.12 provides the details for determining how much of Social Security benefits are taxable. The calculation is based on provisional income, which is defined as modified adjusted gross income (MAGI) *plus* half of the Social Security benefits *plus* any tax-exempt interest from investments such as municipal bonds. Depending on the publication, this provisional income measure may also be called the combined income or the total income. As well, modified adjusted gross income can mean different things each time it is mentioned in the tax code. In this context, it is generally the components of adjusted gross income listed on the 1040 tax form before including the taxable portion of Social Security benefits. This calculation is what determines how much of the Social Security benefits are taxable, which then allows for the calculation of AGI.

Exhibit 10.12
Social Security Benefits Taxation

Provisional Income		Taxable Benefits
Single Filers	Married Filing Jointly	
Under $25,000	Under $32,000	0%
$25,000 - $34,000	$32,000 - $44,000	up to 50%
Over $34,000	Over $44,000	up to 85%

Note: Provisional Income = MAGI + 1/2 Benefit + tax-exempt interest

The dollar values in Exhibit 10.12 were set in 1994 and this is one part of the tax code that is not adjusted for inflation. Congress may change these thresholds at some point, but they have been the same for a long time. This means that over time more and more Americans will pay income tax on their Social Security benefits unless they have built up large non-taxable reserves. The upper thresholds for triggering taxation on 85 percent of benefits are $34,000 for single filers and $44,000 for joint filers.

Calculating taxable Social Security benefits is complex because of these loopy formulas. You do not know your AGI until you know how much of your benefit is taxed, but you do not know how much of your benefit is taxed until you know your AGI. The amount of Social Security benefits that are taxable is calculated as whichever of these three calculations provides the smallest amount:

1) 85 percent of Social Security benefits

2) 50 percent of Social Security benefits plus 85 percent of the amount of provisional income that exceeds the second threshold ($34,000 for singles and $44,000 for joint filers)

3) 50 percent of provisional income beyond the first threshold plus 35 percent of provisional income beyond the second income threshold

These three calculations can create results that may not be intuitive. It also becomes difficult to connect taxable income directly to the marginal tax rates because the results vary by amount of Social Security benefits. There is not just one tax torpedo; its shape is different for different amounts of Social Security benefits. To provide a sense about this, Exhibit 10.13 shows the taxable portion of Social Security benefits for couples who are married filing jointly. The results are shown for different components of the provisional income (Social Security benefits and everything else). Perhaps the most counterintuitive outcome relates to how the taxable portion of Social Security benefits can decrease as the Social Security benefit increases for different levels of MAGI and tax-exempt interest. This is because the taxable portion of the benefit is not growing as fast as the benefit in those cases where the 85 percent rate is playing a role.

Exhibit 10.13
Taxable Portion of Social Security Benefits
for Married Couples Filing Jointly

		Combined Social Security Benefits for the Household					
		$10,000	$20,000	$30,000	$40,000	$50,000	$60,000
	$0	0%	0%	0%	0%	0%	0%
	$4,000	0%	0%	0%	0%	0%	2%
	$8,000	0%	0%	0%	0%	1%	5%
	$12,000	0%	0%	0%	0%	5%	8%
	$16,000	0%	0%	0%	5%	9%	13%
	$20,000	0%	0%	5%	10%	14%	19%
Modified Adjusted Gross Income + tax-exempt interest	$24,000	0%	5%	12%	15%	21%	24%
	$28,000	5%	15%	18%	24%	27%	30%
	$32,000	25%	25%	29%	32%	34%	36%
	$36,000	45%	39%	40%	41%	41%	41%
	$40,000	59%	56%	51%	49%	48%	47%
	$44,000	85%	73%	63%	58%	55%	53%
	$48,000	85%	85%	74%	66%	61%	58%
	$52,000	85%	85%	85%	75%	68%	64%
	$56,000	85%	85%	85%	83%	75%	70%
	$60,000	85%	85%	85%	85%	82%	75%
	$64,000	85%	85%	85%	85%	85%	81%
	$68,000	85%	85%	85%	85%	85%	85%
	$72,000	85%	85%	85%	85%	85%	85%

For Exhibit 10.13, the tax torpedo is at work in any case that taxable Social Security benefits are greater than 0 percent and less than 85 percent. When the taxable portion is still 0 percent, a dollar of additional income does not trigger tax on Social Security. Once the taxable portion becomes 85 percent, then a dollar of additional income does not trigger more Social Security taxes. But for the range in between, the tax torpedo is at work as more income triggers not just taxes on that income but also taxes on more Social Security benefits.

Exhibit 10.14 provides a visual illustration of the tax torpedo for Social Security. In this example, we consider a single filer in 2021, and the assumed

Social Security benefit is $30,000. The exhibit plots the MAGI plus tax-exempt interest against the marginal tax rate on $1 of additional income. I will simply call this amount MAGI to avoid having to keep writing "plus tax-exempt interest" every time as well. When the MAGI reaches $11,700, the marginal tax rate jumps to 15 percent (this is a 10 percent federal tax bracket and a trigger of 50 percent of a Social Security dollar becoming taxable). It jumps to 18 percent at $18,334, 22.2 percent at $19,000, and 40.7 percent at $34,987. It then drops to 22 percent at $43,706. The MAGI of $43,706 is the point which serves as the upper limit of the tax torpedo with the $30,000 benefit, as now 85 percent of Social Security is taxed. Subsequent increases in taxable income do not also cause more Social Security taxation. With this benefit, a MAGI of $43,706 represents an AGI of $69,206 with 85 percent of Social Security added. With a standard deduction of $14,200 for single filers over 65, this represents a taxable income of $55,006.

Exhibit 10.14
The Social Security "Tax Torpedo" for a Single Filer in 2021
with a $30,000 Social Security Benefit

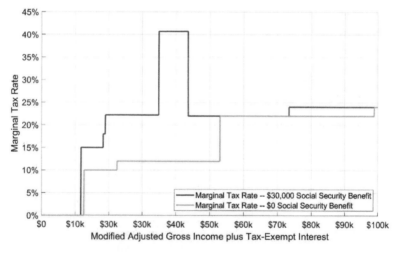

For tax bracket management, the MAGI of $43,706 becomes an important threshold where there can be extra advantages to stay below it as possible. Otherwise, once getting past this threshold, taxpayers then experience a range where the marginal tax rate is back down to 22 percent. Understandably, it can be very clunky to move this discussion back and forth between MAGIs, AGIs, and taxable incomes, but at least I hope this discussion has helped to provide a sense about how this tax torpedo can uniquely increase marginal tax rates for retirees as income triggers taxes on itself as well as on more of Social Security.

Social Security taxation creates a case for more than just tax bracket management; it also can add greater after-tax value for delaying Social Security benefits. If one is already retired at age 62, delaying Social Security benefits to 70 could help to provide a foundation for making more Roth conversions before Social Security benefits begin, which could then help keep taxable income lower after age 70 so that Social Security then does not experience as much of the tax torpedo. If Social Security is delayed until age 70, then pre-70 taxable income is reduced. Those waiting to age 70 will have more opportunity to conduct Roth conversions and realize long-term capital gains on taxable accounts at lower tax rates. This will also help to reduce taxable income later after benefits begin. Subsequent Roth distributions do not count when determining how much of Social Security is taxable. Those with the capacity to get a large portion of their IRAs converted to Roth accounts prior to beginning Social Security could enjoy substantial tax improvements. Not only will Social Security benefits be larger, but less, or at least a smaller percentage, of those benefits count as taxable income. These strategies may also help later in retirement to lower the amount of RMDs, to increase the cost-basis for taxable accounts, and to create less pressure to make taxable withdrawals to meet retirement spending needs. Social Security delay frequently complements strategies to support more after-tax spending power.

The tax torpedo can apply for couples as well, and its specific shape does depend on the level of Social Security benefits. The torpedo has the biggest impact when it is adding Social Security taxes on top of the 22 percent tax bracket, getting the marginal rate up to 40.7 percent for a portion of income. If the old tax code returns in 2026, the tax torpedo could impact the 25 percent tax bracket, which would amplify the marginal tax rate to 46.25 percent with Social Security's impact included.

That is not even the whole story. These tax rates could be even higher if there were long-term capital gains that further get pushed from the 0 percent tax bracket to the 15 percent tax bracket as Social Security becomes taxable. For this to be relevant, the household would need to still be in the 12 percent tax bracket and in a range where a dollar of income is taxing 85 percent of a dollar of Social Security. If this also then pushes $1.85 of long-term capital gains from the 0 percent to the 15 percent tax bracket, then suddenly the marginal tax rate is 49.95 percent. With the tax rates scheduled to return in 2026, the 12 percent tax bracket becomes 15 percent, which then increases the overall marginal tax rate to 55.5 percent for this perfect tax storm. Retirement tax rates will not always be lower in retirement, especially when a dollar of income leads to tax on that income, tax on more of Social Security, and tax on more of long-term capital gains or qualified dividends.

Increased Medicare Part B and Part D Premiums

Another part of the tax code that can create tricky planning implications relates to how Medicare Part B and Part D premiums are determined. This is known as the Income Related Monthly Adjustment Amounts (IRMAA) for Medicare premiums. The level of premiums paid depends on modified adjusted gross income, which in this context is defined more simply as adjusted gross income plus tax-exempt interest. Note again, as with Social

Security, that while tax-exempt interest is not taxable, it can generate higher taxes on other sources of income. An additional issue for Medicare, though, is that the relevant measure of MAGI is from two years prior, which is what you have stated on your prior year tax returns. For example, determining Medicare premiums in 2021 means using the MAGI from 2019 included on your 2020 tax forms. For those starting Medicare at 65, this means that tax planning begins accounting for impacts on Medicare premiums at age 63. For those experiencing life changing events that lower current year MAGI relative to two years prior, which does include retiring, it is possible to file a petition with form SSA-44 to have a smaller premium applied. It is important to note that Roth conversions are not considered as a life changing event and any higher premiums a Roth conversion generates should be viewed as an additional tax.

Exhibit 10.15
Medicare Premiums in 2021 (Based on Income in 2019)

Single Filers Modified Adjusted Gross Income	Married Filing Jointly Modified Adjusted Gross Income	Part B Monthly Premium per recipient	Part D Monthly Premium per recipient	Combined Annual Amount per Individual
$88,000 or less	$176,000 or less	$148.50	$33.06 (base premium)	$2,178.72
$88,001 - $111,000	$176,001 - $222,000	$207.90	base + $12.30	$3,039.12
$111,001 - $138,000	$222,001 - $276,000	$297.00	base + $31.80	$4,342.32
$138,001 - $165,000	$276,001 - $330,000	$386.10	base + $51.20	$5,644.32
$165,001 - $500,000	$330,001 - $750,000	$475.20	base + $70.70	$6,947.52
Over $500,000	Over $750,000	$504.90	base + $77.10	$7,380.72

Note: The average base plan premium ("base") for Part D prescription drug coverage is $33.06 per month in 2021, but it can vary between insurers.

Exhibit 10.15 provides the details for 2021 Medicare Part B medical insurance and Part D drug coverage. It shows the MAGI income thresholds for a single and for a married-filing-jointly couple as the associated monthly premiums and combined annual values. These are per-person premiums, which doubles the cost for a couple who are both enrolled in Medicare. The costs for Medicare can increase in quite noticeable ways at higher income levels. And it is important to understand that these thresholds are firm. A single person with a MAGI of $88,000 would experience annual premiums of $2,179. With one more dollar of income ($88,001), the annual premium jumps by $860 dollars, representing an 86,000 percent marginal tax rate on that dollar. This effect gets even larger at other thresholds, and with couples the premium jump is multiplied by two. This is a more extreme type of tax torpedo, and those who are using tax bracket management as part of tax planning should take care to make sure that the MAGI does not exceed a particular threshold by even $1. Leave yourself a buffer for surprises with tax projections that get you close to any of these thresholds. Because these tax brackets are significantly higher than with the Social Security tax torpedo, this issue will affect fewer retirees, but it is important to monitor for Roth conversions.

Affordable Care Act Subsidies for Health Insurance Before Medicare

Another issue impacting anyone who buys health insurance through healthcare.gov or the state insurance exchanges under the Affordable Care Act, including early retirees who are yet qualified for Medicare, are the subsidies available for such health plans. Premium subsidies are available for those whose modified adjusted gross incomes fall between 100 percent and 400 percent of the federal poverty levels, which vary based on household size. Also, in some states, these percentage thresholds may be different. For a two-person household, 100 percent of the federal poverty line in 2021 is $17,420, and the 400 percent level is $69,680 in most states. This is another case in which having $1 of additional income beyond the 400 percent threshold could result in potentially thousands of dollars of lost subsidies to help cover the cost of insurance, which can make this a very important matter. This non-linear part of the tax code has been called the "subsidy cliff" due to the steep drop in subsidies at the top threshold. This measure of modified adjusted gross income includes AGI plus other categories like untaxed foreign income, non-taxed Social Security benefits, and tax-exempt interest.

The American Rescue Plan Act of 2021

The American Rescue Plan Act passed in March 2021 has temporarily changed the contents of this section for 2021 and 2022. I have provided explanations for how things will be again in 2023, but temporarily one does not have to be as cautious about the impacts of taxable income on health care subsidies. There is no subsidy cliff at the 400 percent threshold as now taxpayers are expected to cover insurance costs at up to 8.5 percent of their income even when exceeding this threshold, making subsidies possible. For those facing the subsidy cliff, this may provide a short-term opportunity to do more strategic tax planning.

The health insurance subsidy amount available is based on a percentage of income one is deemed to be able to afford based on income and the cost of the benchmark Silver insurance plan in the region where one lives. The subsidy is the cost of the insurance plan exceeding the percentage of modified adjusted gross income one is deemed able to pay. That percentage ranges from 2.06 percent for those with incomes up to 133 percent of the federal poverty line, up to 9.78 percent for those with incomes between 300 percent and 400 percent of the federal poverty line. An individual could still choose a lower or higher cost plan, which would impact out of pocket costs without impacting the subsidy. Plans range from bronze, silver, gold, and platinum, in terms of the lowest premium cost and more co-pays and deductibles with bronze plans, shifting to a higher premium and less additional costs with other plans.

For those who may exceed the top poverty threshold, it may be possible to reduce the modified adjusted gross income with tax deductible contributions to employer plans or IRAs. Only above-the-line deductions like this will help. This is a situation in which a strategic Roth conversion could backfire as it reduces subsidy eligibility. At the other extreme, an income of 100 percent of the poverty line is required to qualify for the subsidy, which could generate a need to have more taxable income for those who might have designed their plans well to avoid income sources that show up in AGI. In this case, generating taxable income could be achieved through Roth conversions, realizing capital gains on taxable accounts, or taking other taxable distributions from retirement plans.

Net Investment Income Surtax

Another source of taxes that can be impacted by having higher taxable incomes is the 3.8 percent Medicare surtax on net investment income. It applies for those whose modified adjusted gross incomes exceed $200,000 for singles and $250,000 for those married filing jointly. These income thresholds are not inflation adjusted. They have been fixed since this tax was created in 2013. I wish I could provide an easy explanation for how AGI is adjusted to determine this version of MAGI. Alas, here is how the IRS defines this MAGI in their FAQ on the topic:

> For the Net Investment Income Tax, modified adjusted gross income is adjusted gross income (Form 1040, Line 37) increased by the difference between amounts excluded from gross income under section 911(a)(1) and the amount of any deductions (taken into account in computing adjusted gross income) or exclusions disallowed under section 911(d)(6) for amounts described in section 911(a)(1). In the case of taxpayers with income from controlled foreign corporations (CFCs) and passive foreign investment companies (PFICs), they may have additional adjustments to their AGI. See section 1.1411-10(e) of the final regulations. (https://www.irs.gov/newsroom/questions-and-answers-on-the-net-investment-income-tax)

Once this MAGI is determined by tax software or an accountant, an additional 3.8 percent tax applies on whichever is less: the modified adjusted gross income exceeding these thresholds or the net investment income. Net investment income includes items such as capital gains, interest, and dividends on assets in taxable accounts, as well as royalties, rents, and the taxable portion of nonqualified annuity distributions.

As mentioned, this tax only becomes relevant when incomes get up to the $200,000 range for singles and $250,000 for married filing jointly, so it will not be relevant for many retirees. But when it applies, it will add an additional 3.8 percent marginal tax rate to some components of income. When the net investment income is smaller, this raises the preferential long-term capital gains and qualified dividend tax rates by 3.8 percent.

Pushing Long-Term Capital Gains and Qualified Dividends into Higher Tax Brackets

Another potential concern is that additional taxable income can also push long-term capital gains and qualified dividends into higher tax brackets as well, raising the effective marginal tax rate. This topic was introduced at the end of the Social Security tax torpedo discussion, and it exists more broadly. Long-term capital gains and qualified dividends have a separate set of tax rates and tax brackets, and these income sources are added on top of other income sources to determine their taxation. The impact is largest when shifting this income from the 0 percent tax rate to 15 percent, but the matter does apply more generally with the 20 percent tax rate and the net investment income tax. Suppose $1 of income is generated in the 12 percent tax bracket, which in turn pushes $1 of long-term capital gains from the 0 percent bracket to the 15 percent bracket. The effective tax rate on that dollar of income, even though it was in the 12 percent tax bracket, is now 27 percent. Because of the unique properties and stacking of these income sources, it is also important to consider how they are impacted when generating additional income elsewhere.

Additional Medicare Tax

A related tax that passed in 2013 is an additional 0.9 percent surtax on wages and self-employment income that exceeds certain thresholds. This tax is similar to the net investment income tax in terms of how it is structured, but it applies to different types of income. It applies to wages and self-employment income that exceeds the fixed thresholds of $200,000 for singles and $250,000 for married filing jointly. As this only applies to income from working, it may be less relevant for retirees.

Alternative Minimum Tax

A complicated part of the tax code that still exists but impacts fewer people since the Tax Cuts and Jobs Act of 2017 is the alternative minimum tax. It is a separate way for calculating taxes, and it applies if the calculations lead to a higher tax bill than with the standard tax code. For retirees, the most likely way that one might incur the alternative minimum tax is when taking large, itemized deductions. The need to manage the alternative minimum tax in retirement is rare and beyond our scope here.

Other Considerations

If the 2017 tax code returns in 2026, this would likely include a return of the personal exemption phaseout and Pease limitations on itemized deductions for higher income individuals that were suspended by the Tax Cuts and Jobs Act. For singles, in 2017, Pease limitations and the personal exemption phaseout both began at an AGI of $261,500. For married filing jointly, these phaseouts began at $313,800. Though this is not an issue at the present, it is another factor whose practical impact is to raise marginal tax rates by about 1 percent for incomes past these levels until the full phaseout has occurred.

A final idea relates to maintaining some holdings in a tax-deferred account later in retirement to possibly take advantage of large deductible expenses such as late-in-life itemized medical expenses that fall above 7.5 percent of AGI. One must be careful because larger IRA distributions raise the AGI, which makes less of the health expense tax deductible, but at the same time the deductions would reduce taxable income and possibly allow such distributions to come out at a lower tax rate.

Other Planning Ideas

There are a few more tax planning ideas worth considering as well. First, though we just considered pitfalls with generating more taxable income as a part of tax planning, there are some reasons to further frontload tax payments at the start of retirement. We also offer the idea of tax loss harvesting as part of an ongoing strategy to offset gains and losses in the taxable portfolio to increase the cost basis without generating tax. We then consider deduction bunching and donor advised funds as ways to take advantage of the ability to itemize tax deductions in some years.

Reasons to Further Frontload Taxes

Though there are pitfalls to monitor when generating more taxable income, there are also reasons why it may be particularly advantageous to frontload some taxes to the early part of retirement. The first reason relates to the idea that there are many unknowns about public policy, including a lack of visibility as to future tax changes. Many fear that Congress could raise taxes in the future. With this view, retirees may wish to take more advantage of the lower tax rates available now. We are in an odd period where the presently legislated tax code has lower rates through 2025, and then the higher tax structure from 2017 is scheduled to return in 2026 if Congress takes no further action on this matter. With the costs of the global pandemic that arrived in 2020, even more uncertainty is created about what could happen with future tax policy.

The tax implications that accompany the death of a spouse in retirement should be considered as well. In the year after the death takes place, the household's filing status will switch from married filing jointly to single. To the extent that expenses may not fall as rapidly after the death of a spouse, and as RMDs are not impacted by the size of the household, married couples may plan to do Roth conversions more aggressively in anticipation of this tax impact. Single filer status could lead to facing a higher marginal tax bracket, a greater percentage of Social Security being taxed, and more vulnerability to experiencing heightened Medicare premiums.

Another matter to further emphasize is that the early retirement period may provide an opportunity to frontload taxes before Social Security and Medicare begin. For those retiring by their early 60s, a systematic tax planning strategy could be accompanied by delaying Social Security to set in motion a plan that could subsequently avoid a large part of the Social Security tax torpedo. We will have an example about this in the following section. As well, before income becomes relevant for Medicare premiums, which happens with income at age 63 for those starting Medicare at 65, one could work on tax planning strategies that will avoid the need to pay higher Medicare premiums. Remember, as well, the health insurance used prior to Medicare may have premiums or subsidies based on taxable income levels that would need to also be considered.

A further matter to consider relates to thinking about if leftover assets will go to beneficiaries rather than being spent for retirement expenses. The SECURE Act ended lifetime stretches for many recipients of inherited IRAs. These beneficiaries will have to distribute the assets and pay taxes during a ten-year window. When beneficiaries are adult children receiving assets from their parents, this could end up leading to RMDs taking place during the children's peak earnings years, which could push up the marginal tax rate paid on the inheritance. For retirees thinking ahead about bequeathing assets, the tax bracket management problem for paying taxes at the lowest rates includes comparing tax rates for the retiree against tax rates for the potential beneficiary. Roth conversions by the retirees may allow for the taxes to be paid at a lower rate. Beneficiaries would then receive Roth assets instead, and though they will have to take RMDs from the inherited Roth, this would not create taxable income for these potential peak earning years. These legacy-related issues are explored in the next chapter.

Tax Loss Harvesting

For taxable accounts, tax loss harvesting can also be used to raise the cost basis of taxable investments at times that do not trigger additional taxes. Tax loss harvesting is a portfolio management technique to systematically realize losses from the investment portfolio that can be used to offset the gains from the portfolio, or to even offset some regular income. When determining taxes around taxable gains and losses, short-term losses are first deducted against short-term gains, and long-term losses are first deducted against long-term gains. Then they are netted from each other. If there is an overall loss, up to $3,000 of losses can be used to offset other taxable income, and further losses can be carried forward to future tax years. With tax loss harvesting, one must be careful about the wash sale rule, which says that the loss cannot be realized if a substantially identical investment is purchased within 30 days before or after the sale. After that time passes, the same investment can be purchased, but otherwise one can look for something that is similar to the asset sold for a loss.

Deduction Bunching

Another technique for tax management is deduction bunching. With the increase in the standard deduction and limitations on some categories for itemized deductions created by the Tax Cut and Jobs Act of 2017, it will be increasingly difficult for taxpayers to itemize instead of taking the standard deduction. The standard deduction wastes possible deductible expenses from the perspective of their impact on reducing taxes: without itemizing, such allowed deductions do not have any impact on taxable income. One must itemize to receive a financial benefit for allowed below-the-line deductions such as charitable giving.

This has led to the popularity of the bunching strategies. The idea behind deduction bunching is to generate large deductible expenses in one tax year to cover spending that would have otherwise been spread over several years. This is done to exceed the standard deduction threshold in one year to create a tax deduction for things like charitable giving, state and local taxes, or medical expenses. This works by bunching deductible spending into one year and skipping this spending in subsequent years.

For example, if you plan to donate $10,000 a year to charity for each of five years, you may be in a situation where you do not exceed the standard deduction in each of these five years. However, if you front-load your five-year contribution into one year as a $50,000 gift, then you will be able to deduct the $50,000 against your income in the current year. The amount that exceeds the standard deduction would provide a true tax benefit, and then the standard deduction can be used in the other four years. For those with state and local taxes below the $10,000 limit and who live in places that allow it, it may be possible to pay for two years of these taxes in one year when otherwise eligible to itemize. Another idea is to focus these deduction bunching strategies into tax years with unusually high taxable income to have a bigger impact on taxes due. This higher income could be for natural reasons in a particular year, such as the sale of a business, or it could be because of a large strategic Roth conversion.

Donor Advised Funds and Other Charitable Tools

In recent years, donor advised funds have become a simple and effective way to get assets transferred to charities using a deduction bunching approach. These funds can separate charitable planning from tax planning for those who want to make charitable contributions, but who have not figured out exactly how much should go to each of multiple charities. This also helps to offset unexpected income near year end, as a donor can quickly shift funds at the end of the year without having to figure out which charity should receive the donation. It is important to note that this would not avoid the tax torpedo for Social Security or Medicare premiums, because those are determined by MAGI measures before this below-the-line deduction is taken.

When assets are moved to the donor advised funds, the full tax deductions are available immediately for the current tax year. The funds then grow tax free until they are distributed to qualified charities. Though the funds must eventually be donated, there are no specific requirements about when.

In addition to allowing for itemizing, this strategy can also provide the benefits associated with donating appreciated shares instead of cash. It is important to recognize that for those with appreciated shares in their taxable accounts, it can be much more effective from a tax perspective to donate appreciated shares rather than cash. The tax savings could then be leveraged to provide an even larger gift, if desired. For instance, consider an individual wishing to donate $30,000. By donating cash, and when itemizing deductions, this contribution reduces taxable income by $30,000 if we ignore the standard deduction. Suppose this individual also owns $30,000 worth of shares in a taxable account with a cost basis of $10,000. These are appreciated shares with unrealized capital gains of $20,000. By donating these shares instead, this person gets the same $30,000 tax deduction PLUS there is no need to pay capital gains taxes on the $20,000 of gains associated with a later sale of these assets.

By donating the appreciated shares, and then using the available cash to repurchase those shares, we have erased $20,000 of taxable capital gains from the investment portfolio. In practice, it can be a real hassle for individuals to donate appreciated shares directly to charities, but a donor advised fund can help facilitate this process. Assuming you itemize your tax return, there are also AGI limitations for how much of a charitable gift is deductible. It is important to work with an accountant when making a large charitable gift to make sure it is structured in such a way that the full tax benefits can be received.

For those with charitable inclinations, a charitable gift annuity is another alternative. With charitable gift annuities, a charitable organization receives the premium. In turn, the charity provides a protected lifetime income. Charitable gift annuities will offer lower payout rates than competitive commercial annuities (i.e. their money's worth measures will be lower) to better ensure that the average participant leaves something for the charity. Charitable gift annuities provide the opportunity to receive a charitable tax deduction for a portion of the premium in the year that the premium is paid, which reflects an estimate of the amount that will eventually be available for the charity after lifetime payments are provided. The premium can also be paid with appreciated stock, but long-term capital gains tax may then have to be paid on income received through the annuity. Charitable gift annuities use unisex rates, which can be relatively helpful for longer-living women. They may also help to satisfy concerns people have about dying early with annuities, as one could view the charity as receiving the benefit in these cases instead of an insurance company. The American Council on Gift Annuities provides more information at their website, www.acga-web.org.

An Example for Tax Bracket Management

We can put these ideas together with an example that quantifies how strategic tax planning and delayed Social Security claiming can increase portfolio longevity in retirement. I have created an example for a 60-year-old single individual who has just retired in 2021. She has $2 million of investment assets, divided between $400,000 in a taxable account, $1.3

million in a traditional IRA, and $300,000 in a Roth IRA. The cost basis for her taxable assets is also $400,000. Her goal is to spend $95,000 a year in retirement net of any federal income taxes and she lives in a state that does not tax income. For Social Security, her primary insurance amount is $30,000 if she claims at her full retirement age of 67. She will get $21,000 if she claims at 62 and $37,200 if she claims at 70.

This example does not incorporate asset location issues and long-term capital gains management, as I simplify investment returns to be 2 percent annually with no inflation. This implies that investments are held in bonds and provide 2 percent taxable interest payments annually without potential for capital gains or losses. While investment returns are simplified, the full tax code has been built into the example. Taxes for 2021 to 2025 are based on present law, and the 2017 tax code (with inflation adjustments through 2021) is used for 2026 and later.

Exhibit 10.16 summarizes the results for this example. It shows five different strategies for this individual. The first is to claim Social Security at age 62 and to follow the conventional wisdom for spending down assets: take any RMDs, then spend the taxable portfolio, then the tax-deferred portfolio, and then the tax-exempt portfolio. This strategy supports 28.99 years of retirement spending, and the details are provided in Exhibit 10.17. It is the baseline. When the portfolio covers a fraction of the year, that represents the percentage of the overall spending goal that can be funded in the year.

Next, to show the value of delaying Social Security, if this retiree claims Social Security at 70 and uses the same conventional wisdom spend-down strategy, portfolio longevity increases by 1.86 years to 30.85 years. The remaining strategies in the exhibit also use Social Security claiming at 70. The next strategy is to use tax bracket management at a pre-determined level of AGI without using Roth conversions. I test various AGI levels to manage and find that an AGI target of $60,000 provides the most benefit for this example, with portfolio longevity of 32.82 years (see Exhibit 10.20). If we follow the same strategy and include strategic Roth conversions as well, portfolio longevity increases to 33.54 years (see Exhibit 10.21). Coincidentally, an AGI target of $60,000 also creates the greatest portfolio longevity with Roth conversions. Finally, I provide an example of front-loading taxes to a higher level in the early retirement years and then targeting a lower AGI level for later in retirement. After several different permutations, I find that managing AGI to $111,000 until age 70, which is the threshold just before a second layer of IRMAA-related Medicare premium increases kick in for earnings starting at 63, and then switching to manage an AGI of $25,000 for age 70 and later (when Social Security starts) can increase portfolio longevity by more than another year to 34.62 years (see Exhibit 10.22). This is 5.63 years longer than following convention wisdom on spenddown strategies and claiming Social Security early. After raising the claiming age to 70, this more tax-efficient strategy still adds 3.77 years of portfolio longevity to the convention wisdom tax strategy. The topics described in this chapter can add significantly to the longevity of retirement distributions.

Exhibit 10.16
Tax-Efficient Retirement Income for a 60-Year-Old Single Retiree

Singles	Years of Longevity	Increase from (1)	
(1) Conventional Wisdom, Social Security at 62 (Taxable, Tax-Deferred, Tax-Free) [EXHIBIT 10.17]	28.99	---	
Conventional Wisdom, Social Security at 70 (Taxable, Tax-Deferred, Tax-Free)	30.85	1.86	
Tax Bracket Management, AGI= $60,000 Social Security at 70 [EXHIBIT 10.20]	32.82	3.83	
Tax Bracket Management with Roth Conversions, AGI=$60,000 Social Security at 70 [EXHIBIT 10.21]	33.54	4.55	
Tax Bracket Management with Roth Conversions Manage 2nd IRMAA Threshold Through 2029, then Manage AGI=$25,000 Social Security at 70 [EXHIBIT 10.22]	34.62	5.63	

Married Filing Jointly	Years of Longevity	Increase from (1)	Bonus over Single Rates
(1) Conventional Wisdom, Social Security at 62 (Taxable, Tax-Deferred, Tax-Free)	32.65	---	3.66
Conventional Wisdom, Social Security at 70 (Taxable, Tax-Deferred, Tax-Free)	35.62	2.97	4.77
Tax Bracket Management, AGI= $65,000 Social Security at 70	36.9	4.25	4.08
Tax Bracket Management with Roth Conversions, AGI=$63,000 Social Security at 70	37.41	4.76	3.87
Tax Bracket Management with Roth Conversions Manage 2nd IRMAA Threshold Through 2029, Social Security at 70	33.92	1.27	-0.7

As a further note, this exhibit also shows the five corresponding strategies assuming that everything is the same except that the discussion is about a married couple instead of a single person. The point for including results for the couple is to demonstrate how much impact the differing tax brackets between singles and couples can have on retirement sustainability. For the different strategies, applying tax brackets for married filing jointly could extend portfolio longevity by more than 3.66 years. This does speak to the planning idea mentioned about how those who are married filing jointly may seek more balance by frontloading taxes in anticipation of an inevitable point when the surviving spouse will face the tax brackets for singles. We can also note that the strategy for managing the second IRMAA threshold for couples ($222,000) is too aggressive and results in worse outcomes. It forces too much taxes to be paid early on, such that tax capacity is wasted later in retirement.

Moving now to the specific lifetime patterns for different strategies, Exhibit 10.17 provides the results for claiming Social Security at age 62 and following the specific distribution strategy of spending taxable assets first, then tax-deferred assets, and then tax-exempt assets. In this case, she can meet her full spending goals for 28.99 years until just before her 89th birthday. At this point her investment assets deplete and she only has a $21,000 Social Security benefit to cover the rest of her life. I show the details of this strategy to contrast it with more efficient spending strategies.

In Exhibit 10.17, we can identify some of the inefficiencies with the standard withdrawal recommendations. First, by only spending from the taxable portfolio at the start, she wastes space in her tax brackets to trigger taxes when tax rates are low. Her adjusted gross income in the early retirement years consists only of the 2 percent interest payments being generated by her remaining taxable assets each year. Her income does not even rise to the level of the standard deduction until age 65, when her taxable assets deplete, and she switches to spending from the tax-deferred account. Though she does not pay taxes during the first 5 years of retirement, she is heading toward a bigger tax bill later that will have a profound effect on her portfolio longevity.

From ages 65 to 81 her adjusted gross income is more than $100,000 because she spends only from the tax-deferred account and Social Security benefits. This inefficiency is leading her to have tax payments on 85 percent of her Social Security benefits between the ages of 65 and 82. In addition, from ages 66 to 81 her Medicare MAGI (I assume no tax-exempt bonds so this MAGI matches the AGI) exceeds the second Medicare threshold ($111,000), which causes her Medicare premiums to increase by $2,164 per year from ages 68 to 84. Remember, Medicare premiums have a two-year lag related to income. I include these IRMAA increases as part of her taxes. Her annual tax bill between ages 68 and 82 is $23,670, which represents an effective tax rate of 24.9 percent of her $95,000 pre-tax spending goal. As discussed at the outset of the chapter, this is a meaningful way to describe the effective tax rate in retirement.

Later in retirement, after she depletes the tax-deferred account, spending is sourced to the Roth IRA and Social Security. Her taxes eventually fall back to $0 as her adjusted gross income is $0 starting at age 83. That year she just has one more IRMAA adjustment to pay. Roth distributions do not create any taxable income, and her Social Security benefits are not taxable at this stage. While taxes are $0 as of age 84, the damage has already been done and there is 0 percent tax rate capacity being wasted by not having income to cover the standard deduction.

One other harmful possibility that was not an issue with this example is that required minimum distributions were never binding in terms of forcing a higher distribution from the tax-deferred account than the retiree otherwise wanted, but this could also be an issue for those whose IRA balances are too high relative to their spending goals. This distribution strategy simply missed opportunities to pay taxes at lower rates and ended up paying too much tax at higher rates.

Exhibit 10.17
Outcomes for Claiming Social Security at 62,
Following Conventional Withdrawal Order Sequencing Strategy

Age	Remaining Wealth			Spending			
	Taxable	Tax-Deferred	Tax Exempt	Taxable	Tax-Deferred	Tax Exempt	Social Security
60	$311,100	$1,326,000	$306,000	$95,000	$0	$0	$0
61	$220,422	$1,352,520	$312,120	$95,000	$0	$0	$0
62	$149,350	$1,379,570	$318,362	$74,000	$0	$0	$21,000
63	$76,857	$1,407,162	$324,730	$74,000	$0	$0	$21,000
64	$2,915	$1,435,305	$331,224	$74,000	$0	$0	$21,000
65	$0	$1,371,517	$337,849	$2,915	$90,681	$0	$21,000
66	$0	$1,302,389	$344,606	$0	$94,665	$0	$21,000
67	$0	$1,230,659	$351,498	$0	$95,860	$0	$21,000
68	$0	$1,155,649	$358,528	$0	$97,670	$0	$21,000
69	$0	$1,079,138	$365,698	$0	$97,670	$0	$21,000
70	$0	$1,001,097	$373,012	$0	$97,670	$0	$21,000
71	$0	$921,495	$380,473	$0	$97,670	$0	$21,000
72	$0	$840,302	$388,082	$0	$97,670	$0	$21,000
73	$0	$757,484	$395,844	$0	$97,670	$0	$21,000
74	$0	$673,010	$403,761	$0	$97,670	$0	$21,000
75	$0	$586,847	$411,836	$0	$97,670	$0	$21,000
76	$0	$498,960	$420,072	$0	$97,670	$0	$21,000
77	$0	$409,316	$428,474	$0	$97,670	$0	$21,000
78	$0	$317,878	$437,043	$0	$97,670	$0	$21,000
79	$0	$224,612	$445,784	$0	$97,670	$0	$21,000
80	$0	$129,481	$454,700	$0	$97,670	$0	$21,000
81	$0	$32,447	$463,794	$0	$97,670	$0	$21,000
82	$0	$0	$423,998	$0	$32,447	$48,110	$21,000
83	$0	$0	$354,791	$0	$0	$76,164	$21,000
84	$0	$0	$286,407	$0	$0	$74,000	$21,000
85	$0	$0	$216,655	$0	$0	$74,000	$21,000
86	$0	$0	$145,508	$0	$0	$74,000	$21,000
87	$0	$0	$72,938	$0	$0	$74,000	$21,000
88	$0	$0	$0	$0	$0	$72,938	$21,000
89	$0	$0	$0	$0	$0	$0	$21,000
90	$0	$0	$0	$0	$0	$0	$21,000
91	$0	$0	$0	$0	$0	$0	$21,000
92	$0	$0	$0	$0	$0	$0	$21,000
93	$0	$0	$0	$0	$0	$0	$21,000
94	$0	$0	$0	$0	$0	$0	$21,000

Exhibit 10.17 continued…

Age	RMDs	Roth Conversion	Adjusted Gross Income	Taxable Income	Taxable Social Security	Federal Income Taxes
60	$0	$0	$6,100	$0	$0	$0
61	$0	$0	$4,322	$0	$0	$0
62	$0	$0	$2,928	$0	$0	$0
63	$0	$0	$1,507	$0	$0	$0
64	$0	$0	$57	$0	$0	$0
65	$0	$0	$108,531	$96,581	$17,850	$19,595
66	$0	$0	$112,515	$100,565	$17,850	$20,665
67	$0	$0	$113,710	$101,760	$17,850	$21,860
68	$0	$0	$115,520	$103,570	$17,850	$23,670
69	$0	$0	$115,520	$103,570	$17,850	$23,670
70	$0	$0	$115,520	$103,570	$17,850	$23,670
71	$0	$0	$115,520	$103,570	$17,850	$23,670
72	$33,631	$0	$115,520	$103,570	$17,850	$23,670
73	$31,710	$0	$115,520	$103,570	$17,850	$23,670
74	$29,705	$0	$115,520	$103,570	$17,850	$23,670
75	$27,358	$0	$115,520	$103,570	$17,850	$23,670
76	$24,761	$0	$115,520	$103,570	$17,850	$23,670
77	$21,789	$0	$115,520	$103,570	$17,850	$23,670
78	$18,605	$0	$115,520	$103,570	$17,850	$23,670
79	$15,065	$0	$115,520	$103,570	$17,850	$23,670
80	$11,119	$0	$115,520	$103,570	$17,850	$23,670
81	$6,674	$0	$115,520	$103,570	$17,850	$23,670
82	$1,754	$0	$44,552	$32,602	$12,105	$6,556
83	$0	$0	$0	$0	$0	$2,164
84	$0	$0	$0	$0	$0	$0
85	$0	$0	$0	$0	$0	$0
86	$0	$0	$0	$0	$0	$0
87	$0	$0	$0	$0	$0	$0
88	$0	$0	$0	$0	$0	$0
89	$0	$0	$0	$0	$0	$0
90	$0	$0	$0	$0	$0	$0
91	$0	$0	$0	$0	$0	$0
92	$0	$0	$0	$0	$0	$0
93	$0	$0	$0	$0	$0	$0
94	$0	$0	$0	$0	$0	$0

As we shift to more efficient strategies, Exhibits 10.18 and 10.19 helps us identify how the AGI target choice impacts portfolio longevity. These exhibits become the source of the strategies we consider in greater detail in subsequent exhibits. The strategy we just described is represented as "Conventional Wisdom, SS@62" in these two exhibits. We can contrast the conventional wisdom approach to tax bracket management either as the source of retirement spending (Bracket Manage) or to conduct strategic Roth conversions (Roth Conversions). For these strategies, the level of AGI managed impacts portfolio sustainability and the charts can be used to find the income level linking to the longest sustainability.

Exhibit 10.18
Portfolio Longevity and Tax-Efficient Distribution Strategies
Managing a Fixed Level of Adjusted Gross Income in Retirement

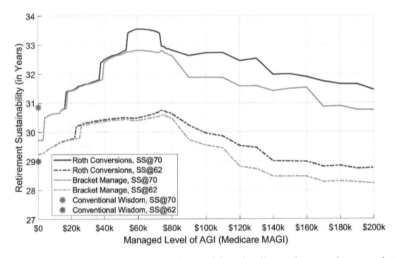

In Exhibit 10.18, we consider a variety of fixed adjusted gross income levels to manage and study portfolio longevity as we vary income targets. Generally, allowing Roth conversions can support greater portfolio longevity. The exhibit shows that for this example, using Roth conversions and managing an adjusted gross income of $60,000 per year allows for the greatest portfolio longevity. It is the sweet spot to provide the best balance for lifetime taxes. Lower AGI levels will not be able to get enough moved to the Roth account and can lead to too much later taxes. Higher levels mean moving assets to the Roth account too quickly such that some of the lower tax bracket space is eventually wasted by a lack of taxable income.

Exhibit 10.19 takes matters a step further to show how managing to the $111,000 AGI level for the years before Social Security begins and then managing to a lower subsequent level may support even better outcomes. This front-loading of taxes reduces the impact of the Social Security torpedo later in retirement, as by that time managing an AGI of $25,000 can support the most long-term sustainability. Using the optimal outcomes from these two exhibits give us the sources for additional examples to explain how tax bracket management can improve portfolio sustainability.

Exhibit 10.19
Portfolio Longevity and Tax-Efficient Distribution Strategies
Managing $111,000 of Adjusted Gross Income for the First Ten Years
And then Managing a Fixed Level of AGI for the Rest

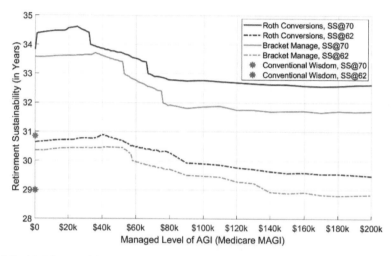

Exhibit 10.20 provides a more complete picture about how the optimal "Bracket Manage" strategy plays out with a fixed $60,000 AGI target. Compared to the previous strategy in Exhibit 10.17, this strategy adds 3.83 years of portfolio longevity by increasing Social Security benefits, shifting income from the high-tax middle years of retirement to earlier and later years when lower marginal tax rates apply, reducing the portion of Social Security that gets taxed, and eliminating IRMAA-related Medicare surcharges until later in retirement. Specifically, the strategy works by first sourcing spending gaps from the tax-deferred account until the AGI target is reached, and then filling the remaining need from the taxable account while assets remain and then from the Roth account after taxable assets deplete. The taxable account now lasts until age 69 since spending from it is slowed. This leads to taxes of $6,188 for the first five years, and then $7,483 starting in 2026 with the reversion to the pre-TCJA tax code. Taxes then stay at this level until age 81 when an RMD becomes binding for three years and forces more out of the tax-deferred account. By age 84, the Roth account depletes and the subsequent greater distribution need from the IRA pushes up taxable income from that point. Social Security begins at age 70 with a benefit of $37,200, which helps reduce the portfolio distribution need. This strategy keeps the taxable portion of Social Security lower at 61.6 percent of benefits, until later in retirement when the AGI is forced to increase as tax-deferred assets become the only available investment resource in those later retirement years.

Exhibit 10.20
Outcomes for Claiming Social Security at 70,
Managing $60,0000 Adjusted Gross Income (no Roth Conversions)

Age	Remaining Wealth			Spending			
	Taxable	Tax-Deferred	Tax Exempt	Taxable	Tax-Deferred	Tax Exempt	Social Security
60	$358,813	$1,271,976	$306,000	$48,223	$52,964	$0	$0
61	$317,625	$1,242,568	$312,120	$47,415	$53,772	$0	$0
62	$276,438	$1,211,748	$318,362	$46,608	$54,580	$0	$0
63	$235,250	$1,179,488	$324,730	$45,800	$55,387	$0	$0
64	$194,063	$1,145,759	$331,224	$44,993	$56,195	$0	$0
65	$151,600	$1,110,507	$337,849	$45,435	$57,027	$0	$0
66	$109,138	$1,073,699	$344,606	$44,602	$57,860	$0	$0
67	$66,675	$1,035,307	$351,498	$43,770	$58,693	$0	$0
68	$24,213	$995,297	$358,528	$42,937	$59,525	$0	$0
69	$0	$954,003	$347,083	$24,213	$60,000	$18,250	$0
70	$0	$935,266	$325,274	$0	$37,076	$28,187	$37,200
71	$0	$916,154	$303,029	$0	$37,076	$28,187	$37,200
72	$0	$896,660	$280,339	$0	$37,076	$28,187	$37,200
73	$0	$876,776	$257,196	$0	$37,076	$28,187	$37,200
74	$0	$856,495	$233,589	$0	$37,076	$28,187	$37,200
75	$0	$835,807	$209,510	$0	$37,076	$28,187	$37,200
76	$0	$814,706	$184,950	$0	$37,076	$28,187	$37,200
77	$0	$793,183	$159,898	$0	$37,076	$28,187	$37,200
78	$0	$771,230	$134,346	$0	$37,076	$28,187	$37,200
79	$0	$748,837	$108,282	$0	$37,076	$28,187	$37,200
80	$0	$725,997	$81,697	$0	$37,076	$28,187	$37,200
81	$0	$702,346	$54,771	$0	$37,423	$28,000	$37,200
82	$0	$677,669	$27,603	$0	$37,965	$27,709	$37,200
83	$0	$652,170	$68	$0	$38,286	$27,536	$37,200
84	$0	$586,198	$0	$0	$77,466	$68	$37,200
85	$0	$518,814	$0	$0	$77,557	$0	$37,200
86	$0	$448,901	$0	$0	$78,715	$0	$37,200
87	$0	$377,589	$0	$0	$78,715	$0	$37,200
88	$0	$304,852	$0	$0	$78,715	$0	$37,200
89	$0	$230,659	$0	$0	$78,715	$0	$37,200
90	$0	$154,983	$0	$0	$78,715	$0	$37,200
91	$0	$77,793	$0	$0	$78,715	$0	$37,200
92	$0	$0	$0	$0	$77,793	$0	$37,200
93	$0	$0	$0	$0	$0	$0	$37,200
94	$0	$0	$0	$0	$0	$0	$37,200

Exhibit 10.20 continued…

Age	RMDs	Roth Conversion	Adjusted Gross Income	Taxable Income	Taxable Social Security	Federal Income Taxes
60	$0	$0	$60,000	$47,450	$0	$6,188
61	$0	$0	$60,000	$47,450	$0	$6,188
62	$0	$0	$60,000	$47,450	$0	$6,188
63	$0	$0	$60,000	$47,450	$0	$6,188
64	$0	$0	$60,000	$47,450	$0	$6,188
65	$0	$0	$60,000	$48,050	$0	$7,463
66	$0	$0	$60,000	$48,050	$0	$7,463
67	$0	$0	$60,000	$48,050	$0	$7,463
68	$0	$0	$60,000	$48,050	$0	$7,463
69	$0	$0	$60,000	$48,050	$0	$7,463
70	$0	$0	$60,000	$48,050	$22,924	$7,463
71	$0	$0	$60,000	$48,050	$22,924	$7,463
72	$33,436	$0	$60,000	$48,050	$22,924	$7,463
73	$33,836	$0	$60,000	$48,050	$22,924	$7,463
74	$34,383	$0	$60,000	$48,050	$22,924	$7,463
75	$34,817	$0	$60,000	$48,050	$22,924	$7,463
76	$35,266	$0	$60,000	$48,050	$22,924	$7,463
77	$35,577	$0	$60,000	$48,050	$22,924	$7,463
78	$36,054	$0	$60,000	$48,050	$22,924	$7,463
79	$36,551	$0	$60,000	$48,050	$22,924	$7,463
80	$37,071	$0	$60,000	$48,050	$22,924	$7,463
81	$37,423	$0	$60,642	$48,692	$23,219	$7,623
82	$37,965	$0	$61,645	$49,695	$23,680	$7,874
83	$38,286	$0	$62,240	$50,290	$23,953	$8,022
84	$38,820	$0	$109,086	$97,136	$31,620	$19,734
85	$36,637	$0	$109,177	$97,227	$31,620	$19,757
86	$34,133	$0	$110,335	$98,385	$31,620	$20,915
87	$31,174	$0	$110,335	$98,385	$31,620	$20,915
88	$27,561	$0	$110,335	$98,385	$31,620	$20,915
89	$23,632	$0	$110,335	$98,385	$31,620	$20,915
90	$18,906	$0	$110,335	$98,385	$31,620	$20,915
91	$13,477	$0	$110,335	$98,385	$31,620	$20,915
92	$7,203	$0	$109,413	$97,463	$31,620	$20,676
93	$0	$0	$0	$0	$0	$860
94	$0	$0	$0	$0	$0	$860

Though retirees may be wary about unnecessarily generating more taxable income in the early retirement years, we have another example about how short-term sacrifice with retirement income planning can lead to long-term efficiencies. This strategy has smoothed taxes at a lower level throughout retirement. Tax bracket space is not wasted by paying some taxes during the earlier retirement years. Altogether, this strategy added 3.83 years of portfolio longevity as compared to the baseline strategy. As well, even if assets deplete, the retiree benefits from still having a Social Security benefit that is 76 percent larger than when claiming at 62.

Next, in Exhibit 10.21 we allow for strategic Roth conversions as part of tax-bracket management. The optimal AGI target is $60,000 again, and this increases portfolio longevity by another 0.72 years over the previous strategy. Roth conversion strategies tend to support the same or better outcomes than simple bracket management. For Roth conversions, the early retirement years consist of spending down taxable assets like in the conventional strategy, but also generating more taxable income by converting assets from the tax-deferred account into the Roth account to cover the target. The first four years of retirement witness Roth conversions of more than $50,000 per year. Roth conversions continue until the taxable portfolio depletes. The additional taxes on the conversions are also funded by the taxable account, which depletes it more rapidly.

At age 64, the taxable account depletes, Roth conversions end, and distributions from the tax-deferred account are instead used to fund retirement expenses up to the $60,000 AGI target. The remainder of spending is covered by distributions from the Roth account, allowing for the AGI target to continue being managed. This keeps taxable income lower. Again, 61.6 percent of Social Security benefits are taxed during the middle period, which provides additional tax relief relative to when 85 percent of benefits are taxed.

With the same pre-tax spending goal, the combined effects of this strategy maintain investment assets until age 93. After assets deplete, Social Security continues to provide $37,200 of annual spending. This example highlights the value of tax-efficient retirement planning, as portfolio longevity extends by 4.55 years relative to the first strategy. We moved away from the conventional wisdom by first blending distributions from the taxable and tax-deferred accounts while taxable assets remain, and then blending distributions from the tax-deferred and tax-free accounts. This blending process provides greater control over AGI and marginal tax rates.

As a final example, Exhibit 10.22 provides a case in which taxes are even more strongly front-loaded into the early retirement years before Social Security begins. This helps to better manage the Social Security tax torpedo. Even though tax bills are higher in the early retirement years, the strategy can increase portfolio longevity by more than a full year relative to the previous strategy. This strategy allows the retirement spending goal to be met for 34.62 years.

In this case, Roth conversions are used to manage a $111,000 AGI level for the first ten years of retirement before Social Security begins. As I am assuming there is no tax-exempt interest from municipal bonds to be counted, the AGI matches the MAGI used to calculate IRMAA-related premium increases for Medicare. This AGI target is right at the level that accepts one hike in Medicare premiums but just avoids the second hike. In practice, one must be especially cautious about managing income around one of the Medicare brackets, because going over by just $1 will trigger a substantial additional premium hike.

This strategy allows for larger Roth conversions in the early years of retirement until the taxable portfolio depletes at age 63. Roth conversions exceed $100,000 for three years but are limited in the fourth year by the small remaining balance for taxable assets. The spending is then sourced to a combination of tax-deferred and Roth distributions to continue managing the same AGI level through age 69.

At age 70, Social Security begins and a new AGI target of $25,000 is used for the remainder of retirement. Though the tax bill reaches $21,101 for ages 65 to 69, it is only $2,320 at age 70 and 71 and then never exceeds $1,460 for the remainder of retirement. Required Minimum Distributions are never binding to force more from the IRA than is desired for spending and tax-efficiency purposes. This $1,460 tax number provides an effective tax rate of 1.5 percent of the retirement spending goal for ages 72 and later, which may seem shocking for someone who began their retirement with $2 million of investment assets and is managing $95,000 of pre-tax spending. The reason this strategy is so effective is because it worked to further reduce the Social Security tax torpedo, as only 18.4 percent of Social Security benefits are counted as taxable income throughout retirement. Portfolio assets last for 34.62 years until the retiree is almost 95 years old. This is an increase of 5.63 years over the baseline, showing the real value that can be obtained for retirement plans by combining a delay in Social Security with an aggressive Roth conversion strategy in the early retirement years.

A Caveat About the Results

Strategies that extend portfolio longevity involved aggressively consuming the taxable portfolio to cover spending needs and taxes on Roth conversions. This is partly due to the assumption that portfolio returns are realized and taxed annually at ordinary income tax rates. With preferential treatment for long-term capital gains and qualified dividends, there may be reason to slow spending from the taxable portfolio, as keeping some assets may allow for future distributions that can be taxed at preferential rates, though that would also make more of Social Security taxable. I aim to explore this further in my next iteration of research on this topic.

Exhibit 10.21
Outcomes for Claiming Social Security at 70,
Managing $60,0000 Adjusted Gross Income (Using Roth Conversions)

Age	Remaining Wealth			Spending			
	Taxable	Tax-Deferred	Tax Exempt	Taxable	Tax-Deferred	Tax Exempt	Social Security
60	$304,789	$1,270,896	$361,104	$101,188	$54,024	$0	$0
61	$207,673	$1,239,267	$425,373	$101,188	$55,928	$0	$0
62	$108,615	$1,205,025	$492,908	$101,188	$57,870	$0	$0
63	$7,577	$1,168,077	$563,815	$101,188	$59,851	$0	$0
64	$0	$1,130,238	$540,808	$7,577	$60,000	$33,611	$0
65	$0	$1,091,643	$508,312	$0	$60,000	$42,463	$0
66	$0	$1,052,276	$475,167	$0	$60,000	$42,463	$0
67	$0	$1,012,122	$441,358	$0	$60,000	$42,463	$0
68	$0	$971,164	$406,874	$0	$60,000	$42,463	$0
69	$0	$929,387	$371,699	$0	$60,000	$42,463	$0
70	$0	$910,158	$350,383	$0	$37,076	$28,187	$37,200
71	$0	$890,544	$328,640	$0	$37,076	$28,187	$37,200
72	$0	$870,537	$306,462	$0	$37,076	$28,187	$37,200
73	$0	$850,131	$283,841	$0	$37,076	$28,187	$37,200
74	$0	$829,316	$260,767	$0	$37,076	$28,187	$37,200
75	$0	$808,086	$237,232	$0	$37,076	$28,187	$37,200
76	$0	$786,430	$213,226	$0	$37,076	$28,187	$37,200
77	$0	$764,342	$188,740	$0	$37,076	$28,187	$37,200
78	$0	$741,811	$163,764	$0	$37,076	$28,187	$37,200
79	$0	$718,830	$138,289	$0	$37,076	$28,187	$37,200
80	$0	$695,390	$112,304	$0	$37,076	$28,187	$37,200
81	$0	$671,480	$85,800	$0	$37,076	$28,187	$37,200
82	$0	$647,093	$58,765	$0	$37,076	$28,187	$37,200
83	$0	$622,217	$31,190	$0	$37,076	$28,187	$37,200
84	$0	$596,844	$3,063	$0	$37,076	$28,187	$37,200
85	$0	$533,839	$0	$0	$73,473	$3,063	$37,200
86	$0	$465,408	$0	$0	$77,557	$0	$37,200
87	$0	$394,427	$0	$0	$78,715	$0	$37,200
88	$0	$322,026	$0	$0	$78,715	$0	$37,200
89	$0	$248,177	$0	$0	$78,715	$0	$37,200
90	$0	$172,851	$0	$0	$78,715	$0	$37,200
91	$0	$96,018	$0	$0	$78,715	$0	$37,200
92	$0	$17,649	$0	$0	$78,715	$0	$37,200
93	$0	$0	$0	$0	$17,649	$0	$37,200
94	$0	$0	$0	$0	$0	$0	$37,200

Exhibit 10.21 continued…

Age	RMDs	Roth Conversion	Adjusted Gross Income	Taxable Income	Taxable Social Security	Federal Income Taxes
60	$0	$54,024	$60,000	$47,450	$0	$6,188
61	$0	$55,928	$60,000	$47,450	$0	$6,188
62	$0	$57,870	$60,000	$47,450	$0	$6,188
63	$0	$59,851	$60,000	$47,450	$0	$6,188
64	$0	$0	$60,000	$47,450	$0	$6,188
65	$0	$0	$60,000	$48,050	$0	$7,463
66	$0	$0	$60,000	$48,050	$0	$7,463
67	$0	$0	$60,000	$48,050	$0	$7,463
68	$0	$0	$60,000	$48,050	$0	$7,463
69	$0	$0	$60,000	$48,050	$0	$7,463
70	$0	$0	$60,000	$48,050	$22,924	$7,463
71	$0	$0	$60,000	$48,050	$22,924	$7,463
72	$32,502	$0	$60,000	$48,050	$22,924	$7,463
73	$32,850	$0	$60,000	$48,050	$22,924	$7,463
74	$33,338	$0	$60,000	$48,050	$22,924	$7,463
75	$33,712	$0	$60,000	$48,050	$22,924	$7,463
76	$34,096	$0	$60,000	$48,050	$22,924	$7,463
77	$34,342	$0	$60,000	$48,050	$22,924	$7,463
78	$34,743	$0	$60,000	$48,050	$22,924	$7,463
79	$35,157	$0	$60,000	$48,050	$22,924	$7,463
80	$35,586	$0	$60,000	$48,050	$22,924	$7,463
81	$35,845	$0	$60,000	$48,050	$22,924	$7,463
82	$36,296	$0	$60,000	$48,050	$22,924	$7,463
83	$36,559	$0	$60,000	$48,050	$22,924	$7,463
84	$37,037	$0	$60,000	$48,050	$22,924	$7,463
85	$37,303	$0	$105,093	$93,143	$31,620	$18,736
86	$35,121	$0	$109,177	$97,227	$31,620	$19,757
87	$32,320	$0	$110,335	$98,385	$31,620	$20,915
88	$28,790	$0	$110,335	$98,385	$31,620	$20,915
89	$24,963	$0	$110,335	$98,385	$31,620	$20,915
90	$20,342	$0	$110,335	$98,385	$31,620	$20,915
91	$15,031	$0	$110,335	$98,385	$31,620	$20,915
92	$8,891	$0	$110,335	$98,385	$31,620	$20,915
93	$1,747	$0	$24,061	$12,111	$6,412	$2,180
94	$0	$0	$0	$0	$0	$860

Exhibit 10.22
Outcomes for Claiming Social Security at 70,
Managing $111,0000 Adjusted Gross Income for the First Ten Years,
And then $25,000 of AGI for the Rest (Using Roth Conversions)

Age	Remaining Wealth			Spending			
	Taxable	Tax-Deferred	Tax Exempt	Taxable	Tax-Deferred	Tax Exempt	Social Security
60	$293,098	$1,218,642	$413,358	$112,649	$105,253	$0	$0
61	$184,058	$1,133,476	$531,164	$112,649	$107,391	$0	$0
62	$71,960	$1,044,365	$653,568	$113,509	$109,589	$0	$0
63	$0	$952,032	$737,479	$71,960	$111,000	$0	$0
64	$0	$857,853	$749,669	$0	$111,000	$2,509	$0
65	$0	$761,790	$759,459	$0	$111,000	$5,101	$0
66	$0	$663,805	$769,444	$0	$111,000	$5,101	$0
67	$0	$563,862	$779,630	$0	$111,000	$5,101	$0
68	$0	$461,919	$790,019	$0	$111,000	$5,101	$0
69	$0	$357,937	$800,616	$0	$111,000	$5,101	$0
70	$0	$346,576	$773,825	$0	$18,157	$41,964	$37,200
71	$0	$334,988	$746,499	$0	$18,157	$41,964	$37,200
72	$0	$323,168	$719,504	$0	$18,157	$41,103	$37,200
73	$0	$311,111	$691,969	$0	$18,157	$41,103	$37,200
74	$0	$298,813	$663,883	$0	$18,157	$41,103	$37,200
75	$0	$286,270	$635,235	$0	$18,157	$41,103	$37,200
76	$0	$273,475	$606,014	$0	$18,157	$41,103	$37,200
77	$0	$260,425	$576,209	$0	$18,157	$41,103	$37,200
78	$0	$247,113	$545,808	$0	$18,157	$41,103	$37,200
79	$0	$233,536	$514,799	$0	$18,157	$41,103	$37,200
80	$0	$219,687	$483,170	$0	$18,157	$41,103	$37,200
81	$0	$205,560	$450,908	$0	$18,157	$41,103	$37,200
82	$0	$191,152	$418,001	$0	$18,157	$41,103	$37,200
83	$0	$176,455	$384,435	$0	$18,157	$41,103	$37,200
84	$0	$161,464	$350,199	$0	$18,157	$41,103	$37,200
85	$0	$146,173	$315,277	$0	$18,157	$41,103	$37,200
86	$0	$130,577	$279,658	$0	$18,157	$41,103	$37,200
87	$0	$114,669	$243,326	$0	$18,157	$41,103	$37,200
88	$0	$98,442	$206,267	$0	$18,157	$41,103	$37,200
89	$0	$81,891	$168,467	$0	$18,157	$41,103	$37,200
90	$0	$65,009	$129,911	$0	$18,157	$41,103	$37,200
91	$0	$47,789	$90,584	$0	$18,157	$41,103	$37,200
92	$0	$30,225	$50,470	$0	$18,157	$41,103	$37,200
93	$0	$12,310	$9,554	$0	$18,157	$41,103	$37,200
94	$0	$0	$0	$0	$12,310	$9,554	$37,200

Exhibit 10.22 continued…

Age	RMDs	Roth Conversion	Adjusted Gross Income	Taxable Income	Taxable Social Security	Federal Income Taxes
60	$0	$105,253	$111,000	$98,450	$0	$17,649
61	$0	$107,391	$111,000	$98,450	$0	$17,649
62	$0	$109,589	$111,000	$98,450	$0	$18,509
63	$0	$69,450	$111,000	$98,450	$0	$18,509
64	$0	$0	$111,000	$98,450	$0	$18,509
65	$0	$0	$111,000	$99,050	$0	$21,101
66	$0	$0	$111,000	$99,050	$0	$21,101
67	$0	$0	$111,000	$99,050	$0	$21,101
68	$0	$0	$111,000	$99,050	$0	$21,101
69	$0	$0	$111,000	$99,050	$0	$21,101
70	$0	$0	$25,000	$13,050	$6,843	$2,320
71	$0	$0	$25,000	$13,050	$6,843	$2,320
72	$12,226	$0	$25,000	$13,050	$6,843	$1,460
73	$12,195	$0	$25,000	$13,050	$6,843	$1,460
74	$12,200	$0	$25,000	$13,050	$6,843	$1,460
75	$12,147	$0	$25,000	$13,050	$6,843	$1,460
76	$12,079	$0	$25,000	$13,050	$6,843	$1,460
77	$11,942	$0	$25,000	$13,050	$6,843	$1,460
78	$11,837	$0	$25,000	$13,050	$6,843	$1,460
79	$11,712	$0	$25,000	$13,050	$6,843	$1,460
80	$11,561	$0	$25,000	$13,050	$6,843	$1,460
81	$11,324	$0	$25,000	$13,050	$6,843	$1,460
82	$11,111	$0	$25,000	$13,050	$6,843	$1,460
83	$10,800	$0	$25,000	$13,050	$6,843	$1,460
84	$10,503	$0	$25,000	$13,050	$6,843	$1,460
85	$10,092	$0	$25,000	$13,050	$6,843	$1,460
86	$9,617	$0	$25,000	$13,050	$6,843	$1,460
87	$9,068	$0	$25,000	$13,050	$6,843	$1,460
88	$8,370	$0	$25,000	$13,050	$6,843	$1,460
89	$7,631	$0	$25,000	$13,050	$6,843	$1,460
90	$6,712	$0	$25,000	$13,050	$6,843	$1,460
91	$5,653	$0	$25,000	$13,050	$6,843	$1,460
92	$4,425	$0	$25,000	$13,050	$6,843	$1,460
93	$2,993	$0	$25,000	$13,050	$6,843	$1,460
94	$1,296	$0	$15,265	$3,315	$2,955	$331

I conclude this example with Exhibit 10.23, which could serve as the guiding emblem for this book. It tracks remaining wealth in retirement for the longest surviving strategy from Exhibit 10.22 against the baseline strategy from Exhibit 10.17. This image shows the tradeoff between short-term costs and long-term benefits for the two strategies. We described how delaying Social Security to 70 and aggressively making Roth conversions allows for retirement assets to last 5.63 years longer while meeting the same pre-tax spending goal, as compared to a strategy in which Social Security is claimed at 62 and assets are spent in order from taxable, tax-deferred, and then tax-exempt accounts. The exhibit shows how obtaining these long-term benefits requires short-term sacrifice, as the tax-efficient strategy will lag with its remaining wealth for the first 17 years of retirement. For the largest early gap, the baseline strategy supports $286,283 more at age 69, as the long-term winning strategy has been spending investment assets faster to cover missing Social Security benefits and higher tax bills. After age 70, the trend reverses. The crossover happens at age 77 when there is about $840,000 left with both strategies. The more efficient long-term strategy provides the largest advantage at age 88 with $323,057 left when the baseline strategy runs out of assets.

Exhibit 10.23
Portfolio Longevity and Tax-Efficient Distribution Strategies
Comparing Wealth for Two Retirement Distribution Strategies

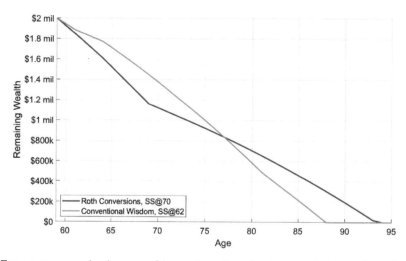

For someone who is more focused on the short-term, the baseline strategy could have appeal. Legacy values will be larger if death happens before age 77. But age 77 is before life expectancy so that there is more than a 50 percent chance that life will continue to an age where the efficient strategy performs better. As well, in both cases legacies will be relatively large with an early death. If death happens at 69, the baseline strategy provides $1.44 million of legacy. But the $1.16 million remaining with the efficient strategy is still quite large. Retirees might focus more on the legacies with a longer retirement, where dollar values are less, and each dollar of legacy can have a bigger impact. For instance, with death at age 88, one strategy provides $323,057 of legacy while the other provides $0. For those living beyond 88, reverse legacies may come into play as retirees outlive their assets and come to rely on the support from others. A case can be made for either strategy, though I would suggest serious consideration should go to the strategy creating the most long-term benefit. It is important to consider these trade-offs when thinking about the right approach.

Action Plan

This chapter has shown how the progressive nature of the tax code makes planning important. Strategies that keep taxes in mind can dramatically improve retirement asset sustainability. The action plan for this chapter consists of accumulation strategies for the pre-retirement years followed by tax-efficient distribution strategies during retirement.

- ☐ While still in the accumulation phase, retirees can take many steps to prepare for tax management in retirement.
    - o Understand the basics of the tax code in terms of values for tax brackets, how marginal tax rates work, how taxable income is determined, and the differences between ordinary income tax rates and preferential rates for long-term capital gains and qualified dividends.
    - o When saving for retirement, build tax diversification for the asset base by saving with taxable, tax-deferred, and tax-exempt accounts.
    - o Understand how to choose between saving in tax-deferred and tax-exempt accounts based on whether the marginal tax rate will be higher now or in the future, and after considering the advantages of having some assets in tax-exempt accounts.
    - o Work through asset location decisions to position assets based on their tax efficiency and long-term growth prospects.
    - o Determine whether there are other ways to obtain tax advantages, such as with education 529 plans, health savings accounts, tax-advantaged bonds, nonqualified annuities, and life insurance.
- ☐ With a strong base built in the pre-retirement years, additional strategies can help with tax management during retirement.
    - o Understand the rules for taking distributions from tax-advantaged retirement plans, including required minimum distributions, early withdrawal penalties, rules for qualified distributions from Roth accounts, making rollovers and conversions, and managing net unrealized appreciation on any employer stock.

- o Understand withdrawal sequencing strategies based around managing adjusted gross income and using strategic Roth conversions.
- o Identify the impact of the various retirement pitfalls when generating taxable income, including the Social Security tax torpedo, heightened premiums for Medicare, the loss of subsidies for health insurance, the net investment income surtax, and the impact of pushing preferential income sources into higher tax brackets.
- o Also consider the benefits of front-loading taxes in retirement, including the potential to improve the eventual tax situation for a surviving spouse or to manage future tax increases.
- o Consider tax-efficient strategies for charitable giving, including qualified charitable distributions, deduction bunching for gifts, donor advised funds, and charitable gift annuities.

Further Reading

Olsen, John L., and Michael E. Kitces. 2014. *The Advisor's Guide to Annuities, 4th Edition*. Cincinnati: The National Underwriter Company.

Piper, Mike. 2019. *Taxes Made Simple: Income Taxes Explained in 100 Pages or Less*. Simple Subjects.

Reichenstein, William. 2019. *Income Strategies: How to Create a Tax-Efficient Withdrawal Strategy to Generate Retirement Income*. Retiree Inc.

Chapter 11: Legacy and Incapacity Planning

As we discuss various facets of retirement income planning, this chapter turns toward how to properly prepare you and your family for end-of-life issues. We first discuss how to get your finances organized. This will certainly be helpful during your own lifetime, but we discuss it here specifically to help guide those you love. You will better understand your finances and how the different pieces fit together. And you will also have your financial affairs collected in one place with easy access for those who need it after an emergency. Often there is one member of the household who manages the family finances, and obvious problems can arise when that person is no longer able to continue these tasks following either incapacity or death. During a stressful time, family members who do not understand the financial picture will experience even greater stress and may be prone to making mistakes or falling victim to financial abuse in ways that could quickly overturn the benefits created through years of careful planning. This process will help to prepare family members to take control.

We need to address how to prepare your family for managing the household finances. Taking time to properly prepare instructions and explanations around these matters, and to collect the relevant documentation so it is accessible to those who need it, is key to making these transitions as smooth as possible. This involves collecting and organizing your personal and family information, contact information for professionals and service providers you work with, insurance information, medical history, and details about various financial accounts and other assets.

After describing how to get organized, we shift to a discussion of estate planning issues. Estate planning begins with the process of tracking and organizing assets. As part of that process, take a careful look at how each asset is titled and whether beneficiary designations are included. This is important because asset titles and beneficiary designations always take precedence over whatever is stated in a will. But creating a will is a vital part of this process as well, as it indicates how you would like your property to be disbursed upon death. As a part of creating a will, consider whether the creation of a trust would be a useful tool for managing the estate. Other aspects of an estate plan include deciding on both a financial power of attorney and on advance health care directives to help manage your finances and health care in the event of incapacity. Who can make medical and financial decisions for you if you are unable? One may also want to provide final wishes, which can include matters such as funeral arrangements, lists of who should be contacted, messages to family members, words of wisdom, and so forth.

When assigning different powers and roles, be sure to discuss the roles and responsibilities with those who will be asked to act in the event of your incapacity or death. You can make everyone's situation easier by working to make sure that your wishes are known and to develop agreement and acceptance around your choices. Your family will thank you for having everything organized for them as it will avoid countless hours of additional hassle during already stressful periods.

After addressing these preparations, we continue the discussion regarding tax-efficiency and tax-planning considerations as it relates to legacy. The tax planning discussion of the previous chapter explained matters related to sustaining a spending objective for as long as possible by maximizing retirement spending after-tax efficiency. Naturally, greater tax efficiency will be correlated with providing a larger legacy because there is less chance of spending all available resources as a part of managing longevity risk. But legacy was not a specific objective in the previous chapter. This chapter continues by explaining how decisions may change if supporting a legacy goal is an explicit part of retirement planning, or as it becomes clear that a retiree will not be spending all available assets and there will be a legacy to coordinate. Tax planning for legacy includes updates to withdrawal ordering decisions and managing estate taxes, as well as understanding required minimum distribution rules for various inherited tax-deferred assets. Estate taxes are possible, but currently the exemptions exceed what most families need to worry about. Nonetheless, estate tax rules could change in the future, and this chapter will introduce a few concepts to contemplate with estate planning professionals.

I must emphasize that I am not providing legal advice in this chapter, or anywhere else in this book. The matters discussed here are particularly sensitive to legal considerations, and state laws do vary widely on how these decisions should be made. While I attempt to explain the main issues for you to think about, developing a personalized estate plan should occur with the guidance and advice of a qualified estate planning attorney knowledgeable about the laws in your state. My hope is that this chapter will leave you better prepared to understand your options and to make the decisions needed when working with a professional.

Getting Your Financial House in Order

Getting your finances organized is important for both you and those who depend on you. It is also important for when you may depend on others in the event of cognitive decline or other impairments or illness. It is important so that family members know where things are and what needs to be done. For instance, there is little use in paying life insurance premiums if no one knows about the policy after your death. This section provides a summary for a topic on which entire books have been written. Three books that I found valuable for those seeking a deeper dive into getting your affairs organized include Sally Balch Hurme's *Checklist for My Family*, Tony Steuer's *Get Ready!*, and Melanie Cullen's *Get It Together*. While I attempt to provide a summary of what you need to consider, you may wish to consult an additional resource for more comprehensive explanations about how to build and store a complete set of documents and instructions.

Personal Information, Family History, and Financial Information

Getting organized first involves getting your key personal information and documents gathered and stored in a safe and accessible place. A checklist of personal items in this category include:

- ☐ Birth certificates
- ☐ Adoption papers
- ☐ Marriage license
- ☐ Prenuptial agreement
- ☐ Divorce documentation
- ☐ Immigration or citizenship documents
- ☐ Social Security cards
- ☐ Military DD-214 service record
- ☐ Driver's license (copy)
- ☐ Health insurance cards (copy)
- ☐ Passports

As well, in terms of priority, very near the top of your to-do list should be organizing your emergency contacts and important medical details. Who needs to be contacted and what information should be quickly accessible in the event of emergencies? Important considerations include:

- ☐ Who to contact after emergencies
- ☐ Contact information for close friends and neighbors
- ☐ Medical and health information, list of current medications and dosages, allergies, blood type, immunization records, doctors and physicians, and medical history
- ☐ Employer details: who to contact at your employer, availability of paid time-off, available employer benefits
- ☐ School and day care contacts if children are attending
- ☐ Pets: contact information for veterinarian, details about who should care for pets

Most individuals will work with a variety of financial and medical professionals that may need to be contacted. It is important to provide the names and contact information for any of these professionals:

- ☐ Financial advisor
- ☐ Attorney
- ☐ Estate plan attorney
- ☐ Insurance agent
- ☐ Banker

- ☐ Accountant
- ☐ Trust officer
- ☐ Executor
- ☐ Guardian
- ☐ Power of attorney for finance
- ☐ Power of attorney for health care
- ☐ Family physician and other relevant medical professionals

Some of these details, such as emergency contacts and medical information, should also be kept in your wallet or purse. Speaking of what you may carry in your wallet or purse, maintaining a separate list of credit cards or other items contained therein can be helpful in the event these items become lost or stolen.

Your Online Life

As more of our lives move onto the internet, it is worth taking the time to build and maintain a list of your online accounts that includes the website URL for the login page, username, password, security question answers, and basic details about the account such as if automatic payments have been set up. Ideally this file will be password protected as well, but it is important that the right people can obtain access when necessary. This file can include all of one's online life, including bank accounts, brokerage accounts, retirement plans, insurance, credit cards, as well as utilities, social media, streaming television, and shopping sites.

Though of less immediate priority, other financial details should be collected to ease the tasks of anyone assigned to help. Without a stack of paper bills, the convenience of using automatic bill payment for yourself can be a hindrance for others to unravel if you have not provided clear instructions about how payments are structured. In addition to knowing how to pay your bills, some of these items will also include online accounts requiring usernames and passwords. Cross-checking this bill payment list with the budgeting process efforts described in Chapter 3 can help to ensure that nothing important is missed. Considerations here include:

- ☐ Utilities: electricity, heating/fuel, water, sewage, telephone, etc.
- ☐ Service providers: electrician, plumber, handyman, housekeeper, lawn service, roofer, snow plowing, car repair, security system, babysitter, home health agency, etc.
- ☐ Ongoing expenses: anything with reoccurring bills or automatic bill payment, such as magazine subscriptions, gym memberships, season tickets, cell phones, cable and streaming TV, internet, retail memberships like Costco or Amazon Prime, etc.
- ☐ Credit cards and debit cards: a list of cards, annual fees, website and login information, account numbers, expiration dates, rewards programs, and automated bill payments.

In addition, basic biographical details that you may wish to collate and share with family members or others include:

- [ ] For yourself, spouse, and children: name, legal name changes, address, phone number, email, birth date
- [ ] Education and degrees
- [ ] Employment history
- [ ] Military service
- [ ] Past residences
- [ ] Awards
- [ ] Membership organizations (professional, religious, political, trade unions, veterans, civic rights, educational, fraternal, hobbies, etc.)
- [ ] A booklet or other written or recorded materials to provide family members that details the events of your life, your values, your interests and passions, words of wisdom, and other remembrances. This is also known as an ethical will.

Furthermore, collecting information about your family's medical history could prove useful to help other family members with prevention, diagnosis, or early treatment for various hereditary conditions. This type of information is often asked when visiting a new medical facility.

Regarding family, for those with an interest in genealogy, it may also be fun to include a family tree and lists of relatives, family history documents or news clippings, as well as a collection of family photos and videos with descriptive comments about who is featured, and where and when they were taken. If this information is not identified on the photos or in the filenames, it will eventually be lost to coming generations. Though such details are not needed for the estate plan, it might be something that you wish to consider organizing at the same time.

Assets and Liabilities

We next describe the information needed to access the relevant accounts related to constructing the household's net worth statement. For various asset and liabilities, information needed by others includes firm names, contact information, website, username and password, account numbers, account owners and title information, account types, and beneficiary details. In collecting this information, it is important to review how accounts are titled and if the beneficiary designations are up-to-date and appropriate. Titling for bank accounts involves knowing who has ownership, who has access, and what happens in the event of the owner's incapacity or death. With bank accounts, there may also be ATM card numbers and pin numbers to monitor. You may wish to provide further instructions about what you want done with various assets or liabilities and such matters should also be formally addressed within your estate plan.

While this is by no means a comprehensive list, potential assets or benefits to gather include:

☐ Bank accounts – checking, savings, money market, CDs
☐ Credit union accounts
☐ Savings bonds (series, denomination, serial number, issue date)
☐ Treasury Direct account
☐ Brokerage accounts
☐ IRAs, Roth IRAs, and other individual retirement plans
☐ 401(k), 403(b), and employer-based qualified retirement plans
☐ Social Security statement and benefits
☐ Executive deferred compensation or other benefits
☐ Pensions
☐ Veteran benefits
☐ Workers' compensation
☐ Business interests, stock options, contracts
☐ Royalties – copyrights, trademarks, patents
☐ Education savings accounts (529 plans)
☐ ABLE accounts for children and young adults with disabilities
☐ Health Savings Accounts
☐ Real estate: home, second residences or vacation homes, time-shares, investment properties, farmland, etc.
☐ Real estate rental contracts related to long-term care, such as an assisted living facility or continuing care retirement community
☐ Vehicles, including cars, trucks, boats, planes, RVs, etc.
☐ Uncollected legal judgments
☐ Other property you expect to receive from others
☐ Collectibles inventory, including receipts and appraisals
☐ Significant special possessions with documentation including photos or video recordings
☐ Jewelry, antiques, artwork
☐ Reward and loyalty programs: credit cards, airlines, hotels, rental cars, etc.
☐ Storage units
☐ Digital assets: email, ebooks, music, videos, blogs, Facebook, LinkedIn, Twitter, etc.
☐ Crypto-currency accounts

Meanwhile, liabilities related to debt holdings include:

☐ Mortgage
☐ Home equity line of credit
☐ Reverse mortgage
☐ Vehicle loans
☐ Student loans, including those for others on which you co-signed
☐ Personal loans
☐ Lawsuits or claims against you
☐ Credit card balances
☐ Money borrowed informally from others

We can also view taxes as a liability, and there are a variety of tax records to keep organized, including past returns and supporting documents for:

- ☐ Federal income taxes
- ☐ State income taxes
- ☐ Property taxes
- ☐ Other local taxes

To organize this information, you may wish to maintain separate folders or sections for each account and then refer to a master index list of accounts in the main letter of instructions to be used by others.

Business Ownership and Succession

Owning a business can create some unique complications for estate planning. Questions to consider include succession planning for who will run the business, whether the estate will have sufficient liquidity to protect the business and keep it operating while also covering other estate expenses, and how to bequeath or sell one's stake in the business at the highest possible valuation. Keeping a business outside of the probate process may be important and ownership by a living trust is one method to handle this.

Insurance Policies

Households also generally hold a variety of insurance policies. It is important to collect information about each insurance policy, including the company name, policy number, insurance agent contact details, website, username, password, policy amounts and other benefit or beneficiary details. This will ease the process of filing claims. It is worthwhile to also conduct an insurance review to make sure that the right types of policies and coverage are held, that the beneficiary designations on any policies reflect current wishes, and that unnecessary policies are terminated to save on premiums. Potential insurance policies to get organized include:

- ☐ Life insurance
- ☐ Annuity contracts
- ☐ Long-term care insurance
- ☐ Disability insurance
- ☐ Health insurance
- ☐ Medicare coverage (Medicare Advantage, Medigap, Part D)
- ☐ Dental insurance
- ☐ Vision insurance
- ☐ Property insurance – homeowner or renter insurance
- ☐ Vehicle insurance
- ☐ Umbrella insurance

Regarding life insurance, in addition to standard policies, life insurance may also be provided through employers and some credit cards may offer life insurance benefits if death happens during travel paid for with the credit card.

To be complete with updating records about available insurance policies, it is important to keep any of these additional possibilities in mind as you want to ensure that nothing is overlooked by your heirs.

Organizing and Storing Information and a Letter of Instruction

The purpose of collecting and organizing these documents is to simplify life for those who will need it as a part of managing your incapacity or death. Your family or other professionals will need to have convenient access and explanations about your household finances. Be clear about where they can find the necessary documents and who should be contacted. You want to help them avoid overlooking anything. The next matter is deciding where to keep this information and to provide an accompanying letter of instructions and guidance.

Important documents could be kept in a binder or storage box with paper copies and stored in a safe and accessible place, as well as having electronic copies on a flash drive or stored in a secure account on the cloud. The originals should be kept safe in the event of a fire or flood, such as in a secure safe or fireproof box.

A safe deposit box at a bank is an option for important documents and valuables that may not be needed immediately in an emergency, but it should not be where you keep everything. There are mistakes that can happen with a safe deposit box that include making it hard for the needed individuals to access it. A safe deposit box is not the right place to keep a will or advanced directives, as this may hinder access to these documents when they are needed. For any safe deposit boxes, make sure that the core information you make available includes its location, box numbers, and the location of keys or other means of access. Make sure that those you intend to be able to access it will be allowed by the bank.

As for distinguishing what should be kept where, items that you may wish to keep in a home safe to provide for quicker access include:

- ☐ Household net worth statement listing all assets and liabilities, as well as information on ownership and beneficiary designations, asset values, and cost basis
- ☐ A list of ongoing bills, as well as automatic payment details or whether payments must be made manually
- ☐ A list of websites, usernames, passwords for important accounts
- ☐ Insurance policies
- ☐ Your will
- ☐ Durable financial power of attorney documentation
- ☐ Advance health care directives
- ☐ Documentation for trusts
- ☐ Passports
- ☐ Social Security cards
- ☐ Access instructions for your phones, computers, tablets
- ☐ Safe deposit box details and content inventory

Meanwhile, items that are appropriate for your safe deposit box include:

- [ ] Copies of items in home safe
- [ ] Copy of financial instructions
- [ ] Personal documents: birth, adoption, marriage, divorce
- [ ] Financial documents (non-emergency)
- [ ] Household inventory
- [ ] Collectibles
- [ ] Jewelry
- [ ] Family photos
- [ ] Computer back-up files

For anything kept behind a lock, including a digital lock on an electronic device, it is important to make sure the lock combinations or other information is accessible. Something that may be forgotten but is highly important is how to access and unlock smartphones, tablets, and other computers that may contain important details for the family. It is also important to provide instructions for disarming home and vehicle alarms.

Along with collecting these items and documents, you will likely want to create a letter of instruction that explains everything needed for managing the household finances. The letter can include explanations for how to find everything we have described as well as summarizing the key information that needs to be known for a smooth transition. You may include suggestions about asset allocation, withdrawal order sequencing, or other helpful advice that could improve financial outcomes. This letter should be kept very secure and should be updated at least annually. Here is an example for a table of contents you may wish to use when organizing your letter of instructions:

1. Overview and Key Instructions, Including People to Contact
2. Secured Places and Passwords
3. Letters to Loved Ones
4. Biographical Information
5. Health Care Directives
6. Durable Power of Attorney for Finances
7. Final Wishes
8. Will
9. Trusts
10. Insurance Policies
11. Bank Accounts
12. Service Providers and Automatic Bill Pay
13. Credit Cards and Debts
14. Brokerage Accounts and Retirement Plans
15. Social Security and Government Benefits
16. Real Estate, Vehicle, and Other Real Property
17. Employment History
18. Business Interests
19. Taxes
20. Memberships and Other Miscellaneous Items

As you collect this information and create your letter, make sure your family knows how to find it. Of course, having things organized in one place does not help if no one knows where to look. At the same time, having all this information gathered in one place can create a real security risk if this information falls into the wrong hands. It would be quite dangerous to keep the full passwords alongside everything else, and only a few key individuals should know how to connect the two pieces needed for this full access. You could instead include a code about how different passwords are organized, and then include the actual passwords in a separate location. You might also handwrite passwords on your letter after printing it, so the passwords are not included in the electronic version. The goal will be to balance having the information accessible when needed, but not so accessible that it leads to identify theft. Finally, for some less important documents you may decide whether to provide printed paper copies or just digital copies. Make sure that your letter clarifies the locations (both physical and digital) where you keep everything discussed here.

Components of an Estate Plan

Now that the financial picture is organized, estate planning is the process for determining how to manage and distribute one's net worth upon death. For ease of discussion, we will also mix in issues for incapacity planning as well, since there is a large overlap about what needs to be done.

Estate planning will help you and your family members be prepared. It involves developing answers for three questions about distributing assets – to who, when, and how? You want to design mechanisms that will accomplish your goals in a tax- and cost-efficient manner. This process includes properly titling assets and making beneficiary designations, maintaining a will and other related instructions, determining whether there is a role for trusts, identifying an agent with financial powers of attorney, creating advance health care directives, and providing final wishes.

Some of these tasks can be accomplished on your own, while others include more complex legal issues that will benefit from professional advice. Working with the right professionals, rather than trying to accomplish everything in a do-it-yourself manner, will become important especially for the matters addressed in this chapter.

Everyone has a default estate plan, even if it means dying without a will and having property distributed by the state. Before going further, you might assess the outcomes of your current estate plan. Have you identified your assets and liabilities and organized them so they can be found and understood by others? Do you understand how your relevant property is titled or registered? Do you know the beneficiary designations you have made for relevant assets? Do you know what will happen to your finances and who will decide about your health care if you are incapacitated? Do you know what property will be subject to the probate process after death? Do you have a will? Do you have any trusts, and have they been properly executed and funded? Have you made your final wishes known? Does the distribution of your assets under your current plan accomplish what you intend, or could there be big mistakes related to unequal distributions, mistaken distributions (such as to someone you have divorced), distributions to those unready or unable to handle immediate full receipt, unnecessary costs, or other unintended consequences?

Goals that we outline in this section include:

- Identify the entirety of your assets and debts
- Determine your wishes for asset disbursement: to who, when, and how? What is the right breakdown between providing for heirs and for charitable causes?
- Clarify that assets are titled and beneficiary designations are made in the ways you intend
- Provide survivors with sufficient assets for their lifetime as well as for covering expenses while the estate is in probate
- Simplify the probate process as much as possible to reduce fees and maintain privacy
- Minimize estate taxes (if applicable) and manage estate distributions with other tax consequences in mind
- Ensure that financial and health care decisions are handled as you wish if you become incapacitated

When it comes time to settle your estate, the first step is to identify the entirety of your assets and debts. This is everything we have been describing in the previous section, and by going through this process and providing these details you will surely make things much easier (and less expensive) in the future. Your estate executor will only need to double-check your work and make sure everything has been accounted for and there are not outstanding issues to be resolved, rather than trying to undergo a full forensic investigation about what you owned and owe. Assets can then be divided between those in your probate estate and those which can be distributed outside of the probate process. As well, asset values can be assessed for estate tax purposes.

The probate estate includes everything that will be distributed according to your will, if one exists, or otherwise according to state law. Assets falling outside of a will and the probate estate include assets with joint ownership and right of survivorship, assets owned by a trust, or assets with beneficiary designations. The taxable estate are the assets counted to determine federal and state estate taxes. Your trust estate included assets you have included in your trust. After thinking about general goals regarding how much to provide to family, friends, and charity, it is time to structure the plan.

The Titling of Assets

Though it may not feel like estate planning, an essential component of planning happens when you decide how to title or register the ownership of assets as you proceed through life. This includes financial assets such as bank or brokerage accounts, and real assets such as homes and vehicles. You have different options available for defining asset ownership, and you may want to revisit what you have done in the past to make sure it is what you intend for the present and future. For those who are married, the defaults for asset ownership also depend on state laws and whether you are in a common law or community property state. The titling or registration of assets refers to the process of documenting how the asset is owned, and this can include options for how to disburse the asset in the event of the owner's death. These decisions always take priority over anything stated in a will or trust document, and so it is important to be careful with these titling decisions along with beneficiary designations.

To re-emphasize this point, since it is so important, it does not matter what you say in a will or trust if you have not also formally updated the asset titles to be aligned with what you want to have happen in your will or trust. As a part of getting your affairs in order, you can review and update ownership as appropriate. There are numerous options.

First, assets can be owned *individually* without reference to how they will be disbursed upon death. For such assets, the probate process will determine the asset's fate, either as documented by a will when one exists, or by the state's probate laws. Certain relatives such as spouses may have rights that supersede the will, but otherwise this is the only type of ownership that would allow a will to take over and handle the asset disbursement at death as part of the probate estate.

There are other ways to title assets that will allow them to avoid the probate process by outlining who receives the property upon an owner's death. Assets can be held jointly with one or more other individuals, for instance. If an asset is owned *jointly with right of survivorship*, then when one owner dies, his or her share of the asset automatically transfers to the surviving owners. The last surviving owner becomes the sole owner of the asset.

This type of titling may be a natural default for spouses. However, there could potentially be problems if there are children from previous marriages that an individual would like to receive a portion of the asset. A will cannot redirect what the account title indicates; the living spouse would receive the full asset value and instructions from the deceased spouse's will to have a portion of the asset go to those children may not be obeyed.

People sometimes think to add a child as a joint owner to a bank account to help manage household finances, but there are risks to choosing this titling option. These include that the child then has full ownership and will essentially inherit what is left, that this ownership change constitutes a gift that could have tax implications, and that creditors for the children will be able to go after the account. As well, particularly with real estate, any step-up in basis that may be allowed at death will not take place. Having a younger owner could also complicate attempts to use a reverse mortgage. Alternatives to joint ownership include allowing the child to be a signer on the account without having ownership (called a *convenience account)*, moving the account to a trust in which the child is a trustee, or providing the child with control over the account by acting as an agent through a durable financial power of attorney.

Another option for titling an asset is called *joint ownership in common*. In this case, joint owners own portions of the asset and may maintain rights over their share of ownership, such as to sell or bequeath it, that do not require agreement among all owners. In the context of estate planning, the important distinction for ownership in common is that the share of the asset owned at an owner's death is transferred to the deceased owner's estate rather than to surviving owners. This avoids having the last surviving owner become the sole owner of an asset, and it may be a popular option with vacation homes owned by a larger family with multiple siblings.

For states with *community property* laws (Arizona, California, Idaho, Louisiana, Nevada, New Mexico, Texas, Washington, and Wisconsin), real assets purchased during a marriage are automatically titled as ownership in common shared equally between the spouses. Each spouse can use a will to assign ownership of their share of the asset upon death. Another possibility is ownership in common with rights of survivorship, in which when one spouse dies, his or her share automatically transfers to the surviving spouse.

Other ownership options include the possibility of adding *transfer at death (TOD)* or *payable at death (POD)* provisions to the account title. These work in the same manner as beneficiary designations. The beneficiary is not an account owner but will receive the asset upon the owner's death outside of the probate process. A TOD option can be especially useful with real assets such as a home or vehicle. This option is also commonly available for bank and brokerage accounts. Again, having these provisions in place overrides whatever may be stated in a will and keeps the asset out of probate.

For real estate, another option to consider is to create a *life estate* for a property. This allows one to sell a property, likely at a discount, while maintaining the right to continue living in the property until death. This could be another way to free up some home equity to be used within a retirement income plan.

A final option we consider is to title property to be transferred to and owned by a trust. A trust can be drafted calling for ownership of the asset, but it is important to follow through with updating the title so it can be transferred to the trust. We describe trusts in more detail later.

Beneficiary Designations

Related to how some accounts and real estate are titled, certain types of assets will pass directly to stated beneficiaries outside of what is indicated in a will. These are accounts with beneficiary designations. It is important to make sure that beneficiary designations are up to date and account for life changes, such as births of children or grandchildren, deaths of existing beneficiaries, marriages, divorces, or other changes in relationships, and that these are aligned with what you want to have happen with your will or trust. If an asset has a beneficiary designation assigning it to person A while the will includes directions to assign the asset to person B, it is person A who will receive the asset.

Beneficiary designations are available for different types of financial accounts including life insurance policies, annuities, IRAs, company retirement plans, deferred compensation plans, pensions, education savings accounts, and other transfer-on-death securities accounts. Often beneficiary designations are made as accounts are opened without much thought or coordination over the years, and so it is worthwhile to include a complete beneficiary designation review as part of your planning and to create a list of all assets along with their beneficiary choices. Maintaining a list of all your assets along with their beneficiary designations or ownership titling could prove invaluable to uncovering mistakes.

When making beneficiary designations, there are a few types of beneficiaries to identify. First are primary beneficiaries. When alive, primary beneficiaries are the first in line to receive the assets. There can be multiple primary beneficiaries, in which case the assets are divided among them in the shares specified on the designation form.

Contingent or secondary beneficiaries can also be identified. This is who is next in line only if all primary beneficiaries are deceased before the original account owner or otherwise disclaim their right to receive the assets. Contingent beneficiaries do not maintain any rights once the account has passed to a primary beneficiary, as the primary beneficiaries can then decide on their own subsequent beneficiaries as desired.

There is also another type of beneficiary called a successor beneficiary. The successor would become the beneficiary for anything left after a primary or contingent beneficiary has received the asset and then later has died. The original account holder could attempt to add a successor beneficiary. The choice for a successor beneficiary may not always be enforceable, but it is a way to at least indicate one's wishes. Usually instead of the original owner identifying a successor beneficiary, the new primary or contingent beneficiary will be able to decide about their own primary or contingent beneficiaries for the asset after it is received.

It is also important to note that minor children, such as children or grandchildren, cannot own more than a de minimus amount of financial assets. One should appoint a guardian or create a trust to oversee the assets until the children reach the "age of majority" in their state. Trusts can also serve as beneficiary designations, and this can provide a way to fund a trust intended for minor children after death.

If there are no living beneficiaries, either because no one was named or the beneficiaries have already died, then the assets will pass to the estate and be subject to the probate process to be distributed through the will.

As part of your beneficiary review, you can help those implementing your estate plan by creating a list within your broader instructions that provides the information about the ownership and beneficiaries for each account. Record the beneficiary names and contact information, Social Security number, primary or contingent status, and share of the account to be received. Having this information collected in one place will also help with determining a more strategic plan for bequeathing assets.

Creating a Will

Upon death, your financial affairs will need to be settled. Preparing a will allows you to provide your input and desires into the process. A will is a legal document outlining how to transfer property and assets after your death. It will guide the probate process and it covers what are known as probate assets. Probate assets refer to any assets subject to a will or to state intestacy laws if no valid will is available. Preparing a will involves deciding on a plan of action and preparing a legal document for how you wish to have your probate estate distributed after your death. It includes three major items:

- Identifies an executor to manage the probate process
- Identifies how probate property will be distributed to beneficiaries
- When relevant, designates a guardian for minor children

Not all assets are probate assets. Assets that are jointly owned with rights of survivorship, have valid beneficiary designations or payable on death provisions, or are held in a trust or life estate will pass to their beneficiaries without becoming a probate asset that is directed by the will. For those who can effectively manage the titling and beneficiary process for their assets and accounts, or who have positioned most assets within a trust, the remaining assets to be covered by the will in the probate process could be quite small. Even if careful to move assets outside the probate process governed by a will, the will may still be important as a backup to account for anything else that you may have missed, and it is needed if you care for minors. Relatedly, a pour-over will serves to redirect property into a trust at death, though such property directed by the will to a trust is still treated as part of probate first.

The probate process can have downsides. Heirs may be restricted from receiving their inheritance for a significant amount of time, such as a year or more for complicated estates. Probate can also be expensive when accounting for various court and attorney fees. Probate is also public, reducing the level of privacy available to the estate. For small probate estates, different states may provide workarounds to avoid the time and costs associated with large estates. Otherwise, as noted, steps can be taken to keep most assets outside of the probate process through property titling, beneficiary designations, and use of trusts.

The probate process is run through a court to determine your will's validity and identify who is charged with settling your affairs. The will names an *executor* who is to carry out the wishes of the deceased person by managing the estate and its distribution. This could be a spouse, sibling, adult child, or other relative or friend. It could also be a professional, such as an attorney, a bank employee, or a professional fiduciary. Being an executor can be a significant undertaking requiring organization, honesty, assertiveness, and interpersonal skills.

When relevant, arrangement can be made to pay the executor for their services from the estate assets. However, if the executor is someone who will be receiving most of the assets as an inheritance anyway, it can be better to avoid receiving payment that would count as taxable income. These instructions can be included in the will and any professional executor will expect payment.

The executor's tasks including contacting heirs, cataloguing the assets, having relevant assets appraised to determine their value, paying bills, settling debts, settling business affairs, posting notices, notifying relevant parties of the individual's death, filing tax returns, closing out accounts, canceling subscriptions and other ongoing expenses, and then distributing remaining property to heirs in accordance with the will. The will can be specific in terms of identifying who receives specific items or assets, or assets can be distributed on a percentage basis. Beneficiaries of the will can include individuals as well as institutions.

If you have not identified an executor, then the probate court will appoint an administrator to carry out these tasks. Not having a valid will means dying intestate, and then state law will govern the process for how assets are distributed. State laws vary and are based on trying to guess what an owner's desires would be. The order for distributing assets would typically follow spouse, children, parents, siblings, and so forth to find the next of kin, until the first people on the list can be identified. If no next of kin can be identified, the state will typically keep the property. Cases where state intestacy laws may lead to different outcomes than you intend include if you have charitable intentions, wish to make unequal distributions between heirs, wish to disinherit someone, or have other tax planning considerations with respect to the estate.

The will is also the only place to appoint a guardian to care for any minor children, such as children or grandchildren in your care. The guardian is a person designated to act as a representative to oversee personal affairs and finances, including caring for minors until they reach the age of majority. Guardians can be named in a will or be appointed by a judge if necessary. Having the courts manage this process will be costly and time consuming with respect to limitations a court appointed property guardian would receive. Minors cannot inherit assets, so trusts or custodial accounts should be created to manage any probate assets meant for them until they are old enough to receive it. Such a trust can be set up and funded as part of the will and only comes into being after your death.

Creating a will can be done on one's own with online tools and software, but it is worthwhile to also work with an estate planning attorney to review the documentation and make sure that everything conforms with state law so that your wishes can be met as intended. The will should be signed and dated with the number and types of witnesses and notary needs as required by your state. After completing your will, you need to make sure that it is easy for your executor to find the original copy.

A will should be updated every several years, or after any changes in family circumstances or tax laws. A codicil can be used to amend your will without starting from scratch. Codicils should be arranged and executed professionally, as directly editing your will could result in it becoming invalid. While codicils are an option, the fact that they must be executed in the same way as a will means that it may be just as simple to redo the will with the change. The old will and its copies can then be destroyed.

In the context of the will, you may create an additional letter of instruction to the executor of the will. While not having legal authority, the letter can provide more details about your wishes. This can include how to divide personal possessions of lesser financial value (but perhaps greater emotional value) that would not necessarily be included in a will, desires about your funeral or memorial service, and other aspects we will cover in the final wishes section. You might also state your intentions about how you wish certain property to be used, such as for family members to keep the vacation home instead of selling it. Since this is not a legal document, it is less formal and can be changed easily. It is also not legally enforceable, and you should include a note in the letter that you understand it is not legally enforceable to help prevent any potential challenges to your will. Just be sure to sign and date the document so that people can determine the most recent version to use, and it will be helpful to discard older versions to reduce potential confusion.

A Role for Trusts in Distributing an Estate

Trusts can be a particularly complex subject that benefit from receiving professional advice to determine their efficacy as well as in guiding their creation and management. A trust provides a way for a trustee to hold the legal title to property for a beneficiary. Not everyone will need a trust, though it is also the case that trusts are not just for the ultra-wealthy. Trusts have lots of potential uses outside of estate tax management.

There are two general reasons one might consider for creating trusts: to provide greater control over the process of distributing an estate while also avoiding probate, especially if there are minor children involved as beneficiaries, and to help reduce estate taxes. In this section we focus on the first consideration, which is using a trust to manage an estate when the estate is not large enough for estate taxes to be a concern. This means we will discuss revocable trusts here, which can be changed during the lifetime of their grantor. Later in the chapter we will look creating an irrevocable trust to help manage estate taxes.

It is possible to create trusts in a do-it-yourself manner, but there are many potential pitfalls and unanticipated outcomes. It is important to also speak to professionals about the best approach to take and to make sure the documentation is legally valid and will have the intended effects. I aim to help you become an educated participant in these discussions.

Some examples of cases where a trust may be helpful in achieving planning goals not directly related to reducing estate taxes include:

- Worries about asset management after your incapacity
- Probate is avoided for assets held in a living trust at death, which can reduce costs to the estate and maintain privacy
- Beneficiaries are minors and unable to inherit assets directly
- Control disbursement of assets to beneficiaries who may not be responsible enough to manage full receipt (spendthrift trust)
- Own real estate in different states and want to avoid the probate process for those states
- Married more than once with children from previous marriages
- Protect assets from the beneficiary's creditors
- Protect assets for children in the event your spouse remarries
- Protect assets from children's spouses in the event of their divorce
- Provide for a special needs family member in a way that does not impact eligibility for government benefits (special needs trust)

If you determine that a trust will be a helpful part of your estate planning, an important decision is whether to use a living trust or a testamentary trust. A living trust is set up and funded during one's lifetime, while a testamentary trust is set up and funded after death through the provisions outlined within your will. A living trust may also call for the creation of new trusts at death.

With any type of trust, there are several key parties to keep in mind. A *grantor* creates the trust and shifts ownership of property to it. The trust then assumes legal ownership of property it receives. Assets held in a trust may be referred to as the trust property, trust assets, or trust principal. The grantor also determines a *trustee* to manage the property of the trust and determines how and when the trustee will transfer that property and any income or other considerations it generates to the trust *beneficiaries*. The trustee serves as a fiduciary working toward the best interest of the grantor and beneficiaries. Beneficiaries are those who receive benefits from the trust and who may eventually fully inherit the trust assets. Life estate or income beneficiaries may have a limited interest in the trust property that lasts for a fixed period or until that beneficiary dies, and final beneficiaries are those who will ultimately receive trust property after the terms for income beneficiaries have ended. A corporate trust is a bank or trust company that is chosen to serve as the trustee.

A living trust, which also goes by the names of revocable living trust, or a settlor, grantor, or donor trust, provides a framework for transferring your property to a trust while alive so that it can be managed by a trustee other than you in the event of incapacity as well as including provisions for what happens at death. A revocable living trust can be designed either for one person or to be shared between spouses to manage both co-owned and separately owned property. With a living trust, the grantor, trustee, and beneficiary can be the same person, and a successor trustee can be identified to take control if the original trustee (i.e. you) is incapacitated or dies. A secondary beneficiary can also be added for when the primary beneficiary (i.e. you) is deceased, and the grantor (i.e. you) can design the instructions for how to disburse assets to various successor beneficiaries and over what time frame.

A revocable living trust allows the grantor to modify the trust and remove property or revoke it entirely while alive and maintaining mental capacity. The grantor continues paying taxes on trust property as though he or she is still the owner of the property in the trust, as a revocable living trust is not registered as a separate legal entity. Living trusts generally change from revocable to irrevocable upon the death of the grantor. With living trusts, assets remain as part of the grantor's estate, and so when used by themselves do not reduce potential estate taxes. A revocable living trust may be understood as an invisible or passthrough entity in this regard. This is different for irrevocable trusts, which we will discuss later.

A living trust is created with a "declaration of trust" that names the creator as the trustee. Property can then be transferred to the trust which you can still manage and fully control as the trustee. You may also identify yourself as primary beneficiary during your lifetime, with secondary beneficiaries to subsequently inherit the assets outside of probate after your death. Your will may also direct additional probate assets to be transferred to the trust upon your death. A successor trustee is also named who then takes over management when you are no longer willing or able to continue self-management as trustee. An independent method of determining incompetency for a successor trustee to take control can be included, such as the determination of two physicians.

To summarize this process, we can think of three phases for a living trust. During the first phase the grantor is alive and has mental capacity. The grantor serves as the trustee and beneficiary of the living trust. The second phase is if the grantor loses capacity. Then the successor trustee takes control of management for the benefit of the grantor who is still the beneficiary of the trust. The third phase is when the grantor dies. Then the successor trustee manages the trust for the disbursement of assets to its secondary beneficiaries.

A wide variety of assets and property can be shifted to a trust. Options include bank accounts, brokerage accounts, real estate, vehicles, and so forth. In many cases, a choice can be made about whether to shift assets to the trust during one's lifetime, or to use beneficiary designations, transfer-on-death provisions, or a will to move the assets to the trust at death. Two advantages of transferring during one's lifetime is so the successor trustee could manage the assets during times of incapacity, as well as helping to keep assets out of probate before transferring to the trust in cases where the assets would go through probate first.

When determining assets for a living trust, a few additional comments are relevant for IRAs and other qualified retirement plans. First, they cannot be owned by trusts during the owner's lifetime, so placing these assets in a trust can only be done through a beneficiary designation at death. As well, it may not be wise to use a trust as a beneficiary for retirement accounts, especially if your spouse is alive. This will eliminate the benefits a spouse can receive from inheriting these assets and may even lead to the poor treatment that non-person beneficiaries obtain for required minimum distributions. The inherited account may need to be drained within five years unless the trust is set up in a specific way. This is covered further later in the chapter.

For distributions, the value of a trust over a will and probate is that more detailed instructions can be provided about the post-death distribution process. Assets do not have to be disbursed all at once, which can be helpful for managing disbursements to those who are minors, who are adults but may not be mature enough to receive everything at once, or to provide other creditor protections for beneficiaries. Instead, the living trust can call for the creation of irrevocable trusts at death to help manage the distribution process for trust assets. With a will, the probate assets are fully disbursed to the beneficiaries at the time that probate business has been handled and the process is closed.

Trust for minors, such as children or grandchildren, can spell out that assets are not available until a chosen age that can occur well past the age of majority, except for allowed expenses like education, medical needs, and living expenses approved by the guardian. These trusts can be established as a testamentary trust through the will, or as part of a living trust that is designed to become an irrevocable children's trust after death.

These trusts could be set up as a single trust, or each child could receive a separate trust. With a single trust, one may have "sprinkling" provisions that provide discretion about the distribution of trust income and property in a non-equal way between beneficiaries. For a simple example, if the trust supports education expenses for multiple children facing different education costs, the grantor may not necessarily want offsets made elsewhere for those with higher education expenses. The grantor may also want provisions for a spendthrift trust that are designed to stop beneficiaries from squandering trust assets or to protect the assets from the beneficiary's creditors.

As well, this type of property control provided by a trust can be useful for those who have been married more than once. The grantor may wish to balance concerns for supporting a surviving spouse while also providing an inheritance to children from previous marriages. A trust can be designed so that the surviving spouse is a life-estate beneficiary of a trust, with rules defining the amount and type of support received during the survivor's lifetime, and with any remaining property then being directed to final beneficiaries defined by the trust creator when that surviving spouse dies. Surviving spouses may be able to receive income generated by the trust, be able to use property owned by the trust, and may be able to invade principal of the trust in certain situations such as for health care expenses. With this approach, a surviving spouse can receive support from a trust without owning or having control over it. The trust becomes irrevocable after the grantor's death.

Having a living trust does not override the need for a will, and of course a will is necessary to direct the creation of a testamentary trust. But even if most of one's assets are held in a living trust, a will can provide backup for any other loose ends or property not in the trust. For example, a pour-over will simply gathers up any remaining assets at death and calls for them to be transferred into the trust. A will is also necessary if you wish to name your own executor or a guardian for minor children.

A living trust provides support for three phases of life: when the grantor is alive an able to be in control of trust assets, when the grantor is incapacitated and needs someone else to manage the trust assets, and when the grantor has died and would like to direct the trust assets to beneficiaries. A testamentary trust, on the other hand, only serves this final role as the trust only comes into effect through the will as part of the probate process. Assets held in a living trust do not become part of the probate estate since they are already owned by the trust instead of the individual who died, which is one of the main advantages of a living trust over a testamentary trust. A living trust is also helpful for those who are worried about their will being tested by unsatisfied potential heirs.

A living trust could be compared to having granted a "financial power of attorney" for trust assets to the successor trustee. Then the successor trustee would be like the "executor" for the trust assets at death, as both roles involve managing the distribution of assets. You will probably want to name the same person as the successor trustee for living trusts, the agent with financial power of attorney, and the executor for the estate. For each role, you should also name an alternative to serve as backup if your first choice is not available or unwilling to serve the role.

There are potential risks or downsides to keep in mind about living trusts. These include potential costs, as creating and maintaining a trust can be expensive. Another disadvantage of a trust over a will relates to your creditors who would otherwise only have a fixed amount of time to lay claim to probate assets. Also, placing one's home in a trust can impact property taxes and Medicaid eligibility and these types of matters can be reviewed by a qualified accountant in addition to an estate planning attorney. Testamentary trusts are usually less expensive and do not require maintenance since they are not created until death. However, assets that will be used to fund the trust may be included in the probate process if they do not have other ways to be transferred outside of probate.

Creating a trust involves more than just creating its legal documents. It is also necessary to re-title or update beneficiary designations for any assets that are meant to be held in the trust. You must engage in the work to retitle assets and transfer the ownership of assets you want to be owned by the trust, as the desires expressed by creating a trust do not override the legal ownership rights created in the titles of assets you had intended to be held by the trust. The trust is just an empty shell if you do not follow through with the process to fund it. This point does get forgotten in the real world. As well, remember that property owned by the trust is no longer legally owned by you and is not part of the probate process. Though this does not have significant implications during your lifetime, a practical implication is that a will cannot override trust documents when the property has been transferred to the trust. We return to the topic of trusts later in the chapter to cover their uses with managing estate taxes.

The Financial Power of Attorney

The power of attorney is a legal process in which a principal (you) can delegate the decision-making authority over your affairs to an agent or attorney-in-fact. An important part of planning is to identify agents to handle your financial and medical affairs in the event of your incapacity. We first consider the financial power of attorney. It is important to clarify that this power is meant to apply to incapacity during one's lifetime; it ends at death when the executor of the estate would take over this control. This provides an alternative to placing assets into a living trust where a successor trustee plays the same role for the trust assets.

The alternative to identifying agents to have these powers is to go through the potentially costly and cumbersome process of having a court-appointed guardian or conservator to handle your affairs if you have been deemed incompetent and become a "ward" of the state. The guardianship process is called living probate, and it is something you will likely wish to avoid by creating the appropriate legal documents in advance. Identifying an agent with this power in advance not only to reduces stress and potential fighting among family members, but it also allows the principal to be in control of the process and choose the person and the specific duties and responsibilities they are empowered to perform.

A power of attorney can be made general to manage all financial affairs in the same manner as its creator. Courts may interpret the power of attorney narrowly to help protect the principal from abuse, so you may wish to be specific about the types of powers to include. This can include managing investments and real estate, paying bills, managing insurance contracts, collecting debts, engaging in lawsuits, applying for government benefits, making gifts, hiring caregivers, signing tax returns, managing digital assets, operating a small business, and creating, funding, or revoking living trusts. You can limit any of these powers if you wish.

Two types of powers of attorney are durable and springing. A *durable* power of attorney begins as soon as it is signed, with control handed over for the remainder of one's lifetime unless it is canceled. To create a durable power of attorney, some states may require language to also include that the power stays in effect if one is incapacitated. This is an important point, because the common law traditions from which the power of attorney originates did not allow the agent to act when the principal became incapacitated, but the entire point of having this power is that the agent be able to act at the time of incapacity. Make sure you have created a durable power of attorney with this detail about incapacity spelled out as necessary in accordance with your state's law.

Another option is to create a *springing* power of attorney, which delays when it goes into effect until some triggering event happens such as a physician identifying that one has become incapacitated. This may sound more attractive, but having a durable power of attorney in effect does not mean that one loses control of their financial affairs at the present. It only means that now two individuals have legal authority to handle the affairs. A power of attorney can also be changed or even revoked at any time while the principal maintains his or her capacity.

Choosing an agent for the power of attorney can be complicated. It should be someone both trustworthy and experienced at managing financial matters, though the person does not have to be a financial professional. It is also best for the agent to live nearby as many tasks may need to be accomplished in person. You may also name an alternative agent as well to be covered for any reason that your primary agent is not able to fulfill the role. To simplify matters, your financial agent can be the same person as the executor for your will, the successor trustee for any living trust, and your health care agent (discussed in the next section). Because of the vulnerability it creates, you need to feel completely confident that the individual can be trusted. The starting point would be to choose one's spouse for this role for those who are married, unless there are valid reasons to choose someone else such as another close relative or friend. It is also possible to have a professional serve in this role and be compensated, such as a lawyer or banker you work with. If you cannot think of anyone to play this role, it may be best to allow the guardianship process to play out with court supervision if the need ever arises.

You can create a financial power of attorney on a do-it-yourself basis for a low cost using online tools such as those found at nolo.com, but it is a good idea to have an estate planner review to make sure what you have created conforms with your state laws and has been properly executed so that it will work as intended. This is especially important if you are worried that a family member will challenge your decision. Your agent will need to know how to find the original copy as well. You will also want to inform your key financial institutions that you have authorized an agent to act on your behalf and make sure these institutions will honor it. They may have additional paperwork for you to complete. Regarding bank accounts, it is important to also set up the power of attorney with the bank by filling out in advance the authorization forms and signature card for the agent with the power of attorney. This does not make the agent into an owner of the account, but the individual will have authorization to pay bills and make other distributions. Otherwise, the bank may not be willing to honor actions taken by the agent with these powers.

Advance Health Care Directives

Advance health care directives are documentation for making health care decisions when a person is unable to make such decisions on his or her own. This includes a living will and a health care power of attorney. When you are unable to communicate your wishes related to medical treatment, your advance health care directive can be helpful in outlining the types of treatment you may or may not want. This can help family members and health care providers to better meet your wishes when you cannot communicate them.

Creating these documents will avoid the slower, costlier, and more cumbersome process of having a legal guardian appointed to make these decisions at the time of your incapacity. Such an individual would then be following state laws in absence of understanding your preferences for care, leaving you without input into the process.

The portion of the advance health care directive outlining your wishes is the *living will*. It provides details about the types of medical treatment you wish to receive. This can include whether to receive life-prolonging treatments such as intravenous nutrition, resuscitation, the use of respirators, and a statement about the quality-of-life you find acceptable. Of course, many people may not really know what types of decisions might need to be made with end-of-life care. Different groups have created helpful materials to outline the potential types of decisions to be made as well as the implications of different choices. In the further reading section, I have included helpful materials from the American Bar Association.

The advance health care directives can also assign a health care power of attorney to an agent who can then make these health care decisions on your behalf. As with a financial power of attorney, you can provide guidance and instructions about how broad the power of attorney will be, but generally you may want to allow authority for all health care decisions to address whatever issues are not covered by the living will. It can be especially useful to have an advocate for communicating your wishes to medical professionals. This power is always springing in the sense that you will be asked to make your own decisions when possible, and the agent only steps in when you are not capable. Of course, defining when you are capable can be subjective and you may include instructions for this.

Choosing someone you trust is critical. That person should meet several criteria, including availability to help in the future, a willingness to carry out your wishes, ability to meet your state's criteria for who can serve in this role, and an ability to act as an assertive advocate as needed. You should avoid naming a committee, and you may wish to avoid naming your child. You should also identify a successor agent if your primary agent is not available when needed. It is important to have conversations with these individuals and to provide written explanations so that the person is best equipped to fulfill your wishes around medical care and when to stop attempts to prolong life. You and your proxy should agree on what you view as an acceptable quality of life. At what point would you be willing to let go, or do you want to be kept alive at all costs even without realistic prospects for recovery. How do your personal values or religious beliefs affect this? Does your agent understand your wishes and is willing to respect them?

The Health Insurance Portability and Accountability Act (HIPAA) tightened privacy rules around health care records. HIPAA restricts access to information about health care except to the patient or those who have been granted access. As a part of developing your advance health care directives, you should fill out the additional HIPAA paperwork needed to grant access to key family members, the health care power of attorney, the financial power of attorney, and/or the trustee under a living trust.

After creating this documentation, it is important to share it with your chosen agent and with your health care providers. You should also make sure your agent knows how to find the original version. You may also include a card in your wallet indicating that this documentation exists and providing contact details for the agent. You can also take comfort in knowing this document can be amended or revoked while you maintain your decision-making capacity.

This advanced directive can be prepared without a lawyer in many states. This service may also be included as part of an overall package when working with an estate planner. For those seeking a do-it-yourself approach, the AARP provides a list of state-specific advanced directive forms. This information is at www.aarp.org/advancedirectives. States have different laws; make sure to use the right documents and advice.

Final Wishes

A final part of your estate plan includes more personal items that you wish to communicate to family and friends, including documentation and instructions about your final wishes. You may identify who should oversee funeral arrangements, information on whether a burial plot is owned, or a funeral has been pre-paid, desired funeral home and service locations, and details such as who should speak or what songs should be played. With final wishes, these are the main details to include:

- ☐ Letters written to be given to friends and family
- ☐ An ethical will or other personalized messages

- ☐ Desires for organ or body donation
- ☐ Obituary details
- ☐ Burial or cremation choice and location of final resting place
- ☐ Documentation about any pre-payment made for funeral or burial
- ☐ Plans and ideas for funeral and memorial services
- ☐ Items to be destroyed
- ☐ Other people to contact
- ☐ Pet care

Wills, Living Wills, and Ethical Wills

Three types of "wills" are described in this chapter. Each describes something quite different. A *will* is a legally binding document that describes how an individual would like their probate assets to be disbursed upon death. A *living will* outlines your wishes regarding your health care, which can be followed in the event of your incapacitation. An *ethical will* shares your beliefs, values, inspirations, life lessons, favorite memories, expressions of love and gratitude, and other personal communications with your family after your passing. It is comparable to letters prepared for families and friends, and it provides another option for how you may wish to communicate with loved ones.

Tax Planning with Legacy and Estate Considerations

With the basic components of an estate plan in place, we now shift our attention toward tax issues related to legacy. First, we consider important matters for tax-efficient retirement distributions with a legacy in mind when estate taxes are not an issue. Then we explain how estate taxes work and describe different strategies to help manage them related to gifting, life insurance, and trusts.

Tax-Efficient Retirement Distributions with Inheritance in Mind

We now shift to a discussion of taxes and legacy when estate tax is not a concern because asset levels are below the estate tax exemptions. We described tax-efficient retirement distributions in Chapter 10 as the process of using tax-bracket management and strategic Roth conversions. Tax-efficient distributions generally involve spending from a blend of taxable and tax-deferred assets first, and then from a blend of tax-deferred and tax-free assets once the taxable accounts have been depleted. When considering how to position financial assets also for inheritance, we include:

- The step-up in basis available for taxable assets at death means that bequeathing appreciated securities can avoid capital gains taxes compared to if those assets are sold during one's lifetime.
- Tax-bracket management should also incorporate the marginal tax rates that heirs will pay on any inherited assets.

- When multiple heirs face different tax rates, the inheritance can be designed to improve efficiency by having unequal pre-tax inheritance amounts that are equalized after tax payments to provide more after-tax value for all recipients.

Addressing these matters in order, an important aspect of the tax code is that capital assets receive a step-up in basis at death. This means that the cost-basis for determining taxes is reset to the fair market value of the asset at the time the owner dies. This is relevant both for taxable assets held in brokerage accounts as well as for real estate and other related assets that track a cost basis for tax purposes. As for exceptions, annuities and retirement plan assets do not receive a step-up in basis. For assets experiencing large appreciations, the step-up in basis can imply a huge reduction in potential capital gains taxes. Sell the asset while alive and capital gains taxes are due; leave it for an inheritance and those capital gains taxes disappear. Joint ownership of assets such as real estate can eliminate the possibility of receiving a step-up in basis at death, though for community property a complete step-up may be possible at the death of either owner. Losing the potential for a step-up in basis can create a costly tax mistake for appreciated assets.

To consider a simple example, suppose you have a long-held mutual fund in a taxable brokerage account worth $100,000 with a cost-basis of $40,000. You could sell it to cover retirement spending and then pay long-term capital gains rates on the $60,000 of gains. However, if you instead leave this asset for heirs, its cost basis resets to the $100,000 fair market value at the time of death. If then sold at this price, there will be no capital gains taxes to be paid by the heirs.

This possibility speaks to the idea that it may not always be wise to fully spend down taxable assets first. In some cases, as legacy planning becomes realistic, it may prove wise to hold on to some highly appreciated taxable assets so that their embedded capital gains can avoid taxation when inherited. As for a related point, some assets may experience losses and be worth less than their cost basis. It might be wise to sell those assets while alive to receive a tax deduction on the losses that would be lost at death when there is a step-down in basis.

The next point relates to the marginal tax rates paid on distributions from IRAs and other tax-deferred retirement plans. We spoke in Chapter 10 of reducing the marginal tax rates paid through tax-bracket management and strategic Roth conversions. Taxes must be paid at some point, and the strategy is to trigger taxable income when the tax rates applied to that income are relatively low. The extension to consider here is that when these IRA assets are inherited, tax-bracket management also extends to include the marginal tax rates paid by the account beneficiaries.

Peak earnings years often happen at around age 50, and this age may also coincide with when beneficiaries are inheriting IRAs from their parents. The

SECURE Act speeds up the process for many beneficiaries to take required distributions, allowing for ten years to fully distribute an inherited tax-deferred account and pay taxes on the proceeds. This eliminates the previous ability to stretch distributions from inherited accounts over one's lifetime (we discuss this further later in the chapter). With the SECURE Act's ten-year window on distributions, beneficiaries may increasingly be forced to take distributions during peak earnings years and, therefore, at higher marginal tax rates. The implication is that the advice to pay taxes when the tax rates are lowest might increasingly suggest Roth conversions to retirees who may be in lower tax brackets than their beneficiaries.

It is also quite possible that multiple beneficiaries may be in different tax brackets. Perhaps one adult child is a high earner facing high marginal tax rates while another adult child has a more modest income and faces lower tax rates. A desire to be fair might suggest dividing all accounts equally between the two children. But a more tax-efficient approach would be to lean toward leaving taxable accounts and Roth accounts to the high earning child and leaving IRAs to the low earning child. This way, lower tax rates can be applied to the IRA distributions.

One can also consider what is meant by "equal" inheritances. Should the amounts be equal before tax or after tax? In this scenario, the low earner will be stuck paying taxes on IRA distributions while the tax bills will be less for the high earner receiving assets that are not taxed. This speaks to providing a larger monetary amount to the low-earning child such that after taxes are paid, the inheritance values will be more equalized. When strategizing in this way, it is worthwhile to explain to your heirs what you are doing so that they do not view it as unfair and understand that this can lead to a larger after-tax inheritance value for each of them than a simple equal splitting of each account value. We generally view monetary amounts in gross terms rather than in the more relevant after-tax terms, and that thinking can lead to less after-tax value for beneficiaries.

This concept is complex and is worth providing a simple illustration. An estate consists of $100,000 in an IRA and $100,000 in a Roth IRA. Two adult children will be the beneficiaries of these accounts. One child will be in the 37 percent marginal tax bracket while the other child will be in the 12 percent marginal tax bracket. First consider if these accounts are split evenly between the children, with each receiving $50,000 from the IRA and $50,000 from the Roth IRA. The $100,000 pre-tax values will not be the same after taxes. For the high tax child, the after-tax value of the inheritance is $81,500. This consists of $50,000 from the Roth IRA and $31,500 net-of-taxes from the IRA. For the low-tax child, the after-tax inheritance is $94,000 after paying 12 percent taxes on the IRA component. The combined after-tax inheritance value is $175,500.

But consider a different distribution. The high-tax child receives an inheritance of $94,000 from the Roth IRA, while the low-tax child receives the $100,000 from the IRA and $6,000 from the Roth IRA. As the low-tax child received $12,000 more than the high-tax child, this may not seem fair. But consider the after-tax impact. The high tax child still has $94,000 after taxes. The low-tax child has $88,000 from the IRA after paying 12 percent taxes and $6,000 from the Roth IRA, for a total of $94,000. They both received $94,000 after paying taxes, for a combined after-tax value of $188,000. This is $12,500 more combined after-tax inheritance than in the case where accounts were split equally. Even though the pre-tax inheritance values were not equal, both children should be understanding of the situation once the after-tax implications are made clear.

A final variation on this applies to those with charitable intentions as part of their legacy and who own a variety of account types. IRAs and other tax-deferred accounts may be the best suited for charitable donations. IRAs carry embedded income tax requirements for their distributions that qualified charities do not have to pay. Roth IRAs and taxable assets with a step-up in basis will then be better suited for receipt by individuals. As a related point, it would not make sense to engage in Roth conversions for assets that you intend to donate to a tax-exempt charity.

Estate Taxes

The other wrinkle with estate planning is the existence of estate taxes, which are applied to the value of the assets an individual owns at death. These taxes exist at the federal level as well as in some states. Currently, most people will not need to worry about paying federal estate taxes. In 2021, the estate tax exemption for an individual is $11.7 million. Since 2011, unused exemption amounts can be passed to a US citizen spouse, using a concept called portability. To take advantage of this portability between spouses, an estate tax return (IRS Form 706) must be filed within nine months of an individual's death, even if no estate tax is otherwise due. This process effectively doubles the exemption to $23.4 million for a couple in 2021. Estate taxes are due only if the net value of the estate exceeds these exempt amounts. An estate tax return must be filed if the gross value of the estate exceeds the thresholds, even if the net value after deductions is less. For asset values exceeding the exemptions, estate tax rates range from 18 percent to 40 percent. The 40 percent rate applies on any amount of the taxable estate above $1 million.

If these exemption levels seem unimaginably high for your potential estate, and you otherwise live in a state that does not have estate taxes, you may be thinking to skip ahead to the next section. But estate taxes are still something to be aware of, as the exemptions and other rules could be changed by Congress in the future. In fact, even the current exemption amounts, which adjust annually for inflation, are set to be expire after the 2025 tax year like other provisions of the Tax Cuts and Jobs Act of 2017. Current law has the exemptions set to be cut in half starting for deaths in 2026. But Congress can change the estate tax laws at any time, and the exemptions could possibly be made much lower. As recently as 2001, the individual estate tax exemption was $675,000, and it was still only $2 million in 2008. If Congress decides to return to these levels as part of a tax reform package, you may suddenly be in a situation where estate taxes become relevant. You may want to be ready to revisit these issues should the exemption amounts ever be lowered to levels that could impact you.

Thus, it is worth understanding how estate taxes work. These taxes are due on the net value of the estate. The gross value of the estate is the total value of all assets owned by the deceased. There are several deductions available to determine the net value. First, there is a marital deduction for any portion of the estate bequeathed to a surviving spouse who is a US citizen. As well, a charitable deduction is available for all property left to a tax-exempt charity. Deductions are also available for funeral expenses, expenses for settling the estate, claims against the estate, and a percentage of state or foreign estate or inheritance taxes. An annual gift tax exclusion is also available prior to death and will be discussed further in the next section. Lifetime gifts made above the annual exemptions are added to the estate, and any gift taxes already paid are deducted.

Income taxes are not paid on the value of the estate by those who receive it. The exception is when beneficiaries receive retirement plan assets or annuities that were provided with tax advantages and still require taxes on their required distributions. As well, if inherited property then generates further income or gains, then the new owner becomes responsible for those taxes. If the estate is large enough that estate taxes are paid on the value of retirement accounts, then it is possible for the beneficiary to receive a pro-rata deduction on the income taxes due for their distributions to offset the estate taxes paid. Nonetheless, the embedded income taxes due on retirement accounts like IRAs can make them great assets to leave to charities as part of the estate plan, as this avoids both income and estate taxes for these assets.

Residents of some states may also find themselves exposed to state-level estate or inheritance taxes. Estate taxes are imposed on the estate, while inheritance taxes are imposed on individual beneficiaries. For inheritance taxes, the tax rate can differ by the type of beneficiary, with close relatives often receiving lower rates. Some states have deduction thresholds matching federal levels, while others have lower thresholds. States with an estate tax include Connecticut, Hawaii, Illinois, Maine, Maryland, Massachusetts, Minnesota, New York, Oregon, Rhode Island, Vermont, and Washington, as well as the District of Columbia. As well, states with an inheritance tax include Iowa, Kentucky, Nebraska, Maryland, New Jersey, and Pennsylvania. Maryland is the only state with both estate and inheritance taxes.

Gifting

Aside from taking advantage of exemptions and deductions, the general concept of estate tax planning involves trying to remove assets from the estate at current valuation levels so that any subsequent appreciation takes place outside of the taxable estate. This is the idea guiding strategies around gifting, life insurance, and irrevocable trusts, which we now consider in turn.

Gifting can play an important role in reducing the size of a taxable estate and probate is avoided for gifts made during one's life. Gift decisions are often made for personal reasons unrelated to taxes, and gifting strategies are only relevant when the gifts do not threaten the sustainability of a retirement plan. When other aspects of the retirement plan are set, one may also find value in providing gifts while alive to enjoy seeing their receipt, rather than waiting to leave everything as an inheritance.

As well, the gift tax exemption can be quite valuable. Assets can be permanently removed from the estate for valid gifts of up to $15,000 per recipient in 2021. Recipients who may trigger gift taxes include individuals and non-charitable organizations. Gifts made beyond the exemption level in a tax year are taxable for the giver and a gift tax return (IRS Form 709) must be filed. The gift tax is not immediately due, as it instead works to reduce the exemption amount for the estate by the taxable portion of the gift. Actual payment of gift taxes begins once taxable gifts exceed the estate tax exemption. This may still help to reduce eventual estate taxes by taking property and its subsequent appreciation out of the estate.

Even just taking advantage of the gift exemption each year can add up over time. This exclusion is per individual giver. A couple could jointly gift $30,000 to one recipient before reaching the exemption limit. And if a couple makes that gift to five individuals each year, that is $150,000 removed from the estate without creating tax. This process can be repeated annually. Other gift exemptions are also available for the full amount of a gift to a spouse, a gift of tuition or eligible medical expenses that are paid *directly* to the institution or provider, or gifts to political organizations and qualified charities. Educational 529 plans also have a special provision that allows up to five years of the gift-tax exclusion to be taken at one time for a large gift of up to $75,000. One might consider paying education expenses for grandchildren, or perhaps taking the entire family on a vacation.

Assets that are better suited for gifting include those with a high cost-basis and limited embedded capital gains, assets with strong appreciation potential for the future, and assets that produce large amounts of income, which could be gifted to someone paying taxes at lower marginal tax rates. The idea of gifting assets that are expected to appreciate is to freeze the value of an asset at its current level so that any subsequent appreciation occurs outside of your estate. Relatedly, there may be value for individuals in higher income tax brackets to gift income-producing assets to those in lower tax rates to reduce the tax rate on that income. This consideration may not work for gifts to minors, though, as income generated by those assets is generally taxed at the same higher rates as for irrevocable trusts.

As for less useful assets for gifting, appreciated assets that are eligible for a step-up in basis at death are not as suitable for giving away while alive. The gift would sacrifice the potential step-up in basis and elimination of capital gains at death. Conversely, gifting property with embedded losses would mean losing the ability to deduct those losses for yourself first, and there would be a step-down in basis at death. One might sell assets with losses, take the deduction, and then gift the value of those assets.

The issue of asset appreciation can become a source for mistakes. For example, someone might consider adding a child as a joint owner on the deed to one's home for personal reasons unrelated to taxes. This action would allow the child to eventually become the homeowner without going through the probate process. However, there can be negative consequences to this decision. First, the child's consent is now needed for any actions related to selling the home or opening a mortgage or home equity loan on the home. The home could also become entangled in any proceedings related to the child getting divorced, sued, or entering bankruptcy. As well, adding the child to the deed counts as a gift of the home value to the child, which could trigger gift taxes. It will also mean that the child does not receive a step-up in basis on the home value upon your death and so may be exposed to greater capital gains taxes on a subsequent home sale. The gifting may also be penalized and delay the process of gaining Medicaid eligibility for long-term care, whereas home equity may otherwise be an excluded asset for Medicaid eligibility.

As for other issues, some gifts must be made at least three years before death for the gift to be allowed to reduce one's estate. This can be an issue with life insurance, as the cash value of the gift is typically much smaller than the value of the death benefit. If death happens within three years of gifting a life insurance policy, then the gift is not recognized, and the death benefit is added to the estate. But after three years, the gift is allowed and only the cash surrender value is treated as a taxable gift. This provides a way to leverage legacy assets to get them outside the reach of estate taxes. For example, suppose a life insurance policy with a cash surrender value of $100,000 and a death benefit of $1 million is provided as a gift in 2021. Should that individual survive for three more years, the taxable portfolio of the gift ($85,000) is all that impacts the estate. However, the estate would grow by $1 million should the giver die within that three-year period. It may be useful to note that the three-year rule does not apply to gifts made from a living trust.

To qualify for the gift tax exclusion, the gift must have a "present interest," which means that it is immediately available for the recipient to use. Gifts to irrevocable trusts may not meet this requirement. For minors, such as children or grandchildren, who are not legally able to receive gifts of value, the gift tax exclusion is still available if certain conditions are met. These include that the gift is retained in a proper child's trust, in a custodial account conforming to the requirements of the Uniform Transfer to Minors Act (UTMA) or Uniform Gifts to Minors Act (UGMA), or in a 529 Education savings plan. The custodian manages the assets for the minor's benefit and the account control transfers fully to the child at the age of majority. For

UTMA and UGMA accounts, the gift must be made available outright when the minor reaches the age of majority, which is between 18 and 21 in most states. The "present interest" rule can also be met by creating a "Crummey" trust which makes the gift immediately available, but if it is not accepted within a limited time then the gift becomes owned by an irrevocable trust. When comparing trusts to UTMA accounts, trusts can have multiple beneficiaries, different tax treatment, and the ability to defer the distribution of assets beyond the age of majority.

Selling an asset for less than its fair market value can also be counted as a gift. Gifts can also complicate Medicaid eligibility for long-term care benefits. Gifts or transfers at less than fair market value during the previous five years can impact Medicaid eligibility by creating a penalty period before benefits begin. This is an area in which a knowledgeable estate planner can help identify allowed ways to transfer assets.

Life Insurance

Life insurance can provide a tax-efficient way to support legacy goals in the estate plan. Life insurance can be used to pay final expenses, to cover estate taxes or unpaid debts, to fund business continuation agreements, or to provide financial support to a spouse or other beneficiaries. Beneficiary designations can be used to keep the proceeds out of probate, which can help the death benefit become quickly available to support immediate liquidity needs. Life insurance can provide an important way to create liquid assets for paying estate taxes or final expenses so that illiquid assets do not need to be sold for this purpose. The death benefit will not be subject to income taxes, and irrevocable life insurance trusts (ILITs) can be designed to keep the proceeds of a life insurance policy outside of an estate to avoid estate taxes. The smaller cash surrender value of the policy at the time of the trust creation becomes the gift amount. As well, the death benefit for life insurance provides a method to meet a legacy goal using risk pooling and tax advantages that is distinct from preserving investment assets for this purpose. This can allow the retiree to potentially enjoy a higher standard of living in retirement, while also ensuring that assets have been earmarked to meet the legacy goal.

A life insurance policy can also be gifted to an individual or organization. This also has the same effect of freezing the value of the policy for the estate at its current cash surrender value rather than the larger death benefit it will eventually provide. Gifts of life insurance do have to meet the same three-year rule described previously. As well, if you are using the policy as part of your retirement income strategy, which requires keeping control to borrow against the policy or take other actions, then the IRS would not recognize the gift for estate tax purposes. That is because the IRS requires giving up any retained interest in an asset for it to be accepted as a completed gift. An advantage of using an ILIT over gifting a policy is that the trustee may better manage premium payments or may prevent the beneficiary from cashing out the policy before your death.

Life Insurance for Retirement Income

Aside from estate planning, permanent life insurance can also play a role in retirement income strategies. Permanent life insurance with cash value providing stable growth can serve as a volatility buffer for the investment portfolio (whole life insurance joins cash reserves and reverse mortgages as the three types of buffer assets). It can provide a source of funds to support legacy, liquidity, and even long-term care if a rider is added for that purpose. With the support of a death benefit as backup for the annuity premium, the retiree may also feel more comfortable using an annuity with lifetime income protections as part of a retirement plan. Another use of permanent life insurance is as a supplemental source of retirement income. To be effective, the policy must provide net benefits so that the tax-advantages of life insurance contribute more value than the insurance costs of the policy. If tax rates increase in the future, this would increase the relative advantage of life insurance. As well, when viewed as an investment, life insurance cash value can provide an attractive alternative to holding bonds in a taxable investment portfolio. In addition to tax deferral and the potential for tax-free distributions, premiums are invested in the insurance company's general account, which can provide advantages by holding higher-yielding fixed-income investments relative to what a household can obtain on its own by accepting more maturity, credit, and illiquidity risk. Using life insurance as part of a retirement income plan is discussed in much greater detail in my book, *Safety-First Retirement Planning*.

A Role for Trusts in Managing Estate Taxes

Our earlier discussion of trusts focused on avoiding probate and controlling the distribution of property after death. For estate taxes, those matters are not mutually exclusive as trusts can be designed both to manage estate taxes and control trust property. But now the focus is directed toward estate tax issues rather than property control issues. The basic idea for this section is that irrevocable trusts can be used to provide gifts at their current value such that any subsequent asset appreciation or income generation occurs outside of the estate and is not counted as part of the taxable estate. Revocable trusts do not have any impact on reducing estate taxes because assets held in a revocable trust are included as part of the grantor's estate. Revocable trust assets are still controlled by the grantor, so they do not count as taxable gifts. Revocable trusts may create irrevocable trusts at death to control the disbursement of assets. But for estate taxes, this discussion is about creating irrevocable trusts during one's lifetime to gift assets, or in some cases to create irrevocable trusts at death to take better advantage of personal estate tax exemptions. This discussion of irrevocable trusts and estate taxes introduces basic concepts. You should seek professional legal guidance to determine the appropriateness of these approaches and to draft the legal documentation to create an irrevocable trust provided that is the optimal approach.

Irrevocable trusts are permanent and cannot be changed once created. Unlike revocable trusts, they become independent legal entities with their own tax IDs, tax rules, and tax filing requirements. The trust pays taxes and holds ownership of its assets once they have been transferred. Property cannot be returned to the grantor, and the grantor cannot serve as a trustee for the irrevocable trust if the goal is to keep assets outside the estate. This is necessary to ensure that the property has truly been gifted away from the estate and to be compliant with gift tax rules. Grantors can be income beneficiaries of the trust with rules defining how much access is available to trust assets and income.

As separate legal entities, irrevocable trusts face their own set of tax rules. For those who are living when transferring property to the trust, that property is treated as a gift and is subject to the gift tax. As noted, taxable gifts are offset against the estate tax exemption. This becomes the main point of these strategies: to transfer property out of an estate when it may be valued at lower levels to reduce the subsequent taxable estate. For instance, if property is gifted to a trust when it is worth $1 million, and that property is worth $2 million when the grantor dies, this strategy allows for $1 million to be counted when determining estate taxes. If property is transferred at death, the whole $2 million is counted as part of the taxable estate.

When an irrevocable trust generates income from trust property as part of its ongoing operation, trust income tax rates apply for any income that is retained at the end of the tax year. The tax rates on trust income quickly escalate, with a top marginal tax rate of 37 percent already applying to retained trust income above $13,050 in 2021. If the trust instead distributes that income to its beneficiaries before year end, then it instead becomes part of the beneficiary's income tax return.

An important type of irrevocable trust that can be designed with estate tax management in mind is an AB disclaimer trust. Before portability of the personal estate tax exemption became available for spouses, these trusts were popular for married couples who expected to be subjected to estate taxes. Now this design is less necessary for married couples, but it still may be used for those who are not married, who are subject to state-level estate taxes, or who are worried that the portability of the deduction may be eliminated. The objective of an AB disclaimer trust is to keep the property of the first-to-die individual out of the estate of the surviving individual in this joint set up. When the first individual dies, an existing joint living trust is split into Trust A and Trust B. Trust A is an irrevocable trust for the deceased individual's assets and Trust B is the separate revocable living trust for the survivor. That survivor is a life beneficiary of Trust A, which means that the survivor can receive trust income, use trust property, and spend trust principal if it covers basic needs through a standard "health, education, support, and maintenance" clause. For the trust to work for its intended estate tax purpose, the survivor cannot have full access to or ownership of the property in Trust A. When the survivor dies, the remaining property in Trust A goes to its final beneficiaries as had been defined by the first-to-die individual, but the goal was not necessarily to save property for those final beneficiaries. Property in Trust A is part of the deceased individual's estate used to take greater advantage of that individual's estate tax exemption. The disclaimer aspect of the trust allows the survivor to have control over which property is kept outright by the survivor and which property is disclaimed by the survivor and therefore goes into Trust A. Disclaiming property means it is never owned by an individual and does not become part of that individual's estate.

A second similar type of trust is a qualified terminable interest property (QTIP) trust. Its basic setup is comparable to an AB Disclaimer Trust, though a QTIP trust is only available for married couples. The basic difference for this trust is that it uses the marital deduction for estate taxes to delay the payment of estate taxes until the second spouse dies. When the first spouse dies, the trust property is exempt from estate taxes by passing it to the spouse, and the remaining property is included in the second spouse's estate to be taxed at that time. The surviving spouse has access to money and property in the trust, but does not have outright ownership, and remaining trust property will go to the final beneficiaries after the surviving spouse has also died. This can be useful for those in second marriages to support a surviving spouse while also ensuring that some assets will also go to children from a previous marriage. The tradeoff involves determining just how much the life beneficiary (surviving spouse) can use, as controls against too much use will better protect property for the final beneficiary. A QDOT trust can play a similar role for married couples in which one spouse is not a US citizen.

Irrevocable trusts can also be used in the context of giving to charity and can provide both income and estate tax benefits. A Charitable Remainder Trust (CRT) provides an annual payment to an income beneficiary (typically you or a family member) during his or her lifetime or for a set number of years and then the remaining property is passed to the charity as the final beneficiary. Income payments are either defined as fixed amounts (annuity trust) or as a fixed percentage of remaining assets (unitrust). A Charitable Lead Trust (CLT) works in the opposite way by providing distributions to a charity for a specified period and the remainder is then available for other beneficiaries (typically you or a family member). These trusts are irrevocable, can be used with eligible tax-exempt charities, and are often set up during one's lifetime to take advantage of income tax deductions for the charitable donation. The IRS uses tables to estimate the portion of the donation that will remain with the charity as opposed to being returned as payments to the income beneficiary. An income tax deduction for the donated portion can then be spread over a five-year period and is subject to limitations on the percentage of one's adjusted gross income that can be donated for a tax deduction. Appreciated assets can be used to set up these trusts to avoid capital gains taxes as well, though a portion of payments received back will return some capital gains to you. The trustee is typically the charity, but you or someone else might serve as trustee if the charity allows this. Assets in a CRT are no longer part of your estate once they go to the final beneficiary. Charitable gift annuities, which we discussed in the previous chapter, are streamlined and standardized forms of CRTs. CLTs do require income taxes to be paid on the distributions to charities, which can offset the value of the tax deduction, but this approach may still be attractive to avoid capital gains taxes on appreciated assets.

Charitable Giving after Death

When charitable giving is an important goal, besides the obvious questions of whom to give to and how to balance the desires between family and charity, important questions for givers include when to give and with what assets. In this and the previous chapter we discuss tools for giving when alive to obtain income tax deductions in addition to reducing the subsequent size of the taxable estate. Many may prefer to give while still alive once they feel the gifts are affordable and will not disrupt their retirement sustainability. Charitable giving after death is still possible and it will reduce the size of the taxable estate for those whom estate taxes are a consideration, even though income tax deductions are no longer possible. But even for the vast majority who will not pay estate taxes, charitable giving may be a goal and coordinating it properly can help to save on taxes. With their embedded income tax liabilities, we noted that IRAs and retirement plan assets can be great candidates for charitable giving, because tax-exempt charities will not have to pay income taxes. One might even use life insurance policies to replace the value of the IRA assets as a gift for family members, with the possibility that the income tax savings from not paying taxes on IRA distributions could help to fund the life insurance premiums.

The discussion of CRTs also has a parallel set of trusts when the final beneficiary is not a charity. These include Grantor Retained Annuity Trusts (GRATs) that pay fixed amounts, and Grantor Retained Unitrusts (GRUTs) that pay fixed percentages. These are irrevocable trusts that maintain some ability for you to use trust property for a set period as an income beneficiary before the property goes to the final beneficiary. During the period you use the property, you remain as a trustee. A downside for these is that if you die before your period of use has ended and before the trust assets have been transferred to the final beneficiary, then the estate planning benefits about removing the asset from the estate are lost. Even though the trust is irrevocable, you have a retained interest in the trust while serving as the income beneficiary. You must outlive the period of property use to have the trust assets valued as a gift from the time the trust was established, which is a disadvantage if the trust property had further appreciated in value since that date. The value of the gift is adjusted downward from the amount of assets placed in the trust to estimate the value of your retained interest in the same manner as with CRTs and the gift tax exclusion is not applicable at the time of the trust creation. These trusts are also established so that any income and capital gains from the trust are taxed to you as the grantor, even though the trust is a separate legal entity.

A related type of trust is the Grantor Retained Income Trust (GRIT). These are designed to provide use of the property, such as living in a home, rather than to provide income generated from the trust property. GRITs are now generally used as qualified personal residence trusts (QPRTs) to own a personal residence for a specific number of years and to provide use of the home to the grantor during that time. After that time, the property's title passes to the remainder beneficiaries. The original grantor might remain in the house after that time if a fair market rental value is paid to the beneficiary who serves as owner.

For another example, Irrevocable Life Insurance Trusts (ILITs) are an option to help keep a life insurance death benefit out of the estate for the purpose of determining estate taxes. Though life insurance death benefits are not exposed to income taxes, they do become part of the taxable estate. The ILIT provides a way to remove the policy from the estate by transferring its ownership to an irrevocable trust. This may be useful in cases where you do not wish to gift the policy directly to another person. There are many rules that must be met to ensure the estate tax benefits are received, including that you cannot be the trustee or otherwise have any decision-making control over the policy. As noted earlier, the trust must be in place for at least three years before your death for it to be effective in keeping the death benefit out of your estate. The policy may still require premium payments, and there are a variety of techniques that can be used to pay premiums that do not imply retained control over the policy from the IRS's perspective.

Other types of complicated trusts are also available to help manage estate taxes. These include generation-skipping trusts which treat one's children as income beneficiaries and grandchildren as final beneficiaries to avoid a second round of estate taxes from having to be paid by the grandchildren when the children die. This skipping ability only applies up to the level of the generation-skipping transfer tax exemption, which is currently the same as the personal estate tax exemption amount. There are other options as well, as the limits relate to the creativity of estate planning professionals and their abilities to convince the IRS that the efforts to reduce the estate's size are legitimate.

Required Minimum Distributions for Inherited Assets

In this section, we continue the discussion of tax issues related to legacy by extending the discussion of required minimum distributions during one's life to what happens after the death of the original owner. Beneficiaries of IRAs and other qualified retirement plans and annuities will face required distributions from these assets. The SECURE Act from December 2019 changed how these rules work, creating many possible scenarios for any embedded income tax liabilities in these accounts that remain after the death of the original account owner.

RMDs on Inherited IRAs and Qualified Plans

Upon the IRA account owner or qualified plan participant's death (which, to simplify the language, I will refer to as "owner" from this point forward), IRAs and retirement plan assets will pass to the beneficiaries indicated on the account beneficiary forms, or to the estate (or what the plan documents otherwise require with qualified plans) if beneficiaries are not otherwise listed. Required minimum distributions for beneficiaries work differently than for the original owners. The nature of the rules used depend on the type of beneficiary, on whether the death happens before or after the owner had reached the required begin date for distributions, and on whether the death took place before or after January 1, 2020. Exhibit 11.1 provides a summary of these details. We also note that if the beneficiary has details about non-deductible contributions that had been made to the IRA, then it is not necessary to pay tax on that portion as was also the case during the owner's lifetime.

I will walk through the process to explain the details in Exhibit 11.1. The first step is to identify the required minimum distribution in the year of the owner's death. If the owner dies before April 1 in the year after reaching the RMD starting age (this is the required beginning date), the RMD is not due and the first set of rules in the exhibit is applied. If the owner has already made that first payment before dying, then nothing happens. The payment is not refunded, and it does not shift the beneficiary to the bottom half of the exhibit. The RMD starting age was 70.5 in 2019 and before, and it is now 72.

Once we get past the required beginning date, the regular RMD for the owner is due as usual by December 31. If the owner has not made the RMD for the year yet, beneficiaries need to make sure they complete this task by December 31 to avoid the large 50 percent penalty tax on the distribution amount. A death in December, for instance, with everything else going on for the family, becomes one more matter to get addressed quickly. Though waiting until the end of the year provides the most tax-deferral potential, individuals may wish to take their RMDs earlier in the year to protect their families regarding this matter.

In the year after the death takes place, matters diverge as based on the date of death and type of beneficiary. And there may be multiple beneficiaries, in which case the RMD rules will be linked to the beneficiary with the least favorable RMD status.

The process for determining RMDs is to first identify all beneficiaries of an account at the owner's death. Then we look toward determining whether any of the beneficiaries cease to have an interest by September 30 of the following year. A beneficiary could cease to have an interest by receiving their full payout or by disclaiming their benefit. Non-person beneficiaries such as the estate, charities, and some types of trusts, will receive the least favorable RMD status by needing to apply a five-year rule to distributions. To avoid that impacting other beneficiaries, a charity or other non-person beneficiary could receive its full payout by the following September 30 and cease to be a beneficiary at that point.

Exhibit 11.1
Required Minimum Distributions (RMDs) for Inherited Retirement Plans

Owner or Participant Dies before Required Beginning Date for RMDs		
Type of Beneficiary	Death took place in 2019 or earlier	Death took place in 2020 or later (SECURE Act)
No RMD in the year of owner's death. In subsequent years:		
Spousal beneficiary	Spouse may rollover or otherwise treat the account as his or her own, such that RMDs are based as though the spouse is the owner; Spouse may leave in name of decedent and distribute using the single life table (annually updated) beginning when owner would have turned 70.5.	No changes, except RMD start age is now 72.
Non-spousal beneficiary	Lifetime stretch: RMDs based on smaller of beneficiary's age and owner's age at end of the year in the year following death using the single life table (fixed).	End of lifetime stretch. Now a 10-year rule, except for "eligible designated beneficiaries"
Non-person beneficiary (estate, charity, some trusts)	5-year rule	No changes
Owner or Participant Dies after Required Beginning Date for RMDs		
Owner's same RMD in the year of death (must be paid by beneficiary if not paid yet). In subsequent years:		
Spousal beneficiary	Spouse may rollover or otherwise treat the account as his or her own such that RMDs are based as though the spouse is the owner; Spouse may leave in name of decedent and base RMDs on smaller of beneficiary's age and owner's age at end of the year in the year following death using the single life table (annually updated).	No changes
Non-spousal beneficiary	Lifetime stretch: RMDs based on smaller of beneficiary's age and owner's age at end of the year in the year following death using the single life table (fixed).	End of lifetime stretch. Now a 10-year rule, except for "eligible designated beneficiaries"
Non-person beneficiary (estate, charity, some trusts)	RMDs based on owner's age at end of year of death using the single life table (fixed). Some trusts may be able to be set up to use single life expectancy (fixed) of beneficiary.	No changes

With multiple beneficiaries, the RMD rules for the beneficiary with the least favorable treatment (i.e. the shortest distribution period) are applied to all beneficiaries. Younger individuals could be hurt by the rules for an older beneficiary, and every person could be hurt by the presence of a non-person beneficiary. The account could be divided into separate accounts with one beneficiary per account, which may work, for instance, if multiple children are beneficiaries. This would also allow each beneficiary to use a different asset allocation and distribution strategy. See-through trusts may also be used to avoid applying the non-person treatment to all beneficiaries. More on this in a moment.

There are three types of beneficiaries to consider. The spouse is first. Spouses receive the most favorable treatment which make them a natural beneficiary choice for retirement accounts. In addition, for employer plans the spouse must be the beneficiary and needs to specifically waive this protection for the owner to choose a different primary beneficiary. The spousal right does not automatically apply for IRAs, except in community property states.

Next are non-spousal beneficiaries. These are people who represent anyone other than the spouse. For this category, the SECURE Act also creates a subset of "eligible designated beneficiaries." Rights are more limited for non-spousal beneficiaries, such as they can only use direct rollovers into inherited IRAs, whereas spouses have more flexibility. Finally, there are non-person beneficiaries. Technically, a non-person beneficiary means that there was no designated beneficiary. These include the estate, charities, and some types of trusts. Regarding trusts, proper structuring can be used to provide treatment more along the lines of the non-spousal beneficiary. These are pass-through or see-through trusts that meet various requirements under state law, including that the trust is irrevocable and has a list of clearly defined beneficiaries that can be provided to the IRA custodian by October 31 in the year following death. Even in this case, the beneficiary with the worst RMD treatment will be applied for all beneficiaries. A master trust may also create sub-trusts for each beneficiary to use the separate rules for each as a non-spousal beneficiary.

Regarding these types of beneficiaries, first consider if the owner dies before the required beginning date for RMDs. Spouses have flexibility about their choice at this point. One option is to simply treat the inherited account as their own, or to roll it over into their own IRA. For spouses doing this, the account is subsequently treated as his or her own account and the RMD discussion reverts to the previous chapter about how RMDs work for the original owner.

Another option for spouses is to leave the account in the name of the decedent and then take RMD distributions using the single life table beginning when the owner would have reached the age that RMDs begin. In the exhibit, this is referred to as single life table (annually updated). The annually updated aspect refers to the same idea as how RMDs are calculated during the owner's lifetime. Each year a new life expectancy factor is used based on the individual's age in that year. An important difference, though, is that the single life table is used here unlike the uniform life table during the owner's lifetime. This distinction was described in Chapter 10. This single life table has shorter life expectancies and higher distribution rates than the uniform life table used during the lifetime of owners. The single life table draws down the account faster and will lead to larger RMDs and more taxable income. As for deaths in 2020 and later, the SECURE Act did not change the treatment for spouses. The only difference for spouses is that the RMD starting age is now 72.

The next group is non-spousal designated beneficiaries. In other words, people other than the spouse. In 2019 and earlier, when the owner died, non-spousal beneficiaries could stretch the RMDs over the beneficiary's lifetime. This "lifetime stretch" rule worked by identifying the beneficiary's age at the end of the year following the year of the owner's death. Usually, we think of the beneficiary as younger, but technically, the RMDs are based on the smaller age of the beneficiary and owner. That age is used to find the life-expectancy from the single life table. This life expectancy is then fixed, with the terminology in Exhibit 11.1 of "single life expectancy (fixed)." In this case, the life expectancy is not updated each year with the life table, but instead one is subtracted from the fixed life expectancy each year until the remainder gets to zero. At that point, the account is fully distributed through RMDs. This will deplete the account faster than with annual updating.

The SECURE Act removed this lifetime stretch for deaths happening in 2020 and later. Instead, there is now a ten-year rule. The new ten-year rule is not technically an RMD in terms of specific amounts being taken in each calendar year. The rule only requires that the full account value be distributed by December 31 in the year with the tenth anniversary of the owner's death. For instance, if the death happens in October 2021, the account will need to be depleted by the end of 2031. This ten-year window can speed up the process for distributions, reducing the attractiveness of inherited retirement plan assets, but it does at least provide flexibility about how much is taken each year as there is no ongoing RMD during the ten years. If desired, the full amount could be taken in the tenth year. Planning around seeking lower tax rates on distributions can help with developing strategies for how to distribute during this ten-year window.

The SECURE Act also creates eligible designated beneficiaries who can potentially apply the old rules for a lifetime stretch instead of the new ten-year window. These include the spouse, disabled or chronically-ill individuals, beneficiaries who are not more than ten years younger than the owner, and minor children of the owner. When any of these beneficiaries dies, the subsequent beneficiary will face a ten-year window. As well, when minor children reach the age of majority, the ten-year rule applies to them starting at that point. One final change is that before the SECURE Act, when a non-spousal beneficiary died, their new successor beneficiary would continue using the same remaining fixed life expectancy. Under the SECURE Act, these individuals would now shift to a ten-year window.

Regarding non-person beneficiaries, the non-person beneficiary has a five-year window to take distributions in situations where the owner had not yet reached the required beginning date. The five-year window applies the same flexibility about when to take distributions as was described for the ten-year window. Only having five years to deplete the account is the least favorable treatment applied. The SECURE Act did not change this rule for non-person beneficiaries.

An additional point can be made about assets from qualified plans. Plan sponsors may require that all beneficiaries use the five-year rule instead of whichever rules they might have otherwise been eligible to use. It is important to check the plan documents regarding this point. This problem can be avoided through a rollover into an inherited IRA.

Next, we consider the situation for beneficiaries when the owner died after the required beginning date for the RMDs. As noted, the usual RMD for the owner must be taken in the year of death as though the owner was still alive. Then, in the following year, the situation varies by type of beneficiary.

We start with spouses. For spouses, the rules are the same as when the death took place before the required beginning date. Except, since we now know that the owner passed the required begin date already, that would begin the lifetime stretch in the following year when the spouse left the account in the name of the decedent. The SECURE Act keeps this.

As for non-spousal beneficiaries, the rules are mostly the same. With deaths before January 1, 2020, the lifetime stretch applied in which RMDs are based on the smaller of the beneficiary's age and owner's age at end of the year in the year following death with the single life table (fixed). The SECURE Act did change this, replacing the lifetime stretch with the ten-year rule except for some types of eligible designated beneficiaries as noted earlier. For any successor beneficiaries, the same rules applied as mentioned when the owner died before their required beginning date on RMDs. Before the SECURE Act, successor beneficiaries continued using the same fixed life expectancy, but in 2020 or later they switch to using the ten-year rule.

Non-person beneficiaries take distributions based on the remaining single life expectancy (fixed) of the owner based on his or her age at the end of the year of death. This value then reduces by one in each subsequent year, so the first RMD in the following year does use that calculated amount less one. As noted, switching from the uniform to single life table will increase the RMDs. The SECURE Act did not change these rules for non-person beneficiaries. With trusts, there are possibilities to structure the trust in a way that RMDs are applied more in line with non-spouse persons rather than with non-persons. That could support a switch to using the life expectancy of the beneficiary instead, which would help if the beneficiary is younger and is an eligible designated beneficiary or is otherwise able to switch to the ten-year rule.

We should make a further caveat about pass-through trusts that could follow the person beneficiary rules. There was some panic after the SECURE Act passed as many trusts have provisions to distribute only the RMD amount to an income beneficiary, which was designed for the lifetime stretch rules. When the treatment for the beneficiary changes from a lifetime stretch to the ten-year rule, this could lead to a very large distribution made just in the tenth year, potentially generating a very large tax bill and high marginal tax rates. Estate attorneys were scrambling to update trust documents to avoid this outcome and you may wish to check any older trusts you have to see if this is an issue.

RMDs on Inherited Roth IRAs

For inherited Roth IRAs, beneficiaries do have required minimum distributions. These distributions follow the same rules as just discussed for inherited tax-deferred retirement assets. The difference, of course, is that the distributions are not taxable. They are qualified distributions triggered by the death of the owner. They can simply be reinvested in a taxable account at the time of distribution, and they do not add to the adjusted gross income of the beneficiary. Their relevance, then, is just the timetable created in which subsequent asset growth is no longer tax-deferred and tax-free for the beneficiary.

A Caveat for Inherited Health Savings Accounts

In Chapter 10, we noted the incredible role that health savings accounts (HSAs) can play for providing tax deductions, tax-deferral, and tax-free distributions for eligible medical expenses. There is a caveat for this if the accounts are inherited. When going to a spouse, there is no problem. The spouse can treat the account as his or her own. But for other non-spouse beneficiaries, the account ceases to be an HSA. It behaves like an inherited IRA with a one-year window. The entire account value must be distributed to the non-spouse beneficiary in the year of the owner's death, such that the entire account value becomes taxable income in one year. This suggests an importance for HSA owners to use their accounts to cover eligible medical expenses and to avoid targeting the assets to be part of legacy.

With taxes not being paid, for cases when the ten-year rule applies, it would generally make sense to simply wait until year ten and then withdraw the entire Roth account value when the distributions were not otherwise needed for spending purposes. This would provide the most tax-deferral. The asset value could then be reinvested in a taxable account. As we described before, the reductions to the ability to use a lifetime stretch triggered by the SECURE Act increases the value of receiving an inheritance as a Roth instead of a traditional IRA. The new ten-year stretch period can force faster and larger distributions for beneficiaries when they may be in their peak earnings years, and this can trigger higher marginal tax rates than the retiree may have needed to pay with Roth conversions. With the ten-year window, forced distributions from an inherited Roth IRA may be more favorable than forced distributions from an inherited IRA for those beneficiaries in peak earnings years. This will make Roth conversions more popular in the future.

Taxation Issues for Inherited Annuities

Inheriting an annuity can create tax complications for beneficiaries. Annuities share characteristics with inherited IRAs as they are exposed to both estate and income taxes and have rules for required distributions by beneficiaries. At a very superficial level, the rules treating inherited retirement plan assets and inherited annuities are similar. But the rules do have important differences and there are many specific complications for annuities that go well beyond what we present here. Those with tax questions about inherited annuities should seek further guidance from a tax professional. We only cover the issue with broad strokes.

We have four basic scenarios to consider that involve whether the annuity is held in a qualified retirement plan or whether it is a non-qualified annuity purchased using taxable assets, and whether the contract has been annuitized or whether it is still in the deferral stage. Because rules around annuities held inside of qualified retirement accounts require taxes to be paid in the same manner as with other plan assets, we will focus the discussion on non-qualified annuities. There are also additional complications if the owner and the annuitant for an annuity contract are not the same person, as this can trigger different outcomes for whether the beneficiary receives the annuity when the annuitant dies or when the owner dies. Tax rules also vary based on when the annuity contract was created, with different rules for before and after dates that often fall in the 1980s. For this section, we will describe the rules in general terms for contracts created in the past thirty-plus years. These contracts are owner driven. In any case, due to the complexity of these tax rules, which could fill an entire book (see further reading by John Olsen and Michael Kitces), I must emphasize again the importance of consulting with a professional when inheriting an annuity.

For estate taxes, the relevant idea is that the value of the annuity provided to a beneficiary is included in the deceased owner's estate. For annuitized contracts, this would include any lump-sum cash refund payment. If the death benefit is structured as a series of payments, such as period-certain, installment refunds, or a remaining payment based on the life of an annuitant, then the estate value would be equivalent to the cost of purchasing a similar payment structure from an insurance company at the time of the owner's death. For deferred annuities, the value of the annuity death benefit would be included in the estate.

Inherited non-qualified annuities are also subject to income taxes, and these assets do not receive a step-up in basis at death. Like Roth IRAs, nonqualified annuities are not subject to required minimum distributions during the lifetime of the owner. The basic idea is that for annuitized contracts, payments will continue under the terms of the contract using an exclusion ratio, and that these pre-defined distributions will satisfy distribution requirements for the beneficiary. A portion of the payments will be classified as taxable income, while a portion continues to reflect the return of premium.

Owner-driven contracts and Annuitant-driven contracts

As a reminder from Chapter 5, the owner of an annuity makes decisions about it. The annuitant is the individual whose mortality is used to drive payments from mortality-based annuity contracts. If the owner and annuitant are the same individual, then the death of that individual will clearly pass any remaining annuity proceeds to the beneficiary. The problem is determining when the proceeds go to the beneficiary if the owner and annuitant are not the same person. If the contract is annuitant driven, then the beneficiary receives the contract proceeds when the annuitant dies, even if the owner is still alive. That might surprise the owner who would not necessarily expect to lose control of the death benefit. If the contract is owner driven, then the beneficiary receives the contract on the owner's death, even if the annuitant is still alive. This might also be a surprising outcome to an annuitant. Annuitant-driven contracts were more common before 1985, but since that time owner-driven contracts are the norm. Much of this problem can be solved by having the owner and annuitant be the same person.

But this issue can create complications with jointly-owned annuities. When we described a GLWB providing a joint lifetime income to a couple owning a deferred annuity, the natural expectation for the couple is that payments would continue to the surviving spouse upon the death of the first spouse. It is important that the insurance company designs the contract carefully to ensure this happens by identifying each spouse as the sole beneficiary in case the death of an owner triggers the passing of the contract to the beneficiary. A secondary beneficiary could then be added to receive any remaining death benefit after the deaths of both owners.

As for nonqualified deferred annuities, there are five possible options to guide required distributions that vary based on the type of beneficiary (spouse, non-spouse person, and non-person) and rules of the insurance company. These possibilities include receiving as a lump-sum, distributing over five years from the date of the owner's death, annuitizing the contract, stretching the contract out over a fixed life expectancy, and having a spouse who is the sole-beneficiary stepping in and treating the contract as his or her own. Spouses have the best option available to take over as owner and then do not have to worry about required distributions. Depending on the rules of the insurer, non-spousal beneficiaries may have to use the five-year rule, may annuitize the contract, or may use the lifetime stretch based on their fixed life expectancy that does not annuitize the contract and maintains flexibility to take out more than the minimum. This latter option is based on private letter rulings from the IRS that do not give universal authorization and is not accepted or used by all insurance companies. It is also not impacted by the SECURE Act, which removed this option for inherited IRAs. Non-person beneficiaries (such as estates, trusts, or charities) have up to five-years to take distributions. Deferred annuities continue to use the last-in first-out tax rules in which any contract gains are removed as taxable income before removing non-taxable principal, though private letter rulings have also been used to allow the lifetime stretch approach to also apply an exclusion ratio. For beneficiaries choosing the annuitization option, that would also trigger the use of the exclusion ratio for taxation. These matters are especially complicated, but I hope this introduction can give you a basic idea about the relevant issues.

Action Plan

As a review for the chapter, an action plan that incorporates the key aspects of legacy and incapacity planning includes:

- ☐ Collect personal information
- ☐ Create an inventory of household assets and liabilities
  - ○ Account numbers
  - ○ Values
  - ○ Ownership details
  - ○ Existing beneficiary designations
  - ○ Whether asset will be part of the probate estate
- ☐ Assemble information on all insurance policies
- ☐ Assign a durable financial power of attorney
- ☐ Create advance health care directives
  - ○ Living will
  - ○ Health care power of attorney
  - ○ HIPAA releases
- ☐ Decide how assets should be distributed: what, to whom (family, friends, charity, others), and when
- ☐ Write a will
  - ○ Identify executor
  - ○ Implement asset distribution plan
  - ○ Identify guardian for minors in your care
- ☐ Create and fund trusts to meet potential goals including incapacity planning, avoiding probate, managing property distribution at death, providing asset protection, and reducing estate taxes
  - ○ Identify trustees
  - ○ Ensure ownership and beneficiaries of assets are updated to include trust

- ☐ Review completely all ownership titles and beneficiary designations to ensure they are aligned with your goals and other estate planning documents such as wills and trusts
- ☐ Decide and share final wishes
- ☐ Create letter of instructions for family members, executor, trustees, and attorneys-in-fact to help simplify their process as much as possible by describing your whole financial situation and providing your wishes about a course of action
- ☐ Store these documents safely and let the relevant individuals know how to access the information when they need it, as well as discussing matters with those individuals and providing them with copies of appropriate documents
- ☐ Discuss your plans with family members so that everyone knows what to expect and potential conflicts are managed regarding your intentions, the disbursement of assets, access to key documents, and the roles and responsibilities of each person
- ☐ Review your estate planning at least every several years to see if updates are needed. Certain life triggers that should prompt reviews sooner include:
  - o Significant changes to household balance sheet
  - o Changes in family: births, deaths, marriages, divorces
  - o Move to a new state
  - o Changing relationships or death of individuals holding key roles in the estate plan
  - o Changes in law and tax code that impact the plan

Further Reading

American Bar Association. 2020. Tool Kit for Health Care Advance Planning. [https://www.americanbar.org/content/dam/aba/administrative/law_agi ng/2020-tool-kit-hcap.pdf]

Clifford, Denis. 2020. *Plan Your Estate*. 15th Edition. NOLO.

Cullen, Melanie. 2018. *Get It Together: Organize Your Records So Your Family Won't Have To*. 8th Edition. NOLO.

Hurme, Sally Balch. 2015. *Checklist for My Family: A Guide to My History, Financial Plans, and Final Wishes*. American Bar Association.

Olsen, John L., and Michael E. Kitces. 2014. *The Advisor's Guide to Annuities, 4th Edition*. Cincinnati: The National Underwriter Company.

Steuer, Tony. 2019. *Get Ready! A Step-by-Step Planner for Maintaining Your Financial First Aid Kit*. Alameda, CA: Life Insurance Safe Press.

Chapter 12: The Non-Financial Aspects of Retirement Success

Much of this book focuses on retirement finances. But finances are only one component for achieving retirement success. Equally important is crafting a plan to manage your retirement transition in a way that allows you to flourish and enjoy these years. Improved finances can help lay a foundation to make a great retirement possible. But if other non-financial aspects of retirement have been neglected, then having more money is not going to create a satisfying life.

It is important to cultivate a proper balance between work and other life pursuits, investing in your life as well as your career. If work is all that matters in your life, then retirement can mean death. For some, the proper balance can easily include working in retirement. Work and retirement can be compatible, as retirement is more about a state of mind.

Retirement is associated with having financial independence so that you can do what you want with your time. You do not have to be compelled to do certain things by a need to earn income. If working is what you want to do, then that is fine, but retirement provides a sense of freedom and flexibility to change your mind and do the things that bring you the most life satisfaction.

When looking beyond finances, a study by Merrill Lynch and Age Wave identified seven life priorities for retirees: Health, Home, Family, Work, Giving, Finances, and Leisure. Finances, which we cover throughout the book, are just one of these seven considerations. Home was also the topic of Chapter 9. This leaves five priorities for us to explore in this chapter: health, family, work, giving, and leisure. In this chapter we shift the question from "how can we efficiently fund our retirement goals?" into "what will I do in retirement?"

To provide more context, there are two general styles of books about retirement planning: those mostly focused on the financial side and those mostly focused on the non-financial side. Many of the non-financial books were written by recent retirees who developed a passion for sharing their experiences with navigating the day-to-day personal aspects of retirement by writing a book about it. I would suggest that if you are seeking a deeper exploration of the issues discussed in this chapter, you might also read Mike Bellah's *The Best is Yet to Be*, Don Ezra's *Life Two: How to Get to and Enjoy What Used to Be Called Retirement*, Fritz Gilbert's *Keys to a Successful*

Retirement, and Ernie Zelinski's *How to Retire Happy, Wild, and Free*. This chapter benefits from their experiences.

Money has value, but only up to a point. Planning on how to have a fulfilling and satisfying retirement lifestyle may only be tangentially related to finances. Once getting your basic life expenses covered, which is often possible to do with just a Social Security benefit, other aspects become more important. These include having purpose and passion, strong relationships, and a healthy lifestyle. The non-financial aspects may end up being more important than the finances, as people have a capability to adapt to their financial circumstances.

No matter income levels, people tend to report that they would feel very satisfied with 40 percent more income. But while further increases can lead to temporary satisfaction, we quickly return to our baseline satisfaction levels. That is why having 40 percent more continues to be the target. If not careful, this can put us on a hedonic treadmill where one needs more and more just to continue feeling the same. It is an attitude that is important to avoid. Money is often not the solution to dissatisfaction with retirement.

The financial and non-financial sides must strike a balance and can reinforce each other, as creating a stable financial situation is meant to provide the time and resources to focus on the non-financial considerations that make life worth living. Enjoying better health, stronger relationships, a sense of worth, and opportunities for fun make it easier to provide enough focus on work to build up the finances and to save on potential retirement costs.

Since this book is mostly about finances, another type of analogy may be helpful. With the financial side, the question becomes how to best position our resources to avoid running out of money during retirement. There are other types of non-financial assets that we also wish to avoid depleting, such as physical health, mental health, friendships, relationship with a partner or spouse, and maintaining a sense of purpose and satisfaction with life. With finances, we discuss things like asset allocation, Social Security claiming, whether to use an annuity and so forth, to create sustainability and efficiencies. But we also need to make sure to "invest" our time and energy into the non-financial aspects as well.

Exhibit 12.1 summarizes the types of changes that one can expect in retirement. Some of these may seem obvious, but it is worth identifying them to ensure they are not overlooked. For each change, the response could be viewed as positive or negative depending on your perspective, background, and attitude. Your feelings are legitimate either way. As well, some changes could initially be negative but gradually change to become positive, or the change could start out positive but then gradually become more negative. The objective of this chapter is to identify issues that could be negatives and to find ways to transform them into something positive to create the conditions for a better retirement.

Exhibit 12.1
Lifestyle Changes for Retirees

Retirement Change	Positive Response	Negative Response
Lose Work Identity and Sense of Purpose	Identify activities or goals that create purpose and passion for retirement to forge a new identity and become who you truly wish to be	Loss of work identity with no alternative interests can lead to depression and worsening health
Increase in Unstructured Time	Opportunity for new pursuits and interests, to be spontaneous, and to focus on health, hobbies, passions, and relationships	Lack of structure and focus leads to boredom and results in increased television watching, internet surfing, or other passive activities
Change in Routines	Focus on developing new routines to provide any needed structure to your days	Retirement is a life transition with the loss of habits and routines that can create great stress and reduced life satisfaction
Increased Time with Spouse	Opportunity to re-connect and pursue common interests as well as respect a separation for individual pursuits	Time together leads to greater conflict and worsening relationship with potential for grey divorce
Reduced Social Connections Through Work	Use additional time as opportunity to build and enhance relationships	Increased social isolation and loneliness risk depression and worsening health
Health and the Aging Process	Recognize aging as a natural part of life and maintain positive outlook, while also exercising and pursing activities to support physical and mental health	Less active lifestyle and worsening health status creates a negative feedback loop with stress and depression causing further physical and mental health decline

It is important to also address the emotional and quality of life aspects of retirement. Think about what you will do in retirement before you get there. Retirement happiness does extend beyond just having your financial situation under control. Adequate retirement finances are only part of the story for a successful retirement. We begin by discussing how to find a purpose or passion that will get you motivated to get up in the morning and getting going with the day. Then we look at the relationship between work and retirement, ways to strengthen relationships, and promoting an active and healthy lifestyle.

Finding Your Purpose and Passion

Retirement brings freedom to spend your days in a very different manner than before. A retiree is no longer required to be at work, performing work-related tasks. For successful retirements, this freedom will serve as a blessing and opportunity to become your true self. For unsuccessful retirements, this freedom may reflect a loss of routine and purpose that will become a curse. Creating a plan to manage the newfound freedom of retirement may ultimately determine whether a retirement is successful or unsuccessful. Unless work will be part of your retirement, you need to cultivate a life outside of work (activities, interests, relationships) before you get there.

It is a simple statement to make, but it is extremely important to recognize that being able to retire **to** something, instead of retiring **from** something, is a key starting point to retirement success. Retiring because you have grown tired of working, without having a clear idea about what you are going to do with your time after retiring can lead to depression and a lack of fulfillment for many new retirees. Not everyone is able to retire on his or her own terms, and we must consider the important distinctions between voluntary and involuntary retirements, but in either case you must find motivation to start each day. This is about understanding your passions and interests to create the best retirement experience.

Retirement offers the time and opportunity to do what you want and what you love. Finances can facilitate, but they are only part of the story. Retirement is a time in life designed to fulfill dreams. You want to find ways to spend time that will keep you engaged and feeling good while providing you with a sense of purpose and accomplishment. The hours of the week previously spent with work will need to be redirected. The novelty of retirement can wear off quickly in the absence of engaging activities.

The need to find a new purpose or passion in retirement may not become evident at the beginning of retirement. There can be a honeymoon phase early on as you enjoy your newfound freedoms to sleep in and not need to adhere to a specific schedule. As well, there may be a list of activities, such as specific trips or home renovation projects, that keeps you occupied for even the first year of retirement. But at some point, treating retirement as an extended vacation will grow tiresome for most retirees. The thrill of being retired will gradually wear off. There will need to be something else beyond simple leisure. If you do not know what that something will be, then you will need to figure it out. Ideally, planning for what you want to do in retirement will begin long before the time that being retired is your reality.

Before retirement, think carefully about your life dreams so you are better prepared to transform those dreams into reality with the time and opportunities afforded by retirement. You can begin this brainstorming process now. You may do a lot of daydreaming as you read through this chapter. What do you view as a perfect retirement? How would you spend a perfect day and a perfect week? What will you do and experience? Where will you be? How will you feel? What resources would it take to ensure this can happen? Try to map this out on a schedule or calendar to make it more concrete in terms of where the hours will go.

George Kinder identified similar thought exercises as part of his development of life planning. He says to imagine that at the start of retirement, a doctor informs you that you have five years left to live. The nebulous potential of living 30 to 40 years in retirement is shortened in a concrete way. What would this news do to your focus in retirement? What would you want to do, to accomplish, to see, to say, and to be during these final years? Even further, suppose the doctor informs you that you have just 48 hours left to live. In this case, what hopes and dreams can you let go, what would you wish you had accomplished or experienced, and what regrets would you have? Naturally, thinking through these matters can help to create a priority and emphasis to guide your actions in retirement. Make sure to do the things you identify as most important and make sure you will not have regrets about things left undone. We never know just how long our health and life will last, and though *on the financial side we must plan for the possibility of a long retirement, it is the non-financial side where we also need to plan for the possibility of a short retirement.* We need to prioritize what matters most and work from there.

How will you know what you want to do in retirement? An idea that Ernie Zelinski offers in his retirement book is to create a get-a-life tree. This is a mind map where you list out as many brainstorming ideas as you possibly can. The idea is to work from the center of the page by branching off at least three general concepts to which you link your ideas. One way to organize this is to identify things that interested you in the past, things that interest you now, and things you have considered doing. There could be sub-branches as well, such as for different types of physical activities, different trip destinations, or different types of classes that interest you. It is important to include all the main areas within this for a happy retirement, such as relationships to strengthen, activities that fulfill your purpose, and activities to keep you healthy. This brainstorming can prove valuable to clarify what will make your retirement a success.

Write down any dreams that cross your mind. Think about what gives you a feeling of "being in the zone," where you are focused on completing a goal and feel a sense of accomplishment afterward. Not everything you list must be realistic or affordable. But having a complete list will allow you to then focus on an action plan regarding what is truly the most important to you and for what can truly be accomplished. As a part of this, revisit your childhood dreams. With such dreams, if it is something you have put off doing for 50 years, recognize that you might not be likely to start, but there could be something from your childhood that can again capture your interest and heart.

Ernie's book lists hundreds of possible activities, but this brainstorming may work better if it comes from your own thoughts, as that may suggest it is something you will truly follow-through with rather than just being something that sounds nice. To give just a brief overview to get your thinking started, there may be hobbies or interests that you wish to re-devote yourself to in retirement, or there could be new activities that you have dreamed about and finally have the time to pursue. Examples may include playing a musical instrument, learning a new language, reading classical literature, playing a favorite sport, spending more time with friends, playing a more active role at civic or religious organizations, sitting in on college courses, creating art, cooking new recipes, committing to an exercise regime, writing a book, or maintaining a blog or website. You may also want to fulfill certain travel experiences, such as RV trips, international trips, cruises, staying at a cabin in the woods, or seeing different oceans, mountains, and cities. Figure out what truly matters to you, and what you have always wanted to do but never had the right opportunity to make it happen. As a side benefit, this process of planning and anticipating events can be just as important to creating life satisfaction as actually experiencing the event itself.

Defining legacy can also be an important part of determining your purpose. We considered the financial aspects of legacy planning in Chapter 11, but there are many other non-financial aspects of legacy as well. How would you like to make the world a better place? Possibilities include passing down family values to grandchildren, supporting worthy causes with your time, mentoring young professionals in your industry, tutoring children, writing a memoir or a recipe book, and so forth. You may volunteer with your time as well as your money. To consider your charitable intentions, you might think about where you have given in the past, where you wish to volunteer your time, and what you would like to change or preserve in the world. In addition to injecting passion and purpose, volunteering can create social connections which helps to improve health and life satisfaction in other ways as well.

When it comes to purpose and passion, for many individuals approaching retirement, it is entirely possible that continuing to work or coping with the loss of work will be an important part of the retirement landscape. Individuals whose lives revolve around work will have a hard time if retirement means not working. Work can be an important part of your purpose or passion, and we explore this further in the next section.

The Relationship between Work and Retirement

In the popular view, the key act that defines retirement is leaving work behind for a life of leisure. But there are many life changes related to stopping work, and so this version of retirement may not be best for everyone. Changes include the loss of work identity, the increase in unstructured time each day, and the loss of daily routines and structure associated with work. The purpose and identity provided by a career can disappear quickly after leaving. The social connections, camaraderie, responsibilities, income, structure, routines, and status provided through work will need to be replaced in other ways. This is especially true for those whose personal identity is closely linked to their careers and whose retirements may not have started voluntarily. If possible, try a test run of retirement before leaving work. Ideally you could try this for at least a month, but even if it is only a week, try as best as you can to avoid anything work related and see how you feel about the increased free time and lack of structure and whether retirement might be best for you. Retirement does not have to mean stopping work entirely.

An important additional consideration is the possibility that you might not be able to work for as long as you planned. Surveys consistently find that about half of retirees ended up retiring sooner than they had anticipated, as discussed in Chapter 2. These estimates were created before the global pandemic in 2020, which has also forced countless individuals into an early retirement. Retiring early was voluntary for some, but more common reasons include retiring due to poor health, involuntary job loss, or needing to provide care to other family members. Involuntary retirement can be traumatic for both the financial and non-financial aspects of life.

There is potential for any of the lifestyle changes associated with the end of work to create depression and stress for new retirees. The Holmes-Rahe Life Stress Inventory identifies 43 stressful life events and ranks "retirement from work" as the tenth most stressful event on their list. With a 45 point-score, the act of retiring gets one about a third of the way toward a score that suggests a 50 percent chance for a major health breakdown within the next two years. The loss of work identity and daily structure, as well as a paycheck, can create stress and requires adjustments. If retirement begins involuntarily, then it may be associated with "major personal injury or illness" (ranked 6th), "being fired at work" (ranked 8th), or "major change in the health or behavior of a family member" (ranked 11th). These events compound the stress of retirement.

Retirement is a stressful event because it involves change and new patterns. It is an end but also a beginning. The natural changes that accompany retirement can trigger uncertainty and stress as new ways of living are adopted. Not everyone is equally equipped to manage these transitions. While on this topic, moving can also be stressful, and moving at the start of retirement can compound this stress, and so you might not rush a move, or another major life change right at the start of retirement.

It is worth dwelling more on some of the negatives of leaving work. First is the impact of losing one's work identity. Many new retirees may feel a sense of loss as an important aspect of their identities is tied up with their work. Retirement can naturally disrupt this part of identity. The title shown on one's business card can be very important. Giving up that title can create a real sense of loss and even trauma. New retirees can feel as though they have lost power, status, and respect, changing overnight from somebody important into a nobody. Work also provides a routine and structure. It can be scary to deviate from these routines. This sense of loss can easily lead into depression. Retiring can be a mistake in situations where losses to prestige and stature cannot be recovered. The psychological stress and sense of loss related to retiring can lead to depression, addiction, and declining health.

It is important to recognize that these are normal feelings. The sense of loss is valid, and the response is important. Are you able to find new challenges and opportunities to replace the psychological benefits from work? If possible, try not to think about losing a work identity, but to focus more on what you can become. Retirement provides an opportunity to reimagine your identity and to reinvent yourself.

Traditional retirement may not be best for everyone. For some it may be best not to leave work. For others, after the initial honeymoon period of retirement has past, the best decision may be to return to some type of work. This can be a bigger issue for those whose work ends involuntarily. Having a job may be necessary for mental health even if the finances are otherwise under control. If what you do is who you are, then it can make sense to simply not want to retire from who you are. That is the sense where retirement is more about the freedom to do as you wish, and so working can provide a sense of purpose while having financial independence can give a sense of being retired at the same time. You do not have to feel compelled to leave work just because you reach a particular age or meet a wealth target. You still have the freedom to decide that you would like to keep working, understanding that it is what you want to do and not because of economic necessity.

As we consider our interests and habits, an important step in the transition toward retirement is to consider your relationship with work. It can be too limiting to think that retirement always means the cessation of work. Some individuals will want to retire and never look back. Some individuals will want to keep working. Some will be excited to retire but soon find themselves wanting to go back to work once the initial exhilaration of retirement has passed. Some will plan all along to continue working but in a different capacity. It is important to understand that work can provide a source of enjoyment, a sense of purpose, a way to stay active and involved, a way to develop social connections, a way to maintain routines, and a source of additional spending money.

Some people enjoy working and do not wish to stop, at least not entirely. There is no judgment. You will not receive a call from the retirement police if you decide to return to work. It is fine to do what brings you fulfillment. For some, work can be an important part of one's identity, and losing this can be quite difficult. In addition to the obvious monetary benefits, working can also provide a sense of importance, status, and self-worth, social interactions, and routines and activities to get through each day. The social engagement and activity of work can be good for one's health. Those who have reached financial independence have more flexibility to make decisions about these issues. One may decide to leave work entirely, to just cut back on hours, to switch to a completely unrelated field, or perhaps to become more active with volunteer work as an alternative.

Working and Retirement Finances

Though I am trying to keep financial considerations out of this chapter, it is worth recognizing that continued work is one of the most powerful ways to improve the sustainability of a retirement income plan for those who may be falling short. Working longer allows for more savings, and for existing savings to grow for longer before being tapped. Because wealth is at its largest, hopefully, in the pre-retirement years, the compounded returns from investments before distributions begin can have a huge impact on the number of dollars available for retirement. And then, as one works longer, the subsequent retirement period will be shorter and easier to fund. Working longer may also make it easier to enjoy the benefits of deferring Social Security and it may help increase benefits from any other employer pension plans. Working longer also maintains more options for managing a market downturn. For those receiving health insurance through work, these benefits may also help manage retirement costs. Stanford University released a study in 2018 which showed that working 3-6 months longer has an equivalent impact as increasing one's savings rate by 1 percent for 30 years. Even working for just one additional month has the same impact as a 1 percent increase in the savings rate for the last 10 years before retirement. Many of these advantages can also be realized through part-time work in retirement, which reduces the pressure to take distributions from investments in the early retirement years. Those who are thinking that they may wish to work longer before retiring can also take comfort in knowing the benefits this will have for their finances.

To better understand the connections between retirement and work, Lynda Gratton and Andrew Scott describe three types of intangible assets in their book, *The 100-Year Life*. Intangible assets are aspects of our lives that extend beyond financial wealth. First are productive assets, such as skills, knowledge, and investments in human capital. Second are vitality assets, which include aspects of mental and physical health, such as family and friends, personal fitness, and mental well-being. Third are transformational assets. These relate to having options to make changes or adjustments in life, such as a broad network of contacts and an openness to new experiences. All three categories of intangible assets are important for transitioning into a successful retirement. It is not about accumulating financial assets alone.

We can think more broadly about work. Retirement as the end of working may be antiquated. It may be better viewed as achieving *financial independence* such that one no longer feels compelled to engage in a certain type of work because of financial concerns. In this framework, retirement does not necessarily mean retiring from work. It just expands the opportunities available to find a new balance that allows for even more emphasis to be placed on the non-financial aspects of life. And it is important not to ignore these non-financial aspects while still working; you need to "invest" in them as well or your satisfaction with retirement could be at risk. As lifespans increase, there will more time and opportunities to achieve this balance in different ways.

This discussion about balancing work and retirement is relatively new in human history. Even the concept of retiring completely in one's 60s may turn out to be a unique circumstance of the late 20th century. For most of human history, retirement did not really exist. People worked until they no longer could, and if still alive but physically unable to work, they may have spent a few final years in the care of family members. Suddenly, then, with the expansion of pension systems and improved longevity, a more enjoyable 10-to-15-year retirement became possible.

With the prosperity created after World War II, there was a growth in motivations to retire and enjoy leisure activities at the end of life. Employers facilitated this through defined-benefit pensions as an employee benefit that pooled longevity and market risk for their retired employees. Now as traditional pensions decline in availability and as 10 to 15 years of retirement change into the possibility of 30 to 40 years, the burden of saving enough to fund retirement may be too great for many individuals to manage. As people continue to live longer, the concept of retirement may change. Retirements may evolve to incorporate work in different ways. On the non-financial side, 30 to 40 years is also a long time to fill up with purely non-work activities.

People quickly shifted from not living long enough to have much worry about funding retirement, to living too long and being unable to save enough to drop completely out of the workforce. For those falling behind, continuing part-time work, or maintaining the option to return to the work force are also important building blocks for retirement income.

Lynda Gratton and Andrew Scott write in *The 100-Year Life* that as longevity improves people may find themselves working into their 70s or 80s. But they describe how changes to our traditional model of retirement may make this idea less potentially shocking than it seems. As people live even longer, lives will shift away from the three phases of education, work, and retirement, into a more dynamic and multi-state process in which breaks may be taken throughout life to rest and to learn new skills with the possibility of having multiple different careers. Working until one is in their 70s or 80s will be hard if there is no time to balance work with the non-financial considerations of life, which may lead to taking short "retirement" breaks throughout life and perhaps even start new careers after each break. Those already at retirement age today may be at the start of these trends, as we do already see many cases of having an "encore" career in retirement.

Even when earning income no longer is a primary motive for working, many people choose to return to work, perhaps after the honeymoon phase of retirement has concluded. For those in retirement, voluntarily wanting to work is more common than needing to work for the money. Many people simply find that they enjoy working, and they miss the aspects of life that work provided. Working in retirement could be full time or part time, and it could be paid or voluntary. Returning to the same employer could be done on a part-time or temporary basis, as a consultant, or in other ways dreamed up with the employer. Returning to the same full-time work is not necessarily needed to obtain the social aspects and sense of accomplishment that one had with their work. As well, qualifying for Medicare at age 65 means there is no need to stay bound to a full-time career for the purpose of obtaining health insurance.

A first possibility is a phased retirement. Phased retirements are formal arrangements with your current employer to allow a shift from full-time to part-time work. It is still uncommon for employers to have these employment models in place, but those with valuable skills may be able to create a suitable arrangement that can combine the best aspects of work with an increase in leisure time and opportunities to pursue non-work interests as well. While phased retirements imply a temporary transition into retirement with the same employer, holding a bridge job or other temporary position provides another possibility to support a gradual transition to retirement.

Another possibility is to develop an encore career that may be more related to personal satisfaction than to making money. You may wish to consult in the same industry where you built your career and have developed strong professional skills. But encore careers could relate to something entirely different. Pursuing a new line of work could relate to an interest or hobby. You might serve as a mentor or teacher. You might provide leadership to a non-profit organization.

The encore career could be a way to unleash your entrepreneurial spirit. Perhaps you have assembled a portfolio of investment properties to manage. You might even want to take advantage of opportunities in the gig economy, setting your own hours for a task that will provide some income as well as a broader range of social connections. You may also wish to engage in seasonal work, which allows for a clearer delineation between time for retirement and time for work. Seasonal jobs could also relate to one's interests, such as working in a national park or other vacation destination. Volunteer work could be another outlet if the goals for work relate more toward pursuing passions than to the need for financial remuneration. There are many possibilities available.

For those interested in continuing to work, there are important steps to take to better ensure the marketability of one's skills. This can involve keeping up to date with new technologies and acquiring new skills. As well, maintaining work networks can be an important way to keep current with potential opportunities. As well, though many near retirement will find it hard to replace work lost to the pandemic, there may be some opportunities that emerge. As remote working becomes more common and accepted, this may fit into the retirement lifestyle more easily as it will be increasingly possible to continue with some types of work from anywhere, such as while traveling in an RV. Geography is not a constraint.

Strengthening Relationships and Social Connections

Maintaining social connections and having a network of social support in place is an important aspect of retirement. Loneliness can create negative health and cognitive impacts and can shorten lives. For those with partners or spouses, a lot more time may be spent together after retiring. As well, as children grow up and leave the home, there may be new strains for a couple to manage their newfound time together. Beyond the household, retirees have fewer naturally occurring ways to be socially connected. Greater effort will be needed for social interactions in the absence of work. These are issues to address before retiring.

For social relationships, an important starting point is the relationship between spouses. Spousal relationships can change dramatically with the increased amount of time spent together after retirement. New strains can develop as well during a transition period where one member of the couple retires while the other continues work. A stay-at-home spouse can also be impacted by having their routines changed with a retired spouse now at home all day. Spending more time together can have positive or negative impacts depending on circumstances.

Relationship strains are a real risk at the start of retirement. Grey divorce is on the rise. Couples may tend to grow apart over time. Childrearing may have bonded them with common purpose, but this is no longer a consideration once the children have grown. As well, spouses are less financially dependent on each other, and spouses may have different visions about retirement that become irreconcilable.

Communication between spouses will be important. Spouses may need to reacquaint themselves. Spouses need to understand each other's dreams for retirement and to find common ground on how both sets of dreams can be achieved. Further issues for discussion including retirement timing, finances, changing roles, ideas about spending time together as well as time apart, thoughts about social life and how outgoing each spouse wishes to be (especially if moving in retirement), other family obligations, where to live, where and when to travel, legacy plans, and end-of-life care.

Don Ezra describes a simple Venn diagram illustrated in Exhibit 12.2 that I found to be a very insightful way to approach the impact that retirement can have on the relationship with one's spouse. What do you want from retirement? What does your partner or spouse want from retirement? Which aspects can be accomplished together? Which aspects are separate? How can the couple work together to make sure that each spouse's independent goals and dreams also receive sufficient attention?

Create a shared vision for retirement and then figure out which aspects overlap to be done together as a couple, and which aspects may be done separately as individuals. Each circle represents an individual in the couple. For the parts of the circles that do not overlap, this reflects time and activities spent apart from one another. The middle overlapping part is where to list the time and activities that will be spent together. How much of the circles overlap can vary, but it is important to at least have a sense that both spouses are comfortable with the portions spent alone and the portions spent together.

Exhibit 12.2
Time Management for a Couple

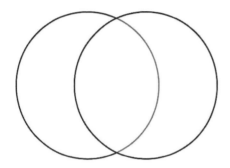

There are many other relationships with family and friends for retirees to also consider. Retirees need to feel a sense of community and belonging. Friendships can provide continuity in life to help manage negative life events such as the death of loved ones or the development of health problems. But it can be more difficult to maintain connections after retirement, especially those flowing from work.

A helpful way to plan for social connections is to maintain and update a friends list, identifying friends, family, co-workers, or other connections that remain important in retirement. You can identify the strengths of these relationships and think about which relationships you may like to strengthen further. Think about how you can reach out and strengthen these relationships starting now. Perhaps you could arrange weekly meetups for a meal or other socializing. Do not wait until after retiring to get started on this. It is an area where you may think that having more time available after retiring will make it possible to fill in gaps and fix problems that develop during the working years. But neglected relationships are not always easy to repair.

It does seem like a lot of the books about the non-financial aspects of retirement were written by extroverts. Not everyone will have an easy time making new friends at this stage of life. Those who may have been devoted to their work may enter retirement without many friends and may have lost the skills for finding new friends. This may also impact decisions around moving in retirement, as some may find it more difficult to create new social networks at this stage in life. As well as actively seeking to reach out to new neighbors, perhaps joining organizations designed around a common interest or investigating the potential for making connections at an active adult community could be helpful.

On these points, the global pandemic and its need for social distancing have changed aspects for how people connect. New technologies have made it easier to keep in touch remotely, when in-person meetings would create greater risk. But these technologies over the longer term could increase isolation by providing more remote monitoring that reduces need for human contact. These possibilities include health monitors, driverless cars, and smart homes. For many, a digital connection will have less value than in-person connections. As well, social media and the internet enhance addiction risks with algorithms designed to keep you scrolling, reducing the strength of real-world connections. Loneliness can worsen health and lead to an early death. Retirees must fight this rising tide to maintain their personal relationships.

Healthy and Active Lifestyle

Though more time may be available each day, retirees also need to make greater effort to be active and to engage in a healthy lifestyle. There will be fewer naturally occurring opportunities for physical and mental activity without taking the initiative to make things happen. Falling into the trap of spending too much time watching television is a risk. As well, though the idea of declining health can be overblown, it is the case that the natural aging process can lead to reduced mobility and declining vision, hearing, and cognitive skills, among other possibilities. Recognizing and adapting positively to these natural changes is important for ongoing health.

There is an important distinction between mortality and morbidity. Mortality regards the length of life, while morbidity refers to health during life. As people live longer, are they doing so in good health, or do they experience more years of bad health? The objective of a healthy and active lifestyle is to better support the conditions for a longer *and* healthier life.

It is not too late to improve health habits through diet and basic exercise, even if these are areas that you have been neglecting. Benefits from exercise and diet can arrive quickly. But that is not an invitation to continue to procrastinate on health matters. Invest in your health, including exercise, nutrition, sleep, and preventative care. Work on maintaining your health before you retire so that you will still have as much of it as possible after retiring. Do not wait until retirement to begin an exercise regime. This is another topic where the idea that retirement will provide the extra time needed to accomplish items on your to-do list may not be the case. Matters could get worse without making the necessary initiative and effort.

Exercise does not have to be overly strenuous to yield powerful benefits. Frequent moderate exercise that focuses on distance rather than speed is fine to get the basic health benefits of exercise. Work to get outside and engage in activities like walking, biking, or swimming. Having simple daily exercise routines can also be important for mental health. A daily exercise routine can be a source of structure in retirement that may help replace the structure that had been provided through work.

Exercise can also apply to one's mind. Exercising the brain may help to maintain cognitive abilities. Not providing challenges for your brain can cause it to atrophy in the same way that a lack of exercise can lead to physical decline. Ways to stimulate your brain include writing, reading, studying a language, attending classes, playing word games, playing a musical instrument, volunteering, and seeking new experiences.

As well, taking care of health means getting appropriate health screenings and taking advantage of other preventative care benefits through Medicare or other health insurance. Seek treatment to help with any reduced functions related to vision, hearing, or other matters. It is important to remember that aging does not automatically lead to illness and dependency, and though a degree of physical decline is inevitable, staying fit and active can help prolong the healthy portion of one's life. Focusing on health can create positive reinforcements to have more energy and motivation to be successful with other aspects of retirement.

Mental health is another important aspect of retirement. Retirement can create many pitfalls that can lead to depression, loneliness, addiction, and even suicide. This may especially be the case when retirement is triggered by poor health, involuntary job loss, or a need to provide care to a partner or aging parents. Those who retired before they were ready may go through a grieving process. These can be stressful events. Retirement can intensify stress and increase feelings of depression, and it is important to have strategies to help manage these feelings. There is always a risk for negative life events, and this continues for retirees who may be subject to age discrimination, illness, or the loss of a friend or loved one.

Even beyond these stresses, part of the difficulty of a retirement transition is that much of the popular culture presents it as a wonderful time in life with walks along the beach and spending happy time with grandchildren. An important component of retirement satisfaction relates to the expectations for retirement one has developed beforehand. Those whose experiences do not live up to these expectations may feel a sense of isolation and feeling that something is wrong with them. It is important to understand that it is very common to have mixed feelings about retirement, either right away or with a delay after the honeymoon portion.

It is tempting to think that retiring will provide the time needed to solve existing problems, but it is also possible that the extra time provided by retirement can make existing problems worse. Retirement does not necessarily solve lingering or ongoing issues. Procrastination can still occur, and retirees may feel even more guilty about not getting things done after retiring. This can intensify feelings of uselessness and not having anything interesting to do.

Understand that transitioning into retirement can take time and energy. It is okay if things do not click right away, though it is important not to let negative feelings become overwhelming in a way that makes it hard to improve one's situation. This does not all have to be negative. On average, mental health and life satisfaction tends to improve with age once people get to their 50s. Older individuals have more life experiences to help provide resilience for coping with negative events. Retirement can also provide more opportunity to focus on religious faith and spiritual health. Experience and wisdom grow with age. Being optimistic about aging can help manage some of the potential downsides related to cognitive and physical decline, and it is important to try and maintain a positive outlook.

Retirement Spending – Ants and Grasshoppers

This chapter has emphasized that having a balanced life portfolio is just as important as a balanced financial portfolio. For seeking a life balance, it is worth revisiting the old parable of the ants and the grasshopper. In the context of retirement, ants are those who tend to over save and underspend. They may become overly prepared for retirement, and their innate focus on preservation may make it difficult to fully enjoy their retirement years. Grasshoppers, meanwhile, tend not to worry about the future. They may not have sufficient savings for retirement, though they may be able to adapt their finances and be okay overall.

Readers of this book will have a natural tendency to be ants. Saving and preserving wealth may be a source of satisfaction, but ants may still worry about whether they are striking the right balance between enjoying the present and feeling comfortable about the future. This is a reminder for ants that there is more to retirement than finances, and it is important not to neglect these non-financial aspects of life. Investing in a more diversified "portfolio" of life experiences can lay the foundation for the most overall satisfaction with retirement.

Action Plan

Quality of life in retirement is an important topic existing side-by-side with finances. The focus on the financial side of retirement implicitly assumes that the personal and psychological aspects of retirement have been addressed elsewhere. However, it is important to make sure these issues have indeed been addressed. Retirees seek purpose and satisfaction. These are key steps to guide the way:

- ☐ Find purpose and passion to guide your retirement
  - o Identify expectations for a good retirement life
  - o Retire *to* something, not *from* something
  - o Identify fulfilling activities to replace work identity
  - o Develop leisurely interests while still working
  - o Prioritize your activities to make sure the most important items get accomplished while you have time and health

- o   Consider your legacy beyond financial gifts
- ☐ Strike the right balance with work
  - o   Understand the importance of your work identity
  - o   Buy into retirement as a new lifestyle and new identity
  - o   Maintain your skills and networking to create flexibility
  - o   Consider whether work will play a role in your retirement
  - o   Prepare for an unexpected jolt into an early retirement
- ☐ Strengthen your relationships with others
  - o   Reconnect with spouse and identify retirement dreams
  - o   Focus on friendships and other relationships
  - o   Engage in activities to maintain social ties
- ☐ Promote an active and healthy lifestyle
  - o   Develop exercise routines and a healthy diet
  - o   Keep your body and mind active
  - o   Take care of physical and mental health
  - o   Have appropriate expectations for gradual decline
  - o   Focus on spiritual and religious needs
  - o   Build structure into your day as needed to feel comfort

Further Reading

Bellah, Mike. 2019. *The Best is Yet to Be: Discovering the Secret to a Creative, Happy Retirement*. Canyon, TX: BestYears Press.

Ezra, Don. 2019. *Life Two: How to Get to and Enjoy What Used to Be Called Retirement*. Don Ezra Consulting Services.

Gilbert, Fritz. 2020. *Keys to a Successful Retirement: Staying Happy, Active, and Productive in Your Retired Years*. Emeryville, CA: Rockridge Press.

Gratton, Lynda, and Andrew Scott. 2016. *The 100-Year Life: Living and Working in an Age of Longevity*. London: Bloomsbury Information.

Zelinski, Ernie. 2019. *How to Retire Happy, Wild, and Free: Retirement Wisdom You Won't Get From Your Financial Advisor*. Edmonton: Visions International Publishing.

Chapter 13: Putting It All Together

We have worked through the important decisions for navigating a successful retirement. To review, these include:

- [ ] Determine your retirement income style
- [ ] Assess exposure to various retirement risks, including choosing your planning age and discount rate
- [ ] Quantify your financial goals (your budget, legacy, reserves) and assess your preparedness with the funded ratio
- [ ] Understand strategies for sustainable spending from investments
- [ ] Understand strategies using annuities with risk pooling
- [ ] Develop a claiming strategy for Social Security
- [ ] Manage health care and Medicare decisions
- [ ] Plan for long-term care risks
- [ ] Decide about retirement housing and housing wealth
- [ ] Build tax-efficient retirement distribution plans
- [ ] Create plans for legacy and incapacity
- [ ] Prepare for the non-financial aspects of retirement
  - o Find your purpose and passion
  - o Understand your relationship with work
  - o Strengthen social relationships
  - o Maintain a healthy and active lifestyle

Now it is time to fit these pieces together into an overall planning approach to achieve financial and non-financial success in retirement. In this chapter I organize the previous discussions into an integrated series of steps to be prepared for your best retirement. It is time to implement and monitor your retirement plan. The simple act of proactively planning for retirement can improve satisfaction and happiness. Risks become less nebulous, and comfort can be taken knowing you have a plan in place.

Getting Started Now

Some readers may still be twenty years away from retirement. Others may be just on the precipice. Some may have retired several years ago. In addition to everyone facing different circumstances and situations, it is not possible to provide a universal checklist that applies equally for everyone. What I aim to do in this chapter is to organize retirement planning steps as best I can under the basic assumption that the reader is still several years away from retiring. As you work through the tasks of this chapter, please keep in mind that it may be necessary to make some adjustments in the ordering of these tasks, and some matters may not be relevant or may have already been accomplished. In this section we address some initial steps as one begins the transition toward retirement.

Organizing your Finances and Preparing Estate and Incapacity Plans

The legacy and incapacity planning discussion in Chapter 11 provides an important initial step for retirement planning. Not only does it help with risk management for your family if you tend to be the one who manages the finances, but it also provides you with the opportunity to get your finances organized. This becomes very important when taking a subsequent step to determine your funded ratio for retirement. If you have procrastinated on developing your estate plan, it is important to get started on this as soon as possible. The action plan for legacy and incapacity planning includes:

- ☐ Collect personal information for family members
- ☐ Create an inventory of household assets and liabilities
  - o Account numbers
  - o Values
  - o Ownership details
  - o Existing beneficiary designations
  - o Whether assets will be part of the probate estate
- ☐ Assemble information on all insurance policies
  - o Review whether each policy is still needed
  - o Review whether some insurance need has not been fulfilled (life insurance, health, long-term care, disability, homeowner, vehicle, umbrella)
  - o Ask insurer for in-force illustrations on life insurance policies to assess the current situation
- ☐ Assign a durable financial power of attorney
- ☐ Create advance health care directives
  - o Living will
  - o Health care power of attorney
  - o HIPAA releases
- ☐ Decide how assets should be distributed: what, to whom (family friends, charity, others), and when
- ☐ Write a will
  - o Identify executor
  - o Implement asset distribution plan
  - o Identify guardian for minors in your care
- ☐ Create and fund trusts to meet potential goals including incapacity planning, avoiding probate, managing property distribution at death, providing asset protection, and reducing estate taxes
  - o Identify trustees
  - o Ensure ownership and beneficiaries of assets are updated to include trust
- ☐ Fully review ownership titles and beneficiary designations to ensure they are aligned with your goals and other estate planning documents such as wills and trusts

☐ Decide and share final wishes

☐ Create letter of instructions for family members, executor, trustees, and attorneys-in-fact to help simplify their process as much as possible by describing your whole financial situation and providing your wishes about a course of action

☐ Store these documents safely and let the relevant individuals know how to access the information when they need it, as well as discussing matters with those individuals and providing them with copies of appropriate documents

☐ Discuss your plans with family members so that everyone knows what to expect and potential conflicts are managed regarding your intentions, the disbursement of assets, access to key documents, and the roles and responsibilities of each person

Planning for How to Claim Social Security

Choosing your Social Security claiming strategy is a key part of building a retirement income plan. The benefit application can be done online, by phone, or in person at a Social Security office. Though Social Security claiming is just one step in building a retirement income plan, the value of lifetime Social Security benefits can dwarf many other retirement assets. Thought and care are needed to determine how to claim Social Security in the most effective manner for the household. Here are key steps to take:

☐ Obtain your updated Social Security Statement at ssa.gov

☐ Check your statement's earnings history for accuracy and understand the assumptions used for estimating your benefits
  o future covered earnings
  o economy-wide wage growth and inflation

☐ Familiarize yourself with the basic claiming philosophies

☐ Collect the relevant information for making a claiming decision
  o Benefits from your earnings record: spouse & dependents
  o Your eligibility for benefits from other's earnings records: spouse, ex-spouse, survivor
  o Role of earnings test, windfall elimination provision, government pension offset, disability benefits
  o Availability of resources to support delayed claiming
  o Dependence on Social Security as reliable income
  o Risk tolerance
  o If you already claimed and regret this, identify possibilities for suspending benefits

☐ Use software to calculate the optimal claiming strategy and compare with other options

☐ Build a strategy to support deferring benefits when applicable
  o Identify how to meet spending goals before benefits begin (portfolio distributions, part-time work, reverse mortgage, life insurance, period-certain annuity, bond ladder)
  o Consider tax planning opportunities while deferring

Tax Planning Steps

The progressive nature of the tax code makes tax-planning strategies important to sustaining retirement assets. When you still have the opportunity in the pre-retirement accumulation years, there are steps you can take to prepare for tax management in retirement:

- ☐ Understand the basics of the tax code, including marginal tax rates and tax brackets, how taxable income is determined, and the differences between ordinary income tax rates and preferential rates for long-term capital gains and qualified dividends
- ☐ Build tax diversification for the asset base by saving with taxable, tax-deferred, and tax-exempt accounts
- ☐ Understand how to choose between saving in tax-deferred and tax-exempt accounts as based on whether the marginal tax rate will be higher now or in the future, and after considering the advantages of having some assets in tax-exempt accounts
- ☐ Work through asset location decisions to position assets based on their tax efficiency and long-term growth prospects
- ☐ Determine usefulness of other ways to obtain tax advantages, such as education 529 plans, health savings accounts, tax-advantaged bonds, nonqualified annuities, and life insurance

Retirement Housing Decisions

Housing decisions are also very important for retirement planning. The following action plan relates to making the right housing decisions:

- ☐ Identify the aspects of retirement housing that are most important
- ☐ Begin thinking about housing options in advance of retirement and determine whether a move will be part of your plan
- ☐ Conduct trials in any new area to make sure it is the right decision
- ☐ Make housing decisions in anticipation that physical and mental impairments associated with aging will impact your needs
- ☐ Understand how housing decisions could be impacted by long-term care needs and how moving becomes more difficult with age
- ☐ Consider how frequently you want to move and at what point you want or need to consider a last, permanent move. When you reach the point where the current or next home is likely to be permanent, assess the following factors:
  - o The home is affordable and the home-related costs, as well as how they may change with age, are budgeted
  - o The home is near family, friends, or a social network that can help prevent growing isolation at later ages
  - o The home provides an agreeable climate with the right blend of activities and opportunities to have an enjoyable retirement lifestyle
  - o The home is in a location that supports any desired work or volunteer opportunities

- o The home is accessible to health facilities and long-term care opportunities
- o The community provides diverse transportation options
- o Home renovations are done to support aging in place
- o For those owning an eligible home, consider whether to incorporate a HECM early on as part of an overall strategy rather than treating it as a last-resort option

Assess your Financial Situation for Retirement

The next steps relate to getting a big picture view for how you will approach retirement planning and whether you have sufficient funds to meet your financial goals, or whether you are at least on track with projected future income included. Working toward this, it is quite important to first have a sense of your retirement income style. You can assess this on your own, or you may take up my offer to use the Retirement Income Style Awareness® tool. You aim to:

- ☐ Understand the factors to identify retirement income preferences and how they interact to define retirement income styles
- ☐ Determine your RISA Profile, which is your preferred style for generating retirement income

The next matter is to assess your risks for retirement income. The amount of assets required to fund your financial goals in retirement depends on how long you live, your investment returns, and your exposure to various shocks. You will want to choose a planning age and a discount rate as an assumed investment return. Greater conservatism for your assumptions is suggested for those with a Distribution mindset and a preference for Back-Loading. You will also want to think about your exposure to different types of retirement shocks. Begin thinking about your retirement risk exposure:

- ☐ Obtain longevity estimates using a tool such as the Longevity Illustrator [www.longevityillustrator.org]
  - o Those with a front-loading preference may prefer to use numbers closer to the 25th percentile of outcomes
  - o Those with a back-loading preference may prefer numbers closer to the 10th percentile of outcomes
- ☐ Market and sequence-of-return risk
  - o Understand your comfort level with market risk as it relates to your retirement income style
  - o Decide on reasonable net-return assumptions for your retirement portfolio. The starting point is the current yield on long-term Treasury Inflation-Protected Securities
- ☐ Assess exposures to various retirement spending shocks and other surprises. As part of this assessment, consider the potential costs or impacts that these risks could create:
  - o Long-term care risks
  - o Health care and prescription costs

- Inflation
- Death of a spouse
- Unexpected family-related financial responsibilities
- Divorce
- Changing public policy and tax rules
- Business risk for annuities and pensions
- Excess withdrawal risk
- Frailty and declining cognitive abilities
- Financial elder abuse
- Changing housing needs
- Forced early retirement and reduced earnings capacity

Two of the largest spending shocks for retirement relate to long-term care and health expenses. You will want to settle on estimates about additional desired reserves to manage these shocks. Those with a true liquidity preference will wish to be more explicit about setting aside specific reserve assets for these risks. These are the key steps related to long-term care:

☐ Identify the long-term care options and costs in your community
☐ Consider how other budgeted expenses, such as travel, may be reduced if long-term care is needed
☐ Decide where you would like to receive care. Are CCRCs a consideration?
☐ Understand what your default plan of care will be if you do not take further action. This includes taking an inventory of what you have:
  - Traditional long-term care insurance policies
  - Permanent life insurance with long-term care benefits
  - Family members and friends who may be willing and able to help without creating too much burden
  - Reserves earmarked to cover long-term care expenses
  - The level of countable assets that would be spent before reaching Medicaid eligibility in your state
☐ Identify the potential to self-fund long-term care expenses and the impacts this could have on other family members
☐ Identify a reasonable amount of reserve assets to set aside as a funding source for long-term care
  - Is this amount realistic?
  - How will it be invested?
  - Do family members understand and accept the obligation if you are expecting them to provide care?
☐ Determine whether Medicaid may be unavoidable as part of your long-term care plan. Consult with an elder-law attorney to assist with Medicaid planning as needed
☐ If interested to offset some of the spending risk related to self-funding, explore a variety of options to include traditional long-term care insurance or hybrid approaches
  - Will your health allow you to qualify for coverage?

- How much of the long-term care spending risk would you like to offset through insurance?
  - How much of the risk can you afford to offset?
  - Will you pay for coverage with investment assets or through the exchange of existing insurance policies?
  - How much would the coverage lower your need to hold reserves for self-funding while still feeling comfortable?
- ☐ When considering insurance, determine what makes the most sense regarding the tradeoffs between premiums and the periodic benefit amounts, total coverage, inflation adjustments, and elimination period
  - Traditional long-term care insurance may appeal to those who can obtain tax deductions for premiums, may use a partnership plan to provide further asset protection for Medicaid, and wish to include inflation protection riders
  - Hybrid policies may appeal to those seeking stability for premium amounts, protections for the use-it-or-lose-it aspect, have health issues that make it hard to qualify for traditional insurance, and have existing insurance available that could be exchanged to these policies
- ☐ Provide family members with your written plan for long-term care so they can easily implement it if you are cognitively impaired. The plan includes details about sources of care, sources of funds, insurance policies, and any professionals who may be available to answer questions, such as a care coordinator provided by an insurance policy

Health expenses are also a major component of retirement spending. Precise expenses can be hard to estimate and become more uncertain through health spending shocks not covered through insurance. The action plan for health care in retirement relates to finding the appropriate health care and prescription drug coverage and having a plan to cover health care related expenses. At this stage:

- ☐ Develop estimates for a baseline health care budget, how it may grow, and potential cost shifting from other categories
- ☐ Make sure you have budgeted for dental, vision, hearing, or other types of health-related needs that may not be covered by your insurance choices
- ☐ Decide how much in reserves you want to set aside to help with higher than anticipated expenses
- ☐ Review the "Leaving employment" section if you are transitioning away from employer-based insurance before Medicare eligibility

Now we can look more directly at providing an overall determination of your funded status by calculating the funded ratio of assets to liabilities. The following action items summarize the key steps for quantifying your goals and assessing your retirement preparedness:

- [ ] Estimate the Four Ls of retirement: longevity, lifestyle, legacy, and liquidity
    - o Collect data on spending over the previous few years
    - o Use past spending and analyze what will change in retirement to develop a baseline retirement budget
    - o Organize the retirement budget as essential longevity expenses and discretionary lifestyle expenses
    - o Project how spending needs may evolve
    - o Determine legacy goals
    - o Assess exposure to spending shocks to determine a target for reserves
- [ ] Build a retirement balance sheet by collecting household finances and determining all assets and liabilities, including the present value for income and expenses that happen in the future
- [ ] Choose a planning age and conservative discount rate to apply to the funded ratio calculations, and then calculate the funded ratio
- [ ] Take special care to also note the level of funded ratio with reliable income for longevity goals, along with other categories of the RIO-Map. For styles other than total return, seek to fill gaps in reliable income (annuities, bond ladders)
- [ ] In situations where a plan is underfunded, consider taking one or more of these steps to ensure a reasonable funded ratio:
    - o Delay retirement or otherwise add a greater role for work
    - o Reduce projected future spending goals
    - o Those with styles that de-emphasize the role for market growth and use more conservative assumptions will generally find an improved funded ratio with annuities
    - o Reassess the role for home equity in the plan
    - o Assume a higher discount rate (with caveats about risk)

A Note about Online Retirement Calculators

There are many online retirement calculators intended for use by do-it yourself individuals. I have not discussed them for three reasons.

First, I simply prefer to do my own calculations and have not spent much time investigating other options.

Second, I hold the view that the funded ratio method is good enough for most situations. Once you have made the effort to estimate your budget, your Social Security strategy, your collection of assets and liabilities, and a way to estimate taxes, then a simple spreadsheet to calculate the relevant present values to create a funded ratio tells you what you need. There is not much need to also worry about Monte Carlo simulations and the probability of plan success. The equivalent for success rates with the funded ratio would be to increase the discount rate above the level of TIPS yields, which will imply a chance of underperformance for your assets relative to the discount rate and, therefore, a risk of failure. But if the assumed discount rate is a conservative number that you are comfortable with, then this is enough.

There are fixed return assumptions that correspond to probabilities of success, so a funded ratio without all the other complexities can work effectively. If you use average historical stock returns for your funded ratio, recognize that this will correspond to a probability of success that is under 50 percent. Moving closer to bond yields will imply a greater success rate.

The third reason is that there are countless calculators available, and it is hard to know which one to choose. Several studies have attempted to enter the same user inputs into different calculators and have found widely divergent results in terms of whether the plan is expected to work. At least for calculators that do not also make complete guesses about your spending goals (by using a simple replacement rate on your salary) and Social Security benefits, the two most important factors that explain these differences surely relate to the underlying assumptions about market returns and longevity. Some calculators may assume that bonds will earn 5 or 6 percent returns with even higher returns for stocks, or that retirees will die by 85. These calculators will report high success rates. But the assumptions are questionable.

Many of these calculators represent black boxes, as it is not always easy to know what is being assumed about underlying variables such as market returns, inflation, spending goals, how spending adjusts over time, Social Security decisions and benefits, other income sources outside of investments, the use of annuities, the role of the home, household composition, tax calculations at the federal and state level, the retirement age, asset allocation, asset location, investment fees, withdrawal order sequencing, legacy goals, planning for contingencies, and accepted risk for investment depletion.

I think a funded ratio analysis can allow for more control over these variables. Estimating taxes is hard, but at least a simple spreadsheet can provide more control over cash flows related to retirement assets and liabilities. Assuming a conservative effective tax rate on your spending should get you in the right direction for tax estimates. Any lack of precision with this assumption should be more than offset by the greater control you have with the other assumptions for your plan. Anyway, I do not think that many of the online calculators available to consumers are doing sophisticated tax planning either. Calculators which do not allow you to control your planning inputs could provide misleading outcomes based on incorrect guesses.

I do plan to eventually compare various retirement calculators to see if I can find one that I feel comfortable suggesting to do-it-yourself retirees. Until then, I suggest using the funded ratio. You might then compare your funded ratio with other online calculators to double-check your results. I personally just use the funded ratio approach.

Retirement CARE Analysis™: Product & Asset Allocation Decisions

So much of the focus for retirement income rests on the idea of a "safe" withdrawal rate for retirement, which is especially tied into probability-based approaches. I tend to be quoted in the media with a number in the ballpark of 2.8 percent. But recently Bill Bengen (the founder of the 4 percent rule) suggested that 5 percent is a more reasonable estimate when inflation is low. The problem with estimating withdrawal rates is that they depend on so many underlying assumptions, as we explored in Chapter 4. How long should the funds last? How much risk of depletion is acceptable? What is the asset allocation? What are the assumptions about future market returns? Will spending keep pace with inflation or otherwise decline over time? Does the lumpiness of real-world spending negate the usefulness of thinking in terms of withdrawal rates? Is there any flexibility to adjust the distributions in response to market performance? Are there buffer assets to coordinate with portfolio spending? Is there desire to build in a safety margin for assets to preserve something for contingencies or legacy? How important are these distributions in the overall plan? This makes it hard to have an underlying baseline for the conversation.

More broadly, any estimate for a withdrawal rate does have a one-to-one correspondence with an underlying fixed market return. The specific connection depends on the details about future portfolio distributions and how that impacts sequence risk. If you are seeking a high enough probability of success when using a volatile investment portfolio, at some point your plan may be assuming an underlying market return that is less than TIPS yields. However, Monte Carlo based financial planning software does not report the results in this way, so the detail gets obscured. I have tried to make this book less technical, but the underlying mechanics of this issue I did explore further in *How Much Can I Spend in Retirement?*

Withdrawal rates can be fraught with peril, as it does seem to be difficult to understand how a "safe" withdrawal rate must assume a low underlying investment return. Because of the complex underlying relationships between market returns and withdrawal rates, I have concluded that it will be easier for individuals to think about their plans in terms of a market return. That return is then reflected in the discount rate used for the funded ratio. Rather than debating about a "safe" withdrawal rate, just focus on whether your discount rate will be based on bond yields alone, or whether you are comfortable including some degree of risk premium into it. Then, with your chosen discount rate, is your plan sufficiently funded?

This viewpoint is still not widely shared. Heated debates about withdrawal rates have continued since the concept gained recognition in the 1990s. People want to know what the right withdrawal rate is for their plan. So, to help manage one's thoughts about this decision, I now turn to the Retirement CARE Analysis™. This analysis pre-dates the Retirement Income Style Awareness®. It provides a set of considerations to guide decisions around withdrawal rates, asset allocation, and the use of annuities. How aggressive should spending and asset allocation be in your retirement income plan? Would you like to use an annuity and how does this impact your decisions about asset allocation and withdrawal rates? This framework is based on

Capacities, Aspirations, Realities, and Emotions. Exhibit 13.1 provides the factors to keep in mind.

First are capacities, which relate to the idea of risk capacity. Risk capacity is the ability to experience portfolio losses without suffering a major life setback or a major reduction to your standard of living. How important are the withdrawals from your investment portfolio to your overall standard of living in retirement? The less that lifestyle is impacted by market downturns, the greater is the capacity to bear financial market risk. Risk capacity can diminish rapidly at retirement to the extent that work becomes less of an option to respond to risks. The investment horizon is shorter, the ability to generate new income sources reduces, more liquidity may be needed for unplanned expenses, and alternative options to reduce expenses or change lifestyle may decline with increasing age.

There are four factors that can increase risk capacity. These include having more spending covered through reliable income resources (Social Security, pensions, annuities, individual bonds) that are not exposed to market downturns, being flexible with spending so that cuts can be made in response to a market downturn without overly hurting the living standard, having a higher funded ratio such that there is greater discretionary wealth which can experience losses without impacting goals, and having more reserves to protect from the need to sell assets at inopportune times to cover expenses.

The funded ratio speaks to whether a retiree even needs to take risk in retirement. Those who are funded when TIPS yields are used as the discount rate do not require risk. They have won the game and can stop playing if they wish, to avoid the risk of losing their successful funded ratio. When plans are underfunded, a discussion can then proceed about whether it is acceptable to add risk with a hope of achieving a better funded ratio through investment growth while accepting the risk of falling further behind as well.

Next are aspirations, which relate to your goals for spending and legacy. With the funded ratio, the specific withdrawal rate from investments is not so important, but much of retirement planning is still based around the concepts for finding a "safe" withdrawal rate. Naturally, your choice for withdrawal rates will relate to what it takes to meet your goals. A starting point for the withdrawal rate decision is to first determine what rate would satisfy your overall lifestyle goals. You do not need to use a higher withdrawal rate than what is needed to cover your spending. In some cases, you might decide to accept greater risk by using a higher withdrawal rate than deemed "safe" if there are important spending needs it will cover. How your future spending patterns will link to inflation is also important, as is a desire to preserve investment assets for legacy goals.

Exhibit 13.1
The Retirement CARE Analysis™

CAPACITIES (Resiliencies)	
Reliable Income	What proportion of your spending goals are covered through reliable income sources from outside the investment portfolio that will not be diminished by market downturns?
Spending Flexibility	Is it possible to reduce portfolio distributions by making simple lifestyle adjustments without significantly harming your standard of living?
Funded Ratio	Are there sufficient assets to meet retirement goals without taking market risk? Is there excess discretionary wealth, or are you underfunded with respect to goals?
Availability of Reserves and Exposures to Spending Shocks	How much exposure is there to large and uncertain expenses? What insurance policies or other reserves are available to manage these shocks? Are there reserve assets?
ASPIRATIONS (Goals)	
Lifestyle	What is the retirement budget? How does it change over time? How closely connected is it to consumer price inflation?
Legacy	What are the legacy goals? How important is legacy, relative to other goals?
RETURNS (Assumptions)	
Capital market expectations	What are reasonable market return assumptions for different asset classes and inflation to guide simulation of the retirement income plan? How are returns impacted by investor behavior, fees, taxes, and investment vehicle choices?
EMOTIONAL COMFORT (Constraints)	
Traditional risk aversion	How much short-term portfolio volatility can you stomach before it affects your sleep and leads you to panic and change course if markets are down?
Longevity risk aversion	How fearful are you about outliving your investment portfolio? Greater concern means more longevity risk aversion, implying that one should choose a higher planning age.
Financial tool aversion	Are you willing to consider different types of retirement tools, such as annuities and reverse mortgages, or are some tools simply nonstarters for you?
Susceptibility to behavioral mistakes	When it comes to investing and long-term planning for complex situations, how prone are you to making a variety of behavioral mistakes? Will you be able to stick to your financial plan?
Financial plan complexity	What is the acceptable degree of complexity and involvement needed to manage your finances? Do you enjoy the planning process, or would you prefer to outsource management to others? Would you prefer more simple set-it-and-forget-it types of solutions?

The third category is returns. These are your capital market expectations, or your assumptions about net portfolio returns and inflation. Net returns are important and are determined as gross returns less the impacts of fees, investor behavior, and investment vehicle choices. Taxes could also impact your net returns, or you may account for them separately. With the funded ratio, you begin with TIPS yields and decide whether you are comfortable assuming a higher net return. With traditional Monte Carlo based financial planning tools, you make your best guess about average market returns and their volatility, and then test your plan with randomized return simulations and calibrate a desired probability of success to manage downside risks. Either approach uses market return assumptions to estimate your plan feasibility. Your choice for assumptions is important. Naturally, the higher your assumed returns, the easier it will be for your plan to work, with the caveat that assuming higher returns also entails accepting greater risk that those returns will not be met.

The final category is your emotional comfort with different aspects of planning. Your comfort represents potential limitations regarding your planning and is often related to behavioral factors. The first of these is traditional risk aversion, or, conversely, risk tolerance. How much short-term market volatility can you stomach before it starts affecting your sleep with undue stress or causes you to panic and sell stocks after a market downturn? Risk tolerance implies comfort in managing your portfolio volatility and being able to "stay the course" and not panic after a market drop. It represents a willingness to use a more volatile asset allocation.

In this behavioral context, risk tolerance is defined in its traditional way regarding short-term portfolio volatility. But it is important to recognize that true risk tolerance is different for retirees. Risk tolerance in retirement relates to how well one can deal with the prospect of reducing their spending. Being more aggressive in this case means understanding and accepting that lifestyle may have to be reduced if things go poorly. Aggressiveness can be manifested both by spending at a higher rate and by using a more aggressive asset allocation. For those with greater risk tolerance, spending well above the "safe" withdrawal rate could be perfectly acceptable.

For those with less risk tolerance, spending conservatively, investing more conservatively (without overdoing it), and considering annuities as protected income sources are all alternatives. For the Accumulation vs Distribution factor, risk-averse retirees will accept a strategy with lower but more stable spending over retirement, compared to a strategy that might support higher average spending, but with greater volatility and more occasions for annual spending to dip to uncomfortably lower levels. Risk aversion links to the Distribution preference. The more risk averse will prefer the lower average but less volatile spending path, while those with more flexibility and risk tolerance might be willing to accept the higher average but more volatile spending path.

Nonetheless, though traditional accumulation-based risk tolerance may not be important at this lifestyle level if short-term downturns do not impact spending, it is still an important behavioral constraint on choices. If someone is not comfortable with short-term portfolio volatility, then none of these broader considerations matter.

A second emotional constraint is longevity risk aversion. How worried are you about outliving your assets? How strongly do you wish to avoid spending reductions in the event you live well beyond your life expectancy? Those with a preference for Front-Loading have lower longevity risk aversion. They use a higher withdrawal rate and more aggressive asset allocation because they want to focus more on the present and worry less about reduced spending in the future. A preference for Back-Loading implies higher longevity risk aversion and a lower spending rate.

The third constraint is aversion to certain retirement income tools. How willing are you to consider various retirement income tools, such as annuities or a reverse mortgage? If the thought of using such tools strikes you negatively on an emotional level, then such options can simply be non-starters for your planning purposes. It may be fruitless to try and convince you otherwise. In the end, you need to be comfortable with your choices.

Next is your susceptibility to making behavioral mistakes that could harm the long-term prospects for your financial plan. Can you stick to the spending and investment objectives for your financial plan without arbitrarily changing course? Probably the most damaging behavioral mistake made by real-world investors is succumbing to the greed-and-fear cycle that causes someone to buy into the market at its peak and sell out at its lows. This natural cycle happens thus: when markets are doing well, investors get excited and pour more money into the market with the hope that this trend will continue indefinitely. But it usually does not. Investors on the sidelines may become jealous of neighbors' gains and may worry that they are missing out, leading them to pile in at the market peak. It is tough to rebalance to your strategic asset allocation that matches your risk tolerance when markets are rising, because this requires you to sell shares of the biggest gainers. Do you have the discipline to stick with your plan?

Conversely, sometimes markets plummet, as we saw most recently in February and March 2020. Investors get nervous, and some, after seeing significant declines, become scared enough that they start selling off holdings. Staying the course is an even greater challenge if you are experiencing cognitive decline. Unfortunately, downturns also call for rebalancing to your strategic asset allocation, which would require buying assets with falling prices, rather than selling them. This is also a challenge, both emotionally and intellectually. Unfortunately, investors in financial markets tend to do the opposite of what happens in most other markets: they buy more when prices are high and sell when prices are low. This causes returns to drag behind what a "buy, hold, and rebalance" investor could have earned. The 4 percent rule assumes that investors do stick with a "buy, hold, and rebalance" strategy. Those more susceptible to behavioral biases should reflect on the implications this will have for portfolio returns and net sustainable spending.

A further issue of emotional comfort relates to financial plan complexity. Can your plan run on autopilot or be facilitated by a trusted financial professional, or does it require ongoing complex decision-making on your part? It is important that retirees find manageable approaches.

Finally, how financially savvy are different members of your household? Would surviving household members be able to carry on financially if you were incapacitated due to illness or death? This also has implications for strategy choices, asset allocation decisions, and withdrawal rates.

The Retirement CARE Analysis provides a way to begin thinking about an appropriate personalized withdrawal strategy in retirement. It provides the details for how to decide on the aggressiveness of both spending and asset allocation within a retirement income plan. It also helps to identify the role that annuities can play within the plan. A more conservative retiree will generally experience fewer reliable income sources outside the investment portfolio to help cushion the impact of market volatility on lifestyle, less flexibility to make spending reductions because spending goals are fixed and rise with inflation, fewer reserves, buffer assets, or insurance policies to help cushion spending shocks, a desire to build in a margin of safety for the financial plan, and greater worry and stress about short-term market volatility and about outliving your retirement assets.

Meanwhile, a more aggressive retiree will tend to fall in the opposite direction on these matters, highlighting the highly personal and complex nature of determining asset allocation and withdrawal rates for retirement. Retirees need to consider carefully about the threat to their quality of life should they happen to deplete their investment portfolio at some point while still alive. With a sufficient base of reliable income, those who tend toward relative frugality may find that it is reasonable to go ahead and occasionally splurge a bit without feeling guilty about it.

The Retirement CARE Analysis also helps with thinking about annuities. For income protection and risk wrap retirement income styles, annuities can also provide a tool to improve plan funding by providing additional risk pooling. The lower your discount rate and the higher your planning age, the better an annuity with lifetime income will look in your plan. This is because the annuity income stream will have a higher present value, and therefore you will see a larger asset on your balance sheet. As you increase the discount rate or lower the planning age, an annuity will begin to lose its attractiveness. As a series of future cash flows, its present value declines and there are less assets on your balance sheet. The caveat, though, is that a higher discount rate or lower planning age creates risk.

Whether you find this risk to be worrisome is a personal matter that relates to your style. Probability-based versus safety-first determines whether you are more comfortable basing your retirement income on market growth or on contractual protections. Market-based approaches also tend to be correlated with front-loading and accumulation preferences, while safety-first preferences are more aligned with back-loading and distribution. Either approach has merit if it is the right approach for you.

Not everyone will need or want an annuity. For some, it will not fit their style. Others may already have plenty of lifetime income through Social Security and traditional defined-benefit pensions. The action items for determining whether and how to include annuities within your retirement income plan include:

☐ Your RISA Profile suggests that your preferences align with income protection and risk wrap strategies

☐ You have an income gap in which there is not enough reliable income to cover your longevity expenses

☐ Your risk tolerance limits your comfort with stocks in retirement. The case for annuities is stronger for those with less stocks

☐ You have greater longevity risk aversion. Concerns about outliving retirement assets lead to more relative benefits from annuities as the alternative is to spend even less from investments

☐ You view annuities as a replacement for bonds and are comfortable using a higher stock allocation with remaining investments

☐ You seek protection from making behavioral mistakes with your investment portfolio, you lack self-control for spending, or you find investments intimidating

☐ Choosing a joint annuity can also help to protect less financially savvy family members

If you do decide that an annuity may be worthwhile, then additional considerations include:

☐ Learn about the features and mechanics of different annuities

☐ Determine the income gap you are seeking to fill and decide whether the amount of assets needed to fill that gap with annuities is reasonable. Decide on a premium amount

☐ Take your time with making this purchase decision: consider various options and make sure you understand them, discuss with family members, and only include benefits that you intend to use

Planning for the Non-Financial Aspects of Retirement

Quality of life in retirement is an important topic existing side-by-side with finances. The focus on the financial side of retirement implicitly assumes that the personal and psychological aspects of retirement have been addressed. However, this is not always the case. These are key steps:

☐ Find purpose and passion to guide your retirement
  o Identify expectations for a good retirement life
  o Retire *to* something, not *from* something
  o Identify fulfilling activities to replace work identity
  o Develop leisurely interests while still working
  o Prioritize activities to accomplish what is most important
  o Consider your legacy beyond financial gifts
☐ Strike the right balance with work
  o Understand the importance of your work identity
  o Buy into retirement as a new lifestyle and new identity
  o Maintain your skills and networking to create flexibility

- o Consider whether work will play a role in your retirement through phased retirement, consulting, a part-time position, starting a new business, or an encore career
  - o Prepare for an unexpected jolt into an early retirement
- ☐ Strengthen your relationships with others
  - o Reconnect with spouse and identify retirement dreams
  - o Focus on friendships and other relationships
  - o Engage in activities to maintain social ties
- ☐ Promote an active and healthy lifestyle
  - o Develop exercise routines and a healthy diet
  - o Keep your body and mind active
  - o Take care of physical and mental health
  - o Have appropriate expectations for gradual decline
  - o Focus on spiritual and religious needs

Determining Whether to Seek Financial Planning Help

Retirement requires making complicated decisions that can benefit from the guidance of various financial professionals. A financial planner can coordinate these interactions to ensure a consistent strategy. Other professionals who may be part of your team include accountants, elder-law or estate planning attorneys, insurance agents, Medicare specialists, reverse mortgage originators, and long-term care coordinators.

As for financial planners, not everyone will wish to have an ongoing engagement. Another aspect of the Retirement Income Style Awareness process that I described in Chapter 1 investigates your preferred implementation style for retirement planning. We found two factors that prove to be quite instructive about the preferences for working with a financial advisor. These include your self-efficacy for implementing your retirement plan, and your degree of perceived advisor usefulness. Those with high self-efficacy believe they can be successful with personally implementing the steps outlined in this book. These individuals will not procrastinate, will view themselves as having the resolve to overcome behavioral hurdles, and can cope with the natural stressors of aging. Though not conclusive, the fact that you have made it this far into the book suggests you may have high self-efficacy for retirement income. But it is okay if you feel overwhelmed. Meanwhile, perceptions may vary about whether financial advisors provide value beyond their fees.

For the Financial Implementation Matrix in Exhibit 13.2, we find four quadrants that combine these two sets of attitudes and preferences. Starting in the upper right are individuals with high self-efficacy and high perceived advisor usefulness. These are *collaborators* who value working with an advisor and intend to be active participants in their planning process. In our initial RISA study, we found that 19 percent of respondents were collaborators. The lower-right quadrant identifies individuals with high self-efficacy and low perceived advisor usefulness. This is the *self-directed* or do-it-yourself community, representing 34 percent of respondents. These individuals are confident in their abilities to implement their plan and do not see any reason to pay an advisor for these services. Some self-directed individuals may view personal finance as a hobby.

Exhibit 13.2
Financial Implementation Matrix™

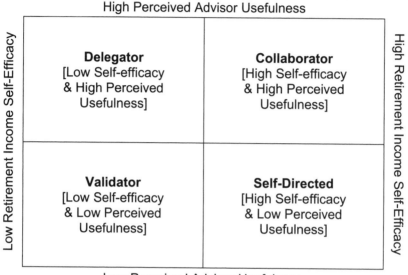

The lower-left quadrant includes individuals with low self-efficacy and low perceived advisor usefulness. These are *validators* who will aim to implement the plan themselves but may seek an occasional second opinion as they are generally unsure about both themselves and advisors. Rather than seeking an ongoing advisory relationship, these individuals might prefer a one-time plan or may seek specific advice at key decision points. Overall, though, they will assume ownership of their plan even though they do feel less comfortable about it. Our survey identified 13 percent of respondents as validators. Finally, the upper-left quadrant includes those with low self-efficacy and high perceived advisor usefulness. These are *delegators* who are most likely to seek a traditional ongoing financial planning relationship with an advisor. These individuals do not feel confident about implementing their financial plans and believe that a trusted advisor can be of benefit to obtain a better retirement outcome. Among our respondents, 34 percent were delegators.

With retirement, it is important to consider how declining cognitive skills associated with aging will make it increasingly difficult to self-manage your investment and withdrawal decisions. As well, for households where one person handles money matters, surviving household members will be especially vulnerable to making mistakes when they outlive the family financial manager. Developing a strong relationship with a trusted financial planner can help with both matters. Beyond this, not everyone wants to work with an advisor. The rest of this section provides a bit more background for those who want to learn more about financial planners.

Though the financial services profession is highly regulated at both the state and national levels, use of the terms financial advisor or financial planner as job titles is hardly regulated. Regulation generally focuses on the nature of business activities rather than job titles. Pretty much anyone can use these terms without any further oversight about training, competency, education, or qualifications. Financial designations have developed to train advisors and to signal quality. Well respected general planning designations include the CFP and ChFC, and for retirement-specific training there is the RICP, RMA, or CRC. Finding advisors with these designations can help as a starting point.

Generally, those calling themselves financial planners or advisors represent one of three types: registered investment advisors, stockbrokers, or insurance agents. When investigating an advisor, you will want to examine their credentials, complaint records and other background details, as well as the advisor's fit with your preferred style.

Among different types of advisors, there are three types of compensation models used:

- ☐ Fee-only: only paid through fees from the client, which could involve paying a percentage of the assets managed, paying fixed fees for planning services, or paying an hourly rate for advice
- ☐ Fee-based: paid through a mix of fees from clients as well as commissions from selling financial products
- ☐ Commissions: paid through commissions earned on selling financial products such as loaded mutual funds or insurance policies

With the debate about fees, fee-only advisors have held themselves out as the "good guys" by not having a conflict of interest in their recommendations since they only receive fees from their clients. But to the extent that many fee-only advisors charge their fees as a percentage of assets under management, this reduces incentives to recommend insurance products which the advisor could not collect fees on. Such advisors tend to be more aligned with total-return and time segmentation styles as they build investment portfolios and charge on the assets they manage. Annuities and other insurance fell outside their business models because they could not be paid for suggesting such products and they might lose control over some of the assets covered by their fees. This matter is being remedied partly with the growth of fee-only insurance products that do not compensate through commissions. But more broadly, if you are willing to accept that there are multiple legitimate retirement income styles, and that not everyone is best served with total-return or time-segmentation strategies, then fee-only advisors who live in this narrow world may not be appropriate for everyone.

Nonetheless, fee-only advisors are more likely to provide comprehensive planning opportunities than other types of advisors. There are exceptions, so it is important to inquire and discuss further before committing to an engagement. Some fee-only advisors simply focus on investments, and there is still a popular perception that a financial advisor is mainly tasked with such a role. But a good comprehensive fee-only financial planner should assist their clients with eight core planning areas: investments, taxes, debt management, education planning, retirement planning, estate planning, insurance, and household budgeting. Those charging an ongoing assets-under-management fee will also generally provide portfolio management, while other fee-only approaches such as one-time plans or hourly rates may involve the presentation of recommendations that the client would them implement on their own.

Next, fee-based advisors may have more potential to serve different retirement styles by having the ability to incorporate both investment management and insurance solutions within the same firm. Nonetheless, there is always a danger with commissions. Advisors who do not serve as fiduciaries may base their product recommendations more on personal profitability than on what is best for the client. Commissions lend themselves to abuses and it is good to be skeptical about advice provided when commissions are at stake. But in an ideal world, commissions can be an attractive compensation model that costs less to the client over time than paying an ongoing percentage of assets under management.

As well, purely commissioned advisors may be fine to work with when you have done your homework and know the specific product that you want. Though non-commissioned insurance products are growing in popularity, some products are still only available to be sold through a commission-based advisor.

Returning to the three types of advisors (registered investment advisors, stockbrokers, and insurance agents), traditionally only the registered investment advisors were required to serve as fiduciaries for their clients, at least when they are wearing their "investment advisor" hat. The fiduciary standard of care requires investment advisors to act in the best interests of clients and disclose any material conflicts of interest to clients for the advice they provide. Regulations are changing to require more types of advisors to also make decisions in the best interest of their clients.

Many advisors are registered dually as investment advisors and as brokers or agents. This is how they become fee-based instead of fee-only or commission-only. In such cases, it may not always be clear when advisors are wearing the hat of a fiduciary, and when they are making recommendations under other requirements. You are always welcome to ask questions about how an advisor is compensated.

As well, if you are specifically seeking a comprehensive planner, there are some questions you might ask to get a sense about the breadth and depth of their advice. First, simply ask questions and see if the advisor is patient and provides answers in a straightforward manner. You might also ask about the assumptions used in their planning projections (or whether they are even creating a plan for you, rather than just selling products). As well, potentially a good litmus test for an advisor is to simply ask about reverse mortgages. Some firms still prohibit their advisors from discussing them, which suggests a lack of emphasis on comprehensive planning.

Are you working with a comprehensive financial planner who does more than just manage investment portfolios and can help you to implement good financial planning decisions? A comprehensive planner can support your effort to make and coordinate key retirement decisions and will do much more than just designing investment strategies that aim to "beat" the market. A good planner can serve as a sounding board for ideas and as a behavioral coach to help avoid making rash decisions and to overcome inertia or biases. A good planner can also help you manage incapacity risk and provide a resource to help transition other family members into taking control of the finances. A good planner can help to free up time for you to better enjoy your retirement years. Finally, a good advisor who is also right for you will be comfortable with serving your preferred style for implementing your retirement income strategy and will not try to pigeonhole you into a different style that the advisor views as better. A financial advisor can be cost-effective for those who do not see personal finance as a hobby that they enjoy spending time and energy to handle, those who may experience inertia when it comes to implementing and updating their plan, and those who worry that other family members may not be able to handle taking over the reins.

Decisions at Specific Ages or Moments

Next, we consider items that connect to specific inflection points. First, we look at important ages with retirement planning and then consider key decisions when leaving employment and reaching Medicare eligibility.

Some Meaningful Ages

- ☐ Age 50: catch-up contributions allowed for retirement plans
- ☐ Age 59.5: End of early withdrawal penalties for retirement plans
- ☐ Age 62: Earliest age for Social Security claiming
- ☐ Age 62: Eligible borrowing age for HECM reverse mortgage
- ☐ Age 65: Medicare eligibility
- ☐ Age 66 to 67: Full retirement age for Social Security
  - ○ End of earnings test
  - ○ Possibility to suspend benefits to earn delay credits
  - ○ Full survivor and spousal benefits are available
- ☐ Age 70: End of delay credits for claiming own Social Security
- ☐ Age 70.5: Qualified charitable distributions from IRAs are allowed
- ☐ Age 72: Required minimum distributions begin

Leaving Employment

Leaving employment is a key milestone. For some, retirement will be voluntary. Others will experience an involuntary retirement after job loss, health problems, or the need to care for a family member. For those with the option, a phased or partial retirement may be possible. Those seeking to learn more about new possibilities for working in retirement may visit websites such as Encore.org. The following action items are important when approaching your date for leaving work.

- ☐ Meet with human resources to get an accurate understanding about employer benefits and other decisions to be made
    - ○ Pension decisions
    - ○ Retirement health benefits
    - ○ Inventory of other employer benefits
- ☐ Defined-benefit pensions: lump-sum or lifetime income choices
    - ○ Timing retirement to obtain an additional pension credit
    - ○ Identify distribution options for the pension
    - ○ Analyze need for additional reliable income
    - ○ Compare to annuity options if lump-sum goes to IRA
    - ○ Consider credit risk of employer and whether pension is fully covered by Pension Benefit Guaranty Corporation
    - ○ Determine if pension choice impacts other retirement benefits such as retiree health insurance
    - ○ Assess risk tolerance for investing a lump-sum amount
    - ○ For lifetime income, consider tradeoff between joint lifetime income and higher income for single recipient
- ☐ Defined-contribution plans: rollover to IRA or keep in plan
    - ○ Compare investment options and fees in plan and IRAs
    - ○ Determine value of having more discretionary control over withdrawals in an IRA
    - ○ Compare annuity options in and out of employer plan
    - ○ Consider if rollover will disrupt plans for Roth conversions through pro-rata rule on non-deductible contributions
    - ○ Determine opportunities for net unrealized appreciation
- ☐ Actions that may be easier before leaving employment
    - ○ Obtaining a mortgage may be easier if still employed
    - ○ Consider paying off existing mortgage before retiring
    - ○ Obtaining a home equity line of credit may be easier
    - ○ Take advantage of health insurance benefits such as getting exams or other preventative care
    - ○ Coordinate personal emails that go to your work address to go to a personal email address
- ☐ Opportunity to consolidate accounts when rolling over
    - ○ Work toward one IRA and one Roth IRA per spouse
    - ○ Consolidate bank and brokerage accounts to simplify

- [ ] If retiring before Medicare eligibility:
  - o Consider how to obtain health insurance and what healthcare costs you will face until reaching Medicare eligibility age
  - o Coverage may be available through an employer, a spouse's plan, the Affordable Care Act marketplace, other private insurance, retirement health insurance, a healthshare plan, or COBRA
  - o Make sure that spouses and dependents have coverage if you are retiring and leaving your employer plan

---

FIRE Movement: Financial Independence Retire Early

The FIRE community is growing in popularity. These folks focus on achieving financial independence and retiring early. Much of the discussion in this book can also apply to younger retirees, but there are a few additional considerations. First, the 4 percent rule was not designed for early retirees as it was calibrated to just 30 years of retirement. Early retirees must manage a longer retirement horizon, which suggests using both a lower withdrawal rate and higher stock allocation. This also suggests a need for more flexibility to adjust spending over time and to make cuts if the portfolio is not performing as expected. Early retirees should also make careful plans for health care with the recognition that they are on their own until qualifying for Medicare at 65. Finally, early retirees may emphasize strategies for drawing from retirement accounts without incurring the early withdrawal penalties or otherwise have sufficient taxable assets to get them through age 59.5 before needing such distributions.

Tax Planning Opportunities After Employment

Depending on your retirement age, a window of opportunity may open after retiring with some lower income years before Social Security and required minimum distributions begin. For those who have built a strong base in the pre-retirement years, this can provide an opportunity to deploy strategies for tax-bracket management and tax-efficient distributions:

- [ ] Understand the rules for taking distributions from tax-advantaged retirement plans, including required minimum distributions, early withdrawal penalties, rules for qualified distributions from Roth accounts, making rollovers and conversions, and managing net unrealized appreciation on any employer stock
- [ ] Understand withdrawal sequencing strategies based around managing adjusted gross income and Roth conversions

- ☐ Identify the impact of the various retirement pitfalls when generating taxable income, including the Social Security tax torpedo, heightened premiums for Medicare, the loss of subsidies for health insurance, the net investment income surtax, and the impact of pushing preferential income sources into higher tax brackets
- ☐ Consider reasons in favor of front-loading taxes in retirement, such as how that will help the eventual tax situation for a surviving spouse or to create the opportunity to better manage future tax increases
- ☐ Consider tax-efficient strategies for charitable giving, including qualified charitable distributions, deduction bunching for gifts, donor advised funds, and charitable gift annuities
- ☐ Be mindful of cost-basis and capital gains tax for portfolio changes

Reaching Medicare Eligibility

As you reach the Medicare eligibility age:

- ☐ If you would like professional assistance, identify an independent broker specializing in Medicare to guide you
- ☐ If you or your spouse is still actively employed, determine whether your employer health insurance can be counted as primary insurance after you reach age 65
- ☐ If Medicare will become your primary insurance, plan for timely Medicare enrollment to avoid penalties and a lapse in coverage
  - o Read *Medicare and You* booklet at Medicare.gov
  - o Choose Original Medicare or Medicare Advantage
  - o Choose a Part D drug plan, drug coverage through Medicare Advantage, or coverage through other secondary health insurance with creditable coverage
  - o With Original Medicare, decide whether to purchase a Medicare supplement plan or whether other secondary retirement health insurance can play this role
  - o Determine whether there are any impacts from Medicare decisions on any of your other employer benefits
  - o If you are considering switching from secondary coverage to a supplement later, determine if you will potentially be eligible for a special enrollment period at some point to provide access to some plans without underwriting
  - o Use Plan Finder tool at Medicare.gov/plan-compare
- ☐ Make sure that your spouse and dependents have coverage if you are switching your coverage to Medicare
- ☐ Enroll in Medicare online, by phone, or at your local Social Security office
- ☐ Open account at MyMedicare.gov to keep track of your Medicare claims and obtain information about your coverage

- [ ] Medicare personnel are available 24 hours a day by phone for counseling (1-800-633-4227), and you can also talk to knowledgeable volunteers through the Medicare Rights Center (www.medicarerights.org) and your state's State Health Insurance Assistance Program (www.shiptacenter.org)

Ongoing Monitoring and Adjustments

This section is intended for those who are already retired and have worked through the steps from the previous sections. I have attempted to provide a month-by-month list of annual activities to keep your retirement plan updated. There is flexibility to adjust this calendar of activities, and not all items may be relevant. This organization is based on placing activities when they make the most sense, or otherwise spreading activities throughout the year in cases where the timing does not matter.

January

- [ ] Gather account balances and asset values at year end to update your household net worth statement.
- [ ] Use online tools to finalize household spending from the previous year. Add spending to your ongoing budget numbers and adjust your future retirement budget as needed based on what you learned with your past year's spending. Make note of any surprises that should be used in plan updates.
- [ ] Make a final estimated tax payment for the previous year as needed. (January 15)
- [ ] Take note of what your RMDs will be for the year as a starting point for tax bracket management.

February

- [ ] Check annual credit reports. (www.annualcreditreport.com)
- [ ] Revisit your financial instructions documentation and make any needed updates.
- [ ] Obtain updated Social Security statement. (usually available in mid-February)

March

- [ ] Review legacy goals.
- [ ] Revisit estate planning steps to make any necessary updates.
- [ ] Outside of this annual review, be mindful of other life events that could trigger a quicker response for estate planning documents:
    - o Significant changes to the household balance sheet
    - o Change in marital status, births or deaths, family relations
    - o Open or close important financial accounts or policies
    - o Move to a new state
    - o Changes to tax or estate laws
    - o Change in relationship with those serving key roles

☐ Review estate plan and associated documents, asset titles, and beneficiary designations.

April

☐ Prepare and submit tax return for the previous tax year.
☐ Pay estimated taxes. (April 15)
☐ Review your discount rate and update your funded ratio analysis.
☐ Consider any planning adjustments based on funded ratio update.
  o Appropriateness of overall funded level
  o Appropriateness of funding for reliable income and longevity expenses
  o Adjustments to assets or liabilities
  o Possibility for making gifts when becoming more overfunded or more potential to be exposed to estate tax

May

☐ Review asset allocation and rebalance portfolio. Include decisions about re-filling buffer assets or upcoming spending with time segmentation strategies.
☐ Make sure your emergency fund is sufficiently funded.
☐ Schedule annual opportunities to use preventative care benefits with health insurance.

June

☐ Pay estimated taxes. (June 15)
☐ Review insurance policies. (life, homeowner, vehicle, umbrella)

July

☐ Ponder your passions, activities, and relationships to find areas for improvement.
☐ Review physical activities and diet to maintain a healthy lifestyle.

August

☐ Reconnect with important players in your estate plan: executor, trustees, those with power of attorney, etc.

September

☐ Pay estimated taxes. (September 15)
☐ Update your assessment about housing decisions and the ability to age in place.
☐ Review local long-term care facilities and options, and review for any updates to your long-term care plan.

October

☐ Revisit health insurance decisions for the Medicare open enrollment period lasting from October 15 to December 7.

- Update health care budget and reserves based on recent spending and health care usage
- Update your list of prescription drugs to use with testing for the best personalized prescription drug plan during each open enrollment
- Review choices for Part D prescription plan, Medicare Advantage, Original Medicare, and supplements (be aware of underwriting with supplements)
- ☐ When relevant, review annual decisions and coverage options for employer open enrollment season.

November

- ☐ Review asset allocation and rebalance portfolio.
- ☐ Revisit asset location, withdrawal order sequencing, and tax-planning decisions.

December

- ☐ Charitable giving plans: RMDs or QCDs, contributions to donor advised funds
- ☐ Make sure that any RMDs have been taken by December 31.
- ☐ Make any desired gifts for which you wish to benefit from the annual gift tax exclusion.
- ☐ Engage in any strategic Roth conversions or other tax planning to manage your taxable income at the desired level for the year.

Avoiding Mistakes

Many things can go wrong with retirement planning. A significant mistake could unravel years of hard work. To conclude, I highlight key pitfalls to summarize the book's lessons.

Investment Decisions

- ☐ Using an inappropriate asset allocation for your risk tolerance or risk capacity
- ☐ Letting emotions take control and drive asset allocation changes during periods of market volatility, and related behavioral mistakes
- ☐ Assuming too high of return for your portfolio
- ☐ Believing that higher-cost investments must be better
- ☐ Assembling investments piecemeal without an overall strategy
- ☐ Using an excessive number of accounts or funds
- ☐ Holding concentrated positions, especially in your employer stock
- ☐ Falling victim to a sales pitch for an investment product without understanding clearly about the role it will play in your plan
- ☐ Missing deadlines for making required minimum distributions
- ☐ Being overly exposed to losses if interest rates rise
- ☐ Not being emotionally prepared for multiple bear markets through-out your retirement

Insurance Decisions

- ☐ Purchasing annuities or life insurance in a haphazard manner without a clear plan for how the policies fit into your plan
- ☐ Lacking needed insurance or carrying unnecessary insurance
- ☐ Falling victim to a sales pitch for an insurance product
- ☐ Forgetting to pay a premium and unintentionally lapsing on an insurance policy

Social Security Decisions

- ☐ Not testing your claiming decision with software
- ☐ Missing out on eligible dependent, ex-spouse, or survivor benefits
- ☐ Thinking that the act of retiring means you must also claim
- ☐ Being overly excited to have both spouses claim at 62
- ☐ Finalizing divorce just before ten years of marriage

Medicare Decisions

- ☐ Not understanding that Medicare becomes the primary payer for health coverage upon reaching the age of eligibility except for those who can maintain coverage through active employment (by yourself or a spouse) at a firm with at least 20 employees
- ☐ Not understanding that if you do not have primary coverage by law after turning 65 and do not enroll in Medicare, you may find yourself without health coverage and may have to wait up to 15 months to begin coverage during a general enrollment period
- ☐ Not understanding that Medicare coverage is based on individuals and does not provide benefits to younger spouses or dependents
- ☐ Not realizing that Medicare enrollment is not automatic if you are delaying Social Security past age 65
- ☐ Not enrolling at least in Parts A and B for those with secondary coverage through other health insurance

- ☐ Not understanding that using only Medicare Parts A, B, and D can lead to significant exposure to uncapped medical expenses
- ☐ If you have secondary coverage that provides primary coverage for other family members, be careful about making decisions that could have unintended consequences as based on the rules of your health plan
- ☐ Making decisions based solely on which option has the lowest premiums or deductibles, rather than considering the full costs of various options
- ☐ Assuming that Medicare is set-it-and-forget-it and not reviewing your options during each year's open enrollment period
- ☐ Not recognizing that outside of the initial enrollment period and somewhat with special enrollment periods, applications for Medicare supplements will be underwritten and potentially denied
- ☐ Thinking that Medicare will cover long-term care needs

Tax and Estate Planning

- ☐ Lacking an estate plan
- ☐ Lacking a plan for incapacity
- ☐ Having out-of-date beneficiary designations
- ☐ Forgetting to fund your trusts
- ☐ Creating unequal or unintended inheritances
- ☐ Paying unnecessary costs and taxes for estate distribution
- ☐ Missing important strategies to save on taxes
- ☐ Not filling up zero percent tax brackets with taxable income
- ☐ Donating cash instead of appreciated securities
- ☐ Doing Roth conversions for funds you will otherwise donate

Non-Financial Aspects

- ☐ Thinking you will figure things out with the extra time after retiring
- ☐ Lacking a purpose and passion for retirement
- ☐ Not communicating with your spouse about your retirement vision
- ☐ Not considering how important work is to your identity
- ☐ Engaging in too many passive activities: television, internet surfing
- ☐ Using retirement funds to start a new business based on a hobby
- ☐ Neglecting your health and avoiding preventative care

Opportunities for Further Engagement

As we finish, please let me outline a few ways to continue engaging together as you prepare for your best retirement. First you can visit **www.retirementresearcher.com** and sign up for our weekly newsletter with our latest articles, invitations to webinars, Q&A sessions, and more. The newsletter arrives to your inbox each Saturday morning.

I created Retirement Researcher as a blog in September 2010. As it developed beyond a blog over the years, I have tried to maintain the original mission: RetirementResearcher.com provides independent, data-driven, and research-based information about retirement income planning. The website is geared toward providing unbiased information about building efficient retirement income strategies and endeavors to bridge between the various retirement income styles.

Our most recent innovation regarding this bridging is the Retirement Income Style Awareness I described in Chapter 1. If you are interested to obtain your RISA Profile as an initial step toward retirement, you can sign up without cost at **www.risaprofile.com/guidebook**.

As well, returning to the topic of financial implementation preferences discussed in this chapter, we are working hard to provide support that works for everyone. For self-directed retirees, we now have the **Retirement Researcher Academy** membership site. It empowers members with a clearinghouse of knowledge that provides an extension to these contents.

For those who are collaborators, validators, or delegators, Retirement Researcher also provides opportunities to work with its sister firm, McLean Asset Management. McLean offers various **one-time planning options** for validators that do not require commitment for ongoing wealth management. These range from undertaking a **Funded Ratio Analysis** and discussing it with an advisor, engaging in a reliable income analysis, a base financial plan, or a comprehensive one-time financial plan. As well, for collaborators and delegators, McLean offers traditional financial planning relationships that includes portfolio management with ongoing **comprehensive planning** and update meetings. I can help you arrange an introductory call to learn more about these options (**wade@retirementresearcher.com**).

Finally, I am also a Professor of Retirement Income at The American College of Financial Services and the director for the **Retirement Income Certified Professional® (RICP®)** designation. It is a three-course sequence intended for financial professionals wanting to learn more about retirement income.

The door is opening to a wonderful phase of life. I wish you all the best for your retirement! Thank you for reading, and I hope you now have the skills needed to make the retirement you want.

Make an Author Happy!

If you found this information helpful, I would truly appreciate it if you left a brief review of the book at your favorite book retailer. Perhaps you could mention the most useful item you learned. As the book is self-published, it can be a challenge to get the word out to a wider audience and every review helps to get this information in front of more readers. Thank you!

The Retirement Researcher's Guide Series

The Retirement Researcher's Guide Series includes four volumes. This book provides an overall investigation of retirement income planning. For most readers, this may be sufficient. The other three volumes offer a deeper dive into specific aspects of a retirement income plan. These books are available at most major retailers. I can also arrange discounted bulk orders for any of the four volumes in this series. Please contact me directly about bulk orders at **wade@retirementresearcher.com**.

Safety-First Retirement Planning	*How Much Can I Spend in Retirement?*	*Reverse Mortgages (2nd Ed.)*
A deeper exploration of strategies for those with income protection and risk wrap styles.	A deeper exploration of strategies for those with total return and time segmentation styles.	A deep dive on reverse mortgages and different roles they can plan in a retirement plan.

Index

tax loss harvesting, 337-338
taxable income, 21, 280, 286-294, 297-300, 303-308, 311, 314-315, 321-322, 325-329, 331-340, 343, 346-347, 350-351, 357-358, 374, 385, 400, 402, 404-405, 427, 447, 450, 452
tax-deferred - see tax deferral
tax-exempt, 21, 88, 94, 247, 250-251, 290, 294-307, 309, 319, 322, 324-325, 327-334, 339, 341-343, 350-351, 356-357, 384, 387-389, 392-396, 402, 427
technical liquidity, 6, 8, 10, 13, 33, 65, 145
tenure payment, 279, 282, 284
testamentary trust, 376, 378-379
Time Segmentation, 9-10, 14, 18, 31, 83, 100-103, 109-110, 442, 449
total benefit pool, 246-247, 252-254
Total-Return, 9-12, 14, 17, 35, 88, 93-94, 100-103, 431, 442
transfer at death (TOD) provision, 371
Treasury bonds, 30-31, 36, 184, 277, 290, 364
Treasury Inflation Protected Securities (TIPS), 30-32, 36, 43-44, 72, 74, 77-78, 81, 123, 173, 176, 179, 181, 428, 431, 433-435
Trinity study, 86-87, 108
true liquidity, 8, 11, 14, 69, 140-142, 145-146, 429
trustee, 49, 371, 375-381, 383, 391, 393, 395-396, 405-406, 425-426, 449

underwriting, 206-207, 211-216, 220, 227-229, 246, 249, 251, 255, 257, 447, 450, 452
unexpected expenses - see spending shock
Uniform Transfer to Minors Act (UTMA) - see custodial account
unstructured time, 409, 412

volatility, 1, 7, 10-11, 14, 16, 24, 28-29, 33-36, 38, 40, 67, 77, 79, 80, 83-87, 99-101, 103-106, 109-110, 115-117, 129-130, 135, 137, 142-143, 223, 230, 271-274, 282, 392, 435-438, 450
volatility buffer, 110, 392
volunteer work, 414, 417

whole life insurance, 109-110, 250, 392
will, 373-375, 384, 406, 425

Windfall Elimination Provision (WEP), 19, 151, 159-160, 167-168, 186, 426
work identity, 409, 412-413, 423, 439

Zelinski, Ernie, 408, 411

About the Author

Wade D. Pfau, PhD, CFA, RICP® is a professor of retirement income and the director of the Retirement Income Certified Professional® (RICP®) designation program at the American College of Financial Services in King of Prussia, Pennsylvania. He also serves as a principal and the director of retirement research for McLean Asset Management. He is the founder of Retirement Researcher, which is an educational resource for individuals and financial advisors on topics related to retirement income planning.

He holds a doctorate in economics from Princeton University and has published more than sixty research articles in a wide variety of academic and practitioner journals. His research has been discussed in outlets including the print editions of the *Economist, New York Times, Wall Street Journal, Time, Kiplinger's,* and *Money* magazine.

Wade is a past selectee for the *InvestmentNews* Power 20 in 2013 and inaugural 40 Under 40 in 2014, the Investment Advisor 35 list for 2015 and 25 list for 2014, and *Financial Planning* magazine's Influencer Awards. In 2016, he was chosen as one of the Icons and Innovators by *InvestmentNews*. He is a two-time winner of the *Journal of Financial Planning* Montgomery-Warschauer Editor's Award, a two-time winner of the Academic Thought Leadership Award from the Retirement Income Industry Association, and a Best Paper Award winner in the Retirement category from the Academy of Financial Services. Wade served for four years as a coeditor of the *Journal of Personal Finance*.

Wade is a contributor to *Forbes* and an Expert Panelist for the *Wall Street Journal*. He has spoken at the national conferences of organizations such as the CFA Institute, the CFP Board, the FPA, NAPFA, and the Academy of Financial Services.

He is also author of three other books in the Retirement Researcher's Guide Series: *Reverse Mortgages: How to Use Reverse Mortgages to Secure Your Retirement, How Much Can I Spend in Retirement: A Guide to Investment-Based Retirement Income Strategies,* and *Safety-First Retirement Planning: An Integrated Approach for a Worry-Free Retirement.*

Twitter: @WadePfau

Website: RetirementResearcher.com